LEMON-AID
CAR GUIDE
2000

LEMON-AID
CAR GUIDE
2000

PHIL EDMONSTON

Published in 2000 by Stoddart Publishing Co. Limited
180 Varick Street, 9th Floor, New York, New York 10014

Distributed by:
General Distribution Services Inc.
4500 Witmer Industrial Estates, Niagara Falls, New York 14305-1386
Toll-free tel. 1-800-805-1083   Toll-free fax 1-800-481-6207
Email gdsinc@genpub.com

U.S. Cataloguing in Publication Data
(Library of Congress Standards)

Edmonston, Louis-Philippe, 1944–
Lemon-aid car guide 2000/Phil Edmonston .—
1st ed.
[496]p. : cm.   (Lemon-Aid Car Guide)
Originally published: Lemon-aid used cars, 1999.
Summary: Everything consumers need to know about cars.
ISBN 0-7737-6084-9 (pbk.)
1. Automobiles — purchasing. 2. Consumer education.
3. Used Car — purchasing. I. Title. II. Series.

629.22/ 22 21 2000   CIP

ISBN 0-7737-6084-9

Cover design: Bill Douglas @ The Bang
Typesetting and text design: Wordstyle Productions
Editing: Greg Ioannou/Colborne Communications

Printed and bound in Canada

CONTENTS

SMALL CARS
127

MEDIUM CARS
191

SPORTS CARS
386

MINIVANS
436

Key Documents

Introduction
COSTLY LITTLE SECRETS!

The 2000 edition of the *Lemon-Aid Car Guide* is unlike any other auto book on the market. Its main objective, to inform and protect consumers in an industry known for its dishonesty and exaggerated claims, remains unchanged. However, this guide also focuses on secret warranties and confidential service bulletins that automakers swear don't exist. That's why you'll be interested in the "Key Documents" list found on the previous pages. There you'll find the page number of the exact bulletin, memo, or news clipping reproduced from the original so neither the dealer nor the automaker can weasel out of its obligations.

Lemon-Aid's information is culled mostly from U.S. and Canadian sources and is gathered throughout the year from owner complaints, whistleblowers, lawsuits, and judgments, as well as from confidential manufacturer service bulletins.

Each year, we target abusive auto industry practices and lobby for changes. For example, in last year's guide, we:
- blasted General Motors for ABS brakes that don't brake;
- exposed engine defects on 1991–97 Saturns;
- highlighted Chrysler's automatic transmission, engine head gasket, paint, and brake problems;
- took Ford to task over its failure-prone 3.8L engine head gaskets, automatic transmissions, ACs, and brakes;
- blew the whistle on deadly airbags, using unpublicized U.S. and Canadian government studies that showed death and severe injuries are the prices women and seniors routinely pay for airbags that deploy during fender-bender accidents or inadvertently when the vehicle is started.

Following *Lemon-Aid*'s urging, the federal government and automakers have agreed to make airbag on-off switches more readily available. Chrysler has set up a special review committee (see Part Two, "Fighting Back!") to compensate owners even if their warranty had expired or they had been refused a refund in the past. Ford has paid off many 1993–96 Taurus, Sable, and Windstar owners beset with the above-mentioned powertrain failures under its "after warranty adjustment" (AWA) programs and by empowering dealers through its P-05, P-06, and P-07 claims procedures. GM has also reacted by extending the warranty on 1994–96 Saturns and recalling millions of vehicles with faulty ABS brakes.

The above successes have come about because *Lemon-Aid* publishes *in toto* secret warranty memos, internal service bulletins, and bulletin summaries showing many parts failures are factory related and are *not* the owner's responsibility. This year's guide expands its service bulletin

1

listings and updates which vehicles are covered by "goodwill" programs long after the base warranty has expired.

This guide also makes a critical comparison of 1991–98 cars and minivans. Furthermore, comprehensive crash ratings, troubleshooting shortcuts taken from actual service bulletins, and sample complaint letters with jurisprudence are included.

Our goal for almost 28 years: to keep ownership costs low and make automakers and dealers more honest and accountable—even if it does make them kick and squeal!

Phil Edmonston
February 2000

Part One
STEALS AND DEALS

Clyde, Have You Driven a Ford, Lately?

Courtesy of the Corbis collection.

Tulsa Okla.
10th April 1934
Mr. Henry Ford
Detroit Mich.

Dear Sir:

While I still have got breath in my lungs I will tell you what a dandy car you make. I have drove Fords exclusively when I could get away with one. For sustained speed and freedom from trouble the Ford has got ever other car skinned, and even if my business hasen't been strickly legal it don't hurt enything to tell you what a fine car you got in the V8.

Yours truly
Clyde Champion Barrow

Accused of committing 12 murders during a two-year crime spree, Bonnie and Clyde were gunned down together by police six weeks after Clyde wrote this letter. He would have been caught much sooner had he driven a Taurus or Windstar.

Do You Feel Lucky?

"Out of 100 vehicles, we're apt to build 10 that are as good as any that Toyota has ever built, 80 that are okay and 10 that cause repeated problems for our customers."

Robert Lutz, President
Chrysler U.S.
Chrysler Times, 17 July 1995

I wish I could have as much faith in American car quality as Clyde Barrow had in his Ford V8. But the sad reality is closer to what Chrysler's president describes: the majority of American Big Three cars and trucks are of average quality and 10 percent might be dubbed "lemons" by their owners.

It's hard to believe I've been writing *Lemon-Aid* guides for almost 28 years. Imagine, when the first guides were written, Volkswagen had a monopoly on cold, slow, and unsold Beetles and minivans; Ford was selling biodegradable pickups (and denying it had a secret "J-67" warranty to cover rust repairs); and a good, three-year-old used car could be found for less than $2,000. The average price now tops $15,000.

Chrysler owners' protest against paint peeling led to the creation of CLOG (Chrysler Lemon Owners Group). Chrysler cars and minivans are examples of a good idea gone bad. Although they're reasonably priced, spacious, and loaded with convenience features, chronic automatic transmission, brake, electrical, and paint defects can easily put a $5,000–$7,000 dent in your wallet. When faced with paint peeling or discoloring claims, Chrysler usually blames its workers, bird droppings, or the sun and then settles out of court.

Garbage in, garbage out: 1970–90

Japanese and European cars imported into North America during the early '70s were junk—as thousands of owners of rust-cankered Fiats, Hondas, Toyotas, and Nissans will confirm.

Nissan, called Datsun at the time, proved to be both incompetent and dishonest in manufacturing and marketing its product line during its first decade of operation. Not only was its attractively styled 240Z sporty coupe a junk car with multiple brake failures and a rust-weakened chassis, but Nissan had the audacity to add insult to injury by scamming buyers with two-year-old Datsun 510 sedans marketed as the latest model—a fraudulent practice later stopped by the courts. Other importers saw the pickings were easy and followed Nissan's example. And matters went downhill from there. For example, when Hyundai came along in the early '80s, they set a new benchmark for lousy quality control and a "go to hell" approach to customer relations.

This begs the question as to how foreign automakers peddling unreliable and rust-prone junk got a toehold in the North American car market. The answer is quite simple: as bad as their vehicles were, the Big Three's products were worse. Seizing the opportunity, foreign automakers smartened up within a remarkably short period of time and quickly built reliability and durability into their cars and trucks and offered them fully loaded and reasonably priced.

In the meantime, American automakers pumped out junk—small cars like the Chevy Vega and Pontiac Fiero; Chrysler's Omni and Horizon; and the Ford Pinto and Bobcat. The Pinto was Ford's rolling Molotov cocktail, catching fire and trapping occupants when hit from the rear. Ford knew of the danger before the first Pinto rolled off the assembly line but bowed to its accountants, who figured it would cost less to stonewall each future death and burn injury than to recall and redesign the fuel tank. They projected losses based upon 180 people burned to death and another 180 persons severely burned over the Pinto's life span. Their figures showed that it would cost $137 million to recall the cars already sold and $10 per car to modify each Pinto in production. But should Ford not fix the cars, its projected losses would be $200,000 for each burn death and $67,000 for each burn injury, for a total of $48.1 million. Ford executives concluded it would be more "cost effective" to let drivers and passengers burn.

Throughout the '80s, the quality of imports improved dramatically (Hyundai, Audi, and VW excepted), with Toyota and Honda leading the pack. American quality, on the other hand, improved at a snail's pace over the same period. Today, American cars' quality control is about where Japanese cars' was in the mid-'80s. Where the gap hasn't narrowed (and a case can be made that it's actually gotten wider) is in engine, automatic transmission, airbag, and anti-lock brake reliability and fit and finish.

For example, take a look at the following three confidential internal service bulletins depicting serious automatic transmission problems with Chrysler, Ford, and GM cars and trucks. Note how the Big Three domestic automakers have allowed the same defect to be carried over year after year.

Chrysler's "Limping" Transmissions

NO: 18-24-95
GROUP: Veh. Performance
DATE: Jun. 23, 1995
SUBJECT:
Improved Transmission Shift Quality

MODELS:
1989-1995	(AA) Acclaim/Sprit/LeBaron Sedan
1989-1993	(AC) Dynasty/New Yorker/New Yorker Salon
1990-1993	(AG) Daytona
1990-1994	(AJ) LeBaron Coupe/LeBaron Convertible
1993-1994	(AP) Sundance/Shadow/Shadow Convertible
1990-1991	(AQ) Chrysler TC
1989-1995	(AS) Caravan/Voyager/Town & Country
1990-1992	(AY) Imperial/New Yorker Fifth Avenue
1993-1995	(ES) Chrysler Voyager (European Market)
**1995	(FJ) Sebring/Avenger/Talon**
1995	(JA) Cirrus/Stratus
1993-1995	(LH) Concorde/Intrepid/Vision/LHS/New Yorker

NOTE: THIS BULLETIN APPLIES TO VEHICLES EQUIPPED WITH THE 41TE OR 42LE TRANSAXLE.

SYMPTOM/CONDITION:

1992 AC. & AY VEHICLES BUILT AFTER FEB. 15, 1992 (MDH 02-15-XX). **1995 FJ VEHICLES** AND ALL OTHER 1993-1995 SUBJECT VEHICLES BUILT BEFORE OCT. 24, 1994, (MDH 10-24-XX) ARE VEHICLES EQUIPPED WITH AN ELECTRONICALLY MODULATED CONVERTOR CLUTCH (EMCC).

Vehicles that operate at speeds where EMCC usage is engaged (vehicle speeds 34 – 41 MPH) may experience early deterioration of the transmission fluid (15,000 – 30,000 miles), exhibit a pronounced shudder during EMCC operation, harsh upshifts/downshifts, and/or harsh torque converter engagements. Performing REPAIR PROCEDURE # 2, which includes updates to the Transmission Control Module (TCM) calibration and eliminates EMCC, will resolve these symptoms/conditions. However, if an overheat condition is identified by the PCM or TCM, EMCC operation will be temporarily enabled.

ALL 1995 FJ VEHICLES AND ALL OTHER 1989-1995 SUBJECT VEHICLES BUILT BEFORE OCT. 24, 1994 (MDH 10-24-XX).

The TCM calibration used in the 1995 model year 41TE and 42LE TCM is being made available for all vehicles dating back to the 1989 model year. The shift quality improvements and default issues that will be corrected by the new TCM calibration are:

1. COASTDOWN TIP-IN BUMP: Vehicle is decelerated almost to a stop (less than 8 MPH), then the driver tips back into the throttle to accelerate, a noticeable bump may be felt.
2. COASTDOWN SHIFT HARSHNESS: Harsh coastdown shifts on some 4-3, 3-2, 2-1 downshifts.
3. 1995 LH WITH 42LE TRANSAXLE – SLUGGISHNESS/LACK OF RESPONSE: On some early 1995 LH vehicles built prior to Oct. 24, 1994, a perceived lack of power or transmission responsiveness may be encountered under normal operating conditions. The transmission may not release the converter clutch as desired with increased throttle. This occurs in 4th gear 35–50 MPH.
4. 1989-1994 WITH 41TE & 42LE TRANSAXLES: Harsh shifts and/or vehicle shudder during 3-2 or 2-1 kickdowns at speeds less than 25 MPH.
5. 1993 WITH 41TE TRANSAXLE: Harsh 3-4 upshifts may occur, especially at highway speeds, while using the speed control.
6. 1989-1994 WITH 41TE TRANSAXLE – HARSH/DELAYED GARAGE SHIFTS: Delay is less than 2 seconds and the shift is harsh after the brief delay. NOTE: Delays greater than 2 seconds are caused by transmission hardware malfunction, i.e., valve body, pump, failed lip seals, or malfunctioning PRNDL or neutral start switch.
7. 1989-1994 WITH 41TE & 42LE TRANSAXLES – POOR SHIFT QUALITY AFTER A BATTERY DISCONNECT: All transmission learned values are reset to the factory default values if battery power is lost to the TCM. The new 1995 calibration will now retain all learned values in memory after battery disconnect. However, if a transmission is rebuilt or a new transmission or TCM is installed, the Quick Learn procedure must be performed to calibrate Clutch Volume Indexes (CVI) on 1993 and later vehicles (1992 and prior vehicle cannot be Quick Learned).
    NOTE: BEFORE PERFORMING THE QUICK LEARN PROCEDURE, THE TRANSMISSION MUST BE SHIFTED INTO OVERDRIVE (OD) WITH THE ENGINE RUNNING AND THE TRANSMISSION FLUID SET TO THE CORRECT LEVEL. THIS PROCEDURE WILL PURGE THE AIR IN THE CLUTCH CIRCUITS TO PREVENT ERRONEOUS CLUTCH VOLUME VALUES WHICH COULD CAUSE POOR INITIAL SHIFT QUALITY.
8. EARLY 1993 WITH 41TE & 42LE TRANSAXLE – INTERMITTENT SPEED CONTROL DROP OUT: The new service calibration change corrects this condition (this condition was also covered in Technical Service Bulletin 08-09-93 dated Mar. 12, 1993).
9. 1989-1993 WITH 41TE & 42LE TRANSAXLES: New fault code 35 (failure to achieve pump prime) has been added for improved diagnostic capability, and fault codes 21, 22 and 24 are desensitized to reduce erroneous limp-in conditions.

Chrysler's problems are caused by both hardware and computer software glitches that affect almost its entire product line. Owners of 1991–97 vehicles should claim a "goodwill" repair refund from Chrysler. Hundreds of Chrysler claimants have received compensation up to 75 percent of the repair amount on vehicles not exceeding 100,000 miles when the transmission failed (see Part Two).

Ford's "Biodegradable" Aluminum Transmissions

SUBJECT: Forward Piston Change
APPLICATION: Ford
DATE: 1995
Forward Piston Change
• No forward or reverse engagement.
• Delayed forward and/or reverse engagement.
• Shifts out of gear when coming to a stop.

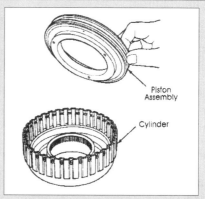

Piston Assembly

Cylinder

All of these complaints can be attributed to a cracked or broken forward piston clutch. There have been three different versions of the aluminum piston in this location (the original plus two updates). Problems with cracking still persist.
A steel version of this part has been released that should prevent this from happening.
The Ford part number is F4DZ-7A262-A. The aluminum piston should always be replaced with the steel piston.

Failures with Ford's aluminum forward piston clutch affect most of the company's products made since 1986, though complaints on the most recent models target mainly the Taurus, Sable, and Windstar.

GM's "Neutral" Transmissions

File In Section: 7 - Transmission
Bulletin No.: 67-71-64
Date: February, 1997
Subject:
Intermittent Neutral or Loss of Drive at Highway Speeds or from Fourth Gear
(Replace Control Valve Body Assembly)
Models:
1995–96 Buick Skylark Regal, Century, Park Avenue, Riviera, LeSabre
1997 Buick Skylark, Regal, Century, LeSabre
1995 Cadillac DeVille
1995–96 Chevrolet Beretta, Corsica, Lumina APV, Lumina, Monte Carlo 1997 Chevrolet Lumina, Monte Carlo, Venture
1995–96 Oldsmobile Cutlass Ciera, Cutlass Cruiser, LSS, Ninety Eight, Ninety Eight Regency, Eighty Eight, Achieva, Silhouette, Cutlass Supreme
1997 Oldsmobile Eighty Eight, Achieva, Cutlass Supreme, LSS, Silhouette
1995–97 Pontiac Bonneville, Grand Am, Trans Sport, Grand Prix with HYDRA-MATIC 4T60-E Transaxle (RPO M13)

How's this for a scary scenario: you're cruising down the highway or in city traffic and the transmission of your 1995–97 GM front-wheel-drive car or minivan drops into "neutral." Another traffic fatality blamed on driver's error?

Good buys are out there

If you are careful in your choice, this is an excellent year to buy a used car or minivan. Most vehicles are now equipped with many of the essential safety features that were ignored by automakers two decades ago;

overall reliability and durability have improved and are backed by longer warranties that are still in force; and millions of reasonably priced leased vehicles are now entering the used-car market. Right now, for example, Ford's popular and reliable Crown Victoria, Mercury Grand Marquis, and Lincoln Town Car are coming off two- and three-year leases and are in abundant supply from both dealers and private parties.

You can reduce your risk of buying a lemon by getting a recommended vehicle that has some of the original warranty in effect. Not only will this protect you from some of the costly defects that are bound to crop up shortly after your purchase, but the warranty allows you to make one final inspection before it expires and requires both the dealer and the automaker to compensate you for all warrantable defects found at that time. The ultimate irony is that because Chrysler dropped its seven-year warranty on its 1995 models, your used '93 Chrysler will be under warranty until the year 2000—surpassing the 1996 models' three-year guarantee.

Five Reasons to Buy Used

How popular are used vehicles in North America? Estimated private U.S. car sales in 1996 were 11.5 million vehicles valued at $50.2 billion, according to CNW Marketing Research. Why are people buying used? Mostly to save money, but there are other important reasons as well:

1. Less initial cash outlay, slower vehicle depreciation, and better and cheaper parts availability.
New-vehicle prices that hover around an average $18,000 payout are priced out of reach for many first-time purchasers. Insurance for young drivers runs about $4,000 a year—probably more than the monthly vehicle payment. And once you add financing costs, maintenance, taxes, and a host of other expenses, expect to shell out about $3,000–$5,000 annually in overall operating costs. Minivans are a bit cheaper to own and operate due to their slower rate of depreciation—the biggest expense for most vehicles.

Be practical. In buying a used car or minivan, keep in mind you're simply buying transportation and function: principally, no-surprise handling, a comfortable ride, reliable performance, and interior, cargo, and passenger capacity. Because you need only about one-half the cash or credit required for a new vehicle, it's easy to see that you won't have to invest as much money in a depreciating investment and may be fortunate enough to forgo a loan.

Depreciation savings
If someone were to ask you to invest in stocks or bonds guaranteed to be worth about half their initial purchase value after four or five years, you'd probably head for the door. But this is exactly the trap you're falling into when you buy a new vehicle that could depreciate 20 percent in the first year and 15 percent each year thereafter (minivans and

other specialty vehicles like trucks and sport-utilities depreciate about 10 percent each subsequent year). Here's how a new car adds up:

New-Car Cost

Purchase price	$20,000
Sales tax (5%)	$1,000
Total price	**$21,000**

Now, the motorist buying a new vehicle is certain that the warranty and status far outweigh any inconvenience. He or she forks over $21,000 and takes possession of a new car or minivan. If he or she had a trade-in, its value would be subtracted from the negotiated price of the new vehicle and sales tax would be paid on the reduced amount.

When you buy used, the situation is altogether different. That same vehicle can be purchased three years later, in good condition and with much of the manufacturer's warranty remaining, for about one-half of its original cost (in the red-hot truck and sport-utility market, depreciation may be much less). Look at what happens to the price:

Used-Car Cost

Purchase price (3 years old, 60,000 miles)	$10,000
Sales tax (5%)	$500
Total price	**$10,500**

In this conservative example (some savings exceed 50 percent), the used-vehicle buyer saves $500 in sales tax and gets a reliable, guaranteed set of wheels for about one-half of the vehicle's original price. Furthermore, the depreciation "hit" will be much less in the ensuing years.

Parts
A new 1999 Ford Taurus SE equipped with typical options would cost about $25,000. Rebuilding it with factory parts would cost over $72,000. No wonder insurance companies prefer to scrap rather than repair.

Generally, a new gasoline-powered vehicle can be expected to run at least 125,000 miles to 200,000 miles in its lifetime; a diesel-powered vehicle can easily triple those figures. Some repairs will crop up at regular intervals and, along with preventive maintenance, your yearly running costs should average about $500. Buttressing the argument that vehicles get cheaper to operate the longer you keep them, the U.S. Department of Transportation points out that the average vehicle requires one or more major repairs after every five years of use. However, once these repairs are done, it can then be run relatively trouble-free for another five years or more.

Time is on your side in other ways, too. Three years after a model's launching, the replacement-parts market catches up to consumer demand, due to dealers stocking larger inventories and parts wholesalers and independent parts manufacturers expanding their output. Used replacement parts are unquestionably easier to come by, through bargaining with local garages or through a careful search of auto wreckers' yards. A reconditioned or used part usually costs one-third to one-half the cost of a new part. There's generally no difference in the quality of reconditioned mechanical components, and they're often guaranteed for as long as new ones. Also, buying from discount outlets or independent garages or ordering through mail order houses can save you big bucks (30–35 percent) on the cost of new parts and another 15 percent on labor when compared with dealer charges.

Body parts are a different story, however. Buyers would be wise to buy only original equipment manufacturer (OEM) parts supplied by automakers in order to get body panels that fit well, protect better in collisions, and have maximum rust-resistance, says *Consumer Reports* in its February 1999 study. Although insurance appraisers often substitute cheaper, lower-quality aftermarket body parts in collision repairs, *Consumer Reports* found that 71 percent of those policyholders who requested OEM parts got them with little or no hassle. It suggests consumers should complain to state insurance regulators if OEM parts aren't provided. If that doesn't produce the desired results, take out a small claims action or file a class action similar to the one recently filed and won in the state of Illinois against State Farm (see page 119).

There are generally no problems with parts distribution for American vehicles, unless a particular unit has been off the market for some time or a specific component has experienced a high failure rate (such as electronic control units that regulate engine, transmission, and braking performance). In these cases, though, there are many independent suppliers who can find the missing parts and price them far below dealer cost. Components can also be more easily interchanged on American and Japanese vehicles than on European models.

With some European models, you can count on a lot of aggravation and expense caused by the unacceptably slow distribution of parts and the high markup. Because these companies have a quasi-monopoly on replacement parts, there are few independent suppliers you can turn to for help. And auto wreckers, the last-chance repository for inexpensive car parts, are unlikely to carry foreign parts for vehicles more than three years old or manufactured in small numbers.

Finding parts for Japanese and domestic cars is hardly a problem, though, due to the large number of vehicles produced, the presence of hundreds of independent suppliers, the ease with which relatively simple parts can be interchanged from one model to another, and the large reservoir of used parts stocked by junkyards. Incidentally, when a part is hard to find, the *Mitchell Manual* is a useful guide to substituting parts that can be used for many different models. It's available in some libraries, most auto parts stores, and practically all junkyards.

Auto clubs listed on the Internet are often helpful sources for parts that are otherwise unobtainable. Club members trade and sell specialty parts, keep a list of where rare parts can be found, and are usually well informed as to where independent parts suppliers are located. Most car enthusiast magazines will put you in touch with auto clubs and suppliers of hard-to-find parts.

2. There are lower insurance rates.
The difference in annual insurance costs between a new car or minivan and a used one may be only a few hundred dollars, but by carefully negotiating the deductible, the smart shopper can further reduce insurance premiums by another couple hundred dollars. For example, as an automobile gets older, the amount of the deductible should increase. It may reach a maximum of $500–$1,000 per collision. As the deductible increases, the annual premium for collision coverage decreases.

By agreeing to a higher deductible, the motorist agrees to repair the vehicle for all damages where costs do not exceed the deductible. Generally, purchasing used parts (remember, you bought a used vehicle) from a local auto wrecker and having the work done by small, specialized garages keeps repair costs down. What may have been an estimated loss of $500 may be significantly reduced by sharp repair bargaining.

3. There are fewer "hidden" defects.
Have your choice checked out by an independent mechanic (for $50–$75) before paying for a used vehicle. This examination before purchase protects you against any hidden defects the vehicle may have. It's also a tremendous negotiating tool, since it allows you to use the cost of any needed repairs to bargain down the purchase price.

It's easier to get permission to have the vehicle inspected if you promise to give the seller a copy of the inspection report should you decide not to buy it. If you still can't get permission to have the vehicle inspected elsewhere, walk away from the deal, no matter how tempting the selling price. The seller is obviously trying to put something over on you. Ignore the standard excuses that the vehicle isn't insured, the license plates have expired, or the vehicle has a dead battery.

4. You know the vehicle's history.
Smart customers will want to get answers to the following questions before paying a cent for any used vehicle: What did it first sell for and what is its present value? How much of the original warranty is left? How many times has the vehicle been recalled for safety-related defects? Are parts easily available? Does the vehicle have a history of costly performance-related defects that can be corrected under a secret warranty, through a safety recall campaign, or with an upgraded part? (See Part Three, "Secret Warranties/Service Tips.")

5. Litigation is quick, easy, and relatively inexpensive.
A multitude of federal and state consumer protection laws go far beyond
whatever protection may be offered by the standard new-vehicle warranty. Furthermore, buyers of used vehicles don't usually have to conform to any arbitrary rules or service guidelines to get this protection.

Let's say you do get stuck with a lemon. Most small claims courts have
a jurisdiction limit of $3,000–$10,000, which should cover the cost of most
used cars or minivans. Therefore, any dispute between buyer and seller
can be settled within a few months, without lawyers or excessive court
costs. Furthermore, you're not likely to face a battery of lawyers standing
in for the automaker and dealer. Actually, you may not have to face a
judge since many cases are settled through court-imposed mediators.

Safety Features

Before buying any used "bargain," determine what degree of active and
passive safety the vehicle provides. Passive safety assumes that you will
be involved in life-threatening situations and should be warned in time
to avoid injury. Daytime running lights and a third, center-mounted
brake light are two passive safety features that do this job extremely
well. In fact, the National Highway Traffic Safety Administration
(NHTSA), an arm of the U.S. Department of Transportation, estimates
that center brake lights—a required safety feature in Canada and the
U.S. since 1986—reduce the number of rear-impact crashes by 4.3 percent, thereby preventing 92,000 crashes, 58,000 injuries, and $655 mil-
lion in property damage annually. The annual cost to the consumer of
the center brake lamp is about $13.60 a car and about $20 for vans,
pickups, and sport-utilities.

Passive safety features also assume some accidents aren't avoidable and
that when that accident occurs, the vehicle should provide as much protection as possible to the driver, the vehicle's other occupants, and other
vehicles that may be struck—without depending on the driver's reactions.
Passive safety components that have consistently proven to reduce vehicular deaths and injuries are safety belts and vehicle structures that absorb
or deflect crash forces away from the vehicle's occupants.

Advocates of active safety stress that accidents are caused by the
proverbial "nut behind the wheel" and believe that safe driving can best
be taught through schools or by private driving courses. Active safety
components are generally those mechanical systems that may help
avoid accidents, such as high-performance tires and traction control, if
the driver is skillful and mature.

The theory of active safety has several drawbacks. First, there's no
independent proof that safe driving can be taught successfully. Even if
a young driver learns how to master defensive-driving techniques,
there's still no assurance that this training will be of any use in an emergency. Second, 40–50 percent of all fatal accidents are caused by drivers who are under the influence of alcohol or drugs. Surely all the
high-performance options and specialized driving courses in the world

will not provide much protection from impaired drivers who take a bead on your vehicle. Finally, because active safety components get a lot of use—you're likely to need anti-lock brakes 99 times more often than an airbag—they have to be well maintained to remain effective.

Some safety features may kill

In the late '60s, Washington forced automakers to include essential safety features like collapsing steering columns and safety windshields in their cars. As the years have passed, the number of mandatory safety features has increased to include seatbelts, airbags, and crashworthy construction. These improvements met with public approval until four years ago, when reports of deaths and injuries caused by ABS and airbag failures showed that defective components and poor engineering negated the potential life-saving benefits associated with these devices.

For example, one out of every five ongoing NHTSA investigations into possible defects in cars and light trucks concerns inadvertent airbag deployment, failure of the airbag to deploy, or injuries suffered when the bag did go off. In fact, airbags are the agency's single largest cause of current investigations, exceeding even the full range of brake problems, which runs second.

Anti-lock brake system (ABS)

Essentially, ABS prevents a vehicle's wheels from locking when the brakes are applied in an emergency situation, thus reducing skidding and the loss of directional control. When braking on wet and dry roads, your stopping distance will be about the same as with conventional braking systems. But in gravel, slush, or snow, your stopping distance will be greater.

A particularly important feature of ABS is that it preserves steering control. As you brake in an emergency, ABS will release the brakes if it senses wheel lockup. Braking distances will lengthen accordingly, but at least you'll have some steering control. On the other hand, if you start sliding on glare ice don't expect ABS to help you out very much. The laws of physics, particularly the coefficient of friction, still apply on ABS-equipped vehicles. You can decrease your stopping distance, however, by installing four snow tires that are the same make and size.

Anti-lock brakes are impressive on the test track but not on the road. In fact, the Insurance Institute for Highway Safety (IIHS) says that cars with anti-lock brakes are more likely to be in crashes where no other car is involved but a passenger is killed. Insurance claim statistics show that anti-lock brakes aren't producing the overall safety benefits that were predicted by the government and automakers. The latest IIHS study found that a passenger has a 45 percent greater chance of dying in a single-vehicle crash in a car with anti-lock brakes than in the same car with old-style brakes. On wet pavement, where ABS supposedly excels, the chance of being killed increases to 65 percent. In multi-vehicle crashes, ABS-equipped vehicles have a passenger death rate 6 percent higher than vehicles not equipped with ABS.

The high cost of ABS maintenance is one disadvantage that few safety advocates mention, but consider the following: 1) original parts can cost five times more than regular braking components, and 2) many dealers prefer to replace the entire ABS unit rather than troubleshoot what is a very complex system.

Keep in mind that anti-lock brakes are notoriously unreliable. They often fail completely, resulting in no braking whatsoever, or they may extend stopping distance by 30 percent. While General Motors continued to blame drivers for ABS brake failures, *AutoWeek* magazine reported three years ago that NHTSA knew GM had secretly bought back hundreds of vehicles equipped with failure-prone Kelsey-Hayes anti-lock brakes the automaker couldn't fix. Interestingly, GM ditched the Kelsey brakes and began using Lucas-Varity designed systems, which soon developed problems. (Remember Lucas? It was dubbed the "Prince of Darkness" by the British motoring press when the company supplied electrical components to the British auto industry). Presently, GM is shopping for other suppliers.

General buyback. While publicly blaming drivers for problems with the antilock braking systems on millions of pickup trucks and sport/utility vehicles, General Motors was quietly buying some trucks back from consumers whose dealers could not repair the systems, according to documents filed with the National Highway Traffic Safety Administration.

NHTSA has been investigating ABS defects on 1991-94 Chevy Blazer, GMC Jimmy and Typhoon, and Olds Bravada sport/utes, as well as on Chevy S-10 and GMC Sonoma and Syclone pickups for three years. The agency has received more than 15,000 consumer complaints. In late 1995, NHTSA added 1992-94 Chevy/GMC Suburbans to the probe. In dozens of cases, when owners threatened to contact attorneys or file lemon law claims, GM either bought vehicles back or offered vehicle trade-in assistance to get customers into new vehicles.

Fed up with GM's mendacity and secret buybacks after a five-year investigation, NHTSA this past July forced the automaker to recall 3.5 million 1991–96 sport-utilities, vans, and pickups.

Car Guide 2000 15

GM Offers to Repair 3.5 Million Vehicles

Recall Over Brake Defects In Pickup Trucks, SUVs Paired With Lesser Fix

By ANNA WILDE MATHEWS
And JEFFREY BALL
Staff Reporters of THE WALL STREET JOURNAL

General Motors Corp. said it will offer free repairs for 3.5 million light trucks, vans and sport-utility vehicles because of potential problems with their anti-lock brakes.

The action ends one of the federal government's biggest safety-defect investigations. The vehicles sometimes didn't come to a stop as fast as drivers expected.

GM will recall 1.1 million GMC and Chevrolet four-wheel-drive pickup trucks and SUVs, model years 1991 through 1996, to fix a safety defect. It also will offer free repairs on 2.4 million vehicles from the model years 1992 through 1996, including certain two-wheel-drive Chevrolet Blazer and GMC Jimmy sport utilities, Chevrolet S-10 and GMC Sonoma pickup trucks, and Chevrolet Astro vans, GMC Safari vans and G-vans.

A safety defect is generally considered a more serious problem that can lead to accidents, while service issues like the one involving the 2.4 million vehicles are of less concern to regulators.

The four-wheel-drive trucks and SUVs contain a safety defect in a brake-sensor switch that could increase the vehicles'

Fixing the Brakes
GM agrees to provide free repairs for 3.5 million vehicles.

	Model years 1991-1996		Model years 1992-1996
Number	1.1 million	**Number**	2.4 million
Models	Chevrolet S-10 and GMC Sonoma model four-wheel drive pickups and sport utility vehicles.	**Models**	Chevrolet Blazer and GMC Jimmy sport utilities; 1994-1996 Chevrolet S10 and GMC Sonoma pickup trucks; 1992-1995 Chevrolet Astro vans and GMC Safaris; 1993-1996 G-vans.
Problem	The anti-lock braking system may mistake two-wheel drive operation for four-wheel drive operation, a problem that could extend stopping distances.	**Problem**	Vehicles can experience extended stopping distances when they are traveling over more than one surface with different textures and levels of slickness.
Fix	GM will replace or fix a switch that signals to the braking system whether the vehicle is in 4-wheel or 2-wheel mode.	**Fix**	GM will reprogram software controlling the antilock brake system.

Sources: National Highway Traffic Safety Administration, GM

dent of Union Park Pontiac GMC in Wilmington, Del., and a member of a national committee of GM dealers, estimated that the safety-recall repair might cost less than $50 per vehicle.

In New York Stock Exchange composite trading, GM shares closed unchanged at $66.50. John Casesa, an analyst at Merrill Lynch, said that even such large recalls rarely affect an auto maker's stock price, because manufacturers generally have set aside enough reserve funds to cover the costs.

Still, the recall could be a public-relations blow for the company at a time when

plaints pouring in from consumers. Overall, the agency said, it received 10,861 complaints about the brakes on the pickups and smaller SUVs, and unconfirmed reports of 2,111 crashes and 293 injuries related to brake problems.

The agency got another 2,400 reports of brake problems on GM Suburbans. The investigation of Suburbans from model years 1992 through 1994 was not closed, but GM told the agency it would "develop field action that would address customer satisfaction issues."

The problems with the trucks, vans and SUVs are highly technical. The four-wheel-

This massive recall addresses only the extended stopping distance complaint up to 1996; the allegations on complete loss of braking haven't been addressed. Additionally, Suburbans and later-model GM vehicles are still "under investigation" along with other automakers' vehicles. Nevertheless, ABS failures remain one of the top safety problems for 1997–99 models, according to NHTSA's complaints database.

Airbags

Well-publicized American and Canadian safety studies show convincingly that airbags save lives in high-speed collisions, but equally thorough, though little-publicized, government and university studies show that airbags can maim or kill through inadvertent deployment (1 chance in 30) or in collisions at speeds as low as 7 mph.

The chance of injury increases if you are a woman, are a senior, are not of average size, have had upper torso surgery, or use a tilt steering wheel. In fact, the dangers are so great that a 1996 Transport Canada and George Washington University study of 445 drivers and passengers concluded:

While the initial findings of this study confirm that belted drivers are afforded added protection against head and facial injury in moderate to severe frontal collisions, the findings also suggest that these benefits are being negated by a high incidence of bag-induced injury. The incidence of bag-induced injury was greatest among female drivers. Furthermore, the intervention of the air bag can be expected to introduce a variety of new injury mechanisms such as facial injuries from "bag slap," upper extremity fractures, either directly from the deploying air bag module or from arm flailing, and thermal burns to the face and arms.

A frightening admission. The above study can be found in its entirety on NHTSA's website at www.nhtsa.dot.gov/esv/16/98S5OO7.PDF. *Incidentally, GM now claims competitors' side airbags on '99 and year 2000 models are equally hazardous to children.*

Federal legislation makes it a crime to disable an airbag without government permission, and automakers won't sell you a shut-off switch without NHTSA approval. To get that approval (a three- to eight-week process), owners have to show that they meet the following criteria:
• they are unable to sit at least 10 inches away from the airbag housing;
• they have a medical condition that would put them at risk (such as osteoporosis);
• they have a rear-facing child safety seat that must be used in the front passenger seat;
• they must routinely place children in the front seat (as with car pools).

Adding insult to potential injury, cut-off switches are estimated to cost $200–$300 (an Alabama class action lawsuit winding its way through the courts says automakers should pay for the switch installation) and won't be installed by most independent garages. In the meantime, don't be surprised to find dealers reluctant to touch the devices until they get clear instruction from automakers and insurers. In fact, the American Automobile Association (AAA) estimates that 84 percent of the repair facilities it has surveyed won't install cut-off switches. NHTSA's website (*www.nhtsa.dot.gov*) has an extensive listing of garages/dealers willing to install switches in the United States.

As I fit together all the recent accident reports and emergency-room studies it became obvious to me that for over two decades engineers, automakers, and government bureaucrats have lied to us about airbag dangers. Instead of the promised billowing protective cloud that would gently cushion us in an accident, we discover that the airbag's 200 mph deployment is more like a Mike Tyson right cross. Front airbags have killed 131 people in low-speed collisions or otherwise survivable accidents since 1990. Many of these deaths came from accidents with speeds as slow as 7 or 8 mph, and three-quarters of the adults killed were women. Seven of the first 28 recorded deaths involved 1994–96 Chrysler minivans.

Sexist federal regulations governing automobile airbag design are the main reason why the safety devices put women, children, and the aged at risk. The auto industry and government engineers have set federal regulations that aim to protect the average-sized unbelted adult male in a 35 mph frontal crash. Meeting that rule requires that the airbag inflate with sufficient force to kill or seriously injure women, children, and seniors who don't fit the engineering norm.

A campaign of misinformation

The safety establishment, composed of government, automakers, and safety advocates, hasn't leveled with the public about airbag dangers inherent in the 60 million airbag-equipped vehicles on North American highways. For example, their admonition that children under the age of 13 should sit in the rear is nonsense, since it's a question of size, not age (a small 18-year-old could be more vulnerable). Actually, no one who is of small stature, child or adult, should sit behind an airbag. The government also has yet to explain why airbags are of little benefit to seniors 70 and older, and why there have been 25,000+ injuries from airbag deployment between 1988 and 1991, according to NHTSA. There have also been thousands of incidences of airbag malfunctions, causing late deployment or inadvertent deployment, reported to American federal safety regulators; these led to the recall of over two million vehicles (1 out of every 38 on the road) since 1993. If the five ongoing investigations also result in recalls, 1 out of 30 vehicles will be affected.

Most importantly, we have to stop blaming the victims of airbag deployment for sitting too close, not buckling up, or allowing their children to ride in the front seat. The above-cited Canadian/American airbag study clearly demonstrates that most of the belted drivers and passengers who were injured did nothing to put themselves at risk, except, perhaps, having the wrong gender and a federal Department of Transportation that passed regulations without fully researching their deadly consequences.

Federal regulators' efforts to explain away airbag hazards have been a deliberate policy decision; they didn't want to lose their own credibility, alarm the public, or undermine the acceptance of airbags as a supplementary restraint. Well, guess what? The public is more than alarmed; it's clamoring for retrofitted cut-off switches and looking for new vehicles in which airbags aren't a standard feature. In fact, recent surveys show that the public's confidence in airbags has plummeted following the spate of news stories reporting airbag-induced deaths and injuries.

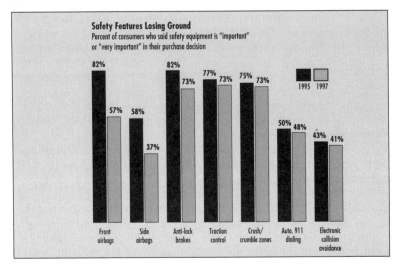

Safety Features Losing Ground
Percent of consumers who said safety equipment is "important" or "very important" in their purchase decision

Inadvertent airbag deployment

Airbags frequently go off for no apparent reason due to what Ralph Hoar, an Arlington, Virginia, safety adviser to plaintiffs' attorneys, blames on cheap sensors. Causes of sudden deployment include: passing over a bump in the road in your GM Cavalier or Sunfire, slamming the car door, having wet carpets in your Cadillac (no kidding), or, in some Chrysler minivans, simply putting the key in the ignition. This happens more often than you might imagine, judging by the frequent recalls and thousands of complaints recorded on NHTSA's website (*www.nhtsa.dot.gov/cars/problems/complain/compmmy1.cfm*). Incidentally, insurers are refusing to pay for damage to the car or for airbag replacements unless there has been a collision. Meanwhile, automakers deny responsibility on the grounds that the vehicle collided with something. In the end, the driver is faced with a hefty repair bill and no means of proving the automaker's liability.

Airbag deployment for no apparent reason is bad enough if the vehicle is parked; however, if the airbag explodes while the vehicle is being driven, it will likely cause an accident and then be of no use during the ensuing impact because it has already deflated. Says Michael Leshner, a U.S. forensic engineer, "The airbag knocks them silly—*then* they have an accident."

Side airbags

Side airbags protect drivers and passengers in side-impact crashes, which account for an estimated 30 percent of vehicular deaths. About three-quarters of automakers offer side airbags on some of their models.

NHTSA is concerned that rear side airbag systems offered by Audi, BMW, and Mercedes may be too powerful for rear seat occupants, notably children, who must sit there to escape the deployment dangers of front-seat airbags. Following these findings, BMW has turned off the rear airbags prior to delivery, although it offers owners the option of having them reconnected by the dealer. Side airbags aren't required by federal regulation in the States or in Canada and neither government has developed any tests to measure their safety to children and adults of smaller stature.

There's also the problem of inadvertent deployment of side airbags. The NHTSA has just launched an investigation of 1998–99 Cadillac DeVille side airbags following reports of injuries to three people when the airbags suddenly deployed for no apparent reason. This is all the more ironic since GM has branded as "unsafe" side airbags made by its rivals.

Protect yourself
You should take the following steps to lessen the danger from airbag deployment:
• don't buy a vehicle with side airbags until the federal government comes up with standards;
• make sure that seatbelts are buckled and all head restraints are properly adjusted (about ear level);
• make sure the head restraints are rated Good by IIHS;
• insist that passengers who are frail, short, or have recently had surgery sit in the back;
• make sure that the driver's seat can be adjusted for height and has tracks with sufficient rearward travel to allow short drivers to remain a safe distance away from the bag's deployment (about 10 inches) and still reach the accelerator and brake (buy pedal extensions, if needed);
• have a retrofitted cut-off switch installed by a dealer for your make of vehicle;
• buy a vehicle that comes with passenger-side airbag disablers;
• buy a vehicle that uses sensors to detect the presence of an electronically tagged child safety seat in the passenger seat and disables the airbag for that seat (already used in the Mercedes SLK);
• if you are short-statured, consider the purchase of aftermarket pedal extensions from auto parts retailers or optional adjustable accelerator and brake pedals to keep you a safe distance away from a deploying airbag.

Crashworthiness
The most important safety features are those that reduce the risk of death or serious injury when a crash occurs. This aspect of vehicle design is referred to as crashworthiness. Purchasing a used vehicle with the idea that you'll be involved in an accident is not unreasonable—according to the Insurance Institute for Highway Safety (IIHS), the average car will likely have two accidents before ending up as scrap.

The vehicle's structural design is the starting point for protecting you during a serious crash. A good structural design should have a strong occupant compartment, or safety cage, and "crush zones"—

front and rear ends designed to buckle and bend to absorb crash forces during serious crashes. It's important for these crush zones to keep damage away from the safety cage because the likelihood of injury increases rapidly once this cage begins to collapse. If effectively designed, a longer crush zone lowers both the likelihood of damage to the occupant compartment and the crash forces inside it.

Not all vehicles are equally well designed. Some have crush zones that are too stiff and/or too short and safety cages that aren't strong enough. Such poorly designed crush zones can contribute to the collapse of the occupant compartment in serious crashes. Crash tests demonstrate differences in structural design among vehicles in the same weight class.

Two Washington-based agencies monitor how vehicle design affects crash safety. They are the U.S. National Highway Traffic Safety Administration (NHTSA) and the Insurance Institute for Highway Safety (IIHS), an insurance research group that collects and analyzes insurance claims data. Crash information from these two groups doesn't always agree because, while the insurance research group's results incorporate all kinds of accidents, the NHTSA figures relate only to 35 mph frontal and some side collisions. The frontal tests are equivalent to two vehicles of equal weight hitting each other head-on while traveling at 35 mph or to a car slamming into a parked car at 70 mph. Bear in mind that a car providing good injury protection often produces the highest damage claims because its structure, not the occupants, absorbs most of the force of the collision.

Large vs. small
Occupants of large vehicles have fewer severe injury claims than do occupants of small vehicles. This was proven conclusively in a 1996 NHTSA study that showed collisions between light trucks or vans with small cars resulted in an 81 percent higher fatality rate for the occupants of the small cars than occupants in light trucks or vans.

Vehicle weight protects you, principally, in two-vehicle crashes. In a head-on crash, for example, the heavier vehicle drives the lighter one backwards, which decreases forces inside the heavy vehicle and increases forces in the lighter one. All heavy vehicles, even poorly designed ones, offer this advantage in two-vehicle collisions but may not offer good protection in single-vehicle crashes.

IIHS figures show that for every thousand pounds added to a vehicle's mass, driver injury risk is lowered by 34 percent for the unrestrained driver and 25 percent for the restrained driver. GM's recent two-car crash tests dramatically confirm this fact. Its engineers concluded that if two cars collide, and one weighs half as much as the other, the driver in the lighter car is 10 times as likely to be killed as is the driver in the heavier one, no matter how many crash stars the smaller car was awarded in government crash tests.

Interestingly, a vehicle's size doesn't *always* guarantee that you won't be injured in an accident. U.S. government crash tests show, for example, that a 1991 Ford Escort small car gives better full-front collision protection than a 1994 Mercury Villager or Nissan Quest, two large minivans that could have been easily engineered to crash safely at moderate speeds of 35 mph. Some small vehicles are designed better than larger ones to absorb crash forces. VW's New Beetle is a good example. So far, it's the only small car to win a good crash rating from IIHS, while a handful of sport-utilities and even some Cadillacs rate poorly at protecting their occupants. Also, different years of the same model or size variation can produce startlingly different scores. For example, Chrysler's 1995 Caravan and Voyager minivans earned better driver crash protection scores than did the 1996 and 1997 Grand Caravan and Grand Voyager.

There are some factors that can skew crash scores, such as size, height, and frame rail placement. If your Ford Taurus (five-star rating) is clobbered by a Dodge Durango 4X4 (two stars), chances are you'll still fare much worse than the sport-utility's occupants simply because their car is so much heavier and will likely ride over the Taurus's protective frame. Other factors: whether or not occupants are wearing seatbelts and airbag and head restraint design.

Unsafe designs

Although it sounds hard to believe, automakers will deliberately manufacture a vehicle that will kill or maim simply because in the long run it costs less to pay off victims than to make a safer vehicle. I learned this lesson after reading the court transcripts of *Grimshaw v. Ford* and listening to court testimony of GM engineers who deliberately placed fire-prone "side-saddle" gas tanks in millions of pickups to save $3 per vehicle.

More recent examples of corporate greed triumphing over public safety: airbag designs that maim or kill women, children, and seniors; anti-lock brake systems that don't brake (a major problem with GM minivans, trucks, and sport-utilities, and Chrysler sport-utilities and minivans); flimsy front seats; the absence of rear head restraints; and fire-prone GM pickup fuel tanks and Ford ignition switches. All are examples of hazardous engineering designs that put profit ahead of safety. Incidentally, State Farm Insurance has filed a lawsuit against Ford to recoup the millions of dollars in claims it paid out for fire damage caused by Ford's fire-prone ignition switches.

Top 15 safety defects reported by owners

The federal government's on-line safety complaints database contains well over a hundred thousand entries, going back to vehicles made in the late '70s. Although originally intended to record incidents of component failures that only relate to safety, you will find every problem imaginable recorded by dutiful clerks working for NHTSA.

A perusal of the listed complaints shows that some safety-related failures occur more frequently than others and often affect one manufacturer more than another. Here is a summary of some of the more commonly reported failures in order of frequency:

1. airbags not deploying when they should; deploying when they shouldn't
2. ABS total brake failure; wheel lockup
3. sudden acceleration
4. sudden stalling
5. sudden electrical failure
6. transmission fails to engage or suddenly disengages
7. transmission jumps from Park to Reverse or Neutral; vehicle rolls away when parked
8. steering or suspension failure
9. seatbelt failures
10. collapsing seatbacks
11. defective sliding door, door locks, and latches
12. poor headlight illumination
13. dash reflects into windshield
14. hood flies up
15. tire falls away; steering wheel lifts off; transmission lever pulls out

Recalls
Vehicles are recalled for one of two reasons: they may be unsafe or they may not conform to federal and state pollution control regulations. Whatever the reason, though, recalls are a great way to get free repairs—if you know which ones apply to you.

On average, about 800,000 motor vehicles are recalled each year because of safety problems. More than 200 million unsafe vehicles have been recalled by automakers for the free correction of safety-related defects since American recall legislation was passed in 1966. During that time, about one-third of the recalled vehicles never made it back to the dealership for repairs. Auto Service Monitor, a firm that tracks recalls, estimates this means there are close to 20 million vehicles, still on North American roads, that could suddenly careen out of control, catch fire, or fail to brake. Surprisingly, motorists aren't generally motivated to bring in their recalled vehicles—even when the result of the defect is as life-threatening as fire. For example, NHTSA figures show that Ford's recall of 1.4 million Pintos and Bobcats in the late '70s to correct the much-publicized exploding gas tank defect received a response rate of just 52 percent. According to NHTSA, the average completion rate is 68 percent. This lack of public concern can be blamed partly on apathy, but automakers must also bear much of the blame because they downplay the defect's safety implications (see "Safety summary/Recalls" for the Chrysler Caravan in Part Three) and send out only one recall letter to the first recorded owner of the vehicle. If the owner has moved or leased the vehicle, or is not the first owner of record, he or she likely won't be notified.

Choosing the Right Seller

When to buy
Used-car sales are seasonal, depending where you live. In the northern and western states, fewer used vehicles are sold in the winter months of December through March than in the spring or summer. Dealers see few customers, and used vehicles generally show their worst characteristics: they won't start, have defective heating and defrosting systems, reveal poor suspensions, etc. On the other hand, in fall and spring, dealer stocks of good quality trade-ins and off-lease returns are at their highest level and private sellers are more active. It's precisely for these reasons that smart consumers shop during these months for real bargains.

Should you use a broker?
My answer is a qualified yes. Even with my 30 years' experience as a consumer advocate and automotive expert, I have used brokers and found them to be well worth the money spent for their services when I considered the runaround time they saved me.

Brokers are independent agents who try to find the new or used vehicle you want at a price below what you'd pay at a dealership (including the extra cost of the broker's services). Broker services appeal to buyers who want to save time and money while avoiding most of the stress and hassle associated with the dealership experience, which for many people is like a swim in shark-infested waters.

According to *Automotive News*, automobile brokers represent only about 5 percent of new- and used-car transactions even though their numbers have grown perceptibly in the past few years. Because their services aren't effectively regulated throughout the country, it's difficult to determine how many brokers are operating in any one area.

Brokers get new vehicles through only dealers, while used vehicles may come from dealers, auctions, private sellers, and leasing companies. Basically, a broker finds an appropriate vehicle that meets the client's expressed needs and then negotiates the purchase (or lease) on behalf of the client. The majority of brokers tend to deal exclusively in new cars, trucks, or vans, with a small percentage dealing in both new and used vehicles. Ancillary services vary among brokers and may include such things as comparative vehicle analysis, price research, and battling dealers and insurance adjusters to ensure their clients are treated fairly.

The cost of hiring a broker ranges anywhere from a flat fee of a few hundred dollars to a percentage of the value of the vehicle. Sometimes a broker may offer his services for a nominal fee, or even tell the buyer that the service is free. In such cases, it's best to remember that nothing is free in the auto business. If the customer isn't paying the fee directly, then the broker's fee is being paid by the dealer, who simply buries that commission in the total price of the vehicle. Ultimately, the customer pays, either way. While it's not impossible to get a reasonable deal under such an arrangement, beware: the broker may be unduly biased towards a certain dealer or manufacturer. Reputable brokers are not beholden to any particular dealership or make and will disclose their flat fee up front or tell the buyer the percentage amount they charge on a specific vehicle.

Finding the right broker
Buyers who are looking for a broker should first ask friends and acquaintances if they can recommend one. Word-of-mouth referrals are often the best, because people won't refer others to a dissatisfying service provider. If a referral isn't an option, try a broker that's used by your local AAA, Costco, or Price Club store. This will give you some important leverage if you aren't treated fairly.

Obviously, buyers should use a broker they trust, but trust must be earned. Ask about the benefits of the buying service above and beyond the usual "locate and negotiate." Does the broker have industry experience? Is the broker well informed? Impartial? Sympathetic to your needs? The broker should provide full disclosure of all charges related to the service at the time of your first interview. If the broker seems vague or evasive on this point, you should probably choose someone else.

Private sellers
Private sellers are your best source for a cheap and reliable used vehicle, because you're on an equal bargaining level with a vendor who isn't trying to profit from your inexperience. This translates into a golden opportunity to negotiate a fair price, which isn't common in many dealer transactions.

Apart from newspaper classified ads, you can track down good private deals and get a good idea of prices through the following:
• word of mouth;
• grocery store bulletin boards;
• specialty publications (e.g., *Auto Trader, Auto Mart,* or *Buy and Sell Bargain Hunter)*;
• the *NADA Official Used Car Guide,* the *Kelley Blue Book,* and *Edmund's Price Guide:* these are three of the most popular guides used throughout the States, offering comprehensive ratings and prices. They are sold at newsstands and bookstores for less than $10, are available from the reference section of your local library, and can be consulted, gratis, through the Internet: *Kelley Blue Book* at *www.kbb.com* and *Edmund's* at *www.edmunds.com.*

The best way to determine the price range for a particular model is to read the publications or surf the websites listed above before you buy the vehicle. This will give you a reasonably good idea of the top asking price. Remember, nobody expects to get his or her asking price, be it a dealer or private party. A 10–20 percent reduction from the advertised price is common. The fact is that these values are very volatile and no one source can be considered completely accurate. For example, I find the *Kelley Blue Book*'s prices more accurate than the other two guides and I especially like its listing of the MSRP (Manufacturer's Suggested Retail Price) for each model year going back to 1983. *Edmund's,* on the other hand, only goes back 10 years; it gives vehicles the lowest values, but does include a short summary of what was new each year, in addition to a bar graph rating safety, reliability, performance, and comfort. The *NADA* guide is sanctioned by the National Automobile Dealers Association, covers 10 years, and lists values comparable to those in *Kelley*.

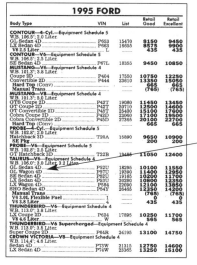

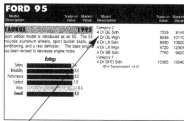

Imagine, Kelley *says your* '95 Taurus GL *is worth between* $10,100 *and* $11,550 *but* Edmund's *says don't pay a cent more than* $9,145. My suggestion: use Kelley *if you're selling, and* Edmund's *if you're buying.*

Don't be surprised to find that many national price guides have a northeastern bias that often results in unrealistically low price quotes for buyers in the southern and western states or residents in rural areas, where good used cars are often sold for outrageously high prices or simply passed down through the family.

Most price guides have three prices listed, from left to right: the MSRP, showing what the vehicle sold for new; the wholesale price negotiated between dealers; and the retail price charged by dealers to walk-in customers. Used vehicles purchased from dealers over the Internet or from private sellers will sell for somewhere between the wholesale and resale prices.

When you compare dealer ads with the price guides, you'll see the dealers have added incredible markups that ensnare unsuspecting buyers. Take the *Lemon-Aid* guide along and bargain down the markup by about one-third.

Be wary

As a buyer, you should get a printed sales agreement, even if it's just handwritten, that includes a clause stating there are no outstanding traffic violations or liens against the vehicle (a lien is a debt for which the vehicle is used as collateral). It doesn't make a great deal of difference whether the vehicle will be purchased "as is" or as certified under state regulation. A vehicle sold as safety "certified" can still be dangerous to drive or turn into a lemon. The certification process can be sabotaged by incompetent mechanics or poorly calibrated instruments, or if a minimal number of components were checked. "Certified" is not the same as having a warranty to protect you from engine seizure or transmission failure. Certified means only that the vehicle has met minimum safety standards on the day tested.

Make sure the vehicle is lien-free and hasn't been written off after an accident or been flood-damaged.

TELL-TALE SIGNS OF FLOOD DAMAGE

Car experts agree buying a flooded vehicle is a bad idea, even if the price seems right and the car looks like new. Used-car buyers should have their mechanics check for these warning signs of flooding.

Damp or musty odor inside the vehicle or trunk.

Newly shampooed or replaced carpet or upholstery in a vehicle that is old enough to show wear and tear.

Dampness under carpeting or between seat cushions.

Rusty brackets and/or screws under dash.

Watermarks under the hood.

Dried mud in cracks and crevices under the hood, behind trim panels inside the car, inside door joints or wheel wells, or under the dashboard.

Traces of water in engine, transmission or axle lubricants.

SOURCE: The American Automobile Association

Spotting a flood-damaged car.

Some states with lax reporting laws are dumping grounds for rebuilt wrecks and write-offs shipped from states where there are stringent disclosure regulations. In most states, you can do a lien and registration search yourself. If a lien does exist, you should contact the creditor(s) listed to find out whether any debts have been paid. If a debt is outstanding, you should arrange with the vendor to pay the creditor the outstanding balance. If the debt is larger than the purchase price of the vehicle, it's up to you to decide whether or not you wish to complete the deal. If the seller agrees to clear the title personally, make sure that you receive a written relinquishment of title from the creditor before paying any money to the vendor. Also, make sure the title doesn't show an "R" for "restored."

Even if all documents are in order, ask the seller to show you the vehicle's original sales contract and a few repair bills in order to ascertain how well it was maintained. The bills will show you if the odometer was turned back and will also indicate which repairs are still guaranteed. If none of these can be found, *run, don't walk, away.* If the contract shows that the vehicle was financed, verify that the loan was paid. If you're still not sure that the vehicle is free of liens, ask your bank or credit-union manager to make a check for you. If no clear answer is forthcoming, look for another vehicle.

Repossessed vehicles
Repossessed vehicles are usually found at auctions but they're sometimes sold by finance companies or banks—institutions that have been held by the courts to be as legally responsible as dealers for the defects found in the vehicles they sell. The biggest problem with repossessed vans, sport-utilities, and pickups, in particular, is that they're likely to have been abused by their financially troubled owners. The full extent of the abuse can't always be ascertained in one brief examination by a mechanic. Before buying a repossessed vehicle, try to find out something about the previous owner and what care the vehicle received. A visit to the local dealer for that particular make, with the vehicle's identification number and a small gratuity in hand, will get you a vehicle history printout from the dealer's PC link with the manufacturer.

Cross-border shopping
In spite of the depressed value of the Canadian dollar, there's no iron-clad guarantee that you'll save money by purchasing a used vehicle in Canada and bringing it into the States. Safety and pollution control regulations differ considerably between the two countries and it may be impossible to upgrade your used vehicle to American standards. Find out which vehicles pass muster by accessing NHTSA's website.

Buyers of used Canadian vehicles should also be wary of the following: the odometer registers in kilometers instead of miles; safety-related defects may not have been corrected because Canada doesn't have a cross-border owner notification system; and engine calibrations may not be set for American emissions control standards, thereby putting you in violation of some state pollution control regulations. Furthermore, vehicles that are exported to the United States may have rolled-back odometers; as a buyer, you will have no legal recourse worth pursuing, once you add up the cost of civil litigation.

If you do decide to import a used vehicle from Canada, be careful to check for liens and make sure the vehicle wasn't stolen. Unfortunately, there's little cooperation among provincial registrars and no effectual link-up between U.S. and Canadian registrars, so your chances of getting the required information are pretty slim.

Rental and leased vehicles

The second-best choice for getting a good used vehicle is a rental company or leasing agency. Budget, Hertz, Avis, and National sell cars, minivans, vans, and sport-utilities that have one to two years of service and approximately 50,000 to 60,000 miles. These rental companies will gladly provide a vehicle's complete history and allow an independent inspection by a qualified mechanic of the buyer's choice, as well as arrange competitive financing, without "boosting" the price.

Rental vehicles are generally well maintained, sell for a few thousand dollars more than a privately sold vehicle, and come with a strong guarantee. Rental car companies also usually settle customer complaints without much of a hassle so as not to tarnish their image with rental customers.

Vehicles that have just come off a three- or five-year lease are much more competitively priced, generally have less mileage, and are usually as well maintained as rental vehicles. You're also likely to get a better price if you buy directly from the lessee rather than going through the dealership or an independent agency, but remember, you won't have the dealer's leverage to extract post-warranty "goodwill" repairs from the automaker.

New-car dealers

Although going to a new-car dealer is the most expensive way to get a used vehicle (prices are 20–30 percent higher than those for vehicles sold privately), they aren't a bad place to pick up a good used car or minivan if you don't mind paying top dollar. For example, new-car dealers are insured against selling stolen vehicles or vehicles with finance owing or other liens. New-car dealers offer financing, occasionally allow a prospective buyer to have a used vehicle inspected by an independent garage, and offer a much wider choice of models. Repair facilities are also available for warranty work, and if there's a possibility of getting post-warranty "goodwill" compensation from the manufacturer, your dealer can provide additional leverage. Plus, if you have to take the dealership to court, dealers have deeper pockets than private sellers, so there's a better chance that you'll get paid should the judge rule in your favor.

"Certified" vehicles

Try to get a vehicle that the dealer's had certified by an auto association or an automaker. Buying one of these independently certified vehicles allows you to sue both the dealer and the certifier if things go wrong.

The Big Three American automakers and many importers have begun to refurbish and certify used vehicles sold by their dealers. They guarantee the vehicle's mechanical fitness and provide a warranty where length depends on the age of the vehicle. But these vehicles don't come cheap, mainly because automakers force their dealers to bring them up to better-than-average condition before certifying them.

Automaker and dealer leasing

Automakers and dealers are now leasing three-year-old cars, trucks, sport-utilities, vans, and minivans for additional two- to three-year periods. For a relatively low monthly payment (relative to leasing new), you can get a better-equipped vehicle with some of the automaker's original warranty in effect and a used warranty that kicks in afterwards.

Leasing has been touted as a method of making the high cost of vehicle ownership more affordable, but for most people the pitfalls (whether you lease new or used) far outweigh any advantages. Keep in mind that leasing is costlier than an outright purchase. If you must lease, do it for the shortest time possible and make sure the lease is closed-ended (meaning that you walk away from the vehicle when the lease period ends). Also, make sure there's a maximum mileage allowance of at least 15,000 miles a year and that the charge per excess mile is no higher than 6¢.

Used-car dealers

Used-car dealers usually sell their vehicles for a bit less than what new-car dealers charge, but their vehicles may be worth a lot less, too, because they don't get the first pick of top-quality trade-ins. They're usually marginal operations that can't invest much money in reconditioning their vehicles, which are often collected from auctions and new-car dealers reluctant to sell the vehicles to their own customers. And they don't always have repair facilities to honor what warranties they do provide. Often, they may offer easier (but more expensive) credit terms than franchised new-car dealers.

Used-car dealers operating in small towns are an entirely different breed. These small, often family-run businesses recondition and resell cars and trucks that usually come from within their community. Routine servicing is often done in-house and more complicated repairs are subcontracted out to specialized garages nearby. These small outlets survive by word-of-mouth advertising and would never last long if they didn't deal fairly with local townsfolk. On the other hand, their prices will likely be higher than elsewhere due to the better quality of used vehicles they offer and the cost of reconditioning and repairing under warranty what they sell.

Superstores

Used-car "superstores" like CarMax are nationally franchised operations backed by Circuit City and other investors. Although for the past few years they have been expanding slowly, they are expected to pick up steam once differences with automakers have been ironed out.

These aren't the places to find "super" bargains when compared with what's offered by traditional new- or used-car dealers. The

December 1995 issue of *Smart Money* magazine, for example, found that
CarMax's prices and warranties came up short 25 out of 26 times when
compared to used vehicles sold by local dealers. Furthermore,
Automotive News reports that more recent studies show used-car superstores tend to drive up prices in the regions where they are established.
On the plus side, however, their emergence makes existing dealers
more consumer sensitive when it comes to warranties and disclosure.
In fact, CarMax's 5-day/250-mile money-back guarantee and 99-day
warranty put most dealers to shame.

Auctions
You need patience and smarts to pick up anything worthwhile at an
auction. Government auctions—places where the mythical $50 Jeep is
sold—are fun to attend, but are risky ventures because you can't determine the condition of the vehicles put up for bid and government
employees often pick over the stock before you ever see it.

You swim with the piranha, however, at commercial auctions. They
are frequented by "ringers" who bid up the price and professional dealers who pick up cheap, worn-out vehicles unloaded by new-car dealers
and independents who are afraid to sell them to their own customers.
There are no guarantees, cash is required, and quality is apt to be as low
as the price. Remember, too, that auction purchases are subject to state
sales taxes and the auction's sales commission (3–5 percent), and an
administrative fee of $25–$50 may also be charged.

Say what? This Chicago Times *ad promises there's no need to purchase
anything in order to win one of three $1,000 prizes—to be used only with
the purchase of an auctioned vehicle. Watch out! Like phony carpet
"Customs auction" scams, there are many false auto auctions run by used-
car dealers and independent brokers. Make sure you're dealing with a
legitimate auctioneer.*

If you are interested in shopping at an auto auction, remember that certain days are reserved for dealers only, so call ahead. You'll find the vehicles locked in a compound but you should have ample opportunity to inspect them and, in some cases, take them for a short drive around the property before the auction begins.

Paying the Right Price

Get ready for "sticker shock" when pricing popular used cars and mini-vans—most of these vehicles don't depreciate very much and it's easy to get stuck with a cheap one that's been abused through lack of care. Furthermore, it's such a seller's market out there that even those vehicles with worse-than-average reliability ratings, like early GM Cavaliers, Ford Tauruses, and Chrysler minivans, still command ridiculously high resale prices simply because they're popular.

If you don't want to pay too much when buying used, you've got the following four alternatives.

• Buy an older vehicle. Choose one that's five years old or more and has a good reliability and durability record, and buy extra protection with an extended warranty. The money you save from the extra years' depreciation and lower insurance premiums will more than make up for the extra warranty cost.

• Look for off-lease vehicles sold privately by owners who want more than what their dealer is offering. If you can't find what you're look-ing for in the local classified ads, put in your own ad asking for lessees to contact you if they're not satisfied with their dealer's offer.

• Buy a vehicle that's depreciated more than average simply because of its bland styling, lack of high-performance features, or its discontinu-ation by one of its distributors. For example, many of the Japanese pickups cost less to own than their American-made counterparts yet are more reliable and more than adequate for most driving chores. And, now that the Dodge Stealth has been dropped by Chrysler, used versions can be picked up for a song and servicing is easily found at Mitsubishi dealerships who sell the Stealth's twin, the 3000GT.

• Buy a twin or re-badged model. Listed below are some of the better-known cars, minivans, vans, sport-utilities, and trucks that are nearly identical but sold under other nameplates. They usually share the same basic design, appearance, dimensions, and mechanical com-ponents but their resale values may differ considerably.

"Twin" Savings

Chrysler

Chrysler Sebring, Dodge Avenger

Chrysler Cirrus, Dodge Stratus

Chrysler Concorde, LHS, New Yorker, Dodge Intrepid, Eagle Vision

Chrysler Town & Country, Dodge Grand Caravan, Plymouth Grand Voyager

Dodge Caravan, Plymouth Voyager

Dodge Colt, Eagle Summit

Dodge Dart, Duster, Plymouth Valiant, Duster

Dodge Omni, Plymouth Horizon

Dodge Spirit, Plymouth Acclaim

Dodge Stealth, Mitsubishi 3000GT

Dodge Volaré, Plymouth Aspen

Eagle Talon, Mitsubishi Eclipse, Plymouth Laser

Ford

Ford Pinto, Mercury Bobcat

Ford Escort, ZX2, Mercury Tracer, Lynx, Mazda 323

Ford Tempo, Mercury Topaz

Ford Contour, Mercury Mystique

Ford Taurus, Mercury Sable

Ford Mustang, Mercury Capri

Ford Probe, Mazda MX-6

Ford Thunderbird, Mercury Cougar

Ford Crown Victoria, Mercury Grand Marquis

Ford Explorer, Mazda Navajo, Mercury Mountaineer

Ford Ranger, Mazda B-Series

Mercury Villager, Nissan Quest

General Motors

Buick LeSabre, Olds 88, Pontiac Bonneville

Buick Century, Regal, Olds Intrigue, Pontiac Grand Prix

Chevrolet Cavalier, Pontiac Sunfire (Sunbird)

Chevrolet Corsica, Beretta, Pontiac Tempest

Chevrolet Lumina, Monte Carlo

Chevrolet Malibu, Olds Cutlass

Chevrolet Camaro, Pontiac Firebird

Chevrolet Astro, GMC Safari

Chevrolet Express, GMC Savana

Chevrolet Lumina APV minivan, Olds Silhouette, Pontiac Trans Sport

Chevrolet Metro, Pontiac Firefly, Suzuki Swift, Sprint

Chevrolet Prizm, Toyota Corolla

Chevrolet Venture, Olds Silhouette, Pontiac Trans Sport

The Cavalier (shown above), Sunbird, and Sunfire: identical cars, different prices.

Chevrolet S-10 pickup, GMC Sonoma pickup
Chevrolet Blazer, GMC Jimmy, Olds Bravada
Chevrolet Blazer, Tahoe, GMC Yukon

Chevrolet C/K pickup, GMC Sierra pickup
Geo Tracker, Pontiac Sunrunner, Suzuki Sidekick
Olds Achieva, Pontiac Grand Am
Saturn SC, Sl

Imports

Acura Integra, Honda Civic
Acura CL, Honda Accord
Acura SLX, Isuzu Trooper
Honda Odyssey, Isuzu Oasis
Honda Passport, Isuzu Rodeo
Hyundai Elantra, Tiburon
Infiniti I30, Nissan Maxima

Infiniti QX4, Nissan Pathfinder
Lexus ES 300, Toyota Camry
Lexus LX 450, Toyota Land Cruiser
Toyota Paseo, Tercel

Prices will vary

In spite of what many guide books say (including *Lemon-Aid*), cars and minivans have no "official" selling price. Most dealers will charge as much as the market will bear and use any pretext they can to boost prices—if you let them. Although they pretend to have abandoned negotiated prices and high-pressure sales tactics in favor of "no-haggle prices," dealers will negotiate and it's in your best interest to make sure they do.

Consumer Reports, for example, found that its expert shopper saved hundreds of dollars buying from a conventional dealership as opposed to one which displayed the dealer's invoice cost and a "no haggle" selling price.

There are several price guidelines, however, and dealers use the one that will make the most profit on each transaction. The most common quoted price is from the *NADA Official Used Car Guide*, which shows the full retail price (similar to the Manufacturer's Suggested Retail Price, or MSRP). The wholesale price, thousands of dollars less, is more likely what the dealer paid. Never mind that few people ever pay the MSRP; the fact that it's there is sufficient reason for most dealers to charge the

higher rate. Both price indicators leave considerable room for the
dealer's profit margin and some extra padding—inflated preparation
charges and administration fees that shouldn't exist for a used vehicle.

Just as with new cars, dealers know that last-minute add-on charges
to used cars are their last chance to stick it to you before the contract
is signed. They therefore try to extort extra profits through so-called
preparation and documentation fees and charge extra handling costs
that give you nothing in return. These charges should have no place in
a used vehicle transaction—but wait until the opportune moment
before objecting. Patiently await management's approval of the vehicle's bottom-line price and then reject these add-on charges; otherwise,
the dealer may try to pad the price to get its normal add-on profit.

Financing Choices

No one should spend more than 30 percent of his or her annual gross
income on the purchase of a used vehicle. By keeping the initial cost of
a used vehicle low, the purchaser may be able to pay in cash, a key bargaining tool to use with private individuals selling vehicles directly.
Used-car dealers are not all that impressed by cash sales because they
lose their kickback from the finance companies, which is based on the
volume and amount of finance business they write up. Furthermore, a
portion of the life insurance premium tacked on as a rider to the loan
may also be remitted to the dealer as part of the sales commission.

*Dealer greed knows no bounds. This buyer was charged a $99 "adminis-
tration fee" for a used car!*

In spite of the lower costs involved (as compared to a new-vehicle purchase), not everyone can pay cash for a used car or minivan. If you need a loan, consider the advantages and disadvantages of going through the following lending institutions.

Credit unions

A credit union is the preferred place to borrow money at low interest rates and with easy repayment terms. You'll have to join the credit union or have an account with them before the loan is approved. You'll also probably have to come up with a larger down payment relative to what other lending institutions require.

Banks

Banks want to make small loans to consumers who have average incomes and appear to be financially responsible. Their interest rates are very attractive and can be negotiated downwards if you have a good credit history or agree to give them other business. Auto club members can benefit from lower interest rates at banking institutions recommended by the association. Bank loans are seldom made for more than 36–48 months.

Dealers

Dealers can finance the cost of a used vehicle at rates that compete with those of banks and finance companies because they get substantial rebates from lenders and agree to take back the vehicle if the creditor defaults on the loan. Some dealers mislead their customers into thinking they can get financing at rates 3–4 percentage points below the prime rate. Actually, the dealer jacks up the base price of the vehicle to compensate for the lower interest charges.

Finance companies

With their excessive interest rates, finance companies should be the last place to go for a small, short-term loan, but the fact remains that these lenders fill a consumer need created by the restrictive policies of other institutions. The advantages of relaxed credit restrictions and quick loans appeal to many people who can't get financing elsewhere or who may wish to extend their payments for up to 60 months.

Dealer Scams

Used vehicles are subject to the same deceptive sales practices that are employed by dealers who sell new vehicles. One of the more common tricks is to not identify the previous owner, either because the vehicle was used commercially or had been written off as a total loss from an accident. It's also not uncommon to discover that the mileage has been turned back, particularly if the vehicle was part of a company's fleet. These scams can be thwarted if you demand the name of the vehicle's previous owner as a prerequisite to purchasing the vehicle.

It would be impossible to list all the dishonest tricks employed in used-vehicle sales. As soon as the public is alerted to one scheme, crooked sellers use other, more elaborate frauds.

Here are some of the more common fraudulent practices you're likely to encounter.

Failing to declare full purchase price
This tactic, used almost exclusively by small, independent dealers, involves the buyer being told by the salesperson that he or she can save on sales tax by listing a lower selling price on the contract. But what if the vehicle turns out to be a lemon or the sales agent has falsified the model year or mileage? The hapless buyer will usually be offered a refund on the fictitious purchase price indicated on the contract only. If the buyer wanted to take the dealer to court, it's quite unlikely that he or she would get any more than the contract price. Moreover, both the buyer and dealer could be prosecuted for making a false declaration to avoid paying sales tax.

Sales agents posing as private parties ("curbsiders")
Independent scam artists and some crooked dealers get agents to pose as private sellers in order to get a better price for their vehicles and avoid giving a warranty. Once again, this scam is easy to detect if the seller can't produce the original sales contract or if few repair bills are made out in his or her own name. You can also identify a dealer in the want ads section of the newspaper by checking to see if his or her telephone number is repeated in different ads.

Most new-car dealers get very angry when one of these scamming teams hits town. Unfortunately, they don't get angry enough, because they continue to sell used vehicles at wholesale prices to curbsiders who they know are stealing their business and cheating consumers and tax authorities in their communities.

If you get taken by one of these scam artists, don't hesitate to sue, through small claims court, both the newspaper carrying the ad (the papers know these are scammers from the volume of ads placed each week) and the state agency responsible for dealer registration and consumer protection. These parties could be considered negligent for allowing these rip-off artists to operate.

"Free-exchange" privilege
Dealers get a lot of sales mileage out of this deceptive offer. The dealer offers to exchange any defective vehicle for any other vehicle in stock. What really happens, though, is that the dealer won't have any other vehicles selling for the same price and thus will demand a cash bonus for the exchange, or he or she may have nothing but lemons in stock.

"Money-back" guarantee
Once again, the purchaser feels safe in buying a used car with this kind of guarantee, because what could be more honest than a money-back

guarantee? Dealers using this technique often charge exorbitant handling charges, rental fees, or mechanical repair costs to the customer
who's bought one of these vehicles and then returned it.

"50/50" guarantee
This means that the dealer will pay half the repair costs over a limited
period of time. It's a fair offer if an independent garage may do the
repairs. If not, the dealer can always inflate the repair costs to double
their actual worth and write up a bill for that amount. The buyer winds
up paying the full price of repairs that would probably have been much
cheaper at an independent garage. The best kind of used-vehicle warranty is 100 percent with full coverage for a fixed term.

"As is" cars
Buying a vehicle "as is" means that you're aware of mechanical defects,
you're prepared to accept the responsibility for any damage or injuries
caused by the vehicle, and that all costs to fix it shall be paid by you. The
courts have held that the "as is" clause is not a blank check to cheat buyers and, therefore, must be interpreted in light of the seller's true intent.
That is, was there an attempt to deceive the buyer by including this
clause? Did the buyer really know what the "as is" clause could do to his
or her future legal rights? It's also been held that the courts may consider
oral representations ("parole evidence") made by the seller as to the fine
quality of the used vehicle but never written into the formal contract.
Courts generally ignore "as is" clauses when the vehicle has been misrepresented, when the dealer is the seller, or when the defects are so serious that the seller is presumed to have known of their existence.

Odometer tampering
It's often too dangerous for the dealer or "curbsider" to turn back the
mileage, so independent outfits are hired to pick up the vehicle or visit
the dealership and "fix" the odometer. Still, the seller is taking a big
risk since this scam can lead to jail time for fraud, and consumer protection statutes allow citizens to sue for triple damages, plus lawyers'
fees and court costs, if they find their odometer has been rigged.
Nevertheless, the best protection is prevention, and that can be
achieved by simply demanding that the seller (dealer or private party)
put the mileage figure on the contract and give you the name and
address of the previous owner as well as all repair receipts.

Misrepresentation
Used vehicles can be misrepresented in a variety of ways. A used airport
commuter minivan may be represented as having been used by a
Sunday school class. A mechanically defective pickup that's been rebuilt
after several major accidents may have sawdust in its transmission to
muffle the "clunks," heavy oil in the motor to stifle the "clanks," and
cheap retread tires to eliminate the "thumps." These fraudulent practices may lead to the seller being charged with civil or criminal fraud.

The best protection against these dirty tricks is to have the vehicle's quality completely verified by an independent mechanic before completing the sale.

Private Scams

A lot of space in this guide has been used to describe how used-car dealers and scam artists cheat uninformed buyers. Of course, private individuals can be dishonest too, so in either case protect yourself at the outset by keeping your deposit small and getting as much information as possible about the vehicle you're considering buying. Then, after a test drive, you may sign a written agreement to purchase the vehicle and give a deposit of sufficient value to cover the seller's advertising costs, subject to cancellation if the automobile fails its inspection.

After you've taken these precautions, watch out for these private sellers' tricks.

Used vehicles that are stolen or have finance owing

A lot of used vehicles are sold without free title because the original auto loan was never repaid. Here's where car dealers have a net advantage over private parties. Dealers aren't easily fooled and they have insurance to compensate buyers if they do inadvertently sell a stolen vehicle. When buying from a private party, you have to contact the state agency that registers property and pay a small fee for a computer printout that may or may not be accurate. You'll be asked for the current owner's name and the vehicle's 17-character identification number (VIN), which is usually found on the driver's side of the dashboard and on title or insurance documents.

There are two other high-tech ways to get the goods on the seller. First, have a "vehicle history" check done by a dealer of that particular marque through a computer link-up with the automaker's main frame. That check will tell you who the previous owners and dealers were, what warranty and recall repairs were carried out, and what other free repair programs may still apply. Second, you could use Carfax (*www.carfax.com;* tel.: 1-888-422-7329) to carry out a background check to see if the vehicle has been wrecked, had flood damage, is stolen, or shows incorrect mileage on the odometer. The $20 fee by telephone is cut to $12 if the order is placed via the Internet. A typical search takes only a few minutes.

Both amateur and professional crooks sell vehicles that haven't been paid for because it's so easy to do and the profits are enormous. They skip town after sticking you with the finance payments and, by the time the lender tracks you down, most legal recourse is ineffective. Your best bet may be to buy the car again from the lender at a discount and take a tax loss.

This racket can be avoided by asking for proof of purchase and payment from any individual who offers to sell a used vehicle for an incredibly low price. Check the sales contract to determine who granted the original loan and call the lender to see if it's been repaid. Place a call to the Department of Motor Vehicles to ascertain whether the vehicle is registered in the seller's name. Also, find out if a finance company is named as a beneficiary on the auto insurance policy. Finally, call up the original dealer to determine whether there are any outstanding claims.

Misrepresentation (wrong model year)
That bargain-priced car or truck you just bought may be a year older than you think. That's why you should check its true age by looking at the date-of-manufacture plate found on the driver's side door pillar. If the date of manufacture reads 7/96, it was one of the last 1996 models made before the September changeover to the 1997 models. Exceptions to this rule are those vehicles that are redesigned or relatively new to the market, which arrive at dealerships in early spring or mid-summer. They're considered to be next year's models but depreciate more quickly due to their earlier launching (a difference that narrows over time).

Now, one last word on protecting yourself from legal liability if you are selling a vehicle to a private individual. Normally, once you take the tags and give the buyer a bill of sale, you're no longer the registered owner. Unfortunately, though, if you don't personally go down to the registry office and make sure the title has changed, you could be sued by an insurance company for damages arising from an accident if you're still the owner of record.

Choosing the Right Kind of Vehicle

Import or domestic model?
Forget all the popular mythology about what is "North American–made" and what is "foreign-made." DaimlerChrysler has dramatically altered the rules of interpretation. Furthermore, the seesawing of foreign currency values has led to a rush of foreign automakers moving production facilities to the U.S., Canada, and Mexico, in addition to importing major components from offshore. Surprisingly, this has been accomplished without a corresponding drop in quality control. On the other hand, it has made it practically impossible to designate many vehicles as American-made.

Whether you buy domestic or imported, overall vehicle quality has improved a great deal during the past decade. Premature rusting is less of a problem and factory-related defects aren't as numerous as they once were. But problems remain. Owners of American-made vehicles still report serious deficiencies, often during the first three years in service. These include electrical system failures caused by faulty computer modules, malfunctioning ABS, failure-prone air conditioning and automatic transmissions, as well as defective powertrains, fuel systems, suspensions, steering, and paint. Further evidence that American cars are more failure-prone than their Japanese-made counterparts can be seen in the service bulletins sent out each month by the automakers. For this guide, I've compared the bulletins of a 1994 Ford Taurus and Sable to those of a 1994 Toyota Camry.

1994 Ford Taurus V6
DSB SUMMARY

1. SEP-89 20 STEPS TO SUCCESSFUL AUTO TRANSMISSION REPAIR
2. JAN-94 A/C - BLOWER MOTOR INOPERATIVE IN AUTOMATIC MODE
3. JAN-94 A/C - MANIFOLD AND TUBE ASSEMBLY REPLACEMENT
4. JUL-95 A/C EVAPORATOR CORE-ON VEHICLE-LEAK TEST
5. OCT-94 A/C SERVICE TIP - OIL VISIBLE AT SPRING LOCK COUPLERS
6. JUL-96 A/C SYSTEM SERVICE TSB LIST
7. MAR-94 A/T (AX4N) - SERVICE PROCEDURE FOR ORANGE TAGGED UNITS
8. MAR-94 A/T (AXOD/AXODE/AX4S) - LEAK AT TORQUE CONVERTER
9. JAN-96 ACCELERATOR CABLE - DIAGNOSTIC PROCEDURE
10. JAN-95 ACCUMULATOR SPRINGS - IDENTIFICATION
11. MAR-96 ADDING REFRIGERANT OIL PROCEDURE
12. MAR-96 AIR BAG - DIAGNOSTIC FAULT CODE 51
13. OCT-95 AIR BAG MODULES - DISCOLORED/MARRED COVERS
14. AUG-97 AIR COMPRESSOR MOAN
15. SEP-95 AIR CONDITIONING - FORD APPROVED FLUSHING
16. FEB-98 AIR CONDITIONING MUSTY AND MILDEW TYPE ODORS
17. SEP-96 AIR CONDITIONING O-RING AVAILABILITY AND APPLICATIONS
18. JAN-95 AIR CONDITIONING O-RING REMOVAL - SERVICE TIP
19. SEP-96 AIR CONDITIONING THICK O-RING APPLICATIONS
20. DEC-93 AIR IN POWER STEERING SYSTEM
21. SEP-87 ALL AUTOMATICS - FRONT BUSHING WEAR
22. MAY-95 ANTENNA - BOWED CONDITION ONLY - WARRANTY REVISION
23. MAR-94 ANTI-LOCK BRAKES - PEDAL FEELS LIKE IT HAS EXTRA TRAVEL
24. OCT-95 ANTI-LOCK BRAKES CYCLING ON ROUGH ROADS
25. JAN-94 AUTOMATIC TRANSMISSION - AX4S - DO NOT SERVICE TAG
26. FEB-90 AUTOMATIC TRANSMISSION FLUID
27. AUG-89 AUTOMATIC TRANSMISSION MATH FORMULAS
28. OCT-89 AUTOMATIC TRANSMISSION MATH PART 2
29. AUG-96 AX4S TRANSAXLE - NEW MAIN CONTROL COVER AND PAN GASKET
30. NOV-94 AX4S TRANSAXLE EXCHANGE PROGRAM
31. FEB-98 AX4S/AX4N NEW TRANSAXLE FLUID
32. NOV-97 AX4S/AX4N, TROUBLE CODES STORED AFTER TRANSAXLE REPLACED
33. JAN-96 AXLE NUT/LUG NUT TIGHTENING SPECIFICATIONS
34. SEP-92 BATTERY REPLACEMENT 72AH TO 84AH
35. MAR-95 BLOWER MOTOR - CHIRP/SQUEAK FROM BLOWER MOTOR
36. NOV-93 BLOWER SPEED CONTROL - AUTOMATIC TEMPERATURE CONTROL
37. SEP-97 BRAKE AND ROTOR SERVICE TIPS
38. DEC-94 BRAKE ROTOR MACHINING EQUIPMENT AND WARRANTY INFORMATION
39. OCT-95 BRAKES - PETROLEUM BASED LUBRICANT CAUSES SWELLING
40. MAR-96 BRAKES - REAR BRAKES NOISE/SQUEAL
41. MAR-95 BRAKES - ROUGHNESS DURING BRAKE APPLICATION
42. NOV-93 BUMPER COVER REPAIR MATERIALS
43. APR-94 BUMPERS - ISOLATOR AND BRACKET ASSEMBLY REPLACEMENT
44. MAY-96 CALIFORNIA REFORMULATED GASOLINE (CARFG) SERVICE TIP
45. JAN-96 CASE BREAKAGE AT REAR PLANET SUPPORT
46. DEC-97 CHIRPING/SQUEAKING FROM BLOWER MOTOR AT LOW SPEEDS
47. JAN-98 CODES 327, 332, MIL LAMP ON, 32 DEGREES F OR BELOW, 3.0L
48. JUL-94 COOLING SYSTEM BY-PASS HOSE LEAK
49. FEB-98 CUSTOMER ASSISTANCE-TELEPHONE NUMBERS FOR TIRE COMPANIES
50. JAN-95 DELAYED ENGAGEMENT, SHIFT ERRORS, POSSIBLE MLPS CODES
51. NOV-93 DRIVEABILITY CONCERNS - DAMAGED FUEL PUMP
52. MAY-94 DRIVER'S SEAT SENSOR CAUSES DOORS TO LOCK WHEN EXITING
53. NOV-93 EGO SENSORS - SILICONE CONTAMINATION
54. NOV-96 ELECTRICAL DIODE IDENTIFICATION AND REPLACEMENT
55. JUN-93 ELECTRICAL INFORMATION - AXOD/E
56. AUG-95 ELECTRONIC SHIFT SOLENOID APPLICATIONS

Look at this service bulletin summary for a 1994 Ford Taurus and Mercury Sable. Out of a total of 162 bulletins, 53 bulletins concerned a factory-related defect, often related to the powertrain.

57. OCT-96 ELIMINATION OF SANDING BRAKE ROTORS AND DRUMS
58. MAY-97 ENGINE COOLING FAN MODULE SERVICE INFORMATION
59. OCT-90 ENGINE TESTING WITH A VACUUM GAUGE - AUTO TRANS.
60. JAN-95 ERRATIC/HIGH LINE PRESSURE
61. OCT-93 FAILSAFE MODES - COMPUTER SHIFTED TRANSMISSIONS
62. JUL-96 FILTERING REFRIGERANT AFTER REPLACING A/C COMPRESSOR
63. OCT-96 FOG/FILM ON WINDSHIELD/INTERIOR GLASS
64. JUL-96 FORD'S POSITION ON PROPYLENE GLYCOL COOLANT
65. JAN-95 FORWARD PISTON CHANGE
66. JAN-94 FORWARD SPRAG UPGRADE
67. NOV-94 FORWARD/REVERSE ENGAGEMENT CONCERN - AXOD, AXOD-E, AX4S
68. DEC-97 FRONT END ACCESSORY DRIVE BELT SLIP, 3.0L 2-VALVE
69. FEB-96 FUEL INFORMATION OF GASOLINE - SERVICE TIP
70. MAR-97 FUEL ECONOMY - CUSTOMER EXPECTATIONS VS. VEHICLE USAGE
71. JAN-96 FUEL PUMP BUZZ/WHINE THROUGH RADIO SPEAKER
72. OCT-97 FUEL SYSTEM - FUEL ODOR INSIDE PASSENGER COMPARTMENT
73. OCT-94 FUEL TANK - FUEL SLOSH NOISE
74. OCT-93 GLASS - IRIDESCENCE OR MOTTLING IN TEMPERED GLASS
75. OCT-95 GROANING NOISE FROM POWER WINDOWS
76. JAN-94 HARSH SHIFTS, NO 3-4 SHIFT, ERRATIC SHIFTS
77. JUL-97 HEADLAMPS OPERATE INTERMITTENTLY
78. AUG-94 HEATED EXHAUST GAS OXYGEN SENSOR APPLICATION CHART
79. JAN-95 HEATER TO ENGINE COOLANT BYPASS HOSE REPLACEMENT
80. JUN-94 HEATER/ A/C - COLD ENGINE LOCKOUT OPERATION
81. MAR-96 HESITATION/NO START/STALLING - INTERMITTENT (HOT)
82. NOV-91 HOW TO USE A PRESSURE GAUGE - AUTOMATIC TRANS.
83. JAN-98 HUB-MOUNT BRAKE ROTOR MACHINING EQUIPMENT AVAILABILITY
84. SEP-97 IDENTIFICATION OF NON-FORD APPROVED REFRIGERANTS
85. APR-94 IGNITION CONTROL MODULE CONNECTOR UPDATE
86. MAR-95 INCORRECT PCM USAGE WILL CAUSE TRANSAXLE DAMAGE
87. FEB-98 INTERMITTENT NEUTRAL CONDITION, NO FORWARD/REVERSE, AX4N
88. AUG-97 LOOSE CATALYST OR MUFFLER HEAT SHIELDS
89. DEC-94 LOW TRANSAXLE FLUID LEVEL IMPROPERLY SETTING DTC
90. AUG-87 METAL SEALING RINGS - AUTOMATIC TRANSMISSIONS
91. JAN-94 MODIFICATION TO IMPROVE GEAR LUBRICATION
92. AUG-95 NEW ROTUNDA FLUID CHANGER - SERVICE TIP
93. JAN-96 NEW TORQUE SPECS FOR INSTALLING NEW DESIGN TIE RODS
94. DEC-94 NO CRANK - POSSIBLE CORROSION AT STARTER SOLENOID
95. FEB-96 NOISE - CLICK FROM TRANSAXLE DURING REVERSE ENGAGEMENT
96. JUL-96 NOISE - FUEL PUMP GURGLING AFTER HOT RESTART
97. DEC-96 NOISE FROM REAR TENSION START - WAGONS ONLY
98. SEP-94 NON-MATING CONDITION - HARNESS CONNECTOR/IGNITION SWITCH
99. SEP-97 ON-VEHICLE HEATER CORE PRESSURE TEST FOR WARRANTY CLAIM
100. NOV-93 PAINT - REGULAR PRODUCTION OPTION PAINT CODES
101. MAR-95 PAINT - IRON PARTICLE REMOVAL
102. NOV-93 PAINT CODES AND SUPPLIER STOCK NUMBERS
103. NOV-94 PAINT PREPARATION PROCEDURE AND MSDS INFORMATION
104. JUL-94 PASSENGER SEAT BACK RATTLES WHEN UNOCCUPIED
105. JUL-94 POWER DOOR LOCK ACTUATORS
106. AUG-97 PREVENTING BRAKE VIBRATION SERVICE TIP
107. JUN-94 PROGRAM 94B48 - FUEL TANK CONTAMINATION
108. JAN-95 RADIATOR - NEW MANUFACTURING PROCESS
109. SEP-97 RADIO AM BAND STATIC WHILE DRIVING
110. MAR-95 REAR SUN GEAR AND DRUM BEARING SERVICE - TRANSAXLE
111. JAN-96 REAR SUN GEAR BEARING - UPDATE
112. DEC-96 REAR TIRE INNER EDGE WEAR
113. AUG-94 REAR VIEW MIRROR - DETACHES FROM WINDSHIELD
114. AUG-97 REAR VIEW MIRROR REATTACHMENT
115. DEC-95 RECALL 95S22 ENGINE COOLING FAN
116. SEP-95 RECYCLED ENGINE COOLANT - SERVICE TIPS
117. DEC-94 RELEASE OF R-134A FLUORESCENT DYE
118. NOV-97 REMOTE KEYLESS ENTRY (RKE) DIAGNOSTIC SERVICE TIPS
119. NOV-93 REMOTE KEYLESS ENTRY SYSTEM

120. FEB-94 REMOTE KEYLESS ENTRY SYSTEM - SERVICE TIPS
121. JAN-95 REMOTE KEYLESS ENTRY SYSTEM TRANSMITTERS
122. OCT-96 REPLACEMENT OF THE MASS AIR FLOW SENSOR AS AN ASSEMBLY
123. NOV-94 REPLACEMENT PROCEDURE FOR FRONT DOOR MOULDING
124. DEC-93 RETURN OF OBSOLETE STARTER SOLENOIDS AND STARTER DRIVES
125. JAN-96 REVISED FORWARD SPRAG RACE
126. JAN-96 REVISED SPLINE DRIVE JOINT - OVERDRIVE DRUM
127. JUL-95 REVISED TORQUE CONVERTER IDENTIFICATION CODES
128. AUG-95 REVISED TRANSAXLE CLUTCH CLEARANCES
129. SEP-94 ROUGH IDLE, HESITATION/STUMBLE, BUCKS/JERKS ON COAST
130. NOV-93 ROUGH IDLE/HESITATION/ POOR HEATER OUTPUT
131. MAR-97 SAFETY REGAL 97S66 ENGINE COOLING FAN MOTOR CIRCUIT
132. JUL-97 SEAT LEATHER CLEANING PROCEDURE
133. JAN-94 SERVICE PARTS RETURN OF OBSOLETE FUEL PRESSURE
134. JUN-94 SERVICE PARTS RETURN OF OBSOLETE FUEL TANKS
135. MAY-97 SERVICE TIP - REFRIGERANT OIL REFILL CAPACITY
136. NOV-96 SERVICE TIP - TORQUE CONVERTER LEAK TEST PROCEDURE
137. APR-97 SERVICE TIPS - ELECTRONIC AUTOMATIC TEMPERATURE CONTROL
138. JUL-97 SERVICE TIPS - WINDNOISE AROUND DOORS
139. AUG-94 SHIFT CONCERNS OR TRANSAXLE DAMAGE - INCORRECT PCM
140. JUN-97 SPEEDOMETER NEEDLE WAVERS AND STICKS
141. NOV-95 SQUEAKS FROM REAR WINDOW AREA
142. SEP-96 SUSPENSION RIDE HEIGHT MEASUREMENT AND ADJUSTMENT
143. SEP-95 TEMPERATURE GAUGE - FLUCTUATION/INACCURATE
144. JUL-95 TEMPERATURE GAUGE READS LOW/ERRATIC
145. DEC-94 THROTTLE POSITION SENSOR - FUNCTION AND DIAGNOSTIC II
146. NOV-94 THUMPING/CLACKING NOISE WHILE BRAKING
147. FEB-94 TORQUE CONVERTER - CHANGE FROM 23 TO 25 TEETH
148. DEC-94 TORQUE CONVERTER CLEANING AND REPLACEMENT GUIDELINES
149. OCT-94 TRANSAXLE - AX4S/AXOD - NEW LUBE TUBES
150. OCT-94 TRANSAXLE (AXOD, AXODE, AX4S) - RETAINING RING ORIENTATION
151. OCT-94 TRANSAXLE LUBE TUBE BRACKET
152. JUL-94 TRANSAXLE - AX4N - FLUID PAN EMBOSSED WITH SHO
153. APR-96 TRANSAXLE - AX4S/AX4N DRIVELINE NOISES
154. DEC-95 TRANSAXLE - BONDED MAIN CONTROL SEPARATOR PLATE GASKETS
155. FEB-96 TRANSAXLE - REVISED GROB SPLINE DRIVE JOINT
156. JUL-95 TRANSAXLE REAR PLANET SUPPORT RETAINING RING I.D
157. JAN-95 TRANSMISSION CONTROLLED CLUTCH PULSING ON/OFF
158. MAR-97 TRANSMISSION FLUID USAGE CHARTS
159. FEB-95 TURBINE SHAFT SPEED AIR GAP MEASUREMENTS CHANGE
160. JUL-95 WHEEL COVER DISTORTED OR MELTED
161. JUN-95 WINDSHIELD, URETHANE MOUNTED, MATERIAL USAGE TIP
162. NOV-97 WIRE HARNESS TERMINAL REPAIR KIT AND WIRE SPLICE REPAIR

1994 Toyota Camry Sedan 4-Door V-6
DSB SUMMARY

1. APR-94 1994 TOYOTA SPECIAL SERVICE TOOLS
2. JAN-95 1995 TSB BINDERS
3. SEP-89 20 STEPS TO SUCCESSFUL AUTO TRANSMISSION REPAIR
4. MAY-96 A/C COMPRESSOR MAINTENANCE FOR STORED VEHICLES
5. OCT-93 A/C COMPRESSOR OIL APPLICATION
6. NOV-94 A540E SECONDARY REGULATOR MODIFICATION
7. MAY-97 AIR CONDITIONING EVAPORATOR ODOR
8. MAR-95 AIRBAG ASSEMBLY REPLACEMENT PROCEDURE
9. SEP-93 ALIGNMENT SPECS - 94 YEAR MODELS
10. SEP-87 ALL AUTOMATICS - FRONT BUSHING WEAR
11. NOV-96 ALTERNATIVE REFRIGERANTS AND RETROFITS
12. JUN-93 APPLYING CAUTION LABEL TO R-12 AIR CONDITIONING SYSTEMS

Look at this service bulletin summary for a 1994 Toyota Camry. Out of a total of 79 bulletins, only 13 covered a manufacturing defect.

13. MAY-95 ATM TRANSMISSION FLUID SEEPAGE
14. FEB-90 AUTOMATIC TRANSMISSION FLUID
15. AUG-89 AUTOMATIC TRANSMISSION MATH FORMULAS
16. OCT-89 AUTOMATIC TRANSMISSION MATH PART 2
17. DEC-96 AUTOMATIC TRANSMISSION SERIAL NUMBERS
18. JAN-95 AXLE NUT/LUG NUT TIGHTENING SPECIFICATIONS
19. FEB-95 BATTERY MAINTENANCE FOR IN-STOCK VEHICLES
20. SEP-97 BRAKE BOOSTER PUSH ROD GAUGE
21. JUN-94 BRAKE PAD KITS - NOW AVAILABLE WITHOUT HARDWARE
22. OCT-94 BRAKE REPAIR
23. FEB-94 BRAKES - CAUSE AND REPAIR OF VIBRATION AND PULSATION
24. DEC-96 CARPET CLEANING PROCEDURES
25. JAN-96 CHECKBALL WEAR
26. JUN-95 EMISSION CONTROL LABEL ORDER FORM
27. JUN-94 EMISSION CONTROL LABELS - ORDERING FORM
28. OCT-95 ENGINE SUPPORT BAR IMPROVEMENTS
29. OCT-90 ENGINE TESTING WITH A VACUUM GAUGE - AUTO TRANS
30. JUN-96 EXHAUST PIPE HEAT SHIELD
31. MAR-96 FRONT BRAKE GROAN NOISE
32. SEP-93 FRONT STABLIZER - NEW LINK NUTS
33. AUG-95 GROOVED B CLUTCH DISC ON AS40E ATM
34. NOV-91 HOW TO USE A PRESSURE GAUGE - AUTOMATIC TRANS.
35. JAN-96 IMPROVED POWER WINDOW REGULATOR ASSEMBLY INSTALLATION
36. AUG-95 INTRODUCTION OF BRAKE SHIM/FITTING KITS
37. JAN-97 MAIN BEARING CHANGES
38. AUG-87 METAL SEALING RINGS - AUTOMATIC TRANSMISSIONS
39. APR-96 MOONROOF PANEL WIND NOISE
40. SEP-93 NEW PDS FOR 1994 MODEL YEAR VEHICLES
41. AUG-94 NEW WIRE HARNESS REPAIR KIT AVAILABLE
42. SEP-94 OVERDRIVE CLUTCH BEARING - IMPROVED DURABILITY
43. DEC-93 PAINT AND REFINISHING FORMULA CODES
44. SEP-95 PAINT REPAIRS ON POLYURETHANE BUMPER
45. OCT-94 POWER WINDOW REGULATOR - NEW PARTS OPTIONS AVAILABLE
46. SEP-93 PRE-DELIVERY SERVICE - SHORT PIN INSTALLATION (NON USA)
47. JUN-94 PRE-DELIVERY SERVICE - SPRING SPACER REMOVAL
48. NOV-94 PROTECTIVE FILM REMOVAL PROCEDURES
49. APR-96 PUBLICATION CORRECTION - GENERAL INFORMATION
50. MAY-95 PUBLICATION CORRECTION INFORMATION
51. JUN-93 R-12 CAUTION LABEL - APPLICATION INSTRUCTIONS
52. MAR-97 REAR BRAKE SQUEAK
53. SEP-93 REAR SUSPENSION - NEW MEMBER NUT
54. MAR-96 REFRIGERANT LEAK DETECTION - SERVICE HINTS
55. JUL-94 REPLACEMENT BATTERY PART NUMBERS
56. JUL-97 REPLACEMENT CERTIFICATION LABELS
57. MAR-94 REPLACEMENT REFRIGERANTS DAMAGE TO SYSTEM
58. JUL-97 REPLACEMENT VIN PLATES
59. OCT-96 SEAT BELT EXTENDER
60. APR-94 SEAT BELT EXTENDER - AVAILABILITY
61. NOV-95 SEAT BELT EXTENDERS
62. OCT-97 SEAT BELT EXTENDERS
63. NOV-94 SPOILER LAMP SENSOR REPLACEMENT
64. AUG-96 STAIN ON PAINT
65. JUL-95 STANDARD BOLT TORQUE SPECIFICATIONS
66. SEP-94 STEERING COLUMN CLICKING NOISE - CORRECTION PROCEDURE
67. MAY-96 STEERING GEAR/WHEEL REMOVAL WITH SRS
68. APR-95 SUSPENSION SQUEAK/GROAN NOISES
69. JAN-94 TIRES CHANGE IN ORIGINAL EQUIPMENT
70. AUG-94 TOYOTA CHECKER APPLICATIONS (REFERENCE GUIDE)
71. DEC-94 TRUNK FINISH PLATE LOOSE
72. OCT-95 TRUNK LID TORSION ROD ADJUSTMENT
73. NOV-93 WATER LEAKAGE - NEW SEALS

74. MAY-95 WATER PUMP SEAL IMPROVEMENTS
75. MAR-96 WHEEL BALANCE ADAPTER KIT
76. SEP-96 WHEEL BALANCE ADAPTER KIT UPDATE
77. JUL-94 WIND NOISE FROM WINDOW - NEW PARTS AVAILABLE
78. NOV-95 WIPER MOTOR CIRCUIT BREAKER INSPECTION
79. JUL-94 WOOD DASH - REPAIR PROCEDURES

Japanese vehicles hold up fairly well, until their fifth year. Then the engine head gasket will probably have to be replaced, the front brakes will need reconditioning, and the rack-and-pinion steering system will likely have to be overhauled. Furthermore, the front-wheel-drive constant-velocity joints will probably need replacing—at a cost of about $200 each. Unfortunately, used Japanese-built vehicles are seldom priced reasonably, because their owners paid inflated prices when they were new and want to get some of their money back when they're resold.

Japanese automakers redesign their vehicles every three to four years, while American automakers often wait a decade or longer. The Big Three American automobile manufacturers know that the Japanese and their dealers build, market, and service vehicles to a higher standard than the Americans do. That's why the Big Three gave up much of the small-car market to Asian producers in the late '80s; it was easier and more profitable for them to buy high-quality Asian products and market them as homegrown. Today, the small, compact, and luxury car markets have been literally conquered by Japanese imports.

Don't buy the myth that parts for imports aren't easily found. It's actually easier to locate parts for Japanese vehicles than for domestic vehicles, due to the large number of units produced, the presence of hundreds of independent suppliers, the ease with which relatively simple parts can be interchanged from one model to another, and the large reservoir of used parts stocked by junkyards. Incidentally, when a part is hard to find, the *Mitchell Manual* is a useful guide to substituting parts that can be used for many different models. It's available in some libraries, most auto parts stores, and practically all junkyards.

Where used vehicles are concerned, the following American-made rear-drive cars are better choices than many imports: Chrysler's V8 New Yorker; Ford's Mustang, T-Bird, Cougar, Crown Victoria, Mercury Grand Marquis, and Lincoln Town Car; and GM's Camaro, Caprice, and Cadillac Fleetwood. Their depreciated prices are more competitive than the inflated values of Asian and European imports, they're cheap and easy to service almost anywhere, they support lots of power-hungry accessories, and they sustain high mileage with fewer major breakdowns. The only problem is that American rear-drives have become an endangered species, with Ford being the only automaker still churning them out in large numbers.

South Korean cars are poor imitations of Japanese vehicles. They start to fall apart after their third year due to poor-quality body construction, cheap and unreliable electrical components, and parts suppliers who put low prices ahead of reliability and durability. This is particularly evident when one looks at the failure-prone Hyundai Excel and low-quality Daewoo and Kia models.

Hyundai's Sonata—you know Hyundai has serious quality-control problems when late-night talk show host David Letterman likens Hyundai reliability to the Russian space station Mir.

European cars and minivans deserve much of the bad-mouthing they've received over high parts costs and limited parts availability. With some European models, you can count on lots of aggravation and expense due to the unacceptably slow distribution of parts and their high markup. Because these companies have a quasi-monopoly on replacement parts, there are few independent suppliers you can turn to for help. And auto wreckers, the last-chance repository for inexpensive car parts, are unlikely to carry European parts for vehicles older than three years or manufactured in small numbers.

Sport-utilities, trucks, and vans
As far as reliability and dependability are concerned, sport-utilities, vans, and pickups are more problem-prone than cars, simply because there are more things that can go wrong. Nevertheless, they often cost less to repair because key components are easily accessible—many vehicles are actually modified trucks, parts have been around for years and can be purchased from independent jobbers, and knowledgeable do-it-yourself manuals abound. Furthermore, reliability and durability have improved considerably during the past decade. In a 1995 J. D. Power study ranking customer satisfaction after the first year of ownership, multipurpose vehicles had a 29 percent improvement in owner satisfaction since the study was first done, in 1988. Dealer servicing improved 30 percent, compared to a reported 12 percent improvement in product quality over the same period.

As a rule, 4X4s, minivans, vans, and pickups have more squeaks and rattles and engine, transmission, electrical system, brake, and paint problems than cars. Separated into vehicle classes, owners of small pickups and compact sport-utilities submitted the best customer satisfaction evaluations, according to the Power survey.

Take the phrase "carlike handling" with a large grain of salt. Since many rear-drive models are built on a modified truck chassis and use steering and suspension components from their truck divisions, they tend to handle more like trucks than cars, in spite of automakers' claims to the contrary. What you see is not necessarily what you get when you buy or lease a new 4X4, minivan, van, or pickup, because multipurpose vehicles seldom come with enough standard features to fully exploit their versatility. Additional options are usually a prerequisite to making them safe and comfortable to drive. Consequently, the term "multipurpose" is a misnomer unless you are prepared to spend multi-bucks to outfit your 4X4, van, or pickup. Even fully equipped, these vehicles don't always provide the performance touted by automakers. Bear in mind that off-roading requires suspension, engine, and drivetrain packages and other components, such as off-road tires and a skid plate, that may not come as standard equipment on the vehicle.

Front-drives handle better than rear-drives, but the size and weight of multipurpose vehicles still require a whole new set of driving skills when cornering under moderate speeds, parking, or turning. A moment's inattention can easily lead to a deadly rollover when driving a sport-utility or pickup—vehicles that are two to three times more likely to roll over than passenger cars.

The following is a summary listing of some of the vehicles rated in *Lemon-Aid Used 4X4s, Vans and Trucks 2000*. The list has been compiled after reviewing owner complaints, automaker internal service bulletins and memos, government complaints data, court judgments, and out-of-court settlements.

Ratings may contradict *Consumer Reports* or the AAA's ratings due to the weight *Lemon-Aid* gives owner complaints and internal service bulletins. Cars and minivans are rated in Part Three of this guide.

Sport-Utilities

Recommended
Explorer, Mountaineer (1995–98)
Ford (Lincoln) Expedition, Navigator (1997–98)

Infiniti QX4 (1997–98)
Lexus LX 450, LX 470 (1997–98)
Toyota 4Runner (1996–98)

Above Average
Chrysler (Jeep) CJ, Wrangler, TJ Wrangler (1997–98)
Ford Explorer (1993–94)

Mercedes ML 320 (1998)
Subaru Forester, Outback (1995–98)

Honda CR-V (1997–98)
Honda Passport/Acura SLX/
  Isuzu Rodeo, Trooper (1998)

Toyota 4Runner (1988–95)
Toyota RAV4 (1997–98)

Average

Chrysler Durango (1998)
Chrysler Ramcharger (1990–93)
Chrysler (Jeep) Cherokee
  (1995–98)
Chrysler (Jeep) Grand Cherokee
  (1995–98)
Chrysler (Jeep) CJ, Wrangler, YJ
  Wrangler (1987–96)
Ford Bronco (1994–96)
GM Blazer, Bravada, Envoy,
  Jimmy (1995–98)

GM Blazer, Tahoe, Yukon
  (1995–98)
GM Chevrolet Tracker, Suzuki
  Sidekick (1994–98)
Honda Passport/Acura SLX/
  Isuzu Rodeo, Trooper (1993–97)
Nissan Pathfinder (1987–98)
Suzuki Samurai (1992–94)
Toyota Land Cruiser
Toyota RAV4 (1996)

Below Average

Chrysler Ramcharger (1985–89)
Ford Bronco (1988–93)
GM Blazer, Jimmy, Tahoe, Yukon
  (1990–94)

GM Chevrolet Tracker, Suzuki
  Sidekick (1989–93)
GM Suburban (1995–98)
Honda Passport/Isuzu Rodeo,
  Trooper (1986–92)

Not Recommended

AM General Hummer (1996–98)
Chrysler(Jeep) Cherokee
  (1985–94)
Chrysler(Jeep) Grand Cherokee
  (1993–94)
Chrysler(Jeep) Wagoneer, Grand
  Wagoneer (1985–93)
Ford Bronco (1979–87)
Ford Bronco II (1983–90)
Ford Explorer (1991–92)

GM Blazer, Jimmy (compacts)
  (1983–94)
GM Blazer, Jimmy (full-sized)
  (1985–89)
GM Escalade (1998)
GM Suburban (1985–94)
Lada Cossack, Niva
Land Rover Discovery
  (1994–98)
Suzuki X-90 (1997–98)
Suzuki Samurai (1986–91)

Full-Sized Vans

Recommended
GM Chevy Van, Express, Savana (1996–98)

Above Average
Chrysler Ram Wagon (1995–98)
Ford Club Wagon, Econoline
  (1997–98)

GM Chevy Van, Vandura
  (1980–95)

Average

Chrysler Ram Wagon   Ford Club Wagon, Econoline
   (1985–94)   (1991–96)

Not Recommended

Chrysler Ram Wagon (1980–84)
Ford Club Wagon, Econoline (1980–90)

Pickup Trucks

Recommended

Ford Ranger (1996–98)   Toyota Pickup, Tacoma
Mazda B-series* (1993–98)   (1995–98)
Nissan Frontier, Pickup (1985–98)

Above Average

Chrysler Dakota (1995–98)   Mazda B-series (1984–92)
Chrysler Ram D-150, 1500,   Toyota Pickup, Tacoma (1987–94)
   2500, 3500 (1997–98)   Toyota T100 (1997–98)

Average

Chrysler Dakota (1993–94)   Ford Ranger (1994–95)
Chrysler Ram 50 (1991–93)   GM C/K, Sierra (1994–98)
Chrysler Ram D-150, 1500,   Isuzu/Passport Hombre, Pickup
   2500, 3500 (1986–96)   (1992–98)
Ford F-series (1996–98)   Toyota T100 (1995–96)

Below Average

Chrysler Dakota (1987–92)   GM S-10, Sonoma, T-10
Ford F-series (1990–95)   (1996–98)

Ford Ranger (1980–93)   Isuzu/Passport Pickup (1989–91)
GM C/K, Sierra (1988–93)   Toyota T100 (1993–94)

Not Recommended

Chrysler Ram 50 (1985–90)   GM S-10, Sonoma, T-10 (1986–95)

*Although similar to the Ranger, Mazda's pickups elicit fewer owner complaints.

Other Buying Considerations

Front-wheel drive

Front-wheel drives direct engine power to the front wheels, which *pull*
the vehicle forward, while the rear wheels simply support the rear. The
biggest benefit of front-wheel drive (FWD) is foul-weather traction. With
the engine and transmission up front, there's lots of extra weight pressing down on the front-drive wheels, increasing tire grip in snow and on
wet pavement. However, when driving up a steep hill or towing a boat or
trailer, the weight shifts and there's no longer a traction advantage.

Although I recommend a number of FWD vehicles in this guide, I don't like them. Granted, front-wheel drives give a bit more interior room (no transmission hump), provide more carlike handling, and provide better fuel economy than rear-drives, but damage from pot-holes and fender-benders is usually more extensive and maintenance costs (premature front tire and brake wear, in particular) are much higher than with rear-wheel drives.

Servicing front-wheel drives can be a real nightmare. Entire steering, suspension, and drivetrain assemblies must be replaced when just one component is defective. Downtime is considerable, the cost of parts is far too high, and the drivetrain and its components are not designed for the do-it-yourself mechanic. A new FWD transmission assembly, called a transaxle, can cost about $2,000 to repair, compared to $700 for a rear-drive transmission.

Accident repairs are a unique problem. Front-wheel-drive transmissions and steering and suspension components are easily damaged and alignment difficulties abound. Repair shops need expensive, specialized equipment to align all four wheels and square up a badly smashed unibody chassis. Even if you can get all four wheels tracking true, the clutch and transaxle can still be misaligned. No wonder many insurance companies prefer to write off a FWD car rather than repair it. And when that happens, you wind up eating the difference between what you paid for the vehicle and what the insurance company says your vehicle is worth—minus your deductible, of course.

I also feel front-wheel drives are unsafe because braking requires a whole new set of reflexes than what we've developed over the years with rear-wheel drive vehicles. You remember the routine from driving school: *When in a skid, pump the brakes lightly and turn into the direction of the skid.* Well, if you pump the brakes of a FWD in a skid, you've bought the farm.

Rear-wheel drive

Rear-wheel drives direct engine power to the rear wheels, which *push* the vehicle forward. The front wheels steer and support the front of the vehicle. With the engine up front, the transmission in the middle, and the drive axle in the rear, there's plenty of room for larger and more durable drivetrain components. This makes for less crash damage, lower maintenance costs, and higher towing capacities than front-wheel drives.

On the other hand, rear-drives don't have as much weight over the rear wheels as front-drives do (and putting cement blocks in the bed or trunk will only void your transmission warranty). As such, they can't provide as much traction on wet and icy roads unless equipped with an expensive traction-control system.

Four-wheel drive

Four-wheel drives direct engine power through a transfer case to all four wheels, which *pull and push* the vehicle forward, giving you twice as much traction. The system is activated with a floor-mounted shift lever or dashboard button. When 4X4 drive isn't engaged, the vehicle is essentially a rear-drive truck. The large transfer case–housing makes the vehicle sit higher, giving you additional ground clearance. Two-wheel rear-drive vehicles have some of the highest payload and towing capabilities, usually slightly more than four-wheel drives.

Many 4X4 customers have been turned off by the typically rough and noisy driveline; a tendency for the vehicle to tip over when cornering at moderate speeds (a Bronco specialty); vague, trucklike handling; high repair costs; and poor fuel economy. Also, extended driving over dry pavement with 4X4-drive engaged will cause the driveline to bind and result in serious damage. Some buyers are turning instead to rear-drive pickups equipped with winches and large, deep-lugged rear tires.

All-wheel drive
Essentially, this is four-wheel drive *all the time*. Used mostly in sedans and minivans, all-wheel drive (AWD) never needs to be deactivated when running over dry pavement and doesn't require the heavy transfer case (although some sport-utilities and pickups do use a special transfer case) that raises ground clearance and cuts fuel economy. AWD-equipped vehicles aren't recommended for off-roading because of their lower ground clearance and fragile driveline parts, which aren't as rugged as four-wheel drive components.

Diesels
Diesel engines become more efficient as the engine load increases, whereas gasoline engines become less so. This is the main reason diesels are best used where the driving cycle includes a lot of city driving, with slow speeds, frequent stops, and long idling times. At full throttle, both engines are essentially equal from a fuel-efficiency standpoint. The gasoline engine, however, leaves the diesel in the dust when it comes to high-speed performance. Many owners of diesel-equipped vehicles are frustrated by excessive repair costs and poor road performance on vehicles that lack turbo. Bear in mind that before the fuel savings can outweigh the high cost of a diesel purchase, the average owner would have to drive 30,000–40,000 miles per year.

Fuel economy fantasies
Fuel economy figures are supplied by the federal government and are based on data supplied by the automakers following U.S. Environmental Protection Administration (EPA) testing guidelines. These figures are often off by 10–20 percent due to the testing method chosen. In fact, a recent Ford bulletin warns dealers: "Very few people will drive in a way that is identical to the EPA tests.... These [fuel economy] numbers are the result of test procedures that were originally developed to test emissions, not fuel economy."

Rustproofing
First off, remember, the best rustproofing protection is to keep your vehicle in a dry unheated garage or outside. Never bring your car in and out of a heated garage during the winter months. The months where temperatures are just a bit above freezing are the worst for rust promotion; especially during that time, keep your vehicle clean and dry.

If you live in an area where roads are heavily salted in winter, or in a coastal region, make sure you regularly have undercoating sprayed on the rocker panels (door bottoms), the rear hatch's bottom edge, and the wheel wells. This annual treatment, costing less than $100, will protect vital suspension and chassis components, make the vehicle ride more quietly, and allow you to ask a higher price at trade-in time. The only downside, which can be checked by asking for references: the undercoating may give off an unpleasant odor for months and drip, soiling your driveway.

A full rustproofing job doesn't offer that much protection—no matter how long the guarantee. In fact, you have a greater chance of seeing your rustproofer go belly-up before he makes good on your warranty than of having your untreated vehicle ravaged by premature rusting. Even if the rustproofer stays in business, you're likely to get a song-and-dance about why the warranty won't cover so-called "internal" rusting or why repairs will be delayed until the sheet metal is actually rusted through.

"Beaters," "collectibles," and "chick magnets"
If an independent mechanic says that the more common and costly defects listed in *Lemon-Aid* have been repaired, and if you have the time, knowledge, and parts suppliers to do your own maintenance and repairs, you may find an old, beat-up-looking vehicle that runs well (most of the time) in the $500–$1,000 range. Look for one of the recommended vehicles from the following list, avoid the non-recommended ones, take your time, and insist upon an independent check-up. Be wary of the trouble areas listed in parentheses.

If you have a bit more money to spend and want to take less of a risk, look up the recommended vehicles found at the beginning of each vehicle category in Part Three.

Recommended Beaters
(Cars to Get You through the Next Millennium)

Checker—Last made in 1982, the **Checker** is the poor man's Bentley. Its rear-drive configuration, sturdy, off-the-shelf mechanicals, and thick body panels all add up to bulletproof reliability. Beware of corrosion along door rocker panels and wheel wells.

Chrysler—Dart, **Valiant**, **Duster**, **Scamp**, **Diplomat**, **Caravelle**, **Newport**, **rear-drive New Yorker Fifth Avenue**, and **Gran Fury** (engine, electrical system, suspension, brakes, body and frame rust, plus constant stalling when humidity is high).

The **Caravelle**, **Diplomat**, and **New Yorker Fifth Avenue** are reasonably reliable and simple-to-repair throwbacks to a time when land yachts ruled the highways. Powered with 6- and 8-cylinder engines, they will practically run forever with minimal care. The fuel-efficient "slant 6" powerplant was too small for this type of car and was changed to a gas-guzzling, but smooth and reliable, V8 after 1983. Handling is vague and sloppy, though, and emergency braking is often accompanied by rear-wheel lockup. Still, what do you want for $500–$2,500 for a 1984–89 "retro rocket"?

Overall reliability is fairly good, and inexpensive parts are available anywhere. Carburetor, ignition, electrical system, brake, and suspension (premature idler-arm wear) problems predominate. It's a good idea to adjust the torsion bars frequently for better suspension performance. Doors, windshield pillars, the bottoms of both front and rear fenders, and the trunk lid rust through more quickly than average.

Chrysler's 1991–93 **2000GTX** is an above average buy that may cost $4,000–$6,000, depending upon the model year. It's a reliable Japanese-built sedan that was discontinued in 1994. It has a competitive price, modern styling, and high-performance options that put it on par with such benchmark cars as the Honda Accord and Toyota Camry. The base engine provides uninspiring yet adequate performance, but this car is distinguished by its high-performing optional powerplant—a 16-valve version that's smooth and powerful. The manual transmission and clutch are exceptionally smooth. Handling is acceptable in all situations. Excellent braking with anti-lock brakes, but mediocre without. The ride is firm but fairly comfortable on most roads, especially with the adjustable suspension. Interior room is generous for four people and you can carry a fifth passenger in a pinch (in the literal sense).

There are some reports of automatic transmission failures around the 40,000-mile mark. The front brakes need more attention than average. The car hasn't been crash-tested.

Ford—Maverick, Comet, Fairmont, Zephyr, Tracer, Mustang, Capri, Cougar, Thunderbird V6, Torino, Marquis, Grand Marquis, LTD, and **LTD Crown Victoria** (trunk, wheel well, and rocker panel rusting; brakes, steering, and electrical system). The 1991–93 **Festiva** can also be a good buy as long as you check out the brakes, exhaust system, and body panels for rust and paint; stay away from the 1989–90 versions.

General Motors—Chevette and **Acadian** (steering, and brakes you have to stand on to stop); rear-drive **Nova, Ventura, Skylark**, and **Phoenix** (suspension); front-wheel drive **Nova** and **Spectrum; Camaro, Firebird, Malibu, LeMans, Century, Regal, Cutlass, Monte Carlo**, and **Grand Prix**

(suspension and brakes); **Bel Air**, **Impala**, **Caprice**, **Laurentian**, **Catalina**, **Parisienne**, **LeSabre**, **Bonneville**, and **Delta 88** (suspension and brakes).

Nissan—The **Micra** is a subcompact commuter car that was sold 1985–91. It uses generic Nissan parts that are fairly reliable and not difficult to find, except for body panels that are more problematic. (Electrical shorts, premature front-brake wear, and body rusting along the door rocker panels and wheelwells are the more common deficiencies).

The 1991–95 **Nissan minivan** is an excellent choice that's fairly reliable and easily serviced (electrical system, brakes, manual transmission, and resonator).

Pulsar and **NX** models are good small-car buys ($500–$3,500, depending upon the year), as long as you pick the right years and stay away from failure-prone and expensive-to-repair turbo models. The **Pulsar** was replaced by the 1991 **NX**, a similar small car that also shares Sentra components. For 1983–86 models, overall reliability is poor to very poor. As with other discontinued Nissans, the 1987–93 models have shown remarkable performance improvement and are all the more attractive due to their depreciated prices. Crash test scores were below average for the 1990 and earlier models, while the 1991 and later versions scored quite well. All Pulsars built before 1991 are prone to premature wear on the front brake pads and discs and faulty air conditioners. From 1991 on, the only problems reported concern minor AC malfunctions, premature wearout of front brakes and suspension components, and exhaust systems that don't last very long (two years, tops). Complaints of premature rusting and paint peeling are legion for the 1983–90 models.

Subaru—Sold 1988–95, the **Justy** does everything reasonably well for an entry-level Subaru. Pairing smooth and nimble handling with precise and predictable steering, the 4X4 system is a boon for people who often need easy-to-engage extra traction and an automatic transmission. Prices range $500–$3,000.

The **Justy**'s reliability record has been about average from the 1991 model onwards. Some owners complain about poor engine idling and frequent cold-weather stalling, manual and automatic transmission malfunctions, premature exhaust system rust-out, catalytic converter failures, and paint peeling. With the exception of the CVT, servicing and repairs are made easy due to a very straightforward design.

Toyota (late '80s and early '90s)—All models, except the LE Van (brakes, chassis, and body rusting). Chassis rusting and V6 engine head gasket failures are common problems with the 1988–94 sport-utilities and pickups (Toyota will pay for the engine repairs up to eight years).

Volvo—The 1989–93 **240 series** is an average buy costing $3,000–$4,500. Problems with entry-level Volvos like the 240 mirror the quality control problems manifested by Saab, the other Swedish automaker, except for the fact that Volvo styling is more bland than bizarre. The 240 is a solid and spacious car. Unfortunately, it doesn't live up to Volvo's advertising as an automotive longevity wonder.

The V6 is an honest, though imperfect, engine. Avoid the turbocharged 4-cylinder engine and failure-prone air conditioning systems. Diesels suffer from cooling system breakdowns and leaky cylinder head gaskets. The brakes on all model years need frequent and expensive servicing, and exhaust systems are notorious for their short life span. The GL and GLE suffer from occasional electrical bugs.

"Beaten" Beaters
(Cars That Won't Get You through the Next Month)

American Motors—Hornet, Gremlin, Concord, Spirit, Pacer, and **Eagle 4X4** (faulty engines, transmissions, and steering).

Audi—Fox, 4000, and **5000** (engine, transmission, and fuel system; a combination of sudden acceleration and *no* acceleration).

British Leyland—Austin Marina, MG, MGB, and **Triumph** (electrical system, engine, transmission, clutch, and chassis rusting).

Chrysler (all years)**—Cricket, Omni/Horizon, Volaré/Aspen** (engine, brakes, steering, chassis rusting); **Charger, Cordoba**, and **Mirada** (brakes, body, and electrical system).

The 1985–89 **Lancer** and **LeBaron GTS** may only cost $500–$1,000, but they're no bargain. In fact, they suffer from many of the same problems as the **Aries** and **Reliant** K cars and their 1989 replacements, the **Spirit** and **Acclaim**. Although the interior will seat five comfortably and offers all the advantages of the hatchback design, road performance is merely passable with the standard engines and suspension.

Poor reliability causes maintenance costs to mount quickly. The manual transmission is balky and its clutch has a poor durability record. Turbo models are especially risky buys at all times. Head gaskets are prone to leaks, on all engines. Shock absorbers, MacPherson struts, and brakes wear out quickly. Front brake rotors are prone to rusting and warping. The electrical system is troublesome: the distributor pickup and computer modules malfunction constantly, causing stalling and hard starting. Air conditioning components have a short life span, and body hardware is fragile. Crash test scores are below average.

Although they don't cost much—$500–$2,000, depending on the year—steer clear of 1983–89 **Aries** or **Reliants**. Uncomplicated mechanical components and a roomy interior made these cars attractive buys when new, but once in service they quickly deteriorate. Both cars use dirt-cheap, low-tech components that tend to break down frequently. They have also performed poorly in crash tests.

All cars have a problem with idle shake caused by the transverse-mounted 4-cylinder engine, as well as driveability problems, especially in cold or damp weather. The "gutless" 2.2L Chrysler-built 4-cylinder motor is a bit more reliable than the 2.6L Mitsubishi engine, which has a tendency to self-destruct. It also suffers from premature wear of the timing belt guide and piston ring, and leaky camshaft oil plugs. The 2.2L powerplant has multiple problems, the main ones being a weak cylinder head gasket and timing belt failures. The turbocharged version often requires expensive repairs. The MAP sensor fails frequently and is costly to replace.

Carbureted engines are renowned for stalling and poor driveability. Exhaust systems, wheel bearings, and air conditioning components aren't durable. Water infiltration around the windshield and into the trunk is common. Serious corrosion generally starts along the trunk line and the edges of the rear wheel wells. Perforations tend to develop along the bottom door edges, around the windshield, and on the floor.

Datsun/Nissan—210, **310**, **510**, **810**, **F-10**, and **240Z** (electrical system, brakes, and rusting).

Eagle—Medallion, **Monaco**, and **Premier**. These bargain-priced French imports—$700–$800 for the **Medallion** and $1,000–$3,000 for the **Premier**—had a 1988–1992 model run. Sold through Chrysler's Renault connection, they are two of the most failure-prone imports to ever hit our shores. Powertrain, fuel system, electrical system, AC, suspension, and brakes are the worst offenders. The '91 and '92 **Monaco** and **Premier** are covered by a 10-year ABS brake warranty.

Fiat—"Fix it, again, Tony." All Fiat models and years are known for temperamental fuel and electrical systems and biodegradable bodies. **Alfa Romeos** have similar problems.

Ford—Cortina, **Pinto**, **Festiva**, **Fiesta**, **Bobcat**, and **Mustang II** (electrical system, engine, and chassis rusting); fire-prone **Pintos/Bobcats** are mobile Molotov cocktails.

The German import **Fiesta** and the **Festiva** built in South Korea are two small imports that only survived a few years on the North American market. Parts are practically unobtainable for both vehicles. The 1978–80 **Fiesta** was a fairly well made, inexpensive small car that's now worth $300–$500. Highway driving isn't recommended due to its weak engine and brakes. The slightly larger and more refined 1988–90 **Festiva** is an $500–$1,000 subcompact that's two feet shorter than the Escort, and weighs about 1,700 lb. Acceleration is slow, but the manual transmission is precise and easy to use. The post-'90 **Festiva** is only adequate for city use and with one passenger at best. Floorboards, body panels, and exhaust components quickly rust out, brakes and electrical components frequently need replacing, and the tall body and tiny tires make highway cruising a scream. Crash tests of an '89 **Festiva** showed the driver and passenger would sustain only minor injuries, however.

General Motors—Vega, **Astre**, **Monza**, and **Firenza** (engine, transmission, body, and brakes); **Cadillac Cimarron** and **Allanté** (poor-quality components and overpriced); all front-wheel drives (engine, automatic transmission, electronic modules, steering, brakes, and rust/paint peeling); **Citation**, **Skylark**, **Omega**, and **Phoenix** (engine, brakes, electronic modules, and severe rust canker).

The Pontiac **Fiero**, sold 1984–88, snares lots of unsuspecting first-time buyers through its attractive, sports-car styling, high-performance pretensions, and $700–$1,500 price. However, one quickly learns to both fear and hate the **Fiero** as it shows off its fiery disposition (several safety recalls) and "I'll start when I want to" character.

Buick's **Reatta**, a luxury two-seater sold only 1988–91 (present value: $5,500–$8,500 for the convertible), has higher-than-average maintenance costs, although repairs aren't that dealer-dependent, except for the electronically controlled fuel system. The **Reatta** also has higher-than-average parts costs and body parts are tough to find. GM improved the quality somewhat with its 1991 models, but then discontinued production.

The Geo **Storm** was GM's Japanese-made small car that only had four model years (1990–93). Owners report serious body hardware deficiencies (not paint or rust, however), in addition to brake, exhaust, electrical, and ignition problems. Prices vary between $2,500 and $4,000, depending on the model chosen.

Hyundai—Pony and **Stellar** (electrical system, brakes, poor-quality body components, and no parts). Hyundai's first imports into Canada during the early '80s, these cars were shooting stars that captured lots of sales during their first few years on the market—and then crashed once word got around that they were unsafe and unreliable.

Jaguar—All models (poor body assembly/paint, electrical system, and service).

Lincoln—Versailles (electrical system, suspension, and rusting) and early front-wheel drive Continentals (transmission, electrical system, brakes, and fuel system).

Passport/Isuzu—The **I-Mark**, **Stylus**, and **Optima** compacts were sold from 1988 until 1992 and can be bought for $1,000–$2,000, depending upon the year and model. Repair costs are higher than average due to the cars' mediocre reliability and the difficulty in finding parts at a reasonable cost. 1988–89 models garnered below-average crash test scores, while the last three model years (1990–92) did quite well.

Renault—All models (fuel and electrical systems, CV joints and brakes, no parts, and few mechanics).

Saab—All models (electrical fires, short circuits, hard-to-find parts, and few competent mechanics).

Volkswagen—Beetle (unsafe front seats, heater that never worked, hazardous fuel tank placement, wheels, and seat tracks); **Camper** minivan (engine, transmission, fuel system, and heater); **Rabbit/Dasher** and **411/412**: these cars are full of surprises, parts are rare, and the slow and expensive dealer servicing would give anyone nightmares (engine, electrical system, front brakes, and cooling system).

Sold during 1987–93, and now costing $1,500–$3,000, the **Fox**, with its old design, can't offer the mechanical or interior efficiency that newer small cars provide. Other failings are the absence of power steering and an automatic transmission. It's true that these cars are fun to drive, but they have a checkered reputation as far as reliability and durability are concerned. Furthermore, as time goes on, these cars become more troublesome and difficult to repair. Crashworthiness, as tested by NHTSA, is way below average.

Owners report common failures with engine timing belts, starter motors, the heating system, and brake cylinders. Other problem areas include electrical, engine cooling, and fuel systems. The manual transmission shift linkage needs frequent adjustment, and the front brakes and shocks, as on most VWs, need more frequent servicing than those of comparable makes.

VW's **Scirocco** is fun to drive, but risky to own. You'll like its nimble handling, strong, responsive engine, and tight steering. You'll like a lot less the car's chronic breakdowns, parts shortages, and poor crashworthiness. Electrical short circuits, chronic fuel supply problems, premature front brake wear, and fragile body parts are common owner complaints. Sold 1985–89, expect to pay $1,000–$2,000, depending upon the model year.

Collectibles?

Be wary of investing in recent high-performance American and Japanese sports cars. For example, GM took the Corvette ZR-1 off the market due to poor sales after only four years of production. Although 3,000 vehicles were to be produced annually, that figure dropped to fewer than 500 units. Owners who paid $59,555 for a new 1990 ZR-1 now own a car worth about $25,000. Today, you would likely do much better investing in a used Dodge Viper or Plymouth Prowler.

Discontinued Japanese sports cars have fared no better, with the possible exception of the limited-production 1965–70 Toyota 2000 GT. Datsun's 1961–69 1500/1600/2000 sports cars, for example, were better made, more reliable, and better equipped than the MGBs and MGAs, yet the English roadsters sell for about $15,000, while Nissan's barely go for a third of that price. The 240Z/260Z/280ZX used values decreased in direct proportion to their increased heft. What's the outlook on the axed 1990–96 300ZX? More of the same.

If you're seriously interested in collecting cars, remember that most vehicles jump in value after their 20th birthday. So you probably won't lose money if you buy a car of this vintage, especially if it's a convertible (trucks, sport-utilities, and vans are riskier investments). Shop the Internet and car shows—they're good places to contact wholesalers and restorers. Car clubs also offer a wealth of information and are regularly listed in major auto magazines like *AutoWeek, Car and Driver, Motor Trend,* and *Road and Track. Hemmings' Motor News* and *Old Cars Weekly* out of Iola, Wisconsin, are two other excellent sources of collector news.

Saving Money and Keeping Safe

You can get a good used vehicle at a reasonable price—it just takes lots of patience and homework. You can further protect yourself by becoming thoroughly familiar with your legal rights as outlined in Part Two and buying a vehicle recommended in Part Three. Following is a summary of the steps to take to keep your risk to a minimum.

Summary

1. Keep your vehicle for at least 10 years.
2. Trade in your vehicle if the dealer's sales tax reduction is more than the potential profit of selling privately.
3. Sell to a private party (10 percent premium).
4. Buy from a private party (10 percent savings).
5. Use an auto broker to save time and money.
6. Buy a *Lemon-Aid*-recommended vehicle for depreciation, parts, and service savings.
7. Buy a three- or four-year-old vehicle with lots of original warranty that can be transferred (35–50 percent savings over a new vehicle).
8. Choose a vehicle that's crashworthy and cheap to insure.
9. Carefully inspect Japanese-built vehicles that have reached their fifth year (engine head gasket, CV joints, steering box, and front brakes).
10. Don't buy an extended warranty ($500–$1,000 savings) unless it's recommended in this guide.
11. Have non-warranty repairs done by independent garages offering lifetime brake and exhaust repairs (50 percent savings).
12. Install used or reconditioned mechanical parts (30–50 percent savings).
13. Keep all the previous owners' repair bills to facilitate warranty claims and help mechanics know what's already been replaced or repaired.
14. Upon delivery, adjust mirrors to eliminate blind spots and adjust head restraints to prevent your head from snapping back in the event of a collision. On airbag-equipped vehicles, move the seat backwards more than half its travel distance and sit at least

10 inches away from the airbag housing. Make sure the spare tire and tire jack haven't been removed from the trunk. Get shoulder/lapbelts for the rear seats; lapbelts alone can be deadly.

15. Make sure the dealer and automaker have your name in their computers as the new owner of record. Ask for a copy of your vehicle's history, stored in the same computers.

Japanese vehicles that have a reputation for bulletproof reliability, like the '96 Honda Civic (shown above), are usually way overpriced. Look instead for a Japanese product sold by an American automaker.

Part Two
FIGHTING BACK!

Chrysler Battles Paint Blemishes by Banning Deodorant

"Paint-line workers at Chrysler Corp.'s Jeep plant were asked to stop using antiperspirant after the company discovered that falling flakes left costly blemishes on the new Jeep...General Motors officials contacted late yesterday said they didn't believe they had a similar problem....

One woman filed a grievance last year after her supervisor asked to check her armpits...."

Newsday, 1991

Ford Admits Its Paint Mistake (Privately)

"In June 1990, a field survey of about 1,000 F-series trucks (1985–1990 models) was conducted in three locations by Body and Chassis Engineering to assess paint durability. Results showed that about 13% of the F-series trucks displayed peeling paint, which would represent about 90,000 vehicles annually...."

Memo to members of the Finance Committee from
A. J. Trotman, Executive Vice President
Ford North American Automotive Operations

Ford customer relations has awesome, uncanny powers. It turned the owner of this Windstar from a dutiful wife and mother into a sign-carrying, service manager–chasing, letter-writing consumer activist in just a few weeks.

Invest in Protest

Few people really like to complain and even fewer are willing to make their dissatisfaction public. However, with 10 percent of cars estimated by Runzheimer International to be "lemons," and automakers promising more quality than they deliver and then cutting back on warranty coverage, consumers have discovered that they must either "act up" or get shut out—even if this means carrying signs or going to court to get compensation.

Getting Your Money Back

When letter writing and public protests fail to elicit a satisfactory response, your only recourse is to sue or at least threaten to sue. Yet we all know that you can win in court and still end up losing your shirt. That's why this section of the book is dedicated to helping you get your money back—without going to court or getting frazzled by the broken promises and "benign neglect" of the seller. But if going to court is your only recourse, you'll find here the jurisprudence you need to get an out-of-court settlement or to win your case without spending a fortune on lawyers or research.

First of all, forget about the seller's claim that "there's no warranty" or "because it was sold 'as is' you can't claim a refund." This is all hogwash. Any sales contract for a used vehicle can be canceled for one or more of the following reasons:
• The vehicle was misrepresented.
• The vehicle was unfit for the purpose for which it was purchased.
• The vehicle was not reasonably durable, considering its selling price, how well it was maintained, the mileage driven, and the type of driving.
• The vehicle was seriously defective at the time of purchase.

For example, if the seller claims that a minivan can pull a 2,000 lb. trailer and you discover that it can barely tow half that weight, you can cancel the contract for misrepresentation. The same principle applies to a seller's exaggerated claims concerning a vehicle's off-road capability, fuel economy, and reliability; and to "demonstrators" that are in fact used cars with false (rolled-back) odometer readings.

It's essential that printed evidence and/or witnesses (relatives are not excluded) be available to confirm that the false representation actually occurred. These misrepresentations must also concern an important fact that substantially affects the vehicle's performance, reliability, or value.

Some vehicles are meant to be driven hard, but when they fail to live up to the advertised hype, sellers often blame the owner for having pushed the vehicle beyond its limits. Therefore, when you attempt to set aside the contract, the testimony of an independent mechanic is essential to prove that the vehicle's poor performance wasn't caused by negligent maintenance or abusive driving.

Another hurdle to overcome is the "reasonable diligence" rule that requires one to file suit within a reasonable time after purchase or after the defect is discovered. The delay for filing a lawsuit can be extended if there's a secret warranty that extended the parameters of the original warranty, or if the seller has been promising to correct the defects for some time or has done some minor repairs while negotiating a final settlement. In cases of this sort, most courts will accept a four- to six-year delay, particularly with paint delamination claims.

Warranties

Unscrupulous dealers and con artists won't tell you this, but it's true: *every vehicle sold has some kind of warranty that can be enforced in court.* In fact, every new or used vehicle sold is covered by both state and federal warranties that protect you from misrepresentation and a host of other evils. Furthermore, American law and jurisprudence presume that car dealers, unlike private sellers, are aware of the defects present in the vehicles they sell. That's why dealers are paid a commission. The vehicles they sell are expected to be reasonably durable and merchantable. What is reasonably durable depends on the price paid, miles driven, the purchaser's driving habits, and how well the vehicle was maintained by the owner. Judges carefully weigh all these factors in awarding compensation or canceling a sale.

There is no standard warranty period, however, and some states require that dealers provide only minimal warranty coverage. Safety restraints like airbags and seatbelts often have coverage extended for the lifetime of the vehicle. On the other hand, you can lose warranty coverage through abusive driving, inadequate maintenance, or by purchasing aftermarket products and services such as gas-saving gadgets, rustproofing, paint protectors, air conditioning, and van conversions.

The manufacturer's or dealer's warranty is a legal promise that the product sold will perform in the normal and customary manner for which it was designed. This promise remains in force regardless of the number of subsequent owners as long as the warranty's original time/mileage limits haven't expired.

Some dealers tell customers that they need to have original equipment parts installed in order to maintain their warranty. A variation on this theme: a dealer requires that routine servicing, including tune-ups and oil changes (with a certain brand of oil), be done by the selling dealer or the warranty is invalid. Nothing could be further from the truth.

Congress passed the Magnuson-Moss Warranty Improvement Act— under the Federal Trade Commission (FTC)—years ago to protect motorists from this kind of abuse. The act says that whoever issues a warranty cannot make that warranty conditional on the use of any specific brand of motor oil, oil filter, or any other component, unless it's provided to the customer free of charge. If it is not provided for free, the customer should ask the issuer of the warranty to produce a copy of an FTC waiver that exempts the party from the act. If the waiver isn't forthcoming, the repair is free, and the repairer can be fined for violating a federal statute.

Sometimes dealers will do all sorts of minor repairs that don't correct the problem, and then after the warranty runs out they'll tell you that major repairs are needed. You can avoid this nasty surprise by repeatedly bringing in your vehicle to the dealership before the warranty ends. During each visit, insist that a written work order include the specific nature of the problem as *you* see it and that it carries the notation that this is the second, third, or fourth time the same problem has been brought to the dealer's attention. Write it down yourself, if need be. This allows you to show a pattern of non-performance by the dealer during the warranty period and establishes that it's a serious and chronic problem. When the warranty expires, you have the legal right to demand that it be extended on those items that consistently reappear on your handful of work orders.

A retired GM service manager gave me another effective tactic to use when you're not sure a dealer's warranty "repairs" will actually correct the problem for a reasonable period of time after the warranty expires. Here's what he says you should do:

> When you pick up the vehicle after the warranty repair has been done, hand the service manager a note to be put in your file that says you appreciate the warranty repair; however, you intend to return and ask for further warranty coverage if the problem reappears before a reasonable amount of time has elapsed—even if the original warranty has expired. A copy of the same note should be sent to the automaker....Keep your copy of the note in the glove compartment as cheap insurance against paying for a repair that wasn't fixed correctly the first time....

Chrysler's warranty performance

Chrysler's warranty performance is much better in Canada than it is in the U.S. This has come about because of the sustained media and legal pressure the company has felt from well organized, angry consumers north of the border; the creative way Chrysler has energized and empowered its best service advisers; and Chrysler's setting up of an easily accessible, efficient owner-assistance structure that handles appeals for post-warranty "goodwill" adjustments (Ford calls this AWA, for "After Warranty Assistance").

Chrysler paint and automatic transmission complaints have been reduced dramatically, though engine head gasket and AC failures are on the rise. Overall, the customer complaint handling of Chrysler is fairer and more efficient than that of other automakers, including the Japanese. Of course, the company's warranty performance will be closely monitored during the coming years and will be reviewed annually in upcoming *Lemon-Aid* guides.

Chrysler Canada

Here's a brief summary as to how Chrysler Canada's transformation came about—just in case American consumer activists are interested.

A year after Chrysler cut back its base warranty and post-warranty payouts, the 1997 Canadian edition of *Lemon-Aid Used Cars* blasted the company for systematically stonewalling owner complaints concerning automatic transmission, brake, and paint deficiencies that had afflicted the automaker's entire 1986–96 production. Shortly after *Lemon-Aid* hit the bookstores, Chrysler Parts, Service, and Engineering Vice President Robert Renaud and Public Affairs Vice President Othmar Stein agreed that Chrysler did, indeed, have some quality control and owner relations problems (this was a refreshing change from other automaker negotiations I've endured where the first day is wasted with incessant denials that any problem exists), and that the company was prepared to "do whatever it takes" to satisfy any outstanding complaints, whether the vehicle was bought new or used or had an expired warranty. Understand that this was during the period that Chrysler was in talks to merge with Mercedes-Benz, and Chrysler probably didn't want any more bad press.

I told both gentlemen that I would ask the Chrysler owners to band together regionally into CLOGs (Chrysler Lemon Owner Groups) and channel their complaints through a special phone number Chrysler would set up. Renaud agreed to take the calls, but the idea of the owners getting together didn't meet with a great deal of enthusiasm. I argued, however, that it was the only way to have a coherent set of demands, involve the owners directly in the efficient resolution of their complaints, and monitor Chrysler's commitment to fairness. We also agreed to meet again, to review how the complaint resolution process was or was not working.

Several months later, I met with the same two vice presidents and told them there were apparently 600 complaints outstanding; however, the team of customer advisors set up by Renaud, called the Owner Review Committee (bypassing Chrysler's customer relations "hot line," which many owners felt was ineffectual), was successfully whittling that number down. I then gave Renaud a set of powertrain, paint, and brake compensation benchmarks that I felt the company should use in compensating owners. Judging by the cases settled, Chrysler hasn't strayed far from the durability parameters I gave them. The durability chart that includes those benchmarks, which can be used with any automaker, is found on page 85.

In Canada, after almost three years, the committee continues to handle owner complaints relating to automatic transmission, paint delamination, AC, and brake malfunctions on a case-by-case basis for goodwill assistance, even if the claim has been previously refused, the base warranty has been exceeded, or the owner bought the car used.

You are looking at a rare piece of written evidence, showing Chrysler will pay for an AC failure—long after the original warranty has elapsed.

Furthermore, Chrysler customer service staffers still maintain that no claim will be automatically rejected because the vehicle owner had repairs done by an independent repair facility; many other mitigating factors would be weighed before the committee made a final decision to accept or reject a claim.

Owners seeking assistance in the future should initially work through their dealer service manager, request help from a Chrysler regional team representative, or call the Chrysler customer assistance toll-free number. If all these efforts fail, send a registered claim letter and file your complaint in small claims court.

Ford's warranty performance
Like Chrysler's warranty performance, Ford's warranty performance and "After Warranty Assistance" is better in Canada than in the U.S. American Ford owners frequently relate how dealers deny "goodwill" programs exist, or refuse engine head gasket and other extended warranty repairs because the vehicle was bought used or from a rival dealer. Ford USA insiders tell me the company prefers to stonewall post-warranty complaints, unless small claims action is threatened. Then claims are quickly paid off. Presently, Ford is seeking to empower dealers to settle post-warranty claims at the dealer level through P-05, P-06, and P-07 programs, but unless Ford gives clearer guidelines and stops cutting regional backup personnel—functions of field service engineers (FSE) and customer service engineers (CSE) have been merged with disastrous results in Memphis, Tennessee—nothing will have been accomplished.

Ford's customer assistance centers (CAC), in both Canada and the U.S., are contracted out to independent telephone- and letter-answering shops that use underpaid, under-trained employees who are given a prepared script to recite and a computer terminal to type in your complaint. They likely won't know the differences between a recall, an

emissions warranty, an Owner Notification Program, and a Special
Service Message repair. Safety complaints apparently don't fare much
better. After I was assured in a meeting with Ford Canada that safety-
related complaints would be automatically channeled from the CAC to
Ford's Product Liability section, it took me three months to get a simple coil spring failure/accident investigated and then settled.

Ford Canada
Here's a thumbnail summary of my dealings with Ford Canada—for
interested Americans.

The Canadian edition of *Lemon-Aid Used Cars 1999* targeted Ford
Canada for its denial of claims by owners of 1992–96 Tauruses, Sables,
and Windstars who had experienced 3.8L V6 engine head gasket and
automatic transmission failures. Subsequently, Ford formally extended
the warranty on head gasket claims to up to 5 years/100,000 km (letters were sent out under the company's Owner Notification Program)
for 1994–95 Tauruses, Sables, and Windstars, and Ford pledged to
review on a case-by-case basis all engine head gasket and automatic
transmission claims (principally, forward clutch piston failures) not fitting the above parameters.

When I met with Ford Canada executives in February 1999, they
flatly refused my request to formally extend the warranty relating to
forward clutch piston defects, inadequate automatic transmission planetary gear lubrication, clutch slave cylinder, and Villager engine
exhaust manifold stud failures, preferring to treat post-warranty claims
on an individual basis. At that same meeting, they were very forthcoming in providing me with information on a number of free fixes available under a variety of Owner Notification Programs. These free fixes
cover automatic transmission downshifts, front coil springs, engine
head gaskets, engine intake manifolds, engine mount bolts, engine
knocking, engine block heaters, seatbelt buckles, fuel tank stops, fuel
hose replacement, cooling fans, GEM modules, cooling system by-pass
kits, rear brake shields, and air cleaners (see following charts).

"M"
EXTENDED WARRANTY PROGRAMS (AS OF 2/23/99)

PROGRAM #	AFFECTED COMPONENT	VEHICLE LINE	PARAMETERS
98M04	Front Coil Springs	All 1995–1997 4cyl. Contour/Mystique	Through December 31, 2004
98M02	Front Coil Springs	Certain 1993 Taurus/Sable	December 31, 2001, regardless of distance
98M01	Headgasket 3.8L Engine	Certain 1994–1995 Taurus/Sable 3.8L engine	5 years or 100,000 km, whichever occurs first
		*1994 Continental	*6 years or 120,000 km,
		1995 Windstar	whichever occurs first
97M91	Intake Manifold	Certain 1996–1997 Crown Victoria (taxi), Thunderbird, Cougar, Mustang 4.6L Engine	7 years unlimited distance
97M90	Seat Belt Buckles	Certain 1989–1990 Continental Certain 1989 Taurus/Sable	12 years, regardless of distance travelled
96M89	Engine Knock	Certain 1995–1996 Villager	7 years or 160,000 km, whichever occurs first

Owners seeking assistance or compensation for any of the above problems should call one of Ford USA's customer assistance toll-free numbers: 1-800-392-3673 (Ford [Mercury]); 1-800-521-4140 (Lincoln); 1-800-232-5952 (TDD for the hearing impaired).

"B"
EXTENDED WARRANTY PROGRAMS (AS OF 2/23/99)

PROGRAM #	AFFECTED COMPONENT	VEHICLE LINE	PARAMETERS
98B37	Transmission Downshift	Certain 1999 Windstar 3.8L	Through July 31, 1999
98B36	Engine Mount Bolts	Certain 1999 Windstar 3.8L	Through July 31, 1999
98B35	Fuel Tank Stop	Certain 1999 F-800 (33KGVW)	Through July 31, 1999
98B32	Rear Brake Shields	Certain 1999 F250-550 SuperDuty 4x4 Trucks	April 30, 1999, regardless of distance
98B31	Fuel Hose Replacement	Certain 1992–1998 B-series chassis 5.9L	November 30, 1999, regardless of distance
98B30	Cooling Fan	Certain 1998 Contour/Mystique	April 30, 1999, regardless of distance
98B29	GEM Module	1999 F250/350 Super Duty 4x4	Through July 31, 1999
98B26	Cooling System By-pass	Certain 1996–1997 3.0L Taurus Methanol Engine	Through February 28, 1999, regardless of distance
98B23	Cooling System By-pass Kit	Certain 1996–1997 3.0L Taurus/Sable Gas/Ethanol	Through February 28, 1999, regardless of distance
98B21	Engine Block Heater	Certain 1995–1998 Contour/Mystique 1998 ZX2	Through February 28, 1999, regardless of distance
97B16	Air Cleaners	1994–1997 H.D. F-series with 7.3 DIT	Through February 28, 1999, or 160,000 km whichever occurs first

    Since that last meeting, Ford engine head gasket and automatic transmission complaints have continued to pour in, a class-action lawsuit targeting the 3.8L engine has been filed in Chicago (tel: 312-372-8822), and a half-dozen websites that inform and mobilize owners have been set up (see the Appendix, "30 Best Internet Gripe Sites").

General Motors' warranty performance

General Motors' warranty performance is a bit better than Ford's, due mainly to the company's successful dealer empowerment programs allowing dealers in the States and Canada to make substantial warranty and post-warranty refunds. GM quality control has also improved, particularly in its full-sized pickups, though most of GM's front-drive lineup is mediocre, at best. The automaker's customer service staffers aren't very knowledgeable or helpful as far as warranty disputes are concerned, preferring to refer customers back to the dealer.

Like Ford, GM has a codified system of archiving post-warranty payout programs included in its monthly service bulletins. (Interestingly, Chrysler doesn't leave much of a paper trail.) Overall, the GM "goodwill" programs are far more generous than Ford's and about on par with Chrysler's, although, as you can see in the GM service bulletin on the following page, customers are routinely given the third degree before refunds are granted.

FILE IN SECTION: Warranty Administration
BULLETIN NO.: 57-05-01
DATE: April 1995
SUBJECT:
Dealer/Retailer Administration of Case-by-Case individual Goodwill Adjustments
MODELS:
General Motors Passenger Cars and Trucks
All General Motors Marketing Divisions **(Except GM of Canada)**
ATTENTION: Service Manager/Warranty Claims Administrator
Listed below is the definition for goodwill adjustments, general administrative guidelines, identifying the facts
and division claim authorization empowerment information.
DEFINITION:
Individual, case-by-case, goodwill adjustments are intended to recognize that circumstances, outside the parameters of
the written warranty, may exist where special consideration is in order to enhance customer satisfaction and loyalty.
Such goodwill adjustments should not be confused with special policy adjustments provided to all involved owners through a special bulletin and direct mail. Case-by-case individual goodwill adjustments are not legal obligations like the terms of General Motors warranties.
GENERAL ADMINISTRATIVE GUIDELINES:
• Maximum dealer/retailer authorization empowerment, common to all GM divisions, is up to 2
  years/24,000 miles for non-paint conditions and up to 2 years/unlimited mileage for paint, beyond the
  limits of the Bumper to Bumper base new vehicle warranty. Maximum authorization empowerment regarding GMC and Chevrolet medium duty truck authorization empowerment will be 2 years unlimited mileage
  for both non-paint and paint due to the unlimited mileage base warranty.
• Some dealers/retailers may be empowered to limits less than the maximum while a few select
  dealers/retailers may not be empowered at all. Individual dealer/retailer authorization empowerment levels are subject to change upon divisional notification.
• Any claim involving "individual goodwill adjustments" submitted after the effective date of March 15,
  1995, which exceeds the dealer/retailer goodwill adjustment authorization empowerment limit will require
  wholesale review and authorization. This includes work in process for which you may have already com-
  mitted to perform.
• Bumper to Bumper base new vehicle warranty coverage does not include current and past model year warranty
  coverages on specific components that carry warranty coverage longer than the base new vehicle warranty coverage, i.e., "Federal and California Emissions Warranties," "Sheet Metal Coverage" or Diesel Engine Coverage."
• Paint Labor Operations excluded from authorization empowerment. See below:
  Dealer/retailer authorization empowerment for paint claims covers exterior body panels only.
IDENTIFYING THE FACTS:
Your authorization empowerment should be exercised when it appears that the condition could be the result of a
defect in materials or workmanship rather than conditions occurring from aging, physical damage, lack of proper
maintenance or owner abuse. Vehicle concerns should be assessed on their own merits within the context of the cur-
rent owner's reasonable expectations and with appropriate concern for the cost to General Motors.
In exercising your judgment in each case, the following questions are some which should be considered:
• Is the vehicle covered by other service or extended warranty contracts? If "yes," repairs must be performed
  under that contract.
• Does the vehicle show a lack of proper care and maintenance?
• Is the overall condition of the vehicle such that the cost to repair will approximate the vehicle's value?
• If the vehicle was purchased used by the current owner, is it likely the vehicle exhibited the condition before purchase?
• Did the condition occur while the vehicle was in the possession of a second or third owner and no vehicle
  history is available?
• Could the customer have done anything to prevent or cause the condition?
• Has the vehicle been used in ways for which it was not intended?
• Did the condition result from an after market conversion or alteration?
• Did the condition result from use of non-GM parts or accessories?
• Is there evidence of vehicle mileage alteration?
• Is the vehicle condition a normal operating characteristic?
• Is the condition largely a result of normal aging, wear and usage?
• Is the condition a result of unusual localized environmental, geographical or climate factors?
Additional Questions When Paint Condition Is the Concern:
• Is the condition largely the result of normal paint aging or environmental damage (fading, gloss loss, chalk-
  ing, cracking, yellowing)?
• Is the condition only on a physically damaged panel that the customer declines to repair?
The above list is not intended to be all inclusive. However, if the answer to any of these or similar questions is
"yes," then it probably is not a concern you should address at General Motors' expense.
PARTIAL PARTICIPATION:
In situations beyond the warranty period, but within your claim authorization empowerment, customers have received
value from use of the vehicle. It would be reasonable to consider partial payment by the customer. The judgment
belongs to you.
• Determine what the customer expects before making an offer to assist.
• Evaluate the reasonableness of the customer's expectations.
• Determine what offer would satisfy the customer as a fair and equitable adjustment.
• Make your evaluation of the situation through direct communication with the customer.
• Always strive for a mutually acceptable agreement.

*Be prepared to answer the above questions that GM suggests its dealers ask you
before doling out any "goodwill" repair refunds. In fact, you can save time
and improve your chances of getting compensation by incorporating some of the
questions and answers in a fact sheet accompanying your complaint letter.*

Extended (supplementary) warranties

Extended warranties provide extended coverage, may be sold by the manufacturer, dealer, or an independent third party, and are automatically transferred when the vehicle is sold. They cost $500–$1,500 and should be purchased only if the vehicle you're buying is off its original warranty, has a poor repair history (see Part Three), or if you're reluctant to use the small claims courts when trouble arises that is factory related. Don't let the dealer pressure you into deciding right away. Generally, you can purchase an extended warranty anytime during the period the manufacturer's warranty is still in effect.

Dealers love to sell extended warranties because about one-third to one-half of this warranty's cost represents dealer markup. Out of the remainder comes the sponsor's administration costs and profit margin, calculated at another 25 percent. What's left is a minuscule 25 percent of the original amount paid to the dealer. It's estimated that of the auto buyers who purchase an extended service contract, fewer than half actually use it.

It's often difficult to collect on supplementary warranties because independent companies not tied to the automakers frequently go out of business. When this happens, and the company's insurance policy won't cover your claim, take the dealer to small claims court and ask for the repair cost and a refund of the extended warranty payment. Your argument for holding the dealer responsible is a simple one: by accepting a commission for acting as an agent of the defunct company, the selling dealer took on the obligations of the company as well.

Emissions control warranties

These little-publicized warranties come with all new vehicles and are automatically transferred to subsequent owners. They cover the emissions control system for up to 8 years/100,000 miles (California residents will find they may have longer warranties for these same emissions components). Unfortunately, although owner manuals vaguely mention the emissions warranty, most don't specify which parts are guaranteed.

EPA investigators had waged a longstanding battle with Ford over the company's charging its customers for repairs covered by the emissions warranty. Each time customers complained to the EPA, Ford refunded the money or agreed to repair the vehicle—but not to change its warranty practice.

In 1989, the EPA sued Chrysler and Ford for billing customers for emissions-related repairs that should have been done for free. Chrysler was fined $660,000 for denying warranty coverage to 66 car owners for replacement of and repairs and adjustments to carburetors, fuel injectors, and turbochargers. These owners paid from $22 to $645 to have their cars fixed, even though the repairs fell under warranty. Ford was fined $92,000 for charging for similar repairs. The government had proposed a $230,000 fine for denying the warranty to 23 owners but reduced the amount when Ford agreed to repay over 500 consumers.

EMISSIONS COVERAGE

Under the Emissions Control Systems coverage of this warranty, Ford Motor Company of Canada Limited warrants that your vehicle:

1) is designed, built and equipped to conform, at the time it was manufactured, with the Emissions Regulations under the Canada Motor Vehicle Safety Act.

and

2) is free from defects in factory-supplied materials or workmanship which would cause it to fail to conform to those regulations for a period of five years or 80,000 kilometres, whichever occurs first.

Your Ford of Canada dealer will not charge you to adjust, repair, or replace (including labour and diagnosis) an emissions-related part. If the diagnosis reveals no emissions-related defect, the Emissions Control Systems coverage of this warranty does not apply.

The following list of parts is covered under the Emissions Control Systems coverage of this warranty for 5 years/80,000 kilometres.

- Air/Fuel Feedback Control System and Sensors
- Altitude Compensation System
- Catalytic Converter
- Controls for Deceleration
- Electronic Engine Control Processor
- Electronic Engine Control Sensors and Switches
- Electronic Ignition System
- Exhaust Gas Recirculating (EGR) Valve, Spacer, Plate, and Associated Parts
- Exhaust Manifold
- Exhaust Pipe (Manifold to Catalyst)
- Fuel Filler Cap and Neck Restrictor
- Fuel Injection System
- Fuel Tank
- Fuel Vapor Storage Canister, Liquid Separator, and Associated Controls
- Ignition Coil and/or Control Module
- Intake Air Flow Meter/Temperature Sensor Assembly
- Intake Manifold
- Malfunction Indicator Light System (MIL)
- PCV System and Oil Filler Cap
- Spark Control Components
- Spark Plugs and Ignition Wires
- Throttle Air Control Bypass Valve
- Throttle Body Assembly (MFI)
- TWC Air Control Valve

The emissions-related bulbs, hoses, clamps, brackets, tubes, gaskets, seals, belts, connectors, gasoline fuel lines, and wiring harnesses that are used with the components listed above are also covered by the Emissions Control Systems coverage of this warranty.

The above chart was prepared by Ford Canada to give consumers an idea as to which parts can be charged back to the company. American Ford owners have much longer extended warranties that cover essentially the same components.

Dealer service bulletins listed in Part Three, "Secret Warranties/ Service Tips," show some parts failures that are covered under the emissions warranty. If you've paid for repairs that should have been covered by this warranty (3.8L engine head gaskets and Villager, Quest, Maxima, and Pathfinder exhaust manifold bolts, for example), contact the automaker and your dealer and ask for a refund. (Don't be shy about mentioning the EPA lawsuit.)

Secret warranties

Secret warranties have been around since automobiles were first mass-produced. They're set up to provide free repairs to fix performance-related defects caused by substandard materials, faulty design, or assembly-line errors. In 1974, *Lemon-Aid* exposed Ford's J-67 secret seven-year rust warranty, which covered the company's 1970–74 models. After first denying that it had such a warranty, Ford admitted two years later that it was indeed in place and negotiated a $2.8 million settlement with this author to compensate owners of rust-cankered Fords who had formed the Rusty Ford Owners Association. And you know what? Twenty-six years later, hundreds of secret warranties continue to exist among most automakers and *Lemon-Aid* is still the only consumer publication blowing the whistle on hundreds of current programs that secretly allocate funds for the repair of engine, transmission, fuel pump, and paint defects on cars, sport-utilities, trucks, minivans, and vans.

Even mundane little repairs that can still cost you a hundred bucks or more are covered. Take, for example, the elimination of foul, musty, or mildew odors emitted by your air conditioning unit. Despite what the dealer may say, it's covered by the base warranty. In fact, automakers have secret warranty policies that pay for AC service adjustments.

Automakers are reluctant to make secret warranty extensions public because they feel it would weaken confidence in their product and increase their legal liability. The closest they come to an admission is sending a "goodwill policy," "product improvement program," or "special policy" service bulletin to dealers or first owners of record. Consequently, the only motorists who get compensated for repairs to defective parts are the original owners who haven't moved or leased their vehicle, or those who yell the loudest and present automaker service bulletins (see the Appendix, "30 Best Internet Gripe Sites," for an address where you can order bulletins). Connecticut, Massachusetts, New York, Maryland, Texas, and California have enacted laws prohibiting secret auto warranties under penalty of a $2,000 fine, but they're seldom enforced because it's hard to get written proof they exist.

If you're refused compensation, remember that secret warranty extensions are an admission of manufacturing negligence. Try to compromise with a pro rata adjustment from the manufacturer. If polite negotiations fail, challenge the refusal in court on the grounds that you should not be penalized for failing to make a reimbursement claim under a secret warranty you never knew existed!

Here are a few examples of the latest and most comprehensive secret warranties that have come across my desk in the last several years. Keep in mind that an up-to-date listing of service bulletins that provide for free repairs under secret warranties and assorted other service programs can be found in Part Three under the heading "Secret Warranties/Service Tips."

Chrysler, Ford, and General Motors: all years, models
- **Problem:** Faulty paint jobs that cause paint to turn white and peel off of horizontal panels. Ford and GM internal memos and service bulletins admit this is a factory defect. Out-of-court settlements proffered by all three automakers also confirm the six-year benchmark, although Chrysler confirmation is anecdotal, not written. Three small claims judgments that nailed GM to the wall, however, have extended the benchmark to seven years, second owners, and pickups.
- **Warranty coverage:** Automakers will offer a free paint job up to 6 years/no mileage limitation. Thereafter, all three manufacturers offer 50–75 percent refunds on the small claims courthouse steps.

Article No. 93-8-4
April 14, 1993
PAINT - EXTERIOR CLEARCOAT "MICROCHECKING," HAZING OR PEELING

FORD:
1983-93 THUNDERBIRD
1984-93 TEMPO
1985-93 ESCORT
1986 LTD
1986-93 TAURUS
1989-93 CROWN VICTORIA, MUSTANG, PROBE

LIGHT TRUCK:
1983-93 RANGER
1986-93 AEROSTAR
1987-90 BRONCO II
1988-93 F SUPER DUTY, F-47
1991-93 ECONOLINE, EXPLORER
1992-93 F-150-350 SERIES
1993 VILLAGER

LINCOLN-MERCURY
1983-93 COUGAR
1984-92 MARK VII
1984-93 TOPAZ
1985-89 TRACER
1986 MARQUIS
1986-93 SABLE
1988-93 CONTINENTAL, TOWN CAR
1989-93 GRAND MARQUIS
1991-93 TRACER
1993 MARK VIII

ISSUE: The clearcoat layer of the basecoat/clearcoat paint system may "microcheck" (crack and erode), turn white, flake or peel off vehicle. This condition is noticeable on the horizontal surfaces only.
ACTION: Inspect the vehicle and if repair is necessary, refer to the following procedure for service details. This is a wet on wet procedure. Sanding is not required after the seal coat is applied.

Paint delamination afflicts Ford's entire lineup going back to the 1983 model year, according to Ford DSB 93-8-4.

Clearcoat Degradation - Chalking and Whitening
Group Ref.: Body
Bulletin No.: 331708
Date: November, 1993
SUBJECT:
CLEARCOAT DEGRADATION - CHALKING AND WHITENING
MODELS:
PASSENGER CARS WITH BASECOAT/CLEARCOAT
CONDITION:
The vehicle exterior surface may show large chalky or white patches in the clearcoat, usually but not limited to the horizontal surfaces.
Blacks, Dark Blues, Reds, may have potential for this condition. On rare occasions, other colors may be involved.
CAUSE:
The clearcoat (with sunlight and heat) may degrade and turn white or chalky.
IDENTIFICATION:
On a clean surface, at or above room temperature, firmly apply a 2" wide piece of masking tape to the chalky or white area of the clearcoat and pull upward quickly. The adhesive side of the tape WILL NOT HAVE THE PAINT COLOR ON IT. A light shine of reduced tackiness may be noticed on the tape adhesive surface, indicating clearcoat transfer to the tape.
CORRECTION:
Refinish all horizontal surfaces using the following procedure.
- Remove the clearcoat layer from all horizontal surfaces and the top surfaces of fenders and quarter panels.
NOTE:
In some cases, it will be necessary to remove the clearcoat from the upper vertical surfaces of fenders, doors and quarters (approximately 3"), and the top areas directly above the front and rear wheelhouse openings.
- Lightly sand any previously exposed base color to remove any chalky residue from the surface.
- The vertical surfaces should be sanded and colorcoated to the next lower breakline (typically the body side moldings) for color uniformity of the repair.

This General Motors service bulletin not only is an admission of GM's paint delamination problem, it also gives a simple test for identifying the defect.

Preliminary Information
FILE IN SECTION: 10-Body
BULLETIN NO.: 23-10-54
DATE: June 1995
SUBJECT:
Service Procedures for the Repair of Paint Colorcoat Delamination from ELPO Primer (Repair Surfaces Above the Body Side Moldings)
MODELS:
1988-91 Buick Century (Plant Code 6)
1988-92 Buick LeSabre (Plant Code H), Skylark
1988-90 Chevrolet Celebrity
1988-92 Chevrolet Beretta, Corsica, Skylark
1988-90 Oldsmobile Cutlass Supreme
1988-91 Oldsmobile Calais, Ciera (Plant Code 6)
1988-92 Oldsmobile Achieva, Eighty Eight (Plant Code H)
1988-90 Pontiac Grand Prix
1988-91 Pontiac 6000 (Plant Code 6)
1988-92 Pontiac Firebird, Grand Am, Tempest
1988-92 Chevrolet and GMC Truck C/K, R/V, S/T M/L, G Models
1991-92 Oldsmobile Bravada
This bulletin is being revised to provide a process change for the repair of paint delamination from ELPO primer. Please discard previous publications:
Buick   92-10-57
Chevrolet   92-300A-10
GM of Canada   93-10-100
GMC Truck   92-10-134A
Oldsmobile   93-T-05
Pontiac   93-10-59
EFFECTIVE DATE:
THE REVISED REPAIR PROCEDURES, NEW LABOR OPERATION NUMBERS AND REVISED TIME AND MATERIAL ALLOWANCES CONTAINED IN THIS BULLETIN ARE EFFECTIVE WITH REPAIR ORDERS WRITTEN ON OR AFTER JUNE 20, 1995.
CONDITION:
This bulletin is being issued to assure that the correct procedure is followed to repair a condition known as delamination. Some of the listed passenger cars, light duty trucks, and vans may have DELAMINATION (peeling) of the paint colorcoat from the ELPO primer depending upon variable factors including prolonged exposure to sunlight and humidity.
Blues, Grays, Silvers and Black Metallics are the colors that have the highest potential for this condition. On rare occasions, other colors may be involved.
Important:
Delamination is different than other paint conditions and/or damage. A proper problem identification is necessary, and the service procedure that follows is specific to the proper repair of delamination and must be followed. The information in this bulletin covers paint delamination of the colorcoat from the ELPO primer ONLY. It does not address any other paint conditions. Procedures for the repair of other paint conditions (stone chips, scratches, environmental damage, clearcoat peeling, runs, dirt, fading, etc.) will not effectively repair delamination and customer dissatisfaction will result.
CAUSE:
*This condition may occur on vehicles produced in plants where the paint process did not call for application of a primer surfacer. Under certain conditions, ultraviolet light can penetrate the colorcoat, sometimes causing a reaction and separation of portions of the colorcoat from the ELPO (electrocoat) primer.
PROBLEM IDENTIFICATION:
On a clean surface, at or above room temperature, firmly apply a 2" wide piece of masking tape and pull upward quickly. DO NOT USE duct tape, cloth backed tape or other aggressive tapes. If the colorcoat flakes or peels away from the ELPO (leaving the ELPO intact) the colorcoat is delaminating and the vehicle should be repaired.

Judging by the models listed above, paint delamination can occur within the first three years the vehicle's on the road.

Paint Should Last Six Years, Says GM!

 PONTIAC

PONTIAC DIVISION
General Motors Corporation
One Pontiac Plaza
Pontiac, Michigan 48340-2952

October 16, 1992

TO: All Pontiac Dealers

SUBJECT: Partners in Satisfaction (PICS)
Dealer Authorization

Pontiac continually reviews the Warranty Management System to ensure that Warranty Administration achieves its purposes, including high levels of customer satisfaction with after sale treatment.

Following a recent review, Pontiac has decided to provide dealers authorization for cases involving <u>paint repairs</u> for vehicles up to six (6) years from the date of delivery, without regard for mileage. This is a change from the current PICS dealer self-authorization which allows paint repair goodwill adjustments to be made up to 6 years/60,000 miles. Dealers who have a deductible override capabilities may also waive deductibles as they see appropriate on this type of repair.

Paint repairs are only to be authorized beyond the warranty period by the Dealership <u>Service Manager</u> on a case-by-case basis as with any other goodwill policy adjustment.

Assistance should only be considered for cases involving evidence of a defect in materials or workmanship by the manufacturer. Assistance should not be considered for conditions related to wear and tear and/or lack of maintenance (such as fading, stone chips, scratches, environmental damage, etc.).

Please contact your Zone representative if you have specific questions.

Perry S. White

Perry S. White
Director of Service/
Customer Satisfaction

This confidential memo to Pontiac dealers applies to all of GM's vehicles, and can be used as a benchmark for what the automaker considers its obligation when faced with paint claims. Note GM doesn't use any "weasel" words, like "acid rain" or "UV-ray deterioration," to avoid its responsibility. Plus, GM says owners don't have to pay any deductible.

Chrysler: 1995–99 Breeze, Cirrus, Neon, Sebring convertible, Stratus, and minivans

• **Problem:** Engine head gasket failure.

• **Warranty coverage:** Chrysler is quietly paying off owners after the warranty has expired up to 5 years/100,000 miles if they threaten small claims action. For all those owners who are refused compensation, bulletin number 09-05-98 shows that Chrysler's 1995–99 models equipped with 2.0L and 2.4L engines have weak head gaskets that should be replaced with more durable ones. It can be useful as another tool to negotiate an out-of-court settlement.

Chrysler (Jeep): 1991–93 minivans and 1989–93 Cherokee and Wagoneer

• **Problem:** ABS brakes that fail or malfunction.

• **Warranty coverage:** Piggy-backing a service campaign onto a recall, Chrysler extended the warranty to 10 years/100,000 miles on a number of costly ABS components. Owners will also be reimbursed for previous ABS repairs—not applicable to calipers, pads/shoe linings, or other maintenance items. Two other ABS components, piston seals (excessive wear) and the pump motor (deterioration), will be repaired free of charge at anytime during the life of the vehicle (see the recall notice on the following page).

Chrysler (Jeep): 1993–99 Concorde, Intrepid, New Yorker, LHS, Vision, and Grand Cherokee

• **Problem:** AC evaporator failure or malfunction.

• **Warranty coverage:** 7 years/80,000 miles (see page 65 for a copy of the Chrysler warranty addendum).

Ford (Lincoln): all 1992–97 models equipped with automatic transmissions

• **Problem:** Forward clutch piston, planetary gear, and clutch slave cylinder may fail prematurely.

• **Warranty coverage:** Ford will replace the defective components at no charge up to 5 years/80,000 miles.

Ford (Lincoln): 1994 Lincoln Continental; and 1994–95 Taurus, Sable, and Windstar

• **Problem:** Defective 3.8L engine head gaskets may cause loss of engine coolant, engine overheating, or destruction of the engine.

• **Warranty coverage:** Ford will replace the defective components at no charge up to 5 years/80,000 miles. Vehicles that have exceeded the mileage limit will still be covered if the problem was reported or repaired before December 31, 1998. Continentals are eligible up to 6 years/100,000 miles.

1996-12-06   #685
SAFETY RECALL #685 — ANTI-LOCK BRAKE SYSTEM (ABS)

Dear Chrysler Canada Ltd. Vehicle Owner:

PLEASE CALL YOUR SELLING CHRYSLER CANADA LTD. DEALER AS SOON AS POSSIBLE TO ARRANGE FOR A SERVICE APPOINTMENT TO CORRECT A POTENTIAL SAFETY DEFECT ON YOUR VEHICLE, AS SHOWN ON THE ENCLOSED RECALL SERVICE AUTHORIZATION CARD.

Chrysler Canada Ltd. has determined that a defect which relates to motor vehicle safety exists in some **1991 through 1993 Dodge Caravan/Grand Caravan, Plymouth Voyager/Grand Voyager and Chrysler Town and Country; late-1990 through 1993 Dodge Dynasty, Chrysler New Yorker, Fifth Avenue and Imperial; and 1991 and 1992 Eagle Premier vehicles equipped with an anti-lock brake system (ABS).**

The Problem is...	The ABS hydraulic control unit on your vehicle may experience excessive brake actuator piston seal wear an/or pump-motor deterioration. If this occurs, the ABS function may be lost and reduced power assist may be experienced during braking. This *may* result in increased stopping distance that could result in an accident.
What you must do to ensure your safety...	Owners of vehicles that experience any of the following symptoms should contact their dealers *immediately* to schedule a service appointment: • Either the Brake System Warning Light or the Anti-lock Warning Light remains *illuminated more then two minutes* after starting the vehicle; *or if either light comes on* at any other time during vehicle operation; • A *substantial* increase in *brake* pedal force is needed to stop the vehicle; or • Any other ABS malfunction occurs. Contact your Dealer right away to schedule a service appointment. **Bring the enclosed Service Authorization Card with you and give it to your dealer.** NOTE: **If your ABS brake system is operating properly** and none of the above symptoms are present, **no action is necessary at this time**. However, if any of these symptoms appear in the future, contact your dealer immediately for a free repair. *Keep this letter with your vehicle's other owner information in case you notice any of these conditions in the future.*
What Chrysler and your dealer will do...	**Your Selling Dealer will test your vehicle's ABS for excessive piston seal wear and possible pump-motor deterioration.** If problems *with these components* are found at any time during the entire life of your vehicle, *Chrysler* will replace these components free of charge. The test will take about one hour to complete and you will not be charged for it. **Another one to two hours may be required if components must be replaced. However, additional time may be necessary depending on how dealer appointments are scheduled and processed.**
Extended Warranty...	In addition to this recall action, the warranty period on other ABS components in your vehicle is being extended to 10 years or 160,000 km (100,000 miles) whichever occurs first. This means that if any of these other ABS components fail within 10 years or 160,000 km (100,000 miles) your dealer will correct the problem free of charge. This extended warranty is limited to the same conditions defined in the original warranty and does not include any base brake system components (calipers, pad/shoe linings, etc.). Further, Chrysler will reimburse owners for any previous ABS components expenses incurred.
If you need help...	If you are unable to return to your selling dealer, any authorized Chrysler Canada Ltd. dealer can perform this service. Should you experience any difficulty in obtaining the recall service, please contact Chrysler Canada Customer Service at 1-800-465-2001 (English) or 1-800-387-9983 (French). We will take the necessary steps to ensure prompt servicing of your vehicle.

This notice is sent to you in accordance with the Canada Motor Vehicle Safety Act.

American and Canadian owners of sport-utilities, minivans, or cars that experience any kind of ABS malfunction should go to the nearest Chrysler dealer and demand that the ABS be checked at Chrysler's expense.

Ford Motor Company of Canada, Limited   The Canadian Road
Ford du Canada Limitée   P.O. Box 2000
                                                Oakville, Ontario
                                                L6J 5E4

                                                June 23, 1998

As part of our ongoing efforts to increase customer satisfaction, Ford Motor Company of Canada, Limited (Ford) is providing extended coverage under service program number 98M01, to owners of 1994 and 1995 Taurus and Sable and 1995 Windstar vehicles equipped with a 3.8L FWD Engine. Our records show you own the vehicle with the serial number shown above your name and address.

Reason For This Program:	Premature failure of the head gaskets may occur and may result in engine overheating, or, in extreme cases could cause engine failure if the overheat condition is ignored. The extended coverage is Ford Motor Company's commitment to customer satisfaction and we are taking this action as part of our ongoing efforts to maintain your confidence in our products.
No Charge Coverage:	Ford is providing extended coverage for this condition only. If your vehicle's engine should experience this condition, your dealer will verify the condition and replace the engine head gaskets, if necessary.
	The extended coverage for this condition is available on affected Taurus, Sable and Windstar vehicles for 5 years or 100,000 km from the vehicle's original warranty start date and is automatically transferred to subsequent owners.
	On vehicles for which the extended coverage has expired, vehicles are eligible for this program through December 31, 1998, regardless of distance travelled.
What You Should Do:	PLEASE KEEP THIS LETTER. If your vehicle's engine head gasket should exhibit the condition described above within the extended coverage period, contact your dealer. The dealer will replace the engine head gaskets, if necessary, after verification of this specific condition.
Refunds:	If you paid to have this service performed prior to the date of the letter, Ford is offering a full refund. For the refund, please give your paid original receipt to your Ford or Lincoln Mercury dealer. To avoid delays, do not send the receipts to Ford Motor Company.

Continental owners got an extra year and 20,000 extra miles. Hmm, that doesn't seem fair. Ford sent American and Canadian owners the above letter; American owners get extended coverage up to 5 years/80,000 miles.

Ford/Nissan: 1995–96 Villager and Quest minivans and Pathfinders equipped with 3.0L engines

- **Problem:** Excessive engine noise is caused by a poorly designed connecting rod that's insufficiently lubricated. The design on the VG30E was changed in January 1996 to provide a quieter operation.
- **Warranty coverage:** Ford will replace at no charge any 3.0L V6 engine block if customers complain of engine knock following a cold start. Ford is replacing the entire engine, including the cylinder head. Nissan, on the other hand, is in "deep denial" and will stonewall customer complaints, until faced with a small claims lawsuit.

Car Guide 2000

Automotive News

JUNE 24, 1996

Gripers get new Nissan engines

MARY CONNELLY
Staff Reporter

Nissan and Mercury are replacing engine blocks or entire engines in up to 125,000 1995 and 1996 vehicles because of engine knock in Nissan's 3.0-liter V-6.

Vehicles involved are the Nissan Quest, Pathfinder and pickup plus the Mercury Villager.

"Customers may drive the vehicles without causing damage to the engine."

Engines are being replaced because connecting rod designs are not interchangeable. Ford routinely replaces — rather than repairs — engines in new, low-mileage vehicles to increase customer satisfaction and to avoid creating new engine troubles.

Staff Reporter Mark Rechtin in Los Angeles contributed to this report.

Ford/Nissan: 1993–94 Villager and Quest minivans, Pathfinder, and Maxima equipped with 3.0L engines

- **Problem:** Engine exhaust manifold studs fail prematurely and cost over $3,000 to repair.
- **Warranty coverage:** Nissan denies the problem exists ("Bulletin? What bulletin? Oh, that one. It's only for technicians...."), though recent reports indicate the company will refund half the cost of repairs if threatened with small claims action. The defect is covered by the emissions warranty (up to six years), according to Ford bulletin number 98-10-14. Ford usually offers 100 percent "goodwill" refunds within the first six years, if threatened with a small claims action, particularly when owners show up with service bulletins in hand that show the defect falls under the emissions warranty and is a common problem.

Some dealers have tried to cut corners (and costs) by replacing only one of the bolts. Yet the bulletin says *all* bolts must be replaced when the problem is first reported. This means that anyone who has had a partial replacement under warranty has a claim for another free correction if the problem reappears.

General Motors (Saturn): 1994–96 Saturn

- **Problem:** Faulty head gaskets may cause loss of engine coolant, engine overheating, or destruction of the engine.
- **Warranty coverage:** GM will replace the faulty head gasket or repair the engine damage caused by head gasket failure at no charge up to 6 years/100,000 miles, as set out in its June 7, 1999, statement to *Automotive News*. Second owners and repairs done by independent garages are included in this program. This warranty extension can be used in claims against all other GM models/years with similar engine problems and against other automakers. Apparently, this Saturn defect has existed since 1991, according to the GM bulletin reprinted on the following page.

BULLETIN NO.: 96-T-65A
ISSUE DATE: February 1997
GROUP/SEQ. NO. Engine-15
CORPORATION NO.: 686204R
SUBJECT:
Engine Runs Hot and Engine Oil Mixed with Engine Coolant in Engine Coolant Recovery Reservoir (Replace Cylinder Head Assembly)
This bulletin is revised to replace an incorrect part number for the one gallon container of DEX-COOL(TM) and supersedes bulletin 96-T-65, which should be discarded.
MODELS AFFECTED:
1991–1997 Saturns equipped with SOHC (LKO-1991-1994, L24-1995-1997) engines
CONDITION:
Engine may run hot and/or have engine oil mixed with engine coolant. This condition may be noticeable when checking coolant recovery reservoir level.
CAUSE:
Some 1991–1997 SOHC engines may develop a crack on or near the camshaft journals and surrounding casting areas allowing engine oil to mix with engine coolant. These cracks may be caused by "folds" in the aluminum that occur during the head casting process.
CLAIM INFORMATION

Case Type	Description	Labor Operation Code	Time
VW	Replace Cylinder Head Assembly	T9715	11.2 hrs
Add:	with A/C		0.8 hrs
	with power steering		0.3 hrs

To receive credit for this repair during the warranty coverage period, submit a claim through the Saturn Dealer System as shown.

Don't kid yourself. This is a major engine defect that'll take 11-plus hours to correct. GM will pay, if you refuse to go away.

General Motors: 1992–93 Cavalier and Sunbird with 2.2L 4-cylinder engines
• **Problem:** Faulty head gaskets may cause loss of engine coolant, engine overheating, or destruction of the engine.
• **Warranty coverage:** GM will replace the faulty head gasket or repair the engine damage caused by head gasket failure at no charge up to 7 years/100,000 miles, as set out in its March 1996 letter to first owners. Second owners and repairs done by independent garages are included in this program. This warranty extension sets the benchmark at a new high for engine durability and can be used in claims against all automakers whose vehicles reveal similar engine problems.

Dear General Motors Customer:

As the owner of a 1992 or 1993 Chevrolet Cavalier equipped with a 2.2L engine, your satisfaction with our product is of the utmost concern to us. Your vehicle was provided with a new vehicle warranty, which covers certain parts of your vehicle for a specified period. These warranties are of considerable value to you if you should experience problems with your vehicle.

This letter is intended to make you aware that some 1992 and 1993 Chevrolet Cavalier models with 2.2L engines may develop a failure of the cylinder head gasket that allows coolant to leak from the cylinder head gasket to engine block joint. Early evidence of this would be a loss of coolant in the coolant reservoir and an odor of coolant from the engine compartment, or a low coolant lamp. There may also be visible coolant deposits at the cylinder head to engine block joint.

General Motors of Canada Limited is, therefore, taking the following action:

We are providing owners with special coverage. If the above-mentioned condition occurs within seven (7) years of the date your vehicle was originally placed in service or 160,000 km, whichever occurs first, your vehicle will be repaired for you at no charge.

This special policy applies only to repairs requiring cylinder head gasket replacement as a result of cylinder head gasket failure that results in an engine coolant leak. It does not cover engine damage from continuing to operate the engine in an overheated condition after loss of coolant.

This is not a recall campaign. Do not take your vehicle to your GM dealer as a result of this letter unless you believe that your vehicle has the condition as described above. Keep this letter with your other important glovebox literature for future reference.

If you have already paid for some or all of the cost to have the cylinder head gasket replaced and in-service time was less than seven (7) years and 160,000 km, you should contact your GM dealer. You may be eligible for partial or complete reimbursement of costs if genuine GM parts were used in the repair. If the work was done by someone other than a GM dealership the amount of reimbursement may be limited to the amount the repair would have cost GM to have it completed by a GM dealership. Please provide your dealer with your original paid receipts or invoices verifying the repair, the amount charged, proof of payment, and the date of payment of those charges by March 1, 1997.

Repairs and adjustments qualifying under this Special Policy coverage must be performed by your GM dealer.

Honda/Acura: 1995–97 Civic; 1996–97 Accord, Prelude, and Odyssey; 1995 Acura NSX and 2.5 TL; all 1996–97 Acuras, except for the Integra Type R and Passport

- **Problem:** Engine malfunctions cause emissions to exceed the federal norm.
- **Warranty coverage:** In a settlement with the Environmental Protection Agency (EPA), Honda extended its emissions warranty to 14 years or 150,000 miles. The automaker has agreed to the EPA's demand that it provide a full engine check and emissions-related repairs at 50,000 to 75,000 miles and give free tune-ups at 75,000 to 150,000 miles. Judging by Honda's past actions in denying its responsibility for these kinds of problems, don't hesitate to complain to the EPA if you encounter a scintilla of evidence that the company won't keep its promise.

Toyota: 1988–95 compact pickups, T100 pickups, and 4Runner SUVs with 3.0L and 3.6L 6-cylinder engines

• **Problem:** Defective head gaskets may cause loss of engine coolant, engine overheating, or destruction of the engine's short block.

• **Warranty coverage:** Toyota will replace the defective components at no charge up to 8 years/100,000 miles (*Automotive News*, February 10, 1997).

Although some repairs have been attempted, it's recommended that the entire short block be replaced and new head bolts be installed. This has resulted in warranty claims as high as $6,000 among the 36,000 vehicles repaired up to February 1997. While Toyota doesn't mention it, jurisprudence, as well as similar warranty extensions set up by other automakers, leads one to assume that second owners and repairs done by independent garages are included in this program.

Incidentally, there have been some 1996 model head gasket failures reported to the National Highway Traffic Safety Administration (NHTSA); Toyota will likely extend the warranty again.

Confidential service bulletins

These are special warranties confirmed by technical service bulletins (confidential, for the most part) that automakers send to dealers to advise them of special warranties and to help them quickly diagnose and correct factory defects. These bulletins also disclose how much of the repair the dealer can charge back to the manufacturer and which parts are available free of charge. Armed with these bulletins, motorists can use less expensive, independent garages to diagnose and repair their vehicles or motorists can negotiate compensation for defects that the bulletins point out are the manufacturer's fault.

The major problem with these bulletins is that they're difficult to get. Dealers and automakers are reluctant to provide this kind of detailed technical information because it allows customers to second-guess a mechanic's work or to buttress their demands for compensation. However, as long as their involvement isn't disclosed, some dealers will discreetly provide copies of service bulletins to help their customers fight for compensation from the auto manufacturer.

For just a summary of bulletins applicable to 1982–99 vehicles, you have two sources: free summaries from the ALLDATA or the NHTSA sites on the Internet (listed in the Appendix, "30 Best Internet Gripe Sites"). Copies of individual bulletins can be obtained from an ALLDATA $29.95 CD-ROM containing all the bulletins applicable to your vehicle.

GENERAL MOTORS BUSINESS RESOURCE CENTER
LEGAL DEPARTMENT

November 4, 1999

VIA MAIL ONLY
RE: 1990 Chevrolet Corvette

Dear ▉▉▉▉▉ :

Regarding the above case, following is Chevrolet Motor Division's position:

Per our review of this case, Chevrolet Motor Division will not refund the $8000.00 that you are requesting. We have searched through our system and have found no open campaigns or special policies relating to your concern, however you did refer to service bulletin #331708. Service Bulletins are used by the manufacturer as a way of communicating a wide variety of information to the dealerships and are not issued to the public, therefore the public would not be notified of anything contained in them. Service Bulletins would contain things such as updated warranty information, different tools that may be used for different repairs, diagnostic information or service information. They do not contain a list of product defects, good will assistance that is offered or special policy and campaign information. I hope this clears up any confusion you may have had in regards to Service Bulletins.

Sincerely,

Jennifer Hatten
BRC/Legal Dept. Tampa

c: FILE

ATTORNEYS AT LAW

November 12, 1999

BRC/Legal Dept. Tampa
General Motors Division
16 E. Judson Street
Mail Code 483-616-830
Pontiac, Michigan 48342

Dear ██████████ :

Your letter of 11/4/99 is both non-responsive and insulting. The vehicle I own has a doc-
umented factory-related defect in its paint. General Motors is well aware of this significant and pervasive defect in its vehicles. General Motors routinely authorizes paint repair
good-will adjustments of the type I proposed in my 10/26/99 letter up to the present
time.

Your letter states that the public is not entitled to the benefit of warranty or other information contained in technical service bulletins "because the public would not be notified of anything in them". This argument is specious and entirely unsupported in the law.

Please be advised that I have every intention of pursuing this matter to its legal conclu-
sion. I will pend this file for seven (7) days prior to instituting legal proceedings against
General Motors. I trust that this will give you the opportunity to reconsider your decision
and authorize the paint repair to my vehicle in the amount demanded.

Sincerely,

ATTORNEY AT LAW

---

*GM lawyers don't like to deal with GM service bulletins. Notice how they flatly
told this California lawyer the public "would not be notified of anything contained in them." Of course, that's how you keep secret warranties secret.*

How long should parts/repairs last?

Let's say you can't find a service bulletin that says your problem is factory related or covered by a special compensation program. Or a part
lasts just a little longer than its guarantee, but not as long as is generally expected. Can you get a refund if the same problem reappears
shortly after it has been repaired? The answer is yes, if you can prove
the part failed prematurely.

Automakers, mechanics, and the courts have their own benchmarks
as to what's the reasonable period of time or amount of mileage one
should expect a part or adjustment to last. The following table shows
what most automakers consider to be reasonable durability as
expressed by their original warranties and secret warranties that are
often called "goodwill" or "special policy" programs.

Estimated Part Durability

ACCESSORIES

Air conditioner	5 years
Cellular phone	5 years
Cruise control	5 years/ 100,000 miles
Power antenna	5 years
Power doors, windows	5 years
Radio	5 years

BODY

Paint peeling	7 years
Rust (perforations)	7 years
Rust (surface)	5 years
Vinyl roof	5 years
Water/wind/air leaks	5 years

BRAKE SYSTEM

Brake drum	100,000 miles
Brake drum, turn	35,000 miles
Brake drum linings	25,000 miles
Disc brake calipers	20,000 miles
Disc brake pads	25,000 miles
Master cylinder, rebuild	100,000 miles
Wheel cylinder, rebuild	80,000 miles

ENGINE AND DRIVETRAIN

Constant velocity joint	5 years/ 100,000 miles
Differential	7 years/ 140,000 miles
Engine (gas)	7 years/ 140,000 miles
Radiator	4 years/ 80,000 miles
Transfer case	7 years/ 140,000 miles
Transmission (auto.)	7 years/ 140,000 miles
Transmission (man.)	7 years/ 140,000 miles
Transmission oil cooler	5 years/ 100,000 miles
Universal joint	5 years/ 100,000 miles

EXHAUST SYSTEM

Catalytic converter	5 years/ 100,000 miles or more
Muffler	2 years/ 40,000 miles

Tailpipe	3 years/ 60,000 miles

FUEL SYSTEM

Carburetor	5 years/ 100,000 miles
Fuel filter	2 years/ 40,000 miles
Fuel pump	5 years/ 100,000 miles
Injectors	5 years/ 100,000 miles

IGNITION SYSTEM

Cable set	60,000 miles
Electronic module	5 years/ 100,000 miles
Spark plugs	40,000 miles
Tune-up	20,000 miles

SAFETY COMPONENTS

Airbags	life of vehicle
ABS brakes	7 years/ 140,000 miles
ABS computer	7 years/ 140,000 miles
Seatbelts	life of vehicle

STEERING AND SUSPENSION

Alignment	1 year/20,000 miles
Ball joints	80,000 miles
Power steering	5 years/ 100,000 miles
Shock absorber	2 years/ 40,000 miles
Struts	5 years/ 100,000 miles
Tires (radial)	4 years/ 80,000 miles
Wheel bearing	3 years/ 60,000 miles

VISIBILITY

Aim headlights	20,000 miles
Halogen/fog lights	3 years/ 60,000 miles
Sealed beam	2 years/ 40,000 miles
Windshield wiper motor	4 years/ 80,000 miles

The preceding guidelines were extrapolated from Chrysler's payout to hundreds of Chrysler Lemon Owners Group (CLOG) members from December 1997 through March 1998, in addition to Chrysler's original seven-year powertrain warranty applicable from 1991–95.

Other sources for this chart were the Ford and GM transmission warranties outlined in their secret warranties, and Ford, GM, and Toyota engine "special programs" laid out in their internal service bulletins.

Safety features generally have a lifetime warranty, with the exception of ABS brakes, which are a wear item. Nevertheless, the Chrysler 10-year "free service program" portion of its ABS recall announced several years ago (see page 77) can serve as a handy benchmark as to how long one can expect these components to last.

Airbags are a different matter. Those that are deployed in an accident and the personal injury and interior damage their deployment will likely have caused are covered by your accident insurance policy. However, if there is a sudden deployment for no apparent reason, the automaker and dealer should be held jointly responsible for all injuries and damages caused by the airbag. This will likely lead to a more generous settlement from the two parties and prevent your insurance premiums from being jacked up. Inadvertent deployment may occur after passing over a bump in the road, slamming the car door, having wet carpets in your Cadillac (no kidding), or, in some Chrysler minivans, simply putting the key in the ignition. This happens more often than you would imagine, judging by the hundreds of recalls and thousands of complaints recorded on NHTSA's website (for recalls and complaints addresses, see the following section on "Safety defect information").

Finally, the manufacturer's emissions warranty serves as the primary guideline governing how long a vast array of electronic and mechanical components should last. Look first at your owner's manual for an indication of which parts are covered on your vehicle. If you come up with few specifics, use the EPA's guidelines along with GM's bulletins on the matter. Keep in mind that these durability benchmarks, secret warranties, and emissions warranties all apply to subsequent owners.

Recall repairs
Let the automaker know who and where you are. If you've moved or bought a used vehicle, it's a smart idea to pay a visit to your local dealer and get a "report card" on which recalls, free service campaigns, and warranties apply to it. Simply give the service advisor your vehicle identification number (VIN), found on your insurance card or on the dashboard just below the windshield on the driver's side, and have it run through the automaker's computer system ("Function 70" for Chrysler, "OASIS" for Ford, and "CRIS" for GM). Ask for a computer printout of the vehicle's history (have it faxed to you, if you're so equipped) and make sure you're listed in the automaker's computer as the new owner. This ensures that you'll receive notices of warranty extensions and emissions and safety recalls.

Still, don't expect to be welcomed with open arms when your vehicle develops a safety- or emissions-related problem that's not yet part of a recall campaign. Automakers and dealers generally take a restrictive view of what constitutes a safety or emissions defect and frequently charge for repairs which should be free under federal safety or emissions legislation. To counter this tendency, look at the following list of typical defects that are clearly safety related, and if you experience similar problems, tell the dealer you expect your repair to be paid by the manufacturer:

• airbag malfunctions
• corrosion affecting safe operation
• disconnected or stuck accelerators
• electrical shorts
• faulty windshield wipers
• fuel leaks
• problems with original axles, drive shafts, seats, seat recliners, or defrosters
• seatbelt problems
• stalling or sudden acceleration
• sudden steering or brake loss
• suspension failures
• trailer coupling failures

Recall campaigns force automakers to pay the entire cost of fixing a vehicle's safety-related defect. Recalls may be voluntary or ordered by the U.S. Department of Transportation. Voluntary recall campaigns are a real problem, though; they aren't as rigorously monitored as government-ordered recalls, and dealers and automakers routinely deny they exist. Also, the company's so-called "fix" may not correct the hazard, and the company may take its own sweet time in notifying owners. Take, for example, Chrysler's voluntary "service program" to strengthen the rear latches on as many as 4.5 million 1984–95 minivans. Almost 50 percent of affected owners were still waiting for Chrysler to fix their minivans nearly two years after the company volunteered to correct the defect without the government's involvement.

Safety defect information
If you wish to report a safety defect or want recall information, you can access the NHTSA website and recall/complaint database. You can search the database for your vehicle specifically and be thoroughly briefed on recalls, crash ratings, safety defects reported by other auto owners, and a host of other safety-related items. The web address is *www.nhtsa.dot.gov/cars/problems/recalls/* for recalls and *www.nhtsa.dot.gov/cars/problems/complain/* to access the complaint database.
For those of us not fortunate enough to have a computer or who cannot access the Internet, NHTSA's fax-back service provides the same free recall information through its toll-free line (most calls take five to ten minutes to complete). For calls placed within the U.S., the toll-free hot line is 1-888-327-4236 (1-800-424-9153 for the hearing impaired). If you find the toll-free number busy, try the regular long-distance number: 202-366-0123 (202-366-7800 for the hearing impaired). It will get you into the automatic response service just as quickly and can be reached 24 hours a day.

Searches and printouts are available free of charge. Unless your request is complex, you can get the data you need within an hour by calling the hot line. An operator will conduct a search while you're still on the phone and a printout will be faxed or mailed to you within 24 hours.

Office hours are 8:00 a.m.–10:00 p.m. (EST) and an answering machine is available 24 hours a day so that you can leave your name and number for a return call.

Three Steps to a Settlement

Step 1: Informal negotiations
If your vehicle was misrepresented, has major defects, or wasn't properly repaired under warranty, the first thing you should do is give the seller (the dealer and automaker or a private party) a written summary (by registered mail or fax) of the outstanding problems, and stipulate a time period in which the seller must make the repairs or refund your money. Keep a copy of the letter for yourself along with all your repair records. Be sure to check all of the sales and warranty documents you were given to see if they conform to state laws. Any errors, omissions, or violations can be used to get a settlement with the dealer in lieu of making a formal complaint.

At the beginning, try to work things out informally. In your attempt to reach a settlement, keep in mind the cardinal rule: ask only for what is fair and don't try to make anyone look bad.

- Listen. The really tough part of negotiating is listening. Listen to the automaker's representative or the dealership principal and try to understand their problem while thinking of a cooperative solution. This means frequently restating the other side's position so they realize you understand their offer.
- Line up evidence and allies. Be sure to line up your proof (work orders, service bulletins, and independent garage reports) and allies before making your claim.
- Be reasonable and give as well as take. Consumers are frequently given a "Let's Make a Deal" spiel where the initial offer of 50 percent is often boosted to 75 percent compensation if the customer will agree—at that very moment—to pay 25 percent of the repair.
- Keep your demands reasonable but add a request for consequential damages (frustration, inconvenience, rental cars, missed work/ vacation, etc.) and keep it as a throwaway claim to be used at a critical juncture in the talks. You should allege the maximum possible damages in your complaint, so remember to add up all your repair and rental bills. Also, hit them for days you couldn't use the vehicle even if you didn't rent one (the reference for this is *Gent v. Collinsville*, 451 NE2d).
- Don't set up an unrealistic timetable.
- Know when to shut up.

Furthermore, take a close look at the confidential GM bulletin on page 69, which outlines for dealers the strategy they should follow and questions they should ask before offering their clients any goodwill warranty consideration.

Finally, when negotiating, speak in a calm, polite manner and try to avoid polarizing the issue. Talk about how "we can work together" on the problem. Let a compromise slowly emerge—don't come in with a hardline set of demands. Don't demand the settlement offer in writing, but make sure that you're accompanied by a friend who can confirm the offer in court if it isn't honored (relatives may testify in court). Be prepared to act upon the offer without delay so that you won't be blamed for its withdrawal.

Dealer/service manager
If you bought a used vehicle from a dealer who sells the same make new, you stand a good chance of getting free repairs, particularly if the vehicle is still under warranty or is covered by a "goodwill" program, or if you intend to plead premature failure of a specific part based upon the parameters listed in the Estimated Part Durability chart found on page 85.

The service manager is directly responsible to the dealer and manufacturer and makes the first determination of what work is covered under warranty. He is paid to save the dealer and automaker money and to mollify irate clients—almost an impossible balancing act. When a service manager agrees to warranty coverage, it's because you've convinced him he must. This can be done by getting him to access the vehicle's history from the manufacturer's computer and by presenting the facts of your case in a confident, forthright manner with as many supporting dealer service bulletins and NHTSA owner complaint printouts as you can find.

Don't use your salesperson as a runner, since the sales staff are generally quite distant from the service staff and usually have less pull than you do. If the service manager can't or won't set things right, your next step is to convene a mini summit with the service manager, the dealership principal, and the automaker's rep. By getting the automaker involved, you run less risk of having the dealer fob you off on the manufacturer and can often get an agreement where the seller and automaker pay two-thirds of the repair cost.

Independent dealers and dealers selling a different brand of vehicle give you less latitude. You have to make the case that the vehicle's defects were present at the time of purchase and should have been known to the seller, or that the vehicle doesn't conform to the representations made when it was purchased. Emphasize that you intend to use the courts if necessary to obtain a refund—most independent sellers would rather settle than risk a lawsuit with all the attendant publicity. An independent estimate of the vehicle's defects and cost of repairs is essential if you want to convince the seller that you're serious in your claim and stand a good chance of winning your case in court. The estimated cost of repairs is also useful in challenging a dealer who agrees to pay half the repair costs and then jacks up the costs 100 percent so that you wind up paying the whole shot.

Step 2: Send a registered letter or fax
This is the next step to take if your claim is refused. Send the dealer and manufacturer a polite registered letter or a fax that asks for compensation for repairs that have been done or need to be done, insurance costs while the vehicle is being repaired, towing charges, supplementary transportation costs like taxis and rented cars, and damages for inconvenience.

Specify that either party has 5 days (but allow 10 days) to respond. If neither the dealer nor the manufacturer makes a satisfactory offer, file suit in small claims court. Make the manufacturer a party to the lawsuit, especially if the emissions warranty, a secret warranty extension, a safety-recall campaign, or extensive chassis rusting is involved. The two sample claim letters on the following pages can be useful in getting compensation for a defective used vehicle or for unsatisfactory repairs. Include in your letter references to any court decisions you find in this section of the book that support your claim.

Step 3: Mediation and arbitration
If the formality of a courtroom puts you off, or if you're not sure that your claim is all that solid and you don't want to pay legal costs to find out, consider using mediation or arbitration sponsored by the Better Business Bureau (BBB), the American Automobile Association, or state courts (often a prerequisite before a small claims trial is convened or lemon law provisions are applied). Understand too that BBB efficacy and fairness in arbitration is spotty at best, and that arbitration may not be suitable if previous decisions are silenced through gag orders or you are barred from using the courts though you consider the decision to be unfair.

Mandatory arbitration clauses
Automakers and dealers are inserting mandatory arbitration clauses into their new- and used-car contracts as a means to override federal and state legislation that protect buyers. Unfortunately, most consumers miss the significance of binding arbitration clauses. They never realize that they are renouncing their legal right to use the courts; to apply state lemon laws, which give them special protections such as the right to a replacement when their vehicle comes with serious defects; and to apply the federal Magnuson-Moss Act, which establishes strict requirements for consumer warranties.

One recent Supreme Court decision (*Allied-Bruce Terminex Cos. v. Dobson*) held that these arbitration clauses are valid provisions of consumer contracts and can't be prohibited by state law. In other words, if you sign a sales contract that requires binding arbitration, you may be agreeing to undisclosed costs, such as high per-hour arbitrator fees, risky loser-pays provisions for attorneys, and the requirement that the dealer gets to choose the arbitrator.

Used-Car Complaint Letter/Fax

WITHOUT PREJUDICE

Date: _____
Name: _____

Please be advised that I am dissatisfied with my used vehicle,
a _____, bought from you for _____ on _____.

The vehicle has not been reasonably durable and is, therefore, not
as represented to me. You have been given repeated opportunities,
to no avail, to fix the following recurring problems:

1. _____
2. _____
3. _____

In compliance with the federal *Magnuson-Moss Warranty
Improvement Act*, state consumer protection statutes, and the lemon
law, I formally put you on notice to repair the above defects without charge or to refund the purchase price. A summary of the facts
relating to this claim is included on a separate sheet.

Should you fail to repair these defects in a satisfactory manner and
within a reasonable period of time, I may choose to get an estimate
of the needed repairs from an independent source and claim that
amount, plus consequential damages, in court, without further
delay.

A response by fax or phone within the next five (5) days would be
appreciated.

Sincerely,

_____
(signed with telephone or fax number)

Secret Warranty Claim Letter/Fax

WITHOUT PREJUDICE

Date: _____
Name: _____

Please be advised that I am dissatisfied with my vehicle,
a _____, bought from you on _____.
It has had the following recurring problems that I believe are
factory-related defects as confirmed by internal service bulletins
sent to dealers and covered by your "goodwill" policies:

1. _____
2. _____
3. _____

If your "goodwill" program has ended, I ask that my claim be
accepted nevertheless, inasmuch as I was never informed of your
policy while it was in effect and should not be penalized for not
knowing it existed.

I hereby put you formally on notice under the federal *Magnuson-Moss Warranty Improvement Act* and state consumer protection
statutes that your refusal to apply this extended warranty coverage
in my case would be an unfair warranty practice within the purview
of the above-cited laws.

I have enclosed several estimates (my bill) showing that this problem is factory related and will (has) cost $_____ to correct.
I would appreciate your refunding me the estimated (paid) amount,
failing which, I reserve the right to have the repair done elsewhere
and claim reimbursement, plus consequential and punitive damages,
from you in court, without further delay.

A response by fax or phone within the next five (5) days would be
appreciated.

Sincerely,

_____
(signed with telephone or fax number)

Getting a Secret Warranty Settlement

The following settlement advice applies mainly to paint defects, but you can use these tips for any other vehicle defect that you believe is the automaker's/dealer's responsibility. If you're not sure that the problem is a factory-related deficiency or a maintenance item, have it checked out by an independent garage or get a dealer service bulletin summary for your vehicle. The summary may include specific bulletins relating to the diagnosis, correction, and ordering of upgraded parts needed to fix your problem.

1. If you know your vehicle's paint problem is factory related, take your vehicle to the dealer and ask for a written, signed estimate. When you're handed the estimate, ask that the paint job be done for free under the manufacturer's "goodwill" program. (Ford's euphemism for this secret warranty is "Owner Dialogue Program," GM's term is "Special Policy," and Chrysler just calls it "goodwill." Don't use the term "secret warranty" yet; you'll just make the dealer and automaker angry and evasive.)
2. Your request will probably be met with a refusal, an offer to repaint the vehicle for half the cost, or, if you're lucky, an agreement to repaint the vehicle free of charge. If you accept half-cost, make sure that it's based on the original estimate you have in hand, since some dealers jack up their estimates so that your 50 percent is really 100 percent of the true cost.
3. If the dealer/automaker has already refused your claim and the repair hasn't been done yet, get an additional estimate from an independent garage that shows the problem is factory related.
4. Again, if the repair has yet to be done, mail or fax a registered claim to the automaker (send a copy to the dealer), claiming the average of both estimates. If the repair has been done at your expense, mail or fax a registered claim with a copy of your bill. A sample letter/fax can be found on page 92.
5. If you don't receive a satisfactory response within a week, deposit a copy of the estimate or paid bill and claim letter/fax before the small claims court and await a trial date. This means that the automaker/dealer will have to appear, no lawyer is required, costs should be minimal (under $100), and a mediation hearing or trial will be scheduled in a few months followed by a judgment a few weeks later (the time varies among different regions).

Things that you can do to help your case: collect photographs, maintenance work orders, previous work orders dealing with your problem, dealer service bulletins, and an independent expert (the garage or body shop that did the estimate or repair is best, but you can also use a local teacher who teaches automotive repair).

Other situations

- If the vehicle has just been repainted but the dealer says that "good-will" coverage was denied by the automaker, pay for the repair with a certified check and write "under protest" on the check. Remember, though, if the dealer does the repair, you won't have an independent expert who can affirm that the problem was factory related or that it was a result of premature wearout. Plus, the dealer can say that you or the environment caused the paint problem. In these cases, internal service bulletins can make or break your case.
- If the dealer/automaker offers a partial repair or refund, take it. Then sue for the rest. Remember, if a partial repair has been done under warranty, it counts as an admission of responsibility, no matter what "goodwill" euphemism is used. Also, the repaired component/body panel should be just as durable as if it were new. Hence, the clock starts ticking again until you reach the original warranty parameter— again, no matter what the dealer's repair warranty limit says.
- It's a lot easier to get the automaker to pay to replace a defective part than it is to be compensated for a missed day of work or a ruined vacation. Manufacturers hate to pay for consequential expenses apart from towing bills because they can't control the amount of the refund. Fortunately, the courts have taken the position that all expenses (damages) flowing from a problem covered by a warranty or service bulletin are the manufacturer's/dealer's responsibility under both state and federal law. Nevertheless, don't risk a fair settlement for some outlandish claim of "emotional distress," "pain and suffer-ing," etc. If you have invoices to prove actual consequential damages, then use them. If not, don't be greedy.

Very seldom do automakers contest these paint claims before small claims court, opting instead to settle once the court claim is bounced from their customer relations people to their legal affairs department. At that time, you'll probably be offered an out-of-court settlement for 50–75 percent of your claim.

Stand fast and make reference to the service bulletins you intend to subpoena in order to publicly contest in court the unfair nature of this "secret warranty" program (automaker lawyers cringe at the idea of try-ing to explain why consumers aren't made aware of these bulletins). One hundred percent restitution will probably follow.

A good example is the *Shields v. General Motors of Canada* judgment rendered January 6, 1998.

Shields v. General Motors of Canada, No. 1398/96, Ontario Court (General Division), Oshawa Small Claims Court, 33 King Street West, Oshawa, Ontario L1H 1A1, July 24, 1997, Robert Zochodne, Deputy Judge. The owner of a 1991 Pontiac Grand Prix purchased the vehicle used with over 100,000 km on its odometer. Commencing in 1995, the paint began to bubble and then flake and eventually peel off. Deputy Judge

Robert Zochodne awarded the plaintiff $1,205.72 and struck down every one of GM's environmental/acid rain/UV-rays arguments. Other important aspects of this 12-page judgment that GM did not appeal:

1. The judge admitted many of the service bulletins referred to in *Lemon-Aid* as proof of GM's negligence.
2. Although the vehicle had 156,000 km when the case went to court, GM still offered to pay 50 percent of the paint repairs if the plaintiff dropped his suit.
3. Deputy Judge Zochodne ruled that the failure to protect the paint from the damaging effects of UV rays is akin to engineering a car that won't start in cold weather. In essence, vehicles must be built to withstand the rigors of the environment.
4. Here's an interesting twist: the original warranty covered defects that were present at the time it was in effect. The judge, taking statements found in the GM bulletins, ruled the UV problem was factory related, and therefore, *it existed during the warranty period and thereby represented a latent defect* that appeared once the warranty expired.
5. The subsequent purchaser was not prevented from making the warranty claim, even though the warranty had long since expired from a time and mileage standpoint and he was the second owner.

Bentley v. Dave Wheaton Pontiac Buick GMC Ltd and General Motors of Canada, Victoria Registry No. 24779, British Columbia Small Claims Court, December 1, 1998, Judge Higinbotham. This is the third, and most recent, small claims judgment against GM. It builds upon the Ontario *Shields v. General Motors of Canada* decision and cites other jurisprudence as to how long paint should last on a house. If you're wondering why Ford and Chrysler haven't been hit by similar judgments, remember that they usually settle.

Reasons for judgment

In this case the claimant purchased a vehicle, a pickup truck, from a dealership, Dave Wheaton Pontiac Buick G.M.C. Ltd., a new vehicle, in 1991. There was an admitted defect in the paint which did not become apparent until later. General Motors is also a defendant in this action and discovered in a general sense this problem of delamination in the paint on some vehicles in 1992, about one year after the claimant purchased the vehicle in question.

The specific problem with this vehicle was observed early in 1994. It was brought to the attention of Wheaton when the vehicle was brought in for other maintenance two weeks after the warranty expired. At that time the problem was relatively minor. I say relatively in the sense that compared to what later occurred it was minor.

Mr. Palfry, who is the manager of the paint and body shop for the retailer Wheaton, was made aware of the problem. There is no dispute about that, and he sold the claimant a tub of touch-up paint.

The paint continued to deteriorate and in late 1996 was severely peeled.

In January of 1997, the claimant became aware that this problem was general to certain GM vehicles, vehicles of certain colours produced at a certain time by the defendant company.

The claimant took the vehicle back in but was told that it was too late. The warranty had expired and even the discretionary goodwill warranty was over. I do not think the claimant was told about the discretionary goodwill warranty, but in fact it was a policy of GM to extend the warranty for this sort of claim in certain circumstances, but it was discretionary. In any case, the claimant was told that it was too late for it to be fixed under warranty. Neither the dealership nor the manufacturer would accept responsibility at that time. As a result, this action was commenced.

I make the following findings: There was a latent defect in the vehicle relating to the paint, which revealed itself over time and in far less time than a good paint job would be expected to last.

The dealer or the manufacturer, had the manufacturer been informed by the dealer, ought to have advised the claimant in May of 1994 that they were aware of this general delamination problem and ought to have advised as to what warranty extension might be available. I will say more about this in a moment. In any event, the dealer and the manufacturer, if the dealer had notified the manufacturer of the problem, would have known that the delamination commenced within the three year period and ought to have honoured the warranty.

Despite my findings, as I said earlier that the dealer and manufacturer ought to have given guidance to the claimant in May of 1994 as to a possible warranty claim, I do not find any cause of action arising directly from this finding. It would simply have been good business practice for them to have advised the claimant.

If liability is to be found against General Motors, it must be for a breach of the warranty. On the other hand, if liability is to be found against Dave Wheaton, it must be because as a seller the dealership breached an implied condition of the Sale of Goods Act.

On the issue of the warranty supplied by General Motors, I note that it covers "repairs, or adjustments to correct any vehicle defect related to material or workmanship occurring during the warranty period." It appears from the evidence that General Motors' major concern with this particular case was that the problem with this specific vehicle was not brought to their attention during the warranty period, not that the problem with the paint did not actually arise within the warranty period.

I find the claimant has established that the paint problem was brought to the attention of the dealer in mid-May of 1994. The warranty had expired two weeks earlier. I accept that the defect occurred during the warranty period on two bases. First, as submitted by the claimant, Ms. Bentley, the defect occurred at the time of manufacture and continues to this day.

Similar finding was made in *Shields v. General Motors of Canada,* a decision of the Ontario Court, General Division, number 1398 of 1996.

Secondly, in any event, based on the condition of the paint in mid-May 1994, the defect likely became apparent during the three year warranty period. I therefore find that General Motors has breached the warranty and the claimant is entitled to damages.

As for the dealership, defendant's counsel argues that there has been no breach of the Sale of Goods Act in that the vehicle when sold was of merchantable quality and reasonably fit for the purpose for which it was intended.

I agree as to merchantable quality. And as to the other implied condition, I also agree if what is meant by "reasonably fit for the purpose" is that it was a truck that operated and was capable of hauling cargo and passengers, but I am of the view that every seller of new vehicles knows that the purchaser expects the vehicle to be reasonably fit for the purpose of resale at some future time, depending upon the age and quality of the vehicle. This vehicle was not and is not reasonably fit for resale given those factors. It is not reasonably fit due to the latent defect in its quality, a defect which existed in incipient form at the time of sale.

I note that in *McCready Products v. Sherwin-Williams,* (1984) 53 A.R. 304, a decision of the Alberta Queen's Bench, referred to in the article by Fridman submitted by counsel, in that case paint that weathered and faded in less than three years was found unfit for its purpose. That was house paint. The same is true here. Even though the paint in question here was only a component of the item purchased, it was a very important component having a great deal to do with the value of the vehicle.

I therefore find the defendant Dave Wheaton Pontiac Buick G.M.C. Ltd. also liable for damages. The liability of both defendants is joint and several.

I turn now to the question of damages. The claimants have averaged three estimates they have placed before the court and claim the amount of twenty-three hundred seventy-three dollars and sixty-one cents.

The defendant says damages are lower as a different allowance to dealers are made under the warranty. The defendants cannot now get the benefit of this, in my opinion, as responsibility under the warranty was denied by them.

I prefer to assess damages by taking the defendant's estimate or figure of fifteen hundred eighty-eight dollars twenty-six cents, a sum which the dealer could charge under the warranty to GM, and multiply that figure by a factor admitted to by the defendant as to what another body shop would—the number of hours another body shop would employ in order to obtain a realistic assessment.

It was stated in evidence that twenty-two to twenty-five hours is required to repair this damage, of which two hours are the actual painting.

The defendant's estimate is based on sixteen point one hours, because that's all they can claim under the warranty. There is therefore a difference of approximately nine hours in the estimates based on the upper level of twenty-five hours required by another body shop. I accept the proportion of paint to labour as stated by the witness and therefore accept that the defendant's estimate is based on fourteen point one hours of labour.

I also accept that the acceptable labour rate is fifty dollars and fifty-five cents and the painting rate is twenty-three dollars and seventy-one cents. It is the nine hours of labour that is in issue here in the assessment of damages.

The costs of the paint and materials I accept is two hundred and sixty-two dollars and forty-two cents.

I am therefore going to base damages on the defendant's estimate of one thousand eight hundred and ten dollars and sixty-two cents, which includes taxes, plus an additional nine hours labour at fifty dollars and fifty-five cents per hour, plus taxes, or an additional five hundred eighteen dollars eighty-four cents, bringing the total to two thousand three hundred and twenty-nine dollars and forty-six cents, very close to the estimate given by the claimant.

I am making no adjustment for betterment as it is known because, in my opinion, this is offset by the fact that for seven and a half years, or at least most of those seven and a half years, the vehicle was essentially unmarketable, unsaleable without substantial loss.

The claimant will therefore have judgment against both defendants, joint and several, in the amount of two thousand three hundred twenty-nine dollars forty-six cents, plus costs. No interest is awarded as it is inapplicable to this type of claim.

Lemon Laws

Lemon laws protect consumers with warranties for consumer goods. They most often are used when a consumer buys a defective new or used car, and the manufacturer or dealer refuses to buy the car back or give the buyer a replacement vehicle. Although there are different lemon laws in almost every state, they are all quite similar. There's also a federal lemon law that applies to all fifty states; therefore, even if your state doesn't have a separate lemon law, you can still enforce your warranty rights under federal statutes.

Since state lemon laws are updated continually, contact the state Attorney General's office for a copy of the latest state laws or get a summary from the Internet (see the Appendix, "30 Best Internet Gripe Sites").

Do lemon laws apply to used cars?
Yes, if the buyer has bought the vehicle with a warranty. As with new cars, the defect must exist within the warranty period. So, if a used car has a 30-day warranty and a defect doesn't appear until one year later, one may not be able to get help through a lemon law suit.

However, if the defect was a concealed defect (such as undisclosed accident damage), a problem covered by a secret warranty, or if the dealer drags his feet in correcting the problem until the warranty is over, the buyer may yet have rights under the lemon laws. This is because the defect existed at the time of sale, the dealer was advised of the problem during the warranty period and failed to make the necessary repairs, or the dealer attempted to defraud the buyer.

Robert F. Brennan, a Hollywood, California, consumer fraud attorney (tel: 213-463-2547; fax: 213-463-5527; email: *rbrennan@directnet.com*), gives the following advice to attorneys faced with a used-car fraud:

Most automotive consumer fraud occurs in the sale of used cars. There can be fraud in any aspect of the buying transaction. The two which we see the most are undisclosed accident damage and rolled-back odometers. Sometimes we see both in the same car. If you have a client who has purchased a used car and is having particular difficulties with it, you can direct appropriate inspections to determine if your client has been defrauded in either of these ways:

Undisclosed Accident Damage: Often, this shows up as severe alignment problems, premature tire wear and a lot of unexplained noise while the car is executing turns or braking. To determine if your client has been defrauded in this manner, have your client take the car to a certified auto body shop for a complete inspection, along with a complete photographic history if any signs of damage are found during the inspection.

Rolled-Back Odometers: This is indicated by premature wear and failure in brake drums, belts, hoses, transmission and drive-train components. To check this out, a mechanical inspection is useful, but it is better to order the complete ownership history of the vehicle from the Department of Motor Vehicles. By federal law, any time a car is sold the seller must fill out and sign, under penalty of perjury, the "Odometer Disclosure Statement" that provides the amount of miles on the car at the time of sale.

In odometer cases, you will often find, upon ordering the vehicle's history, that the "vehicle sold two years ago with 78,000 miles on it, and then [was] sold to your client with only 21,000 miles on it." In this case you have a rolled-back odometer on your hands.

Tampering with odometers is specifically prohibited by federal and California law, and tampering with odometers also implicates theories of fraud, breach of warranty and California's Consumer Legal Remedies Act....

Do lemon laws apply to minor defects?
Ordinarily, no, unless the consumer specifically bought the vehicle for
a particular feature which is found to be defective. For instance, you
would not normally be entitled to a refund or replacement vehicle
because, say, the radio antenna is bent. However, if you buy a vehicle
for a specific feature—say, air conditioning—and the dealer and manufacturer cannot make it work properly, you could well have an enforce-
able lemon law claim.

As a general principle, lemon laws apply to more serious defects,
such as brakes, transmission, suspension, serious engine problems (oil
burning, stalling, and hard starting), and the like. However, many consumers have enforced their lemon law rights for paint defects (excessive paint peeling that could not be remedied), for repeated instances
of the engine light coming on, for unusual noises and rattles in the
vehicle, and for other defects that do not quite rise to the level of a serious brake or transmission problem, but just the same, produce stress
and anxiety due to their repeated failure or cumulative effect.

How do lemon laws work?
A lemon law gives the buyer of a defective vehicle an opportunity to get
either a refund or a replacement car, plus up to triple damages (a
$15,000 used car could result in a $45,000 award). However, the defect
must have existed within the warranty period.

For example, if a consumer buys a car with a one-year warranty, a
defect which does not manifest until two years after purchase is probably
not covered by the lemon laws, although it can be still be covered under
other state consumer protection laws or the federal Magnuson-Moss Act.

However, any defect which arises during the warranty period (keep
those old work orders) will entitle the buyer to lemon law rights, if the
dealer and manufacturer cannot fix the defect after a reasonable number of repair attempts (usually two or three tries).

How do you get lemon law protection?
When it's obvious the vehicle is defective, the buyer must promptly
bring the vehicle back to an authorized dealership for warranty repairs
and give the dealership and manufacturer a reasonable opportunity to
correct the problem—one repair attempt will not bring the lemon law
into play. However, in cases in which the dealership and manufacturer
have made multiple repair attempts and cannot fix the defect, the
lemon law comes into force.

After the dealership and manufacturer have failed to repair the
defect, demand a refund or a replacement vehicle. Do this in writing
and send a copy to both the dealer and the manufacturer. If you're
lucky, they may give you a refund or replacement. Or, they may request
that you go through the manufacturer's private arbitration system. You
may do so if you wish, but do not be disappointed or surprised if you
encounter a "kangaroo court" where the arbitrators are all-too-
chummy with the dealer or automaker.

If you still do not get any remedy and it looks like everyone is dragging their feet, then it's time to seek out the assistance of an attorney for advice as to your overall strategy and which other state or federal statutes you should use.

Are there any lemon law traps that can catch me?
There sure are. Foremost is the service manager's reluctance to write the same problem on subsequent work orders so you can't prove the dealership had multiple opportunities to correct the same defect. You can counter this little trick by adding your own comments on the work order or appending a separate list (keep a copy).

Another trap is where the dealer or the manufacturer offers a newer car for a bit more money. Unfortunately, the buyer is stuck with paying additional sales taxes, depreciation loss on the returned vehicle, another sales commission, and registration and licensing fees—costs that would not be applicable under most lemon laws.

Finally, the dealer may try to delay servicing until you're no longer under the warranty or the lemon law's protection. Protect yourself by giving a written deadline for the defect to be corrected and stating that legal action will commence if that deadline isn't respected.

Do I have to pay a lot of money to enforce my rights under lemon laws?
Not usually. Most lawyers will take such cases on a contingency or a semi-contingency basis, because a dealer or manufacturer that loses a lemon law claim must pay attorney's fees to the prevailing plaintiff. Generally, a consumer who loses a lemon law case pays minimal costs. However, verify this, because some states, like California for instance, may require that the losing plaintiff pay more substantial court costs.

Involving Other Agencies

Groups like the Ralph Nader–founded Center for Auto Safety (202-328-7700), your state bar association, and Legal Aid can often refer you to local members who specialize in "consumer rights" or "lemon laws." For both automotive cases and consumer fraud cases, the National Association of Consumer Advocates in Boston has a referral panel of consumer attorneys working throughout the United States; their number is 617-723-1239. Chances are these groups won't refer you to either a turkey or a weasel attorney. If they do, you can hold them responsible for their reference, if you believe they were negligent.

To save money when seeing a lawyer, remember that the first interview is free, and you may buy an hour of the lawyer's time for more research or more detailed instruction, or you may hire a lawyer on a contingency basis (nothing up front—about one-third of the settlement or award if you're successful).

Government consumer affairs offices
Investigation, mediation, and some litigation are the primary areas in
which state and federal consumer affairs offices can be helpful. Despite
severe budget restraints, consumer protection legislation has been left
standing in most states and resourceful consumers can use these laws
along with media coverage to prod state consumer affairs offices into
action. Furthermore, state bureaucrats aren't as well shielded from criticism as are their federal counterparts. A call to your state representative or senator's executive assistant can often get things rolling.

On-line services/Internet/websites
America Online and CompuServe are two on-line service providers with
active consumer forums that use experts to answer consumer queries
and to provide legal as well as technical advice. The Internet offers the
same information but uses a worldwide database. If you or someone you
know is able to create a website, you might consider using this site to
attract attention to your plight and arm yourself for arbitration or court.

Five years ago, Debra and Edward Goldgehn's 1985 Ford Ranger
caught fire and burned completely. The couple's suspicions that it was
a factory-related defect were later confirmed by a TV show that
reported a series of similar Ford fires. The couple created their own
website called "Flaming Fords" and began amassing an incredible database containing reports of similar fires, class action lawsuits, expert witnesses, and actions taken in other countries. (For example, Ford had
already recalled a number of its vehicles in order to fix the problem in
Canada.) Shortly thereafter, Ford USA recalled 8.7 million cars and
trucks, representing the largest recall ever announced by a single auto
manufacturer. Ford says that the Internet pressure was coincidental
and not a factor in its decision to recall the vehicles in the U.S. Right,
and Elvis is building Cadillacs in Detroit.

Michael Hos, a dissatisfied Acura owner, became fed up with what he
felt was Acura's stonewalling of his complaints. Rather than get angry,
he got organized and set up a website called "1997 Acura CL 3.0L: My
Lemon" to collect other owners' comments and list some of the most
common Acura problem areas. Within six months, Acura settled.
Here's what Hos has to say:

Phil,
Hi, remember me? I'm the guy that had the 1997 Acura CL
lemon. Well, as it turns out Acura settled with me. I got payoff on
the car, my attorney fees taken care of, and I'm walking away with
$4,000 in my pocket after the experience. I was so glad to get rid
of this car you have no idea.

I have pulled down my "anti-Acura" website and washed my
hands clean of the entire ordeal. I turned in the CL about 2 weeks
ago, and my checks should be here next week....

At any rate, I wanted to say thanks for all your input into the case and the encouragement to continue on. The last few months of driving the car were horrible, I'm glad it's done.

In a follow-up posting:

As far as my website goes, I think it was a major part of them settling early. I had a counter placed on it which showed them how many people had visited the site. Anyone can set up a web page like mine pretty easily. I have web space on my university's computer, so it was free for me to use. Folks without space should expect to spend about $20 a month for space, or if they have their own email account, web space is usually provided for free. If they don't know how to set up their web page, paying someone to do it will be kinda pricey, a few hundred bucks should cover it. The main thing it needs to have is the counter, and it also needs to be libel free. I had only facts on my web page as I didn't want to get involved in a libel suit. They also need to register the site with all the major search engines so it comes up when looking for the manufacturer. Submitit.com offers such services for free. Putting in a <Meta> tag into the page also helps move it up the search engines' list of hits. Posting to newsgroups also is helpful. I also wrote to JD Power, NHTSA, *Consumer Reports*, and any other consumer oriented agency I could think of.

When we settled before going to court, I had to sign the settlement papers saying I would pull down my site. They would not settle with me until I did that. This shows how much power the site can have. I would also put the manufacturer's phone number and address on it so viewers of the site can contact the manufacturer.

For the most part, everyone who read my site took my side of the story and agreed that Acura should pay up. I did have a few folks that were mad I was slamming Acura, but I wasn't concerned with them. I have about 200 email responses that people have mailed to me over the last few months.

As a side note, I think the only real reason they settled with me, in addition to the page being up, was my attorney. I had 7 charges filed against them in Superior Court. Also keep in mind that I paid nothing for my attorney until after we settled. My bill for him is $1,500, but that's included in the settlement. Also, I'm only 23, so anyone can do this if they are persistent.

PROJECTS AND CAUSES

A BAD FIRE occured in our 1994 Jeep Cherokee because of driving with a compact spare tire while in 4WD (could not get out of 4WD). Compact spare is standard equipment but appropriate warning not in Owners Manual. No appropriate answers from Chrysler Canada yet. Seeking others with similar experience.

The Globe and Mail.

Classified ads
Use your local paper's "Personals" column to pressure the seller and to gather data from others who may have experienced a problem similar to your own. This alerts others to the potential problem, helps build a core base for a class action or group meeting with the automaker, and puts pressure on the dealer or manufacturer to settle.

Launching a Lawsuit

When to sue
If the seller agrees to make things right, give him or her a deadline and then have an independent garage check the repairs. If no offer is made within 10 working days, file suit in small claims court. Make the manufacturer a party to the lawsuit only if the original, unexpired warranty was transferred to you, your claim includes extensive chassis rusting, or your claim falls under the emissions warranty, a secret warranty extension, or a safety recall campaign.

Choosing the right court
You must decide upon the remedy to pursue; that is, whether you want the cost of repairs, a partial refund, or a cancellation of the sale. To determine the refund amount, add the estimated cost of repairing existing mechanical defects to the cost of prior repairs. Don't exaggerate your losses or claim for repairs that are considered routine maintenance.

There are practical problems involved in a suit for cancellation of sale. The court requires that the vehicle be "tendered" back to the seller at the time the lawsuit is filed. This means that you are without transportation for as long as the case continues, unless you purchase another car in the interim. If you lose the case, you must then take back the old car and pay storage fees. You could go from having no car to having two, one of which is a clunker.

Generally, if the cost of repairs or the sales contract falls within the small claims court limit, the case should be filed there to keep costs to a minimum and to obtain a speedy hearing. Small claims court judgments aren't easily appealed, lawyers aren't necessary, filing fees are minimal ($50–$100), and trials are usually heard within a few months.

If the damages exceed the small claims court limit and there's no way to reduce them, you'll have to go to a higher court—where costs quickly add up and lengthy delays of a few years or more are commonplace.

Small claims court

Before getting into the details of launching a small claims action, read the following letter from Steve Wheeler and Eleanor Crawley, which describes how they got almost $4,000 (Cdn.) refunded after following *Lemon-Aid*'s court tips:

We purchased an '88 Tempo....Within six days $1,700 [Cdn.] had been spent on repairs (on an emergency trip to Cleveland). The head gasket, a tension pulley, and an axle all had to be replaced during the first few days. The car never made it to Cleveland and my wife was stranded in motels or stuck sitting beside the inter- state or in garages waiting for repairs....The dealer said he would only reimburse us if we signed an agreement which gave up any future legal claims on repair on the Tempo. We wouldn't sign and negotiations ended....

We filed in small claims court for the refund of $2,800, the car's price with tax, $737 we paid for repairs while the car was under warranty (dealer had already paid $1,000 using his credit card over the phone), and expenses incurred while my wife was stranded for a total of $3,796 plus $50 for the small claim. On the advice of the lawyer, we named the company, the dealer (who also owned the company), and the mechanic as defendants.

We had written the dealer using the example of the Used Car Letter in *Lemon-Aid Used Car Guide 1996* during the negotiations, and had cited the Sale of Goods Act and several sample cases from the book.

In the preliminary hearing, the dealer's defence was that my wife had misunderstood the warranty and that he didn't warranty any work not done at his mechanic's garage.

Yesterday, our day in court came. We got there at 9:30 a.m. and left at 5 p.m. We were awarded $3,800 and the dealer had to take the car back. The judge based his decision on the Sale of Goods Act and found that the Tempo was "not fit for the purpose for which it was sold."...

Without the first few chapters of *Lemon-Aid Used Car Guide 1996*, we wouldn't have known where to start or how to proceed.

A few things we noticed which might help someone else stuck with a lemon: Get inspections done as quickly as possible after you realize you don't want the car. Park it and don't drive it as soon as possible. Get a mechanic to accompany you to court to back up his inspection; the judges seem to be more impressed by a personal appearance than a written report. Keep good records of all meetings and communications for the recounting of events in court. We found that the dealer who was trying to confuse the issue had no answers when we itemized clearly the negotiations and attempts at agreement....

I hope that this letter and the case will encourage anyone else who gets stuck with a lemon.

There are small claims courts in every state, and you can make a claim in the county or parish where the problem happened or where the defendant lives and conducts business. The first step is to make sure that your claim doesn't exceed the dollar limit of the court (the limits differ from state to state). Then you should go to the small claims court office and ask for a claim form. Instructions on how to fill it out properly accompany the form. Remember, you must identify the defendant correctly. It's a practice of some dishonest firms to change a company's name to escape liability; for example, it would be impossible to sue Joe's Garage (1998) if your contract is with Joe's Garage Inc. (1984).

At this point, it would be a smart idea to hire a lawyer or a paralegal for a half-hour walk-through of small claims procedures to ensure that you've prepared your case properly and that you know what objections will likely be raised by the other side. If you'd like a lawyer to do all the work for you, there are a number of inexpensive law firms around the country that are experienced in small claims litigation. Get a reference from the state bar association and call the firm to get an estimate of its hourly charges and fees.

Remember, you're entitled to bring any evidence to court that's relevant to the case, including written documents such as a bill of sale or receipt, a contract, or your claim letter. For severe paint or rust problems, take a photograph to court. Have the photographer sign and date the photo. You may also have witnesses testify in court (a family member may act as a witness). It's important to discuss a witness's testimony prior to the court date. If a witness can't attend the court date, he or she can write a report and sign it for representation in court. This situation usually applies to an expert witness, such as an independent mechanic who has evaluated your car's problems.

If you lose your case in spite of all the foregoing preparation and research, some small claims court statutes allow cases to be retried at a nominal cost in exceptional circumstances—if a new witness has come forward, additional evidence has been discovered, or key documents that were formerly not available have become accessible.

Class actions
Class action suits allow a single individual to sue a company, government, or other entity on behalf of hundreds or even thousands of others with similar claims. They have been used successfully for three decades in the United States.

Class actions allow contingency fees, where consumers can enter into no-win no-pay agreements with lawyers. Usually, if you lose, you pay reasonable court cotss and move on. However, in some jurisdictions, judges can require losing class-action plaintiffs to pay the defendant's legal and professional witness fees as well. Another pitfall is the tendency of some plaintiff lawyers to sell out their client's interests in exchange for "coupon" settlements and hefty legal fees paid for by the defendant corporation.

How to file a class action

- Like any other lawsuit, a lawyer files the plaintiff's statement of claim against the defendant and the plaintiff applies to the court to certify the lawsuit as a class action.
- The presiding judge will then decide whether there is an "identifiable class of two or more persons," whether a class action is the "preferable procedure," and whether the plaintiff truly represents the class. If you meet all the above criteria, the judge will issue a certification order and designate you as the Class Representative.
- Other class members must be notified of the lawsuit. Small groups can be contacted by mail, but larger groups may require notification through newspaper ads backed up by a toll-free telephone line. Members of the class must then be given an opportunity to opt out of the lawsuit. If they don't, they remain part of the class.

If the class wins, individual cases may then be heard to assess damages or a notification will be sent to each member to apply for his or her part of the settlement or award.

It may take from three to five years before a final judgment is rendered. However, appeals may double that time. Lawyers typically charge the class one-third of the amount obtained.

Presenting your case

As plaintiff, you will get the first opportunity to rise and state your case to the judge. You should ask for the exclusion of witnesses from the courtroom (this increases the chance that the other side will give contradictory testimony) and then proceed to lay out your proof, concluding within 5 to 10 minutes. Hang your narrative on the documents that you produce (you can call them "P-1," "P-2," for "Proof 1," "Proof 2," and so on) and let them serve as note cards.

The first three documents should be the sales contract, all work orders relative to the problems you've had, and your registered complaint letter or fax. After that, you may wish to produce the dealer's or automaker's response, a report or work orders from an independent garage supporting your position, and copies of your maintenance records and dealer service bulletins in order to show that the problems are factory related and not maintenance items. Conclude your presentation by simply restating the claim as it's written on your court complaint.

On the day of the trial, bring in a mechanic to confirm that the defects exist and to provide an estimate of repair costs. If the repairs have already been carried out, he or she can explain what caused the defects and justify his or her bill for repairing them. This should be done by presenting the defective parts, if possible. The mechanic must convince the judge that the defects were present at the time the vehicle was sold and not caused by poor maintenance or abusive driving habits.

When the dealer gets on the stand, ask for the exclusion of all witnesses and try to ferret out the following facts:

- When and from whom was the used vehicle last purchased?
- For how much was it bought?
- What was done to recondition the vehicle and at what cost?
- What was the *Edmund's* book value of the vehicle when first bought from the previous owner and when sold to the plaintiff?

This line of questioning should show the judge the considerable profits the dealer made by buying the vehicle below the market value, by not spending much to recondition it, and by reselling it far above the *Edmund's* book value.

Before the dealer leaves the stand, get him to confirm whether he or his salespeople made any representations, either verbally or through a newspaper ad, extolling the vehicle's qualities. With the witnesses excluded, it's quite likely that they will contradict the dealer when their turn comes to testify.

Other witnesses who can help your case are the vehicle's previous owner (who can testify as to its deficiencies when sold) and any of your co-workers or friends who can testify as to how well you maintained your vehicle, how you drove it, and the seriousness of the defects.

Dos and don'ts

- Don't sue a car dealer if he or she has no money, isn't bonded, is bankrupt, has changed his company, or is willing to negotiate a settlement.
- Don't sign a false sales tax receipt. Crooked car dealers try to get their customers to take a receipt that indicates a selling price far below the price paid.
- Don't threaten or insult the dealer. This will only gain sympathy for him and hurt your own credibility.
- Do complain to the state Motor Vehicle Bureau and consumer affairs about possible violations of state laws.
- Do bring in the police fraud squad if you suspect the odometer has been tampered with.
- Do contact local consumer groups for used-vehicle jurisprudence and help in mediating the complaint.
- Do publicize any favorable court judgment as a warning to other dealers and as encouragement for other consumers.

Collecting Your Winnings

Settlements

You may be asked to sign a document, called a release, that proves that a final settlement has been made. Generally, once you sign the release, you can't sue the other person for that particular debt or injury. If you're the debtor, it's very important that you make sure the other person signs the release when you pay him or her. If you're the creditor collecting on the debt, you must sign the release, but don't do so until you've received the money. Release the debtor from that particular debt, but don't release him or her from all future debts.

Deadbeat defendants

If you're dealing with a professional crook, the real work begins once you win your case. You may have to garnish (seize) part of the defendant's bank account or wages or ask the sheriff to serve a writ of execution. This writ allows the sheriff to demand full settlement plus court costs and, failing that, to seize the defendant's goods to cover the amount of the judgment. But here's the catch: property that's needed to earn a living (car, tools, machinery, etc.), household goods, and anything encumbered by a lien are exempt from seizure.

Professional deadbeats can tell the sheriff that practically everything they own is exempt—and it will take another action before the regular courts, at the plaintiff's expense, can have the defendant questioned under oath. If he's found to be lying, he can then be sent to jail for perjury or contempt of court. And the small claims court judgment will remain unpaid.

Key Court Decisions

The following lawsuits and judgments cover typical problems that are likely to arise. Use them as leverage when negotiating a settlement or as a reference should your claim go to trial. Additional court judgments can be found in the legal reference section of your city's main public library or at a nearby university law library. Ask the librarian for help in choosing the legal phrases that best describe your claim.

There is a lot you can find out on your own, beginning with West's *Causes of Action*, an encyclopedia for lawyers preparing lawsuits, particularly Volume 11 on Consumer Protection. You will find information there on how to sue a car company for selling you a defective car, references to relevant cases listed by state, and even a sample complaint. Another useful reference is *Blashfield's Automobile Law*, a 15-volume encyclopedia exclusively on automobile-related lawsuits. Sections 485 and 487 are especially helpful in providing jurisprudence. *Automobile Design Liability* by Goodman and the Center for Auto Safety is a 4-volume legal reference that is essential for proving that a safety defect is design or factory related. Finally, you'll want to read the "rules of civil procedure" for your state to find out how lawsuits are filed and argued and to make sure that you won't be tossed out of court on a technicality.

Defects (Body/Performance Related)

When a used vehicle no longer falls within the limits of the warranty expressed by the manufacturer or dealer, it doesn't necessarily mean that the manufacturer can't be held liable for damages caused by defective design. As mentioned before, the manufacturer is always liable for the replacement or repair of defective parts if independent testimony can show that the part was incorrectly manufactured or designed. The existence of service bulletins or a secret warranty extension will usually help to prove that the part has a high failure rate.

Paint delamination/peeling

A defect that first appeared on Ford sport-utilities, vans, and pickups in the '80s, paint delamination occurs when the top coat of paint separates from the primer coat or turns a chalky color, mostly along horizontal surfaces and often as a result of intense sunlight. When the paint peels, the entire vehicle must be repainted after a new primer resurfacer has been added. For some vehicles, the labor alone can run about 20 hours at a cost of $75 an hour.

The same paint problem affects mostly 1986–97 Chrysler, Ford, and GM vehicles equally; however, each company has responded differently to owners' requests for compensation. To help you prepare the best arguments for negotiations or court, each automaker is profiled separately, beginning with an analysis of the problem and a website reference, followed by copies of lawsuits, judgments, or dealer service bulletins that will help your claim. Pay particular attention to GM's "Goodwill Administration" service bulletin (see page 69). It gives you a peek into how all the automakers play mind games with their customers in order to keep their warranty payout as low as possible.

Chrysler

Chrysler's paint deficiencies include paint delamination, cracking, and fading between the third and fifth year of ownership. One Chrysler service bulletin that can serve as a guide for paint claims is bulletin number 23-60-90, "Base/Clearcoat Paint Damage," issued September 10, 1990. It contains a number of illustrations relating to the kinds of paint problems that Chrysler will repair under its base warranty on its vehicles; it puts Chrysler on record as accepting so-called environmental paint damage.

That bulletin and other helpful documents can be downloaded from the Internet at: *www.wam.umd.edu/gluckman/Chrysler/* (Chrysler); *www.goofball.com/keane/badpaint/* (Jeep).

A class action lawsuit has also been filed in the state of Washington, sseking damages for all Chrysler owners who have owned or leased paint-delaminated 1986–97 models. The case is *Schurk, Chanes, Jansen, and Ricker v. Chrysler,* No. 97-2-04113-9-SEA, filed in the Superior Court of King County, Washington on October 2, 1997 (contact Steve Berman or Clyde Platt with the Seattle, Washington, law firm of Hagens and Berman at 206-623-7292).

The 29-page Statement of Claim uses many photos, internal bulletins, and memos to show that Chrysler engaged in

> unlawful, unfair, and fraudulent business practices and unfair competition by treating different members of the class differently with respect to repairs it agrees to perform as "goodwill gestures," and by effecting partial repairs that do not address the true nature and extent of the delamination defect.

In explaining the delamination defect, plaintiffs' lawyers maintain that Chrysler knew the defect also subjects the paint to softening, chipping, and other damage well before the delamination is detected.

Chrysler did not, however, disclose the defect to potential or actual purchasers, and has until recently denied the existence of any defect, blaming the problem on "acid rain," "the environment," or other factors that are beyond Chrysler's control.

Instead, Chrysler has pursued the practice of only selectively repainting vehicles for a few customers. In doing so, the company has turned away many more customers with the same problem explaining that Chrysler bears no responsibility for the condition. It has not notified purchasers or lessors of the defect, or offered them a refund for the difference between what these damaged cars were worth and the actual purchase or leased price. Rather, it has engaged in a uniform course of conduct designed to deceive class members, who have asked about the cause of the delamination, by falsely stating that it was caused by "environmental factors, road conditions, the age of the car, normal wear and tear," and other similar false and misleading responses.

Only a few customers who have repeatedly complained about their defective paint have received offers from Chrysler to pay for repainting their vehicles. Chrysler also sometimes offers "patch" paint jobs, temporary cosmetic cures that don't halt progressive damage. Even then, Chrysler offers to pay for only a portion of the expense of such partial repairs and offers different amounts to different consumers, even though all vehicles concerned show the same extent of damage.

In researching the root cause of Chrysler's delamination defect, the lawsuit quotes Chrysler's Northwest Division Customer Sales Manager, Mr. Michael Mackey.

Mackey identified the cause of the delamination as an "incompatibility between the primer and the paint" that prevented adhesion between the two. He also said that Chrysler had known about the problem for "quite some time." Mackey further stated that Chrysler encountered the problem when it was forced to begin using water-based paints due to a ban on the use of leaded paints. In order to rectify the problem, Mackey said it would be necessary to strip the existing paint and primer and to put on a new primer coat using a process known as "etching."

The Statement of Claim also details the reasons for delamination:

The cause of the delamination and its widespread nature
Beginning in the early 1980s, Chrysler changed the constituents of its exterior car paints in order to enhance corrosion resistance, reduce the expense of the painting process using the new, corrosion-resistant paint, and comply with environmental regulations. In

doing so, Chrysler streamlined the painting process for its vehicles. Up to that time, Chrysler painted its vehicles using a three-coat process: a bottom-layer electrocoat, applied directly to the sheet metal; a spray primer; and a color coat. Chrysler then changed to a two-coat process. It substituted Uniprime ("HBEC" or "Ecoat"), a "high-build electrocoat" manufactured by PPG industries and other paint manufacturers, for the bottom coat and spray primer. By eliminating the intermediate layer of paint, Chrysler partly off-set the cost increase of using Uniprime by reducing the time and expense required for its painting processes and by reducing chemical emissions. One of its competitors, Ford Motor Company, which had also begun to use Uniprime, estimated a savings of $6–$16 per vehicle by eliminating the middle layer of paint. Chrysler made the change without thoroughly testing the process or the integrity of the vehicle finishes it produced.

Contrary to Chrysler's claim that the problem is not wide-spread, a memo to "Members of the Finance Committee" from A. J. Trotman, Executive Vice President, Ford North American Automotive Operations, indicates what others in the automotive industry experienced on one model vehicle made with the same two-step system as on Chrysler vehicles:

> In June 1990, a field survey of about 1,000 F-series trucks (1985–1990 models) was conducted in three locations by Body and Chassis Engineering to assess paint durability. Results showed that about 13% of the F-series trucks displayed peeling paint, which would represent about 90,000 vehicles annually.

In or about 1983–85, Chrysler began to use the new two-stage "enamel electrocoat" process at its plants in Newark, Delaware, Belvedere, Illinois, and Windsor, Ontario; in or about January 1985, the company announced that it intended to coat all of its products with Uniprime.

The new enamel electrocoat process was flawed. Uniprime is typically applied electrostatically, with the result that the topmost (or color) coat did not adhere properly. The Uniprime was further defective because its use rendered the bond with the finish coat subject to progressive deterioration when exposed to ultra-violet radiation produced even in climates with less-than-average sunlight conditions. Ultraviolet light causes the Uniprime to oxidize, which weakens its bond with the color coat of paint. In addition, the painting process was subject to a number of variables—including timing of application and thickness of the topcoat, temperature fluctuations during the painting process, and humidity inside the paint booth—variables which are critical to producing a durable finish, but which were not properly controlled. These conditions added to the progressive bonding failure inherent in the use of Uniprime as the primer and undercoat.

Chrysler knew that its new painting process was flawed almost as soon as it was used in production. The experience of car manufacturers like Ford illustrates that people in the automobile industry knew of the existence and cause of the paint peeling problem.

Chrysler's 1992 Warranty Manual provided that it covered "the cost of all parts and labor needed to repair or adjust any Chrysler supplied item...that proves defective in material, workmanship or factory preparation."

Chrysler's actions and knowledge, as alleged above, constituted a breach of these warranty conditions.

Ford

Louisiana attorney Danny Becknel, along with other lawyers, have filed three separate class action lawsuits against Chrysler, Ford, and GM. He's also filed suit against PPG Industries, a company out of Pittsburgh that he says sold defective car paint to the three companies.

Becknel claims in his suits that in the late '80s to the early '90s, the Big Three bought Uniprime from PPG Industries without thoroughly testing it. He says when the companies bought Uniprime, they switched from a three-coat car painting process (bottom coat, spray primer, color coat) to a two-coat process that eliminated the middle coat (the spray primer). Mr. Becknel claims eliminating that middle layer of spray primer saved from $6 to $16 a car. "This paint seems to be a minor cost but when you multiply it by 10 to 15 million times a year, it's a big number."

Faced with an estimated 13 percent failure rate of its painting process, Ford repainted its delaminated 1983–93 cars, minivans, vans, F-series trucks, Explorers, Rangers, and Broncos free of charge for five years under a secret "Owner Dialogue Program." Ford whistle-blowers say the company discontinued the program in January 1995 because it was proving to be too costly. Nevertheless, owners who cry foul and threaten small claims action are still routinely given initial offers of 50 percent compensation, but eventually receive complete refunds if they press further.

In your negotiations with Ford, be sure to refer to Ford's admission of the delamination problem found in Ford's service bulletin (see page 73) and in the Washington-state Chrysler class action.

Apart from the Becknel class action, Ford hasn't been a party to many lawsuits as it prefers to settle before cases come to trial. You can get the latest information and internal documents relating to Ford's secret warranty for repainting by logging on to the following site set up by dissatisfied Ford owners: *www.ihs2000.com/~peel*.

General Motors

Confidential U.S. dealer service bulletins and memos confirm the 6-year/ unlimited mileage benchmark that GM uses to accept or reject secret warranty paint claims. Of course, GM wants its customers to jump through hoops to benefit from its secret paint warranty, hence the line of questioning contained in its service bulletin reproduced on page 69.

The dealer service bulletin that GM put out several years ago (see page 74) guides dealers in determining whether paint delamination is a factory defect or is due to other external causes like acid rain, stone chips, etc. Pay particular attention to GM's explanation of the cause of the delamination problem. In effect, the automaker admits that it didn't apply sufficient primer to protect the clearcoat from ultraviolet light. Also, look at the masking-tape test GM recommends in its "Problem Identification" section to diagnose clearcoat delamination; it's the same test used by Ford and Chrysler.

Before settling your paint claim with GM or any other American automaker, download whatever info you can find from dissatisfied customers who've banded together and set up their own self-help websites on the Internet. One helpful GM paint delamination site is *www.geocities.com/ihategm/*.

Defects (Safety Related)

Airbags
The National Highway Traffic Safety Administration (NHTSA) says that airbags have saved 2,500 lives and reduce moderate and severe injuries in auto accidents by 25 percent. Unfortunately, says the *Wall Street Journal*, the government's figures are shaky and not based on real-world experiences.

Although safety experts agree that you are likely to need anti-lock brakes 99 times more often than an airbag, the bag's advantage is that it doesn't depend upon driver skill or reaction time and it deploys when it's too late for braking. Nevertheless, there have been thousands of reports of airbags that have failed to deploy or have accidentally gone off and caused massive injuries. In fact, General Motors recalled almost a million Cadillacs, Cavaliers, and Sunfires for just that problem of accidental deployment—caused by wet carpeting in Cadillacs and passing over a bump in the road for the other vehicles.

Safety experts at NHTSA once estimated that 25,000 people were injured by airbags between 1988 and 1991. Additionally, recent NHTSA-run crash tests indicate that all of Chrysler's minivan airbags produced in 1997 and earlier deploy with such excessive force they may cause disabling or fatal injuries. In February 1999 crash tests, the deploying passenger-side airbag in a 1997 Caravan caused neck injuries to a small, belted, female dummy that, according to the agency, would have disabled or killed a person. The suspect airbags may be in as many as 1.9 million minivans. Coincidentally, a national auto safety group, the Insurance Institute for Highway Safety (IIHS), has launched an exhaustive investigation into reports that inflating airbags have seriously injured motorists.

Hundreds of lawsuits have been filed claiming airbags don't function as designed (not deploying when they should, or deploying when they shouldn't) and over 60 suits have been filed claiming the device caused or aggravated injuries after actually deploying as designed. Chrysler, the first automaker to install airbags as standard equipment, is the target of most of these lawsuits. So far, the successful suits against Chrysler relate to poor design rather than malfunctions and fall into two categories: severe burns and premature deployment at low speeds.

Severe burns

Claimants have won substantial jury awards for first- or second-degree burns caused by the Thiokol-designed airbag directing hot gases at the driver's hands and wrists. Used on Chrysler's 1988–91 models, these airbags have vent holes that direct hot gases at the three o'clock and nine o'clock hand positions. In late 1990, the vent holes were relocated to the twelve o'clock position. A class action lawsuit asking for damages arising from the earlier Thiokol design was filed in Philadelphia County and has recently resulted in a verdict of $60 million in compensatory damages, and another $3.75 million in punitive damages, for 80,000 Pennsylvania Chrysler owners who purchased their vehicles between 1988 and 1990. The jury ruled that vehicles sold during that time came with airbags that, when deployed, could severely burn the hands and wrists of drivers. Owners were awarded $730 each to replace the defective airbags, although Pennsylvania's Consumer Protection Law could triple the damages. Martin D'Urso from the law firm of Kohn, Swift & Graf and Isaac Green from Moody & Anderson pleaded the case for the plaintiffs.

Collazo-Santiago v. Toyota, July 1998, 1st Circuit Court of Appeals. The driver of a 1994 Corolla suffered minor facial burns and abrasions when her airbag deployed as her car was rear-ended. The court concluded that the airbag's design caused the injuries. Toyota maintained that the airbag deployed as it should, and that it couldn't change the design without reducing the airbag's effectiveness. The plaintiff was awarded $30,000 compensation.

Premature airbag deployment
All automakers are worried they may face a slew of huge damage awards in the future following a $750,000 jury award for damages in the death of a five-year-old from a deploying airbag. In *Crespo v. Chrysler*, a New York jury concluded that the 1995 minivan's airbag design contributed to the child's death because it deployed too early (at a speed of between 9 and 12 mph). Safety experts contend that the airbag should deploy within a range of 15–20 mph. Chrysler submitted, however, that there are no standards as to what speeds should trigger the airbag's deployment, and claimed most automakers program their airbags to deploy at crash speeds of 8–14 mph. The jury rejected Chrysler's argument and awarded half the damages sought by the child's family, despite the fact that the child was unbelted and not seated in a safety seat.

Failure to deploy
Taylor v. Ford, Wayne County Circuit Court. American courts are taking a harder look at the automakers' liability when airbags fail to deploy, following a recent Michigan Court of Appeals decision to uphold a lower court's $292,000 verdict against Ford. Although the 1990 Lincoln Continental's driver-side airbag failed to deploy during a frontal collision, the jury found no design defect, but awarded damages against Ford for breach of an implied warranty based on defective manufacturing.

Inadvertent deployment
Perez-Trujillo v. Volvo Car Corp. (*www.law.emory.edu/1circuit/mar98/97-1792.01a.html*). This lawsuit involves injuries suffered by a dockworker while parking a Volvo on the dock. The case has just been reinstated by a U.S. Appeals Court and provides an interesting, though lengthy, dissertation on the safety hazards that airbags pose and why automakers are ultimately responsible for the injuries and deaths caused by their deployment.

Brakes (ABS)
Chrysler has come under fire over the past several years for installing defective anti-lock brakes in its minivans. The judgment below is the first of a series of lawsuits (filed but not yet judged) alleging that the company's base braking system is also faulty.

Santos v. Chrysler Corporation, February 1996, Suffolk County Superior Court. The plaintiff's wife and three children were killed when his 1988 Caravan's rear brakes locked as he applied them to avoid rear-ending another vehicle. The jury award for $19.2 million followed Paul Santos's pleadings that Chrysler "knowingly built the vehicle with a deadly defect that caused the rear brakes to lock before the front brakes." Chrysler's defense was that Santos drove the Caravan 100 miles with a broken windshield wiper and steered directly into oncoming traffic.

Fires

Delage vs. Saab, November 1997, San Francisco Superior Court. A jury awarded Jean Delage $1.4 million for damages caused by an electrical fire in his 1988 Saab 9000 even though the car was never examined. After hearing testimony from eight other Saab owners whose cars had caught on fire, the jury concluded that a defective fuse box caused the fire. The *San Francisco Chronicle* had also published a Saab internal memo that indicated a main connection in the 9000 box (located behind the glove compartment) could loosen, overheat, and ignite the insulation.

Seatbelt design/defects

Door-mounted seatbelts, motorized seatbelts, and lapbelts have come under fire during the past decade from safety advocates and the courts after insurance studies and trauma specialists showed that they increase the severity of accident injuries.

Door-mounted seatbelts
Federal safety agencies are currently looking at the reliability and safety of door-mounted seatbelts in light of accident reports showing a high failure rate and increased severity of injuries. GM, for example, has been sued for $33 million over the inadequate performance of the driver's door-mounted seatbelt on a 1990 Pontiac Sunbird, according to the Washington-based Center for Auto Safety. The driver was killed when the car door opened, rendering the seatbelt inoperative. The suit claims that GM was negligent in the design that caused the belt to be undone, leaving the driver unprotected and unrestrained.

Motorized seatbelts
These front seat restraints run along a channel and cross the shoulder when the ignition is turned on. A lapbelt has to be fastened separately. These automatic belts are set so high above the door frame that they're uncomfortable to wear and a nightmare to adjust. Their most serious shortcoming, however, is that they give the driver a false sense of security and the separate lapbelt often goes unfastened (the U.S. government says that only 29 percent of people with motorized seatbelts use the lap portion). This has resulted in a number of accidents where the driver or front passenger has been decapitated or paralyzed by the shoulder belt. Ford was sued for $1.3 million in Akron, Ohio, where the driver of a 1990 Escort was paralyzed in an accident in which only the automatic shoulder belt was fastened (*Pflum v. Ford*). Nissan faces a $10-million suit in Newnan, Georgia, from the father of a woman who didn't have the lapbelt fastened and was decapitated by her 1989 Sentra's motorized shoulder harness (*Smith v. Nissan*).

Three-point seatbelts, failure to provide

In *Garrett v. Ford*, a Baltimore, Maryland, federal court jury rendered a $3.2-million verdict against Ford for installing a dangerously designed lapbelt and for not including back seat shoulder harnesses in a 1985 Escort. The lapbelts were designed to cross at the waist instead of the pelvis, an error that contributed to the passengers' paralysis. If shoulder harnesses had been installed, the lapbelts would not have aggravated the injuries, according to the Center for Auto Safety. Ford is involved in another ongoing trial, under appeal, where the company is being sued for compensatory and punitive damages arising from the death of a 72-year-old nun, Sister Mary Margaret LeGlise. She was riding in the rear seat of a 1987 Ford Tempo with her lapbelt fastened when the accident occurred. At trial, California Superior Court judge Jeffrey Miller attacked Ford for keeping its settlements in other cases secret (referring to a $6-million payout to settle a San Diego case) in order to avoid embarrassment and other lawsuits. Judge Miller noted further that Ford could not claim that the technology to install three-point belts had not been perfected when the company had, for years, put the safer three-point belts in its European models. Judge Miller concluded:

> Ford knew that the rear seat lapbelt not only did not provide adequate protection but actually caused injury to its users. Ford also knew through its own internal engineering analysis and experimentation that the three-point restraint system was vastly superior and would save many lives.

Illegal/Unfair Insurance Company Practices

Inadequate compensation

The following two lawsuits may be helpful in any disputes you may have with an insurance company over its failure to pay a claim or use quality replacement parts in repairs. Don't get the impression that this is just a State Farm problem. These abuses are widespread.

Campbell v. State Farm Mutual Insurance Automobile Insurance Co. This Utah case saw a $147.6 million jury award against State Farm cut to $26 million by the presiding judge who didn't want the case overturned on appeal because the original award may have been considered excessive.

In his December 19, 1997, verdict, Judge William B. Bohling called State Farm "greedy, callous, clandestine, fraudulent, and dishonest" after evidence showed the company refused to pay off a claim until its own policyholder sued State Farm for bad-faith dealings.

The Campbell attorneys successfully asserted that State Farm had a national plan to cheat policyholders, which included using inferior car parts in repairs, low-balling settlements, and misleading consumers about policy benefits.

This evidence led the judge to conclude that State Farm "appeared to have preyed on the weakest of the herd" in cheating "the most vulnerable" policyholders with its "calculated and callous attitude towards settling valid claims." He concluded:

> It became a matter of plain evidence that State Farm has sold as its product, peace of mind, and has used as its advertising slogan, "like a good neighbor." State Farm's action amounts to betraying the trust that it invites its policyholders to place in it.

Poor-quality replacement parts

In a $2-billion Illinois class action, State Farm has been found guilty of breaching its promise to restore policyholders' autos to their "pre-loss condition," after it was found the company used aftermarket bumpers, door panels, and other parts that failed to meet automakers' specifications for fit, finish, corrosion protection, and safety. Over 20 million car owners whose vehicles were repaired since 1980 could be eligible for refunds or repairs.

This is an important judgment in that it allows you to demand original equipment parts whenever you make an insurance company claim. If the insurer balks at your demand, complain to the state Superintendent of Insurance.

Other Court Decisions

Using an expert (whistleblower)

GM v. Elwell, January 1998, U.S. Supreme Court. Auto industry whistleblowers have gained an ally: the U.S. Supreme Court ruled that they are free to testify against their former employers in other states, despite having signed an employee agreement not to help plaintiffs in litigation against their employer. Justice Ruth Bader Ginsburg wrote the majority opinion that the employee-employer agreements were valid only in the state where they were signed. Elwell, a former GM engineer active in assessing product liability lawsuits for the automaker over a 15-year period, has been particularly effective, since he retired, in helping plaintiffs win against GM in cases involving fire-prone fuel tanks in pickups.

Part Three
CAR AND MINIVAN RATINGS

More Chrysler Corinthian Leather, Ricardo?

"What's the difference between a $30,000 car and one that costs $50,000? A lot of wasted money, according to Steve Sharf, a former Chrysler Corp. manufacturing executive. Sharf says the equipment used to make cheaper cars costs the same as the machines that turn out expensive cars, and autoworkers are not paid according to how expensive their products are. All the amenities like heated steering wheels and leather seats just don't add up to that extra $20,000. Sharf suggests it would be better to buy a pair of gloves and forgo the heated steering wheels. If it's prestige you're looking for, he says, 'it would be cheaper and make more sense to buy $20 cigars.'"

Ward's Auto World

A used car or minivan must first live up to the promises made by the manufacturer and dealer. Ideally, it should be crashworthy, reasonably durable (lasting at least 10 years), cost no more than $500 per year to maintain, and provide you with a fair resale value a few years down the road. Parts should be reasonably priced and easily available, and competent servicing shouldn't be hard to find. We also factor into the rating the relative availability of a particular vehicle, those models and years that are the best buys, the estimated annual maintenance and repair costs averaged over five years, and alternative vehicles that will give you as much or more for less money.

Watch the model year! GM's 1984–95 Cavalier is a risky buy, but the 1996–98 models are acceptable.

Models are rated on a scale from Recommended to Not Recommended. *Recommended* vehicles are those that are an excellent choice in their class and promise their owners relatively trouble-free service (like post-1991 Ford Escorts). Vehicles that are given an *Above Average* or *Average* rating are good second choices if a Recommended vehicle isn't your first choice or is too expensive. A *Below Average* vehicle will likely be troublesome; however, a low price and reasonably priced servicing may make it an acceptable buy. Vehicles given a *Not Recommended* rating are best avoided no matter how low the price, even though they may be attractively styled and loaded with convenience features (Chrysler minivans, for example); they're likely to suffer from a variety of durability and performance problems that will make them expensive and frustrating to own. Sometimes, however, a Not Recommended model will improve over several model years and garner a better rating (as the Ford Aerostar and GM Astro and Safari minivans have done). Keep in mind, too, that the reliability and quality averages are rising, so that a newer vehicle rated Average is a far better buy than an older model with an Average rating. Incidentally, for those owners who wonder how I can stop recommending model years I once recommended, let me be clear: as vehicles age, their ratings always change to reflect new information from owners, service bulletins, etc., relating to durability and the automaker's warranty performance. I warn shoppers of the changes in subsequent issues of *Lemon-Aid* or in updates to my website, *www.lemonaidcars.com*. But that's not enough. Throughout the year, I also lobby automakers to compensate out-of-warranty owners through formal "goodwill" programs or on an individual case-by-case basis. This way, I assist my readers in avoiding a bad purchase and provide an additional means to get compensation if that purchase has already been made.

Some enterprising readers of *Lemon-Aid* use the ratings as a buying opportunity. Dave Ingram, a friend from British Columbia, Canada, and founder of Cen-Ta, uses my Not Recommended list as a shopping guide for vehicles: he buys them up at depressed prices and refurbishes them through garages offering lifetime warranties on major components that I rate as weak. He's done that with several used Cadillacs and seems happy with the system. I doubt many buyers possess Dave's mechanical acumen and intestinal fortitude.

Reliability data is compiled from a number of sources: confidential service bulletins; owner complaints sent to the author by the 2,000-plus readers who filled out the readers' survey in previous *Lemon-Aid* guides; vehicle-owners' comments posted on the Internet; and survey reports and tests done by auto associations, consumer groups, and government organizations. Some auto columnists feel this isn't a scientific sampling, and they're quite right. Nevertheless, it seems to have been right on the mark over the past 28 years. Not all vehicles sold during the last decade are profiled; those that are newer to the market or relatively rare may receive only an abbreviated mention until sufficient owner or service bulletin information becomes available. Best and worst buys for each model category (e.g., "Small" or "Medium") are listed in a summary at the beginning of each rating section. Vehicles may also be profiled in the Recommended Beaters and "Beaten" Beaters lists on pages 51–57.

Strengths and weaknesses
Unlike other auto guides, *Lemon-Aid* pinpoints potential parts failures and explains why those parts fail. We also give parts numbers for upgraded parts (why replace poor-quality brake pads with the same ones, for example?) and offer troubleshooting tips direct from the automakers' bulletins, so your mechanic won't replace parts unrelated to your troubles before coming upon the defective component that is actually responsible. To complement the "Secret Warranties/Service Tips" and vehicle "Profile" tables, we look at a vehicle's overall road performance and reliability, providing details as to which specific mechanical, electrical, or body parts fail repeatedly. This helps an independent mechanic check out the likely trouble spots before you make your purchase.

Dealer service bulletins
Imagine spearing your service manager with a confidential bulletin detailing that pesky defect your car has that he always claimed was your fault. Here we summarize problem areas addressed by confidential dealer service bulletins for more recent models. Important bulletins offering substantial repair refunds are reproduced in the "Secret Warranties/Service Tips" section.

Safety summary/Recalls
Data from independent crash tests, insurance claims statistics, ongoing safety investigations, owner safety complaints, and safety recalls make up this section. Vehicles are rated according to how well they performed in U.S. government 35 mph frontal crash tests (the impact is the same as if two identical vehicles, each travelling at 35 mph, collided head-on). Information recorded during the crash tests measures the likelihood of serious injury, and vehicles are classified by the estimated chance of injury for the driver or passenger. For the past several years, vehicles have been given a one- to five-star rating by NHTSA, with five stars indicating the best protection. Cars and minivans that are identical but carry different nameplates from the same manufacturer can be expected to perform similarly in these crash tests. On the other hand, sometimes the same vehicle tested from one year to the next will post dramatically different results even though the model has remained relatively unchanged. Safety experts admit that this happens occasionally and that consumers should look at the trend established over several model years.

Lemon-Aid is unique in that it includes estimated head, chest, and, for some model years, leg trauma as life-threatening factors in determining a model's safety rating. This is why the crash rating scores, as explained below, are often lower in *Lemon-Aid* than in other publications. Also, this guide's safety rating applies to the driver only.

❶	❷	③	④	⑤
Multiple injuries	One injury	Average protection	Above average protection	Excellent protection

Both safety and emissions recalls are listed in chronological order and by model. If your vehicle is listed and hasn't been fixed, the dealer and manufacturer must pay for the inspection and correction of the defect regardless of the vehicle's mileage, model year, or number of previous owners. It's not the law, but it's general practice.

Keep in mind that recalls affecting only a few hundred vehicles haven't been listed, and watch for the cut-off years. Even if your model year isn't listed, it may be currently under investigation or may have been recalled since this year's guide was published. Also, safety probes may be upgraded or dropped—download data files from NHTSA's website at *www.nhtsa.dot.gov/cars/problems/recalls/recmmy1.cfm* for an update.

Secret warranties/Service tips

It's not enough to know which parts on your vehicle are likely to fail. You should also know which repairs will be done for free by the dealer and automaker even though you aren't the original owner and the manufacturer's warranty has long since expired.

Welcome to the hidden world of secret warranties found in confidential dealer service bulletins (DSBs) or gleaned from owner feedback. A summary of all the important DSBs for each model year is listed, along with selected diagrams. These bulletins target defects related to safety, emissions, and performance that service managers would have you believe don't exist or are your responsibility. They also list the upgraded parts that will best repair the vehicle you plan to buy or have just bought.

Service bulletins cover repairs that may be eligible for warranty coverage in one or more of the following five categories:

- emissions warranty (5–8 years)
- safety component warranty (covers seatbelts and airbags and usually lasts the lifetime of the vehicle)
- body warranty (paint: 6 years; rust perforations: 7 years)
- secret warranty (coverage varies)
- factory defects (depends on mileage, use, and repair cost)

Use these bulletins to get free repairs—even if the vehicle has changed hands several times—and to alert an independent mechanic about which defects to look for. They're also great tools for getting compensation from automakers and dealer service managers after the warranty has expired, since they prove that a failure is factory related and, therefore, not part of routine maintenance or the result of an environmental anomaly (like bird droppings and acid rain).

Their diagnostic shortcuts and lists of upgraded parts make these bulletins invaluable in helping mechanics and do-it-yourselfers trouble-shoot problems inexpensively and replace the right part the first time. Auto owners can also use the DSBs listed here to verify that a repair was diagnosed correctly, the correct upgraded replacement part was used, and the labor costs were fair.

Getting your own bulletins
Summaries of service bulletins relating to 1982–99 vehicles can be obtained for free from the ALLDATA or NHTSA sites on the Internet (listed in the Appendix, "30 Best Internet Gripe Sites"). If you want individual bulletins for your car, they can be ordered from ALLDATA; $29.95 will get you a CD-ROM containing all the bulletins applicable to your vehicle.

Vehicle profiles
These tables cover the various aspects of vehicle ownership at a glance. Included for each model year are details on crashworthiness, repair histories for major mechanical and body components (specific defective parts are listed in the "Strengths and weaknesses" section for each vehicle rated), and which model years have secret warranties or should be bought with an extended warranty.

Prices
Dealer profit margins on used cars vary considerably—leaving lots of room to negotiate a fair price if you take the time to find out what the vehicle is really worth. Three prices are given for each model year: the vehicle's selling price when new as suggested by the manufacturer, its maximum price used (↑), and its lowest price used (↓).

Used prices are based on private sales figures current as of February 2000, and are for the lowest-priced standard model that is in good condition with a maximum of 15,000 miles for each calendar year. Be watchful for price differences reflecting each model's equipment upgrades designated by a numerical or alphabetical abbreviation. For example, L, LX, and LXT usually mean more standard features are included. Numerical progression, like the 2300 series of Mazda trucks or the Mercedes 300, usually relates to engine size.

The original selling price (Manufacturer's Suggested Retail Price, or MSRP) is given as a helpful reference point. Sellers overprice some vehicles (mostly Japanese imports, minivans, and sport-utilities) in order to get back some of the money *they* overpaid in the first place.

Why are *Lemon-Aid*'s prices lower than the prices found in dealer guides? The answer is simple: dealer guides inflate their prices so that you can bargain the price down and wind up convinced that you made a great deal. I print a top and bottom price to give the buyer some mar-gin for negotiation, as well as to account for regional differences in prices, the sudden popularity of certain models or vehicle classes (sport-utilities, trucks, minivans, etc.), and the appreciated value of used cars generally.

Car Guide 2000

Depreciation is the biggest (and often most ignored) expe owners encounter when trading in a vehicle, but smart car sh know which good-quality cars and minivans depreciate the m a bundle. Most new cars depreciate 30–40 percent during the first two years of ownership despite the fact that good-quality used cars are in high demand. On the other hand, some minivans and most vans, pickups, and sport-utilities lose little of their value even after four years of ownership.

No evaluation method is foolproof, so check dealer prices with local private classified ads and add the option values listed below to come up with a fairly representative offer. Interestingly, the value of anti-lock brakes in trade-ins has plummeted in the last few years, undoubtedly as a result of insurance studies showing that ABS has failed to reduce collision fatalities and injuries.

	Model Year					
Option	**1993**	**1994**	**1995**	**1996**	**1997**	**1998**
Air conditioning	$300	$300	$400	$500	$600	$900
AM-FM-CD	100	100	150	175	200	300
Anti-lock brakes	100	100	125	150	175	300
Automatic transmission	200	250	275	300	400	500
Cruise control	50	50	75	100	125	225
Electric six-way seat	50	100	125	150	175	300
Leather upholstery	100	200	225	325	400	700
Level control (suspension)	50	75	100	125	150	250
Paint protector	0	0	0	0	0	0
Power antenna	0	25	50	50	75	125
Power door locks	50	100	125	150	175	300
Power windows	50	100	125	150	175	325
Rustproofing	0	0	0	25	25	50
Sunroof	50	50	75	125	150	300
T-top roof	200	300	400	500	700	1,000
Tilt steering	50	50	75	75	100	175
Tinted windows	0	0	0	25	50	50
Traction control	100	125	150	175	275	400
Wire wheels/locks	75	100	125	150	175	275

It will be easier for you to match the lower used prices if you buy privately. Dealers rarely sell much below the maximum prices. They inflate their prices to cover the costs of reconditioning and paying future warranty claims and to make you feel better. If you can come within 5–10 percent of this guide's price, you'll have done well.

Extended warranties and secret warranties
Usually, but not always, an extended warranty is advised for those model years that aren't rated Recommended. In shopping for an extended warranty, don't be surprised to discover that dealers have the

market practically sewn up. You can bargain the price down by getting competing dealers to bid against each other, contacting them by fax or through their Internet sites. Be wary of extended-warranty companies that aren't backed by the major automakers.

Model years that are eligible for free repairs under a secret warranty are listed in the "Profile" section and further detailed in the "Secret Warranties/Service Tips" section. A **Y** signifies that one or more secret warranties exist or that an extended warranty is needed. An **N** means that no secret warranty applies or that there's no need to buy an extended warranty.

Reliability
The older a vehicle, the greater the chance that a major component like the engine or transmission will fail as a result of high mileage and environmental wear and tear. Surprisingly, there's a host of other expensive-to-repair failures that are just as likely to occur in a new vehicle as in an older one. Air conditioners, electronic computer modules, electrical systems, and brakes are the most troublesome components, manifesting problems early in a vehicle's life. Other deficiencies that will appear early, due to sloppy manufacturing and a harsh environment, include failure-prone body hardware (trim, finish, locks, doors, and windows), water leaks, wind noise, and paint peeling/discoloration.

The following legend shows a vehicle's relative degree of overall reliability and which mechanical and body parts are subject to premature failure. Note that the numbers lighten as the rating becomes more positive.

❶	❷	③	④	⑤
Unacceptable	Below Average	Average	Above Average	Excellent

SMALL CARS

The proverbial "econobox," this size of car is for city dwellers who want economy at any price. Small cars offer excellent gas economy, easy maneuverability in urban areas, and a low retail price.

One of the more alarming characteristics of a small car's highway performance is its extreme vulnerability to strong lateral winds, which may make the car difficult to keep on course. Most of these cars can carry only two passengers in comfort—rear seating is limited—and there is insufficient luggage capacity. As well, engine and road noise are fairly excessive.

Crash safety may be compromised by the small size and light weight of these vehicles. Nevertheless, engineering measures that direct crash forces away from occupants and the addition of airbags have made many small cars safer in collisions than some larger cars.

Recommended

Chrysler Colt/Summit, Expo, Mirage, Vista (1993–98)
Ford Escort, Tracer, ZX2 (1994–98)
Honda Civic, del Sol (CRX) (1993–98)
Mazda 323, Protegé (1996–98)

Nissan Sentra (1995–98)
Subaru Impreza (1996–98)
Suzuki Esteem (1996–98)
Toyota Corolla/GM Prizm (1995–98)
Toyota Paseo (1994–97)
Toyota Tercel (1993–98)

Above Average

GM-Suzuki Metro-Swift (1995–98)
Honda Civic, del Sol (CRX) (1992)
Hyundai Accent (1995–98)
Hyundai Elantra (1996–98)
Mazda 323, Protegé (1991–95)
Nissan Sentra (1991–94)

Suzuki Esteem (1995)
Toyota Corolla/GM Prizm (1991–94)
Toyota Paseo (1992–93)
Toyota Tercel (1991–92)
Volkswagen Cabrio, Golf, Jetta (1997–98)

Average

Chrysler Colt/Summit, Expo, Mirage, Vista (1989–92)
Ford Escort, Tracer, ZX2 (1992–93)
GM Cavalier/Sunfire (Sunbird) (1996–98)
GM Saturn S-Series (1997–98)
GM-Suzuki Metro-Swift (1990–94)

Honda Civic, del Sol (CRX) (1989–91)
Hyundai Elantra (1992–95)
Mazda 323, Protegé (1985–90)
Nissan Sentra (1988–90)
Subaru Impreza, Loyale (1993–95)
Toyota Corolla/GM Prizm (1985–90)
Toyota Tercel (1987–90)

127

Volkswagen Cabrio, Golf,
Jetta (1994–96)

Below Average

Chrsyler Colt/ Summit, Expo,
  Mirage, Vista (1985–88)
Chrysler Duster, Shadow/
  Sundance (1993–94)
Ford Aspire (1994–97)
GM-Suzuki Metro-Swift
  (1987–89)

Honda Civic, del Sol (CRX)
  (1984–88)
Hyundai Excel (1992–94)
Subaru Loyale (1984–92)
Volkswagen Cabrio, Golf,
  Jetta (1993)

Not Recommended

Chrysler Charger, Horizon/
  Omni (1983–90)
Chrysler Duster, Shadow/
  Sundance (1987–92)
Chrysler Neon (1995–98)
Ford Escort, Tracer, ZX2
  (1981–91)

GM Cavalier/Sunfire (Sunbird)
  (1984–95)
GM Saturn S-Series (1991–96)
Hyundai Excel (1986–91)
Nissan Sentra (1983–87)
Volkswagen Cabrio, Golf,
  Jetta (1985–92)

CHRYSLER

Charger, Horizon/Omni

Rating: Not Recommended (1983–90). All of these cars are virtually identical and have been off the market for about a decade. **Maintenance/Repair costs:** Inexpensive. Repairs can be done by independents. **Parts:** Except for body parts, easily found and relatively cheap.

Strengths and weaknesses: Gone and best forgotten, these cars are relatively roomy for subcompacts (except for rear seating and an awkward driving position); they give good, but not spectacular, fuel economy; they perform well on the road with the 2.2L powerplant—when it's running properly; and they can be repaired almost anywhere—which is good, because they tend to break down almost everywhere. Expect serious reliability problems with the 2.2L engine (see "Secret Warranties/Service Tips"), in addition to fuel, electrical, and ignition system problems that are difficult to diagnose and even harder to repair due to the poor quality of components. The power-steering rack develops leaks and the exhaust system rusts quickly. Other problems include rapid brake wear and unreliable electronic components. Air conditioners and turbochargers often malfunction and are expensive to troubleshoot and repair.

All 1978–90 models suffer from extensive surface rust, with perforations found around rear wheels and the rear hatch. Many owners also complain of severe underbody rusting that affects safety. All years have such poor body assembly that doors are constantly sticking shut (some owners have had to climb out the windows), locks fall off, handles detach, and water and air leaks are legion.

Safety summary/Recalls: Recalls: All models: 1985–87—The fuel hose connection may leak on turbo models. **1986**—The rear suspension may partially separate from the vehicle, causing a sudden loss of control. **1987**—A faulty pressure regulator may leak fuel. **1989–90**—2.2L and 2.5L engines leak oil at the valve cover; this can be corrected with a new cylinder head cover kit.

Secret Warranties/Service Tips

All models/years—2.2L, 2.5L, and 3.0L V6 engines that surge and buck at 35–55 mph with A413 and A670 transmissions may require driveability kit #4419447. • All front-drives with automatic transmissions that have delayed engagement and no Drive or Reverse after start-up should have the front transmission pump replaced. **All models: 1988–90**—2.2L and 2.5L EFI engines that run roughly at idle may require a new EGR valve. **1989–90**—2.2L EFI engines with a spark knock during hot engine idle in drive may need a new engine controller.

Charger, Horizon/Omni Profile

	1983	1984	1985	1986	1987	1988	1989	1990
Cost Price ($)								
Charger	7,213	7,420	7,522	7,790	7,585	—	—	—
Horizon/Omni	6,675	6,690	6,871	7,146	6,895	7,116	7,719	8,689
Used Values ($)								
Charger ↑	1,100	1,200	1,500	1,600	1,800	—	—	—
Charger ↓	1,000	1,000	1,300	1,500	1,600	—	—	—
Horizon/Omni ↑	900	1,000	1,400	1,600	1,800	2,200	2,400	2,600
Horizon/Omni↓	500	750	1,200	1,300	1,400	1,700	1,900	2,200
Extended Warranty	Y	Y	Y	Y	Y	Y	Y	Y
Secret Warranty	N	N	N	N	N	N	N	N
Reliability	❶	❶	❶	❶	❶	❶	❶	❶
Crash Safety	❷	❷	❷	❷	❷	❷	❷	❷

Colt/Summit, Expo, Mirage, Vista

Rating: Recommended (1993–98); Average (1989–92); Below Average (1985–88). The 1997 and 1998 Mirages are the standouts among these small cars and "mini" minivans. **Maintenance/Repair costs:** Repairs aren't difficult to perform and can be done by cheaper independent garages or Mitsubishi dealers. **Parts:** Easily found and relatively inexpensive, although Summit and Colt wagon body panels may be in short supply.

Strengths and weaknesses: Some of the best small cars and wagons that Chrysler doesn't make (they're all Mitsubishi imports). Although the E and DL models aren't sparkling performers, they remain competitive in the subcompact arena and can be purchased for a lot less than their Japanese cousins. The 1985–88 Colts don't handle as well or offer as much rear leg room and cargo space as the more rounded, aero-styled, contemporary 1993–96 Colts and Mirages. The 1989–92 versions got a small horsepower boost that gives them a more spirited performance; however, passenger and cargo room are still at a premium.

This well-proven design has accumulated few problems over the years, due primarily to good quality control. Body construction and assembly are also quite good, although inadequate soundproofing allows the intrusion of lots of engine and road noise. Early models tend to have some front-brake, electrical-system, and engine problems, while the later 1989–96 versions are mostly beset with fuel supply, electrical-system, and brake malfunctions.

A troublesome turbocharged 1.6L motor was first offered in 1984. The engines on high-mileage cars often burn oil because of worn piston rings. Models equipped with automatic transmissions vibrate badly when idling in gear. Air conditioners are unreliable and expensive to repair. Carburetors can be finicky, too. Front brakes wear rapidly. There are many reports of ignition troubles for the 1984–85 models. Problems carried over to the 1986–92 models are premature engine and exhaust system wear. Since then, Colts and Mirages have shown few serious defects. In fact, the redesigned '97 Mirage (the Colt was dropped in '94) carries an upgraded automatic transmission, uses a stiffer body, and is much quieter and better appointed than its predecessor. Post-'86 LX, Vista, and 4X4 models are plagued by similar defects, with the addition of transmission and fuel-system malfunctions.

The Expo, Vista, and wagon version of the Summit were small minivans with 5- to 7-passenger seating. They are more reasonably priced, practical, and fuel efficient than many other small wagons. The five-passenger Colt wagon is similar to the Summit and Nissan Sentra wagon in that it offers the extra versatility of a third seat in back and a tall body. As such, it makes a great car for a small family, while being able to haul small loads to the cottage or wherever. The wagon series is available in four-wheel drive and uses practically the same mechanical components as the other Colt models. If the wagon's price is too steep, check out the Nissan Sentra wagon, which offers similar advantages. The Summit wagon is essentially a wagon version of the Colt 200 and sells at a premium. The 1.8L or 2.4L engine goes best with the 5-speed manual transmission. With an automatic, there is a significant fuel penalty and the 2.4L takes a while to change gears, particularly when going uphill.

On post-'90 Colts and Summits, the 2.4L head gasket may fail prematurely. Shocks aren't very durable, braking isn't impressive, and the front brakes have a short life span. Emissions components like the oxygen sensor often fail after two years of use. A few owners have reported automatic transmission failures. Be especially wary of the troublesome 4X4 powertrain on 1989–91 wagons and the 16-valve turbo dropped in 1990. Owners of the 1993 Summit wagon complain of poor heating and defrosting. Surface rust is common, as are rust perforations on door bottoms, the front edge of the hood, and the rear hatch.

Owners of 1992–97 models report premature piston ring wear and excessive engine noise caused by carbon buildup on the top of the piston. Front brakes and shock absorbers continue to have a short life span.

Safety summary/Recalls: Colt and Summit: 1989–93—Automatic shoulder belts malfunction. • The wagon's sliding doors have childproof door locks. Unfortunately, some Summit wagons may have defective sliding door latches. **Mirage and Summit: 1994**—Inadvertent airbag deployment killed driver. **Recalls: Colt: 1986–91**—Takata seatbelts need replacing. **Summit: 1989–91**—Takata seatbelts need replacing. **Colt and Summit: 1992–93**—Automatic seatbelts may not move into place. **1993**—Shoulder belt–guide rail cable may jam.

Secret Warranties/Service Tips

All models/years—A common problem with the 1.6L engine is that the exhaust manifold can come loose, causing an exhaust leak. When you first spot the trouble, simply tighten the exhaust manifold bolts. Chrysler may cover costs related to premature engine head gasket, ring, and valve wear if the five-year emissions warranty is applicable. **All models: 1989–90**—Cold-start driveability problems can be fixed by cleaning the engine of carbon deposits and putting in an upgraded valve cover (#MD 118-125). • Squeaky front suspension: replace both stabilizer bar bushings. **1991**—Hard shifting or gear clashing can be corrected by installing an improved 1–2 synchronizer hub and sleeve, a 1–2 synchronizer spring, and a 3–4 synchronizer spring on cars equipped with manual transaxles. **1992**—Wagon fuel tanks may be slow to fill because the in-tank baffle impedes fuel flow. • Wagons may have excessive wind noise around the upper front door frame. **1992–93**—A front-end popping noise means the stabilizer ball joint grease has deteriorated. Add new grease and install an upgraded dust cover. **1992–94**—Carbon buildup on the piston top can be reduced by adding a bottle of Mopar Fuel Injector Cleaner to a full tank of gas. • The sliding door may not open from inside due to a faulty connecting door latch rod clip. **1993**—Wagons with poor heating/defrosting require upgraded distribution ducts.

Colt/Summit, Expo, Mirage, Vista Profile

	1991	1992	1993	1994	1995	1996	1997	1998
Cost Price ($)								
Colt/Summit	8,247	8,640	9,260	10,779	—	—	—	—
Mirage	8,508	8,823	8,822	10,548	11,563	12,422	11,962	12,130
Colt wagon	13,695	—	—	—	—	—	—	—
Summit wagon	—	12,806	12,926	14,565	15,799	16,347	—	—
Expo wagon	—	12,639	12,988	14,627	17,894	—	—	—
Used Values ($)								
Colt/Summit ↑	3,300	3,700	4,100	4,600	—	—	—	—
Colt/Summit ↓	3,000	3,500	3,700	4,000	—	—	—	—
Mirage ↑	3,500	4,000	4,300	4,500	5,500	6,500	8,000	9,000
Mirage ↓	3,000	3,500	4,000	4,300	5,000	6,000	7,000	8,000
Colt wagon ↑	4,000	—	—	—	—	—	—	—
Colt wagon ↓	3,500	—	—	—	—	—	—	—
Summit wagon ↑	—	4,700	6,000	7,000	8,000	9,000	—	—
Summit wagon ↓	—	4,000	5,000	6,000	7,000	8,000	—	—
Expo wagon ↑	—	6,000	7,000	8,000	10,500	—	—	—
Expo wagon ↓	—	5,000	6,000	7,500	9,000	—	—	—
Extended Warranty	N	N	N	N	N	N	N	N
Secret Warranty	N	N	N	Y	N	N	Y	N
Reliability	❷	❷	❷	③	④	④	⑤	⑤
Air conditioning	❷	❷	❷	③	③	③	④	④
Body integrity	❷	❷	❷	❷	❷	❷	③	④
Braking system	❷	❷	❷	❷	❷	❷	❷	③
Electrical system	❷	③	③	④	④	⑤	⑤	⑤
Engines	❷	③	④	④	④	④	④	⑤
Exhaust/Converter	③	③	④	④	⑤	⑤	⑤	⑤
Fuel system	③	④	④	④	⑤	⑤	⑤	⑤
Ignition system	③	⑤	⑤	⑤	⑤	⑤	⑤	⑤
Manual transmission	④	⑤	⑤	⑤	⑤	⑤	⑤	⑤
- automatic	③	③	③	❷	❷	③	③	④
Rust/Paint	③	③	③	③	④	④	⑤	⑤
Steering	④	④	④	⑤	⑤	⑤	⑤	⑤
Suspension	❷	③	③	③	④	③	③	④
Crash Safety								
Colt sedan	—	③	❷	—	—	—	—	—
Colt wagon	—	⑤	—	—	—	—	—	—
Mirage	—	③	❷	—	—	—	—	—
Vista wagon	—	⑤	—	—	—	—	—	—

Duster, Shadow/Sundance

Rating: Below Average (1993–94); Not Recommended (1987–92). 1994 was the last model year, then these cars were replaced by the Neon (somewhat akin to "jumping from the frying pan into the fire"). **Maintenance/Repair costs:** Average. Repairs aren't dealer dependent. **Parts:** Average cost, but can be bought for less through independent suppliers.

Strengths and weaknesses: Fairly rapid depreciation makes these cars relatively inexpensive to buy. They're better built than other Chryslers in their class, but they still have many of the same mechanical and body weaknesses that Chrysler owners have suffered with throughout the years.

On early models, the turbocharged engine isn't very reliable and can be quite expensive to repair. The fuel-injection system can be temperamental and the MacPherson struts leak or wear out prematurely. Front brakes are particularly prone to rapid wear, and parking brake cables need frequent service. Convertible tops on the 1991 Shadow tend to leak profusely, and non-metallic paint chips easily.

Owners of 1989–94 models report cylinder head, oil-pan gasket, and rear crankshaft seal leakage; the air conditioning compressor rarely lasts more than two years; windshield wiper fluid often freezes in hoses; and the power-steering assembly seldom lasts longer than five years. The upgraded 1992 41TE automatic transmission is still problematic: engine head gaskets often need replacing; oil leaks and oil pump failures are common; rear brakes are noisy; the heating, air conditioning, and ventilation systems often malfunction; electrical components (notably electronic modules) aren't very durable; and excessive suspension vibrations are common. Body assembly is sloppy, paint discolors or peels prematurely, door moldings fall off, and doors freeze shut.

Safety summary/Recalls: According to the Center for Auto Safety (CAS), hundreds of owners have complained about engine fires caused by fuel and oil leaks in 1978–90 front-drive Chryslers. • Brake failures are also common, according to the CAS. **Recalls: All models: 1987—** Fuel can leak at supply hose/pressure regulator/fuel rail connections on turbo models. **1988—**The front passenger seatbelt retractor may be faulty, compromising child safety seat protection. **1988–89—**The automatic shoulder restraint system could malfunction in a collision. **1989–91—**The possibility of engine oil leakage means that owners can get a new engine valve cover gasket. **1991—**Guide pin bolts on front disc brake calipers may be too loose. **1991–92—**Steering wheel cracks may cause the wheel to loosen. • The driver's seatback attaching bolt may fail. **1992—**Coupling bolts are faulty in the steering column shaft. **Shadow: 1991—**Both airbag front-impact sensors may be improperly mounted. • Outboard front seatbelts may not latch properly.

Secret Warranties/Service Tips

All models/years—A rotten-egg odor coming from the exhaust is likely the result of a malfunctioning catalytic converter, possibly covered under the emissions warranty. **All models: 1990**—Clearcoat paint delamination cause and cure are outlined in a special bulletin. **1990–91**—Surging or bucking at 35–55 mph with A413 or A670 automatic transmission can be fixed with driveability kit (#4419447). • 2.2L and 2.5L engines with oil leaks at the valve cover need a new cover. **1990–92**—Erratic idle speeds occurring after deceleration from a steady cruising speed can be corrected by replacing the idle air control motor. **1991–93**—The serpentine belt may come off the pulley after driving through snow; install an upgraded shield, screw, and retainers. **1991–94**—Engines that stall following a cold start may need an upgraded Park/Neutral/start switch. • Poor AC performance while the AC blower continues to operate is likely due to the evaporator freezing. **1992**—If the heater and ventilation systems change to the defrost mode during acceleration, trailer towing, or hill climbing, the installation of a revised vacuum check valve should cure the problem. • Long crank times, a rough idle, and hesitation could be corrected by replacing the intake manifold assembly. **1992–93**—A buzzing heard when the 41TE automatic transmission shifts into Reverse can be fixed by replacing the valve body assembly or the valve body separator plate. • A deceleration shudder can be eliminated by replacing the powertrain control module with an upgraded version. • 3.0L engines that burn oil or produce a smoky exhaust at idle can be fixed by installing snap rings on the exhaust valve guides and replacing all of the valve guide stems or the cylinder head. **1992–94**—Rough idling after a cold start with 2.2L and 2.5L engines can be corrected by installing an upgraded powertrain control module (PCM). • Harsh automatic shifts can be tamed by installing the following revised parts: kickdown, accumulator, reverse servo cushion springs, and accumulator piston. **1993**—Failure of the fuel pump check valve can cause start-up die-out, reduced power, or erratic shifting. **1993–94**—Acceleration shudder may be caused by automatic transmission front pump leakage. • Improved automatic shifting can be achieved by installing an upgraded transmission control module. **1994**—Poor AC performance is likely due to defective compressor suction or discharge lines.

Duster, Shadow/Sundance Profile

	1987	1988	1989	1990	1991	1992	1993	1994
Cost Price ($)								
Duster V6	—	—	—	—	—	11,400	12,825	13,985
Shadow/Sundance	9,402	9,795	10,150	11,650	8,995	9,295	10,750	11,170
Used Values ($)								
Duster V6 ↑	—	—	—	—	—	4,000	5,000	6,000
Duster V6 ↓	—	—	—	—	—	3,500	4,000	5,000
Shadow/Sundance ↑	1,200	1,500	2,000	2,500	3,000	3,500	4,000	5,000
Shadow/Sundance ↓	800	1,300	1,500	2,000	2,500	3,000	3,500	4,500
Extended Warranty	Y	Y	Y	Y	Y	Y	Y	Y
Secret Warranty	N	N	N	N	Y	Y	Y	Y

Reliability	1	2	2	2	2	2	2	3
Air conditioning	1	2	2	2	2	2	2	2
Body integrity	1	1	1	1	1	1	2	3
Braking system	1	1	2	2	2	2	3	4
Electrical system	1	1	2	2	2	2	3	3
Engines	1	2	3	3	3	3	3	4
Exhaust/Converter	2	2	2	2	2	3	3	3
Fuel system	1	2	2	2	2	3	3	3
Ignition system	1	2	3	3	2	3	4	5
Manual transmission	3	3	3	4	4	5	5	5
- automatic	2	2	2	2	2	2	2	3
Rust/Paint	1	1	1	1	1	1	2	3
Steering	2	2	2	3	3	3	4	4
Suspension	2	2	3	3	3	3	4	5
Crash Safety	1	—	—	—	4	4	4	—

Neon

Rating: Not Recommended (1995–98). A low-quality econobox that eats engine head gaskets for breakfast. Choose a model with touring suspension for the best ride. The Highline and Sport versions are more feature-laden. **Maintenance/Repair costs:** Higher than average. Repairs must be done by dealers. **Parts:** Easily found and relatively inexpensive.

Strengths and weaknesses: A small, noisy car with big quality problems, the Neon does offer a spacious interior and responsive steering and handling. Nevertheless, it uses an antiquated 3-speed automatic gearbox, a DOHC engine that has to be pushed hard to do as well as the SOHC engine, and a mushy base suspension. A perusal of service bulletins and owner comments clearly shows that these cars have a plethora of serious factory-related defects, including a biodegradable engine head gasket (covered by a 7-year/100,000 miles secret warranty), an abrupt-shifting and unreliable automatic transmission, an air conditioning system that often requires expensive servicing, a multitude of electrical glitches, lots of interior noise and leaks, uneven fit and finish, and poor-quality trim items that break or fall off easily. The finish is not as good as on most other subcompacts; Chrysler uses only two coats of paint versus the Japanese practice of applying three coats. Furthermore, the thickness of the coat varies considerably and can chip easily.

Except for the addition of a cast aluminum oil pan to reduce engine vibrations, redesigned wheel covers, improved sound system, and a center console with armrest for 1997–98 models, the Neon, unfortunately, remains basically unchanged since it was first launched.

Dealer service bulletins: 1995—Engine sags, hesitates, shudders, and surges. • Rough idle especially bad during cold start-up. • Oil leaks at the cam position sensor. • Buzzy manual and automatic gearshift lever,

and harsh-shifting, erratic automatic transmission. • Noisy clutch pedal
and wheel cover. • Rear suspension bottoms out. • Steering wheel
shakes and accelerator pedal vibrates. • Premature front brake-pad
wear. • AC freeze-up, poor performance, and evaporator odors. •
Inaccurate fuel gauge readings, instrument panel glare, and water
leaks. • Water leaks into the passenger compartment on left-hand
turns. • Flickering headlights. • Discharged battery. • Intermittent
wiper operation. • Excessive engine noise in passenger compartment,
exhaust noise/hiss, B-pillar wind noise, power-steering rattles, steering
column and right engine-mount click, and chattering steering column
tilt lever. • More noise: front seat rattle and front seatback squeak, hood
prop-rod rattle, idle air control motor whistle, front brake moan,
poorly fitted deck-lid rattle, and poor AM reception (static). • Glue
oozes out at third-brake-light/windshield molding, and brake-light
molding lifts off. **1996**—Cold-start hesitation, engine misfiring, and
erratic idling. • Excessive engine vibration and exhaust noise. •
Transmission slippage from second to third gear during light acceleration. • Speed control overshoots or undershoots. • Rear brake chirps or
howls. • AC evaporator produces a high-pitched whistle. • Fuel tank
won't fill or is slow to fill. • Delayed windshield washer fluid output. •
Interior-window film buildup. • Water leaks at cowl cover seam. **1997**—
Rear brake howl. • Front footwell creak/rattle. • Scratched door glass.
• Improper AC compressor engagement. • Loss of power steering in
heavy rain or when passing through puddles. • Poor radio reception. •
Warning that premium fuel may cause stalling, long cold-start times,
hesitation, and warm-up sags. • Front suspension popping/creaking
noise. **1998**—AC compressor lockup at low mileage. • Sag, hesitation,
harsh AC operation, and headlight flickers. • Steering wheel/column
rattles and clunks. • Cold-start power-steering noise. • Emissions recall
due to radiator fan malfunction. • Front brake squeal, creep, or groan.
• Paint fogging. • Warning that premium fuel may cause stalling, long
cold-start times, hesitation, and warm-up sags. • Popping noise when
passing over bumps or making turns. • Remote keyless transmitter battery failure. • Sunroof shade rattles in open position. • Vehicle over-
heats or radiator fan runs continuously.

Safety summary/Recalls: 1995–98 models performed poorly in IIHS
40 mph crash tests. NHTSA officials have opened a formal investigation
into reports of oversensitive airbag deployments on 1995 Neons.
1995—Steering column fires. • 98 reports of "inappropriate" airbag
deployment, causing 13 crashes and injuring 28 people. • Sudden
steering loss. • Small horn buttons are hard to find in an emergency. •
Headlight switch is a "hide and go seek" affair. • Axle shafts may suddenly fail, as the owner of a 1995 Neon discovered:

> I was driving in traffic and the car just stopped. I couldn't move
> forward or backwards but the engine was still going. It turned out
> that the left front axle of the car had collapsed. I was just lucky

that I wasn't driving on the highway when this occurred, because I would have been severely injured or killed. I had the car towed to the dealer, and they repaired the broken axle, but I just don't feel safe in the vehicle….

1995–96—Engine compartment fires. • Electrical short in dashboard. • Sudden acceleration. • ABS brake failures. • Inadvertent airbag deployment. • Failure of airbag to deploy. • Seatbelt failed to restrain driver. • Driver's seatbelt tightens uncomfortably. • Driver's side seatbelt pulled out from buckle during collision. • Premature front brake pad/rotor wearout. • Excessive wearout of brake rotors apparently caused by premature pitting of the rotors due to bubbles created during the casting process. • Front brake–caliper sticking. • Chronic engine head gasket failures. • Engine camshaft seal leaks oil • Engine motor mount and exhaust donut gasket failures. • Sticks in idle. • Chronic stalling. • Throttle system failures. • Faulty cruise control. • Chronic transmission failures. • Transmission suddenly downshifts to first gear when accelerating at 50 mph. • Sudden steering loss. • Steering locks up every time it rains. • Trunk springs won't hold lid up. • Door hinge failures. • Premature wheel bearing and steering knuckle wear. • Chronic light and gauge failures. • Faulty Goodyear tires. • Fuel gauge failures. • Defective brake master cylinder. • Window rattles, goes off track, or shatters when door is closed. • AC condenser and compressor failures. • Water leaks in from dash on driver's side. • Poor door fit allows water to enter cabin. **1997**—Circuit board behind dash caught fire. • Sudden acceleration. • Cruise control won't disengage when braking. • Chronic stalling. • Airbag failed to deploy. • Gas tank leaks fuel. • O-ring in the fuel rail leaks fuel. • Chronic sudden brake failures. • Noisy brakes. • Brake rotor failures. • Steering belt failures. • Sudden steering lockup after passing over speed bump. • Engine head gasket failures. • Window seal failures. • Fuel pump failures. • Seatbelt failed to restrain occupant. • Catalytic converter failure. • Hood fell, injuring driver's arm. **1998**—Sudden acceleration. • Airbag failed to deploy. • Driver-side window exploded in warm weather. • Front right wheel bolt fell out, causing wheel to bend. • Trunk lid may fall. • Engine surging and stalling. • Engine loses speed rapidly when going uphill. • Excessive engine carbon buildup. • Timing belt broke, causing extensive engine damage. • Engine mounts broke and head gaskets leaked. • Erratic automatic transmission performance. • There is a partial steering hangup when making a right turn. **Recalls: 1995**—Corroded fuel and rear brake tubes may fail. • Steering columns could snap loose from the car's frame. • Defective master cylinder piston. • Faulty PCM may cause chronic stalling. • Rear brake lines may be out of position. • Faulty rear ABS brake master cylinder seal. **1996**—Engine wiring harness may short, causing stalling. **1997**—Airbag module should be replaced to prevent airbags from deploying while vehicle is parked. **1997–98**—Faulty fan relay could cause engine overheating. **1998**—Rear suspension cross-member may be missing spot welds.

Secret Warranties/Service Tips

1995—Tips on how to fix paint fogging and stained white bumpers are offered. • Faulty radios will be replaced for free under a secret warranty. **1995–97**—If water drips into the vehicle from the roof-rail weather-strip channel, Chrysler will provide, under warranty, a free anti-drip roof-rail retainer channel.

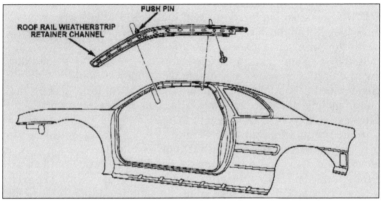

This correction should take one hour and is reimbursable under the warranty.

1995–99—A new Multi-Layer Steel engine head gasket will provide superior sealing characteristics (see bulletin on following page). **1996**—Water could enter the air cleaner housing, be ingested into the engine, and cause serious engine damage. To prevent this from occurring, the dealer will drill a hole in the housing and seal the cowl-to-head weather stripping. This 30-minute correction is free of charge under Chrysler Customer Satisfaction Notice #660. It's not a safety recall, so you may have a hard time getting Chrysler to acknowledge the problem.

Cylinder Head Gasket: Technical Service Bulletins
Multi-Layer Steel Head Gasket Installation Procedures
NO: 09-05-98
GROUP: Engine
EFFECTIVE DATE: Nov. 6, 1998
SUBJECT:
Multi-Layer Steel (MLS)
Head Gasket installation
Procedures
MODELS:

1995–1999	(JA)	Cirrus/Stratus/Breeze
1996–1999	(JX)	Sebring Convertible
1996–1999	(NS)	Town & Country/Caravan/Voyager
1995–1999	(PL)	Neon
1997–1999	(GS)	Chrysler Voyager (International Market)

NOTE:
THIS INFORMATION APPLIES TO MODELS WITH A 2.0L SOHC/DOHC OR 2.4L
ENGINE.
DISCUSSION:
A new Multi-Layer Steel (MLS) head gasket has been developed and is being implemented
into production vehicles. Additionally, it has been approved for service applications.
This new gasket will provide superior sealing characteristics, but will require extra care
in its installation where a composite gasket was previously in place. The following steps
will assist service technicians in the proper installation of this MLS gasket.
CAUTION:
ALUMINUM ENGINE COMPONENTS ARE VERY SUSCEPTIBLE TO METAL TRANSFER
AND SURFACE DAMAGE WHEN OLD GASKET MATERIAL IS REMOVED FROM THEM.
EXERCISE EXTREME CARE WHEN CLEANING THESE COMPONENTS. THE MLS GAS-
KET CANNOT PROPERLY SEAL IF GOUGING OF THE SURFACES, METAL TRANSFER
HAS TAKEN PLACE, OR COMPOSITE GASKET MATERIAL IS LEFT ON THE HEAD OR
BLOCK SURFACES.

1	5014127AA	Package, Head Gasket 1995-1999 2.0L SOHC
		(Includes Head Gasket & Instruction Sheet)
1	5014131AA	Package, Head Gasket 1995-1999 2.0L DOHC
		(Includes Head Gasket & Instruction Sheet)
1	5014173AA	Package. Head Gasket 2.4L
		(Includes Head Gasket & Instruction Sheet)
1	5014132AA	Package, Upper Gasket 1995 2.0L SOHC
		(Includes following seals/gaskets: cam sensor, cam front, head,
		valve cover, spark plug tube, EGR - cover/tube/flange, intake
		manifold, throttle body & instruction sheet)

Premature engine head gasket failures affect Chrysler's entire product line;
this bulletin is an admission that the previous component was inferior.

Neon Profile

	1995	1996	1997	1998
Cost Price ($)				
Base	12,195	11,730	12,430	12,655
Sport 4d	14,393	14,165	—	13,965
Used Values ($)				
Base ↑	4,500	6,500	9,000	10,000
Base ↓	4,000	5,500	7,500	9,000

Sport 4d ↑	5,500	7,500	—	11,000
Sport 4d ↓	4,500	6,500	—	10,000

Extended Warranty	Y	Y	Y	Y
Secret Warranty	Y	Y	Y	Y

Reliability	❶	❶	❷	❷
Air conditioning	❶	❶	❷	③
Body integrity	❷	❷	❷	❷
Braking system	❶	❶	❷	③
Electrical system	❶	❶	❷	③
Engines	❶	❶	❷	❷
Exhaust/Converter	③	④	⑤	⑤
Fuel system	❷	❷	③	③
Ignition system	③	④	⑤	⑤
Manual transmission	③	④	④	⑤
- automatic	❷	❷	③	③
Rust/Paint	❷	❷	③	③
Steering	❶	❷	③	③
Suspension	⑤	⑤	⑤	⑤
Crash Safety	③	④	④	③
Side Impact	—	—	—	❷

FORD

Aspire

Rating: Below Average (1994–97). The Aspire's size, engine, and drive-train limitations restrict it to an urban environment, and its low quality control restricts it to the driveway. The Aspire was discontinued in 1997. **Maintenance/Repair costs:** Higher than average. Repairs are dealer dependent. **Parts:** As with other discontinued models, body panels are rare and expensive.

Strengths and weaknesses: The Korean-built Aspire comes in three- and five-door versions and is powered by a fuel-injected, 4-cylinder engine hooked up to either a standard 5-speed manual transmission or an optional 3-speed automatic. With its smooth-shifting 5-speed manual transmission and fuel-injection, the Aspire's base powerplant is adequate for short, city errands. This car has plenty of front seat room and excellent front and rear visibility. Corrosion protection is enhanced with galvanized steel panels, sealers, and coatings. Except for a minor facelift and upgraded side-impact protection, the 1997 Aspire is much like its predecessors.

The Aspire's engine lacks high-end torque, and the widely spaced gear ratios on the manual shifter rob it of much-needed mid-range power. It takes 13 seconds to reach 60 mph—and an additional 4 seconds with the automatic gearbox, which is jerky when pushed. Air conditioning slows down the car even more. Steering is heavy and vague at high speeds. Unfortunately, the three-door version doesn't offer power steering. Expect excessive low-speed engine and road/tire noise at higher speeds. Its fuel economy is not all that impressive when compared to entry-level Hondas and Nissans, but the higher cost of these vehicles wipes out any fuel savings.

Dealer service bulletins: 1994—Rough idle, hesitation, excessive fuel consumption, and poor heater output likely caused by the thermostat being stuck in the open position or opening before it should. **1995**—Automatic transmission fails to upshift in cold weather. • Brake roughness upon application. • Malfunctioning air conditioning and excessive compressor noise. • No-start due to faulty ignition switch. **1996**—Fog/film on windshield/interior glass. • MTX transmission clicks, clunks, and rattles when in Reverse. • Musty and mildewy odors. **1997**—Excessive manual transmission noise. • Delayed automatic transmission engagement. • Door glass won't roll down.

Safety summary/Recalls: Owners report this car is unstable in a crosswind, and the tiny brakes don't inspire confidence. • NHTSA has opened an official investigation of fuel vapor valve leaks on the 1996–97 Aspires. **1994**—Wiring harness fire. • Driver's airbag deployed and caused fractured eye socket, detached retina, and several dislocated bones. • Airbag deployment caused severe burns. • Airbag failed to deploy. • Stalling caused by malfunctioning throttle position sensor. • Input shaft and Reverse gear failure. • Steering column locks up, causing ignition-switch problems. • Left front window shattered. • Tierod broke and caused accident. • Front brake rotor warpage every 10,000 miles. • Ball joint rusted away. • Frequent headlight switch failures. • Window shatters when door is closed. • Inadequate ventilation; poor defrosting. • Headlights are too dim. • Passenger-side seat unbolted from floor board. **1995**—Under-hood fire. • Frequent complaints that the airbag failed to deploy. • Severe burns and broken wrist when airbag deployed. • Stalling while cruising on the highway with AC operating. • Steering wheel lockup. • Many reports of fuel odor in the interior. • Premature brake pad wearout. • Wheel bearing failure caused vehicle to career out of control. • Several reports of the transmission shift lever breaking off. • Transmission failures. • Cracked bracket causes clutch cable to break. • Rotten-egg smell permeates the interior. • Water enters interior. • Chronic distributor short-circuits. • Lights dim when using defroster. • Headlight failure when switching from low to high beam. • Inside windshield ices up due to faulty defroster. • Rusted-out hatchback hinge. • Rolled-down window shatters when door is closed. **1996**—Inadvertent airbag deployment. • Steering wheel lockup. • Brakes require extended stopping distances. •

Excessive and premature brake pad and rotor warpage. • Front suspension geometry causes premature tire wear. • Gasoline smell in the interior. **1997**—Brake failure. • Wiring harness short caused an underhood fire. • Frequent distributor cap failures cause chronic engine stalling. • Hood flew up and hit windshield. • Chronic fuel vapor odor in car's interior. **Recalls: 1994**—Fuel-supply, return, and vapor hoses or lines may leak. Steel fuel lines will be repositioned; get additional corrosion protection, if needed.

Secret Warranties/Service Tips

1994—The upper steering column cover causes the warning flasher to stick. • Fuel leaks from fuel and vapor hoses/lines. **1996–97**—Fuel odor in the interior may be caused by a cracked seam weld on the vapor vent valve located in the left quarter panel area.

Aspire Profile

	1994	1995	1996	1997
Cost Price ($)				
Base	9,660	9,860	10,225	10,655
Used Values ($)				
Base ↑	3,500	4,500	5,000	6,500
Base ↓	3,000	4,000	4,500	5,000
Extended Warranty	Y	Y	Y	Y
Secret Warranty	Y	Y	Y	Y
Reliability	②	②	②	②
Air conditioning	②	②	③	③
Body integrity	②	②	②	②
Braking system	②	②	②	②
Electrical system	②	②	②	③
Engines	④	④	④	④
Exhaust/Converter	③	④	⑤	⑤
Fuel system	②	②	②	②
Ignition system	④	⑤	⑤	⑤
Manual transmission	②	②	⑤	⑤
- automatic	②	②	②	②
Rust/Paint	②	②	④	⑤
Steering	②	②	②	②
Suspension	③	④	⑤	⑤
Crash Safety	—	④	④	④

Escort, Tracer, ZX2

Rating: Recommended (1994–98); Average (1992–93); Not Recommended (1981–91). The LX became the base Escort during the 1994 model year. Lots of upgraded 1997 Escorts are coming off lease now; they represent an exceptionally good buy. For the 2000 model year, the Escort will be replaced by the Focus. **Maintenance/Repair costs:** Higher than average on pre-1991s; below average for later models. Repairs can be done by independents or Ford or Mazda dealers. **Parts:** Expensive, but easily found.

Strengths and weaknesses: These front-drive small cars are usually reasonably priced and economical to operate, and provide a comfortable though busy ride and adequate front seating for two adults. However, they have a "Dr. Jekyll and Mr. Hyde" disposition, depending on which model year you buy. From 1982 through 1991, these subcompacts were dull performers with uninspiring interiors. Worse, they had a nasty reputation for being unreliable and expensive to repair.

Be wary of early Escorts (1984–87) that use Mazda's 2.0L diesel 4-cylinder; it's weak, noisy, difficult to service, and prone to expensive cylinder head and gasket repairs. From 1987 until 1991, quality continued to go downhill. The 1.9L engine used from 1985 to 1990 gives respectable highway performance but its failure rate is still much higher than average. The radiator and other cooling components, including the fan switch and motor, are failure-prone. Carburetors and fuel-injection systems are temperamental. Ignition modules are often defective. Power steering racks fail prematurely. Front and rear wheel alignment is difficult. Exhaust systems rust rapidly.

The 1991 model's changeover to mostly Mazda 323 components gave it a longer wheelbase, making for a more comfortable ride and a bit roomier interior. The 1.9L engine runs more smoothly as well. The GT and Tracer LTS are equipped with Mazda's powerful 127-hp, 1.8L, 4-cylinder engine, and their overall highway performance and fuel economy are far superior to what previous models offered. Wagon versions are particularly versatile and spacious. The front seats on the Tracer GS and LS are very comfortable and the cargo area is especially spacious in the wagon. Rear seat room is a bit cramped on all other models.

Quality control and reliability improved considerably over the following years but problems remain. Owner complaints relating to the 1991–96 model years concern primarily the automatic transmission and engine, the cooling system, brakes, electrical short circuits, air conditioning, the fuel pump, and ignition system failures.

The 1997 models were significantly improved quality-wise; are more attractively designed; ride and handle better; and featured improved comfort, a quieter interior, and more standard equipment. The car is four inches longer, mostly taken up by a larger trunk. New standard features included power steering; rear heat ducts; intermittent wipers; a battery-saver system; a 24-watt, four-speaker stereo unit that can be upgraded to an 80-watt system hooked to a trunk-mounted CD player, and solar glass. Three-door, five-door, and GT models were dropped and the ZX2—a revived, high-performance coupe—made its debut in late 1997 as a 1998 model.

Safety summary/Recalls: Recalls: Escort: 1983–93—Ford will replace fire-prone ignition switches on designated Escorts and Tracers. **1985**—Rocker arm oil leakage could cause a fire. • Cars with 1.9L engines may fail to return to idle. **1985–86**—Manual gearshift lever may accidentally slip into Neutral in cold weather. **1985–87**—Driver's seat could come loose in an accident. **1986–88**—Fuel line leakage could cause a fire. **1987**—Stainless-steel lug nuts may fracture, causing the wheel to fall off. **1990**—Windshield could come out in a frontal collision. **1991**—Accelerator pedal could stick wide open. • Steering column could lock up. **1991–92**—Fuel vapor could escape from a full fuel tank, causing a fire. **1991–94**—Fuel pump wiring corrosion could cause chronic stalling. **1992**—Faulty brake-light switch. **1993**—Faulty driver's seat could fail in a collision. **1995**—Airbag mounting bolts may be missing or improperly torqued. **Tracer: 1991**—Fuel vapor could escape from fuel tank, causing a fire. **1992**—Steering column may lock up.

Secret Warranties/Service Tips

Escort:1983–94—Hesitation, a rough idle, or poor heater output may all be caused by a faulty thermostat. **1986–89**—Hard starting/stalling may be caused by a defective fuel pump or sender assembly. **1988**—Owner notification M59 says that any fuel pump malfunction that drains the battery, makes for hard starts, or cuts engine performance can be corrected by installing an upgraded fuel pump diode (#E8FZ-14A411-A). **1991–93**—Metallic ticking heard after initial start-up or when returning to idle speed may be caused by a faulty lifter, low amount of oil in the crankcase, incorrect oil filter, or oil deterioration. **1991–94**—Under a recall and Service Program #94B55, Ford will install at no charge a fused jumper harness in the fuel pump electrical circuit. This will prevent short-circuit problems such as stalling, erratic instrument gauge readings, and extensive wiring damage, which are caused by water intrusion. • Fix a timing belt that's noisy during cold weather by installing an upgraded, more rigid belt tensioner. • A missing or loose front valance panel will be replaced or secured with longer bolts free of charge. **1992–93**—A high idle rpm after heavy use may be corrected by installing a new idle air control valve. **1994–98**—Tips on eliminating wind noise around doors are given in DSB #97-15-1. **1997–98**—PCV system may freeze resulting in a serious oil leak through the dipstick tube.

Engine Oil Leak From Dipstick Tube-PCV Freezes, 2.0L SPI
Article No.
98-10-5
05/26/98
ENGINE - 2.0L SPI - PCV FREEZING AT COLD
AMBIENT TEMPERATURES - VEHICLES WITH
SOHC
LEAK - ENGINE OIL LEAK FROM OIL LEVEL
INDICATOR TUBE - PCV FREEZE - VEHICLES
BUILT WITH 2.0L SPI ENGINE
FORD:
1997–98 ESCORT
LINCOLN-MERCURY:
1997–98 TRACER
ISSUE
At cold ambient temperatures, the Positive Crankcase Ventilation (PCV) system may freeze causing the engine to unseat the dipstick and vent crankcase gasses through the dipstick tube. This may result in oil being discharged on some vehicles.
ACTION
Install PCV Service Kit (refer to Parts Block for correct service application) per this TSB. Refer to the Instruction Sheet within the kit for Service Procedure.

PART NUMBER	PART NAME
F8PZ-6A603-CA	PCV Service Kit (1998 Escort/Tracer)
F7PZ-6A603-BA	PCV Service Kit (1997 Escort/Tracer)

OTHER APPLICABLE ARTICLES: NONE
WARRANTY STATUS: Eligible Under The Provisions Of Bumper To Bumper Warranty Coverage And Emissions Warranty Coverage

The above kit doesn't work any better than the original component; Ford says it's still working on a solution to the problem. Remember all losses caused by this defect are Ford's responsibility.

1998—An erratic transaxle shift may simply be caused by a pinched wire.

Article No.
98-21-13
10/26/98
TRANSAXLE - ERRATIC SHIFT WITH DIAGNOSTIC
TROUBLE CODE (DTC) P0712
FORD:
1998 ESCORT
LINCOLN-MERCURY:
1998 TRACER
ISSUE
An erratic transaxle shift with a Diagnostic Trouble Code (DTC) of P0712 may occur on some vehicles. This may be caused
by the Transmission Fluid Temperature (TFT) wire being pinched on the spring clip attached to the valve body.
ACTION
Repair the TFT wire with a plastic wrap. Refer to the following Service Procedure for details.
SERVICE PROCEDURE
1.   Verify that DTC P0712 is stored in memory.
2.   Check the TFT circuit for shorts to ground or opens. If either exist, proceed to Step 3. If neither exist, follow the appro-
     priate Pinpoint Test in the Powertrain Control/Emissions Diagnosis (PC/ED) Service Manual.
3.   Remove the transaxle pan by referring to the 1998 Escort/Tracer Workshop Manual.

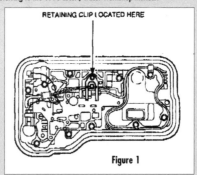

RETAINING CLIP LOCATED HERE

Figure 1

4.   Remove the clip that retains the TFT sensor wire (Figure 1).

Escort, Tracer, ZX2 Profile

	1991	1992	1993	1994	1995	1996	1997	1998
Cost Price ($)								
Escort base/LX	8,586	9,883	8,831	10,510	11,115	11,615	12,225	12,490
GT	12,593	12,800	12,800	12,675	13,530	14,040	—	—
ZX2	—	—	—	—	—	—	—	14,325
Used Values ($)								
Escort base/LX ↑	3,500	4,600	5,200	5,600	6,500	7,500	8,600	10,200
Escort base/LX ↓	3,000	3,700	4,200	4,600	5,400	6,400	7,400	9,200
GT ↑	4,500	5,800	6,700	8,000	9,000	9,500	—	—
GT ↓	4,000	4,800	5,800	6,800	8,000	8,500	—	—
ZX2 ↑	—	—	—	—	—	—	—	10,500
ZX2 ↓	—	—	—	—	—	—	—	9,500

Note: Tracer prices are similar to those of the base Escort.

	1991	1992	1993	1994	1995	1996	1997	1998
Extended Warranty	Y	Y	Y	N	N	N	N	N
Secret Warranty	Y	Y	Y	Y	Y	Y	Y	Y

Reliability	❷	③	③	④	④	⑤	⑤	⑤
Air conditioning	❶	❷	❷	③	③	③	③	④
Body integrity	❷	❷	❷	❷	❷	③	③	③
Braking system	❶	❶	❶	❷	③	③	④	④
Electrical system	❶	❷	❷	❷	❷	❷	③	④
Engines	❷	③	③	③	⑤	⑤	⑤	⑤
Exhaust/Converter	③	④	⑤	⑤	⑤	⑤	⑤	⑤
Fuel system	③	③	③	③	④	⑤	⑤	⑤
Ignition system	❷	③	③	③	④	⑤	⑤	⑤
Manual transmission	⑤	⑤	⑤	⑤	⑤	⑤	⑤	⑤
- automatic	❷	③	③	④	⑤	⑤	⑤	⑤
Rust/Paint	❶	❷	❷	③	③	③	③	④
Steering	③	⑤	⑤	⑤	⑤	⑤	⑤	⑤
Suspension	❷	③	③	④	⑤	⑤	⑤	⑤
Crash Safety								
Escort	⑤	⑤	⑤	④	④	④	③	③
Tracer	—	—	—	④	④	④	③	③
Side Impact								
Escort	—	—	—	—	—	—	③	③
Tracer	—	—	—	—	—	—	③	③
Escort ZX2 2d	—	—	—	—	—	—	—	❶

Note: The low crash scores represent severe leg trauma.

GENERAL MOTORS

Cavalier/Sunfire (Sunbird)

Rating: Average (1996–98); Not Recommended (1984–95). Repair bills will run you bankrupt if you get a pre-1995 model or if maintenance schedules aren't followed to the letter. An incredibly slow depreciation rate means that recent models are no bargains. Still, I'd buy a Cavalier, Sunbird, or Sunfire over a Saturn any day. The base Sunbird became the LE in 1989, and then changed its name to the Sunfire in 1995. The Cavalier Z24 convertible was replaced by the LS in 1995. **Maintenance/Repair costs:** Average; repairs aren't dealer dependent; however, ABS troubleshooting is a real head-scratcher. **Parts:** Reasonably priced; often available for much less from independent suppliers.

Strengths and weaknesses: Snappy road performance (with the right engine and transmission hookup) has been marred by abysmally poor reliability. The basic versions are lackluster performers. The 2.0L 4-cylinder engine gets overwhelmed by the demands of passing and merging. On top of that, major reliability weaknesses afflict all mechanical and body components. Engine, transmission, electronic module, and brake failures are common for all model years. 2.0L engine blocks crack, cylinder heads leak, and the turbocharged version frequently needs expensive repairs. Oil leakage from the rear crankshaft seal is common and oil filters on all model years tend to wear out quickly.

1986–89 model year improvements simply changed the nature, not the frequency, of engine and automatic transmission breakdowns. Power-steering rack and front suspension components aren't durable. Consider replacing the original components with front gas struts and rear cargo coil springs to improve handling and durability. Owners also report that a change to high-octane fuel can help improve engine performance and reduce knocking and engine run-on. The cooling, exhaust, ignition, and fuel systems have had more than the average number of problems. The manifold heat shield tends to be noisy. Front brakes wear out quickly, and rear brakes tend to lock the rear wheels in emergency stops (one cause being the seizure of the rear brake adjusters). The Cavalier's optional 2.8L V6 with 3-speed automatic transmission is the best highway performer, but intake manifold gasket failures, premature head gasket wear, and transmission malfunctions compromise driving pleasure.

For 1990–94 versions, the Cavalier's base 2.2L 4-cylinder and optional 3.1L engines replaced the failure-prone 2.0L and 2.8L power-plants. Unfortunately, the newer engines already have a checkered reputation, highlighted by reports of chronic head gasket failures causing coolant leakage, overheating, engine seizure, hard starting, stalling, and surging—problems covered by a secret warranty. Air conditioning and hood latch failures, seatbelt defects, and a plethora of body deficiencies are also commonplace. Door bottoms and wheel housings are particularly vulnerable to rust perforation. Premature paint peeling and cracking, discoloration, and surface rust have been regular problems since these cars were introduced.

The 1995–98 versions benefited from some engine tweaks, standard dual airbags and ABS, a longer wheelbase (but shorter body), a stiffer structure, and an improved suspension. Unfortunately, though, the engine head gasket failures have apparently been carried over to the later models as well, plus quality control is still woefully deficient.

Dealer service bulletins: All models: 1993—3.1L engines hesitate or stall. • No Reverse or slipping while in Reverse with 3T40 automatic transmissions. • Rear brake squawk. **1994**—Body fit deficiencies. • Premature front brake wear. • Faulty ignition switches. • Electrical short circuits. **1995**—Engine failing to crank and no-start. • Brake vibration and/or pedal pulsation. • Introduction of longer-life front brake linings. • Low voltage reading and dim lights at idle. • Grinding/growling when in Park on an incline. • Knocking noise when traversing rough roads. • Rear window panel squeaking. • Rear quarter-panel road noise. • Loose door trim panel. • Poor paint application and rust spots. **1996**—Excessive engine roll. • Low-speed knocking noise when passing over rough roads. • Air conditioning odors. • Radio frequency interference diagnosis tips. • Water leak diagnostic guide. • Loose door trim panel.

• Tips on silencing rear quarter-panel road noise. • Condensation within exterior light housing. • Rear edge of hood rubs windshield when opening. • Twisted seatbelt webbing. **1997**—Axle seal leakage. • Scuffed interior quarter trim panels on convertibles. • Coolant odor or leakage. • Deck lid hard to open or close. • Automatic transmission failure. • Low-engine-coolant light flashes. • Popping noise originating from the engine compartment. • Rear seatback rattles/squeaks. • Rear shock noise coming from trunk area. • Engine cranks, but won't run.

Safety summary/Recalls: All models: 1995—Steering locks up. • Faulty cruise control. • Windshield wipers fail in cold weather. • **1995–96**—ABS brake failure. • Airbags fail to deploy or deploy accidentally. • Inoperative horn. • Transmission slips out of Park. • Sudden acceleration, stalling. • Passenger-side seatbacks won't stay upright. **1996**—NHTSA has received 96 complaints of inadvertent airbag deployment, which include 10 crashes and injuries to 53 people. • Engine gaskets leak oil. • Mufflers fail frequently. **1997**—Engine fires. • Inadvertent airbag deployment. • Airbag failed to deploy. • During a collision, driver sustained serious leg injuries when the seat pushed her lower body under the instrument panel. • Sudden acceleration. • Chronic stalling and hesitation, particularly when it rains. • Premature engine cylinder failure; leaks oil. • Premature oil pump failure. • Faulty fuel pump relay provokes stalling. • Failure of the engine mounts and ignition switch. • Cruise control failure. • Restart after stalling causes engine to race. • Sudden loss of power. • Steering wheel locked up. • Transmission failures. • Noisy rear end due to faulty suspension struts. • Faulty master cylinder and modulator assembly led to brake failure. • Frequent front brake rotor warpage, premature pad wear, and excessive vibrations when braking. • ABS brake failure. • Horn failed. • Cracked water pump. • Dashboard cracking, rattling, and popping. • Defective instrument panel control module. • Low-beam switch failure. • Inoperative lighting due to rotted-out wiring harness. • Door hinges don't hold door open. • Door came ajar while driving. • Windshield wiper failure. • When turned off, windshield wiper stops in the field of vision. • Lug nuts are easily broken when changing tire. **Recalls: All models: 1984**—The floor pan–anchor on cars with a manually adjusted driver's seat could break, causing the driver's seat to tip backwards suddenly, leading to a potential loss of vehicle control. • Models with 2.0L engines may suddenly accelerate due to a kinked accelerator control cable. **1985**—Air cleaner plastic trim could catch fire. **1986**—A defective headlight switch can cause headlights to flicker or fail. **1987**—It is possible that the fuel feed/return lines will crack, leaking fuel. • Parking brake lever may fail, allowing the vehicle to roll away unexpectedly. • Cars with 2.0L engines may have a frozen accelerator cable that could cause sudden acceleration. **1989**—The fuel tank, which could leak fuel, will be inspected and replaced, if necessary, for free. **1991**—Cracked front-door shoulder belt guide loops could pull loose in an accident. • Front door frames that anchor the seatbelt housing could collapse in an accident, resulting in seatbelt failure. **1992**—The hood could open suddenly, blocking the driver's view. **1992–93**—Vehicles equipped with 2.0L engines may have defective throttle-cable assemblies that could stick open in cold weather. **1993**—Faulty rear brake hoses could cause brake failure. **1993–94**—Horn pad may fall apart. GM has a "safety improvement campaign" to correct the defect for free. **1994**—Loose drive-axle spindle nuts may cause steering knuckle tire-wheel assembly to separate from the axle. **1995**—Front suspension lower control-arm assemblies may be defective. **1995–96**—Front or rear hazard warning lights could be faulty. **1996**—Accelerator cable may be kinked, requiring excessive pedal effort. **1996–97**—Airbag sensor is too sensitive. • Rear suspension trailing arm bolts can fatigue and break. **1997**—Driver's wiper blades may be five inches too short. **Sunbird: 1988**—Backup lights may be inoperative.

Secret Warranties/Service Tips

All models/years—Squeaking front brakes can be silenced by replacing the semi-metallic front brake linings with quieter linings (#12321424). The new linings will be 20 percent less durable (DSB #86-5-20). • A rotten-egg odor coming from the exhaust is probably caused by a malfunctioning catalytic converter; this repair is covered by GM's emissions warranty. **All models: 1985–88**—Premature brake lining wear may be caused by a misadjusted cruise control cutoff or brake light switch. **1985–89**—No first gear and/or slips in first may mean that you need new forward clutch piston seals. **1985–90**—Exhaust boom or moan can be corrected by installing a mass dampener (#10137382). • Noise from rear springs requires the installation of upgraded rear spring insulators (#22555689). **1986–87**—Erratic idle and 2.0L engine surging require the replacement of the PROM or TCC solenoid; another possible cause is a defective mass air flow sensor. **1987–88**—Difficult cold starts with 2.0L engines may require a new drop-in manifold deflector plate (#10112342). • A sagging headliner needs service package #22541347. **1987–90**—A rattle or buzz from the instrument panel may require a new upgraded brake-booster check valve (#18012017). **1988–89**—2.0L engine valve train noise can be reduced by adjusting or replacing the rocker arms. **1988–94**—Water leaks at the front upper door frame are treated in depth in a DSB issued in October 1994. **1989**—Product Campaign 89C16 provides for the free replacement of the 5-speed manual transmission. **1990**—Heater and AC blower noise can be reduced by replacing the blower assembly. **1990–91**—Poor starting may be caused by the spring in early starter drives compressing too easily; install an upgraded starter motor drive assembly (#10473700). **1991–94**—A crunching noise coming from the right side of the dash when turning the steering wheel can be silenced by installing a new steering grommet on the right side. **1992–93**—Engine head gasket failures may cause coolant leakage, overheating, and serious engine failure. GM will repair the defect at no charge under the following secret warranty.

Dear General Motors Customer:

As the owner of a 1992 or 1993 Chevrolet Cavalier equipped with a 2.2L engine, your satisfaction with our product is of the utmost concern to us. Your vehicle was provided with a new vehicle warranty, which covers certain parts of your vehicle for a specified period. These warranties are of considerable value to you if you should experience problems with your vehicle.

This letter is intended to make you aware that some 1992 and 1993 Chevrolet Cavalier models with 2.2L engines may develop a failure of the cylinder head gasket that allows coolant to leak from the cylinder head gasket to engine block joint. Early evidence of this would be a loss of coolant in the coolant reservoir and an odour of coolant from the engine compartment, or a low coolant light. There may also be visible coolant deposits at the cylinder head to engine block joint.

General Motors of Canada Limited is therefore taking the following action:

We are providing owners with special coverage. If the above-mentioned condition occurs within seven (7) years of the date your vehicle was originally placed in service or 160,000 km, whichever occurs first, your vehicle will be repaired for you at no charge.

This special policy applies only to repairs requiring cylinder head gasket replacement as a result of cylinder head gasket failure that results in an engine coolant leak. It does not cover engine damage from continuing to operate the engine in an overheated condition after loss of coolant.

This is not a recall campaign. Do not take your vehicle to your GM dealer as a result of this letter unless you believe that your vehicle has the condition as described above. Keep this letter with your other important glove box literature for future reference.

If you have already paid for some or all of the cost to have the cylinder head gasket replaced and in-service time was less than seven (7) years and 160,000 km, you should contact your GM dealer. You may be eligible for partial or complete reimbursement of costs if genuine GM parts were used in the repair. If the work was done by someone other than a GM dealership the amount of reimbursement may be limited to the amount the repair would have cost GM to have it completed by a GM dealership. Please provide your dealer with your original paid receipts or invoices verifying the repair, the amount charged, proof of payment, and the date of payment of those charges by March 1, 1997.

Repairs and adjustments qualifying under this Special Policy coverage must be performed by your GM dealer.

The same head gasket problem has been reported by owners of 1994–95 models; GM hasn't formally included them in this program yet, probably because most vehicles may still be covered by the base warranty. Whatever the reason, remember this: GM is 100% responsible for repairing this defect.

1992–97—Paint delamination, peeling, or fading: GM lets dealers repaint the entire car at no charge to the owner (up to $650), regardless of whether it was bought new or used. Head office permission isn't needed before work commences (see pages 73–75). **1993–94**—Excessive engine vibrations at idle or a clunk upon acceleration is most likely due to a defective engine mount. **1994**—A squeaking noise heard when going over bumps, accelerating, or shifting can be stopped by replacing the exhaust manifold pipe seal. • Water leaks into the front footwell are discussed in depth in a December 1993 DSB. **1987–88**—Engine stalling in Reverse or Drive with the THM 125C automatic transmission may mean that you need an upgraded auxiliary valve body filter (#8664921). • Poor AC cooling may be caused by a faulty pressure switch O-ring seal. **1992**—Engine hesitation or roughness, particularly at idle, may be corrected by installing a new lower intake manifold gasket (#10103647). **1995–97**—Axle seal leakage may be caused by a pinched transaxle vent hose. • Delayed automatic transmission engagement after a cold soak signals the need to install a revised forward clutch housing assembly. • Repair tips are offered for scuffed interior quarter trim panels on convertibles. • A sticking deck lid may need an upgraded lid release cable. • A dome light that won't shut off probably has a corroded doorjamb switch. • The left-hand mirror may not adjust if the lever has become disengaged. • A popping noise originating from the engine compartment may mean that the torque strut-mount attaching bolts are loose. • Troubleshooting tips on silencing rear shock noise and rear seatback rattles and squeaks are available. **1996–97**—Coolant odor or leakage may occur at the joint where the radiator outlet pipe is connected to the coolant pump cover or at the joint between the cooling system air-bleed pipe and the coolant outlet. **1997**—A low-engine-coolant light may come on to signal that the cooling system surge tank is defective. **Cavalier: 1986–92**—Vehicles equipped with the 3T40 automatic transmission may experience slippage in manual Low or Reverse; install service package #8628222, which includes a Low/Reverse clutch release spring (#8664961) and clutch retainer and snap ring (#656/657).

Cavalier/Sunfire (Sunbird) Profile

	1991	1992	1993	1994	1995	1996	1997	1998
Cost Price ($)								
Cavalier	10,252	11,046	10,667	11082	12,030	12,872	13,357	13,505
Conv.	16,929	17,720	17,110	17,470	17,695	17,995	18,265	20,690
Z24	13,700	14,710	14,215	14,965	14,295	15,490	15,760	16,990
Sunfire	—	—	—	—	12,989	13,514	14,079	14,425
Used Values ($)								
Cavalier ↑	3,500	4,000	4,500	5,500	6,500	8,500	9,500	11,000
Cavalier ↓	3,000	3,500	4,000	4,500	5,500	7,500	8,500	9,500
Conv. ↑	5,500	6,500	7,000	8,000	9,000	11,500	13,000	15,000
Conv. ↓	4,500	5,500	6,000	6,500	8,000	10,000	11,000	14,000
Z24 ↑	4,500	5,500	6,500	7,500	8,500	9,500	10,500	12,500
Z24 ↓	4,000	4,500	5,500	6,500	7,500	8,000	9,500	11,000
Sunfire ↑	—	—	—	—	7,000	9,000	10,500	11,500
Sunfire ↓	—	—	—	—	6,500	8,000	9,500	10,000

Extended Warranty	Y	Y	Y	Y	Y	Y	Y	Y
Secret Warranty	Y	Y	Y	Y	Y	Y	Y	Y
Reliability	❶	❶	❷	❷	❷	③	③	③
Air conditioning	③	③	③	③	③	③	④	④
Body integrity	❶	❶	❶	❷	❷	❷	❷	❷
Braking system	❶	❶	❶	❷	❷	❷	❷	❷
Electrical system	❶	❶	❶	❷	❷	❷	❷	❷
Engines	❷	❷	❷	❷	❷	❷	③	④
Exhaust/Converter	❷	❷	③	③	③	④	④	⑤
Fuel system	❶	❶	❶	③	③	③	④	④
Ignition system	❷	❷	❷	❷	❷	③	③	③
Manual transmission	③	③	③	③	③	④	④	④
- automatic	❶	❶	❶	❷	❷	❷	③	③
Rust/Paint	❶	❶	❶	❷	❷	❷	❷	❷
Steering	❷	❷	❷	❷	❷	③	③	④
Suspension	❶	❶	❶	❷	❷	③	③	④
Crash Safety								
Cavalier 2d	—	—	—	—	—	—	—	③
Cavalier 4d	④	④	④	④	③	③	④	④
Side Impact								
Cavalier 2d	—	—	—	—	—	—	—	❶
Cavalier 4d	—	—	—	—	—	—	❶	❶

Note: NHTSA says the Sunbird and Sunfire safety ratings should be identical to the Cavalier's score.

Saturn S-Series

Rating: Average (1997–98); Not Recommended (1991–96). Don't go anywhere near a used Saturn unless you're armed to the teeth with a comprehensive extended warranty or have thoroughly perused the Saturn owners' website: *saturnexposed.com*. As bizarre as it may appear, the Saturn division has a better reputation than the car it sells. The car's poor quality control is masked by generous amounts of "goodwill" refunds that quickly dry up when the car changes hands. The Geo Storm, Honda Civic LX, and Toyota Corolla perform well and offer better quality for about $1,500–$2,500 more. **Maintenance/Repair costs:** Average. Repairs aren't dealer dependent, unless you're seeking some Saturn "goodwill" refunds. **Parts:** Higher-than-average cost, but not hard to find through independent suppliers.

Strengths and weaknesses: Conceived as an all-American effort to beat the Japanese in the small-car market, the Saturn compact isn't any better built than the other GM home-grown compacts we've learned to dread over the past 30 years. The car is far from high-tech; it's remained virtually unchanged, except for a minor face-lift and a bit more leg room, since it was launched in 1991.

Saturns have exhibited a plethora of serious body and mechanical problems, which GM has masked by generously applying its base warranty. Second owners aren't treated as well, however, and complaints are frequent where owners of used Saturns report they had to pay dearly for GM's powertrain and body mistakes. Servicing quality is spotty. And if the rumors of GM merging Saturn with one of its other divisions are true, warranty claim servicing will become even more problematic, and routine dealer servicing will likely deteriorate as well.

What's so great about Saturn? Its advertising agency.

Granted, these are competitively priced, roomy, and comfortable small cars. They handle nimbly in good weather where acceleration isn't a prime consideration. On the other hand, these lightweight vehicles are tricky to handle in snow or ice.

Powered by a 4-cylinder aluminum engine, and a multi-valve variation of the same powerplant in the coupe, these cars are remarkably fuel-efficient with the base engine hooked to a manual transmission. The rack-and-pinion steering is fairly precise and predictable, while the suspension gives a firm, but not harsh, ride.

The loud, coarse, standard single-cam engine gives barely adequate acceleration times with the manual transmission. This time is increased with the 4-speed automatic gearbox that robs the engine of what little power it produces. Other generic problems affecting all model years are stalling and hard starting. One Ontario, Canada, owner of a 1994 Saturn plagued with chronic stalling problems had this to say:

After stalling in rush hour traffic, car was towed as hazard lights failed after ten minutes; unable to restart. Car was then towed. Cause indicated: bad fuel tank, pump, battery, ECM and ignition module. Replaced probe, module, pump, tank, valve, module, and battery.

Work order indicated that they performed various diagnostic checks, including: updated computer program, checked fuel pressure, checked ignition module circuit for proper operation, checked circuit from ignition switch to PCM for poor connection, and tried good ignition switch. Monitored voltage at back of ignition switch circuit for Fuse #1 PCM, replaced fuel tank and fuel pump as per tac, and replaced ECM. Car returned Feb. 27, 1998, but that evening car stalled again.

Car stalled Feb. 28, March 1, 2, and 3 and finally, after stalling a dozen or so times on my way to work and almost getting into an accident with a bus, I told the Customer Service in Toronto that they could come get the car from my work as I was not driving it home....

The 5-speed manual transmission sometimes has trouble going into Reverse. With the automatic, there's lots of gearbox shudder when the kickdown is engaged while passing.

Dealer service bulletins indicate that four major quality problems are likely to crop up: self-destructing engines; chronically malfunctioning automatic transmissions; myriad electrical short circuits; and a host of body defects, led by paint delamination, rattles, and wind and water leaks. On early models, the doors were poorly fitted, rear seats had to be lowered half an inch to give much-needed headroom, engine mounts were changed to reduce vibrations, the shift mechanism on the manual transmission was unreliable, and the reclining front seats were recalled because they could suddenly slip backwards. Rear head room is a bit tight, and owners report that the headliner in the rear tends to sag. Despite the dent-resistant plastic body panels, Saturn owners complain that the fascia chips and discolors.

GM's minor refinements to the 1997 Saturns don't appear to justify the higher price. The sedans and wagons got upgraded engine mounts to lessen noise and vibration and the coupe was given the sedan's 102-inch wheelbase, providing additional leg room, particularly in the rear. More effective silencing materials were added forward of the dash, and the air inlet was redirected away from the passenger compartment. Upgraded seatbelts on all 1997 models are less likely to trip passengers trying to access the rear seat.

Dealer service bulletins: All models: 1995—Engine flares, loss of power, harsh shifts into Reverse. • Engine knock and/or rattle at normal temperature. • Engine stalls when cold, difficult to restart. • Excessive engine vibration at idle. • ATF leak at automatic transaxle oil pressure filter. • Guide to possible causes of brake pulsation. • More recent info on brake vibration and/or pedal pulsation. • Steering pull, torque steer and wander. • Squealing sound from front of engine during cold starts. • Buzzing noise at rear of vehicle. • Possible other causes of buzzing, rattling, and fluttering noises. • Hoot noise upon light deceleration. • Clicking, ticking noise from instrument cluster odometer. • Ignition noise heard through radio speakers. • Popping noise from front seatback frame. • Rattle or chatter coming from passenger side. • Rattle, pop, or click from front end whenever passing over rough roads. Squeak/squawk noise from rear of vehicle. • Whistling produced by antenna mast. • Troubleshooting tips to silence wind noise at highway speeds. • Low voltage reading or dim lights at idle. • Instrument panel center air outlet closes. • Hard-to-operate sunroof sunshade. • Water drips onto seat/carpet with door open. • Water leaks into right front footwell from front of dash. • Water leak at front upper door frame. **1996**—Excessive engine vibration at idle. • Radio frequency interference diagnosis. **1997**—Automatic transmission malfunctions. • Failure-prone cylinder head. • Cruise control drops out intermittently or won't reset after dropout. • Faulty switch for front doorjamb causes the dome light to stay on and prevents the alarm from arming. • Ignition key can be removed when vehicle is in gear. • Defective ignition lock cylinders wreak havoc with accessories (radio, power windows, AC, etc.). • Ignition key may bind in the ignition's Run position. • Excessive front brake noise or pulsation. • Knocking/rattling from front of floor to front of dash area. • Loose rear exterior door panels. • Vehicle runs out of fuel while fuel gauge reads one-quarter full. • Automatic transmission whine.

Safety summary/Recalls: All models: Owners say horn isn't well positioned for emergency use and isn't sensitive enough. • NHTSA officials have opened an investigation into 1994 Saturn seatback failures. **1992**—Faulty alternators cause vehicle to stall suddenly. • Motorized-seatbelt failure. • Shifter inoperative due to sudden cable breakage. • **1993**—Rear axle broke and wheel flew off. • Rear wheel fell off. • Sudden steering loss. • Airbag failed to deploy. • Driver and passenger seatbacks collapsed in a rear-end collision. • ABS brake failure. • Intermittent cruise control failures. • Driver-side power door lock would not unlock. • Chronic premature transmission failures. **1994**— Airbag failed to deploy. • Severe burns from airbag deployment. • Driver's seatback collapsed several times. • Passenger seatback collapsed in a collision. • Chronic stalling. • Manual transmission jumps out of third and fifth gear when driving. • Windshield wiper failure due to plastic fitting in the linkage pivot drive assembly wearing down. • Automatic seatbelt chokes occupant. • Premature front brake rotor warpage. **1995**—Reports of stuck accelerators. • Plastic fuel line leaks fuel. • Airbag failed to deploy. • Seatbelt failed to restrain driver in collision. • Gear lever slips out of gear and is hard to put into Reverse. • Manual transmission jumps out of third and fifth gear. • Brake rotor warpage and failures. • Steering wheel shakes uncontrollably at 40 mph. • Sudden head gasket failure caused other engine components to self-destruct. • Prematurely worn engine timing chain. • AC fan knob broke in half. • Windshield wiper nut fell out, causing the wiper to fail. • **1996**—Airbag failed to deploy. • Rack-and-pinion steering gear failure. • Frequent brake failures. • Firestone tire blowouts. • Inadequate defrosting. • Engine suddenly accelerates to 3500 rpm at idle or when driving. • Engine suddenly stalls and can't be restarted. • Car slips out of fifth gear. **1997**—Steering wheel came apart while car was being driven. • Several complaints of total loss of steering control. • Engine suddenly loses power while cruising on the highway. • In a rear-end collision, driver's seatback broke, causing serious injuries. **Recalls: All models: 1991**—Seatback recliners will be strengthened at no charge. **1991–92**—The seatbelt retractor may not fully retract the belt. **1991–93**—Faulty trunk lock assemblies will be replaced. • GM dealers will install at no charge a fusible link wiring harness to prevent an engine fire. **1992**—Automatic shift lever may show the wrong gear. **1993**—Sudden brake loss may be caused by faulty brake-booster housing. • The windshield wiper and brake-booster assemblies will be inspected and replaced, if necessary, at no charge under two separate safety recalls. • Battery cable terminal may be defective. **1995**—In models with automatic transmissions, it is possible to shift from Park with key removed or to remove key when lever is in gear. **1996**—Some welds between roof and reinforcement panels on the wagon may not meet specifications. **1996–97**—Horn may not operate or can cause a fire; dealer will replace the horn assembly. **1997**—Belted front passenger's seat not secure during a frontal impact.

Secret Warranties/Service Tips

All models/years—A rotten-egg odor coming from the exhaust is likely the result of a malfunctioning catalytic converter, which you can have replaced free of charge under GM's emissions warranty. • Paint delamination, peeling, or fading (see pages 73–75). **All models: 1991**—Engine misses, surges, or backfires may be caused by a poor ground at the electronic distributorless ignition (DIS). Install another DIS module. • Headlights that stay on when the switch is turned off can be fixed by installing an upgraded switch. • Wind noise from the front and rear doors may be caused by insufficient sealing under the mirror patch gasket, missing sealer at certain locations (for example, the door frame to door assembly at the beltline), insufficient contact of the secondary seals to door openings, or the glass run channels not sealing to the glass at the upper corners. **1991–92**—Owners have reported excessive noise and vibration levels coming from the steering wheel, seat, and floor pan. Saturn officials say that the noise and vibration could be caused by the following: pre-loaded powertrain mounts (1991); a pre-loaded engine strut cradle bracket (1992); improperly positioned or worn exhaust system isolators and muffler band clamp/block (1991–92); lower cooling module grommets and improper positioning of wiring harnesses and upper cooling system module grommets (1991–92); improper routing of AC hoses or hood release cable and air inlet snorkel (1991–92); debris in accessory drive belt pulleys (1991); improper adjustment of hood stop(s) (1991–92); PCV or brake-booster check valve noise (1991); DOHC (LLO) automatic transaxle mount assembly replacement (1991); or a malfunctioning engine, electrical, or fuel system (1991–92). **1991–94**—Rough running or surging after a cold start may signal the need to clean carbon or fuel deposits from the engine's intake valves. • The many causes of hard-to-crank windows are covered in DSB #94-T-19. • Inoperative electric door locks may have been shorted by water contamination. Since the design and positioning of the relay for the power door lock allows this to develop, Saturn is accepting claims on a case-by-case basis. • Water leaks into the front footwell and at the front upper door frame are treated in depth in two DSBs published in August and November 1994. • Whistling noises are also treated in two different bulletins published in June and October 1994. **1991–95**—Erratic cruise control operation can be corrected by replacing the cruise control module assembly. • If the engine stalls within five minutes of starting, or when coming to a stop, or is difficult to restart, the oil viscosity or engine's hydraulic lifters may be at fault. • Engine squealing after a cold start can be corrected by installing an upgraded belt idler pulley assembly. **1991–97**—Excessive front brake noise or pulsation requires the installation of upgraded brake pads, according to DSB #96-T-40A.

• Engines that run hot or have coolant mixed in the engine oil probably have a defective engine cylinder—a factory-related goof, according to GM's service bulletin below. As a partial response to angry Saturn owners, GM has set up a secret warranty to pay for head gasket repairs for 6 years/100,000 miles on all 1994–96 models. Owners of model years not covered will get their refunds from small claims court.

BULLETIN NO.: 96-T-65A
ISSUE DATE: February 1997
GROUP/SEQ. NO. Engine-15
CORPORATION NO.: 686204R
SUBJECT:
Engine Runs Hot and Engine Oil Mixed with Engine Coolant in Engine Coolant Recovery Reservoir (Replace Cylinder Head Assembly)
This bulletin is revised to replace an incorrect part number for the one gallon container of DEX-COOL(TM) and supersedes bulletin 96-T-65, which should be discarded.
MODELS AFFECTED:
1991–1997 Saturns equipped with SOHC (LKO-1991-1994, L24-1995-1997) engines
CONDITION:
Engine may run hot and/or have engine oil mixed with engine coolant. This condition may be noticeable when checking coolant recovery reservoir level.
CAUSE:
Some 1991–1997 SOHC engines may develop a crack on or near the camshaft journals and surrounding casting areas allowing engine oil to mix with engine coolant. These cracks may be caused by "folds" in the aluminum that occur during the head casting process.
CLAIM INFORMATION

Case Type	Description	Labor Operation Code	Time
VW	Replace Cylinder Head Assembly	T9715	11.2 hrs
Add:	with A/C		0.8 hrs
	with power steering		0.3 hrs

To receive credit for this repair during the warranty coverage period, submit a claim through the Saturn Dealer System as shown.

Don't kid yourself. This is a major engine defect that'll take 11-plus hours to correct. GM will pay, if you refuse to go away.

• If your Saturn runs out of fuel while the fuel gauge reads one-quarter full, it's likely you have a plugged EVAP canister vent which should be repaired free of charge under the emissions warranty. • A whistle or groaning noise heard at highway speeds may be caused by the radio antenna mast. **1992—** An engine that stalls, hesitates, or surges during light acceleration may require new PCM calibrations. • Harsh Reverse engagement can also be corrected with new PCM calibrations. • Engine rattling can be fixed by changing the motor mounts. **1993–94—**A popping noise coming from the base of the left-hand A-pillar, hinge pillar, and engine compartment is caused by a slight flexing in the area where the three are joined together. **1993–97—**Troubleshooting tips are available on diagnosing delayed or harsh automatic transmission shifting into Reverse. **1994—**White Saturns may have yellow stains or spotting along the fenders, fender extension, or quarter panel. If so, the company will change the affected part and repaint the area at no charge to the owner. • A Saturn equipped with a manual transmission may have the transaxle stuck in gear due to a defective shift control housing. **1994–95**—Excessive engine knocking can be corrected by changing the clearance between the piston pin and connecting rod bushing. **1995–97**—Electrical accessories may lose power after the car is started or while it's on the road. GM blames the problem on a defective ignition lock cylinder. **1996–97**—If your security alarm won't work properly or your dome light won't go out, GM suggests you change the doorjamb switches.

Saturn S-Series Profile

	1991	1992	1993	1994	1995	1996	1997	1998
Cost Price ($)								
SL	9,045	9,265	10,330	11,210	11,260	11,805	11,925	11,999
SL2	11,345	11,465	12,625	13,010	13,260	13,605	13,825	13,195
SW1	—	—	12,025	12,910	12,960	13,305	13,525	13,695
SC/SC1	12,825	12,945	12,125	12,910	13,130	13,505	13,825	13,995
Used Values ($)								
SL ↑	4,000	5,000	5,500	7,000	8,000	9,000	10,000	10,500
SL ↓	3,500	4,500	5,000	6,000	7,000	8,000	9,000	10,000
SL2 ↑	4,500	5,000	6,000	7,000	8,000	9,000	10,000	12,000
SL2 ↓	4,000	4,500	5,000	6,000	7,000	8,000	9,000	11,000
SW1 ↑	—	—	7,000	7,500	8,500	9,500	10,500	11,500
SW1 ↓	—	—	6,000	7,000	7,500	8,500	9,500	10,500
SC/SC1 ↑	5,000	6,000	7,000	7,500	8,500	9,500	10,500	12,000
SC/SC1 ↓	4,500	5,000	6,500	7,000	8,000	9,000	10,000	11,000
Extended Warranty		Y	Y	Y	Y	Y	Y	Y
Secret Warranty		Y	Y	Y	Y	Y	Y	Y
Reliability	❷	❷	❷	❷	❷	❷	③	④
Air conditioning	❷	❷	❷	❷	③	④	④	④
Automatic transmission	❷	❷	❷	❷	❷	③	③	③
Body integrity	❷	❷	❷	❷	❷	❷	❷	③
Braking system	❶	❷	❷	❷	❷	❷	③	③
Electrical system	❶	❷	❷	❷	❷	❷	③	③
Engines	❶	❷	❷	❷	❷	❷	③	③
Exhaust/Converter	❶	❷	③	③	④	④	④	⑤
Fuel system	❶	❷	❷	③	③	④	④	④
Ignition system	❶	❷	❷	❷	❷	❷	③	③
Rust/Paint	❷	❷	❷	❷	❷	❷	③	③
Steering	❷	③	③	④	④	④	⑤	⑤
Suspension	❷	③	③	④	④	④	④	④
Crash Safety								
SL2	③	④	④	④	④	④	④	⑤
Side Impact	—	—	—	—	—		③	③

GENERAL MOTORS-SUZUKI

Metro-Swift

Rating: Above Average (1995–98); Average (1990–94); Below Average (1987–89). Stay away from AC-equipped versions, unless you want to invest in an AC repair facility. Look at the redesigned 1995 version for better quality, a new body style, standard dual airbags, and a peppier 4-cylinder engine. The convertible version packs plenty of fun and performance into a reasonably priced subcompact body. **Maintenance/Repair costs:** Average. **Parts:** Expensive; sometimes drivetrain and body components are back-ordered several weeks.

Strengths and weaknesses: These tiny, economical, 3- and 4-cylinder, front-wheel drive hatchback econoboxes, equipped with either a manual or an automatic transmission, offer acceptable performance and economy for urban dwellers. In fact, these little squirts should be considered primarily city vehicles due to their small size, small tires, low ground clearance, and high-speed average handling. Interior garnishing is decent but plain, and there's plenty of room for two passengers, with four fitting in without too much discomfort. The turbocharged convertible model is an excellent choice for high-performance thrills in an easy-to-handle ragtop.

Mechanically speaking, the GM-Suzuki partnership hasn't hurt quality control—though it hasn't helped either. Trouble spots on the 1988–95 models: excessive oil consumption after the fourth year of service; automatic transmission and differential failures around 60,000 miles; electrical system shorts; a faulty AC and cooling system (fogging of the side windows and windshield due to inadequate heat distribution is a common complaint); premature brake, clutch, and exhaust system wearout; and minor fuel-supply malfunctions. Body construction is the pits on early models.

Owners of 1990–94 models report that hatches vibrate when windows are open and the rear hatch seems to want to open on its own; push buttons for the lights and wipers tend to fly off the dashboard; fuel economy is often exaggerated by dealers; front metallic brake pads are noisy and the front discs warp easily; occasionally the third gear is hard to engage; and the fuel-injection system performs poorly. Owners also point out that the tiny radiator can't stand up to the rigors of northern climates. If it's not checked, the cooling system will eventually fail, causing great damage to the aluminum engine.

The cars were redesigned for the 1995 model year and were built with more care. Additionally, they gained more horsepower, improved road feel, a more comfortable ride, quieter operation, and more cabin space. Remaining problems are premature front brake wear; electrical system and AC malfunctions; and sub-par body assembly highlighted by paint peeling and discoloration, early rusting, and poorly fitted body panels, leading to rattles and air and water leaks.

Safety summary/Recalls: All models/years: Side window defogging is slow and sometimes inadequate. • Driver's window continually pops out of its mount. **Recalls: All models: 1989–91**—Takata seatbelts will be replaced. **1989–93**—Hood may fly up when car is in motion. **1995**—Faulty rear brake drums may lead to sudden wheel separation. **Metro: 1995**—In hatchbacks without ABS, faulty rear brake drums could cause wheel separation. **1997**—Dealers will replace the shifter assembly on the automatic transmission because the shift lever can move too easily out of Park.

Secret Warranties/Service Tips

All models/years—Paint delamination, fading, peeling, hazing, and "microchecking" (see pages 73–75). **All models: 1989–90**—If you have hard starts or no-starts in cold weather, install Suzuki's cold-start harness set (#36690-60A00). **1989–92**—Stalling or loss of power shortly after starting may be due to high pressure in the hydraulic lifter assemblies. **1991–92**—Excessive vehicle vibration when the vehicle is in Reverse is most likely due to poor insulation between the engine/transaxle assembly and the vehicle's chassis. Install upgraded engine mounts. **1994**—Vehicles that won't start usually have defective oxygen sensors—an emissions warranty item. • When the battery runs down in wintertime, it can set off the car alarm. Buy a heavy-duty battery.

Metro-Swift Profile

	1991	1992	1993	1994	1995	1996	1997	1998
Cost Price ($)								
Metro	7,361	7,585	7,296	7,791	9,481	9,988	10,185	10,110
Swift	6,669	7,184	7,599	7,864	9,029	9,359	9,359	9,479
Used Values ($)								
Metro ↑	2,200	3,300	3,800	4,300	5,000	6,500	7,400	7,900
Metro ↓	1,500	2,800	2,800	3,300	4,000	5,500	6,400	7,200
Swift ↑	2,500	3,500	4,000	4,600	5,200	6,700	7,700	8,200
Swift ↓	1,800	2,700	3,100	3,600	4,200	5,700	6,700	7,400
Extended Warranty	Y	Y	Y	N	N	N	N	N
Secret Warranty	Y	Y	Y	Y	Y	Y	N	N
Reliability	②	②	②	②	③	④	④	④
Air conditioning	②	②	②	②	②	②	②	③
Body integrity	①	②	②	②	②	③	③	③
Braking system	②	②	②	②	②	③	③	③
Electrical system	②	②	②	②	③	③	③	③
Engines	②	②	②	②	②	④	⑤	⑤
Exhaust/Converter	②	②	②	②	③	④	⑤	⑤
Fuel system	②	②	③	③	④	④	⑤	⑤
Ignition system	③	④	④	③	④	④	④	④
Manual transmission	③	③	③	③	④	④	⑤	⑤

- automatic	❶	❷	❷	❷	③	④	④	④
Rust/Paint	❶	❷	❷	❷	❷	③	③	④
Steering	④	④	⑤	⑤	⑤	⑤	⑤	⑤
Suspension	④	④	⑤	⑤	⑤	⑤	⑤	⑤
Crash Safety	—	③	③	③	④	④	④	—

HONDA

Civic, del Sol (CRX)

Rating: Recommended (1993–98); Above Average (1992); Average (1989–91); Below Average (1984–88). Depreciation is so minimal that, if you want to get a good buy at a fair price, the 1993 is your best bet. **Maintenance/Repair costs:** Average. Repairs can be carried out by independent garages, but the 16-valve engine's complexity means that dealer servicing is a must. To avoid costly engine repairs, owners must check the engine timing belt every 3 years/25,000 miles and replace it every 60,000 miles ($300). **Parts:** Parts are a bit more expensive than most other cars in this class, but they aren't hard to find.

Strengths and weaknesses: The quintessential econobox, Civics have distinguished themselves by providing sports-car acceleration and handling with excellent fuel economy and quality control that's better than what American automakers can deliver. Other advantages: a roomy, practical trunk and simple, inexpensive maintenance.

The CRX is a sportier version of the Civic, equipped with a more refined 1.5L and 1.6L engine and stiffer suspension. It gives improved handling at the expense of fuel economy, interior space, and a comfortable ride, and requires valve adjustments every 25,000 miles.

Some other Civic disadvantages: power steering isn't offered with the manual 5-speed transmission; there's no ABS available; you won't find much backseat head room; engine noise may seem excessive when under load; and the Civic's high resale value means bargains are rare.

1984–92 Civics suffer from failing camshafts, crankshafts, and head gaskets and prematurely worn piston rings. The 12-valve engine is prone to valve problems and is costly to repair. Early fuel-injection units were also problematic until the system was redesigned in 1988. Manual transmission shifter bushings need frequent replacement and the automatic version needs careful attention once the 5-year/100,000 miles point has been reached.

The 1988 redesign improved handling and increased interior room, but engine head gasket failures on non-VTEC engines have remained a problem (see following bulletin).

Head Gasket Leaks.
97-047
November 10, 1997
Applies To: 1988 - 95 Civic - All, except VTEC
Head Gasket Leaks
(Supercedes 97-047, dated September 29, 1997)
PROBLEM
The head gasket leaks oil externally or allows coolant into the combustion chambers.
CORRECTIVE ACTION
Install the new style cylinder head gasket and the new head bolts in the Cylinder Gasket
Kit listed under PARTS INFORMATION. Use the cylinder head bolt torque sequence
described in this bulletin.
In warranty:
The normal warranty applies.
Failed part: P/N 12251-PM5-S02 [NEW]
                      H/C 4032470
Defect code: 060
Contention code: B06
Out of warranty:
Any repair performed after warranty expiration may be eligible for goodwill considera-
tion by the District Service Manager or your Zone Office. You must request considera-
tion, and get a decision, before starting work.

The repair is free, if the client squawks.

There isn't a great deal of torque with the 1.6L engine below 3500 rpm, however, and serious generic problems, present since the car's debut, continue to plague the later models. The front brakes continue to wear out quickly and are often noisy when applied, causing excessive steering wheel vibration. Premature constant-velocity-joint and boot wear on all cars is another problem area that needs careful inspection before purchasing. The rack-and-pinion steering assembly often needs replacement around the five-year mark. There have also been reports of premature clutch wear with 4X4 Civics.

A large number of 1988–91 Honda Civics and CRXs have faulty distributor igniters. When the igniter fails, the car stalls, and it may be impossible to restart. The only remedy is to call a tow truck and replace the distributor.

1993–98 Civics continue to be both rugged and reliable. The few problems that are reported concern early engine head gasket failures, front brake noise and premature wear, AC malfunctions, and minor body faults.

What are minor body faults with recent models turn into major rust problems with older Civics, where simple surface rust rapidly turns into perforations. The underbody is also prone to corrosion, which leads to severe structural damage that compromises safety. The fuel tank, front suspension, and steering components, along with body attachment points, should be examined carefully in any Civic more than a decade old. Since 1988, Hondas have been much more resistant to rusting, and overall body construction has been vastly improved. All hatchbacks let in too much wind/road noise due to poor sound insulation. Owners complain of water leaking into the trunk area through the rear taillights on the 1990 DX four-door sedan. The two-piece tailgate rattles and is complicated, for no good reason.

Safety summary/Recalls: Recalls: All models: 1990—Front windshield will be replaced. **1992–94**—The automatic transmission's shift lever position may not match the actual gear that's engaged. **1992–95**—Hood could fly up. **1994**—Passenger-side airbag module may carry a defective inflator. **1996**—Faulty brake-booster vacuum hose. **1996–98**—Passenger-side airbag may not deploy properly. **Civic: 1986–91**—Takata seatbelts will be replaced. **CRX: 1989–91**—Takata seatbelts will be replaced. **Civic, del Sol: 1993**—The automatic transmission's shift lever position may not match the actual gear that's engaged.

Secret Warranties/Service Tips

All models/years—Most Honda DSBs allow for special warranty considera-tion on a "goodwill" basis even after the warranty has expired or the car has changed hands. Referring to this euphemism will increase your chances of getting some kind of refund for repairs that are obviously related to a fac-tory defect. **All models: 1988–90**—Excessive valve noise will be corrected with a cam holder kit (#04101-PM3-308). • The dashboard cracks at the center bolt hole. **1988–91**—Distributor igniters are faulty (see "Strengths and weaknesses"). • New front brake pads that minimize front brake squeal are available for all Civic and CRX models. • A clicking noise heard while making a left or right turn may be caused by a worn outboard drive shaft joint. **1988–93**—A creaking noise coming from the window regulator can be corrected by installing an upgraded regulator spiral spring. **1989–91**—An oil leak around the spark plug well will be corrected with a cam holder kit (#04101-PM3-308). **1990**—The horn sounds by itself when the temper-ature drops. **1992**—A growling noise coming from the wheel area may mean that water has entered the wheel bearing through the hubcap and has damaged the bearing. • A steering wheel shake or body vibration when braking may indicate that the rear brake drum hub is crowned, causing excessive runout when the wheel nuts are torqued. Other factors could be a bent rear wheel, over-torqued wheel nuts, or excessive rust buildup on the brake rotors. **1992–95**—Power steering pump fluid leakage requires a new O-ring, which may be eligible for "goodwill" consideration, says Honda. **1992–97**—Water leaking into the footwell from under the corner of the dash can be stopped by applying sealer to the seam where the side panel joins the bulkhead. • An abnormally long crank time before the car starts may be caused by a leaking check valve inside the fuel pump. **1993**—Poor AM reception or a popping sound coming from the speakers is likely due to a poor ground connection between the antenna collar and car body. **1994–97**—If the AC doesn't blow cold air, Honda will replace both the evap-orator and the receiver/dryer free of charge (see Honda Accord). • When operating a manual or power-assisted front window, the rear edge of the glass comes out of the channel (see Honda Accord). • **1996**—A clunking noise in the front suspension can be fixed by installing upgraded upper arm flange bolts. **1996–97**—In a settlement with the U.S. Environmental

Protection Agency, Honda paid fines totaling $17.1 million and extended its emissions warranty on 1.6 million 1995–97 models to 14 years or 150,000 miles. This means that costly engine components and exhaust system parts like catalytic converters will be replaced free of charge, as long as the 14-year/150,000 mile limit hasn't been exceeded. Additionally, the automaker will provide a full engine check and emissions-related repairs at 50,000–75,000 miles and will give free tune-ups at 75,000–150,000 miles. It is estimated the free checkups, repairs, and tune-ups will cost Honda over $250 million. The story of the settlement was first reported on page 6 of the June 15, 1998, edition of *Automotive News*.

Emissions Warranty Extension
October 16, 1998
98-081
Applies To: 1995 Accord-V6
          1996 - ALL except Passport
          1997 - ALL except Passport
Emissions Warranty Extension
BACKGROUND
The U.S. Environmental Protection Agency (EPA) and the California Air Resources Board (CARB) have asserted that the performance of the On-Board Diagnostic (OBD) system in the vehicles listed below does not fully perform in the manner that they believe is required. Specifically, they allege that the OBD system is not sensitive enough to detect some misfire conditions in the engine.
In an effort to resolve this issue, Honda has agreed to extend the emissions warranty on all the affected vehicles, and to provide emissions-related services during the warranty.
WARRANTY EXTENSION INFORMATION
American Honda is extending the emission warranty on all affected vehicles to 14 years or150,000 miles, whichever comes first. The basic terms of this extended warranty are the same as given with the original Federal end California emissions warranties.
Federal Emissions Warranty - The time and mileage periods for the Emissions-related Design and Defects Warranty and the Emissions Performance Warranty are lengthened from 3 years or 36,000 miles to 14 years or 150,000 miles. All other terms, conditions, and exclusions still apply. All parts on the Emissions Parts List are now covered for 14 years or 150,000 miles, so the 8/80 notations on certain parts no longer apply.
California Emissions Warranties - The time and mileage periods for the Emissions Control Defects and Defects Warranty and the Emissions Performance Warranty are lengthened from 3 years or 50,000 miles to 14 years or 150,000 miles. All other terms, conditions, and exclusions still apply. All parts on the Emissions Parts List are now covered for 14 years or 150,000 miles, so the 7/70 notations on certain parts no longer apply.
File a claim under this extension if:
The MIL comes on, and the cause is diagnosed as an emissions-related component.
The vehicle requires an emissions-related repair because it failed a mandated emissions test.
Any emissions-related component fails.
REPAIR TIME REQUIREMENTS
According to the terms of the agreement, American Honda and the dealer have 45 days from the date the customer first brings the vehicle in to resolve the customer's claim for repair under this warranty. If you decide to refuse a customer's claim for repair under this warranty because you suspect accidental damage, tampering, or lack of proper maintenance, notify American Honda Consumer Affairs immediately at (800) 900-1009. This will allow us to thoroughly investigate the Customer's claim within the 45 day timeline.
ADDITIONAL SERVICES
In addition to the warranty extension, the following services are being provided to owners of affected vehicles.

Between 50,000 miles and 75,000 miles - If an affected vehicle comes in for service within that mileage range, inspect the OBD system. Follow the service manual procedure to read out any Diagnostic Trouble Codes. If any codes are found, replace the affected part or parts. This inspection and any replacements are free of charge to the owner. Between 75,000 miles and 150,000 miles - At this time, the dealer should:
Again inspect the OBD System and replace any parts that have caused a diagnostic trouble code.
Replace the distributor cap, rotor, ignition wires, and spark plugs.
Change the oil and oil filter.
All of the above services are free of charge to the owner. You must use Genuine Honda parts and fluids for this service.
CUSTOMER NOTIFICATIONS
American Honda will send a letter to all owners of affected vehicles notifying them of the terms of the warranty extension. This will be done immediately.
American Honda will send letters to all owners of affected vehicles, reminding them of the 50,000 - 75,000 mile OBD check, five years after the release of their models. This will begin in the latter part of 1999 for the 1995 models, etc.
American Honda will send letters to all owners of affected vehicles, reminding them of the 75,000 - 150,000 mile service, nine years after the release of their models. This will begin in 2005.
WARRANTY CLAIM INFORMATION
The 50,000 - 75 000 mile OBD inspection, 75,000 - 150,000 mile OBD inspection, the 75,000 - 150,000 mile service, and any emissions-related repairs must be filed on separate warranty claims. Warranty claims that combine any of these services will be rejected.

Don't let Honda officials discourage you. These repairs and services are free*!*

Civic, del Sol (CRX) Profile

	1991	1992	1993	1994	1995	1996	1997	1998
Cost Price ($)								
Civic	7,155	8,190	8,730	9,750	10,130	10,360	10,945	11,045
Si/EX	10,555	11,990	12,530	13,520	13,920	15,330	15,645	15,645
del Sol (CRX)	9,405	—	13,530	14,450	15,160	15,475	15,475	15,475
Used Values ($)								
Civic ↑	5,500	6,000	7,000	7,500	8,500	9,000	9,500	10,000
Civic ↓	5,000	5,500	6,000	7,000	7,500	8,500	9,000	9,500
Si/EX ↑	7,000	7,500	8,000	9,000	10,500	12,000	13,000	14,500
Si/EX ↓	6,000	7,000	7,500	8,000	9,500	11,000	12,000	13,500
del Sol (CRX) ↑	6,000	—	9,000	10,000	11,000	12,000	13,000	14,500
del Sol (CRX) ↓	5,500	—	8,000	9,500	10,000	11,000	12,000	14,000
Extended Warranty	Y	N	N	N	N	N	N	N
Secret Warranty	Y	Y	Y	Y	Y	Y	Y	N
Reliability	③	③	④	⑤	⑤	⑤	⑤	⑤
Air conditioning	❷	③	③	④	④	⑤	⑤	⑤
Body integrity	❷	❷	③	③	③	③	④	④
Braking system	❷	❷	③	③	③	④	⑤	⑤
Electrical system	③	③	③	④	④	④	⑤	⑤

Engines	③	③	③	③	③	④	⑤	⑤
Exhaust/Converter	❷	❷	③	③	④	⑤	⑤	⑤
Fuel system	③	③	④	④	④	④	⑤	⑤
Ignition system	③	③	④	④	④	④	⑤	⑤
Manual transmission	③	③	③	④	④	⑤	⑤	⑤
- automatic	③	③	③	④	⑤	⑤	⑤	⑤
Rust/Paint	❷	③	③	③	⑤	⑤	⑤	⑤
Steering	③	③	④	④	④	④	⑤	⑤
Suspension	③	③	④	④	④	④	⑤	⑤
Crash Safety								
Civic 2d	—	—	③	③	③	④	④	④
Civic 4d	④	—	③	③	③	④	④	④
Side Impact								
Civic 2d	—	—	—	—	—	—	—	❷
Civic 4d	—	—	—	—	—	—	③	③

HYUNDAI

Accent

Rating: Above Average (1995–98). Lots of standard features. **Maintenance/Repair costs:** Higher than average. Repairs are dealer dependent. Dealer servicing has been substandard in the past. Hyundai says that the timing chain should be replaced every 80,000 miles. **Parts:** Expensive and not easily found.

Strengths and weaknesses: An upgraded Excel masquerading as a different car, this front-drive, 4-cylinder sedan retains most of the Excel's underpinnings, while dropping the Mitsubishi powerplant in favor of a new home-grown 1.5L 4-cylinder. It's built better than the old Excel, though: upgraded, smoother-shifting automatic transmission; stiffer, better performing suspension; stronger and quieter-running engine; optional dual airbags; and ABS.

Excels have always had a checkered reliability history, so the Accent has a lot of bad karma to overcome, such as mediocre body assembly and poorly applied paint. Past problem areas include the engine cooling system and cylinder head gaskets, transmission, wheel bearings, fuel system, and electrical components, as well as premature front brake wear and excessive noise when braking.

Dealer service bulletins: 1995—The exhaust system has a tendency to release a rotten-egg odor. • Troubleshooting tips for locating and plugging interior water leaks. **1996**—Exhaust rattling. • Shift quality improvements. • Sticking headlight flasher switch.

Safety summary/Recalls: Horn controls may be hard to find in an emergency, rear head restraints appear to be too low to protect occupants, and rear seatbelt configuration complicates the installation of a child safety seat. **Recalls: 1995**—The ECM wiring harness may short on vehicles equipped with a manual transaxle. **1995–97**—Corroded coil spring may break. **1996–97**—Faulty wiper motor.

Secret Warranties/Service Tips

All years—Apparent slow acceleration upon cold starts is dismissed as normal. **1995–96**—Harsh shifting may be fixed by installing an upgraded Transaxle Control Module (TCM). • Clutch drag may be caused by a restriction in the hydraulic line from grease used during the assembly of the clutch master assembly.

Accent Profile

	1995	1996	1997	1998
Cost Price ($)				
L	9,674	8,690	9,014	9,534
Sedan	10,834	11,270	11,819	11,728
Used Values ($)				
L ↑	4,500	5,000	6,000	7,000
L ↓	3,500	4,500	5,000	6,000
Sedan ↑	5,500	6,500	7,500	8,500
Sedan ↓	4,500	6,000	6,000	7,500
Extended Warranty	Y	Y	Y	Y
Secret Warranty	N	N	N	N
Reliability	④	④	⑤	⑤
Crash Safety	—	③	③	③

Elantra

Rating: Above Average (1996–98); Average (1992–95). There's a $1,000–$3,500 difference between the high-end and entry-level models. **Maintenance/Repair costs:** Higher than average. Repairs are dealer dependent. **Parts:** Higher-than-average cost, but not hard to find.

Strengths and weaknesses: This conservatively styled "high-end" sedan is only marginally larger than the Excel, but its overall reliability is much better. It's a credible alternative to the Toyota Corolla, Nissan Sentra, and Saturn, and the redesigned 1996–97 versions actually narrow the handling and performance gap with the Honda Civic. The 16-valve 1.6L 4-cylinder is smooth, efficient, and adequate when mated to the 5-speed manual transmission. It's not very quiet, however. The smooth ride causes excessive body lean when cornering, but overall handling is fairly good, due mainly to the Elantra's longer wheelbase and more sophisticated suspension.

The 4-speed automatic transmission robs the base engine of at least 10 horses. Brakes are adequate, though sometimes difficult to modulate. Conservative styling makes the Elantra look a bit like an underfed Accord, but there's plenty of room for four average-sized occupants. Tall drivers might find rearward seat travel insufficient, making head room a bit tight.

1996–98 Elantras are the better buy due to their additional interior room, improved performance and handling, and quieter-running engine. Still, passing power with the automatic gearbox is perpetually unimpressive and the trunk's narrow opening makes for difficult loading.

Surprisingly for a Hyundai, owners report few serious defects. Nevertheless, be on the lookout for body deficiencies (fit, finish, and assembly), harsh shifting with the automatic transmission, oil leaks, and brake defects.

Dealer service bulletins: 1993—Harsh shifting with the automatic transmission when accelerating or coming to a stop. • Excessive disc brake noise. • Engine has difficulty reaching recommended operating temperature (MPI fault code #21). • Low fuel pressure. • Oil leaks between the oil filter and mounting bracket. • Wheel cover discoloration. **1994**—Excessive front brake noise and premature wear. • Rear speaker whine. • Harsh automatic transmission engagement. • Slow windshield defrosting and defogging. **1995**—The exhaust system releases a rotten-egg odor. • Rear suspension squeaking noises. • An inaccurate fuel gauge. • Trunk water leaks and troubleshooting tips for locating and plugging other interior water leaks. **1996–97**—Automatic transmission won't engage Overdrive. • Clutch pedal squeaking. • Tapping noise coming from the passenger-side dash panel/engine compartment area. • Exhaust system buzz. • Improved shifting into all gears. • Improved shifting into Reverse. • Clutch drag.

Safety summary/Recalls: Recalls: 1992–95—Defective rear suspension trailing arm bolts. **1994–95**—Driver-side airbag could be defective or the warning light could illuminate unnecessarily. **1996–97**—A faulty wiper motor will be replaced.

Secret Warranties/Service Tips

All years—Hyundai has a new brake pad kit (#58101-28A00) that the company says will eliminate squeaks and squeals during light brake application. Hyundai also suggests that you replace the oil pump assembly if the engine rpm increases as the automatic transmission engages abruptly during a cold start. • A harsh downshift when decelerating may require a free transmission replacement, says bulletin #98-40-001. • Bulletin #98–50–001 provides information regarding some brake noises and appropriate services for each condition.**1992**—A harsh shift when coming to a stop or upon acceleration could be due to an improperly adjusted accelerator switch TCU. • Oil leaking from between the oil filter and mounting bracket could be caused by an overly wide mounting surface on the bracket. Correct this by replacing the bracket. **1992–94**—Hyundai has a field fix for manual transaxle gear clash/grind (DSB #9440-004). • The difficult-to-engage Reverse gear needs an upgraded part. **1994**—Rear speaker whine can be stopped by installing an improved noise reduction filter. **1996**—A cold exhaust system buzz can be silenced by installing a sub-muffler resonator. • Improved shifting into all gears can be accomplished by installing an upgraded transaxle control module (TCM). **1996–97**—Tips on eliminating clutch drag and pedal squeaking are offered. **1996–98**—DOHC engine timing chain noise repair.

Elantra Profile

	1992	1993	1994	1995	1996	1997	1998
Cost Price ($)							
Base	11,155	11,749	12,674	13,149	13,434	13,659	13,728
Used Values ($)							
Base ↑	3,500	4,000	5,500	6,500	7,500	8,500	9,500
Base ↓	2,800	3,000	4,500	5,500	6,500	7,500	8,500
Extended Warranty	Y	Y	Y	N	N	N	N
Secret Warranty	Y	Y	Y	Y	Y	Y	Y
Reliability	③	③	③	④	④	④	⑤
Air conditioning	③	③	④	④	④	⑤	⑤
Automatic transmission	❷	❷	❷	❷	③	③	④
Body integrity	❷	❷	❷	③	③	③	③
Braking system	❷	③	③	③	③	③	③
Electrical system	❷	❷	❷	③	③	③	④
Engines	④	⑤	⑤	⑤	⑤	⑤	⑤
Exhaust/Converter	③	④	⑤	⑤	⑤	⑤	⑤
Fuel system	③	③	③	④	④	⑤	⑤
Ignition system	③	③	④	④	③	③	④
Rust/Paint	④	④	④	④	⑤	⑤	⑤
Steering	④	④	⑤	⑤	⑤	⑤	⑤
Suspension	③	③	④	④	④	④	④
Crash Safety	❶	❶	④	④	③	③	③
Side Impact	—	—	—	—	—	—	③

Excel

Rating: Below Average (1992–94); Not Recommended (1986–91). **Maintenance/Repair costs:** Higher than average. Repairs are dealer dependent. To avoid costly engine repairs, check the engine timing belt every 2 years/40,000 miles. **Parts:** Expensive and not easily found.

Strengths and weaknesses: Replaced by the 1995 Accent, the Excel is a low-tech and low-quality economy car that was orphaned in 1995. Resale prices are low, but these cars are no bargain in the long run. Although overall comfort and handling are passable, the engine is distinctly short on power and the carburetor provides uneven throttle response, especially when the car is cold, resulting in difficult starts. Poor interior ventilation, with chronic window fogging and poor defrosting, is particularly irritating.

On early models, likely problem areas are defective constant velocity joints, water pumps, oil pan gaskets, oil pressure switches, front struts, and heat exchange under dash, as well as a leaking head gasket. Excels made after 1989 are noted for their noisy automatic transmissions and engines that fail to start when the weather turns cold or wet. Other problem areas are faulty radiator hoses, alternators, Hyundai radios, and wiper motors. Owners also complain of premature brake wear and temperamental carburetors, electrical problems, poor engine performance, and premature rusting due to poor-quality body parts and paint. Body construction is sloppy, giving rise to wind/water leaks, rattles, and breakage. Mufflers last a little over two years.

Dealer service bulletins: 1993—Harsh shifting with the automatic transmission when accelerating or coming to a stop. • Excessive disc brake noise. • Engine has difficulty reaching recommended operating temperature (MPI fault code #21). • Low fuel pressure. **1994**—Tips for troubleshooting water leaks into the interior.

Safety summary/Recalls: Recalls: 1986—A defective brake pedal cotter pin will be changed. **1986–87**—Excessive brake fade can be improved by installing upgraded metallic pads. **1986–89**—Cruise control operation is erratic. • A malfunctioning emissions control system could cause an engine compartment fire. • Insufficient gear lubrication could cause drive wheels to lock. **1988–89**—A defective heater stem assembly could allow hot coolant leakage. **1990**—Front wheel hub nut lock washer could crack, causing a loss of vehicle control. **1990–94**—In frontal crashes, excessive fuel spillage could pose a fire hazard. **1994**—A short circuit in the crank-angle sensor could cause sudden stalling.

Secret Warranties/Service Tips

1990—A fifth-gear noise can be eliminated by replacing the third- and fourth-shift forks and synchronizer hub and sleeve. • Cranking with no spark may be due to a defective noise filter located between the ignition coil and tachometer. **1990–94**—Difficult-to-engage Reverse gear needs an upgraded part. **1991**—Stalling when shifting into gear immediately after starting a cold engine may be corrected by installing Hyundai's Cold Start Enrichment Kit (#39901-24Q00D). **1994**—A harsh downshift usually means that the accelerator switch is out of adjustment. • A rear suspension groaning noise heralds the need to install upgraded shock absorbers. • A rear suspension squeaking noise can be silenced by retorquing the rear suspension attachment nuts.

Excel Profile							
	1988	1989	1990	1991	1992	1993	1994
Cost Price ($)							
Base	5,520	5,774	7,244	7,965	8,390	8,634	9,140
Used Values ($)							
Base ↑	1,000	1,500	1,900	2,300	2,500	3,000	3,500
Base ↓	800	1,100	1,700	1,900	2,000	2,500	3,000
Extended Warranty	Y	Y	Y	Y	Y	Y	Y
Secret Warranty	N	N	N	N	N	N	N
Reliability	②	②	②	②	②	②	②
Air conditioning	②	②	②	③	③	③	④
Body integrity	②	②	②	②	②	②	②
Braking system	②	②	②	②	②	②	②
Electrical system	②	②	②	②	②	②	②
Engines	①	①	②	③	③	③	③
Exhaust/Converter	①	②	③	③	③	③	③
Fuel system	②	②	②	③	③	③	③
Ignition system	②	②	②	③	③	③	③
Manual transmission	②	②	②	②	②	②	②
- automatic	②	③	③	③	④	④	④
Rust/Paint	②	②	②	②	②	③	③
Steering	③	③	③	④	③	④	④
Suspension	③	③	③	③	③	③	③
Crash Safety	②	②	④	④	④	④	④

MAZDA

323, Protegé

Rating: Recommended (1996–98); Above Average (1991–95); Average (1985–90). If you can't find a reasonably priced 323 or Protegé, look for a Ford Escort or Tracer instead—they're basically Mazdas disguised as Fords. The redesigned 1995–96 Protegé offers fresh styling, a larger wheelbase, standard dual airbags, and a new 4-banger. Along with the 1997–98 versions, which were mostly carried over unchanged with a slightly restyled grille and headlights and interior refinements, they are excellent used-car buys. Plus, they should be plentiful at bargain prices as they come off their two- and three-year leases. **Maintenance/Repair costs:** Higher than average. Repairs are dealer-dependent. To avoid costly engine repairs, check the engine timing belt every 2 years/25,000 miles and replace it every 110,000 miles ($300). **Parts:** Expensive and not easily found outside the dealer network.

Strengths and weaknesses: The GLC was replaced by the 323 in 1986. Both Mazdas are peppy performers with a manual transmission hooked to the base engine. The automatic gearbox, however, produces lethargic acceleration that makes highway passing a bit chancy. Handling and fuel economy are fairly good for a car design this old. However, overall durability is not as good as that of more recent Mazda designs, beginning with the 1991 Mazda 323 and Protegé, both of which were also sold as Ford Escorts. Catalytic converters plug up easily and other pollution-control components have been troublesome. Automatic transmission defects, air conditioner breakdowns, and engine oil leaks are also commonplace. Oil leaks in the power-steering pump may also be a problem.

The fuel-injected 1.6L engine is a better performer than the 1.5L, but you also get excessive engine and exhaust noise. Stay away from the 3-speed automatic transmission. The car's small engine can't handle the extra burden without cutting fuel economy and performance. Both models are surprisingly roomy, but the Protegé's trunk is small for a sedan.

The 1985–90 models offer mediocre reliability. Owners report hard starting in cold weather, in addition to automatic transmission problems and electrical system failures. The engine camshaft assembly and belt pulley often need replacing around 80,000 miles. Clutch failure and exhaust-system rust-out are also common. Other areas of concern are constant velocity joint failures, rack-and-pinion steering wearout, and front brake wear. The front brakes wear quickly due to poor-quality brake pads and seizure of the calipers in their housings. Check for disc scoring on the front brakes. Stay away from models equipped with a turbocharger—few mechanics want to bother repairing it or hunting for parts. Many owners report premature paint peeling.

The 1991–95 models are a bit more reliable and reasonably priced; however, the 1996–98 versions are *la crème de la crème*. When the 323 was dropped at the end of 1994, the Protegé became Mazda's least-costly model and underwent a major redesign the next year. It shares platforms with the Escort and Tracer, but keeps its own sheet metal, engine, and interior styling. Powered by a standard, fuel-efficient, 1.5L engine mated to a manual 5-speed transmission, the Protegé is one of the most responsive and roomiest small cars around.

Nevertheless, these cars aren't perfect and owners report problems with the front brakes (excessive noise and premature wear); weak rear defrosting; rough second-gear engagement; engine stalling; noisy suspension; AC failures; and body defects, including wind and water leaks into the interior, paint defects, and power mirror failures.

Dealer service bulletins: 1995—A tapping, cracking noise that comes from the B- and C-pillars. • Excessive blower motor and brush noise. • Heater and AC unit noise after long storage. • No sound from radio. •

A bump sound when opening the sunroof. • Detached sunroof tilt switch knob. • Power outside mirror glass vibration. • Fuse block cover and glove box hinge breakage. • A slightly off-center steering wheel.

Safety summary/Recalls: Recalls: Protegé: 1992–93—May not meet regulations relative to child restraint tether anchorages. **1995**—The 1.5L engine valve springs are defective.

Secret Warranties/Service Tips

All models: 1990—Cold-weather stalling usually requires the replacement of the ECU, which is under the emissions warranty. **1990–91**—Rough idle or vibration in Drive may require changing the No. 1 and No. 4 engine mounts and the radiator lower mounts. **1990–92**—Noise coming from the front of the car when turning may be due to dirt accumulation in the top strut mount bushing. **1990–94**—Clutch squealing is fixed by installing an upgraded clutch cushioning plate. **1995–96**—A horn noise heard from the exhaust will be silenced with a special tailpipe tip furnished by Mazda.

323, Protegé Profile

	1991	1992	1993	1994	1995	1996	1997	1998
Cost Price ($)								
323	8,243	8,439	9,219	10,220	—	—	—	—
Protegé	11,063	11,769	12,374	10,570	14,010	13,720	14,170	14,170
Used Values ($)								
323 ↑	3,000	3,500	4,000	5,000	—	—	—	—
323 ↓	2,700	3,000	3,500	4,500	—	—	—	—
Protegé ↑	4,000	4,500	5,000	6,000	7,000	8,000	9,000	10,500
Protegé ↓	3,500	4,000	4,500	5,500	6,000	7,000	8,500	9,000

Note: The '94 Protegé's MSRP was cut considerably to boost lagging sales.

Extended Warranty	Y	N	N	N	N	N	N	N
Secret Warranty	N	N	N	N	N	N	N	N
Reliability	②	③	④	④	④	④	④	⑤
Air conditioning	②	②	③	③	④	⑤	⑤	⑤
Body integrity	①	②	②	②	③	③	③	③
Braking system	①	②	②	②	③	③	③	③
Electrical system	①	②	③	③	③	④	④	④
Engines	③	③	③	④	④	④	④	④
Exhaust/Converter	②	②	②	②	③	⑤	⑤	⑤
Fuel system	②	③	③	④	④	⑤	⑤	⑤
Ignition system	③	④	④	④	④	④	⑤	⑤
Manual transmission	④	④	④	④	④	④	⑤	⑤
- automatic	②	②	③	③	④	⑤	⑤	⑤
Rust/Paint	②	②	②	③	③	③	③	④
Steering	③	③	③	④	④	④	④	④
Suspension	③	③	③	③	③	③	③	④

Crash Safety

323	❷	❷	❷	❷	—	—	—	—
Protegé	—	—	—	—	③	③	③	③

NISSAN

Sentra

Rating: Recommended (1995–98); Above Average (1991–94); Average (1988–90); Not Recommended (1983–87). The redesigned 1995 version offers fresh styling, a longer wheelbase, a peppier powerplant, standard dual airbags, and side-door beams. **Maintenance/Repair costs:** Higher than average on early models, but anybody can repair these cars. **Parts:** Reasonably priced and easily obtainable.

Strengths and weaknesses: Late-model Sentras aren't expensive to buy, they're generally reliable, relatively easy and inexpensive to repair, and they give good fuel economy. On the other hand, ride and handling are mediocre and build quality is spotty at best. Until 1991, mechanical and body components suffered from poor quality control, making these cars quite unreliable and sometimes expensive to repair. Clutches and exhaust systems were particularly problematic. The 1.6L engine is much more reliable, but even there the oil pressure switch may develop a leak that can lead to sudden oil loss and serious engine damage. Quality improved considerably with the 1991 version, yet the vehicle's base price rose only marginally, making these later model years bargain buys for consumers looking for a reliable "beater."

1991–94 Sentras are a bit peppier and handle better. Some owner-reported problems: faulty fuel tanks, leaking manual and automatic transmissions, a persistent rotten-egg smell, and noisy engine timing chains and front brakes. With the exception of electronic component failures, repairs are relatively simple to perform.

Redesigned for the 1995 model year, 1995–98 Sentra sedans are much improved, larger, and better-performing vehicles. The seatbelts are more comfortable, and dual airbags are a standard feature. Most owner complaints concern some stalling and hard starting, electrical glitches, premature brake wear and excessive brake noise, and accessories that malfunction. Body assembly is also targeted with some complaints of poor body fits, paint defects, and air and water leaks into the interior.

Dealer service bulletins: 1995—AC compressor leaks or noise. • Excessive brake noise. • C-pillar finisher lifting. • Faulty fuel gauge. • Self-activating horn. • Poor driveability—Code 45. • Power door locks that self-activate during periods of high heat or humidity. • Power windows that won't roll up unless ignition key is cycled. • Front window misalignment. • Front window won't go completely down. • DSB #NTB95-052 addresses all the possible causes and remedies for wind noise intruding into the passenger compartment.

Safety summary/Recalls: Recalls: 1987–88—These model years have been recalled because of cracked fuel tanks. **1987–91**—Takata seatbelts will be replaced. **1990–91**—Frayed front shoulder belts may lead to improper retraction and inadequate protection. **1991–92**—Valve vacuum hose may loosen. **1995**—ABS may be defective. **1995–98**—Dealer will install a water diversion seal to prevent water from entering the windshield wiper linkage.

Secret Warranties/Service Tips

1987–90—Manual transmission fluid leaks can be plugged with upgraded case bolts. **1989**—Install an AIV case assembly if the exhaust smells like rotten eggs. • If the trunk lid is hard to close or latch, install an upgraded latch and a softer weather strip. **1991–92**—Noisy front brakes can be silenced by installing upgraded, non-asbestos front disc brake pads (#41060-63Y90). • Timing chain rattle may be caused by insufficient oil in the chain tensioner. You can correct this by replacing the tensioner with a countermeasure part (#13070-53J03). **1991–93**—The manual transmission has no Reverse gear—install a Nissan upgrade kit. **1991–94**—Stiffer trunk torsion bars will help keep the trunk lid from falling. **1993–94**—Brake and steering wheel vibrations are most likely caused by excessive rotor thickness. **1994**—Door hinges may have received inadequate rust protection; Nissan will apply a sealer at no charge. **1995–96**—DSB #NTB96-001 gives lots of troubleshooting tips on finding and correcting various squeaks and rattles. • Nissan has a special kit to improve brake pedal feel, according to DSB #NTB96-041.

Sentra Profile

	1991	1992	1993	1994	1995	1996	1997	1998
Cost Price ($)								
Base	9,099	9,645	10,310	11,924	11,389	11,904	11,919	11,989
Used Values ($)								
Base ↑	4,500	5,000	6,000	6,500	7,500	8,500	9,500	10,000
Base ↓	3,500	4,500	5,000	6,000	6,500	7,500	8,500	9,500
Extended Warranty	N	N	N	N	N	N	N	N
Secret Warranty	N	N	N	N	N	Y	Y	N
Reliability	❷	③	④	④	④	⑤	⑤	⑤
Air conditioning	③	③	④	⑤	⑤	⑤	⑤	⑤
Body integrity	❷	❷	❷	❷	❷	③	④	④
Braking system	❶	❷	❷	❷	❷	❷	③	④
Electrical system	❷	③	③	❷	❷	❷	③	④
Engines	③	③	④	④	④	⑤	⑤	⑤
Exhaust/Converter	❷	❷	③	③	④	⑤	⑤	⑤
Fuel system	❷	❷	③	③	③	③	③	④

Ignition system	❷	③	③	③	③	④	④	④
Manual transmission	④	⑤	⑤	⑤	⑤	⑤	⑤	⑤
- automatic	❷	④	④	④	④	⑤	⑤	⑤
Rust/Paint	❷	③	③	③	③	③	④	④
Steering	③	③	③	③	④	④	⑤	⑤
Suspension	③	④	④	④	④	④	⑤	⑤
Crash Safety	④	⑤	④	④	—	④	④	③
Side Impact	—	—	—	—	—	—	—	③

SUBARU

Impreza, Loyale

Rating: Recommended (1996–98); Average (1993–95); Below Average (1984–92). The earlier models aren't recommended because of poor-quality emissions components and the premature wearout of major mechanical systems (CV joints, steering, etc.). **Maintenance/Repair costs:** Higher than average, and 4X4 repairs must be carried out by a dealer. Only buy a Subaru if you must have AWD and you're confident you can get dependable service from your local Subaru dealer. **Parts:** Expensive and hard to find. Emissions components are often back-ordered for months, but cheap aftermarket components can be found outside the dealer network.

Strengths and weaknesses: 1984–92 are the years to avoid. Performance, handling, and ride are mediocre. Engine breakdowns and premature clutch and exhaust system wearout are commonplace. Early hatchbacks came with a weak and growly 1.6L flat 4-cylinder motor; later models have a 1.8L version of the same anemic engine. Expensive catalytic converters are often replaced at the owner's cost before the five-year emissions warranty has expired. Subaru will reimburse the cost if you raise a fuss.

On 1988 and later models, steering assemblies, CV joints, and front brakes are the main problem areas. These parts generally need replacing after three to five years and Subaru dealers charge the full rate for replacement.

In the early spring of 1994, the Impreza replaced the unpopular and aging Loyale. The Impreza, too, offered sluggish engine performance, jerky full-throttle downshifts, and mediocre fuel economy. Overall reliability was improved, however.

By 1995, when these small cars went AWD, overall quality control improved as well. Powertrain components are more durable and function more smoothly, and electronic components have fewer glitches. Rusting is less of a problem than with the earlier models, which are particularly susceptible to rapid rusting of the bumpers, door bottoms, rear hatch, and hood.

Safety summary/Recalls: Impreza: 1994–95—Inadvertent airbag deployment is a problem. Airbags could deploy if the underside of the car scrapes the road or if the car drives over a dip in the road, hits a pothole, or is stuck in a ditch in the snow. **Recalls: All models: 1985–87**—Corrosion of the rear suspension inner arms could affect the control of the vehicle. **1989–90**—Automatic transmission may engage abruptly, causing a sudden lurch into Reverse. **Loyale: 1988–90**—Takata seatbelts will be replaced. **1989–90**—Automatic transmission may engage abruptly, causing a sudden lurch into Reverse. **1990**—Vehicles with 3AT transmissions may jump into gear from Park. **1990–93**—5-speed manual transmission may suddenly seize. **XT: 1985**—Improperly installed bumpers will be fixed. **1989–91**—Faulty power steering will be repaired. **1991**—In 4X4 models, 5-speed manual gearbox may leak, causing transmission to suddenly seize. **XT6: 1988–91**—Faulty power steering will be repaired. **DL, GL: 1987**—Faulty carburetor components could pose a fire hazard. **DL, GL, GT: 1985–87**—The rear suspension's inner arms could fail.

Secret Warranties/Service Tips

All models: 1985–90—Correct rear gate door rattle with a plastic sheet buffer. **1987**—An overly rich choke condition during cold starts can be corrected by installing a modified auxiliary choke pull-off spring. **1990–91**—A knocking noise from the exhaust flex joint may require the replacement of an exhaust flange gasket with an upgraded gasket (#44022-GA 191). **1991–92**—Ignition relay failure is the likely cause of no-starts. **1992–94**—The heater mode door actuator may be the culprit of an annoying clicking in the heater area. **Loyale: 1991**—Weak, noisy AM reception can be corrected by installing a modified antenna feeder cable (#86324AA040). • Banging over bumps is likely caused by the struts, strut mounts, and brake cable clamps on trailing arms or by the rear defogger condenser hitting the quarter panel. • A popping noise heard when going over small bumps may be caused by the front stabilizer bar bushing clamps.

Impreza, Loyale Profile

	1991	1992	1993	1994	1995	1996	1997	1998
Cost Price ($)								
Impreza	—	—	11,444	11,645	13,420	—	—	—
Impreza 4X4	—	—	—	—	16,425	13,990	15,290	17,190
Loyale	9,894	10,244	10,923	—	—	—	—	—
Loyale 4X4	—	—	—	13,998	—	—	—	—
Used Values ($)								
Impreza ↑	—	—	5,000	6,000	7,000	—	—	—
Impreza ↓	—	—	4,500	5,000	6,000	—	—	—
Impreza 4X4 ↑	—	—	—	—	10,000	10,500	11,500	14,000
Impreza 4X4 ↓	—	—	—	—	9,000	9,500	10,500	13,000
Loyale ↑	4,000	4,500	5,500	—	—	—	—	—
Loyale ↓	3,500	4,000	4,500	—	—	—	—	—

Loyale 4X4 ↑   —   —   —   8,300   —   —   —   —
Loyale 4X4 ↓   —   —   —   7,500   —   —   —   —
Note: The '95 Impreza 4X4 was outrageously overpriced.

Extended Warranty	Y	Y	Y	Y	Y	Y	Y	Y
Secret Warranty	N	N	N	N	N	N	N	N
Reliability	❷	③	③	③	④	④	⑤	⑤
Air conditioning	❷	③	④	④	⑤	⑤	⑤	⑤
Body integrity	❷	❷	③	③	③	③	③	④
Braking system	❷	❷	❷	③	③	③	④	④
Electrical system	❷	③	③	③	③	④	④	④
Engines	❷	③	③	③	④	⑤	⑤	⑤
Exhaust/Converter	❷	③	④	④	④	④	⑤	⑤
Fuel system	④	④	❷	❷	❷	④	④	⑤
Ignition system	❷	❷	❷	❷	④	④	④	⑤
Manual transmission	④	④	④	④	⑤	⑤	⑤	③
- automatic	③	③	③	③	③	③	③	③
Rust/Paint	❷	③	③	③	③	④	④	⑤
Steering	③	③	③	③	③	④	④	④
Suspension	③	③	④	④	④	④	④	④
Crash Safety								
Impreza/Impreza 4X4	—	—	—	—	—	④	④	—

SUZUKI

Esteem

Rating: Recommended (1996–98); Above Average (1995). An incredibly slow rate of depreciation means that bargains will be rare. Nevertheless, both the base GL and upscale GLX come loaded with standard features that cost extra on other models. The GL, for example, comes with power steering, rear window defroster, remote trunk and fuel-filler door releases, tinted glass, and a fold-down rear seat (great for getting extra cargo space). GLX shoppers can look forward to standard ABS, power windows and power door locks, and a host of other interior refinements. Shop around for a better made, second-series (made after March 1996) 1996 Esteem rather than a 1995 or 1997 version, inasmuch as they're practically identical and a late-model 1996 should be much cheaper. **Maintenance/Repair costs:** Higher than average. Repairs must be carried out by a Geo, Chevrolet, or Suzuki dealer. **Parts:** Average cost, but some long waits reported.

Strengths and weaknesses: The Esteem, Suzuki's largest car, is a small four-door sedan that is a step up from the Swift. Smaller than the

Honda Civic and Chrysler Neon, it has a fairly spacious interior, offering rear accommodation (for two full-sized adults) that is comparable to or better than most cars in its class. Suzuki's top-of-the-line econobox stands out with its European-styled body and large array of such standard features as air conditioning, a fold-down back seat, and remote trunk and fuel-door releases.

The Esteem has been on the market for only five years, but early reports indicate a high level of quality and dependability. In this respect, it competes well with rivals like the Chevy Cavalier, Ford Escort, and Honda Civic. However, some owners complain of premature front brake wear, noisy front brakes, and occasional electrical short circuits.

Safety summary/Recalls: 1998–99—Defective engine block heaters.

Secret Warranties/Service Tips

1996–97—Uneven wear of the front disc brake pads can be corrected by modifying the upper bushing tolerance, says DSB #TS 5-03-04126.

Esteem Profile

	1995	1996	1997	1998
Cost Price ($)				
GL	11,789	11,989	13,319	12,429
GLX	14,789	13,289	14,419	13,529
Used Values ($)				
GL ↑	7,000	7,500	9,000	10,000
GL ↓	6,000	6,500	8,000	9,000
GLX ↑	7,500	8,500	9,500	10,500
GLX ↓	7,000	8,000	8,500	9,500
Extended Warranty	N	N	N	N
Secret Warranty	N	N	N	N
Reliability	④	④	⑤	⑤

Note: The Esteem hasn't been crash-tested yet.

TOYOTA

Corolla/GM Prizm

Rating: Recommended (1995–98); Above Average (1991–94); Average (1985–90). The 1995–96 models combine the best array of standard features, quality control, and "reasonable" (for a Toyota) used prices. Although the 1997 model was "decontented" (less soundproofing, fewer standard features, etc.), there has been little reduction in quality or performance. **Maintenance/Repair costs:** Lower than average, and repairs can be done anywhere. **Parts:** Reasonably priced and easily found.

Strengths and weaknesses: Corollas and Prizms are economical, high-quality, dependable little cars, but age can take its toll, especially in the snowbelt states where rust snacks on these cars. 1985–87 versions may carry the Toyota name and appear to be bargains at first glance, but they're likely to have serious rusting problems and need costly brake, steering, and suspension work. Stay away from the 1.8L diesel version; it lacks performance and parts aren't easy to find. 4X4 versions are also risky. Wiper pivot assemblies may seize due to corrosion. Front shocks on rear-drive models wear out more quickly than average. Exhaust parts aren't very durable.

Post-1987 models are much improved. The two-door models provide sporty performance and good fuel economy, especially when equipped with the 16-valve engine. The engines and drivetrains are exceptionally reliable. Front-drive sedans and five-door hatchbacks offer more room than their rear-drive counterparts. The base engine, however, lacks power and is especially deficient in low-end torque, making for agonizingly slow merging and passing on the highway. Owners report problems with premature front suspension strut and brake wear; brake vibration; faulty defrosting that allows the windows to fog up in winter; and rusting of body seams, especially door bottoms, side mirror mounts, trunk and hatchback lids, and wheel openings.

The 1990–94 Corolla's and Prizm's problems are limited to harsh automatic shifting, early front brake pad and strut/shock wearout, electrical glitches, ignition problems, and some interior squeaks and rattles. They do, however, still require regular valve adjustments to prevent serious engine problems. Less of a problem with later models, rusting is usually confined to the undercarriage and other areas where the moldings attach to sheet metal.

1995–98 models are relatively problem-free, except for some minor brake and electrical problems, and occasional suspension vibrations and body trim imperfections.

Safety summary/Recalls: All models/years: Some owners find the driver's foot room inadequate to safely operate the accelerator, brake, and clutch pedals. **All models: 1993–96**—Researchers are looking into

20 similar incidents where the turn signal failed after the hazard warning light activated. **Recalls: All models: 1993–94**—An unused harness connector for vehicle accessories located under the carpet may cause an electrical short circuit or fire. **1993–95**—Liquid spilled onto the console could make the airbags deploy. **1994**—Seatbelt anchor straps may be faulty. **1995**—Defective terminal could drain the battery or make it explode. Dealer will replace the battery.

Secret Warranties/Service Tips

All models/years—Improved disc brake pad kits are described in DSB #BR94-004. • Brake pulsation/vibration, another generic Toyota problem, is fully addressed in DSB #BR94-002, "Cause and Repair of Vibration and Pulsation." • Complaints of steering column noise may require the replacement of the steering column assembly, a repair covered under Toyota's base warranty. **All models: 1987–88**—Engines that run on, surge, or have flat power spots may need an upgraded carburetor assembly, cold-mixture heater temperature switch, or engine sub-wire harness. **1993–96**—Toyota has upgraded the hazard switch to improve turn signal performance in cold climates. **1993–97**—Inoperative front-passenger side power window switch may be caused by lubricant from the wire harness contaminating the window switch contacts. **1994**—A loose rear seat bolster cover is a common problem, according to DSB #B094-005. • Windshield A-pillar wind noise can be stopped by modifying the molding lip. **1995–96**—To enhance the performance of the rear door glass, Toyota has upgraded the mounting channel rubber insert and offers it as a service part.

Corolla/GM Prizm Profile

	1991	1992	1993	1994	1995	1996	1997	1998
Cost Price ($)								
Base Corolla	10,508	11,123	12,983	13,308	13,782	14,538	15,028	13,443
Prizm	11,555	11,995	11,662	12,480	13,435	14,300	14,375	15,248
Used Values ($)								
Base Corolla ↑	4,700	5,500	6,500	8,000	9,000	10,000	11,000	11,500
Base Corolla ↓	4,200	5,000	5,500	7,000	8,000	9,000	10,000	11,000
Prizm ↑	4,500	5,000	6,000	7,000	8,000	9,000	10,000	11,300
Prizm ↓	3,800	4,000	5,000	6,000	7,000	8,000	9,000	10,500

Note: The '98 Corolla's MSRP was reduced considerably as a result of "decontenting."

Extended Warranty	Y	N	N	N	N	N	N	N
Secret Warranty	N	N	N	Y	Y	Y	Y	Y
Reliability	③	③	③	④	④	⑤	⑤	⑤
Air conditioning	⑤	⑤	⑤	⑤	⑤	⑤	⑤	⑤
Body integrity	❷	❷	❷	❷	③	④	④	⑤
Braking system	❷	❷	❷	❷	③	③	④	④
Electrical system	❷	③	③	③	③	④	④	⑤

Engines	④	④	④	④	⑤	⑤	⑤	⑤
Exhaust/Converter	❷	❷	③	③	④	④	⑤	⑤
Fuel system	❷	③	③	③	③	③	⑤	⑤
Ignition system	❷	❷	③	③	④	④	⑤	⑤
Manual transmission	④	④	④	④	⑤	⑤	⑤	⑤
- automatic	③	③	④	④	⑤	⑤	⑤	⑤
Rust/Paint	❷	❷	❷	❷	③	④	⑤	⑤
Steering	③	④	④	④	④	⑤	⑤	⑤
Suspension	③	③	③	④	④	⑤	⑤	⑤
Crash Safety	❷	❷	③	④	④	④	④	④
Side Impact	—	—	—	—	—	—	③	③

Paseo

Rating: Recommended (1994–97); Above Average (1992–93). 1997 was the Paseo's last model year. **Maintenance/Repair costs:** Lower than average. Repairs can be done anywhere. **Parts:** Reasonably priced and easily found.

Strengths and weaknesses: This baby Tercel's main advantages are a peppy 1.5L 4-cylinder engine, a smooth 5-speed manual transmission, good handling, a supple ride, great fuel economy, and above-average reliability. On the other hand, this light little sportster is quite vulnerable to side winds; there's lots of body lean in turns; there's plenty of engine, exhaust, and road noise; front head room and leg room are limited; and there is very little rear seat space.

Dealer service bulletins show that the 1993s may have defective Panasonic tape and CD players, and a radio hum at low volume caused by fuel pump interference. Later models have fewer reliability problems, except for some brake and drivetrain vibrations.

Safety summary/Recalls: Thick rear pillars reduce rear visibility. **Recalls:** N/A.

Secret Warranties/Service Tips

All years—DSB #B0003-97 recommends the use of a new wind noise repair kit. • DSB #AC002-97 gives lots of troubleshooting tips on eliminating AC odors. • AM radio static is likely caused by a damaged power antenna or by poor grounding due to corrosion. **1992**—Low-volume radio hum can be corrected by installing spacers (insulators) between the radio chassis and the printed circuit board. **1992–93**—Toyota will improve the shift "feel" on its automatic gearboxes by increasing the C1 accumulator control pressure. **1996**—Toyota has developed an upgraded thermostat to improve heater performance. **1997**—Fujitsu radios may not eject/accept CDs.

Paseo Profile

	1992	1993	1994	1995	1996	1997
Cost Price ($)						
Base	14,433	12,663	13,753	14,725	14,383	14,553
Used Values ($)						
Base ↑	6,000	7,000	8,000	9,000	10,000	11,000
Base ↓	5,500	6,000	7,000	8,000	9,500	10,500
Extended Warranty	N	N	N	N	N	N
Secret Warranty	N	N	N	N	N	N
Reliability	④	⑤	⑤	⑤	⑤	⑤
Crash Safety	③	—	—	—	—	④

Tercel

Rating: Recommended (1993–98); Above Average (1991–92); Average (1987–90). **Maintenance/Repair costs:** Inexpensive. Repairs can be done anywhere. **Parts:** Reasonably priced and easily obtainable.

Strengths and weaknesses: Don't buy a Toyota on reputation alone, because many early models (1985–90) can have serious braking, electrical, and rusting problems, and may be overpriced to boot. Also, stay away from the troublesome 4X4 versions made from 1984 to 1987.

All Tercels should be checked for door panel and underbody rust damage. 1987–90 Tercels are rust-prone around the rear wheels and side mirror mounts, and along the bottoms of doors, hatches, and rear quarter-panels. Early models suffer from extensive corrosion of rear suspension components.

1987–88 Tercels give you more for your money with a restyled aero look, a better performing multi-valve, an overhead-cam engine, the impressive performance of a 5-speed manual gearbox, and additional sound insulation. Their main shortcomings are insufficient power when merging into traffic or climbing hills (particularly when shifting from second to third gear with the automatic transmission), cruise control glitches, fuel system malfunctions, excessive carbon buildup on the engine intake valve, occasional air conditioner breakdowns, cracked front exhaust pipes, and exhaust system/catalytic converter rust-out. Tercels are also plagued by pulsating brakes that wear out much too quickly. Owners of the four-wheel drive wagon complain of manual transmission failures and the occasional bug in the transfer case (these repairs are *very* expensive).

The redesigned 1989–90 versions are roomier, better performing, and acceptable in quality and reliability (except for some paint peeling and surface rusting). The sunroof is a frill that cuts head room drastically and causes irritating water leaks and wind noise. Tercels have a great reputation for exemplary durability, but overall performance is not outstanding and the interior is cramped.

1991–94 Tercels are pretty reliable, but they're not perfect. They were the first to be fuel-injected, which makes for livelier and smoother acceleration, and the interior space feels much larger than it is. Owners report faulty clutch-sleeve cylinders, hard shifting with the automatic transmission, premature brake and suspension-component wearout, brake pulsation, defective CD players, leaking radiators, windshield whistling, and myriad squeaks and rattles.

Redesigned 1995–98 Tercels offer a bit more horsepower, standard dual airbags, side door beams, aero styling, and a redesigned interior. They continue, however, to have some minor brake, electrical system, suspension, and body/accessories problems.

Safety summary/Recalls: **Recalls: 1980–82**—Rear control arm could deform from corrosion.

Secret Warranties/Service Tips

All years—DSB #B0003-97 recommends the use of a new wind noise repair kit. • Interior squeaks and rattles can be fixed with Toyota's kit (#08231-00801). • DSB #AC002-97 gives lots of troubleshooting tips on eliminating AC odors. • Older Toyotas with stalling problems should have the engine checked for excessive carbon buildup on the valves before any other repairs are done. • Improved disc brake pad kits are described in DSB #BR94-004. • Brake pulsation/vibration, another generic Toyota problem, is fully addressed in DSB #BR94-002, "Cause and Repair of Vibration and Pulsation." • A damaged power antenna or poor grounding due to corrosion are the most likely causes of AM radio static. **1989–90**—Fix harsh shifting from second to third on automatics by installing a new rubber check ball (#35495-22020). **1994**—A whistling noise coming from the windshield requires a urethane sealant applied at key points. • A steering column that's noisy or has excessive free play may need an upgraded steering mainshaft bushing. **1995**—Troubleshooting windshield molding wind noise is covered in DSB #BO95-005. **1995–96**—Toyota has developed an upgraded thermostat to improve heater performance. • The company will also make available a longer passenger-side seatbelt. **1997**—Fujitsu radios may not eject/accept CDs.

Tercel Profile

	1991	1992	1993	1994	1995	1996	1997	1998
Cost Price ($)								
Base	7,728	8,303	9,223	10,223	11,535	11,981	12,508	13,110
Used Values ($)								
Base ↑	4,000	5,000	5,500	6,500	7,000	8,500	10,000	11,000
Base ↓	3,000	4,000	4,500	5,500	6,000	7,500	8,500	10,500
Extended Warranty	Y	N	N	N	N	N	N	N
Secret Warranty	N	N	N	N	N	N	N	N

Reliability	③	③	③	④	⑤	⑤	⑤	⑤
Air conditioning	③	③	③	④	⑤	⑤	⑤	⑤
Body integrity	③	③	③	④	④	⑤	⑤	⑤
Braking system	**❶**	**❷**	**❷**	**❷**	③	③	③	④
Electrical system	③	③	③	④	⑤	⑤	⑤	⑤
Engines	**❷**	**❷**	**❷**	③	④	⑤	⑤	⑤
Exhaust/Converter	**❷**	③	③	③	④	④	⑤	⑤
Fuel system	③	③	③	④	⑤	⑤	⑤	⑤
Ignition system	④	④	④	④	⑤	⑤	⑤	⑤
Manual transmission	④	④	④	④	⑤	⑤	⑤	⑤
- automatic	③	④	④	④	⑤	⑤	⑤	⑤
Rust/Paint	**❷**	**❷**	**❷**	③	④	⑤	⑤	⑤
Steering	④	④	④	③	④	④	⑤	⑤
Suspension	③	③	③	③	③	③	④	⑤
Crash Safety	**❷**	**❷**	④	④	③	③	④	—
Side Impact	—	—	—	—	—	—	③	③

VOLKSWAGEN

Cabrio, Golf, Jetta

Rating: Above Average (1997–98); Average (1994–96); Below Average (1993); Not Recommended (1985–92). These small imports age particularly badly, and VW is not very generous with "goodwill" repairs. A Jetta is a Golf with a trunk; a Cabrio is a Golf without a roof. There was no 1994 model Cabrio. Interestingly, the early convertibles (Cabriolet) are real bargains inasmuch as they depreciate steeply after their first five years on the market. **Maintenance/Repair costs:** Higher than average. Repairs are dealer dependent. **Parts:** Expensive, but generally available from independent suppliers.

Strengths and weaknesses: On the positive side, these small Europeans are fun to drive and provide great fuel economy. The 1.8L gasoline engine is very peppy and the diesel engines are very reliable and good all-around performers. Both engines are easily started in cold weather. But here's the rub: Golfs and Jettas, like the failure-prone Rabbit they replaced, age badly. What you save in fuel, you lose in the car's high retail price carried over into the used-car market; and the ever-mounting maintenance costs as the vehicle gains years and mileage will easily wear you down.

Reliability is impressive—for the first three years. Then the brake components, fuel, and electrical systems start to self-destruct as your wallet gets lighter. Exhaust system components aren't very durable, body hardware and dashboard controls are fragile, and the paint often discolors and is easily chipped.

Although the 1990–93 models are a tad improved, Volkswagen still has terrible quality problems. Owners report electrical short circuits; heater/defroster resistor and motor failures; leaking transmission and stub axles seals; and defective valve-pan gaskets, head gaskets, timing belts, steering assemblies, suspension components, alternator pulleys, and brake and electrical systems. Body problems are legion, with air and water leaks, faulty catalytic converters, inoperative locks and latches, poor-quality body construction and paint, and cheap, easily broken accessories and trim items.

The redesigned 1994–96 models are a bit more reliable and safer. Nevertheless, problems disclosed in service bulletins for these model years include poor driveability, water leaks, trim defects, and premature rear tire wear. Owners report the following: electric door locks that take a long time to lock; paint that is easily nicked, chipped, and marked; a variety of trim defects; premature rear tire wear; and poor-quality seat cushions. One owner of a 1996 Golf relates this "goodwill" experience with Volkswagen:

> Enclosed is a copy of a work order...to replace both front seat cushions—the second replacement for the driver's side since we purchased the vehicle in January 1996.
>
> The work order states "Goodwill Repair," as we are out of warranty. We feel this statement is rather misleading. Goodwill repair would have been if, when we brought the problem to the dealership's attention, they had offered to have the problem rectified with no hassle and without our having to resort to pressure from an outside source.
>
> The seat cushions have been replaced, but we feel they will only go again. Whether this is a flaw in the design of them or what, we can't say. The store manager seemed to think it was the way we "entered the vehicle" that caused the problem. As someone commented, entry was gained via the door!

For 1997, Golfs and Jettas equipped with the 116-hp 4-cylinder engine got a redesigned cylinder head that cuts engine noise. The Golf GTI VR6 rides lower, thanks to new shocks, springs, and anti-roll bars. The Cabrio Highline received standard AC, 14-inch alloy wheels, halogen driving lights, and leather upholstery. The base convertible lost its standard ABS and a few other goodies in an unsuccessful attempt to keep a lid on price.

Jettas provide slightly more comfort and better road performance than their Golf hatchback counterparts. The 1.6L 4-cylinder found on early Jettas was surprisingly peppy, and the diesel engine is very economical, although quite slow to accelerate. Diesels have a better overall reliability record than gasoline models and are popular as taxis. Jettas are far more reliable than Rabbits, but they, too, suffer from rapid body deterioration and some mechanical problems after their fourth year in service. For example, on post-1988 Jettas, starters often burn out because they are vulnerable to engine heat; as well, sunroofs leak, door locks jam, window cranks break, and windows bind. Owners also report engine head gasket leaks and water pump and heater core breakdowns. It's axiomatic that all diesels are slow to accelerate, but VW's fourth gear can't handle highway speeds above 50 mph. Engine noise is deafening when shifting down from fourth gear.

Factory defects on 1990–96 Golfs and Jettas are so numerous they make these models very risky buys. Problems include automatic transmission, engine, suspension components, and catalytic converter failures; electrical short circuits; AC malfunctions; and fragile trim items. Body assembly and paint are second-class, leading to rattles and air leaks as the vehicles age.

All 1996–98 models are much more reliable, but, nevertheless, owners still report chronic automatic transmission, brake, and electrical system malfunctions problems, in addition to sub-par body construction and paint, leaky sunroofs, malfunctioning gauges and accessories, fragile locks and latches, bumpers that become brittle and crack as the temperature falls, and defective security systems.

Dealer service bulletins: 1995—CD changer skipping or grounding. • Slow or inoperative central locking. • Clutch pedal noise and vibration. • Front-end knock. • Wind noise at A-pillar door glass seal. • Exterior door locks freezing. • Release handle won't open hood. • Faulty instrument cluster control light. • Poor fuel system performance. • Pulsating or clicking noise from engine. • Shifting difficulties. • Rotten-egg odor from exhaust. • Sunroof noise and vibration. • Water leaks from sunroof area. • Noise from 5-speed transmission when cornering. • Vehicle drifts or pulls to one side. • Suggestions for correcting wheel/tire vibrations. • Skipping wiper blades. **1996**—Front-end knock. • Noise in rear center console. • Vehicle drifts to one side. • Skipping wiper blades. **1997**—Anti-theft alarm sounds for no apparent reason and car won't start. • Automatic transmission fluid seeps from final drive breather vent. • Battery cable clamp won't tighten. • Frequent causes for inoperative window regulator motor. • Tips on eliminating front and rear door air leaks. • Excessive vibration or knocking of the shifter lever. • Transmission may not shift in or out of Reverse. • Troubleshooting windshield wiper failures.

Safety summary/Recalls: Recalls: All models: 1983–92—Corrosion may cause the hood to fly up. **1985**—Faulty brake master cylinder. • Front seatbelt retractors on two-door models may not lock properly. **1985–86**—Excessive fuel spillage could occur during a collision. **1985–87**—The engine may suddenly stall due to a seized fuel pump. **1987**—Loose lug nuts on alloy wheels could cause wheel separation. **1987–89**—An incorrectly contoured brake line could result in brake failure. **1987–92**—A de-icing kit will prevent sudden acceleration. **1988**—The seatbelt retractor pawl is weak. • The brake booster is faulty. **1988–91**—The engine preheating tube may interfere with braking. **1988–92**—VW will replace the fuel hose and install new spring-type hose clamps. **1990**— The power-steering pump bracket is faulty. **1991**—Too-short front brake hoses may rupture. **1993**—The windshield wiper motor may fail. **Cabrio: 1983–92**—Hood may fly up. **1985**—The fuel supply hose is faulty. **1987–90**—The fuel tank may leak. **1990**—The airbag harness wire is poorly located. **1990–91**—A bent water separator panel could cause sudden acceleration. **1990–92**—A faulty fuel hose retaining clamp could be a fire hazard. **1991**—Defective track control arms used to support front wheels cause wheel misalignment and steering pull to one side. **Jetta: 1985**—The plastic clip that holds the brake line may be a fire hazard. **Golf, Jetta: 1985–91**—Hot coolant could escape into the passenger compartment. **1990**—Faulty air ducts could cause brake fluid to overheat. **1993–95**—The jack could collapse during use. • Rear brake lines may leak from rubbing against the fuel tank; dealers will reroute and replace damaged lines. • Radiator fan motor could seize. **1993–96**—Hood may fly up.

Secret Warranties/Service Tips

All models: 1988–94—Poor driveability may be caused by a deteriorated oxygen sensor wire shield or poor ground connection. **1990**—Hard winter starting may require the installation of a new high-energy ignition coil, high-tension wires, and spark plugs. **1992–94**—Poor engine performance or a rough idle may be due to a misrouted EVAP vacuum hose. **1993–94**— DSB #95-04 gives simple service tips for frozen door locks. **1994**—Water leaks into the engine bulkhead. **1996–97**—Tape player may have distorted sound or may snack on tapes. • A shifter that's hard to move side-to-side or won't go into Reverse may signal that the selector shaft is binding in the selector shaft housing bearing. **1997**—Erratic electrical functions may be caused by a loose ground at one of two grounding studs located under the battery tray. • If the transmission pops out of gear, check for a hairline crack on the selector shaft shift detent sleeve. • Buzzing noise from right-side air outlet may be caused by loose outlet mounting screws.

Cabrio, Golf, Jetta Profile

	1991	1992	1993	1994	1995	1996	1997	1998
Cost Price ($)								
Cabrio	17,740	18,585	19,665	—	21,215	21,260	20,785	21,455
Golf	10,330	11,135	12,830	13,565	11,915	14,435	14,830	14,855
Jetta	11,355	12,580	14,030	14,365	12,915	15,535	15,930	15,955
Used Values ($)								
Cabrio ↑	6,500	7,500	8,000	—	14,000	15,500	17,000	18,500
Cabrio ↓	5,500	7,000	7,500	—	13,000	14,500	16,000	17,500
Golf ↑	5,000	5,500	6,500	8,000	9,500	10,500	12,000	13,000
Golf ↓	4,000	4,500	5,500	7,000	8,000	9,500	11,000	12,000

| Jetta ↑ | 5,500 | 6,500 | 7,500 | 9,000 | 10,500 | 11,500 | 13,000 | 13,500 |
| Jetta ↓ | 4,500 | 5,500 | 6,500 | 8,000 | 9,500 | 10,500 | 12,500 | 13,000 |

Extended Warranty	Y	Y	Y	Y	Y	Y	N	N
Secret Warranty	N	N	N	N	N	N	N	N
Reliability	❶	❷	❷	❷	❷	③	④	④
Air conditioning	❷	❷	❷	❷	❷	③	⑤	⑤
Body integrity	❶	❶	❶	❶	❶	❷	❷	③
Braking system	❶	❶	❶	❷	❷	❷	③	③
Electrical system	❶	❶	❶	❶	❶	❷	❷	③
Engines	❷	❷	❷	❷	③	④	⑤	⑤
Exhaust/Converter	❷	❷	❷	③	③	④	④	⑤
Fuel system	❷	❷	❷	❷	③	③	③	④
Ignition system	❷	❷	❷	❷	❷	③	④	④
Manual transmission	④	④	④	⑤	⑤	⑤	⑤	⑤
- automatic	③	③	③	③	④	⑤	⑤	⑤
Rust/Paint	❷	❷	❷	❷	❷	③	④	⑤
Steering	③	③	③	③	④	⑤	⑤	⑤
Suspension	③	③	③	③	④	④	④	⑤
Crash Safety								
Golf	—	—	—	—	③	③	③	—
Jetta	—	—	—	—	③	③	③	—
Side Impact								
Jetta	—	—	—	—	—	—	—	③

MEDIUM CARS

A medium-sized car is a trade-off between size and fuel economy, offering more room and comfort but a bit less fuel economy (25–30 mpg) than a small car. These cars are popular because they combine the advantages of smaller cars with those of larger vehicles. As a result of their versatility and upsizing as well as downsizing throughout the years, these vehicles shade into both the small and the large car niches. The trunk is usually large enough to meet average baggage requirements, and the interior is spacious enough to meet the needs of the average family (seating four persons in comfort and five in a pinch). It's the best car for combined city and highway driving.

Recommended

Honda Accord (1992–98)
Mitsubishi Galant (1994–98)
Toyota Camry (1994–98)
Volkswagen Passat (1998)

Above Average

Acura CL-Series (1998)
Acura Integra (1990–98)
Acura Vigor (1992–94)
GM Bonneville/Delta 88/LeSabre, Cutlass/Malibu, Cutlass Supreme, Grand Prix/Intrigue/Regal, Lumina, Monte Carlo (1984–87)
Honda Accord (1990–91)
Mazda 626, MX-6 (1996–98)
Mitsubishi Galant (1990–93)
Nissan Altima (1996–98)
Nissan Stanza (1990–92)
Subaru Legacy (1996–98 AWD)
Toyota Camry (1988–93)
Volkswagen Passat (1995–97)

Average

Acura CL-Series (1997)
Acura Integra (1986–89)
Chrysler Acclaim/Spirit, LeBaron, (1991–95)
Ford Contour/Mystique (1996–98)
Ford Sable/Taurus (1998)
GM Achieva/Grand Am, Skylark (1995–98)
GM Beretta, Corsica (1993–96)
Honda Accord (1985–89)
Hyundai Sonata (1995–98)
Mazda 626, MX-6 (1994–95)
Nissan Altima (1993–95)
Nissan Stanza (1988–89)
Subaru Legacy (1989–98 excluding AWD)
Toyota Camry (1985–87)
Volvo 240 (1989–93)

Below Average

Chrysler Breeze, Cirrus/ Stratus (1995–98)
Ford Contour/Mystique (1995)
GM 6000, Century, Ciera (1998)
GM Achieva/Grand Am, Calais Skylark (1988–94)
Volkswagen Corrado (1992–95)
Volvo 240 (1985–88)

Not Recommended

Chrysler Acclaim/Spirit,
  LeBaron, (1989–90)
Ford Sable/Taurus
  (1986–97)
Ford Tempo/Topaz (1985–94)
GM 6000, Century,
  Ciera (1982–97)
GM Beretta, Corsica
  (1987–92)

GM Bonneville, Delta 88/LeSabre
  Cutlass/Malibu, Cutlass
  Supreme, Grand Prix/
  Inteigue/Regal, Lumina/
  Carlo (1988–98)
Hyundai Sonata (1986–93)
Mazda 626, MX-6 (1985–93)
Nissan Stanza (1985–87)
Volkswagen Corrado (1989–91)
Volkswagen Passat (1989–94)

ACURA

CL Series

Rating: Above Average (1998); Average (1997). Overpriced and hard to find; be wary of the first-year models. The 2.2L CL's engine was upgraded to a 2.3L on the 1998 models. **Maintenance/Repair costs:** Predicted to be higher than average. Repairs are dealer dependent. **Parts:** Expensive, once the warranty expires.

Strengths and weaknesses: The only difference between the 2.2L CL and the 3.0 CL is the 3.0L CL's larger engine, different wheels, and larger exhaust tip. Other vehicles worth considering, but with fewer standard features: BMW 318, Honda Accord, Lexus SC300, Nissan Maxima, and Toyota Camry.

The most distinctive features of the 2.2L CL and its 3.0L CL twin are the engine and wheels. These cars are both stylish, front-drive, five-passenger, American-designed-and-built luxury coupes. They have a flowing, slanted back end and no apparent trunk lock (a standard remote keyless entry system opens the trunk from the outside and a lever opens it from the inside). And while other Japanese automakers are taking content out of their vehicles, Acura has put content into the CL, making it one of the most feature-laden cars in its class.

Sure, we all know that the coupe's mechanicals and platform aren't that different from the Accord's, but when you add up all of its standard bells and whistles, you get a fully loaded medium-sized car that costs thousands of dollars less than such competing luxury coupes as the BMW 318 and the Lexus SC300. Consider this array of standard features: power windows, power mirrors, power moon roof, six-way power driver's seat, remote keyless entry system, ABS, leather-wrapped steering wheel, simulated wood trim, automatic climate control, dual airbags, tilt steering wheel, cruise control, and CD player and AM/FM stereo with six speakers.

Although no one would consider the CL a high-performance car, it gets plenty of power from its quiet and smooth-running 3.0L 24-valve SOHC Variable Valve Timing and Lift Electronic Control (VTEC) V6, as well as from the Accord's 2.2L, single overhead cam 4-cylinder VTEC engine (upgraded to a 2.3L on the '98 models). The latter engine's 145 horses take the CL from 0 to 60 mph in a respectable nine seconds, but the engine works hard and is noisy. Handling is better than average, thanks to the Accord's upgraded suspension, variable assisted steering, and 16-inch wheels, which are one inch larger than the Accord's (I told you there was a lot of Accord in the CL).

Now that I've whetted your appetite with all that's right about these little Acuras, let's look at some of the problems reported with the 1997 models. This is not a car for seating passengers in the rear. Back seat room is insufficient, unless the front seats are pushed all the way forward. And the rear windows don't roll down all the way. Furthermore, owners have become so incensed at what they perceive as Acura's arrogant stonewalling of customer complaints that one owner, Michael Hos, set up his own Acura Lemon website to air Acura gripes and put pressure on the company. He got his money back after a few months and took down his website as part of the bargain. Nevertheless, he shows how others can do the same in Part Two of this guide (see pages 102–103).

Some of the common defects reported on the Hos website: faulty transmission control unit; transmission downshift problems; chronic brake rotor pulsation and other brake problems leading to resurfacing of brake rotors and replacement of brake pads, rotors, calipers, and springs; repeated front end realignments; door and wind noise leading to replacement of door; and a sunroof that won't stop at closed position, requiring replacement of sunroof switch and controller. Honda's 14-year free repair secret warranty applies to all 1996–97 Acuras, except for the type R models.

Safety summary/Recalls: All models: 1997—Complete brake failure; vehicle hit a wall. • Chronic hesitation and stalling. • Passenger-side airbag replaced after sensor indicated it was defective. • Leaky oil pan seals. Premature catalytic converter failure. • Subframe out of alignment, causing vehicle to pull to one side. **1998**—When driving on a flat surface at 30 mph, or 1500 rpms, vehicle will jerk and pull for about 30 seconds. **Recalls: All models: 1998**—Defective shifter/parking pawl may allow vehicle to roll down an incline with shift lever ostensibly in Park. Dealer will put a collar on the pawl.

Secret Warranties/Service Tips

All models: 1997—Acura says it will replace any seatbelt's tongue stopper button for the life of the vehicle. • Remedy for front seat that won't slide forward or backward. • Fix for moon roof seal that sticks up. • Freeing up seatback adjustment lever • Silencing a dash pop or creak. • Fix for incorrect fuel gauge and speedometer readings. • Correction for brake fluid leaking from the ABS modulator.

CL-Series Profile

	1997	1998
Cost Price ($)		
2.2L, 2.3L CL	24,395	24,595
3.0L CL	26,895	27,095
Used Values ($)		
2.2L, 2.3L CL ↑	19,000	22,000
2.2L, 2.3L CL ↓	18,000	21,000
3.0L CL ↑	20,500	23,000
3.0L CL ↓	19,500	21,500
Extended Warranty	N	N
Secret Warranty	Y	N
Reliability	④	⑤

Note: These vehicles have not been crash-tested.

Integra

Rating: Above Average, compromised by a stiff price for the Acura cachet and limited passenger room (1990–98); Average (1986–89). **Maintenance/Repair costs:** Higher than average. Repairs are dealer dependent. **Parts:** Expensive, but can be bought from cheaper independent Honda suppliers.

Strengths and weaknesses: A Honda spin-off, early Integras (1986–89) came with lots of standard equipment and are a pleasure to drive, especially when equipped with a manual transmission. The 4-speed automatic saps the base engine's power considerably. Engine and tire noise are intrusive at highway speeds. The car corners well and is more agile than later 1990–93 models. Its hard ride can be reduced a bit by changing the shocks and adding wide tires. The front seats are very comfortable, but they're set a bit low, and the side wheelwells leave little room for your feet. Rear seat room is very limited, especially on the three-door version.

A large number of 1989–90 Integras have faulty distributor igniters. When the igniter fails, the car stalls and it may be impossible to restart. The only remedy is to call a tow truck and have a garage replace the distributor.

Overall, assembly and component quality are good but not exceptional, as you can see from the "Secret Warranties/Service Tips" list. To avoid costly engine repairs, check the engine timing belt every 2 years/ 30,000 miles.

For model years 1990–93, the high-revving 1.7L powerplant growls when pushed and lacks guts (read, torque) in the lower gears. The 1.8L engine runs more smoothly but delivers the same maximum horsepower as the 1.7L it replaced, until the '94 model year, when it gained 10 extra horses. Surprisingly, overall performance has been toned down and is seriously compromised by the 4-speed automatic gearbox. Interior design is more user-friendly, with the front seating roomier than in previous years, but reduced rear seating is still best left to small children.

Mechanical reliability is impressive, but that's the case with most Hondas that sell for far less, and many mechanical components are so complex that self-service can pretty well be ruled out. The Integra's front brakes may require more attention than those of other Hondas. Surprisingly, what Integras give you in mechanical reliability they take away in poor quality control of body components and accessories. Water leaks, excessive wind noise, low-quality trim items, and plastic panels that deform easily are all commonplace. Owners also report severe steering shimmy, excessive brake noise, premature front brake pad wearout, and radio malfunctions.

In the 1994 model year, the Integra was dramatically restyled with a more aerodynamic profile, and a few more horses were wrung out of the venerable 1.8L 4-banger through variable valve timing. The 1994–98 models also offer a smoother ride than previous versions. On the other hand, the powerful VTEC engine requires lots of shifting and interior room is still problematic. Overall, there are too few improvements to justify the high prices that late-model Integras command.

Owners report that steering wheel shimmy, fit and finish deficiencies, and malfunctioning accessories continue to be problematic on later models. Premature front brake wear is also an ongoing concern. Squeaks and rattles frequently crop up in the door panels and hatches, and the sedan's frameless windows often have sealing problems.

Safety summary/Recalls: Recalls: 1986–87—An upgraded contact unit retainer needs to be attached to the front windshield wiper assembly. **1986–91**—Takata seatbelts will be replaced. **1987–88**—Acura will repair or replace defective heaters for free. **1994**—Automatic transmission retaining clip may show wrong gear.

Secret Warranties/Service Tips

All models/years—Severe and persistent steering wheel shimmy is likely due to an imbalanced wheel/tire/hub/rotor assembly. **1986–89**—A faulty fuel pump check valve or fuel pressure regulator may be the cause of hard starts. Correct this problem by installing an improved fuel pressure regulator (#16740-PG7-663) or fuel pump (#16700-PG7-663). **1990–91**—DSB #91-015 is an excellent troubleshooting guide to the myriad squeaks and rattles in the dash, front doors, hatch, steering shaft, and sunroof. **1990–93**—Poor AM radio reception is likely caused by a poor ground connection between the antenna collar and the car body. **1992–97**—A defective seatbelt tongue stopper will be replaced free of charge with no ownership, time, or mileage limitations. **1994**—Rear hatch rattles are usually caused by a poorly adjusted striker. • Lots of troubleshooting bulletins are offered dealing with in-dash cellular phone problems. • Power door locks that cycle from locked to unlocked require a new power door lock control unit. **1994–95**—Rattling from a partially open window may be caused by excess clearance between the window guide pin and the center sash guide or by the glass run channel having come out of the center channel. These are also likely causes of moon roof chattering or shuddering. **1996–97**—In a settlement with the U.S. Environmental Protection Agency, Honda paid fines totaling $17.1 million and extended its emissions warranty on 1.6 million 1995–97 models to 14 years or 150,000 miles. This means that costly engine components and exhaust system parts, like catalytic converters, will be replaced free of charge, as long as the 14-year/150,000 mile limit hasn't been exceeded. Additionally, the automaker will provide a full engine check and emissions-related repairs at 50,000–75,000 miles and will give free tune-ups at 75,000–150,000 miles. It is estimated the free check-ups, repairs, and tune-ups will cost Honda over $250 million. The story of the settlement was first reported on page 6 of the June 15, 1998, edition of *Automotive News*.

Integra Profile

	1991	1992	1993	1994	1995	1996	1997	1998
Cost Price ($)								
RS	13,870	14,335	14,045	16,695	17,390	18,080	17,335	17,435
Used Values ($)								
RS ↑	7,500	8,500	9,500	10,500	11,500	13,500	15,000	16,500
RS ↓	6,500	7,500	8,500	9,500	10,500	13,000	14,500	16,000
Extended Warranty	N	N	N	N	N	N	N	N
Secret Warranty	N	N	N	N	N	Y	Y	N
Reliability	④	④	⑤	⑤	⑤	⑤	⑤	⑤
Air conditioning	❷	③	④	④	⑤	⑤	⑤	⑤
Body integrity	❷	③	③	③	③	③	③	④
Braking system	❷	❷	❷	❷	❷	③	④	④
Electrical system	③	③	③	③	③	④	④	④
Engines	④	④	④	④	④	⑤	⑤	⑤
Exhaust/Converter	❷	❷	❷	③	④	④	⑤	⑤
Fuel system	③	③	③	④	④	⑤	⑤	⑤
Ignition system	❷	③	④	④	④	④	④	④
Manual transmission	⑤	⑤	⑤	⑤	⑤	⑤	⑤	⑤
- automatic	④	④	④	④	⑤	⑤	⑤	⑤
Rust/Paint	❷	③	③	③	③	③	④	④
Steering	③	③	④	④	④	④	④	⑤
Suspension	③	③	④	④	④	④	④	⑤
Crash Safety	—	—	—	—	④	④	—	—

Vigor

Rating: Above Average (1992–94). **Maintenance/Repair costs:** Higher than average. Repairs are dealer dependent. **Parts:** Expensive, but most mechanical components can be bought more cheaply from independent suppliers. Accord parts can be used for most maintenance chores. Body panels and engine components, however, are more difficult to find.

Strengths and weaknesses: A spin-off of the Honda Accord sedan, the 5-cylinder Vigor went through only three model years (1992–94). Due to its high cost and the absence of a more economical, smoother, and easier-to-repair 6-cylinder powerplant, most buyers chose the cheaper Accord instead. This compact has power to spare, handles well, and has an impressive reliability/durability record. On the other hand, owners report the following problems: lots of engine, tire, and road noise intrude into the passenger compartment at highway speeds; the engine and transmission lack smoothness; and the brakes aren't easy to modulate. The suspension is firm but not harsh, rear leg room is limited, and there have been some complaints of fit and finish deficiencies. Vigors are also notoriously thirsty for premium fuel.

Safety summary/Recalls: Recalls: 1992—Inadequate venting could allow moisture to build up in the distributor cap and prevent the engine from starting.

Secret Warranties/Service Tips

All models/years—Excessive steering wheel shimmy is likely due to an imbalance of the wheel/tire/hub/rotor assembly in the front end. **1992**—DSB #92-034 goes into great detail on ways to silence the Vigor's many squeaks and rattles.

Vigor Profile

	1992	1993	1994
Cost Price ($)			
LS	24,340	25,380	27,485
Used Values ($)			
LS ↑	10,000	11,500	14,000
LS ↓	9,000	11,000	13,000
Extended Warranty	N	N	N
Secret Warranty	N	N	N
Reliability	④	④	④
Crash Safety	❷	—	—

CHRYSLER

Acclaim/Spirit, LeBaron

Rating: Average only with an extended warranty (1991–95); Not Recommended (1989–90). These front-drives are a better choice than the Aries or Reliant (see "Beaten" Beaters list in Part One) due to their more recent vintage and more refined engines and suspension. 1995 was the last model year. **Maintenance/Repair costs:** Lower than average. Repairs can be easily done by independent garages. The ease with which these cars can be repaired and the low cost of most replacement parts add to their attractiveness as relatively inexpensive, five-passenger, fuel-efficient used cars. **Parts:** Reasonably priced, with good availability through independent suppliers.

Strengths and weaknesses: Although these cars have an outdated design, Chrysler improved their assembly quality and backed these cars with a strong base warranty that's transferable to second owners. The 100-hp 2.5L 4-cylinder engine and 3-speed automatic are models of ruggedness. Acceleration is adequate with the standard 4-cylinder engine and quite fast and smooth with the 150-hp Chrysler-bred 2.5L turbo.

The following are all prone to rapid wear: cylinder head gaskets on the 2.5L engine, front suspension, brakes, fuel system, and air conditioning. The Mitsubishi-built V6 has generated complaints about premature oil leaks and fuel system problems. The Ultradrive A604 4-speed automatic transmissions (renamed the 41TE in 1992) were found early in production to have poor shifting, internal fluid leakage leading to clutch burn-out, and sudden second-gear lockup. The problem first becomes apparent when the transmission tries to engage third and fourth gears simultaneously, causing either clutch failure or sticking in second gear. Between 1989 and July 1991, Chrysler tried 28 different changes to resolve the Ultradrive's clutch failures, second-gear lockup, and excessive shifting on hills. The 41TE automatic transmissions on 1992–96 models are also failure-prone.

The air conditioner switches on and off continually. The following parts often need replacing: windshield wiper and interior fan motors; speedometer-sending unit and MAP sensor; and steering rack, bushings, and front stabilizer bar. Owners report that the steering wheel's vinyl coating rubs off on hands and clothing and the plastics used in the seats and dash area give off vapors that collect as a film on inside window surfaces.

All model years have fragile body hardware and sloppy body assembly. Many owners report water infiltration, especially around the windshield and into the trunk. Surface rust is common, especially around the windshield, door bottoms, and rear lip of the trunk lid.

LeBarons are a bit more high-tech, but overall road performance and reliability are just as disappointing. The ride is rough and vibrations and rattles are constant. Automatic transmission torque converters frequently malfunction. The front suspension is particularly trouble-prone, and electrical bugs and major computer module failures are common. Wheel bearings, fuel pumps, and rear window motors tend to wear out prematurely.

Owners of 1991–95 models report that oil leaks and oil pump failures are common; rear brakes are noisy; the heating, air conditioning, and ventilation systems often malfunction; and electrical components (notably electronic modules) aren't very durable. Paint and assembly quality are also below par, characterized by body hardware and trim that rust out, break, or fall off.

Safety summary/Recalls: In all three cars, the front wheels tend to lock prematurely when braking heavily. • According to the Center for Auto Safety (CAS), engine fires due to fuel and oil leaks in 1978–90 front-drive Chryslers have generated hundreds of complaints. • Rear brake lockup and master cylinder failures on 1978–92 models are also common, according to CAS. **Recalls: 1989–90**—Engine oil leakage means a new engine valve cover gasket is needed. **1991**—Pin bolts on the front disc brake caliper guide might be too loose. • Both airbag front-impact sensors might be improperly mounted. • Outboard front seatbelts might not latch properly. **1992**—The coupling bolts on the steering column shaft could be faulty. **1994**—Seatbelt assembly could fail in an accident. **LeBaron: 1990**—Airbag inflator module could be defective.

Secret Warranties/Service Tips

All models/years—Excessive effort required to disengage Park may mean a new Park rod assembly is required (#4431530). • Headlight condensation requires installation of vents in the headlight assemblies. • A rotten-egg odor coming from the exhaust is likely the result of a defective catalytic converter, which should be replaced for free under the emissions warranty. **All models: 1989**—Leaking fuel injectors are a common problem. • If the AC heater check valve freezes, install a new vacuum-control check valve (#5264270). • Models with 3.0L engines that lose power may need a new throttle body base gasket. • 3.0L engines that burn oil, stall, or lack power may have excessive sludge accumulation in the left bank (front) rocker cover baffle oil drain hole. • 2.5L turbo engines that lose power may need the Chrysler driveability kit (#4419460), or, if power loss occurs during hot weather, a new vacuum connector (#5277577). **1989–90**—A604 automatic transmissions with excessive upshifting/downshifting require a new A604 controller (#4557585). • Rough idling might require the replacement of the EGR valve. **1989–91**—A604 automatic transmissions with 1–2 upshift shudder may need the 2–4 clutch replaced. **1989–93**—3.0L engines that burn oil or produce a smoky exhaust at idle can be fixed by installing snap rings on the exhaust valve guides and replacing all of the valve guide stems or the cylinder head. **1989–95**—Intake valve deposits are the likely cause of stalling, loss of power, hesitation, or hard starting. • Failure to go into Reverse is likely caused by faulty low/reverse piston. • Various tips are offered on correcting third-gear shuddering. **1990**—A604 automatic transmissions that limp or fail to shift require the replacement of the PRNDL and Neutral safety switch. **1990–91**—Surging or bucking at 30–50 mph with an A413 or A670 automatic transmission can be fixed with driveability kit (#4419447). **1990–92**—Erratic idle speeds that occur after deceleration from a steady cruising speed can be corrected by replacing the idle air-control motor with a revised motor. **1990–94**—Harsh automatic shifts can be tamed by installing the following revised parts: kickdown, accumulator, reverse servo cushion springs, and accumulator piston. **1991**—Customer Satisfaction Notifications #499 and #521 set out Chrysler's commitment to correct, free of charge, engine oil pump failure. **1991–92**—Engines with a rough idle and stalling following a cold start may require a new Single Board Engine Controller (SBEC). **1991–93**—The serpentine belt may come off the pulley after driving the vehicle through snow. Install an upgraded shield, screw, and retainers. **1991–94**—Engines that stall following a cold start may need an upgraded Park/Neutral/Start switch. **1991–95**—Poor AC performance while the AC blower continues to operate is likely due to the evaporator freezing. **1992**—If the heater and ventilation system changes to defrost mode during acceleration, trailer towing, or hill climbing, the installation of a revised vacuum check valve should cure the problem. • Long crank times, a rough idle, and hesitation may be corrected by replacing the intake manifold assembly. • A low-frequency moan or groan coming from the rear brakes can be reduced by installing an upgraded rear disc pad set (#4423667). **1992–93**—Rough idling after a cold start with 2.2L and 2.5L engines can be corrected by installing an upgraded powertrain control module (PCM). • Some 41TE transaxles may produce a buzzing noise when shifted into Reverse; this problem can be corrected by replacing the valve body assembly or valve body separator plate. • Deceleration shudder can be eliminated by replacing the powertrain control module with an upgraded version. **1992–95**—Tips are offered on eliminating AC odors and tracing likely causes of a rotten-egg exhaust smell. **1993**—Failure of the fuel pump check valve can cause start-up die-out, reduced power, or erratic shifting. **1993–94**—Acceleration shudder may be caused by automatic transmission front pump leakage. • Improve automatic shifting by installing an upgraded transmission control module. **1993–95**—Troubleshooting tips are offered concerning excessive brake noise. **1994–95**—Poor AC performance is likely due to defective compressor suction or discharge lines. **1995**—Transmission limp-in may be caused by an intermittent transaxle input speed-sensor signal.

Acclaim/Spirit, LeBaron Profile

	1989	1990	1991	1992	1993	1994	1995
Cost Price ($)							
Acclaim/Spirit	11,489	12,418	12,852	13,343	13,455	14,154	14,828
LeBaron Sedan	13,256	14,561	16,915	15,253	15,594	17,226	—
Convertible	18,956	18,816	19,160	18,631	19,569	18,239	18,709
Used Values ($)							
Acclaim/Spirit ↑	3,000	3,500	4,000	4,500	5,500	6,000	7,000
Acclaim/Spirit ↓	2,500	3,000	3,500	4,000	5,000	5,500	6,500
LeBaron Sedan ↑	4,000	4,500	5,500	6,000	7,000	8,000	—
LeBaron Sedan ↓	3,000	4,000	5,000	5,500	6,000	7,000	—

Convertible ↑	5,000	6,000	6,500	7,000	7,500	8,000	8,500
Convertible ↓	4,500	5,000	6,000	6,500	7,000	7,500	8,000
Extended Warranty	Y	Y	Y	Y	Y	Y	Y
Secret Warranty	N	N	Y	Y	Y	Y	Y
Reliability	②	③	③	③	③	③	④
Air conditioning	①	①	②	②	②	③	③
Body integrity	①	①	②	②	②	②	②
Braking system	①	①	②	②	②	②	②
Electrical system	②	②	②	②	③	③	③
Engines	②	②	③	③	④	④	④
Exhaust/Converter	③	②	②	④	⑤	⑤	⑤
Fuel system	②	②	③	③	③	④	⑤
Ignition system	②	③	③	④	④	④	④
Manual transmission	—	—	—	—	—	—	—
- automatic	②	②	②	②	②	②	③
Rust/Paint	①	①	②	②	②	②	②
Steering	②	③	③	⑤	⑤	⑤	⑤
Suspension	②	②	③	③	③	④	⑤
Crash Safety							
Acclaim/Spirit	—	—	③	③	③	④	④

Breeze, Cirrus/Stratus

Rating: Below Average (1995–98). Stay away from any model carrying the anemic and failure-prone 4-cylinder engine. Also, be prepared to experience a number of nasty safety-related failures such as blown engine head gaskets, airbags that don't deploy, sudden acceleration, and loss of braking. **Maintenance/Repair costs:** Higher than average, but repairs aren't dealer dependent. **Parts:** Higher-than-average cost (independent suppliers sell for much less), but they are not hard to find. Nevertheless, don't even think about buying any one of these cars without a three- to five-year supplementary warranty.

Strengths and weaknesses: Roomy and stylish, well appointed, comfortable, and smooth, the Chrysler Cirrus and Dodge Stratus are mid-sized sedan replacements for the LeBaron. The Breeze, launched as a 1996 model, is essentially a "decontented" version of the more expensive Cirrus.

Most components have been used for some time on other Chrysler models, particularly the Neon subcompact and Avenger/Sebring sports coupes. Power is supplied by one of three engines: a 2.0L 4-cylinder engine, shared with the Neon; a 2.4L 4-banger; or the recommended optional 2.5L V6. Carrying Chrysler's "cab-forward" design a step further up the evolutionary ladder, these cars have short rear decks, low noses, and massive sloping grilles. A wheelbase that's two inches longer than the Ford Taurus makes these cars comfortable for five occupants, with wide door openings and plenty of trunk space.

These cars aren't all that impressive, either from a performance or a quality control standpoint. Furthermore, owners have serious misgivings as to whether these vehicles can withstand a harsh climate. One radio producer relates the following "adventure" with his 1995 Cirrus:

> ...As I left a shopping mall parking lot, I heard a slight "pop." I instantly lost power steering. I had it towed to Triple Seven. They diagnosed the same problem that the university professor had: it appears Chrysler engineers made the sender hose from the power steering pump too long. In our severe climate, the line freezes, contracts, starves the power steering pump, and sends it into coronary arrest. And the professor and I weren't alone. Two other Cirruses with the same problem were seen Saturday at this dealer alone. Probably, this model was collapsing in large numbers across the West this last week in our record-breaking low temperatures...

Other problems reported by owners include the following: excessive road noise and vibrations, chronic automatic transmission failures, early and frequent engine head gasket failures (no doubt part of the Neon engine legacy) and erratic engine operation, ABS malfunctions and sudden brake loss, paint delamination, electrical short circuits, weak headlights, AC glitches, water leaks into the trunk area and interior, easy-to-break trim items, lots of squeaks and rattles, and poorly located head restraints.

Dealer service bulletins: All models: 1995—Inoperative AC system. • Misaligned windshield washer nozzles. • Faulty deck-lid and door latches. • Rattling exhaust system crossover pipes. • Faulty radios. **1996**—Won't start due to faulty neutral safety switch. • Single cylinder misfire. • Cold engine sag or rough idle. • A number of transmission problems and upgrades, including intermittent control module failures; reduced transmission limp-in default sensitivity; changes to lockup control system; and an upgraded Overdrive clutch hub. • Difficulty going into second gear or Reverse after a cold start. • Shuddering during upshifts or when torque converter is engaged. • Steering noise on right turns. • Vehicle drifts or leads at high speeds. • Cowl plenum leaks water. • Inoperable door glass. • Erratic windshield wiper delay intervals. • Exhaust cover pipe rattle, buzz, and moan. • Ratcheting sound when coming to a stop. • Headlight pattern improvement. • Interior window film buildup. **1997**—Troubleshooting tips are available for poor AC performance. • The powertrain "bumps" when AC engages. • The CD changer rattles. • A low frequency rumbling sound can come from the front of the car while highway cruising. • Transmission shudders. **1998**—Excessive cold crank time, start die-out or weak run-up. • Poor driveability with high-test fuel. • Delayed transaxle engagement. • Clunking or rattling steering wheel/column. • Cold-start power steering noise. • Intermittent front end popping noise. • Low-frequency front end rumble. • Inoperative right headlight high beam. • Seat adjuster rises when seat is unoccupied. • Broken or loose antenna mount.

Safety summary/Recalls: All models: 1995–96—Frequent reports of engine fires. • Chronic engine oil leaks and oil galley plug failures. • Repeated engine head gasket failures, some resulting in engine compartment fires. • Timing belt failure after recall correction. • Chronic stalling or loss of engine power blamed on timing belt tensioner and pulley failure. • Engine sometimes loses power, then quickly accelerates. At other times, while at highway speeds, vehicle won't slow down when foot is taken off the gas pedal; instead, it speeds up. • Engine warning light often alight for no reason. • Reports of sudden acceleration in Drive and Reverse. • Owner claims that sudden acceleration is caused by a design flaw in cable to throttle body. • Airbags often fail to deploy. • Frequent ABS brake failures and prematurely worn rotors, calipers, and pads. • Rear brake failures also reported. • Faulty master cylinders are the cause of some early brake failures. • Floormat can catch the steering shaft clamp and jam the steering column assembly, causing the steering to lock up. • While driving off the freeway at 60 mph, steering tie-rod came apart, resulting in complete steering loss. • Steering components worn out prematurely. • Main computer failed seven times. • Oxygen sensor prone to early failure and fluid leakage. • Alternator burned out. • Child was able to take parked vehicle out of gear without applying brake. • Vehicle jumped out of third gear. • Defective electrical switch causes transmission to stick in second gear. • Sudden transmission lockup. • Transmission won't engage or upshift to third or fourth gear. • Leaking transmission front pump seal. • Prematurely worn strut links and wheel bearings. • Heat is unevenly distributed, causing front and rear passengers to be cold. • Heater failures. • Defogger doesn't adequately defrost windshield. • AC fails to cool interior unless vehicle is traveling at high speed. • AC failures. • Dash reflection into windshield hampers view. • Inadequate headlight illumination. • Windshield wipers don't run fast enough to clear windshield in a heavy downpour. • Rear brake lights and brake switch failure. • Sloping hood design creates poor visibility for parking. • Fuel tank gauge indicates empty when tank is half full. • Trunk lid closes on its own; this gave one owner a mild concussion. • Plastic on seatbelt clinch bar is self-destructing. • Seatbacks collapsed when vehicle was rear-ended. • Seat frame and anchor broke as driver sat down. • Power window motor failures. • Door locks work intermittently. • Binding door hinges make for difficult closing. • Door handle design pinches fingers. • Key sticks in the ignition when vehicle is shut off. • Weak front speakers prevent radio balance. **1997**—Engine compartment fire ignited while car was parked in garage. • Reports of sudden

acceleration in Drive and Reverse. • Chronic stalling at highway speeds.
• Vehicle rolled away while parked with shifter in Park position and keys
pulled from ignition. • Shifter came off in hand when shifting. •
Airbags fail to deploy. • Floormat can catch the steering shaft clamp
and jam the steering column assembly, causing the steering to lock up.
• Frequent engine head gasket failures. • When the head gasket blew,
one driver believes it overheated the transmission causing it to lock up.
• It's common for the engine timing belt idler pulley to fail and damage the timing belt. • Sudden brake and power-steering loss. • Brake
pads and rotors fail prematurely. • Noisy brakes. • AC emits odor and
white flakes through ventilation system, causing headaches, burning
sensation, and congestion. • Noise coming from the high-pressure
power-steering line. • Missing part causes seatbelt to twist. • Seat buckle
design is too short, causing difficulty in latching. • Driver-side shoulder
belt failed to restrain driver in a collision. • Starter short caused fuse to
blow. • Fuel sender for dash gauge often defective. • Inoperative power
door lock motor. **1998**—Airbag exploded rather than inflated. •
Airbags fail to deploy. • Frequent complaints of ABS brake failures; ABS
brakes failed five times on one owner despite dealer attempts to correct
the problem. • There is excessive brake noise whenever brakes are
applied. • Floormat jammed the steering column assembly causing the
steering to lock up. • Automatic transmission (floor console design)
throw from Drive to Reverse to Park is too long, resulting in consumer
thinking vehicle is in Park when it's really in Reverse. • Floor shift indicator
on the dash doesn't give a true reading of which gear is engaged. • Gear
shift lever can be moved into Drive without putting foot on brakes to
engage the transmission/brake interlock system. • High trunk lid makes
it impossible to see directly behind the vehicle. **Recalls: All models:
1995–96**—Rusting in the ABS unit could cause the car to jerk to one
side when stopping. **1995–97**—Dealers may replace, free of charge, prematurely corroded ball joint components. **1996–97**—The hood could
fly up. **Breeze: 1996–97**—An engine oil leak correction will, hopefully,
eliminate fire hazard in the 2.4L engine. • Faulty ignition switches, console shifter, and cables may cause the vehicle to roll away or render the
ignition-park interlock system inoperative. **Cirrus, Stratus: 1995**—
Following an NHTSA lawsuit, Chrysler has been ordered to replace the
rear seatbelt anchor belts. **1995–98**—Faulty ignition switches, console
shifter, and cables may cause the vehicle to roll away or render the
ignition-park interlock system inoperative.

Secret Warranties/Service Tips

All models/years—Anecdotal reports confirm Chrysler has a 7-year/
100,000 mile secret warranty covering engine head gasket failures. **All
models: 1995–96**—Water leaks into the passenger compartment from
behind the door trim panel. Correct the leakage by installing new door
panel clips, door watershields, and additional tape to seal the watershield.
• Front brake lining wears prematurely (see DSB #05-01-96). **1995–97**—

Troubleshooting tips are available to correct poor AC performance. • A powertrain "bump" when the AC engages is normal, according to Chrysler. • Transmission shudder could be caused by using the wrong transmission fluid. **1995–99**—Chrysler will replace faulty 4-cylinder engine head gaskets free of charge. **1997**—Send a rattling CD changer back to the factory. • A low-frequency rumble heard while at highway cruising speed can be silenced by replacing the front hub bearing assemblies. **1997–98**—Excessive cold crank time, start die-out, or weak run-up may be corrected by replacing the powertrain control module (PCM) under warranty, according to DSB #18-18-98.

Breeze, Cirrus/Stratus Profile

	1995	1996	1997	1998
Cost Price ($)				
Breeze	—	15,650	16,380	16,260
Cirrus	17,970	18,895	18,570	19,995
Stratus	15,230	15,820	16,545	16,425
Used Values ($)				
Breeze ↑	—	9,500	11,500	13,000
Breeze ↓	—	8,500	10,000	11,500
Cirrus ↑	11,000	13,000	15,000	16,500
Cirrus ↓	9,500	12,500	14,000	15,000
Stratus ↑	8,500	10,000	12,500	13,500
Stratus ↓	7,000	9,000	11,200	12,500
Extended Warranty	Y	Y	Y	Y
Secret Warranty	Y	Y	Y	Y
Reliability	❷	❷	❷	③
Crash Safety	③	③	③	③
Side Impact	—	—	③	③

FORD

Contour/Mystique

Rating: Average (1996–98); Below Average (1995). Mazda's 626 is a worthwhile alternative to the Contour and Mystique. It's a more stylish, highway-proven sedan with a better-than-average warranty and excellent parts supply, and it's been powered by a 2.0L and 2.5L V6 for the past several years. If you absolutely must have a Contour or a Mystique, choose the much-improved (better seating, upgraded mechanicals) 1996 or a later version. For the latest reports on problems look at the Contour website listed in the Appendix. **Maintenance/Repair costs:** Higher than average. Most repairs are dealer dependent. **Parts:** Higher-than-average cost, and sometimes hard to find.

Strengths and weaknesses: These front-drive, mid-sized twin sedans (Contour has a more angular nose and different dashboard) are based on the European-designed Mondeo, which has met with respectable sales after many years on the market. The four-door, five-passenger Contour sells for a bit less than its practically identical Mercury counterpart.

The main advantages of the Contour and Mystique are exceptional handling and a powerful, limited-maintenance V6 engine. Their drawbacks are an unacceptably high base price; cramped rear seating; a wimpy, noisy 4-banger; and spotty quality control that is most evident with the electrical system, brakes, and poor body assembly.

Both vehicles are set on a wheelbase slightly larger than that of the Taurus and come with a choice of two engines and transmissions: a base 16-valve 125-hp 2.0L 4-cylinder or an optional 24-valve 170-hp 2.5L V6. Either engine may be hooked to a standard 5-speed transaxle or an optional 4-speed automatic. A smooth but firm ride and crisp handling are guaranteed by the standard MacPherson-strut front suspension, an anti-roll bar, and fully independent rear suspension. Other interesting standard features include dual airbags, adjustable head restraints, 60/40 split-fold rear seats, rear heater ducts, and a sophisticated air filtration system for the passenger compartment. Four-wheel disc brakes, a sport-tuned suspension, and high performance tires are standard features on the V6.

These cars have had lots of first-year problems. Owners report frequent computer module failures and a long wait for parts. One CompuServe member had the following to say:

> My '95 Mystique ran fine for six months, but has been in the dealer repair shop—still not fixed—for three weeks now. First the "over-lock" froze, so you couldn't shift out of Park—even with a foot on the brake. The dealer said an "electrical short circuit kept making a module fail." They told me the part was part of a recall that had not yet been announced. No sooner had they fixed that when the Overdrive on-off button on the automatic gearshift stopped working. That's still not fixed after 11 working days. First the dealer claimed they couldn't "locate the cause." They sent the car out to a transmission expert who found another "failed module." The current problem is that the replacement part is "much in demand," and they're "trying to locate one."

Dealer service bulletins: All models: 1995—Fluid leaking from the transaxle pump seal. • Reduced power due to throttle plate icing. • Reduced steering assist during wet weather. • Insufficient AC cooling or excessive clutch end gap. • Delayed transmission engagement and shift errors, or no forward engagement or third gear. • Brake roughness upon application. • PCV tube wear-through. • Excessive vibration upon acceleration. • Noise upon hard acceleration or when turning. • Faulty speedometer. • Stuck fuel-filler door. • Water dripping on floor.

1996—Stalling or hard starts. • Grinding or clashing noise when shifting into third gear. • CD4E transaxle vent right-hand differential leak. • Fluid seeping from CD4E transaxle vent. • CD4E transaxle makes a whistle noise when in Park. • Harsh ride or rubbing noise from rear of vehicle. • Inoperative fuel-filler door. • Fog/film on windshield/interior glass. • Musty and mildew-type odors. • Water dripping on floor from AC condensation leak. • Vehicles with 2.5L engines exhibit a squealing noise from water pump. • Stall or hooting noise from engine compartment. **1997**—Air blows out the defroster ducts only. • AC has a musty odor. • Transaxle fluid seepage. • Harsh transmission shifting. • Chirping or squeaking blower motor. • Fog/film on windshield/interior glass. • Front-end accessory drivebelt slippage. • Parking brakes stick or bind. • Poor carpet fit. • Tips on preventing brake vibration. • Wind noise around doors. • Stall, hooting, or moosing noise from engine compartment. • Stall and/or exhaust sulfur smell.

Safety summary/Recalls: NHTSA has opened an official probe into front-suspension coil spring failures on the 1995 Contour, and headlight switch failures on 1996 models. **Recalls: All models: 1995**—The rear door window will be replaced. • The addition of a ground strap prevents an electrostatic charge from building up and igniting fuel vapors when refueling. • The hardware that attaches the outboard ends of the front seatbelts to the front seat frames may be cracked or fractured. • The passenger airbag may not inflate properly. • The fuel-filler pipe opening reinforcement may leak fuel. Tank replacement includes a new fuel filter and a *free fillup!* The last item in the recall procedure involves filling up the tank (at Ford's expense) in order to confirm that there are no leaks at the tank-to-filler-neck seal. **1995–96**—Faulty traction control throttle cables may prevent the engine from returning to idle. **1996–97**—Natural gas–equipped vehicles may explode in a collision. **1996–98**—The floor shift indicator may give an incorrect reading.

Secret Warranties/Service Tips

All models: 1995–97—Stall and/or exhaust sulfur smell requires a revised power control module. • Stall, hooting, or moosing noise from engine compartment can be fixed by replacing the air intake duct, idle air resonator, and idle air hose with a revised duct and resonator assembly (#F6RZ-9B659-CA). **1995–98**—Air that blows out the defroster ducts only may signal that the defrost actuator door linkage has become disconnected from the crank. • Transaxle fluid seepage can be corrected by servicing with a remote vent kit or by replacing the main control cover. • Parking brakes that stick or bind need a parking brake cable service kit. • Front-end accessory drivebelt slippage can be corrected by installing an upgraded FEAD belt, steel idler pulley, and splash shield kit.

Contour/Mystique Profile

	1995	1996	1997	1998
Cost Price ($)				
Contour GL	15,470	15,980	16,020	17,305
SE V6	18,355	18,865	19,350	19,475
Used Values ($)				
Contour GL ↑	8,000	9,000	10,500	12,000
Contour GL ↓	7,000	8,500	9,500	11,500
SE V6 ↑	9,000	11,000	12,000	13,500
SE V6 ↓	8,000	10,000	11,000	12,500

Note: The Mystique's MSRP was $6,000–$8,000 higher than the Contour, but their resale values are practically the same.

Extended Warranty	Y	Y	Y	Y
Secret Warranty	Y	Y	Y	Y
Reliability	❷	③	③	④
Crash Safety	⑤	⑤	⑤	⑤
Side Impact	—	—	③	③

Sable/Taurus

Rating: Average (1998); Not Recommended (1986–97). An extended powertrain warranty is a prerequisite for any Sable or Taurus. The SHO (Super High Output) version of the Taurus has fewer powertrain defects; however, it shares most of the other generic problems common to the Sable and Taurus.

Sables and Tauruses are aging badly. Serious 3.8L engine head gasket failures, automatic transmission failures, and chronic paint/rust problems are the main reasons the rating has been downgraded this year. I've recommended these cars in the past because Chrysler's and GM's defects were more serious and more frequent. Plus, Ford had set up a number of effective "goodwill" programs to compensate owners for powertrain failures once the warranty had expired. Unfortunately, much of that "goodwill" dried up during the past several years, prompting my meeting with Ford officials early this year to re-prime the "goodwill" pump. I am encouraged by Ford's commitment to me that it will be more generous in settling customers' extra-warranty complaints (see details below); however, I'll maintain my cautious ratings of the Sable and Taurus until I'm convinced all Ford owners are being treated fairly—not just *Lemon-Aid* readers, or owners whose names I pass onto the company. **Maintenance/Repair costs:** Higher than average, but repairs aren't dealer dependent. **Parts:** Average cost (independent suppliers sell for much less) and very easy to find, except for the SHO's Yamaha engine, which is practically indestructible anyhow.

Strengths and weaknesses: Although they lack pickup with the standard 4-cylinder engine, these mid-sized sedans are competent family cars, offering lots of interior room, nice handling, and plenty of safety and convenience features. The best combination of high performance engine and transmission for all driving conditions: the 3.8L V6 hooked to a 4-speed for the family sedan, and the Yamaha powerplant harnessed to a manual gearbox on the high performance SHO.

SHO

The Taurus SHO sedan, debuting in 1989, carries a Yamaha 24-valve 3.0L V6 with 220 horsepower; a stiff, performance-oriented suspension; and 5-speed manual transmission. As of 1993, a 4-speed automatic transmission became available. In mid-1996, a redesigned SHO debuted with a standard Yamaha 32-valve V8. Unfortunately, the manual transmission was dropped at that time, a move that has turned off most die-hard performance enthusiasts.

The SHO is an impressive high-performance car that is apparently better built than regular-production Sable and Taurus versions. In fact, early SHOs escaped Ford's powertrain problems because of their reliance upon Yamaha for their engines and the wide use of a manual gearbox.

Is the SHO a good buy? The answer is yes, but only if you're willing to spend big bucks for your performance thrills. SHOs hold their value well and give impressive performance. On the other hand, they're hard to find (only 10,000 units a year are sold, and only three percent of Taurus buyers opt for an SHO), they're expensive, and engine repairs may become a problem if Ford abandons the model. The SHO's price is likely to remain stable, or even drop somewhat, inasmuch as most buyers feel the vehicle is already overpriced and they are becoming increasingly wary of Ford's reputation for poor quality control.

Reliability in steep decline

Since 1986, Sables and Tauruses (joined by the Lincoln Continental in 1991) have been the object of multiple safety-related recalls, secret warranties, and service adjustments. They've distinguished themselves for being unsafe, unreliable, and costly to maintain and repair (see "Dead Ford" and "Ford Taurus, Sable Automatic Transmission Victims" website links in the Appendix). Their deficiencies fall into the following major categories: powertrain (engines and transmissions), brakes, fuel and air conditioning system, and body.

Automatic transmission failures

Ford's automatic transmissions have always been failure-prone, function erratically, and are slow to shift—an annoying drawback if you need to rock the car out of a snowbank, and fairly dangerous if you need to pull out onto a busy roadway. These problems are caused principally by a cracked aluminum forward clutch piston, although dozens of other causes, including major hardware and software components, have been linked to the above failures. Breakdowns usually occur after three years of use, around the 60,000–80,000 mile mark, and can cost $2,500–$3,500 to repair at the dealer, or half that much at an independent garage.

When Ford modified the automatic transmission in 1991 for easier shifting, it also made it less reliable (Chrysler had a similar experience with its A604 automatic transmission). In fact, *Consumer Reports*' annual member survey shows that almost 20 percent of owners of 1991 Tauruses, Sables, and Continentals experienced a serious transmission failure—four times the average for 1991 vehicles. Ford subsequently extended the warranty on these transmissions for up to six years under a special Owner Notification Program (ONP). Although it's too late for a full refund for 1991–92 models, you should strive for a satisfactory pro rata adjustment; if not successful, challenge Ford's refusal before the small claims court. Obviously 1993 and later models should be eligible for 100 percent repair reimbursements.

Why are we so hard on Ford? Two reasons. First, the automaker has routinely denied that it considers the normal life span for an automatic transmission to be at least 6 years/100,000 miles, judging by Ford's original 1991 ONP parameters. Second, the company's own internal bulletins shout out the fact that Ford has known about the transmission's premature failures and erratic shifting since 1986! Yet the company kept using the cheaper, though failure-prone, aluminum forward clutch piston—which has been principally responsible for the above failures—for over a decade.

Let's take a look at what Ford's bulletins disclose, as background and as arguing points with Ford or in your small claims filing:

Detroit, We Have a Problem! (1986–95)

Article No
94-24-7
11/28/94
TRANSAXLE - AXOD, AXOD-E, AX4S - FORWARD/REVERSE ENGAGEMENT CONCERN - REVISED FORWARD CLUTCH PISTON
FORD:
1986-95 TAURUS
1993-95 TAURUS SHO
LINCOLN-MERCURY:
1986-95 SABLE
1988-94 CONTINENTAL
LIGHT TRUCK:
1995 WINDSTAR
ISSUE:
The forward clutch piston may crack on its outside diameter, seal groove or apply wall (bottom of piston). This condition could allow internal clutch leakage resulting in engagement concerns.
STEEL CLUTCH PISTON PART APPLICATIONS
F4DZ-7A262-A   F4DZ-7A262-B
3.0L TAURUS
3.0L SABLE
3.8L TAURUS
3.8L SABLE
3.8L CONTINENTAL
3.8L WINDSTAR   3.2L TAURUS SHO
ACTION:
Use the chart for proper application if replacement of the forward clutch piston is necessary.
NOTE:
PREVIOUS TSB ARTICLES 91-5-7, 92-1-4, 92-26A-6 AND 93-9-11 SHOULD NOT BE USED DUE TO REVISED PARTS LISTED IN THIS ISSUE.
Use a magnet to verify the forward clutch piston being installed is the new steel piston. The magnet will adhere to the steel piston and not to the aluminum piston.
Do not use any service stock of aluminum forward clutch pistons. Return stock to parts depot for credit.

PART NUMBER	PART NAME	CLASS
F4DZ-7A262-A	Forward Clutch Piston	A
F4DZ-7A262-B	Forward Clutch Piston (SHO)	C

SUPERCEDES: 91-5-7, 92-1-4, 92-26A-6, 93-9-11

This first bulletin updates others going back several years and lists 1986–95 as the model years affected. Note how Ford clearly blames the aluminum piston as the culprit causing what the automaker understates as "engagement concerns."

Surprise! Upgraded Steel Piston Fails, Too (1994–98)

Article No.
98-3-7
02/16/98
TRANSAXLE - AX4N - INTERMITTENT NEUTRAL CONDITION - NO FORWARD OR REVERSE MOVEMENT - VEHICLES BUILT
THROUGH 2/1/98
FORD:
1994-98 TAURUS
LINCOLN-MERCURY:
1994-98 SABLE
1995-98 CONTINENTAL

ISSUE:
Some vehicles may experience an intermittent Neutral condition after driving and coming to a stop. This may be caused by
the bonded seal on the forward clutch piston intermittently not sealing during the 3-2 downshift.
ACTION:
Replace the forward clutch piston with a revised Forward Clutch Piston (F8DZ-7A262-AB). Refer to the following Service
Procedure for details.
SERVICE PROCEDURE
Clean and reseal the transaxle completely including replacement of the forward clutch piston with revised forward clutch pis-
ton and replace the forward clutch plates if darkened or discolored from heat. Refer to the appropriate Continental Service
Manual, Section 07-01, or the appropriate Taurus/Sable Service Manual, Section 07-01B, for details.
Be sure to check end clearance on all three (3) select fit thrust washers (# 16, # 8, 1.02-1.50 mm (0.040-0.059")). Be sure
to clean and inspect the main control (pump and valve body) and servos. Prior to returning vehicle to customer recheck fluid
level at operating temperature.

PART NUMBER	PART NAME
F5DZJ153-AA	Seal And Gasket kit
F8DZ-7A262-AB	Forward Clutch Piston
F8DZ-7B164-AC	Forward Clutch Plates - Friction (4)
F2DZ-7B442-A	Forward Clutch Plates - Steel (4)

Apparently, the move to a steel piston didn't make Ford's transmissions
more reliable or durable, as the above bulletin clearly demonstrates. Hence,
my ratings downgrade Ford's latest models.

3.8L engine failures

Ford's other major powertrain problem is the 3.8L engine's chronic
head gasket failures. Symptoms include engine overheating; poor
engine performance; and a thin film deposited on the inside of the
windshield, thus cutting down night driving visibility. Repairs range
$700–$1,000, depending upon what other damage has occurred from
overheating. Left untreated, the failure can "cook" your engine, requiring $3,000–$4,000 in repairs.

There have been hundreds of cases reported to me of head gasket
failures after three to five years or 45,000 miles of use. Although these
engine repairs are covered by Ford's 98M01 "goodwill" engine warranty
up to five years or 60,000 miles (see page 78 for Ford's ONP letter),
many Sable, Taurus, and Windstar owners have had their claims
rejected because their vehicles fell outside of the 1994–95 limit set out
in the above warranty extension. This makes no sense whatsoever, especially since Ford's own bulletin (see following) traces the problem back
to the 1988 models and through to 1996.

3.8L V6 Engines Blow Their Tops (1988–96)

Article No.
98-4-9
03/02/98
COOLING SYSTEM - OVERHEATING AND/OR LOSS OF COOLANT - 3.8L VEHICLES
FORD:
1988-96 TAURUS
LINCOLN-MERCURY:
1988-94 CONTINENTAL
1988-95 SABLE
LIGHT TRUCK:
1996 WINDSTAR
ISSUE:
Coolant may leak from the head gaskets and/or the vehicle may overheat. There may also be concerns of reduced heater output due to low coolant levels. This may be caused by insufficient sealing of the head gaskets.
ACTION:
Replace the head gaskets and head bolts. The revised head gaskets and bolts provide improved sealing capability and higher clamping force between the cylinder head and block. Refer to the following Service Procedure for details.

PART NUMBER	PART NAME
F5PZ-6051-AA	Head Gasket And Bolt Kit (One Side)

OTHER APPLICABLE ARTICLES: 91-1-8, 94-10-10
WARRANTY STATUS: Eligible Under The Provisions Of Bumper To Bumper Warranty Coverage

OPERATION	DESCRIPTION	TIME
980409A	Verify Coolant Loss	0.3 Hr.
980409B	Replace Cylinder Head Gaskets - Taurus/Sable	8.0 Hrs.
980409C	Replace Cylinder Head Gaskets - Windstar	6.8 Hrs.
980409D	Replace Cylinder Head Gaskets - Continental	8.0 Hrs.

DEALER CODING

BASIC PART NO.	CONDITION CODE
6051	68

OASIS CODES: 208000, 402000, 490000, 499000

Interestingly, the above head gasket failures have also been reported with 3.8L V6 engines equipping Ford's Mustang through 1998.

Paint delamination

Over the past decade, there have been frequent complaints of paint delamination, peeling, and premature rusting. One owner of a 1990 Sable found pinpoint rust spots during the first year of ownership and had the entire car repainted at Ford's expense. Unfortunately, the problem didn't go away. The owner reports the following:

> I have recently noticed continued paint defects causing the car to rust prematurely, specifically under the front edge of the hood…I maintain that the sealer and paint were improperly applied when the car was manufactured and that this is a defect that the Ford Motor Company should correct.

That *Lemon-Aid* reader is right, and that's why Ford is the target of multiple class action paint lawsuits and is settling most small claims court cases, although more class actions may still be imminent.

Ford's warranty performance
In December of 1998, I advised Ford that its handling of owners' complaints was unsatisfactory and requested a meeting with officials to extend the warranty on powertrain problems and improve its customer claims handling procedures.

November 9, 1998

Bobbie Gaunt
President and CEO
Ford Motor Company of Canada Limited
The Canadian Road
Oakville, Ontario
L6J 5E4

Dear Ms. Gaunt,

I am very much concerned over the frequent complaints I have received from Ford Taurus, Sable, and Windstar owners relative to the premature failure of their 3.8L V6 engines and chronic automatic transmission malfunctions.

Having monitored these problems over the past several years and given your company the benefit of the doubt in recommending the above-mentioned vehicles in my *Lemon-Aid* guides, I was convinced your customers would be compensated and the vehicles would be fixed through service campaigns.

Unfortunately, this does not appear to be the case. On the contrary, it appears Ford has taken an unusual hard-line approach.

A perusal of Ford service bulletins and owner complaints show expensive automatic transmission breakdowns (often due to a defective aluminum forward piston, used throughout your entire model lineup since 1985) and engine headgasket failures are still quite common. Furthermore, the 98M01 5-year customer service campaign for 3.8L engines, announced last June, following my first airing of this problem, doesn't compensate owners who fall outside of the program's restrictive model-year parameters ('94 and '95 owners, only), even though your own internal service bulletins show the failures date back to 1988!

As a former Member of Parliament responsible for consumer issues, and thirty-year Canadian consumer advocate, I appeal to your sense of fairness and ask that you extend the warranty retroactively to cover the above transmission and engine defects 100%, up to seven years, without a mileage or prior ownership limitation.

There are many precedents at Ford where similar retroactive compensation has been given to owners. Over two decades ago, I first asked your predecessor, Roy Bennett, to compensate owners for thousands of rust-cankered Fords. Following the formation of Rusty Ford Owners Associations in every province, he agreed, complaints subsided, and Ford gained market share.

I am hopeful we can resolve this issue, as well.

My only regret is that many of the Ford staffers I've enjoyed working with in the past, like Larry Johnson in Service and Tony Fredo in Public Relations, have now retired.

What a sense of timing.

Awaiting your earliest, convenient reply,

Phil Edmonston, *Lemon-Aid*
lemonaid@earthlink.net

After receiving the above letter, Ford officials quickly set into motion a series of meetings between staff and me that culminated, three months later, in the company accepting previously rejected claims, upgrading its customer assistance efforts, and extending on a case-by-case basis the warranty relating to Taurus, Sable, and Windstar engine and transmission failures.

Following a series of meetings subsequent to my letter, most all of my original 75 complaints submitted to Ford were settled. As I see it, Ford is presently paying 50–75 percent on claims that go back to the 1993 models and haven't run up more than 100,000 miles. Other claimants who have been rejected a second time are using the small claims courts and Ford's bulletins in order to get more substantial refunds.

Ford has an uphill battle in its attempts to improve customer assistance because it contracts it out to independent companies, whereas a company like Chrysler, with its own owner assistance staffers, can act and react more quickly. Although Ford has just announced a reorganization to make its customer assistance more accessible, I fear that little will change until the automaker improves its powertrain quality control, empowers customer assistance center (CAC) staffers and dealers to give out more substantial after-warranty assistance, and spends the dough to get competent CAC staffers who have a modicum of automotive knowledge and care about Ford's reputation with its customers.

As always, I'll continue monitoring Ford's customer assistance activities throughout the year, and invite readers to use *www.lemonaidcars.com* for the latest updates and the Appendix to link up with websites specifically oriented toward Ford transmission, head gasket, Windstar, and warranty servicing deficiencies.

In the meantime, anyone seeking assistance should call Ford's toll-free number, found in the Owner's Manual. I have been assured each owner will have his or her claim thoroughly reviewed. I hope this will be the case; however, keep in mind what one Ford customer assistance whistleblower told me recently:

...Ford has just received a J. D. Power report that shows giving out goodwill refunds for repairs doesn't improve car sales. Since then, the company has taken a harder line in reviewing customer claims. THE ONLY THING THAT GETS OUR ATTENTION IS IF A SMALL CLAIMS LAWSUIT IS THREATENED OR HAS BEEN FILED. These we are told to settle right away...

Other problems

The 4-cylinder engine is a dog that no amount of servicing can change. It's slow, noisy, prone to stalling and surging, and actually consumes more gas than the V6.

The 3.0L 6-cylinder is noted for engine head bolt failures and piston scuffing, and is characterized by hard starting, stalling, excessive engine noise, and poor fuel economy. Transmission cooler lines leak and often lead to the unnecessary repair or replacement of the transmission—note the advice given to this vacationing owner of a 1993 Taurus:

...

While in Florida a month ago the local Ford dealer plugged a tester in our car and announced that our problem with the transmission could only be fixed by a new one—at an estimated $2,800 US. Another garage checked the colour of the transmission fluid and came to the same conclusion...a new transmission, but the estimate was lower, about $1,800 US. They added oil which temporarily fixed the problem. On our long drive home, towing a boat, we kept the fluid level topped up.

On arrival, we visited our local CTC station in Port Hope [Ontario], and discovered that a transmission cooling line had been leaking. The two mechanics who listened while I described the problem, immediately guessed what it would likely be. It turns out they have seen a lot these rusted lines on Fords. The fix cost $150, because the radiator had to be removed to get at the line. In fairness to the mechanics in Florida, perhaps this rusting problem is limited to climates where salt is used on roads.

...

Other things to look out for: blown heater hoses, malfunctioning fuel gauge sending units, and brakes that need constant attention—in front, they're noisy, pulsate excessively, tend to wear out prematurely, require a great deal of pedal effort, and are hard to modulate. Master cylinders need replacing around 60,000 miles.

Although these sedans and wagons were redesigned in 1992, quality wasn't improved that much. In fact, only the latest 1996 redesign seems to have tackled some of the cars' quality shortcomings. Owners are keeping their fingers crossed though, because the reduction in quality complaints may simply be caused by the vehicles' low mileage.

1988–95 models continue to have defective ignition modules, oxygen sensors, and fuel pumps, causing rough running, chronic stalling, hard starting, and electrical system short circuits. Other problem areas include the following: defective engine mounts; an automatic transmission that is slow to downshift, hunts for Overdrive, and gives jerky performance; air conditioners that are failure-prone and can cost up to $1,000 to fix; malfunctioning heaters that are slow to warm up and don't direct enough heat to the floor (particularly on the passenger side); a defective heater core that costs big bills to replace (buy from an independent supplier); and noisy, prematurely worn rack-and-pinion steering assemblies. Front suspension components also wear out quickly.

Electrical components, like windshield wipers, fuel pumps, and the rear defroster, interfere with radio reception. The automatic antenna often sticks, electric windows short-circuit, power door locks fail, and the electronic dash gives inaccurate readings. Owners report that electrical short circuits—which illuminate the Check Engine light and cause flickering lights and engine surging—are frequently misdiagnosed. Customers end up paying for the unnecessary replacement of the alternator, voltage regulator, or battery, in addition to unnecessary tune-ups. The speedometer is noisy and often inaccurate in cold weather.

Body/trim items are fragile on all cars (did somebody mention door handles?). Paint adherence is particularly poor on plastic components, weld joints, and the underside—even with mudguards. Owners also report that water leaks into the trunk through the taillight assembly and that 1986–95 versions produce an annoying sound of fuel sloshing when accelerating or stopping.

1996–98 models were radically redesigned with a totally new, more rounded styling that turned off as many buyers as it turned on. Other changes included upgraded engines, new electronic controls for the LX, and a revamped, oval dash panel. Other improvements: better handling and ride quality, more effective soundproofing, and some transmission refinements (beginning with the 1997 models, but ineffective). Despite these changes, owners still report serious safety-related deficiencies (see "Safety summary/Recalls") and other performance-related problems, like the non-upgraded engines being noisy, slow and hard to start; the automatic transmission shifting erratically, or not at all; engine head gaskets still failing; and an assortment of rattles, buzzes, whines, and moans (see following 1998 model bulletin summary).

DSB SUMMARY
1998 FORD TAURUS/SABLE

1. JUN-98	A/C-FILTERING REFRIGERANT AFTER COMPRESSOR REPLACEMENT
2. JUN-98	A/C-IDENTIFYING NON-FORD APPROVED REFRIGERANTS
3. MAY-98	A/C-NO TEMPERATURE CONTROL
4. MAR-98	A/T, BLUE SERVICE TAGGED TRANSAXLES, AX4S
5. JUL-98	A/T-FLUSHING OIL COOLER AND LINES-SERVICE TIP
6. MAY-98	A/T-NO 4TH GEAR AND TROUBLE CODES STORED, AX4N
7. MAR-98	A/T-TORQUE CONVERTER CLUTCH NOT ENGAGING/CODES STORED
8. OCT-98	ADHESIVE BONDING NOT RECOMMENDED FOR BODY PANEL REPAIR
9. APR-98	AUTOMATIC TRANSMISSION FLUID USAGE CHARTS
10. FEB-98	AX4S/AX4N NEW TRANSAXLE FLUID
11. SEP-98	BODY-SOLVENTS REMOVE SAFETY CERTIFICATION LABEL PRINT
12. MAR-98	BRAKE HUB-MOUNT ROTOR MACHINING EQUIPMENT
13. SEP-98	BRAKES-FRONT DISC BRAKE ROTOR PROTECTOR REMOVAL
14. AUG-98	BUMPER-REMOVAL OF TRANSEAL PROTECTIVE COATING
15. OCT-98	BUZZ/RATTLE NOISE-LOOSE CATALYST OR MUFFLER HEAT SHIELD
16. MAR-98	COOLING SYSTEM CONCERNS, 3.0L GASOLINE/ETHANOL
17. AUG-98	EVAPORATIVE EMISSION CANISTER COMPONENTS AVAILABILITY
18. MAY-98	FUEL INJECTORS, NON-WARRANTY REIMBURSEMENT TESTING
19. JAN-98	FUEL PUMP REPLACEMENT PROCEDURE
20. OCT-98	HARD START/LONG CRANK TIME, 3.0L, 3.4L
21. FEB-98	INTERMITTENT NEUTRAL CONDITION, NO FORWARD/REVERSE, AX4N
22. SEP-98	LOCKS-REPLACE/REPAIR LOCK COMPONENTS-INDIVIDUAL LOCKS
23. JUL-98	MOANING NOISE FROM POWER STEERING DURING IDLE, 3.0L, 4V
24. SEP-98	NO START/NO CRANK-BATTERY DISCHARGED/CURRENT DRAIN
25. APR-98	OIL LEAKS-NEW SILICONE GASKET AND SEALANT
26. MAR-98	PAINT ANTI-CHIP STONE ABRASION UNDERCOAT SERVICE TIP
27. SEP-98	PAINT MATERIALS FOR AFTER WARRANTY AND WARRANTY REPAIRS
28. SEP-98	PASSIVE ANTI-THEFT SYSTEM (PATS)-DIAGNOSTIC SERVICE TIPS
29. DEC-97	PROPER DOOR PANEL REMOVAL PROCEDURE-SERVICE TIP
30. DEC-97	RATTLING NOISE DURING ACCELERATION, 3.0L
31. FEB-98	REPAIRS TO VINYL COVERED SURFACES-SERVICE TIP
32. SEP-98	SEAT-LEATHER CLEANING PROCEDURE-SERVICE TIP
33. SEP-98	STEERING WHEEL NIBBLE FELT WHEN DRIVING AT 45 AND 75 MPH
34. FEB-98	SURFACE DEFECT REMOVAL WITHOUT REPAINTING-SERVICE TIP
35. MAR-98	TIRE COMPANY TELEPHONE NUMBERS - CUSTOMER ASSISTANCE
36. DEC-97	TROUBLE CODES P0442, P0455-NO DRIVEABILITY CONCERNS
37. APR-98	WHINING/BUZZING NOISE THROUGH RADIO SPEAKER
38. SEP-98	WINDNOISE AROUND SIDE DOORS-SERVICE TIP
39. JUN-98	WIRE HARNESS TERMINAL REPAIR AND WIRE SPLICE KIT

Dealer service bulletins: All models: 1992–95—Hesitation, no-start, reduced power, stalling, no-crank due to solenoid corrosion. **1993**— Poorly performing air conditioning systems caused by a slipping clutch at high ambient temperatures. • Growling AC FX-15 compressor. • Fuel odors in the passenger compartment. • Noisy power-steering units. • Inoperative power door locks. • Under-hood squeaks, chirps, and knocks; wind noise coming from front door windows. • Intermittent long cranks or no-starts. • A service engine light that has a mind of its own and may go on for no apparent reason. **1994**—A faulty 3.8L engine rocker arm assembly may be the cause of squeaking, chirping, and knocking noises. • A rough idle, hesitation, and excessive fuel consumption. • Defective fuel pumps often produce extraneous noise in radio speakers. • Faulty electric rear window defrosters. • Inadequate AC operation caused by a faulty cold engine lockout switch and hose assembly. **1995**—Delayed transmission engagement and shift errors, harsh shifts, no 3–4 shift, erratic shifts, Forward/Reverse gear malfunctions, and transaxle click when in Reverse. • Insufficient AC cooling or excessive clutch end gap; AC compressor has moans, chirps, or squeaks coming from the blower motor at low speeds. • Fuel pump buzz/whine heard through the radio speaker. • Faulty temperature gauge. • No-crank caused by a corroded starter solenoid (carried over several model years). • Brake roughness upon application and a clacking/thumping noise when braking. • Premature inner-edge wear on the rear tires. • A fuel tank sloshing noise. **1996**—No-start or stall. • Stall or hard start after one- to four-hour soak • Cold engine hesitation/stumble. • Harsh automatic transmission shifting. • Click from transmission when going into Reverse. • Transaxle driveline noises. • Case breakage at rear planet support. • Grunt or groan noise during steering wheel return. • Reduction in power-steering assist. • Door hinge correction. • Fog/film on windshield/interior glass. • Musty and mildewy odors. • Dead battery diagnosis. • Blower motor noise. • Acceleration or deceleration clunk noise. • Wind noise at A-pillar at highway speeds. • A-pillar creaking noise. • Front suspension creak/groan. • Hard starting, long crank, stalling. • Rear headliner sag. • Door handle malfunctions. • High idle, surge, stall, harsh transmission engagement. • Loose catalyst or muffler heat shields. • Click noise when going into Reverse. • AM radio static. • Warm-weather stalling. • Thump, clunk, or chuckle noise from front end. • Troubleshooting driveline noises. • Water leaks onto passenger compartment floor. • Excessive wind noise. **1997**—Harsh automatic shifting. • Chronic dead battery. • Excessive blower motor noise. • Acceleration or deceleration clunk. • Front suspension clunk. • A-pillar creaking noise. • Front end accessory drive belt (FEAD) may slip during wet conditions, causing a reduction in steering power assist. • Steering wheel grunt or honk noise. • Loose catalyst or heat shields. • AM band radio static. • Stall or surging with automatic transmission engagement. • Water leaks onto passenger floor area.

Safety summary/Recalls: All models: 1993—Front coil springs may fracture causing the suspension to collapse. • Windshield wiper failures. **1995**—Sudden windshield shattering. • AC failures. • Headlight failures. **1995–96**—Fuel pump failures. • ABS failures. • Airbag fails to deploy or is accidentally deployed. • Transmission slips out of Park. • Sudden acceleration. • Stalling. • Engine compartment fires. • Defective door locks. **1996**—Chronic stalling. • Sudden acceleration. • Cruise control won't slow vehicle on slopes. • Left front wheel may separate from car. • Frequent ABS brake failures. • Airbag failed to deploy. • Inadvertent airbag deployment. • Loss of steering when it rains. • Loss of power steering. • Frequent engine head gasket failures. • Transmission fails or shifts erratically. • Dash reflects into the windshield. • Faulty door lock switch. • Defective heating/defrosting system causes excessive windshield fogging. **1997**— Sudden acceleration. • Chronic stalling. • Transmission jumps from Park to Reverse. • Sudden steering loss. • Wheels fly off. • Frequent ABS brake failures. • Several engine head gasket failures. • Chronic transmission failures. **1998**—Accelerator and brake pedals are too close to each other. • Vehicle won't slow when accelerator pedal is released. • Faulty cruise control won't slow vehicle down. • Automatic transmission malfunctions. • Chronic brake failures. • Defective rotor and wiring assembly caused ABS failure. • Loss of steering when steering belt pulley and pump failed. • Defective rack and pinion steering spring yoke. • Sudden steering lockup. • Trunk lid fell on owner's head due to defective torsion bar. • Trunk light burned garment in the trunk. • Faulty headlights. • Headlights don't give enough light to the sides. • Daylight running lights flicker due to defective module. • Dashboard reflects in the windshield, causing reduced visibility. • Heater system failed. • Driver's seatbelt won't retract or lock into position. • Hatchback window suddenly exploded while vehicle was parked. **1999**—Frequent complaints of sudden acceleration or high idle. • ABS brakes locked up when applied and vehicle suddenly accelerated. • Front passenger's seatbelt won't retract or lock into position. • Seatbelt broke. • No-start caused by fuel pump failure. • Faulty remote keyless entry. • Defective windshield wiper motor. • In the morning and evening, the light tan dashboard reflects upon the windshield, causing reduced visibility. **Recalls: All models: 1986**—Ignition key can be removed when the ignition switch isn't locked. • Faulty cooling fan motor resistor may cause the air conditioner to malfunction. • Misrouted battery wire may lead to premature radiator leakage. • The right-quarter tinted window on wagons was improperly tempered. **1986–87**—Rear windows may break suddenly. • A faulty spring-lock fuel line coupling is a fire hazard. **1986–91**—The front brake rotors may snap as a result of corrosion. **1986–92**—The rear storage compartment is a hazard to children because it can't be opened from the inside. Owners should deactivate the slam-down latching mechanism with a screwdriver and then get a dealer to install a replacement mechanism. **1986–93**—Vehicles may have detached body mounts at the rear corners of the car's subframe.

This defect could allow the subframe to drop and make steering difficult. The mounts will be inspected and a reinforcement plate installed with new attaching bolts. **1987**—Lower steering shaft may separate. • A defective rear spindle assembly could separate and cause loss of vehicle control. **1988**—The air conditioner compressor shaft seal is faulty in the 3.0L models. • The power-steering pump pulley may fail, causing loss of power steering and other accessories. **1988–89**—A misrouted power seat switch could cause an electrical fire. **1988–90**—Engine mount failure could lead to engine surges, a stuck throttle, or power-steering hose failures. **1989–90**—End release seatbelt buckles may not latch properly. **1991–95**—Cruise control units and throttle control cable are faulty. **1992**—The inner tie-rod may collapse suddenly. The son of a West Coast owner of a 1992 Taurus relates this incident:

> The right inner tie-rod, a piece of the suspension critical to the steering and thus safety of my 1992 Taurus, broke while my father was attempting to make a right turn from a stop sign. The car lost all steering control and the front wheels were seized. Fortunately, the car was barely moving, and no collision occurred...I can tolerate a radio or AC failure on a "medium aged" car but critical safety components should have a longer service life designed into them. I hope you can inform all Taurus/Sable owners of the inherent dangers lurking in their steering system. And for those cars still under warranty, specify that the part be thoroughly inspected by first removing the rubber protecting boot...

1992—Children could lock themselves in the footwell area or storage area of wagons. • The wagon liftgate could open while the vehicle is in motion. **1992–95**—The engine cooling fan may freeze and cause the cooling fan motor to overheat, in turn causing wiring damage and sparking a fire (3.0L and 3.8L engines only). • The throttle can stick and not return to idle if water enters the throttle cable area and freezes (3.8L engines only). **1993**—The following is not a safety problem in accordance with U.S. Federal Regulation 573; however, it is deemed a safety improvement campaign by the NHTSA. Ford is providing an extended warranty through the year 2001 for replacement of front springs due to fracture. The front coil springs can fracture as a result of corrosion in combination with small cracks in the springs. The front tire could deflate due to a broken front coil spring contacting the tire, increasing the risk of a vehicle crash. Dealers will install a spring catcher bracket that will prevent a fractured spring from contacting a tire. Owners can contact Ford at 1-800-392-3673. **1993**—Rear-drive controllers in models with ABS were installed in error. **1995**—Brake master cylinder may be defective. **1996**—Although apparently in Park, the vehicle can roll away. • The brake fluid indicator may malfunction. • Fuel may leak from a faulty fuel pressure regulator. • The brake system fluid level indicator lamp switch may be faulty. **1996–98**—Dealers will replace the dash insulator retainer clip so it doesn't interfere with the accelerator cable or pedal. **1998**—On vehicles equipped with manual seat tracks, the front seatbelt buckle attaching stud may be defective. **SHO: 1996**—Faulty fuel pressure regulator could cause a fire. **Sable, Taurus: 1986–95**—Subframe engine and transmission mounts could fail due to excessive corrosion that could cause the subframe to drop and make steering difficult. **1996–97**—The transmission may not engage. • PRNDL may give a false reading, allowing vehicle to move although it appears to be in Park. • Defective fuel rail may deliver fuel to the injectors at more than 43 psi; it may cause chronic stalling under low-speed deceleration or acceleration. • Transmission fluid leakage could cause a fire. **1998–99**—Dealers will replace the seatbelt buckle mounting bracket and stud assembly on models with manual seats.

Secret Warranties/Service Tips

All models/years—A rotten-egg odor coming from the exhaust probably means that you have a faulty catalytic converter; replacement may be covered under the emissions warranty. • Vehicles equipped with 3.0L engines where piston scuffing is evident (hard starting, stalling, excessive engine noise, poor fuel economy) may be eligible for free engine repairs or replacement on a case-by-case basis. On other engines, Ford has been repairing premature engine head gasket, ring, and valve wear for free when the emissions warranty applies. • Two other components that frequently benefit from Ford "goodwill" warranty extensions are fuel pumps and computer modules. If Ford balks at refunding your money, apply the emissions warranty for a full or partial refund. • Paint delamination, fading, peeling, hazing, and "microchecking" are also candidates for secret warranty compensation (see page 113 for details on claiming a refund). **All models: 1986–89**—If the accessories frequently cut out, install a new ignition switch wire harness. **1986–90**—Extended or no 3–4 shift may require a reassembled direct clutch piston and spring retainer. • No-shifts, harsh shifts, or extended shifts may be due to faulty oil pump body and valve body check balls. • AC evaporator water leaks onto the carpet require a new core and seal assembly (#E9DZ-19860-A). • Poor AM radio reception may be caused by interference from the heated windshield system. **1986–91**—Poor forward shifting may require a new clutch piston. • Engine knocking at idle may require the installation of a new, thicker thrust plate to reduce camshaft end play. **1986–92**—A buzz or rattle from the exhaust system may be caused by a loose heat shield catalyst. **1986–94**—A squeak or chirp coming from the blower motor can be stopped by installing an upgraded blower motor with improved brush-to-commutator friction. • A rear suspension clunk or rattle when a wagon goes over a bump may be caused by a loose rear tension strut. • A speaker whine or buzz caused by the fuel pump can be stopped by installing an electronic noise RFI filter. **1986–95**—A cracked forward clutch piston may cause Forward/Reverse problems. Install the improved clutch piston and ask Ford to cover part of the cost inasmuch as their bulletins confirm it's a design defect. • Premature wear on the inner edges of the rear tires calls for the installation of Ford's rear suspension adjustable camber kit. **1988–92**—Cold hesitation when accelerating, rough idle, long crank times, and stalling may all signal the need to clean out excessive intake valve deposits. **1989–93**—A persistent fuel odor in the interior when the AC is running signals the need to install a new auxiliary vapor-tube service kit and relocate the vapor tube near the rear bumper. **1990–93**—Noise coming from the power-steering pump may be caused by air in the system; purge the system. **1991–93**—Growling from the FX-15 AC compressor can be eliminated by installing a new compressor rubber damped disc and hub assembly. **1991–95**—A sloshing noise from the fuel tank when accelerating or stopping requires the installation of an upgraded tank. Cost may be covered under the emissions warranty. **1992**—A 3.0L engine that stalls or idles roughly after a cold start may require a new EEC IV processor. **1992–95**—A corroded solenoid may be the cause of starter failures. **1993**—Free replacement through the year 2001 of front coil springs that fracture or may fracture due to excessive corrosion (see "Safety summary/Recalls"). **1993–94**—An inoperative AC blower probably needs an improved cold engine lockout switch and hose assembly. • Stalling or hard starts in high ambient temperatures or high altitudes may be due to fuel tank contamination, which causes damage to the fuel pump. Ford paid for a fuel tank flush and a new fuel pump/sender and in-line fuel filter until May 31, 1997, under Service Program 94B48. **1993–97**—If the front end accessory drive belt (FEAD) slips during wet conditions, it can cause a reduction in steering power assist; Ford suggests the belt be replaced. **1994–95**—A thumping or clanking noise heard from the front brakes signals the need to service the front disc brake rotors. **1994–98**—Forward clutch piston returns as the most likely suspect in malfunctioning automatic transmissions. **1996–97**—An acceleration or deceleration clunk is likely caused by the rear lower subframe isolators allowing movement between the mounts and the subframe. • A front suspension clunk may signal premature sway bar wear. • Harsh automatic 1–2 shifting may be caused by a malfunctioning electronic pressure control or the main control valves sticking in the valve body (see following).

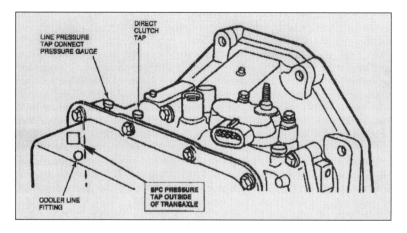

1996–98—Water leaking onto the passenger floor area is likely caused by insufficient sealing of the cabin air filter to the cowl inlet. **1997**—Stalling or surging of 3.0L engines when shifting may signal the need to reprogram the power control module (PCM).

Sable/Taurus Profile

	1991	1992	1993	1994	1995	1996	1997	1998
Cost Price ($)								
L/G/LX	16,075	17,164	19,825	19,825	20,290	18,545	19,000	19,255
GL	16,595	17,619	18,840	18,280	18,295	19,390	19,780	—
GL/SE Wagon	16,986	18,195	18,840	19,360	19,390	20,470	20,995	21,655
SHO	22,551	24,262	25,960	25,240	26,465	27,800	28,220	29,470
Used Values ($)								
L/G/LX ↑	6,000	6,500	7,500	8,500	10,000	10,500	12,000	14,500
L/G/LX ↓	5,500	5,500	7,000	8,000	9,000	9,000	10,500	13,500
GL ↑	5,500	6,000	7,000	8,500	10,500	11,000	13,000	—
GL ↓	5,000	5,500	6,500	7,500	10,000	10,500	11,500	—
GL/SE Wagon ↑	6,000	6,500	7,500	9,000	10,500	12,000	14,000	17,000
GL/SE Wagon ↓	5,500	6,000	7,000	8,500	9,500	11,000	13,000	16,000
SHO ↑	6,000	7,000	8,500	10,000	11,500	14,500	16,500	18,500
SHO ↓	5,500	6,500	8,000	9,500	11,000	13,500	15,500	17,500
Extended Warranty	Y	Y	Y	Y	Y	Y	Y	Y
Secret Warranty	Y	Y	Y	Y	Y	Y	Y	Y
Reliability	❶	❶	❷	❷	❷	❷	❷	③
Air conditioning	❶	❶	❶	❷	❷	③	③	③
Automatic transmission	❶	❶	❷	❷	❷	❷	❷	③
Body integrity	❷	❷	❷	❷	❷	❷	③	③
Braking system	❷	❷	❷	❷	❷	❷	❷	③
Engines	❷	❷	❷	❷	❷	❷	❷	③
Exhaust/Converter	❷	❷	❷	❷	③	③	③	④
Fuel system	❷	❷	❷	❷	❷	❷	③	③
Ignition system	③	③	③	③	③	③	④	④
Rust/Paint	❷	❷	❷	❷	❷	❷	❷	③
Steering	❷	❷	❷	❷	③	③	③	④
Suspension	❷	❷	❷	③	④	⑤	⑤	⑤
Crash Safety	④	④	④	④	④	④	④	④
Side Impact	—	—	—	—	—	—	③	③

Tempo/Topaz

Rating: Not Recommended (1985–94). Be wary of the all-wheel drive's low price—it's no bargain at any price. The V6 is the powerplant of choice, but it's found only on 1992 and later versions. In 1994, these cars were replaced by the 1995 Contour and Mystique. **Maintenance/Repair costs:** Higher than average. Repairs aren't dealer dependent, but troubleshooting usually costs an arm and a leg. **Parts:** Higher-than-average cost, but can be bought for much less from independent suppliers.

Strengths and weaknesses: This front-drive compact's strong points are its attractive, rounded styling; smooth, quiet V6, which works well with the automatic gearbox; and a roomy interior. On the downside, these cars are underpowered with the base 2.3L 4-cylinder engine, fuel-thirsty when coupled with an automatic transmission, and failure-prone. They are riddled with design and manufacturing bugs. The engine, transmission, electrical systems, electronic modules, fuel pump, power steering, suspension components, and cruise control all tend to fail prematurely. The 2.0L Mazda diesel engine is unreliable and doesn't deliver traditional diesel durability.

The 2.3L gas engine isn't much better. Cylinder head gaskets tend to leak and the engine's cooling, fuel, and ignition systems are plagued by a multitude of breakdowns.

For all models, stalling and hard starting are often caused by a malfunctioning catalytic converter. If the car still won't start, mechanics advise owners to tap the solenoid switch behind the battery. The starter motor is weak and the oil pan gasket tends to leak. There are many complaints of prematurely worn front axles and leaking seals. The air conditioning fails frequently and is expensive to repair. Heater noise often signals the need to change the heater motor. Power-steering rack seals deteriorate quickly. Suspension components, such as tie-rod ends and strut bearings, need replacement almost annually. Shocks, for example, last barely 20,000 miles. Front brakes wear out almost as quickly, and rotors are easily damaged. Even though these cars have been dropped, parts are plentiful; but they cost more than the North American average.

Body components are substandard and poorly assembled on all models and all years, with peeling paint and premature rusting being the main offenders. The front door seal tears every time the seatbelt doesn't retract properly, the car's air dam often works loose, and the hood cable-release mechanism tends to jam. Radio reception is mediocre.

Safety summary/Recalls: **All models: 1991–94**—Engine cooling fan motor may overheat and catch fire. • Owners report that their cars' chronic stalling places them constantly at risk. One owner of a 1991 Tempo says:

> The car will stall in all weather conditions and in all driving conditions. The engine failure is most apparent when decelerating or stopping after exiting from highways. The car frequently, and dangerously, stalls in the midst of left-hand turns. There is absolutely no warning. The car engine dies and there is occasionally some difficulty re-igniting the engine.

Other owners report the opposite problem with their 1993 Topaz— the car may suddenly accelerate. **Recalls: All models: 1985**—Rear-suspension control-arm bolts may fail. • 2.3L engine stalling, hesitation, and hard starting is due to a faulty ignition module. **1985–86**—Manual shift lever may accidentally slip into Neutral gear. **1986**—Sudden acceleration on cars with 2.3L engines may be due to a defective electronic control module. **1987**—Again, a faulty 2.3L engine electronic control module may cause high idling, loss of power, and stalling. **1988**—Faulty throttle sensor could cause unintended acceleration. **1988–93**—The ignition switch could experience an internal short circuit, creating the potential for overheating, smoke, and possibly fire in the steering column area of the vehicle. **1989–94**—Cars with 2.3L engines may suffer a frozen PCV system when operated at sustained highway speeds for extended periods in extremely cold weather. • Oil forced out through the dipstick tube or past some other gasket or seal area of the engine could pose a fire hazard. **1990**—Fan motor could overheat and cause engine damage. **1992–94**—Engine cooling-fan motor may overheat and cause a fire. **Tempo: 1987**—Stainless-steel lug nuts may cause stud failure/wheel separation.

Secret Warranties/Service Tips

All models/years—If the transmission seems erratic in shifting from second to third gear, or downshifting from third to second, a newly designed governor spring will have to be installed. • A rotten-egg odor coming from the exhaust is the result of a malfunctioning catalytic converter. • Three components that frequently benefit from Ford "goodwill" warranty extensions are catalytic converters, fuel pumps, and computer modules. If Ford balks at refunding your money, apply the emissions warranty for a full or partial refund. Regarding paint delamination, fading, peeling, hazing, and "microchecking," see page 113 for details on claiming a refund. **All models: 1983–90**—Buzzing or humming coming from the fuel pump when the engine is shut off, a low battery, and hard starts or no-starts signal the need to install an upgraded fuel pump relay (#F19Z-9345-A). **1984–88**—2.3L engines with Duraspark II ignition may have starting problems; correct with a new module (#D9UZ-12A199-A). • Hard starting/stalling is caused by defective TFI modules that link the vehicle's distributor to its microprocessor and signal the plugs. • Coolant and oil leaks that plague 2.3L and 2.5L HSC engines can be stopped by installing an improved cylinder head gasket (#E83Z-6051-A). **1985–94**—An exhaust buzz or rattle can be fixed by installing new clamps to secure the heat shield attachments. • The in-tank fuel pump is the likely cause of all that radio static you hear; squelch the noise by installing an electronic noise RFI filter (#F1PZ-18B925-A). **1986–94**—Ford offers an upgraded wiper motor service kit for wiper motor malfunctions. **1987–94**—Loss of Reverse gear in cold weather may be due to defective inner and outer Reverse clutch piston seals. • A rusty catalytic converter inlet pipe flange may be replaced free of charge with a stainless-steel flange under the emissions warranty. **1989–90**—Owner Notification #B90: Cooling fans on AC may loosen; replace with upgraded fan (#F03Z-8600-B). **1990**—Loss of AC cooling may be due to a cracked spring lock connector. Put in a new discharge manifold and discharge hose. **1990–93**—Noise heard from the power-steering pump may be caused by air in the system. **1992–93**—An inoperative air conditioner may be due to a faulty cooling fan relay (#E93Z-8Z658-A). **1992–94**—If the idle speed fluctuates excessively in cold weather, you may need to change the power-train control module (PCM).

	Tempo/Topaz Profile							
	1987	1988	1989	1990	1991	1992	1993	1994
Cost Price ($)								
GL	9,813	10,311	10,785	11,293	11,376	11,808	11,599	12,065
LX	10,974	11,390	11,884	12,415	12,498	12,936	13,605	13,350
Used Values ($)								
GL ↑	1,500	2,000	2,500	3,000	3,500	4,000	4,500	5,500
GL ↓	1,200	1,700	2,000	2,500	3,000	3,500	4,000	4,500
LX ↑	2,000	2,500	3,000	3,500	4,000	4,500	5,000	6,000
LX ↓	1,600	2,000	2,500	3,000	3,500	4,000	4,500	5,000
Extended Warranty	Y	Y	Y	Y	Y	Y	Y	Y
Secret Warranty	N	N	N	Y	Y	Y	Y	Y
Reliability	①	①	①	①	②	②	②	②
Air conditioning	①	②	②	②	②	②	②	②
Body integrity	②	②	②	②	②	②	③	③
Braking system	①	①	②	②	②	②	②	②
Electrical system	②	②	①	①	②	②	②	②
Engines	①	①	①	①	②	②	③	③
Exhaust/Converter	①	①	②	②	②	③	③	③
Fuel system	①	①	①	①	②	②	②	②
Ignition system	①	①	①	②	②	②	③	③
Manual transmission	④	④	④	④	④	④	⑤	⑤
- automatic	②	②	②	②	②	③	③	③
Rust/Paint	①	②	②	②	②	③	③	④
Steering	①	①	②	②	③	③	③	③
Suspension	①	①	①	①	②	②	②	③
Crash Safety	—	—	—	—	—	—	④	④

GENERAL MOTORS

6000, Century, Ciera

Rating: Below Average (1998); Not Recommended (1982–97). The same failure-prone components have been used year after year. The 1996 Century isn't in the same league as the revised 1997 version. The 1997 Century moved over to the W platform that also serves the Chevrolet Lumina, Pontiac Grand Prix, and 1998 Oldsmobile Intrigue. You'll probably find a cheaper 1996 Ciera, but you won't have the important mechanical and body upgrades offered by its 1997 replacement, the Oldsmobile Cutlass, a new mid-sized sedan similar to the new Malibu. Be careful not to confuse the new Cutlass with the Cutlass

Supreme, a 10-year-old model that was replaced by the Intrigue, which is equipped like the Century. **Maintenance/Repair costs:** Higher than average, but repairs aren't dealer dependent. **Parts:** Higher-than-average cost (independent suppliers sell for much less), but not hard to find. Nevertheless, don't even think about buying one of these front-drives without a three- to five-year supplementary warranty.

Strengths and weaknesses: The A-body line, long a mainstay in GM's family sedan market, has disappeared. This is good news, because these cars are outclassed by the competition and are in desperate need of high-quality components and fresher styling. Overall quality has improved somewhat since the introduction of these cars in 1982, but with the arrival of the Ford Taurus in 1986 and better-quality Japanese imports, these derivatives of the X-bodies aren't really in the running.

Nevertheless, these cars were consistently popular with fleet buyers and car rental agencies because they were useful as comfortable family sedans and wagons. Handling and other aspects of road performance varied considerably depending on the suspension and powertrain chosen.

1988–96 models are particularly unreliable. The 2.5L 4-cylinder engine suffers from engine-block cracking and a host of other serious defects. The 2.8L V6 engine hasn't been durable either; it suffers from premature camshaft wear and leaky gaskets and seals, especially the intake manifold gasket. The 3-speed automatic transmission is weak and the 4-speed automatic frequently malfunctions. Temperamental and expensive-to-replace fuel systems (including the in-tank fuel pump) afflict all models/years, causing chronic stalling, hard starting, and poor fuel economy (use the emissions warranty to get compensation). Fuel system diagnosis and repair for the 3.0L V6 are difficult, and the electronic controls are often defective. Air conditioners frequently malfunction and the cooling system is prone to leaks.

Prematurely worn power-steering assemblies are particularly commonplace. Brakes are weak and need frequent attention due to premature wear and dangerously rapid corrosion, front brake rotors warp easily, excessive pulsation is common, and rear brake drums often lock up. Shock absorbers and springs wear out quickly. Rear wheel alignment should be checked often. Electric door locks frequently malfunction. Premature and extensive surface rust—due to poor paint application, delamination, and defective materials—is common for all years. Far more disturbing are scattered reports of severe undercarriage/suspension rusting, possibly making the vehicles unsafe to drive and costing lots of money to correct, as the owner of a 1990 Century relates:

Recently I was doing an oil change on my car and I noticed a small divot in the engine cradle (or sub frame). I poked at it and put my finger right through it! I discovered that the cradle was rotted on both sides near the idler arm. The car is only 8 years old and has only 112,000 km [75,000 miles] on it. I have had it into two collision repair places and they both said they have never seen a rotted engine cradle. One man has been in the business 25 years!

The 1997 Century received a complete make-over that includes the following: gobs of room and trunk space (rivaling that of the Taurus, Concorde, Accord, and Camry); sleeker styling; a much quieter interior; and an upgraded, standard ABS system that produces minimal pedal pulsation. Engine noise was also reduced. Other new features include a starter that has an anti-grind feature in case you turn the key with the engine running, upgraded door seals, steering-wheel-mounted radio controls, and additional heating ducts for rear passengers. On the downside, you can get only the 160-hp 3.1L V6 engine; the new Century's speed-dependent power steering is too light and vague; and its suspension and handling are more tuned to comfort than performance.

Dealer service bulletins: All models: 1993—Converter seal leaks on 4T60E automatic transmissions (3.3L V6 engines only). • Loss of power. • Unexpected downshifts. • Defective cruise control. • Stalling when decelerating. • Extended cranking. • Faulty Reverse gear on 3T40 automatic transmissions;.additionally, the Century may experience brake drag and loss of power. **1994**—Fuel pumps may fail prematurely. • A front-end squeak may require the replacement of the exhaust manifold pipe springs with dampers. • Excessive noise or vibrations can be caused by defective rear transmission mounts. • Engine wiring harnesses could melt. • Exhaust moan. • Temperature gauges could give false readings. **1995**—The cruise control fails to engage. • Oil leaks at the rocker cover. • Grinding/growling when in Park on an incline. • Popping, banging, and rattling upon hard acceleration. • Engine tick/rattle upon cold start-up. • Cold-start stall, hesitation, and sag; cold rough idle. • Cold-start rattle with the 4T60E automatic transmission. • Brake vibration and/or pedal pulsation. • Low voltage reading or dim lights at idle. • Exhaust manifold seal squeaks and exhaust boom/moan at idle. • Loose windshield garnish molding. • Wind rush at top of doors. • Poor paint application and rust spots. **1996**—Second-gear starts; poor 1–3 shifting. • Vibration at high speeds. • Steering column noise. • Air conditioning odors. • Radio frequency interference diagnosis. **Century: 1997**—Air temperature from HVAC outlets doesn't change. • Rear brake clicking or squealing. • Door glass creaking noise. • Insufficient heater performance on passenger side floor area. • Intermittent Neutral/loss of Drive at highway speeds. • Loose airbag housing door on passenger side dash. • Low voltage reading/dim lights at idle. • Pop, groan, or moan from rear of vehicle. • Remote keyless entry range is shorter than expected. • Slow window operation. • Front brake squealing, grinding noise. • Wiper arms/blades park at incorrect positions.

Safety summary/Recalls: All models: 1996—Vehicle suddenly accelerated on its own. • Cruise control speed increases upon descending a hill. • Sudden brake loss. • Chronic stalling. • Oxygen sensor failures believed to be cause of stalling problems. • Steering radius is too large, and steering response is sluggish. • Dash reflection in windshield causes poor visibility. • Cannot read clock in daylight. • Airbag assembly on steering wheel blocks view of instrument panel. • Back windows often shatter. • Frequent battery failures. • Fuel pump failures. • Transmission failures; gear shift lever fell off in driver's hand. • Front door power motors failed. **1997**—Sudden brake loss. • Car moved forward when put into Reverse. • Battery exploded twice. • Poor design of magnetic variable steering results in difficult handling with vehicle swaying at 40 mph and struts contributing to instability. • Sway bar links failure. • Horn buttons difficult to access and depress due to their small size; must take eyes off the road. • Fuel tank warning system activates prematurely. • Dash reflection in windshield causes poor visibility. • Poor headlight design makes for poor visibility, as well. • Defroster system button breaks easily. • Windshield wipers fail frequently. • Defective airbag cover. • Power door lock failures. • Driver's seatbelt won't fully retract. **1998**—Airbags failed to deploy. • Idle surge after releasing brake due to faulty oxygen sensor. • Leaking lower intake manifold. • Engine oil pan leakage. • Chronic stalling. • Transmission shifts erratically. • Transmission hard to put into Reverse; faulty gear shift lever. • Sudden loss of electrical power. • Climate control switch failures. • Dash reflection on windshield causes poor visibility. • Excessive brake vibrations. • Headlights provide poor visibility. • Headlight switch failure. • Windshield wiper arm failures. • Water leaks into trunk. • Drivers report that the head restraints don't stay up. • Horn buttons hard to access in an emergency because of the airbag located directly under the horn and the radio control on the steering wheel. • Horn blows on its own when car is not running. **Recalls: All models: 1983–87**—The fuel system on the four-cylinder engine may leak fuel, creating a fire hazard. • Some wagons were recalled due to poor braking performance. **1985**—Throttle on V6 engines may stick open, causing sudden acceleration. • Misrouted clutch cable could cause fluid leakage from the brake master cylinder. **1986**—Defective headlight switch can cause headlights to flicker or fail. **1988**—GM will repair a leaking fuel feed hose on vehicles with 2.8L engines. • Dealer will inspect and repair the front suspension. • The lower arm bracket could develop cracks and cause the disengagement of the lower control arm, resulting in steering loss. **1990–91**—A short circuit in the six-way power seat or power recliner could set the seat on fire. **1992**—Automatic 4-speed transmissions were recalled because they performed poorly or remained in Reverse while the indicator showed Neutral. • Wagons may have erratically operating interior lights and suffer a sudden tailgate opening. **1993**—Dealers will install a redesigned intake manifold gasket at no charge on vehicles with rough-running 2.2L engines. • Right front brake hoses are defective. **6000: 1989–91**—Rear seat anchor bolts don't meet federal load standards. **Century: 1986**—Cars with 2.8L engines could suffer an under-hood fire due to misrouted wiring.

1994—Sudden acceleration may occur when the 3.1L primary accelerator spring binds. • Water leakage into the power door lock may cause a short-circuit fire. **Ciera: 1989–96**—Rear seat anchor bolts don't meet federal load standards.

Secret Warranties/Service Tips

All models/years—A rotten-egg odor coming from the exhaust is probably the result of a malfunctioning catalytic converter; replacement cost may be covered by the emissions warranty. • Low oil pressure in 3.8L V6 engines is likely caused by a failure-prone oil pump. A temporary remedy is to avoid low-viscosity oils and use 10W-40 in the winter and 20W-50 for summer driving. • THM 44C-T4 automatic transaxles with V6 engines are particularly failure-prone, due to pinched or kinked vacuum lines that cause oil starvation. • Paint delamination, peeling, or fading (see pages 73–75). **All models: 1984–90**—Frequent loss of Drive with 440-T4 transmissions is likely caused by a maladjusted 1–2 band stop unit. **1986–90**—Vehicles equipped with the 3T40 automatic transmission may experience slippage in manual Low or Reverse gears. Install service package #8628222, which includes a Low/Reverse clutch release spring (#8664961) and a clutch retainer and snap ring (#656/657). **1987–88**—Poor engine performance troubleshooting shortcuts are detailed in DSB #88-T-47B. **1987–90**—A rattle or buzz from the instrument panel may require a new, upgraded brake booster check valve (#18012017). **1989–93**—Vehicles equipped with a 3300 or 3800 engine that experience stalling upon deceleration or hard starts may need a new air control motor. **1990**—Door lock rods that fall off need an upgraded inside handle to lock the rod. **1994**—Loss of Drive or erratic shifts may be caused by an intermittent short to ground on the A or B shift solenoid or an electrical short circuit in the transaxle. • A front-end clunking noise when driving over rough roads may require the repositioning of the diagonal radiator support braces. **1994–95**—DSB #43-81-29 troubleshoots cruise controls that fail to engage. **1995–97**—Intermittent Neutral/loss of Drive at highway speeds can be fixed by replacing the control valve body assembly. **1997**—Rear brake clicking or squealing may be caused by a maladjusted park brake cable. • Insufficient heater performance on the passenger-side floor area can be fixed by installing a new I/P insulator panel and bracket. **Ciera: 1991–92**—Uncomfortable front seat shoulder belts will be replaced at no charge.

6000, Century, Ciera Profile

	1991	1992	1993	1994	1995	1996	1997	1998
Cost Price ($)								
6000	15,628	—	—	—	—	—	—	—
Century	15,798	16,337	16,627	17,325	19,171	18,235	18,590	19,185
Ciera S/SL	15,945	15,855	16,234	17,725	16,595	15,305	—	—
Used Values ($)								
6000 ↑	5,000	—	—	—	—	—	—	—
6000 ↓	4,000	—	—	—	—	—	—	—
Century ↑	5,200	6,700	7,700	8,700	10,000	11,500	16,500	17,500
Century ↓	4,500	5,600	6,500	7,500	9,000	10,000	14,500	16,500
Ciera S/SL ↑	4,500	6,000	7,000	8,000	8,500	9,500	—	—
Ciera S/SL ↓	4,000	5,000	6,000	7,500	8,000	9,000	—	—

Extended Warranty	Y	Y	Y	Y	Y	Y	Y	Y
Secret Warranty	Y	Y	Y	Y	Y	Y	Y	Y
Reliability	②	②	②	②	②	②	③	③
Air conditioning	②	②	②	②	③	③	③	③
Automatic transmission	②	②	②	②	②	②	②	③
Body integrity	①	①	①	①	①	②	②	②
Braking system	②	②	②	②	②	②	②	②
Electrical system	②	②	②	②	②	②	②	③
Engines	②	②	②	②	③	③	③	③
Exhaust/Converter	②	②	③	③	④	⑤	⑤	⑤
Fuel system	②	②	②	②	②	③	③	③
Ignition system	②	②	②	②	②	③	④	④
Rust/Paint	①	①	①	①	①	②	②	②
Steering	②	②	②	②	③	③	③	④
Suspension	②	②	②	②	②	②	③	④
Crash Safety								
Century 4d	④	④	④	④	④	④	—	—
Ciera	—	—	④	—	—	—	—	—
Side Impact								
Century 4d	—	—	—	—	—	—	—	③

Achieva/Grand Am, Calais, Skylark

Rating: Average (1995–98); Below Average (1988–94). The 1992 Achieva replaced the Calais; except for styling, this Achieva is practically identical to the others. There is little to recommend in these cars. More reliable, reasonably priced family haulers and sporty sedans are available from other domestic automakers, principally Ford. **Maintenance/Repair costs:** Higher than average. Repairs aren't dealer dependent. **Parts:** Higher-than-average cost, but can be bought for much less from independent suppliers.

Strengths and weaknesses: These cars come with a standard 150-hp Quad SOHC engine, a 5-speed transaxle, and ABS. The basic front-wheel drive platform continues to be a refined version of the Sunbird and Cavalier J-body. These cars are too cramped to be family sedans (rear entry/exit can be difficult), too sedate for sporty coupe status, and too ordinary for inclusion in the luxury car ranks.

In their basic form, these cars are unreliable, unspectacular, and provide barely adequate performance. An upgraded and more reliable 3.1L V6 powerplant gives you only 5 more horses than the base 4-banger. There's been a lot of hype about the Quad 4 16-valve engine, available with all models, but little of this translates into benefits for the average driver. A multi-valve motor produces more power than a standard engine, but always at higher rpms and with a fuel penalty and excess engine noise. The Quad 4 is rougher than most multi-valve engines when revved to cruising speed and so does little to encourage drivers to get the maximum power from it.

These cars ride and handle fairly well but share chassis components with the failure-prone J-bodies. This explains why engine, transmission, brake, and electronic problems are similar. Water leaks and body squeaks and rattles are so abundant that GM has published a six-page troubleshooting DSB that pinpoints the noises and lists fixes (see "Secret Warranties/Service Tips").

The 2.5L 4-cylinder engine doesn't provide much power and has a poor reliability record. Avoid the Quad 4 and 3.0L V6 engines with SFI (sequential fuel injection) because of their frequent breakdowns and difficult servicing. If you have a blown head gasket or other problems with the Quad 4 engine, keep in mind that GM has a 7-year/100,000 mile secret warranty covering its free repair or replacement; ask for a pro rata refund for the repair, even though the warranty coverage may have expired (see "Secret Warranties/Service Tips," again). Poor engine cooling and fuel system malfunctions are common; diagnosis and repair are more complicated than average, however. The engine computer on V6 models has a high failure rate, and the oil pressure switch often malfunctions. The electrical system is plagued by gremlins. Seals in the power-steering rack deteriorate rapidly. Front brake discs need more frequent replacement than average. Paint defects are common; consequently, surface rust may occur sooner than expected.

Dealer service bulletins: By the way, DSB #43-1007A gives an exhaustive review of all the possible causes and remedies for body squeaks and rattles afflicting 1992–95 models. **All models: 1993**—Achievas and other models equipped with 2.3L engines or 3.1L V6 engines won't continue running after a cold start. • The converter seal leaks on 4T60E automatic transmissions. • Front door windows may be hard to roll up and seal poorly. • Intermittent electrical problems. • Stalling when decelerating. • Hard starting. • Faulty Reverse gear on 3T40 automatic transmissions. • Rear brake squawk. **1994**—V6-equipped models may experience excessive second-gear vibration caused by a defective hub shaft bearing and sleeve assembly. • Loss of engine coolant likely caused by faulty surge tank caps. • Power steering may lead or pull. • A faulty automatic transmission fluid–level indicator could give false readings. • A poorly running 2.3L Quad 4 engine can often be traced to a moisture-contaminated or corroded ECM connector; correction requires the resealing of the engine harness pass-through. **1995**—Oil leaks at the rocker cover. • Engine tick/rattle on cold start-up. • Cold-start stall or tip-in hesitation. • Grinding/growling when in Park on an incline. • AC cut-off after an extended idle. • A cold-start rattle with the 4T60E automatic transmission. • Longer-life front brake linings. • Brake vibration and/or pedal pulsation. • Rear wheel brake drag.

• Inoperative washer pump. • A low voltage reading or dim lights at idle. • Check Oil/Check Gauges light flickers. • Water entering into spoiler (Grand Am). • Poor paint application and rust spots. • Right rear-quarter window wind noise and water leaks. • **1996**—Second-gear starts, poor 1–3 shifting. • Driveability problems, whistling noise, or reduced fuel economy. • Engine overheating/faulty cooling fan. • Excessive engine roll. • Air conditioning odors. • Front seatbelt webbing twists and won't retract. • Fuel-filler door won't open. • Radio frequency interference diagnosis. • Wind noise at front-door outer-belt sealing strip. • Water entering rear compartment at taillight area. • Water leaking into taillight harness. **1997**—Cold-start rattle noise is normal, according to GM, and no fix is planned. • Inoperative power door locks. • Noisy instrument panel. • Intermittent loss of Drive at highway speeds. • No-starts. • Engine popping noises. • Power window malfunctions. • Front suspension squawk noise.

Safety summary/Recalls: All models: 1995—Fire ignited in the engine compartment while vehicle was on the road. • Sudden acceleration due to weak pedal return spring. • Chronic stalling. • Airbag failed to deploy. • Malfunctioning airbag causes horn to suddenly go off. • Driver's seatbelt failed to restrain driver. • Frequent brake failures and extended stopping distance. • Power-steering fluid leak due to high pressure hose chaffing by the two fuel-injector tabs. • Brake caliper seizure damages pads and rotors. • Transmission jumps out of gear. • Shoulder belt rides across driver's neck. • Driver-side door handle popped out. • Erratic fuel gauge operation. • Headlights suddenly shut off. • Passenger seat not anchored securely. **1996**—Inadvertent airbag deployment. • Airbag failed to deploy. • Sudden acceleration and stalling. • When putting car in Reverse, it suddenly accelerated forward. • Left wheel came off after the stud that holds the wheel unbolted from the wheel. • Oxygen sensor failures cause Check Engine light to come on. • Frequent brake failures. • Excessive brake noise. • Defective master cylinder, drums, pads, and rotors. • Engine, transmission, and AC failures. • Seatbelt sticks into driver's side or will not fasten properly. • Insufficient insulation under steering column allows draft to come in under left lower dash area. • Headlight failure. • Water leaks into the trunk. • Cracking around the outside edge of all tires. • Passenger power door lock and window lock do not work properly. **1997**—Many reports of vehicle first losing power and then suddenly accelerating. • Accelerator cable snapped, causing pedal to go to the floor. • While vehicle was being driven, the hood suddenly flipped backwards, hitting the windshield. • Windshield reflection obstructs vision. • Premature brake replacements. • Seatbelt improperly fitted. • Design flaw allows wheels to rub against front fender. • Mirrors aren't adjustable enough to see other vehicles, and seatbacks are too high for some drivers to see over. • Driver-side bucket seat isn't anchored properly; rocks from side to side. • Intermittent windshield wiper failures. •

Headlights sometimes cut out. **1998**—Airbag failed to deploy. • Premature front brake pad wearout and warped rotors. • Seatbelts tend to twist. **Recalls: All models: 1985**—A faulty throttle return spring on 2.5L engines could lead to sudden acceleration. **1985–86**—The door pillar could crack. **1986–90**—Headlights could operate erratically. **1987**—The fuel feed or return hose could leak. **1991**—Power windows could short-circuit and remain in the down position or start an electrical fire. **1994**—Weak fuel tank welds could create a fire hazard in a rearend collision. **1996**—Front or rear hazard warning lights could be faulty. • The airbag could deploy behind the instrument panel. • A loose steering column bolt could cause loss of steering.

Secret Warranties/Service Tips

All models/years—A rotten-egg odor coming from the exhaust may be the result of a malfunctioning catalytic converter—possibly covered by the emissions warranty. Stand your ground if GM or the dealer claims you must pay. • Paint delamination, peeling, or fading (see pages 73–75). **All models: 1988–89**—Power loss in cold weather can be corrected by installing ventilation kit (#12339306). • A whistle or whine coming from the engine is likely caused by a noisy oil pump; replace it with an improved oil pump (#22538689). • The engine wiring harness may have been cut by constant rubbing on the alternator. This will cause a rough-running engine, inoperative air conditioner/alternator, the illumination of the Check Engine light, failure of the ECM module, and excessive white smoke (DSB #88-8-11). **1990–93**—2.3L Quad 4 engine is notoriously bad. Head gasket leaks are covered under GM's 7-year/100,000 mile secret warranty—oops, I mean Special Policy (see following document).

Dear (Buick/Oldsmobile/Pontiac) Owner:

As the owner of a 1992 or 1993 (Buick Skylark/Oldsmobile Achieva/Pontiac Grand Am) equipped with a 2.3L Quad OHC (RPO Code L40, VIN Engine Code 3) engine, your satisfaction with our product is of utmost concern to us. Your vehicle was provided with a new vehicle warranty which covers certain parts of your vehicle for a specified period. These warranties are of considerable value to you if you should experience problems with your vehicle.

Condition: This letter is intended to make you aware that some 1992 and 1993 (Buick Skylark/Oldsmobile Achieva/Pontiac Grand Am) models with 2.3L Quad OHC (RPO Code L40, VIN Engine Code 3) engines may develop a cracking condition of the cylinder head that allows coolant to leak from the cylinder head. Early evidence of this would be a loss of coolant in the coolant reservoir and coolant deposits on the exterior of the cylinder head. These may be combined with the odor of coolant from the engine compartment.

Action: (Buick/Oldsmobile/Pontiac) Division is therefore taking the following action: We are providing owners with special coverage. If the above mentioned condition occurs within seven (7) years of the date the vehicle was originally placed in service or 100,000 miles (160,000 km), whichever occurs first, the condition will be repaired for you at no charge.
This is not a recall campaign. Do not take your vehicle to your (Buick/Oldsmobile/Pontiac) Dealer/Retailer as a result of this letter unless you believe that your vehicle has the condition as described above.

Reimbursement: (Statement for all states except as shown below.)
If you have already paid for some or all of the cost to have the cylinder head replaced and your mileage and in service time was less than seven (7) years and 100,000 miles (160,000 km), you should contact your (Buick/Oldsmobile/Pontiac) Dealer/Retailer Service Department to seek reimbursement. Please provide your retailer with your original paid receipts or invoices verifying the repair, the amount charged, proof of payment, and the date of payment of those charges by November 1, 1996.

Yikes! This is one important free engine fix—just the labor alone is nine hours. Tell your friends before the seven-year limit expires.

1991–95—Front brake linings can be made to last longer by replacing the front brake pads with a new 8100 lining compound (#18022600) **1992–93**—A front-end engine knock troubleshooting chart is found in DSB #306001. **1992–94**—Corrosion of the ECM connectors can lead to a host of driveability problems (DSB #338109A). • DSB #431007 is an excellent troubleshooting guide to finding and correcting squeaks and rattles; it contains six charts that show noise sources and remedies. **1992–97**—Inoperative power door locks may need an upgraded external bumper on the actuator arm. **1994**—Gear whine with the 4T60E automatic transaxle can be stopped by replacing the final drive and updating the PCM calibration. • Insufficient AC cooling may be due to a leak at the low-charge primary-port seal. • Loss of Drive or erratic shifts may be caused by an intermittent short to ground on the A or B shift solenoid or an electrical short circuit in the transaxle. • A front-end clunking noise when driving over rough roads may require the repositioning of the diagonal radiator support braces. **1995–97**—Intermittent loss of Drive at highway speeds may require the replacement of the control valve body assembly. • Engine popping noises can be silenced by tightening the torque strut mount bolts. **1997**—No-starts may be due to an improperly routed and pinched wire from the generator to the wiring harness. • Excessive oil consumption in the 2.5L engine may be caused by one or more damaged intake valve guides. • Hard starting and engine pinging can be fixed by the installation of a new PROM module (#16121217), DSB #88-6E-11. • Frequent engine overheating is caused by a defective thermostat; replace it with an upgraded part (#3059793). **Skylark: 1995–97**—Intermittent Neutral/loss of Drive at highway speeds can be fixed by replacing the control valve body assembly.

Achieva/Grand Am, Calais, Skylark Profile

	1991	1992	1993	1994	1995	1996	1997	1998
Cost Price ($)								
Achieva S	—	14,675	15,009	16,045	14,750	15,790	15,750	18,340
Calais S	12,793	—	—	—	—	—	—	—
Grand Am	12,089	13,859	14,484	14,484	15,084	15,624	15,969	16,209
Skylark	12,036	15,180	14,260	14,914	16,070	15,995	16,495	16,755
Used Values ($)								
Achieva S ↑	—	5,500	6,000	7,000	7,500	8,500	9,500	11,000
Achieva S ↓	—	4,500	5,000	6,000	7,000	7,500	8,500	10,000
Calais S ↑	4,200	—	—	—	—	—	—	—
Calais S ↓	3,500	—	—	—	—	—	—	—
Grand Am ↑	5,000	6,000	7,000	8,000	9,500	10,500	11,500	12,500
Grand Am ↓	4,000	5,000	6,000	7,000	8,000	9,500	11,000	11,500
Skylark ↑	5,000	5,500	6,000	7,000	8,000	8,500	9,500	12,800
Skylark ↓	4,000	4,500	5,000	6,000	7,000	8,000	9,000	11,800
Extended Warranty	Y	Y	Y	Y	Y	Y	Y	Y
Secret Warranty	Y	Y	Y	Y	Y	Y	Y	Y
Reliability	❷	❷	❷	❷	❷	③	④	④
Air conditioning	❷	❷	③	③	④	④	④	④
Body integrity	❷	❷	❷	❷	❷	❷	❷	❷
Braking system	❶	❶	❷	❷	❷	③	③	③
Electrical system	❶	❷	❷	❷	❷	❷	❷	❷
Engines	❷	❷	❷	❷	③	③	③	③
Exhaust/Converter	❶	❷	③	③	③	④	⑤	⑤
Fuel system	❷	❷	❷	❷	❷	③	③	③
Ignition system	❷	❷	③	③	③	③	③	④
Manual transmission	③	③	③	④	⑤	⑤	⑤	⑤
- automatic	❷	❷	❷	❷	❷	❷	❷	④
Rust/Paint	❶	❶	❷	❷	❷	③	③	③
Steering	❷	❷	❷	③	④	⑤	⑤	⑤
Suspension	③	③	③	⑤	⑤	⑤	⑤	⑤
Crash Safety								
Achieva 2d	—	❶	❶	④	④	—	④	—
Achieva 4d	—	—	❶	—	④	④	⑤	—
Grand Am 2d	—	❶	—	④	④	—	④	—
Grand Am 4d	—	—	❶	—	—	④	⑤	—

Skylark 2d	—	—	—	④	④	—	④	—
Skylark 4d	—	❶	❶	—	—	④	⑤	—
Side Impact								
Achieva 4d	—	—	—	—	—	—	❶	❶
Grand Am 4d	—	—	—	—	—	—	❶	❶
Skylark 4d	—	—	—	—	—	—	❶	❶

Beretta, Corsica

Rating: Average (1993–96), if you can adjust to the brakes' poor performance; Not Recommended (1987–92). The Corsica was the entry-level model, followed in price by the Beretta. Best bet is an ABS-equipped and V6-powered version, available 1992–96. The pair was dropped in 1996. **Maintenance/Repair costs:** Higher than average. Repairs aren't dealer dependent. **Parts:** Higher-than-average cost, but can be bought for much less from independent suppliers.

Strengths and weaknesses: These reasonably priced, roomy compacts came with standard anti-lock brakes as of the 1992 model year. Overall road performance is unimpressive, however, and emergency handling is below par. From a quality standpoint, these compact coupes, sedans, and hatchbacks are almost as unreliable as the Skyhawk, Firenza, J2000, and 2000 they replaced. The anemic, failure-prone, and expensive-to-repair 2.0L 4-cylinder engine with its faulty computer modules is a major disappointment. You need to shift into low gear on modest inclines. Owners report frequent no-starts and stalling with all engine variations, mainly due to temperamental electronic modules, particularly in conjunction with multi-port fuel-injection systems. Fuel system and ignition glitches are legion, and cruise control operation is erratic. Servicing is difficult because of the tight engine compartment. The V6 engine is seriously weakened by air conditioning and the automatic transmission's poor quality control. The lockup on the automatic engages and disengages constantly. The 5-speed manual performs better, but it too is unreliable, being handicapped by long clutch-pedal travel and a tendency to stall at light throttle. Owners report some instances where the clutch has shifted into Reverse rather than first gear. Steering is vague and components are unreliable. Braking is terrible and the front brakes rust and wear out quickly. The standard suspension offers poor ride control on bumpy roads, produces excessive body roll in turns, and is characterized by imprecise handling, especially at highway speeds. The sport suspension option (standard on some models) offers better handling and a firm, more comfortable ride. Shock absorbers often begin leaking before 30,000 miles, and the replacement of the suspension struts is sometimes an annual affair. Electrical components often short circuit. Owners report that the windshield wiper motor fails frequently.

1990–96 models also have more than their share of performance problems and factory-related defects. Braking is still scary, even with ABS, and cornering is a white-knuckle affair. The 2.2L engines have a "piston scuffing" problem and the Quad 4 engine's head gaskets fail prematurely. Hard starting, stalling, and engine surging are common, and AC operation is erratic.

Body panels are poorly assembled, paint delaminates and peels away, and rattles are a constant companion. GM announced in the January 18, 1993 edition of *Automotive News* that Corsica and Beretta paint peeling would be covered for six years under a special extended warranty. This change in GM's policy was first communicated to American dealers on October 16, 1992, in a series of letters and bulletins sent to each division's dealers.

Amazingly, GM weasels out of paying many claims for paint repairs by ignoring the *Automotive News* article or by pretending that the extended warranty never existed. Owners who won't take no for an answer and turn to small claims court usually get their cars repainted for free (see "Secret Warranties/Service Tips").

Safety summary/Recalls: There have been many reports of rear-wheel lockup and sudden brake loss on non-ABS equipped models, and ABS brake performance hasn't been impressive. **Recalls: All models: 1987–88**—The hood could fly up. • Replace broken front-door hinges with upgraded hinges (#10092242-3). **1988–89**—Front shoulder belt retractors could fail in a collision. **1989**—Dealers will install a front seat-belt latch plate and buckle for free. • The fuel tank could leak. • Dealers will replace both front seat frames if found defective. • The port fuel injector on 2.8L engines will be replaced for free based on the emissions warranty. **1991**—A loose steering wheel nut may cause steering wheel separation. **1992**—The brake light switch is faulty. **1992–93**—Dealers will install a redesigned intake manifold gasket on vehicles with rough-running 2.2L engines. **1990**—Models with 2.3L Quad 4 engines have faulty ignition coils that cause engine misfiring, and may be replaced under an emissions recall campaign. **1990–94**—Vehicles may have a cracked fuel-hose feed, causing a fuel leak. **1994–95**—The reinforcement panel is missing from the right-side rocker assembly. **Corsica: 1989**—A steel wheel fracture could cause wheel separation.

Secret Warranties/Service Tips

All models/years—A rotten-egg odor coming from the exhaust is probably caused by a malfunctioning catalytic converter, which may be covered by GM's emissions warranty. • Paint delamination, peeling, or fading (see pages 73–75). **All models: 1987–91**—Vehicles equipped with the 3T40 automatic transmission may experience slippage in manual Low or Reverse. Install Service Package #8628222; it includes a Low/Reverse clutch release spring (#8664961) and a clutch retainer and snap ring (#656/657). **1988**—Erratic performance of the window motor may call for a replacement brush package (#22094719). • 2.0L engine valve-train noise can be reduced by adjusting or replacing the rocker arms. • Lack of heat in the rear may require upgraded floor heater outlets. **1988–89**—Product Campaign #89C06 provides for the rewiring of a faulty 2.0L engine coolant switch. • 2.0L engines that fail to run, or stall in cold weather, probably need a new PROM. **1988–95**—A binding or popping noise coming from the front door glass when the glass is rolled down means that the regulator arm stabilizer plate is maladjusted. **1989**—Product Campaign #89C16 provides for the replacement of the 5-speed manual transmission. **1989–91**—A power-steering shudder, moan, or vibration signals the need for a "tuned" power-steering return hose and/or high-expansion pressure hose between the steering pump and gear. **1990**—Engine piston scuffing may cause cold engine knock. GM DSB #90-433-6A recommends a partial engine replacement. **1990–91**—No-starts, stalling, and rough running may be caused by a DIS ignition wiring short circuit. • Poor starting may be caused by the spring in early starter drives compressing too easily. Install an upgraded starter motor drive assembly (#10473700). • Engine overheating or poor AC performance may be due to an inoperative engine cooling fan. • Head gasket leaks in the 2.3L Quad 4 engine were once covered by a secret warranty extension. The first sign of trouble is a loss of power caused by combustion gases mixing with coolant. This is followed by a cloud of steam and coolant loss through the exhaust system. If these warnings are ignored, cylinder bore scoring, a warped cylinder head, and piston seizure will likely result as the engine continues to overheat. **1990–92**—Poor braking may be due to excessive corrosion of the front disc brake caliper bolt bore. **1991–94**—A crunching noise coming from the right side of the dash when turning the steering wheel can be silenced by installing a new steering grommet on the right side. • Water leaking onto the right front carpet from a gap between the air inlet screen and windshield can be stopped by applying a urethane sealing strip. **1992**—Chafing of the engine harness wires can cause hard starting, engine surging, stalling in gear, the display of the "Service Engine Soon" warning, and an inoperative temperature gauge. • Engine hesitation or roughness, particularly at idle, may be corrected by installing a new lower intake manifold gasket (#10103647). **1992–93**—No Reverse or slipping in Reverse can be corrected by installing an upgraded Low/Reverse clutch return spring and spiral retaining ring. **1993–96**—A front suspension squawk noise heard when passing over small bumps can be silenced by using a special GM service kit (see following bulletin).

File In Section: 3 Steering/Suspension
Bulletin No.: 73-33-01
Date: April 1997

Subject:
Squawk Noise Coming From Front Suspension or Engine Compartment Area
(Install Ultra High Molecular Tape)

Models:
1993–97 Buick Skylark
1993–94 Chevrolet Cavalier
1993–96 Chevrolet Beretta, Corsica
1993–97 Oldsmobile Achieva
1993–94 Pontiac Sunbird
1993–97 Pontiac Grand Am

Condition
Some owners may comment on a "squawk" noise coming from the front suspension or engine compartment area. This noise may be more noticeable over small bumps, entering parking lots, and including any irregular road surfaces. This condition may also be more noticeable in cold weather conditions.

Cause
The squawk noise may be caused by the rubber stabilizer bushing material bleeding through the Teflon/Polyester sock (on later models) and coming into contact with the stabilizer shaft. On earlier models, the squawk may be caused from friction when the stabilizer bushing is grabbing and releasing the stabilizer shaft.

Correction
If the above conditions exist, perform the following repair:
1.   Remove front stabilizer bushing clamps and bushings. Refer to Section 3C of the Service Manual.
2.   Inspect stabilizer bushings for excessive wear, replace if necessary.
3.   Use crocus cloth (or equivalent) to sand the stabilizer shaft where the stabilizer bushings contact the stabilizer shaft. Sand all rough corrosion thoroughly.
4.   Install UHM (Ultra High Molecular) tape (provided in kit, P/N 22602686) into stabilizer bushing; adhesive side of tape should be installed onto the bushing. Install UHM tape to the opening of the bushing (the slit) as well as the circumference (this will secure the tape in place). Kit provides enough tape for two bushings (one vehicle).

1994—Insufficient AC cooling may be due to a leak at the low-charge primary port seal. • Automatic transaxle gear whine may be eliminated by installing a redesigned transaxle final drive assembly. • A squeaking noise heard when going over bumps, accelerating, or shifting can be stopped by replacing the exhaust manifold pipe seal. • Harsh automatic transmission upshifts can be corrected by installing an upgraded accumulator valve in the control valve body. • Loss of Drive or erratic shifts may be caused by an intermittent short to ground on the A or B shift solenoid or an electrical short circuit in the transaxle. **1994–96**—If the accelerator pedal is difficult to depress or if the accelerator cable separates, install an upgraded accelerator cable and clip. • Chronic engine miss or a loss of power can be caused by a micro-arcing corroded spark plug wire or ignition coil. **1995–96**—Intermittent Neutral/loss of Drive at highway speeds can be fixed by replacing the control valve body assembly.

Beretta, Corsica Profile

	1989	1990	1991	1992	1993	1994	1995	1996
Cost Price ($)								
Corsica LT	11,650	11,240	11,845	12,834	13,230	13,630	14,385	14,885
Beretta GT/Z	13,600	13,465	14,145	16,620	17,025	15,795	16,790	17,190
Used Values ($)								
Corsica LT ↑	3,000	3,500	4,000	4,500	5,000	6,000	7,000	8,000
Corsica LT ↓	2,500	3,000	3,500	4,000	4,500	5,500	6,500	7,500
Beretta GT/Z ↑	4,000	5,000	5,500	6,500	7,500	8,500	9,500	10,500
Beretta GT/Z ↓	3,500	4,500	4,500	5,500	6,500	7,500	8,500	9,500
Extended Warranty	Y	Y	Y	Y	Y	Y	Y	Y
Secret Warranty	N	N	Y	Y	Y	Y	Y	Y
Reliability	①	②	②	②	②	②	②	②
Air conditioning	②	②	②	②	②	②	②	③
Body integrity	①	①	①	①	①	②	②	②
Braking system	①	①	①	①	①	②	②	②
Electrical system	①	①	②	②	②	②	③	③
Engines	①	①	②	②	②	②	③	③
Exhaust/Converter	②	②	②	②	③	③	③	④
Fuel system	①	①	②	②	③	③	③	④
Ignition system	①	②	②	②	③	③	③	④
Manual transmission	②	②	③	③	③	④	④	⑤
- automatic	②	②	②	②	②	②	②	②
Rust/Paint	①	②	②	②	②	②	②	③
Steering	①	②	②	③	③	④	④	⑤
Suspension	①	②	②	③	③	④	④	⑤
Crash Safety								
Corsica 4d	—	—	⑤	⑤	⑤	③	③	③
Beretta 2d	—	—	⑤	⑤	⑤	—	—	—
Beretta 4d	—	—	—	—	—	③	③	③

Bonneville/Delta 88/LeSabre, Cutlass/Malibu, Cutlass Supreme, Grand Prix/Intrigue/Regal, Lumina/Monte Carlo

Rating: Rear-drives, if you can find them, are Above Average (1984–87); front-drives are Not Recommended (1988–98). Although these GM models are generally classed as medium-sized cars, some of them move in and out of the large car class as well. **Maintenance/Repair costs:** Higher than average, but repairs aren't dealer dependent. **Parts:** Higher-than-average cost (independent suppliers sell for much less), but not hard to find. Nevertheless, don't even think about buying one of the front-drives without a three- to five-year supplementary warranty.

Strengths and weaknesses: Body assembly on all models is notoriously poor and is no doubt one of the main reasons why GM has lost so much market share over the past decade. Premature paint peeling and rusting, water and dust leaks into the trunk, squeaks and rattles, and wind and road noise are all too common. Accessories are also plagued by problems, with defective radios, power antennas, door locks, cruise control, and alarm systems leading the pack.

Rear-drives

The rear-drives are competent and comfortable cars, but they definitely point to a time when handling wasn't a priority and fuel economy was unimportant. Their overall reliability isn't impressive, but at least repairs are easy, defects are obvious, and any independent garage can service them. Models equipped with diesel engines or with the turbocharged gas V6 should be approached with extreme caution. These cars have a higher-than-average incidence of repairs, but parts are inexpensive and all mechanical work is very easy to perform.

Original-equipment shock absorbers and springs aren't durable, and electrical malfunctions increase proportionally with extra equipment. The AC module and condenser and wheel bearings (incredibly expensive) also have short life spans. The 4-speed automatic transmission available in later models isn't reliable. Surface rust caused by poor paint quality and application is common. The rear edge of trunk lids, roof areas above doors, and the windshield and windshield posts rust through easily.

Front-drives

The front-drives are a different breed of car: less reliable and more expensive to repair, with a considerable number of mechanical and electrical deficiencies directly related to their front-wheel drive configuration. Nevertheless, acceleration is adequate, fuel economy is good, and they're better at handling than their rear-drive cousins—except in emergencies, when their non-ABS brakes lock up and directional stability is the first to go. The front-drive's many design and manufacturing weaknesses make for unimpressive high-speed performance, mediocre interior comfort, a poor reliability record, and expensive maintenance costs. That's why most fleets and police agencies use rear-drives when they can get them. They've seen the rear-drive's safety and operating cost advantages.

These aren't driver-friendly cars. Many models have a dash that's replete with confusing push-buttons and gauges that are washed out in sunlight. At other times, there are retro touches, like the Intrigue's dash-mounted ignition, that just simply seem out of place. The keyless entry system often fails, the radio's memory is frequently forgetful, and the fuel light comes on when the tank is below the "1/2" fuel-level mark. The electronic climate control frequently malfunctions and owners report that warm air doesn't reach the driver-side heating vents. Servicing, especially for the electronic engine controls, is complicated and expensive.

Other major problem areas: the engine, automatic transmission, leaking and malfunctioning AC systems (due mainly to defective AC modules), faulty electronic modules, rack-and-pinion steering failure, bursting steering hoses on 1991 models, weak shocks, excessive front brake pad wear, warping rotors, seizure of the rear brake calipers, rear brake/wheel lockup, myriad electrical failures requiring replacement of the computer module (a $500–$750 repair if the emissions warranty has expired), leaking oil pan, and suspension struts.

Owners report that 3.8L engines won't continue running after a cold start, the exhaust system booms, 3T40 automatic transmissions may have faulty Reverse gears, and the instrument panel may pop or creak.

Intrigue

The 1998 Oldsmobile Intrigue is GM's replacement for the Cutlass Supreme and represents the most refined iteration of the W-body shared by the Century, Grand Prix, Lumina, and Regal. It's more luxurious than the Lumina and performs as well as the Accord, Camry, and Maxima. Its rigid chassis has fewer shakes and rattles than are found on GM's other models, and its 3.8L engine provides lots of low-end grunt but lacks the top-end power that makes the Japanese competition so much fun to toss around.

Lumina and Monte Carlo

The Lumina and Monte Carlo are popular two- and four-door versions of Chevy's "large" mid-sized cars, featuring standard dual airbags, ABS, and 160-hp V6 power. The Monte Carlo was formerly sold as the Lumina Z34. Powertrain enhancements have increased horsepower and fuel efficiency. Each car has been given a slightly different appearance and a distinct "personality." A 3.1L V6 is the standard engine, while a 3.8L V6 equips the more upscale versions.

Same old generic front-drive shortcomings as mentioned earlier. In spite of some noise reduction progress, body construction is still below par, with loose door panel moldings, poorly fitted door fabric, and misaligned panels. Other common problems: fuel pump whistling, frequent stalling, vague steering, premature paint peeling on the hood and trunk, heavy accumulation of hard-to-remove brake dust inside the honeycomb-design wheels, and front tires that scrape the fenders when the wheel is turned. Despite its own recent redesign, the 3.1L engine isn't entirely problem-free. Electronic fuel-injection systems and engine controls have created many problems for GM owners. The 4-speed automatic transmission still has bugs. The front brakes wear quickly, as do the MacPherson struts and shock absorbers. Steering assemblies tend to fail prematurely. The electrical system is temperamental. The sunroof motor is failure-prone. Owners report water leaks from the front windshield. Front-end squeaks may require the replacement of the exhaust manifold pipe springs with dampers.

The Lumina's engine is buzzy and anemic, giving out only 140 hp with the V6; the instruments and steering column shake when the car is travelling over uneven road surfaces; and lots of road and wind noise come through the side windows thanks to the inadequately sound-proofed chassis. Seating isn't very comfortable due to the lack of support caused by low-density foam, knees-in-your-face low seating, and the ramrod-straight rear backrest. The ride is acceptable with a light load, but when fully loaded, the car's back end sags and the ride deteriorates.

Malibu and Cutlass
These two front-drive, medium-sized sedans are slotted in between the Cavalier and Lumina in both size and price. This niche was once filled by the long-discontinued Corsica, Beretta, Tempest, Celebrity, and Ciera. Malibu and Cutlass are boringly styled cars that use a more rigid body structure to cut down on noise and improve handling. Standard mechanicals include a 2.4L twin-cam 4-cylinder engine or an optional 3.1L V6. There's plenty of passenger and luggage space. Although head room is tight, the Malibu can carry three rear passengers and gives much more leg room than either the Cavalier or Lumina.

Other points to consider: the base 4-cylinder is loud, handling isn't on par with the Japanese competition, there's lots of body lean in turns, outside mirrors are too small, there's no traction control, and the ignition switch is mounted on the dash (a throwback to your dad's Oldsmobile).

In addition to the generic front-drive problems listed above, owners also report: fuel-injector deposits cause chronic stalling, poor idling, or hard starts; excessive vibration occurs at any speed; transmission doesn't lock when the key is in the accessory position; steering is very loose; and the high-beam light switch is faulty.

Dealer service bulletins: All models: 1993–94—3.8L engine stalls after a cold start. • Converter seal leaks on 4T60E automatic transmissions. • AC hisses from the instrument panel and it becomes too warm on extended idle. • Poor heat distribution. • Door speakers buzz. **1995**— A knocking noise from the accessory drive belt tensioner. • Continuous spark knock. • Excessive oil consumption and oil leaks at the rocker cover. • Coolant leak near the throttle body. • Grinding/growling when in Park on an incline and a cold-start rattle with the 4T60E automatic transmission. • Harsh 1–2 upshifts. • Brake vibration and/or pedal pulsation. • Low voltage reading or dim lights at idle. • Headlights/parking lights remain on. • An upgraded wire protector shield is needed to correct a noisy steering column. • Squeak/creak from rear of vehicle, whistle noise from the heater/AC unit, and excessive radio static. • Door window rattle, popping noise during moderate braking or acceleration, front suspension pop noise, and rear strut–related squeaking/thumping noise. • Left rear door binds. • Poor paint application and rust spots. • Frequent reports of wind noise affecting the 1990–95 Cutlass, Grand Prix, and Regal and the 1988–94 Lumina have led to the publication of

DSB #53-15-16, which outlines the causes of and remedies for persistent wind noise. **1996**—Second-gear starts, poor 1–3 shifting. • Steering column noise. • Air conditioning odors and diagnosis of AC noises. • Whistle noise from HVAC. • Diagnosis and correction of fluttering, popping, ticking, and clunking noises. • Popping noise from the front of the vehicle when turning. • Radio frequency interference diagnosis. • Rear door rattle when closing. • Excessive wrinkles in seat cushion trim. • Condensation on exterior light. **1997**—AC flutter or moan. • Cold-start rattle. Engine cranks but will not run. • Engine oil leak at oil pan sealing flange and rear of engine near flywheel cover. • Engine oil level indicates over-full. • Excessive vibration of electrochromic mirror. • High beams are intermittent. • Inoperative power door locks. • Intermittent AC noise. • Intermittent Neutral/loss of Drive at highway speeds. • Instrument panel buzzes and rattles when the brakes are applied. • Popping or thump noise from the left rear of vehicle is normal, according to GM. • Transmission gear whine at 25–50 mph. **Bonneville: 1995**—Headrest cover splits, loosens, or separates. **Cutlass Supreme: 1995**—Snapping noise from door window, and exhaust manifold seal squeak. • Power door lock/power window switches binding. **1996**—Stalls at low rpm and high loads, extended crank time. • Front suspension popping. • HVAC blower motor noise/vibration. • Loose left side instrument panel access cover. • Inoperative antenna, power mirrors and door locks. **Delta 88: 1995**—Inadvertent low fuel chime. **LeSabre: 1993–94**—Remedies for stalling and hard starts. • Whistling when the AC is in recirculate mode. • Rattling when car passes over bumps. **Regal: 1995**—Left rear door binds when opening. **Delta 88, Bonneville: 1994**—3T40 automatic transmissions have faulty Reverse gears.

Safety summary/Recalls: All models: 1986–88—Brakes either fail or the pedal goes to the floor when depressed. **1988–93**—Corroded brake calipers may cause brake failures. **1990**—ABS is tough to modulate; it doesn't always engage quickly enough or it's sometimes too sensitive. **1990–91**—Wheels may crack and fracture, leading to wheel failure and loss of control. **1991–92**—Damaged fuel lines. **1992**—A poorly aligned PRNDL indicator may allow shifts from Park to Reverse while the engine is running. • There are reports of the driver's seat breaking from its moorings. **1994**—Windshield wiper failures. • When heater is turned on, it emits a strong, irritating odor. **1997**—Airbag failed to deploy. • Seating design forces driver to sit too close to airbag mechanism in the steering column. • Chronic stalling. • Throttle sticks. • Frequent cruise control failures. • Inadequate braking; ABS brake failures are common. • Emergency brake doesn't work properly; it won't remain locked. • Backfires caused by defective ECM. • Premature suspension strut failures. • Vehicle bottoms out with four or more passengers aboard. • Ventilation system emitted fumes that made occupants ill. • Frequent AC compressor failures. • Seatbelt didn't restrain passenger

sufficiently in an accident. • Inoperative rear seat buckles. • Rear seatbelts are too short to secure a child seat or large person. • Plastic part
of buckle came off when trying to buckle up. • Rear seatbelt design
forces user to sit on buckles; they are too close to the seat and difficult
to fasten. • Turn signal lever won't return to neutral position. •
Excessive wind noise comes in around the door openings. • Many
reports that door locks continually engage and disengage while driving.
• Power window motor failure. • Outside rear view mirrors positioned
too far back for a clear view. • Dash reflection in windshield cuts visibility. • Windshield wipers operate erratically. • Water collects in the
headlight lenses, causing them to fog or malfunction. • Headlights
often dim for no apparent reason. • Stop lights and taillights aren't
very durable. **1998**—Airbags failed to deploy. • Sudden acceleration;
faulty fuel pressure regulator suspected. • Power seat puts occupant too
close to airbag. • Headrest can't be raised high enough for someone
over six feet tall. • Engine hesitates when accelerating. • Many reports
of vehicle suddenly stalling in traffic. • Ignition coil failure also causes
engine to stall and backfire. • Flexible hose line from fuel pump rests
against sharp metal edge of the heat shield. • Trunk popped open
while driving. • Excessive wind noise enters the interior. **Recalls: All
models: 1988–91**—Faulty front shoulder belt guide loop. **1989–90**—
Faulty brake lights. **1992**—4-speed automatic transmissions that slip in
Reverse, lock in Reverse when the indicator shows Neutral, or generally
perform poorly. **1993**—The seat back may suddenly recline. **1996–97**—
Backfire can break upper intake manifold, making car hard to start and
possibly starting a fire. **1997**—Seatbelt may not latch properly. **All models with 2.3L Quad 4 engine**—Faulty ignition coils that may cause
engine misfiring will be replaced under an emissions recall campaign.
Cutlass Supreme: 1994—Improperly installed brake hoses could leak
fluid and cause partial brake loss. **1994–95**—Washer wiper may malfunction. **1995**—Seatbelt anchor could fracture in a crash. If cracks
appear in the centre rear seatbelt anchor, the dealer must replace the
entire centre rear seatbelt system. **Delta 88: 1991**—Parking brake may
not hold well enough, allowing the car to roll when the brake is on.
Lumina: 1990—Cracks can develop in the Kelsey Hayes steel wheels.
Delta 88: 1994–95—Headlight switch may not work. **Regal: 1991**—The
fuel-feed hose on vehicles with 3.8L V6 engines may leak fuel; dealer
will install a new fuel-feed hose. **1994–95**—Improperly installed brake
hoses could leak fluid and cause partial brake loss. **1995**—Steering
could fail if the bolts on the steering column support bracket aren't
tightened. **Bonneville, LeSabre: 1992**—Parking brake may not hold
well enough, allowing the car to roll when the brake is on. **Lumina,
Monte Carlo: 1996**—Improperly installed brake booster. **Lumina,
Regal: 1996**—Brake line could rub against the transaxle mounting
bracket. **Cutlass, Grand Prix, Regal: 1988–90**—Cracks can develop in
the Kelsey Hayes steel wheels. **LeSabre, Delta 88, and Bonneville with
4T60-E automatic transmission: 1992–93**—Oil cooler line can leak
transmission fluid, posing a fire hazard.

Secret Warranties/Service Tips

All models/years—A rotten-egg odor coming from the exhaust is probably caused by a malfunctioning catalytic converter (covered by the emissions warranty). • Paint delamination, peeling, or fading (see pages 73–75). **1980–89 front-drives**—First gear malfunctions with the THM 125C transmission may require new forward clutch piston seals (#8631986). **1984–89**—No third gear with the automatic 440-T4 transmission means that a new thrust bearing assembly should be installed. **1985–89**—Wind noise around the doors can be cured by using several kits mentioned in DSB #89-286-10. **1986–87**—Serious stalling problems can usually be traced to a defective PROM module or a malfunctioning TCC solenoid. **1986–88**—Models with anti-lock brakes may have defective hoses. • 3.8L V6 engines have a history of low oil pressure caused by a failure-prone oil pump. A temporary remedy is to avoid low viscosity oils and use 10W-40 in the winter and 20W-50 in the summer. **1987**—Frequent engine stalling may require that a different PROM be put in the ECM (DSB #87-6-17A). **1987–89**—If the engine constantly stalls and won't restart, consider replacing the fuel pump and installing a fuel-sender kit. **1988**—Poor engine performance diagnostic shortcuts are detailed in DSB #88-T-47B. **1988–89**—Poor FM reception can be improved by installing an RFI suppresser harness (#25027405). • If your door hinge breaks, GM will replace it for free up to ten years under a special policy. • Rear suspension thud noise may be reduced by replacing the strut assemblies. **1988–93**—A vehicle equipped with a 3300 or 3800 engine that stalls when decelerating or is hard to start may need a new air control motor (IAC). **1989**—Constant stalling with the 2.8L engine may be fixed by installing a new service MEMCAL (a computer module that regulates powertrain and emissions). **1989–90**—Hard coldstarts may require a new MEMCAL. **1990**—Sunroof failures may be due to static electricity blowing the sunroof's electric module; install a plastic button switch. **1990–92**—A vehicle equipped with a 3.1L or 3.4L engine that is hard to start when cold or that chronically stalls may need an engine calibration or an upgraded MEMCAL module. **1991–94**—Loss of Drive or erratic shifts may be caused by an intermittent short to ground on the A or B shift solenoid or an electrical short circuit in the transaxle. • Harsh automatic transmission upshifts can be corrected by installing an upgraded accumulator valve in the control valve body. **1992–94**—A front-end engine knock troubleshooting chart is found in DSB #306001. • Water leaking from the doors into the passenger compartment has a number of causes and remedies, according to DSB #431003. **1993–94**—Knocking from the accessory drive belt tensioner requires an upgraded replacement. • Owners who complain of automatic transmission low-speed miss, hesitation, chuggle, or skip may find relief with an improved MEMCAL module. **1995–96**—Wind noise around front and rear doors; diagnosis and repair. **1995–97**—Intermittent Neutral/loss of Drive at highway speeds can be fixed by replacing the control valve body assembly. **All models with a 2.3L Quad 4 engine: 1990–91**—Head gasket leaks are a problem that was once covered by a secret warranty extension. The first sign of trouble is a loss of power caused by combustion gases mixing with coolant. This is followed by a cloud of steam and coolant loss through the exhaust system. If these warnings are ignored, cylinder-bore scoring, a warped cylinder head, and piston seizure will likely result as the engine continues to overheat. Up to

7 years/100,000 miles GM has replaced the head gasket with an improved version at no charge. **LeSabre: 1991–92**—Premature bore corrosion of the front brake caliper bolt can be fixed by changing the rubber bushings and honing out the bores. **1991–94**—A scraping noise or increased effort required to open the front doors can be fixed by bending the door's lower check ear. • Water leaking from the doors into the passenger compartment has a number of causes and remedies (DSB #431003). **1995–97**— Transmission gear whine at 25-50 mph means the final drive assembly may have to be replaced. • Intermittent Neutral/loss of Drive at highway speeds can be fixed by replacing the control valve body assembly. **Lumina: 1990**—Vehicles equipped with a 3.1L engine may exhibit piston scuffing, which produces cold engine knock at low ambient temperatures. GM recommends a partial engine replacement rather than changing the pistons. **1990–91**—Late transaxle upshifts may be fixed by resetting the TV cable. **1994**—Excessive brake-pedal effort when cold can be fixed by installing upgraded brake pads. **1994–95**—A steering wheel clicking or scrubbing noise when turning can be fixed by installing an upgraded wire protector shield. **Regal: 1991–94**—Loss of Drive or erratic shifts may be caused by an intermittent short to ground on the A or B shift solenoid or an electrical short circuit in the transaxle. **1992**—Front-door wind noise and water leaks can be fixed by replacing the run channel retainer and adding sealer between the retainer and the door frame. **Grand Prix, Regal: 1997**—Insufficient heater performance on passenger-side floor area can be fixed by installing a new I/P insulator panel and bracket. **Lumina, Regal: 1990–91**—In models with a 3.1L V6 engine, if the starter makes a grinding noise or won't engage the engine, the fault may be a weak starter spring. Replace the starter-motor drive assembly with #10473700. • A defective sending unit will cause a display of high oil pressure or erratic readings. Replace the old pressure sender with #25605389. • Excessive brake-pedal effort can be corrected by replacing the original pads with modified parts. **1990–92**—Vehicles equipped with the 3T40 automatic transmission may experience slippage in manual Low or Reverse. Install service package #8628222, which includes a Low/Reverse clutch release spring (#8664961) and clutch retainer and nap ring (#656/657). **1991–92**—A delayed shift between Drive and Reverse is likely caused by a rolled or cut input-clutch-piston outer seal. **1991–94**—Loss of Drive or erratic shifts may be caused by an intermittent short to ground on the A or B shift solenoid or an electrical short circuit in the transaxle. **1992–93**—No Reverse or slipping in Reverse can be corrected by installing an upgraded Low/Reverse clutch return spring and spiral retaining ring.

Bonneville/Delta 88/LeSabre, Cutlass/Malibu, Cutlass Supreme, Grand Prix/Intrigue/ Regal, Lumina/Monte Carlo Profile

	1991	1992	1993	1994	1995	1996	1997	1998
Cost Price ($)								
Bonneville	18,550	19,677	20,522	21,627	21,584	22,374	22,914	23,215
Cutlass GL	—	—	—	—	—	—	19,500	18,950
Cutlass Supreme	16,812	17,450	17,170	18,830	18,995	17,995	19,500	—
Delta 88	18,969	20,502	21,251	22,480	20,995	21,370	23,100	23,400
Grand Prix	15,869	16,575	16,245	17,094	17,589	18,049	19,250	19,885

Intrigue	—	—	—	—	—	—	—	21,250
LeSabre	19,019	19,615	19,554	22,541	23,481	22,345	23,040	23,265
Lumina	15,200	15,850	15,550	16,650	16,840	17,860	18,480	18,785
Malibu	—	—	—	—	—	—	15,995	16,690
Monte Carlo	—	—	—	—	17,510	18,012	18,220	18,570
Regal	17,295	18,370	18,190	19,670	20,650	20,280	23,495	24,240
Used Values ($)								
Bonneville ↑	5,500	7,500	8,500	10,000	12,000	14,000	16,000	18,500
Bonneville ↓	5,000	7,000	8,000	9,500	11,000	13,500	15,000	17,500
Cutlass GL ↑	—	—	—	—	—	—	13,000	15,000
Cutlass GL ↓	—	—	—	—	—	—	12,500	14,500
Cutlass Supreme ↑	6,500	7,500	9,500	11,000	12,000	13,00	14,000	—
Cutlass Supreme ↓	6,000	6,500	9,000	10,500	11,500	12,000	13,000	—
Delta 88 ↑	6,000	7,000	8,000	9,500	11,000	13,000	15,500	18,000
Delta 88 ↓	5,500	6,500	7,500	9,000	9,500	12,500	14,500	17,000
Grand Prix ↑	5,000	6,000	7,000	8,500	10,000	12,000	16,000	18,500
Grand Prix ↓	4,500	5,500	6,500	8,000	9,000	11,000	15,000	17,500
Intrigue ↑	—	—	—	—	—	—	—	18,500
Intrigue ↓	—	—	—	—	—	—	—	17,500
LeSabre ↑	6,000	7,500	8,500	9,500	11,500	14,000	16,500	18,500
LeSabre ↓	5,500	7,000	8,000	9,000	10,500	13,500	15,500	17,500
Lumina ↑	5,000	5,000	6,500	7,500	9,500	11,000	13,000	15,000
Lumina ↓	4,500	5,000	6,000	7,000	8,500	10,500	12,000	14,000
Malibu ↑	—	—	—	—	—	—	13,000	14,500
Malibu ↓	—	—	—	—	—	—	12,000	13,500
Monte Carlo ↑	—	—	—	—	10,000	12,500	14,000	15,500
Monte Carlo ↓	—	—	—	—	9,500	11,500	13,000	15,000
Regal ↑	6,000	7,000	8,000	9,500	11,000	13,000	16,000	19,500
Regal ↓	5,500	6,500	7,500	9,000	10,000	12,000	15,000	18,500
Extended Warranty	Y	Y	Y	Y	Y	Y	Y	Y
Secret Warranty	Y	Y	Y	Y	Y	Y	Y	Y
Reliability	①	①	①	②	②	③	③	③
Air conditioning	②	②	②	②	③	③	③	③
Automatic transmission	①	①	①	①	①	②	③	③
Body integrity	①	①	①	①	①	②	②	③
Braking system	①	①	①	②	②	②	②	③
Electrical system	①	①	①	②	②	③	③	③
Engines	②	②	②	②	③	③	③	④
Exhaust/Converter	②	②	②	③	③	④	④	④
Fuel system	②	②	②	②	③	③	③	④
Ignition system	②	②	③	③	③	③	③	④
Rust/Paint	①	①	①	①	①	①	②	③
Steering	②	②	②	②	③	③	③	③
Suspension	②	②	②	②	③	③	③	③
Crash Safety								
Bonneville 4d	—	⑤	④	⑤	⑤	⑤	⑤	⑤

Cutlass 4d	—	—	—	—	—	—	④	④
Cutlass Supreme 2d	❷	—	—	—	—	④	—	—
Cutlass Supreme 4d	❷	④	❷	④	—	—	—	—
Delta 88 2d	—	—	—	—	—	—	—	—
Delta 88 4d	—	④	④	—	—	④	—	—
Grand Prix 2d	—	—	—	④	④	—	—	—
Grand Prix 4d	❷	❷	❷	—	—	—	④	—
Intrigue	—	—	—	—	—	—	—	④
LeSabre 2d	—	—	—	—	—	—	—	—
LeSabre 4d	—	④	④	—	—	—	④	④
Lumina 4d	❷	❷	❷	④	—	⑤	⑤	④
Malibu	—	—	—	—	—	—	④	④
Monte Carlo	—	—	—	—	④	④	④	—
Regal 2d	⑤	⑤	—	—	—	④	—	—
Regal 4d	❷	❷	❷	④	—	—	—	—
Side Impact								
Cutlass 4d	—	—	—	—	—	—	❶	❶
Intrigue	—	—	—	—	—	—	—	③
Lumina	—	—	—	—	—	—	④	④
Malibu	—	—	—	—	—	—	❶	❶
Regal 4d	—	—	—	—	—	—	—	③

HONDA

Accord

Rating: Recommended (1992–98); Above Average (1990–91); Average (1985–89). Fast and nimble without a V6, this is the car of choice in the compact sedan class for drivers who want maximum fuel economy and comfort along with lots of space for grocery hauling and occasional highway cruising. Surprisingly, the Accord built during the past few years has racked up an unusually large number of safety complaints, including reports of sudden acceleration, brake failures, and airbag malfunctions that cause the devices to go off when they shouldn't and not deploy when they should. **Maintenance/Repair costs:** Lower than average. Repairs aren't dealer dependent. **Parts:** Higher-than-average cost, but can be bought for much less from independent suppliers. Owners report that Honda frequently charges for parts that should be replaced for free under the emissions warranty and that those charges are far in excess of what other automakers ask.

Strengths and weaknesses: The Accord doesn't really excel in any particular area; it's just very, very good at everything. It's smooth, quiet, mannerly, and competent, with outstanding fit and finish, inside and out. Every time Honda redesigned the line it not only caught up with the latest advances, but went slightly ahead. Strong points are comfort, fit and finish, ergonomics, impressive assembly quality, reliability, and driveability. With the optional 16-valve 4-cylinder engine or V6, the Accord is one of the most versatile compacts you can find. It offers something for everyone, and its high resale value means there's no way you can lose money buying one.

Despite all the foregoing praise, this hasn't always been a great car. During the '80s, Accords were beset with severe premature rusting, frequent engine camshaft and crankshaft failures, and severe front brake problems. Engines leaked or burned oil and blew their cylinder head gaskets easily, and carbureted models suffered from driveability problems through 1986.

Between 1986 and 1989, the brakes, automatic transmission (particularly the 2–4 clutch assembly), rack-and-pinion steering, suspension (coils are practically biodegradable), and electrical system became the major problem areas. Also, water pumps and alternators need replacing about every three years. Rapid front brake wear and frequent brake rotor replacements are common. The automatic transmission shifts a bit harshly upon hard acceleration. Shock absorbers go soft quickly, and replacement prices are often less at independent suppliers. To avoid costly engine repairs, check the engine timing belt every 2 years/30,000 miles.

Early Accords were surprisingly vulnerable to paint chipping, flaking, and premature surface rust. If left untreated, sheet metal perforations develop unusually quickly. Especially vulnerable spots are front fender seams; door bottoms; and areas surrounding side view mirrors and door handles, rocker panels, wheel openings, windshield posts, front cowls, and trunk and hatchback lids.

1990–93 models got more room (stepping up to the mid-sized car niche) and additional power through a new and quieter 2.2L 4-cylinder engine. Nevertheless, rear seating is still inadequate, the added weight saps the car's performance, and the automatic transmission shifts harshly at times. Owners report prematurely worn automatic transmissions, constant velocity joints, and power-steering assemblies. Poor quality control in the choice of body trim and assembly leads to numerous air and water leaks.

Redesigned again for the 1994 model year, the Accord continues to add interior room and other refinements. However, the addition of the V6 powerplant in the 1995 model year gives the Accord plenty of power in reserve without the high rpms. The automatic transmission still works poorly with the 4-banger, producing acceleration times that are far from impressive, and owners still complain of excessive road noise and tire whine. Nevertheless, no significant reliability problems have been reported with the latest redesign.

Confidential dealer service bulletins show that the 1994–98 models are susceptible to AC malfunctions, engine oil leaks, transmission glitches, power steering pump leaks, windows falling off their channels, and numerous air and water leaks. Usually, these problems are simple to repair and Honda customer relations staff are helpful; however, Honda staffers may be getting a bit too arrogant in their dealings with the public. One *Lemon-Aid* reader wrote the following:

> We returned the car to the dealer several times (at least six) to have the doors adjusted to reduce wind noise affecting my 1994 Accord LX sedan. They were finally able to reduce the noise a small amount. A letter written to Honda explaining our dissatisfaction with the car resulted in a response letter with very definite "screw you" overtones.

Dealer service bulletins: All models: 1994—Buzzing when the turn signals are activated. • A clunking noise from the door glass, and instrument panel creaking. • Damaged door handle seals. • Faulty fuel-filler doors. • Rattling moon roof deflectors. • Outside mirror wind noise. • Power door locks that unlock themselves. • Difficulty in closing the trunk lid. • Lots of water leaks and wind noise. **1995**—Noise from the front passenger's footwell, exhaust system, and shoulder belt anchors; rear shelf will buzz. • The dash panel and clutch pedal may creak. • A screeching noise occurs when the driver's window is lowered. • A wind whistle emanates from the top of the windshield. • Heater control indicators may not light. • DSB #95-017 shows which rear brake pads produce less noise and which ones last the longest. **1996**—Instrument panel creaking. • Poor fit of wheel center cap. • Screeching noise when lowering the driver's window. • Seatbelt is slow to retract. **1997**—AC won't blow cold air (we're talking secret warranty here). • Oil seepage from the engine block. • Torque converter won't lock up. • Fifth gear grinds during upshift. • Leak from the power steering pump. • Rear wheel bearing noise. • Static when adjusting the radio volume. • Front door glass comes out of run channel. • Cracking paint on passenger-side airbag cover. • Missing alloy wheel center cap. **1998**—Trunk spoiler damages paint. • Brake system indicator stays on. • Creak from the rear shelf area, headliner, windshield, and rear window. • Front ABS wheel sensor harness rubs against wheel. • Rattle from rear stabilizer bar. • Water leaks from the rear doors. • Wind noise from the top of the windshield.

Safety summary/Recalls: All models: 1995—Rear seatbelt buckle has insufficient slack, preventing buckle from latching. • Airbag warning light stays on. • Excessive windshield glare. • AC failure. • Headlight failure. • Cruise control malfunctions. • Premature front/rear brake wear. **1995–96**—Faulty power windows. • Brake failures/lockup. • Airbag failed to deploy or accidentally deployed. • Injury from airbag. • Sudden acceleration, stalling. • Passenger-side seatbacks won't stay upright. **1996**—Front passenger seatbelt locks up. • The door lock design gives a boost to thieves. • The Check Engine light is always on.

• The defroster could be faulty. • Faulty power door locks. • The steering column separates from the shaft. **1997**—Airbags failed to deploy. • Inadvertent airbag deployment. • Fire caused by faulty wiring harness. • Sudden acceleration while braking. • Cruise control doesn't accelerate properly and won't downshift the transmission. • Transmission shifted into Reverse and vehicle moved forward. • ABS brakes lock up. • Sudden brake failure. • Location of the oil filter allows oil to leak onto the exhaust system and catalytic converter. • Faulty brake master cylinder. • All four front brake pads cracked right down the center. • Power-steering fluid leakage. • Oil plug fell off into the oil pan and sprayed oil everywhere. • Left side seatbelt fails to retract. • Seatbelt tightened and locked up; occupant had to cut belt. • Seatbelt continually ratchets tighter. • When sun visor is opened, it blocks driver's vision due to its large size. • Check Engine light stays on continually. • Defroster fails to defrost side windows, and actually causes them to fog up. • Power windows fail to operate properly in cold weather. • Door continually out of adjustment. **1998**—Sudden acceleration while vehicle stopped in traffic. • Sudden acceleration occurred when vehicle hit from the rear. • Chronic stalling. • ABS brake light comes on continually. • Gas and brake pedals are too close together and often get pressed at the same time. • Airbag failed to deploy. • Frequent brake failures. • Sudden brake lockup. • Brake master cylinder failures. • Floormat bunches under the brake pedal. • Engine oil leakage. • Power-steering fluid leakage, causing sudden loss of steering control. • Vehicle rolled back when parked. • Automatic transmission gears disengage and make a loud noise when engaging. • Transmission fails to engage at slow speeds. • Transmission fails to fully lock up in Overdrive. • Transmission hunts for the right gear. • Clutch pedal failure. • Automatic transmission parking mechanism failure. • Due to design of dashboard lights, it's hard to read odometer, digital clock, and radio indicator. • Can't see high beam indicator light in the daytime. • Light tan dash reflects too much sunlight into the eyes. • Instrument panel lights are too bright at night and can't be dimmed enough. • To activate horn, driver must remove hand from steering wheel. • Fuel gauge shows two-thirds when the gas tank is full, or indicates an empty tank with warning light on while five gallons remain in the tank. • Poor seatbelt design allows for belt to wrap around the release lever and get stuck, or causes seatback to suddenly recline. • Seatbelts get trapped underneath the seatback electric switch. • Seatbelts ratchet too tight, trapping occupants. • Rear passenger-side door won't unlock. • Sunroofs and headliners often need replacing. **Recalls**: **All models**: **1985**—A defective electric control unit could cause the airbags to deploy outside of a crash situation. **1986–1991**—Takata seatbelts will be replaced. **1991**—Power window malfunctions. **1991–93**—Faulty rear seatbelts won't pull out if the car is parked on a steep incline. **1994**—Faulty tire stems may lead to sudden air loss. **1995–97**—Models with 4-cylinder engines (excluding DX version) have improperly routed air conditioning wires that may short and cause fires or other electrical malfunctions; dealers must install protective plastic tubing on the harnesses, reroute the wires, and replace damaged harnesses. **1998**—Vehicle may roll away with transmission lever in Park.

Secret Warranties/Service Tips

All models/years—Steering wheel shimmy is a frequent problem, and is taken care of in DSB #94-025. **All models: 1988–93**—A creaking sound coming from the window regulator can be corrected by installing an upgraded regulator spiral spring. **1990**—Delay after shifting into Drive is corrected by adjusting the cable (#87-040). • A right rear suspension clunking noise can be fixed with a new spring silencer tube. • An interior roaring noise can be silenced by installing blind body plugs (#95550-15000) in the door rocker panels. • If the front inside door handle doesn't work, check for a loose or broken actuator rod clip. • A moaning sound heard when the steering wheel is turned may mean that the steering-pump outlet-hose orifice has slipped out of position or that the outlet hose is faulty. • Water leaks behind the dashboard require sealing near the windshield locating blocks and frame panel seams in the cowl. • Whistling from the front of the car is likely caused by poor hood sealing. • Defective front door handle may prevent entry or exit. Honda will replace the mechanism free of charge. **1990–91**—A faulty automatic transmission countershaft nut was once replaced free under a product update program. • A new distributor body and kit will help cars that have a starting problem. **1990–93**—Poor AM reception or a popping noise from the speakers is likely due to poor a ground connection between the antenna collar and car body. **1992**—A faulty oil pressure switch was once replaced for free under a product update program. **1994**—When operating a manual or power-assisted front window, the rear edge of the glass comes out of the channel. • Damaged door handle seals were once replaced for free under a "goodwill" warranty; try for a partial refund. **1994–97**—If the AC doesn't blow cold air, Honda will consider replacing both the evaporator and the receiver/dryer free of charge under a "goodwill" program. • Oil seepage from the engine block requires sealing and the installation of a new exhaust manifold bracket. (The following three bulletins give more details on the above 1994–97 problems.)

97-060
September 22, 1997
Applies To: 1994-97 Accord 4-door - All
Front Door Glass Comes Out of Run Channel
SYMPTOM
When operating a front window (power or manual), the rear edge of the glass comes out of the B-pillar run channel.
PROBABLE CAUSE
The window regulator is out of adjustment.
CORRECTIVE ACTION
Adjust the window regulator, the front channel, and the glass.
WARRANTY CLAIM INFORMATION
In warranty:
The normal warranty applies.
Failed part: P/N 72250-SV4-A11, H/C 4272282
Defect code: 030
Contention code: B01
Skill level: Repair Technician
Out of warranty:
Any repair performed after warranty expiration may be eligible for goodwill consideration by the District Service Manager or your Zone Office. You must request consideration, and get a decision, before starting work.

This job falls under Honda's "goodwill" policy.

97-031
Applies To: 1994-97 Accord - ALL
1994-97 Civic - ALL
1994-95 del Sol - ALL
August 4, 1997
A/C Does Not Blow Cold Air
SYMPTOM
The air conditioning system does not blow cold air.
PROBABLE CAUSE
The evaporator tubes corrode from ocean salt spray, causing pinholes that allow refrigerant to leak. This problem is limited to areas where a hot, humid climate is combined with ocean air (Florida, Hawaii, Puerto Rico, or Gulf Coast areas).
CORRECTIVE ACTION
Replace only the evaporator if the vehicle comes in with some refrigerant in the high side line. Replace both the evaporator and the receiver/dryer if the vehicle comes in without any refrigerant in the high side line.

MODEL	EVAPORATOR	RECEIVER/DRYER	PAG REFRIGERANT OIL (120 ml) (for ordering only, do not put on warranty claim)	O-RINGS
Accord	P/N 80210-8V1-A11, H/C 4335725 (Use this number only if you are located in Florida, Hawaii, Puerto Rico, or theGulf Coast areas. Otherwise, use the part number in your parts catalog.)	V6 P/N 80351-SV7-A11, H/C 4602330 All except V6 P/N 80351-SV1-A11, H/C 4276267	V6 P/N 38897-P13-AO1AH, H/C 5023627 1994 EX P/N 38897-P0A-AO1AH, H/C 5172663 1994 LX, DX & All 1995-97 P/N 38897-PR8-AO1AH, H/C 5023635	Evaporator (one of each) P/N 80871-ST7-000, H/C 4256103 P/N 80873-ST7-000, H/C 4256129
1994-95 Civic, del Sol	P/N 80210-SR1-A12, H/C 43233242	P/N 80351-ST7-A11, H/C 4255964	P/N 38897-P13-AO1AH, H/C 5023627	Receiver/Dryer (two required) P/N 80873-ST7-000, H/C 4256129
1996-97 Civic	P/N 80210-SR1-A12, H/C 43233242	P/N 80351-SO1-A01, H/C 4809620	P/N 38897-P13-AO1AH, H/C 5023627	

PARTS INFORMATION
WARRANTY CLAIM INFORMATION
In warranty:
The normal warranty applies.
Failed part: P/N 80210-ST7-A21, H/C 4327656
Defect code: 011
Contention code: B02
Skill Level: Repair Technician
Out of warranty:
Any repair performed after warranty expiration may be eligible for goodwill consideration by the District Service Manager or your Zone Office. You must request consideration, and get a decision, before starting work.

This secret warranty pays for major AC components plus two hours of labor needed to get the job done. It also establishes that AC failures are routinely covered by Honda up to four years. Smart owners of other models should argue that any failure of the AC during that time, whether caused by salty air, road salt, or any other defect, falls within these "goodwill" parameters. Repairs required after four years of use should get partial refunds.

```
98-042
May 12, 1998
Applies To: 1994 - 97 Accord - DX, LX, and SE models with L4 engine
Oil Seepage From the Engine Block
SYMPTOM
Oil seepage from the front of the engine at the boss for the exhaust manifold bracket.
CORRECTIVE ACTION
Seal the cracked boss on the engine block, and install a new exhaust manifold bracket onto the A/C compressor bracket.
NOTE:
On DX models without A/C, an A/C compressor bracket must be installed. See PARTS INFORMATION.
WARRANTY CLAIM INFORMATION
In warranty:
The normal warranty applies.
Operation number:    110107
Flat rate time:       2.4 hours
Failed part:          P/N 10002-P0A-A01
H/C 4511465
Defect code:          060
Contention code:      B06
Template ID:          98-042A (DX w/o A/C)
98-042B (All others)
98-042C (LX w/o ABS)
Skill level:          Repair Technician
Out of warranty:
Any repair performed after warranty expiration may be eligible for goodwill consideration by the District Service Manager
or your Zone Office. You must request consideration, and get a decision, before starting work.
```

More "goodwill," we hope.

• Power-steering pump fluid leakage requires a new O-ring, which is also eligible for "goodwill" consideration, says Honda. **1995**—A whistling or howling noise coming from the top of the windshield can be silenced by applying sealant under the upper windshield molding. • Honda will supply an exhaust buzz silencing kit for free on a case-by-case basis. • The Accord's noise problems will be fixed for free only if the dealer makes the request to Honda. **1995–96**—A creaking noise coming from the instrument panel can be silenced through a variety of measures outlined in a series of Honda bulletins. **1996–97**—In a settlement with the Environmental Protection Agency, Honda paid fines totaling $17.1 million and extended its emissions warranty on 1.6 million 1995–97 models to 14 years/150,000 miles. This means that costly engine components and exhaust system parts, like catalytic converters, will be replaced free of charge as long as the 14-year/150,000 mile limit hasn't been exceeded. Additionally, the automaker will provide a full engine check and emissions-related repairs at 50,000–75,000 miles and will give free tune-ups at 75,000–150,000 miles (see Honda Civic rating for full details, page 165).

Accord Profile

	1991	1992	1993	1994	1995	1996	1997	1998
Cost Price ($)								
DX	13,555	14,265	15,030	15,230	15,930	16,280	16,295	16,295
EX	17,805	19,285	20,050	20,650	21,440	21,780	21,895	21,995
Used Values ($)								
DX ↑		7,500	8,800	9,500	10,000	11,500	13,000	14,500	16,000

DX ↓	7,000	8,000	8,500	9,500	10,500	12,000	13,500	15,000
EX ↑	8,500	10,000	11,500	12,500	14,000	15,500	17,500	19,500
EX ↓	8,000	9,500	10,500	11,500	13,000	14,500	16,500	18,500

Extended Warranty	N	N	N	N	N	N	N	N
Secret Warranty	N	N	N	Y	Y	Y	Y	N
Reliability	③	④	⑤	⑤	⑤	⑤	⑤	⑤
Air conditioning	③	③	③	③	③	④	④	④
Body integrity	❷	❷	❷	❷	③	③	③	④
Braking system	❷	❷	❷	❷	❷	③	③	④
Electrical system	❷	③	③	③	④	⑤	⑤	⑤
Engines	④	④	④	⑤	⑤	⑤	⑤	⑤
Exhaust/Converter	❷	❷	❷	④	④	⑤	⑤	⑤
Fuel system	④	④	④	⑤	⑤	⑤	⑤	⑤
Ignition system	③	③	④	⑤	⑤	⑤	⑤	⑤
Manual transmission	⑤	⑤	⑤	⑤	⑤	⑤	⑤	⑤
- automatic	④	④	④	④	⑤	⑤	⑤	⑤
Rust/Paint	③	③	④	④	④	④	④	④
Steering	❷	❷	③	③	③	④	⑤	⑤
Suspension	③	③	③	④	⑤	⑤	⑤	⑤
Crash Safety								
2d	—	—	—	—	—	—	④	④
4d	④	④	④	④	④	④	④	④
LX wagon	④	—	—	—	—	—	—	—
SE	—	—	④	—	—	—	—	—
Side Impact								
4d	—	—	—	—	—	—	❷	④

HYUNDAI

Sonata

Rating: Average (1995–98); Not Recommended (1986–93). The 1994 model year was skipped. These cars aren't rated very high because of their poor quality control. Nevertheless, they haven't registered one-tenth the number of safety complaints as has the higher-rated Honda Accord. If you must have a Sonata, I suggest you buy a 1996–98 version, plan to keep it at least five years to shake off the depreciation, and put some of the savings on the purchase price into a comprehensive supplementary warranty to protect yourself during that period. **Maintenance/Repair costs:** Higher than average. Repairs aren't dealer dependent. **Parts:** Higher-than-average cost, and often back-ordered.

Strengths and weaknesses: This mid-sized front-drive sedan was built under Mitsubishi licensing, but its overall reliability isn't anywhere near as good as what you'll find with Mitsubishi's cars and trucks. Acceleration is impressive with the manual gearbox, but only passable with the automatic. Handling and performance are also fairly good, although emergency handling isn't confidence inspiring, particularly due to the imprecise steering and excessive lean when cornering. As with other Hyundai models, the automatic transmission performs erratically, the engine is noisy, and reliability is a problem: it's way below average for the 1989–93 models; the 1995–98 models are moderately improved (remember, Hyundai skipped the 1994s).

Redesigned for the 1995 model year, the car got additional interior room, more horsepower, and an upgraded automatic transmission. Nevertheless, acceleration with an automatic is still below average with the 4-banger, and the automatic gearbox still downshifts slowly. 1995–97 Sonatas came with more standard features, like air conditioning, power steering, and a 2.0L 16-valve 4-cylinder engine.

Consumer Reports magazine reports that owners of 1990–92 Sonatas had 120 percent more complaints than the average car owner. Sonatas have had body assembly and preparation deficiencies that show that Hyundai doesn't yet have a firm grip on quality control. For example, the sloppily applied paint pits like an orange peel, and the sun visors and headliner look cheap and fragile. If the experience of Stellar and Pony owners is any guide, Sonata owners will notice serious deficiencies by the third and fourth year.

Hyundai dealer service bulletins indicate that the Sonata's automatic transmission could exhibit what Hyundai describes as "shift shock," as well as delayed shifting. Problems reported by owners in the past: poor engine performance (hard starting, poor idling, stalling); the engine runs hot, and when you're stopped at a traffic light, it shakes like a boiling kettle; #3 spark plug often needs replacing or cleaning; rough engine rattle; high oil consumption (one liter every two to three months); excessive front brake pulsation and premature wear; steering defects (when the steering wheel is turned to either extreme, it makes a sound like metal cracking); cruise control malfunctions and electrical short circuits; battery life of only 18 months; malfunctioning lights; radio failures; falling interior roof liner; faulty hood locks; rotten-egg smell coming from the catalytic converter; broken muffler; faulty resonator; defective exhaust pipe; poor door and window sealing (water leaking into the interior when the car is washed); premature paint peeling; and rusting.

The 1995–98 Sonatas haven't elicited as many quality control and safety complaints as previous versions. However, engines, automatic transmissions, brakes, airbags, and electrical system components still top the list of parts most vulnerable to premature failure or malfunctioning.

Safety summary/Recalls: There are reports of electrical fires for the 1989–90 models. • Emergency handling leaves a lot to be desired. **1996**—Tire fell off of car. • Battery blew up while car was idling. •

Airbag light is continuously lit. • Brake malfunctions. • Chronic stalling, particularly when AC is engaged. • Frequent engine valve cover gasket failures. • Poor quality spark plugs cause sluggish acceleration. • Check Engine light is lit continuously. • Frequent automatic transmission failures. • Water leaks from the front of the car. **1997**—Airbags fail to deploy. • Frequent engine failures. • Transmission gear shift will not stay in place. • Power window switch failed. **1998**—Frequent inadvertent airbag deployment. • Sudden transmission failure while driving. **Recalls: 1986–91**—Part of the wiring harness connecting the alternator to the battery could detach, create a short circuit, and cause a loss of electrical power or an engine fire. **1989–90**—Fuel leaks into engine compartment. • Hood could fly up. **1989–93**—The motorized shoulder belt could malfunction. **1995**—There is the potential of loss of rear spring support. **1996–97**—The wiper motor is faulty.

Secret Warranties/Service Tips

All models/years—Harsh shifting when coming to a stop or upon initial acceleration is likely caused by an improperlyh adjusted accelerator pedal switch TCU. • A faulty air exhaust plug could cause harsh shifting into second and fourth gears on vehicles with automatic transmission. • Brake pedal pulsation can be corrected by installing upgraded front discs and pads. **1989–90**—Vibrations caused by excessive hub and brake disc runout require a new hub, machining of the disc, or new brake discs. • Cold-start stalling with the 2.4L engine can be fixed by installing start enrichment kit #39901-326000D. • Engine oil drain-plug leaks are likely caused by a faulty gasket or incorrect gasket installation. **1990**—Difficult shifts into fourth gear require a new transmission restrict ball assembly. **1992**—Oil leaking between the oil filter and mounting bracket could be due to an overly wide mounting surface on the bracket; correct this leakage by replacing the bracket. **1992–93**—Hyundai has a field fix for manual transaxle gear clash/grind (DSB #9440-004). **1992–95**—Difficult-to-engage Reverse gear needs an upgraded part. **1995–96**—Harsh shifting might be fixed by installing an upgraded Transaxle Control Module (TCM). **1995–97**—Lots more tips are offered on getting the automatic transmission to shift properly.

Sonata Profile

	1990	1991	1992	1993	1995	1996	1997	1998
Cost Price ($)								
Base	12,104	12,540	13,130	13,554	14,614	15,204	15,964	15,984
Used Values ($)								
Base ↑	2,500	3,000	3,500	4,500	5,500	8,000	9,500	11,000
Base ↓	2,200	2,500	3,000	3,500	4,500	7,000	8,500	10,500
Extended Warranty	Y	Y	Y	Y	Y	Y	Y	Y
Secret Warranty	N	N	N	N	N	N	N	N
Reliability	❷	❷	❷	❷	③	③	③	③
Air conditioning	❷	❷	③	③	③	③	④	④

integrity	②	②	②	②	②	②	②	③
Braking system	②	②	②	②	②	③	③	③
Electrical system	②	②	②	②	②	④	④	④
Engines	③	③	③	③	④	④	④	⑤
Exhaust/Converter	②	②	③	④	④	⑤	⑤	⑤
Fuel system	③	③	③	⑤	⑤	④	⑤	⑤
Ignition system	③	④	④	④	⑤	⑤	⑤	⑤
Manual transmission	④	④	④	③	③	④	⑤	⑤
- automatic	②	②	②	②	②	③	④	④
Rust/Paint	②	②	②	②	③	③	③	④
Steering	③	③	④	④	④	⑤	⑤	⑤
Suspension	②	②	③	④	④	⑤	⑤	⑤
Crash Safety	—	—	—	—	③	③	③	③
Side Impact	—	—	—	—	—	—	❶	❶

MAZDA

626, MX-6

Rating: Above Average (1996–98); Average (1994–95); Not Recommended (1985–93). 1997 was the last model year for the MX-6 and the Probe, its Ford twin. **Maintenance/Repair costs:** Higher than average. Repairs aren't dealer dependent. Mazda suggests changing the engine timing chain after 60,000 miles. **Parts:** Surveys show that parts for the 626 cost twice as much as parts for other cars in its class. Although Mazda has promised to cut prices, still compare prices with independent suppliers.

Strengths and weaknesses: Although far from being high-performance vehicles, these cars ride and handle fairly well and still manage to accommodate four people in comfort. The 1988–92 versions incorporated a third-generation redesign that added a bit more horsepower to the 4-banger. Apart from that improvement, these cars are still easy riding, fairly responsive, and not hard on gas. On the downside, the automatic transmission downshifts roughly, the power steering is imprecise, and the car leans a lot in turns.

Four-wheel steering was part of the sedan's equipment in 1988, and it was added exclusively to the MX-6 a year later. Wise buyers should pass over this option and look instead for anti-lock brakes and airbags on 1992 LG and GT versions. The manual transmission is a better choice because the automatic robs the engine of much-needed horsepower, as is the case with most cars this size.

A mid-sport and mid-compact hybrid, the MX-6 is a coupe version of the 626. It has a more sophisticated suspension, more horsepower, and better steering response than its sedan alter ego. The 1993 model gained a base 2.5L 165-hp V6 powerplant. Overall reliability and durability are on par with the 626.

Through 1995, 626s have sub-par body construction, electrical system glitches, brakes that wear out prematurely, and automatic transmissions that shift poorly and are prone to premature failure. Expect jerky downshifts when the 4-cylinder is at full throttle. Shocks and struts (MacPherson) are expensive to replace (especially when the model is equipped with the electronic adjustment feature). The electronically controlled shock absorbers haven't been durable and they, too, cost a lot to replace. Body problems include door and hatch locks that often freeze up, headliner rattles, and the metal surrounding the rear wheel wells, which is prone to rust perforation, as are hood, trunk, and door seams. The paint seems particularly prone to chipping. The underbody and suspension components on cars older than five years should be examined carefully for corrosion damage. The exhaust system will rarely last more than two years, and wheel bearings fail repeatedly within the same period.

You will want to buy a 1996–98 626 for the improved performance, handling, and overall reliability, plus reasonable fuel economy (premium grade, though).

Dealer service bulletins: 1993—Door glass rattles. • Vibrating hood. • Water leaking into the trunk. • Engine misses during hard cornering. **1994**—Air conditioning defects. • Head gasket leaks. • Automatic transmission malfunctions. • Excessive engine hydraulic lifter noise. • Brake vibration and premature wearout of the front brakes. • Steering gear could produce a clunking noise or be off-center. • Door glass pulls out of its track. • Inside rear view mirrors fall off the windshield. • Driverside power seat might not work. • Lots of wind noise around the side mirrors and A-pillars. **1995**—Camshaft friction gear noises. • 3–4 shift hunt. • Door side molding detaches in cold weather. • Expansion valve whistling noise. Front strut squeaks on turns. • Heater and AC unit noise after long storage. • Loose, rattling sunroof and outer door handles. • Creak/rattle noise from passenger-side wiper. • Steering wheel slightly off-center. **1996**—3–4 shift hunt. • Front strut squeaks on turns.

Safety summary/Recalls: All models: 1995–96—Inadvertent airbag deployments. **626 ES: 1997**—Head restraints are too low. One Canadian neurologist says the 626's head restraints are set too low and cannot extend to a safe level. He says there is an additional two inches required for a six-foot-tall occupant. When informed of his assessment, the dealer replied that Mazda "cannot help you with your problem." The doctor maintains his Mazda 626 cannot be safely operated by a driver over five feet and ten inches in height. He concludes: "As a result of my occupation, I see many motor vehicle accident neck injuries and have a keen interest in making my new vehicle, and those of others, safe." **Recalls: All models: 1986**—The throttle could stick open due to a defective nylon rotor. **1986–87**—An ignition switch failure will result in faulty wipers, washer, engine fan, heater blower, and air conditioner compressor. **1988**—Automatic shoulder belt could break. • The floor-mat could interfere with the gas pedal. • Frost could accumulate in the throttle body. • A rear brake shoe could separate from a wheel cylinder piston. • Band flexing could cause the fuel tank to leak. **1988–91**—Mazda will replace original door handles with new handles that are more durable so that door won't fly open. **1995**—Airbags malfunction. **1998**—Faulty computer module causes stalling. **626: 1997**—Inadvertent airbag deployment when passing over bumps in the road. **MX-6: 1988–89**—Takata seatbelts will be replaced. **626, MX-6: 1995–96**—Inadvertent airbag deployment when passing over bumps in the road. Sensors will be reprogrammed. **1997**—Tensioner spring may break and get caught in the engine timing belt, stalling the engine; dealers will replace the tensioner.

Secret Warranties/Service Tips

All models/years—Non-turbo models that idle roughly after a warm restart could have fuel vaporizing in the distribution pipe (DSB #023/87R). • Excessive rear brake squealing can be reduced with improved brake pads (DSB #015/89-11). • Excessive vibrations felt in the brake pedal, steering wheel, floor, or seat when applying the brakes can be fixed by installing a redesigned brake assembly. • DSB #50901898 gives tips for eliminating wind-noise around doors. **All models: 1993–94**—Freezing door and hatch lock cylinders are addressed in DSB #021/94. • Headliner rattles can be fixed by using Mazda's fastener kit. • The driver-side power seat might not work if the wiring harness touches the seat frame. • A clunking noise coming from the steering gear is caused by excessive backlash in the steering gear assembly. **1993–97**—Engine camshaft noise may be corrected with a new friction gear spring and lock nut. **1995–96**—A 3–4 shift hunt is probably caused by failure in the 3–4 shift solenoid hydraulic circuit. • Front strut squeaks on turns could be caused by interference between the upper seat spring and the strut dust cover or between the dust cover and the rubber bump stopper. **1996–97**—Unwanted 4–3 downshifts or intermittent shifting into Overdrive is covered in bulletin #015/98. **1998**—Tips on fixing faulty sunroofs, a seat-belt warning buzzer that sounds for no reason, rough automatic transmission shifts, excessive idle vibration, rear brake squeal, coolant leaks, and hard-to-close trunk lid.

626, MX-6 Profile

	1991	1992	1993	1994	1995	1996	1997	1998
Cost Price ($)								
626	14,448	15,685	17,495	15,450	17,630	17,960	18,160	18,690
MX-6	14,384	15,475	18,300	19,540	20,713	21,745	22,345	—
Used Values ($)								
626 ↑	6,000	7,000	8,000	9,000	10,000	11,000	12,500	14,500
626 ↓	5,500	6,000	7,000	8,000	9,000	10,000	11,500	14,000
MX-6 ↑	6,500	7,100	8,000	9,200	10,500	11,500	13,500	—
MX-6 ↓	6,000	6,200	7,000	8,200	9,500	11,000	12,500	—

Extended Warranty	Y	Y	Y	Y	Y	N	N	N
Secret Warranty	N	N	N	N	N	N	N	N
Reliability	②	②	②	②	②	③	④	④
Air conditioning	②	②	③	③	③	③	④	④
Body integrity	②	②	②	②	②	③	③	④
Braking system	②	②	②	②	②	③	③	③
Electrical system	②	②	②	②	③	③	③	④
Engines	④	④	④	⑤	⑤	③	③	④
Exhaust/Converter	⑤	⑤	⑤	③	④	⑤	⑤	⑤
Fuel system	④	④	③	④	④	④	⑤	⑤
Ignition system	④	④	④	④	⑤	⑤	⑤	⑤
Manual transmission	④	④	④	④	⑤	⑤	⑤	⑤
- automatic	②	②	②	②	②	③	④	④
Rust/Paint	②	②	②	②	②	③	③	④
Steering	③	③	③	④	④	⑤	⑤	⑤
Suspension	②	②	②	③	③	④	④	④
Crash Safety								
626 4d	—	—	④	④	④	④	④	—
Side Impact								
626 4d	—	—	—	—	—	—	②	③

MITSUBISHI

Galant

Rating: Recommended (1994–98); Above Average (1990–93).
Maintenance/Repair costs: Higher than average, but repairs aren't dealer dependent. **Parts:** Parts are relatively inexpensive when compared with other cars in this class. Parts availability is about average.

Strengths and weaknesses: The Galant is a recommended family-car buy because of its reasonable price, comfortably spacious interior, good fuel economy, and better-than-average reliability and durability.

1990–93 models have few problems, except for premature brake wear, and excessive noise and vibrations. Add to this poor body assembly, and you can see the Galant is far from perfect.

Totally redesigned, the 1994–98 Galant got larger—now rivaling the Mazda 626, Nissan Altima, and Toyota Camry. It's powered by a potent base 2.4L 141-hp 4-cylinder engine and an optional twin-cam variant that unleashes 160 horses. Either engine will be mated to a 5-speed manual or an electronically controlled 4-speed automatic. The latest redesign has improved the car's overall reliability, however, brakes and body deficiencies continue to be its Achilles heel.

Safety summary/Recalls: Recalls: 1989—Front seatbelt release button may fail. **1994**—Brake lights may fail and cruise control may not disengage due to faulty stop light switch. **1994–97**—After the ignition key is turned off, the sunroof immediately stops when opening the driver's door. This meets the requirements of FMVSS No. 118, "Power-operated Window Systems." However, the sunroof does not stop when the passenger's door is opened and the government has issued a recall order, which Mitsubishi is fighting. **1995**—Vehicle suddenly caught fire; believed to be caused by an electrical short. • Sticking accelerator pedal. • Floormat slips under accelerator pedal. • Sudden stalling. • Airbag failed to deploy. • Airbag deployed for no reason. • Sudden brake failure. • Brakes suddenly lock up when driving. • Parking brake fails to hold, vehicle rolled downhill. • Doors lock when brakes are applied. • Premature brake wear. • Driver-side seatbelt failure. • Seatbelt wouldn't loosen, had to be cut off. • Transmission frequently downshifts. • Transmission slippage, lockup and premature failure. • Gear shift lever fails to go from Park to Reverse or Drive. • Control arm failure. • Window fogging. • Instrument light failure. • Excessive vibration when AC is engaged. • AC emits a foul odor. • Fuel odors in the interior. **1996**—ABS brake failure. • Airbag failed to deploy. • Hard to secure child safety seat due to excessive length of seatbelts. • Front axle collapsed when passing over a bump, causing loss of steering. • Transmission gasket failure. • Defective electric door locks. • Excessive windshield fogging. • Faulty rear door rubber seals.

Secret Warranties/Service Tips

All models/years—Troubleshooting tips to correct spark plug fouling and window fogging. **1994–96**—If the ABS warning light comes on for no apparent reason, it's likely the ABS ECU needs replacing under warranty. • Door trim panel gaps or peeling can be fixed by following the tips given in DSB #96-52A-001. **1995–96**—Sunroof water leaks are tackled in DSB #964-42A-008. **1996**—Rough automatic transmission shifting can be corrected by installing an upgraded transmission control module under warranty.

Galant Profile

	1991	1992	1993	1994	1995	1996	1997	1998
Cost Price ($)								
Base	14,098	15,487	16,024	16,204	17,017	18,535	17,964	18,222
Used Values ($)								
Base Coupe ↑	6,000	6,500	7,000	8,000	9,000	10,000	12,500	13,000
Base Coupe ↓	5,000	6,000	6,500	7,500	8,500	9,000	11,500	12,500
Extended Warranty	N	N	N	N	N	N	N	N
Secret Warranty	N	N	N	N	N	N	N	N
Reliability	⑤	⑤	⑤	⑤	⑤	⑤	⑤	⑤
Air conditioning	④	④	④	⑤	⑤	⑤	⑤	⑤

Body integrity	②	②	②	②	③	③	③	④
Braking system	②	②	②	②	③	③	③	④
Electrical system	③	③	④	④	④	⑤	⑤	⑤
Engines	③	④	④	④	⑤	⑤	⑤	⑤
Exhaust/Converter	②	②	④	④	④	⑤	⑤	⑤
Fuel system	③	③	③	④	④	③	④	⑤
Ignition system	③	③	③	④	④	④	⑤	⑤
Manual transmission	④	④	④	⑤	⑤	⑤	⑤	⑤
- automatic	③	③	③	⑤	⑤	④	④	⑤
Rust/Paint	②	②	②	②	③	③	③	④
Steering	③	③	③	③	③	⑤	⑤	⑤
Suspension	③	③	④	④	④	⑤	⑤	⑤
Crash Safety	②	②	②	—	—	—	④	④
Side Impact	—	—	—	—	—	—	③	③

NISSAN

Altima

Rating: Above Average (1996–98); Average (1993–95). The 4-cylinder engine barely provides the necessary versatility needed to match the competition: the Toyota Camry, Mazda 626, updated Ford Probe, or larger Ford Sable and Taurus. Although the SE gives the sportiest performance, the less-expensive GXE is the better deal from a price/quality standpoint. **Maintenance/Repair costs:** Higher than average. Repairs are dealer dependent. **Parts:** Owners complain of parts shortages, and parts may be more expensive than those for most other cars in this class.

Strengths and weaknesses: The Altima's wheelbase is a couple of inches longer than the Stanza's, and the car is touted by Nissan as a mid-size, even though its interior dimensions put it in the compact league. The small cabin seats only four, and rear seat access is difficult to master due to the slanted roof pillars, inward-curving door frames, and narrow clearance.

The base engine gives average acceleration and fuel economy. Maneuverability is good around town. There are no reliability problems reported with the 16-valve powerplant or transmission. The uncluttered under-hood layout makes servicing easy, and it has good body assembly.

With its noisy and rough engine performance, this car cries out for a V6 like the one used in the Maxima. The 4-banger has insufficient top-end torque and gets buzzier the more it's pushed. In order to get the automatic to downshift for passing, for example, you have to practically stomp on the accelerator. The 5-speed manual transmission is sloppy. The Altima's sporty handling is way overrated; there's excessive body roll and front-end plow in hard cornering, tires squeal at moderate speeds, and steering isn't as precise or responsive as befits a car with performance pretensions. In spite of the car's independent suspension, it gives a busy, uncomfortable ride that's punishing over bumps. Lots of engine, road, and tire noise.

Dealer service bulletins: 1993—A creaking, squeaking, or tapping noise coming from the window and door areas. • Water leaks. • Electrical system, heater, air conditioning, and defrosting malfunctions. • Body/trim deficiencies. **1994**—No Reverse (automatic). • Excessive brake and steering wheel vibration. • Inaccurate fuel gauges. • Rear suspension noise. **1995**—Front cover oil leakage. • No or low line pressure rise (control valve). • Poor driveability—Code 45. • AC compressor leaks or is noisy. • Troubleshooting excessive front and rear brake noise. • Some windshield cracks are covered under warranty.

Safety summary/Recalls: 1997—Fire ignited in the engine compartment while vehicle was parked. • Fire started by fuse box in passenger compartment. • Sudden acceleration. • Frequent reports that the airbag failed to deploy. • Poor braking performance. • Poor design causes electronic control unit failure. • Defective automatic transmission solenoid. • Windshield wiper fails periodically. • Water leaks into trunk area, causing premature rusting. • Automatic door lock failure. • Seat and shoulder belts lock up and don't retract. **1998**—Stalling when accelerating. • Rear seats won't lock upright. • Windows rattle excessively. • Wheel cover failure. **Recalls: 1993–94**—Throttle cable may not return to idle. **1995**—Automatic shift lever plate can break, causing unintended vehicle movement. • Brake hose may leak. **1996**—AC refrigerant leaks. • Leaking AC evaporator drain hose causes ECM damage. **1997**—Defective seatbelt buckles.

Secret Warranties/Service Tips

1993—Center caps on alloy wheels may not fit properly; order upgraded caps (#40315-D9000). • An exhaust rattle during acceleration can be resolved by installing an upgraded muffler-exhaust assembly (#203000-IE860). • Inadequate defrosting on vehicles made before February 1993 can be resolved by following Nissan's suggestions in its #NTB93-059 bulletin. • #NTB93-086, a lengthy Nissan bulletin sent out May 25, 1993, troubleshoots the Altima's most common water leaks into the interior. • Poor AC performance can be corrected by installing a thermal control unit (TCU). • An inoperative AC and heater may have a kinked heater/water valve cable that has damaged the air mix door actuator. **1993–94**—No Reverse gear with the manual transmission: install a Nissan upgrade kit. • Fuel gauge is inaccurate or it may be difficult to fill the fuel tank; can be fixed with upgraded parts. **1993–96**—DSB #NTB96-046 gives lots of useful tips for troubleshooting squeaks and rattles.

Altima Profile

	1993	1994	1995	1996	1997	1998
Cost Price ($)						
XE	16,229	16,904	17,848	18,783	18,798	18,179
Used Values ($)						
XE ↑	7,500	9,000	10,000	11,500	12,500	14,000
XE ↓	6,500	7,500	9,000	10,000	11,500	13,000
Extended Warranty	N	N	N	N	N	N
Secret Warranty	N	N	N	N	N	N
Reliability	③	③	④	④	④	⑤
Air conditioning	❷	③	④	④	④	⑤
Body integrity	❷	❷	③	③	③	③
Braking system	❷	❷	③	③	③	③
Electrical system	❷	❷	❷	③	③	③
Engines	④	⑤	④	⑤	⑤	⑤
Exhaust/Converter	③	④	④	⑤	⑤	⑤
Fuel system	③	③	④	⑤	⑤	⑤
Ignition system	④	⑤	⑤	⑤	⑤	⑤
Manual transmission	④	⑤	⑤	⑤	⑤	⑤
- automatic	④	⑤	⑤	⑤	⑤	⑤
Rust/Paint	❷	❷	③	③	③	③
Steering	③	③	③	④	⑤	③
Suspension	③	③	③	③	③	③
Crash Safety	④	④	—	④	④	③
Side Impact	—	—	—	—	—	③

Stanza

Rating: Above Average (1990–92); Average (1988–89); Not Recommended (1985–87). The Stanza was replaced by the Altima in 1993. **Maintenance/Repair costs:** Lower than average. Repairs aren't dealer dependent. **Parts:** Average cost, but can be bought for much less from independent suppliers.

Strengths and weaknesses: The 1988–89 Stanzas were mini Maximas in that they were redesigned along luxury Maxima lines. Unfortunately, they were underpowered, the automatic transmission was reluctant to downshift, the engine was noisy, and the base suspension allowed the car to bounce about. This is not the car for a full passenger or cargo load.

1990–92 Stanzas are roomy, reasonably priced, four-passenger compacts that offer peppy performance, more responsive steering, nimble handling, and good fuel economy. Overall reliability has been fairly good during the past seven years. Except for some road noise, suspension thumps, starting difficulties, transmission malfunctions, and a biodegradable exhaust system, no major problems have been reported on 1988–92 Stanzas.

Owners complain that the automatic transmission vibrates annoyingly when the car is idling in gear, clutches are noisy, and steering wheel vibrations are frequent. Power antenna malfunctioning, premature front brake wear, and surface rust problems are common for all years. Especially prone to rust perforation are wheel openings, the front edge of the hood, the rear hatch, and door bottoms.

Safety summary/Recalls: Recalls: Wagon 2X4: 1986—Cover the fuel-filler pipe for increased accident protection.

Secret Warranties/Service Tips

All models/years—A rotten-egg smell could be caused by a defective catalytic converter; have it replaced free of charge if the emissions warranty still applies. **All models: 1982–88**—Improved brake pad material will cut brake noise and add to pad durability. Upgraded semi-metallic pads carry the Hitachi HP12 FE designation. **1987–89**—Trunk lid torsion bars won't fall off if you install a torsion bar spacer (#84449-D4060). **1989–92**—Clutch shudder and steering wheel vibration can be eliminated by checking brake rotor thickness or installing an upgraded pressure plate release lever. **1990**—Starting in D4 or delayed downshifting requires a new valve body separator plate. **1990–91**—Starting difficulties can often be traced to an ECU connector not fully seated in the ECU. **1990–92**—Clutch whine or screech in cold temperatures requires the installation of an upgraded clutch disc.

Stanza Profile

	1987	1988	1989	1990	1991	1992
Cost Price ($)						
Base	12,144	12,869	13,654	13,335	13,900	14,000
Used Values ($)						
Base ↑	3,000	3,500	4,500	5,500	6,000	6,500
Base ↓	2,500	3,000	3,500	4,500	5,500	6,000
Extended Warranty	Y	Y	Y	Y	N	N
Secret Warranty	N	N	N	N	N	N
Reliability	❷	③	③	③	④	④
Air conditioning	③	④	④	④	⑤	⑤
Body integrity	❷	❷	③	③	③	③
Braking system	❷	❷	③	③	③	③
Electrical system	❷	❷	❷	③	③	③
Engines	❷	③	④	④	④	④
Exhaust/Converter	❷	❷	❷	❷	③	③
Fuel system	❷	③	③	③	③	③
Ignition system	③	③	③	③	③	③

Manual transmission	③	④	④	④	④	④
- automatic	❷	③	③	③	③	③
Rust/Paint	❷	❷	③	③	③	③
Steering	❷	③	③	④	④	④
Suspension	❷	③	③	③	③	④
Crash Safety						
Stanza 4d	—	—	—	❷	④	④

SUBARU

Legacy

Rating: Above Average for AWD models only (1996–98); Average (1989–98). The 1995–98 AWD models are way overpriced considering they don't offer much more than AWD. Before buying a front-drive Subaru, first consider what Honda, Mazda, or Toyota have to offer. The only reason to buy a Subaru is for its 4X4 capability, and on most used models you'll have to pay a $1,500–$2,000 premium to get it. If it's not what you need for your basic driving requirements, pick a car with a conventional drivetrain. **Maintenance/Repair costs:** Higher than average. Repairs are dealer dependent. **Parts:** Higher-than-average cost can't be attenuated through purchasing from independent suppliers.

Strengths and weaknesses: First launched in 1989 as front-drives, these compacts are a bit slow off the mark. The 5-speed is a bit notchy, and the automatic gearbox is slow to downshift and has difficulty staying in Overdrive. Early Legacys are noisy, fuel-thirsty cars with bland styling that masks their solid, dependable AWD performance. Actually, the availability of a proven 4-wheel drive powertrain in a compact family sedan and wagon makes these cars appealing for special use. In spite of their reputation for dependability, though, Subarus are not trouble-free—engine, clutch, turbo, and driveline defects are common on the early models through to the 1994 models.

The redesigned 1995–98 models have sleeker styling, additional interior room, a bit more horsepower with the base engine, and a new 2.5L 4-cylinder driving the 1996 AWD GT and Lsi. The Outback, a Legacy Madison Avenue spin-off, was transformed into a sport-utility wagon with a taller roof. Even with the improvements noted above, acceleration is still only passable (if you don't mind the loud engine), but handling and ride are remarkably good. Overall, it's a competent car with few faults and only one outstanding feature—AWD. If you don't need that feature, there are better-performing, less-expensive vehicles available. Another word of warning: *Consumer Reports* says that the Outback upgrade isn't worth the extra money. They point out that Subaru's ads are misleading when they show Paul Hogan zipping around off-road. The publication also reports that the Outback's handling isn't as competent as that of the regular Legacy (something to do with the higher center of gravity, no doubt).

Subaru's overall product lineup for 1997 marked a return to the company's four-wheel drive roots with the repackaging of its Legacy and Impreza 4X4 lineup as Outbacks (half of all Legacys sold are Outbacks). A Legacy 2.5L GT all-wheel drive sporting sedan, or wagon variant, also joined the group that year. In addition to these redesignated models—and the squeezing out of a bit more horsepower from its limited range of engines—Subaru continued to tap the sport-utility craze through lower prices for its AWD and ABS options and by offering a greater variety of AWD vehicles.

Are Subarus good buys? Devotees will insist that there's no other car as versatile, and the manufacturer is justifiably proud of the high J. D. Power owner satisfaction rating earned in the U.S. On the other hand, I have found that a Subaru can be a good used-car choice only if its AWD feature is essential for your driving needs, it's been maintained carefully, the body hasn't begun to rust, and dealer servicing is easily available. This last point is crucial because these cars are very dependent on the dealer network for parts and servicing.

Through 1995, premature exhaust system rust-out and automatic transmission (front seals, especially) and clutch breakdowns are the more common complaints. Brakes require frequent attention. Shock absorbers, constant velocity joints, and catalytic converters often wear out prematurely. Other problems that appear over many model years include starter and ignition relay failures and front-end suspension noises. Subarus are rust-prone: fenders, door bottoms, rocker panels, wheel openings, bumpers and supports, rear quarter-panels, tailgates, trunk lids, and hoods are particularly vulnerable. Additionally, the underbody and chassis components should be examined very carefully for corrosion damage.

1996–98 Legacys are much improved, with few problems except for some minor brake, electrical, clutch, and body integrity shortcomings.

Safety summary/Recalls: 1996—Sudden acceleration. • When the vehicle is being driven, transmission may suddenly jump out of Drive into Neutral. • Inadvertent airbag deployment. • Airbags failed to deploy. • ABS brakes locked up. • Brake failures. • ABS performs poorly on snow and ice. • Floor carpet prevented brake pedal application. • Complete engine failure at 15,000 miles. • Chronic stalling. • Computer sensor control unit failure. • Excessive shaking at highway speeds. • Windshield wiper bolt failure. • Alternator failures while driving. • Left turn signal fails intermittently. • Climate control button sticks. • AC seizure. • O-ring failure causes AC to leak freon. • Bridgestone tires frequently blow out. • Keyless entry failed due to pinched wire in driver's door. • New design headlights give poor illumination. **1997**—Airbags deployed but failed to inflate. • Airbags failed to deploy. • Sudden acceleration. • Cruise control failed to disengage when brakes were applied. • Igniter failed, allowing unburned fuel to flow into catalytic converter. • AC blew fumes into interior, causing driver to black out. • Stalling caused by igniter failure. • Complete engine failure due to defective valves and pistons. • Sudden loss of steering. • Poor braking performance; ABS brakes frequently fail or lock up. • Front brake pad failure. • Premature wearout of all brake components. • Transmission surges when cold, or shifts into Neutral at low speed or when descending a small hill. • Transmission failures. • Frequent electronic control unit failures. • Rear seatbelts are too long to properly secure child safety seat, and the locking mechanism doesn't lock properly. • Brake and engine lights continually on. • Three alternators replaced by one owner. • Shorted hazard switch drained battery. • Alternator belt snapped, causing battery and brake warning lights to come on and making car hard to steer. • Alternators frequently quit while vehicle is under power. **1998**—Many instances where the airbags failed to deploy. • Oil leak from oil filter seam caused fire. • Sudden brake loss after linings, calipers, and master cylinder had been replaced. • Cruise control failed to disengage when brakes were applied. • Excessive shaking at highway speeds. • Seatback collapsed when vehicle was rear-ended. • Subaru told car owner that tendency to pull to the right was a design feature. **Recalls: 1989-93**—Frost could build up in the manual transmission dipstick vent, causing transmission oil leakage and eventual wheel lockup. **1990-91**—The defroster is faulty. • Door might not open from the inside. • Automatic transmission could engage abruptly, causing a sudden lurch into Reverse. **1990-93**—Cold weather or high humidity could cause the manual transmission in the 4X4 to seize. **1993**—The top of the fuel tank could leak. **1998**—Due to poor welds, ignition keys can stick, shift levers and linkages can break, and shift levers can move; dealers will replace the automatic transmission shift lever assembly.

Secret Warranties/Service Tips

All models/years—A rotten-egg smell could be caused by a defective catalytic converter. It will be replaced, after a bit of arguing, free of charge under the emissions warranty. **1990-91**—The defroster is faulty. • Front door malfunction could make it impossible to open the door from the inside. • The 4EAT automatic transmission Park gear might not engage properly. **1990-93**—The manual gearbox in the AWD could leak, causing the transmission to seize. **1993**—Legacys could have a headliner droop, which is addressed in a March 1994 DSB. **1994**—Torque converter squeaking is addressed in a June 1993 DSB. **1995**—Tips are provided on silencing excessive front strut noise and engine oil pump leaks. **1995–96**—If the antenna won't fully retract, Subaru suggests cleaning the antenna mast and replacing the dress nut. **1995-97**—Troubleshooting tips on a sticking antilock brake relay are offered. **1997**—Troubleshooting tips are offered on transfer clutch binding and/or bucking on turns.

Lemon-Aid

Legacy Profile

	1991	1992	1993	1994	1995	1996	1997	1998
Cost Price ($)								
Legacy	12,444	15,259	16,220	17,495	17,395	16,517	—	—
4X4	19,294	21,029	22,095	22,295	17,643	18,075	18,490	18,524
Used Values ($)								
Legacy ↑	5,500	6,500	7,000	8,000	9,500	11,000	—	—
Legacy ↓	4,500	5,500	6,500	7,000	8,500	10,500	—	—
Legacy 4X4 ↑	7,000	8,000	9,500	10,500	11,500	13,000	15,000	16,500
Legacy 4X4 ↓	6,500	7,500	8,500	10,000	10,500	11,500	14,000	15,500
Extended Warranty	Y	Y	Y	Y	Y	Y	Y	Y
Secret Warranty	N	N	N	N	N	N	N	N
Reliability	②	③	②	②	③	④	④	④
Air conditioning	②	②	③	③	④	⑤	⑤	⑤
Body integrity	②	②	②	②	②	③	③	③
Braking system	②	②	②	②	②	③	③	③
Electrical system	②	②	②	②	③	③	③	④
Engines	③	④	④	⑤	⑤	⑤	⑤	⑤
Exhaust/Converter	①	①	②	②	③	④	⑤	⑤
Fuel system	③	③	④	④	④	④	⑤	⑤
Ignition system	②	②	③	③	④	⑤	⑤	⑤
Manual transmission	③	③	③	④	⑤	⑤	⑤	⑤
- automatic	②	②	③	③	③	③	⑤	⑤
Rust/Paint	②	②	②	③	③	③	④	⑤
Steering	③	③	④	④	⑤	⑤	⑤	⑤
Suspension	③	③	③	③	⑤	⑤	⑤	⑤
Crash Safety								
Legacy 4d	③	③	④	④	④	④	④	④
Side Impact	—	—	—	—	—	—	—	③

TOYOTA

Camry

Rating: Recommended (1994–98); Above Average (1988–93); Average (1985–87). 1996 was the wagon's last model year. For the past four years, Camrys have elicited an unusual number of safety complaints that are carried over from one model year to the next. The complaints include: severe wandering at highway speeds; sudden acceleration; engine-compartment fires; brake failures; poor headlight illumination; and transmission interlock failures, which allow a parked vehicle to roll away. **Maintenance/Repair costs:** Higher than average, but repairs aren't dealer dependent. **Parts:** Parts are more expensive than for most other cars in this class (alternator and ignition module, for example). Parts availability is excellent.

Strengths and weaknesses: Safety complaints, aside, the Camry is an excellent family-car buy because of its spacious, comfortable interior, good fuel economy, and impressive reliability and durability.

1987–93 models have few problems, although they're far from perfect. Main areas of concern are failure-prone cylinder head gaskets; suspension and electrical system failures; defective starter drive and ring gear; leaking low pressure and high pressure power-steering lines and outer CV boots that split, causing grease to leak; premature brake wear; and some paint peeling and rusting. Mufflers last only two years on earlier models, and sunroofs are rattle-prone.

Persistent problems with all Toyota vehicles are premature brake wear, excessive noise, and vibrations. Stung by consumer criticism that these problems haven't been fixed for over a decade and that owners are charged for useless repairs, Toyota published a "Brake Repair" service bulletin (POL94-18) in October 1994, which defines those repairs that will be done under warranty. Toyota states that premature brake wear and noise will be fixed under warranty for the first 12 months/ 12,500 miles, and that vibrations will be attended to, under warranty, up to 3 years/36,000 miles.

Front suspension bushings wear out quickly, leading to clunking and squeaking noises when going over bumps or when stopping quickly. There's also the so-called Camry chop (exceptionally rough rides when passing over uneven roadways) reported by owners of 1992–94 models. Cruise control fails frequently on all years. Owners of the 1992 Camry have reported that a chronic drone noise, along with a vibration felt from the floor and the gas pedal, occurs mostly when the automatic transmission changes from second to third gear at 1800–2000 rpm.

1994–98 Camrys aren't perfect: owners report premature brake failures, faulty window regulators, smelly ACs, and myriad rattles, clunks, and groans that seem to come from everywhere. There is also an annoying surging and shuddering when decelerating, which appears to be more common with the 1995–96 models. It seems as though it's a sticking throttle position sensor, but mechanics say that the problem is intrinsic to the way the engine/transmission computer module is calibrated. Other deficiencies reported by owners: brake vibrations, premature brake pad wear, AC malfunctions, and defective automatic transmissions that slip out of gear when parked. 1994–98 model body problems include excessive wind noise coming from the front windshield, back doors, and sunroof. Trim items rust and fall off, door handles pull away, and mufflers have a short life span. No reports of rust perforation problems, but weak spots are door bottoms, rear wheel openings, and trunk and hatchback edges. There are complaints concerning premature rusting on cars painted white. Toyota generally corrects these rust/paint deficiencies for free.

Totally redesigned, the 1997 Camry is taller, longer, wider, more powerful, and cheaper, in both a literal and a figurative sense. Gone are the coupe and station wagon variants. The wheelbase was extended by two inches, giving backseat passengers more room. Other changes: it's powered by a base 2.2L 133-hp 16-valve 4-cylinder engine (taken from the Celica) and an optional 3.0L 24-valve V6 that unleashes 194 horses. Either engine will be mated to a 5-speed manual or an electronically controlled 4-speed automatic. ABS and traction control are standard on all V6-equipped Camrys, rear seats have shoulder belts for the middle passenger, brighter low beam lights, optional heated mirrors, more cup holders, a sunglasses holder, and an additional power port in the center console.

"Decontenting" hit Toyota's 1997 lineup hard, resulting in many changes that cheapened the Camry through less sound insulation (when more was needed, I'd say) and less durable trim and accessories. Although Toyota admits to engine head gasket leaks for the first time (see "Secret Warranties/Service Tips"), reliability doesn't appear to have been affected, notwithstanding a sharp increase in noise complaints. The changes include: less expensive S-rated tires on models with 4-cylinder engines, cheaper heating/ventilation system components, no more assist handles for front occupants, no more chrome trim around the windshield, one door seal instead of three (greater chance for wind and water leaks), fewer airbag sensors, an LCD odometer, a distributorless ignition with the 4-cylinder, and a windshield-embedded antenna. Owners report the 1997 models have limited rear visibility (due to the side pillars and high trunk lid), less steering "feel," and more squeaks and rattles than previous versions.

Dealer service bulletins issued so far for the 1998 Camry show fewer trim problems and no engine head gasket alert, but noise concerns relating to the suspension, steering, and power front seat still remain (see following bulletin).

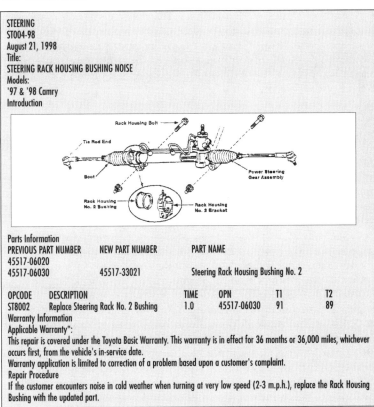

STEERING
ST004-98
August 21, 1998
Title:
STEERING RACK HOUSING BUSHING NOISE
Models:
'97 & '98 Camry
Introduction

Parts Information

PREVIOUS PART NUMBER	NEW PART NUMBER	PART NAME
45517-06020		
45517-06030	45517-33021	Steering Rack Housing Bushing No. 2

OPCODE	DESCRIPTION	TIME	OPN	T1	T2
ST8002	Replace Steering Rack No. 2 Bushing	1.0	45517-06030	91	89

Warranty Information
Applicable Warranty*:
This repair is covered under the Toyota Basic Warranty. This warranty is in effect for 36 months or 36,000 miles, whichever occurs first, from the vehicle's in-service date.
Warranty application is limited to correction of a problem based upon a customer's complaint.
Repair Procedure
If the customer encounters noise in cold weather when turning at very low speed (2-3 m.p.h.), replace the Rack Housing Bushing with the updated part.

Toyota won't give you the upgraded steering component unless you ask for it.

Dealer service bulletins: 1994—Improved durability of Overdrive clutch bearing. • Rear brake squeak. • Rear suspension noise. • Steering column clicking noise. • New seals to prevent water leakage into interior. • Water pump seal improvements. • Wind noise from window. • AC evaporator odor. • Brake pad kits. Cause and repair of brake vibration and pulsation. • Front brake noise. • Improved power window regulator. • Moon roof panel wind noise. **1995**—Front brake noise. • AC evaporator odor. • Moon roof panel wind noise. • Improved power window regulator. • Rear brake squeak. • Rear suspension noise. **1996**—Front brake noise. • AC evaporator odor. • Charcoal canister humming noise. • Rear window rattle. • Rear brake squeak. • Rear suspension noise. • Moon roof panel wind noise. **1997**—Engine head gasket coolant leak. • AC evaporator odor. • Charcoal canister humming noise. • Difficulties with moon roof operation. • Exterior rear view mirror improvement. • Steering rack housing bushing noise. • Front shoulder belt anchor buzzes. • Front suspension groans. • Suspension rattle and popping. Tailpipe contact with heat shield. • Headliner buzzes or rattles.

• Moon roof rattles. • Manual front seat movement/noise. • Power front seat chattering. • Radio volume control too sensitive. • Rubbing noise from door trim. • Seatcover loose at lower rear corners. • Seat movement field fix procedure. • Armrest bum improvement. • CD player won't accept/eject CDs. • Fuel door operation improvement. • Wind noise repair kit.

Safety summary/Recalls: Owners report that the Dunlop D60 A2 tire is a poor wet-weather performer. **1987–91**—Leaking fuel tanks. **1995**— Injury from airbag. • Premature front/rear brake wear. • Defective, poor performance (when wet) Goodyear Invicta tires. • Windshield reflects dashboard image. **1995–96**—Brake failure. • Noisy, vibrating brakes. • Premature front and rear brake wear. • Excessive engine noise. • Transmission lever can slip from Drive to Neutral. • Airbag fails to deploy or is accidentally deployed. • Sudden acceleration, stalling. • Passenger-side seatbacks won't stay upright. • Passenger seatbelts over-retract. • Defective radio antenna. • Taillight and turn signal bulbs frequently burn out. • **1996**—Vehicle wanders over road. • Door bottom/ undercarriage rusting. • Airbag warning light and Check Engine light always on. • Windshield film buildup. • Window water leaks. **1997**— Engine compartment fire following ABS brake failure. • Airbags failed to deploy. • Violent deployment of airbag during an accident caused death. • Sudden acceleration when brakes were applied. • Tendency for car to wander all over the roadway. • Steering wheel suddenly locked up, causing an accident. • Many reports of transmission interlock system failures. • Many other reports, probably related to the interlock system, that vehicle was put in Park and keys taken out of ignition and car then proceeded to roll away. • Century infant seat won't fit in the center of rear seat. • Seatbelts continually ratchet tighter; rear seatbelt was strangling child, who had to be cut free. • Plastic part fell behind the dash and lodged behind the brake pedal arm, causing an accident. • Frequent brake failures. • Premature brake pad and caliper wear or failure. • Loud grinding brake noise when braking. • Excessive noise coming from underneath the car at highway speeds. • Vehicle sits too low, has minimal ground clearance. • Driver's knee can hit the steering wheel adjuster lever, making steering wheel go up and down. On several occasions, steering wheel suddenly tilted all the way up while on the highway. • Very poor headlight illumination; headlight safety cap cover design cuts visibility severely; there's a blind spot on the driver-side headlights. • Low beam lights aren't bright enough. • Dash indicator lights are too small and low in intensity. • Inoperative rear window defroster. • Driver's seatback rocks back and forth. • Power door lock relay failure. • Car locks and unlocks on its own. • Fuel door doesn't open fully when lever is pulled. • Rear windshield exploded while car was parked overnight. **1998**—Several reports of engine fires. • Vehicle stalled, oil light came on, and fire ignited in engine compartment. • Sudden acceleration. • Many reports that airbags failed to deploy. • Frequent complaints that vehicle wanders at highway speeds and is difficult to control in a crosswind. • Overly soft suspension allows the chassis to scrape the roadway when passing over a small bump. • Frequent ABS brake failures. • Excessive brake noise and extended stopping distances. • Transmission gear shift lever went from Neutral to Drive without pressing button. • Airbag service indicator light stays on. • Engine malfunction light stays on. • Inadequate night illumination from headlights; low beam halogen headlights don't carry very far; dark spot cast from left headlight results in poor visibility; metal deflector inside the concealed headlights blocks out all light beyond 30 feet. • Electrical system failure; running lights won't shut off. • Lock design allows for occupants to be temporarily locked in vehicle if someone gets out before them and locks the doors. • Power door locks fail intermittently. • Front restraints lock up when vehicle is parked on an incline. • Sun visors are too small to block the sun, and cut visibility. • Back windshield shattered. • Fumes from inside the vehicle fog up the windshield. • Gas tank makes sloshing noise when brakes are applied. • General Tire wears excessively on the inside tread. • Frequent complaints of moon roof leaks, which may cause electrical short. • Doors have to be slammed shut. **Recalls: 1987**—Liquid spilled on console could short out the automatic seatbelt motor. **1987–89**—Front seatbelt guides that stay retracted will be changed. **1987–90**—Malfunctioning power door locks. **1988**—Original equipment jack in station wagon may collapse. **1991**—Dealer will replace faulty electrical components in Fujitsu Ten radios to eliminate the chance of fire. **1994**—Steering wheel may disengage from the steering column or shaft assembly. One owner of a 1992 Camry reports that her car suddenly went out of control. She found that the left rear tire was turned to a 45 degree angle: the front control arm that holds the tire in alignment had completely broken off at the tire end of the arm. **1996**—Taillight assembly lacks sufficient heat resistance. **1997**—Ignition key can be removed when vehicle not in Park. • Brake failure may occur due to moisture freezing in the brake vacuum hose.

Secret Warranties/Service Tips

All models/years—A decade-old brake pulsation/vibration problem is fully described and corrective measures are detailed in DSB #BR94-002, issued February 7, 1994. Sometimes only the parts are covered; and the owner has to pay for labor. • To reduce front brake squeaks on ABS-equipped vehicles, ask the dealer to install new, upgraded rotors (#43517-32020). • Owner feedback over the last decade plus dealer service managers who wish to remain anonymous tell me that Toyota has a secret warranty that will pay for replacing front disc brake components that wear out before 2 years/ 25,000 miles. If you're denied this coverage, threaten small claims court action. • A wind noise repair kit is now available. **All models: 1987–90**—Engine ping, surging, or jerk can be fixed with an upgraded ECU. **1987–91**—A front inner shoulder belt guide is available to keep the belt away from the neck and face. This free accessory is covered under the seatbelt warranty.

1988—Harsh 2–3 shifts may require the replacement of worn valve body rubber check balls. **1988–89**—Hard starting may require a new cold-start time switch. **1989–90**—A rattling sunroof will be silenced with an upgraded sliding mechanism and new cables and shoes. • Wind noise coming from the upper windshield molding requires that sealant be injected underneath the molding. **1992**—Noisy rear brakes can be silenced by installing upgraded brake pads identified by the letter "N" stamped on the part number label. **1992–93**—Upgraded brake rods will reduce front brake groan/grind. **1993**—Under a special program, Toyota has paid for the repair of AC units that fail to cool due to a faulty expansion valve. Ask for partial compensation. **1993–96**—Suspension squeaks and groans are addressed in DSB #SU95-003. **1994**—A steering column clicking noise calls for the replacement of the steering main shaft assembly and steering column tube assembly. • Rear window wind noise can be stopped by replacing the front centering-type bolt with a non-centering-type bolt and a washer. **1995–96**—Use upgraded brake pad material to eliminate brake groaning, according to DSB #BR002-96. **1996–97**—A charcoal canister humming noise can be silenced by installing an upgraded vacuum hose. **1997**—Head gasket leaks are covered by a special Toyota program that is applied only if the customer complains. • A front suspension groan can be fixed by replacing the front spring bumper under Toyota's three-year warranty. • If the driver's seat "rocks," Toyota has an upgraded assembly that will secure the seat. **1997–99**—Fuel door operation improvement, tips on reducing steering and front suspension noise. **1997–98**—New front brake pad kits will reduce brake grinding or groaning, says bulletin #BR001-99. • To enhance headlight performance, the alignment process has been modified.

Camry Profile

	1991	1992	1993	1994	1995	1996	1997	1998
Cost Price ($)								
Base Coupe	—	—	—	18,963	19,430	19,458	—	—
Base Sedan	14,513	16,713	17,578	19,293	19,815	19,850	19,918	20,464
LE	16,242	17,293	18,235	19,613	19,955	20,588	20,288	20,858
4X4	17,010	—	—	—	—	—	—	—
Wagon	15,837	19,095	19,553	20,703	21,370	22,030	—	—
LE Wagon V6	18,483	—	—	—	—	—	—	—
Used Values ($)								
Base Coupe ↑	—	—	—	11,000	12,000	14,000	—	—
Base Coupe ↓	—	—	—	10,500	11,500	13,000	—	—
Base Sedan ↑	6,500	8,500	10,000	11,500	13,000	14,500	16,000	17,500
Base Sedan ↓	6,000	7,500	9,000	11,000	11,500	14,000	14,500	16,500
LE ↑	7,000	9,000	10,500	12,000	13,500	15,000	16,500	18,800
LE ↓	6,000	8,000	9,000	11,000	12,500	14,500	15,000	16,500
4X4 ↑	7,500	—	—	—	—	—	—	—
4X4 ↓	6,500	—	—	—	—	—	—	—
Wagon ↑	7,000	10,000	11,000	12,500	14,000	16,000	—	—
Wagon ↓	6,000	9,000	10,000	11,500	12,500	14,500	—	—
LE Wagon V6 ↑	8,500	—	—	—	—	—	—	—
LE Wagon V6 ↓	7,000	—	—	—	—	—	—	—

Extended Warranty	N	N	N	N	N	N	N	N
Secret Warranty	N	N	N	N	N	Y	Y	Y
Reliability	⑤	⑤	⑤	⑤	⑤	⑤	⑤	⑤
Air conditioning	④	④	❷	⑤	⑤	⑤	⑤	⑤
Body integrity	❷	❷	❷	❷	③	③	③	③
Braking system	❷	❷	❷	❷	❷	❷	❷	❷
Electrical system	③	③	③	③	③	③	③	④
Engines	③	④	④	④	⑤	⑤	③	⑤
Exhaust/Converter	❷	❷	④	④	④	⑤	⑤	⑤
Fuel system	③	③	③	④	④	③	④	⑤
Ignition system	③	③	③	④	④	④	⑤	⑤
Manual transmission	④	④	④	⑤	⑤	⑤	⑤	⑤
- automatic	③	③	③	③	③	③	③	③
Rust/Paint	③	③	③	④	④	④	⑤	⑤
Steering	③	③	③	③	③	⑤	⑤	⑤
Suspension	③	③	④	④	④	⑤	⑤	⑤
Crash Safety	—	④	④	④	④	④	④	④
Side Impact	—	—	—	—	—	—	③	③

VOLKSWAGEN

Corrado

Rating: Below Average (1992–94); Not Recommended (1990–91).
Maintenance/Repair costs: Way higher than average, and only a VW
dealer can repair these cars. 1994 was the Corrado's last model year.
Parts: Frequently back-ordered; outrageously high cost for parts.
Owners complain that the alloy wheels are easily damaged and can cost
a fortune to replace.

Strengths and weaknesses: The Corrado is an attractive, mid-sized, two-
door coupe with a comfortable interior for the driver and front passenger. It gives good all-round performance, with the accent on smooth
acceleration, a firm but not harsh ride, and excellent handling with little body roll.

The manual transmission's long shift throw is annoying and rear
passenger room is quite limited. The following systems can be troublesome: heating, defrosting, brake, electrical, and fuel. Although the
V6 engine runs quietly, there's lots of road/wind noise intrusion into
the passenger compartment.

Dealer service bulletins: 1993—Excessive diagonal tire wear. •
Excessive brake noise. • Faulty windshield wipers. **1994**—AC expansion
valve noise. • An erratic idle. • Abnormal rear tire wear due to the rear

axle having too much positive toe. • CD changer could skip or be grounded. • Difficulty shifting the manual transmission.

Safety summary/Recalls: Rear visibility is seriously compromised by the high tail and spoiler. • One Canadian owner of a 1993 Corrado reports that his car suddenly fishtailed out of control while rounding a curve at a moderate speed. **1992**—NHTSA is looking into reports of heater cores that rupture and spew hot coolant into the passenger compartment. **Recalls: 1990**—Hot water could leak onto driver's feet and steam up the vehicle's interior.

Secret Warranties/Service Tips

All models/years—Poor driveability (hard starts, surging, stalling, low fuel economy) could be due to a deteriorated oxygen sensor (02S) wire shield or an improper oxygen sensor wire shield ground; ask that it be replaced under the emissions warranty. • Manual transmissions that are difficult to shift in or out of gear could require the installation of a clutch disc with a nickel-plated hub. **All models: 1990-91**—Abnormal engine noise that occurs when the engine is warm can be corrected by installing an upgraded crankshaft (#026-105-101E). • If the radiator fan stays on high speed when the ignition is off and thus discharges the battery, replace the radiator fan high-speed relay with part number #321-919-505A. **1990-95**—On Corrados equipped with an automatic transmission, an engine that won't start could have a loose contact in the ECM power supply relay; if so, replace the power supply relay. **1991-93**—AC expansion valve noises require the installation of an upgraded expansion valve. **1992-94**—Poor 2.8L engine performance or a rough idle could be due to a misrouted EVAP vacuum hose or an improperly routed positive crankcase ventilation hose that causes a vacuum leak. **1993**—If the ABS warning light won't go out, a faulty start switch/lock is the likely culprit. **1993-94**—AC expansion valve noise can be silenced with an upgraded expansion valve. • Troubleshooting tips are offered for insufficient AC cooling. • If the ABS light won't go off, you might have a faulty ignition switch/lock.

Corrado Profile

	1990	1991	1992	1993	1994
Cost Price ($)					
Base	18,220	19,440	20,230	23,260	25,540
Used Values ($)					
Base ↑	6,000	7,000	8,000	11,500	13,500
Base ↓	5,000	6,000	7,000	10,000	12,000
Extended Warranty	Y	Y	Y	Y	Y
Secret Warranty	N	N	N	N	N
Reliability	❷	③	③	③	③
Air conditioning	③	④	④	④	④
Body integrity	❷	❷	③	④	④

Braking system	❷	❷	❷	❷	③
Electrical system	❷	❷	❷	❷	③
Engines	❷	③	③	⑤	⑤
Exhaust/Converter	⑤	⑤	⑤	⑤	⑤
Fuel system	❷	❷	③	③	④
Ignition system	③	③	④	④	⑤
Manual transmission	⑤	⑤	⑤	⑤	⑤
- automatic	❷	❷	❷	❷	❷
Rust/Paint	❷	❷	❷	④	⑤
Steering	⑤	⑤	⑤	⑤	⑤
Suspension	③	③	④	④	⑤

Note: No crash tests have been carried out on the Corrado.

Passat

Rating: Recommended (1998); Above Average (1995–97); Not Recommended (1989–94). Don't buy any Passat without a comprehensive extended warranty. If you must have a Passat, wait until the Audi spin-off 1998 Passats come off their two-year leases. The higher cost for the '94 base version is due to the inclusion of a base V6. The more reliable recent models stick you with a high cost price due to their slow depreciation. **Maintenance/Repair costs:** Much higher than average. Most major repairs are dealer dependent. **Parts:** Parts and service are more expensive than average.

Strengths and weaknesses: This front-drive compact sedan and wagon uses a standard 2.0L engine and other mechanical parts borrowed from the Golf, Jetta, and Corrado. Its long wheelbase and squat appearance give the Passat a massive, solid feeling, while its styling makes it look sleek and clean. As with most European imports, it comes fairly well appointed.

As far as overall performance goes, the Passat is no slouch. The multivalve 4-cylinder engine is adequate, and its handling is superior to that of most of the competition. The 2.8L V6 provides lots of power when revved and is the engine that works best with automatic transmission.

The redesigned 1995 version came with standard dual airbags, a restyled interior, rear headrests, a softened suspension, and a much-improved crashworthiness rating. The 1998 Passat, however, is practically an entirely different car, based upon the Audi A4 and A6, and offers much better performance and reliability.

Passats are infamous for transmission malfunctions that are costly to repair. Even when they're operating as they should, Passat's manual and automatic gearboxes leave a lot to be desired. For example, the 5-speed manual transmission gear ranges are too far apart: there's an enormous gap between third and fourth gear, and the 4-speed automatic shifts poorly with the 4-banger. Also, owners report problems with the front brakes, MacPherson struts, and fuel and electrical systems as the car ages. Interior trim and controls are fragile.

Competent servicing and parts aren't easy to find away from the larger cities, and many of the above-mentioned deficiencies can cost you an arm and a leg to repair.

Dealer service bulletins: 1993—AC expansion valve noise. • Faulty ABS warning lights. • Excessive diagonal tire wear. • Frequent windshield wiper failures. **1995**—Skipping CD changer. • Instrument cluster loss of memory. • Poor fuel system performance. • Excessive rear tire wear. • Drifting, pulling to one side. • Skipping wiper blades. • Engine won't start. **1996–97**—Transmission fluid seepage. • Shifter is hard to move or won't go into Reverse. • Knocking/vibrating shift lever. • Transmission pops out of gear. • Vehicle will not move into any forward gear. • Eliminating musty odor from AC. • Malfunctioning CD player. **1998**—Eliminating musty odor from AC.

Safety summary/Recalls: 1996—Many complaints that transmission slips out of third gear into Neutral. • Vehicle suddenly accelerated forward as lever was put into Reverse. • Intermittent stalling due to electronic control module failure. • Check Engine light constantly goes on and off. • Engine valve cover gasket failures. • Plastic shroud on top of engine rubs against the fuel line. • Leaking windshield and door seals. • Premature wheel bearing failure on the driver's side. • Door lock failure allows door to open while under power, or makes doors difficult to open. • Instrument cluster wiring harness failures. • Repeated trunk switch failures. • Chronic trunk water leaks. • Premature brake pad wearout. • All dash gauges suddenly stop working. **1997**—When manual transmission lever is put into Reverse, it often goes into first gear instead. • Sudden steering wheel lockup. • Cooling fan control module failure. • Rear window defroster power button works only when held in the ON position. • Door handle failures. • Frequent window regulator failures. **1998**—Engine head gasket leaks. • Erratic transmission performance. • Gas tank can't be filled without the pump shutting off repeatedly. • AC recirculation switch failure. • Serious blind spots caused by the small size and narrow view of the three mirrors. • Front seats move back and forth when braking or accelerating. • Total electrical system failure. **Recalls: 1989–90**—Hot water could leak onto driver's feet and steam up the vehicle's interior. **1993**—Axle could separate from struts, causing loss of vehicle control. **1993–95**—Faulty radiator fan motor could cause engine to overheat and stall in models equipped with a VR6 engine.

Secret Warranties/Service Tips

All models/years—Vehicles that won't move into any forward gear could have broken retaining lugs for selector plugs of B2/K1, which causes the selector valve to partially protrude or fall out of the valve body. **All models: 1990–91**—If the radiator fan stays on high speed with the ignition off and thus runs down the battery, replace the fan's high-speed relay with part number #321-919-505A. **1990-95**—On Passats equipped with an automatic transmission, an engine that won't start could have a loose contact in the ECM power supply relay; fix this by replacing the power supply relay. **1991-93**—AC expansion valve noises require the installation of an upgraded expansion valve. • Poor driveability could be caused by magnetic interference due to a deteriorated oxygen sensor wire shield or improper oxygen sensor wire shield ground connection. **1992-94**—Poor 2.8L engine performance or a rough idle could be due to a misrouted EVAP vacuum hose or an improperly routed positive crankcase ventilation hose, which will cause a vacuum leak. **1993**—If the ABS warning light won't go out, a faulty start switch/lock is the likely culprit. **1995-96**—Troubleshooting tips are offered on automatic transmission fluid seepage. **1996-97**—If the transmission pops out of gear, check for a hairline crack on the selector shaft shift detent sleeve.

Passat Profile								
	1991	1992	1993	1994	1995	1996	1997	1998
Cost Price ($)								
Base	17,355	16,955	19,125	24,340	19,215	19,715	19,930	22,325
Used Values ($)								
Base ↑	5,500	6,500	8,000	12,500	10,500	12,000	18,000	20,500
Base ↓	5,000	5,500	6,500	11,000	9,000	10,500	16,500	19,000
Extended Warranty	Y	Y	Y	Y	Y	Y	Y	
Secret Warranty	N	N	N	N	N	N	N	
Reliability	❷	❷	❷	③	③	③	④	⑤
Air conditioning	❷	❷	❷	③	④	④	④	④
Automatic transmission	❶	❶	❶	❷	❷	③	③	④
Body integrity	❷	❷	❷	❷	③	④	④	④
Braking system	❷	❷	❷	❷	❷	③	③	④
Electrical system	❷	❷	❷	❷	③	③	③	③
Engines	⑤	⑤	⑤	⑤	⑤	⑤	⑤	⑤
Exhaust/Converter	⑤	⑤	⑤	⑤	⑤	⑤	⑤	⑤
Fuel system	❷	❷	❷	③	④	⑤	⑤	⑤
Ignition system	❷	❷	❷	③	④	⑤	⑤	⑤
Rust/Paint	③	③	⑤	⑤	⑤	⑤	⑤	⑤
Steering	③	③	③	③	④	④	⑤	⑤
Suspension	③	③	③	③	④	④	⑤	⑤
Crash Safety	❷	❷	❷	—	④	④	④	—

VOLVO

240

Rating: Average (1989–93); Below Average (1985–88). **Maintenance/ Repair costs:** Higher than average; repairs are dealer dependent. **Parts:** Higher-than-average cost and hard to find.

Strengths and weaknesses: Problems with entry-level Volvos like the 240 mirror the quality-control problems manifested by Saab, the other Swedish automaker, except for the fact that Volvo styling is more bland than bizarre. The 240 is a solid and spacious car. Unfortunately, it doesn't live up to Volvo's advertising as an automotive longevity wonder. Volvo reliability is, in fact, a bit below average, if you consider the Japanese competition.

The V6 is an honest, though imperfect, engine. Avoid the turbocharged 4-cylinder engine and failure-prone air conditioning systems. Diesels suffer from cooling system breakdowns and leaky cylinder head gaskets. The brakes on all model years need frequent and expensive service and exhaust systems are notorious for their short life span. The GL and GLE suffer from occasional electrical bugs. Volvos are fairly rust-prone and the front and rear wheel openings are especially susceptible to perforation. The lower edges of the side cargo windows on station wagons rust prematurely, as do the lower tailgate lips.

Confidential dealer service bulletins address the following deficiencies affecting models over the past few years: hard cold starting, electronic module defects, excessive brake and cruise control noise, knocking sway bar bushings, and leaking sunroofs.

Safety summary/Recalls: 1986–91—Interestingly, when a '79 Volvo 240 was crash-tested, researchers concluded both the driver and passenger would have sustained severe head trauma. Nevertheless, the 240 had the lowest rate of driver deaths among popular passenger vehicles on U.S. roads during 1989–93, says an IIHS study. Furthermore, the 240 didn't record a single driver death during the five years of the study. **Recalls: 1985–86**—A low-speed frontal collision could cause unintended sudden acceleration. **1986–87**—Erratic cruise control operation is caused by a voltage drop. **1992**—The ball joint and strut could separate, leading to loss of vehicle control.

Secret Warranties/Service Tips

All models/years—An April 1993 DSB lists front and rear brake pad kits that have been specially developed to eliminate brake noise. **All models: 1988–90**—Brake pulsation, a common problem, is addressed in DSB 51/111.
• If you're having problems starting your Volvo on cold mornings, see DSBs 23/135 and 23/21A. **1989–93**—To improve cold starting, Volvo will install an improved fuel injection control module for free if the emissions warranty

still applies. Under another program, Volvo will replace the MFI EPROM to improve cold starting and idle quality. **1990–93**—Noise coming from the cruise control vacuum pump can be stopped by modifying the pump bracket mounting. **1991–93**—Under Service Campaign 62, Volvo will replace the sway bar bushing. The bushing can pull away from the retainers and create a knocking noise; Volvo says the problem isn't safety related. Cost is to be borne by the owner, but Volvo sometimes makes pro rata "goodwill" adjustments.

240 Profile								
	1986	1987	1988	1989	1990	1991	1992	1993
Cost Price ($)								
240 DL	14,370	16,025	16,920	17,600	17,735	19,680	21,220	22,215
Used Values ($)								
240 DL ↑	3,000	4,000	5,500	6,500	8,500	10,000	11,500	13,500
240 DL ↓	2,500	3,500	4,000	5,500	7,000	8,500	10,500	12,000
Extended Warranty	Y	Y	Y	Y	Y	Y	Y	Y
Secret Warranty	N	N	N	N	N	N	N	N
Reliability	③	③	③	③	③	③	③	④
Air conditioning	❷	❷	❷	③	③	③	③	③
Body integrity	❶	❶	❶	❶	❷	③	③	④
Braking system	❶	❶	❶	❷	❷	③	③	③
Electrical system	❶	❶	❶	❶	❶	③	❷	③
Engines	③	③	③	③	③	③	③	④
Exhaust/Converter	❷	❷	❷	❷	③	③	③	④
Fuel system	❶	❶	❶	❷	❷	❷	③	③
Ignition system	④	④	④	④	③	③	④	⑤
Manual transmission	③	③	③	③	③	③	③	④
- automatic	④	④	④	④	③	③	③	④
Rust/Paint	❷	❷	③	③	③	④	④	⑤
Steering	❶	❶	④	④	④	⑤	③	④
Suspension	④	④	④	④	④	③	③	③
Crash Safety	—	—	—	—	—	—	⑤	⑤

LARGE CARS/WAGONS

For motorists who can write off relatively high gasoline consumption, maintenance, and insurance premiums, these are excellent cars for extensive highway driving.

The term "large car" is relative. It once designated vehicles that had a wheelbase of more than 114 inches and that weighed about 3,200 lb. But now that the automakers have shortened most of the wheelbases of their large cars, reduced their weight, and switched to front-wheel drive, traditional definitions of "large" may no longer be accurate indicators of a car's size. Some large cars, like GM's Caprice and Roadmaster, bucked this trend, however, and remained long and heavy.

Owners have to pay a premium for these vehicles, which usually come fully loaded with performance and convenience features, but they are happy to do so because these vehicles offer considerable comfort and stability at high speeds. Large cars also depreciate slowly, can seat six adults comfortably, and are ideal for motoring vacations.

These vehicles generally incur less damage from front, rear, and side collisions, although recent U.S. government crash tests show that some smaller cars absorb frontal crash just as well.

Recommended

Ford Crown Victoria/Grand Marquis (1997–98)

Above Average

Ford Cougar/Thunderbird (1995–97)
Ford Crown Victoria/ Grand Marquis (1994–96)

GM Caprice, Impala SS, Roadmaster (1995–96)

Average

Ford Crown Victoria/Grand Marquis (1984–93)

GM Caprice, Impala SS, Roadmaster (1994)

Below Average

Chrysler Concorde/Intrepid/ LHS/New Yorker/Vision (1995–98)

Ford Cougar/Thunderbird (1985–94)

Not Recommended

Chrysler Concorde/Intrepid/
 LHS/New Yorker/Vision
 (1993–94)

Chrysler Dynasty, Fifth Avenue,
 Imperial, New Yorker (1985–93)
GM Caprice, Impala SS,
 Roadmaster (1985–93)

Station wagons (full-sized)

If passenger and cargo space and carlike handling are what you want, a large station wagon may not be the answer—a used minivan, van, light truck, or compact wagon can fill the same need for less cost and will probably still be around a decade from now. Popular (though troublesome) wagons—like the Caprice and Roadmaster (both axed in 1996)—in which you could cram a Little League team are an endangered species, losing out to the van and minivan craze.

Some disadvantages of large station wagons: difficulty in keeping the interior heated in winter, atrocious gas consumption, sloppy handling, and poor rear visibility. Exterior road noise is also a frequent problem, since the vehicle's interior has a tendency to amplify normal road noise. Rear hatches tend to be rust-prone. Crash safety is variable.

No full-sized station wagons are recommended.

CHRYSLER

Concorde/Intrepid/LHS/New Yorker (1994–98)/Vision

Rating: Below Average (1995–98); Not Recommended (1993–94). If you want maximum passenger room, choose the 1995–96 LHS or New Yorker. They're about five inches longer and use the larger engine. Whichever vehicle you're considering buying, before paying a cent, make sure you get an extended warranty and take a test drive at night to assess the efficacy of the headlights. **Maintenance/Repair costs:** Higher than average, but most repairs aren't dealer dependent. **Parts:** Higher-than-average cost (independent suppliers sell for much less), but not hard to find. Only vehicles that still carry Chrysler's seven-year powertrain and body warranty are worthy of any consideration.

Strengths and weaknesses: These sleek-styled front-wheel drives are Chrysler's mid-size cum large-size flag bearers. They're roomy, fuel efficient, and highly maneuverable. The base engine is a 3.3L 153-hp 6-banger, but 70 percent of buyers chose the 3.5L for its 61 extra horses. Both engines provide plenty of low-end torque and acceleration; they blow the Camry and Accord away with a 0–60 time of 8.9 seconds. This advantage is lost somewhat when traversing hilly terrain: the smaller V6 powerplant strains to keep up. You'll find good or better handling and steering response than in the Sable and Taurus, and the independent suspension maximizes control, reduces body roll, and provides lots of suspension travel so that you don't get bumped around too much on rough roads.

With all these positives, why aren't these cars recommended? Simple: they're unsafe, unreliable, and cheaply made. One 1994 Intrepid owner's comments posted on the Internet sum it up: "The lack of over-all quality and dangerous headlights made me dump the car after only 15 months' use."

A perusal of dealer service bulletins and comments from car rental agencies and other owners tells me that these cars continue to have many serious safety- and performance-related shortcomings that can no longer be explained away as the "first series" teething problems that all new cars experience.

The automatic climate control system operates erratically, blowing cold air when it's set for warm, and warm air when it's set for cool. The instrument panel must be removed before servicing the ventilation system because the AC ducts are molded into the plastic panel. The shift console needs lighting, the radio and climate controls are too small, the trunk release is hidden in the glove compartment, the hood release is on the floor, the rear view mirror is too narrow, and the fuel-filler door needs a lock. The trunk has a high deck lid, making for difficult loading and unloading, and there's no inside access by folding down the rear seat, as in the Camry.

Owner reports confirm that there are chronic problems with leaking 3.3L engine head gaskets and noisy lifters that wear out prematurely around 30,000 miles. Water pumps often self-destruct and take the engine timing chain along with them (an $800 repair). Other common complaints: a poor fit between the exhaust manifold and the engine block often results in oil leaks and noisy engine operation; if you wash your car during extremely cold weather, the resulting ice buildup and leaking deck lid seals can easily damage the heater fan motor.

AC malfunctions and failures abound. The problem has become so prevalent that Chrysler has a little-known warranty extension that will pay for the replacement of the evaporator up to seven years.

Dear Valued Customer:

Chrysler Canada continuously strives to maintain the highest level of customer satisfaction. For that reason, we are extending the Basic Warranty coverage for the air conditioning evaporator in your vehicle to 7 years or 115,000 kilometres, whichever occurs first, from your vehicle's warranty start date. All owners of the vehicle are covered. We have enclosed an addendum card showing your extended coverage and we suggest that you keep the card in your warranty information booklet.

The air conditioning evaporator's function is to cool the interior of the vehicle when the air conditioner is turned on. Poor interior cooling or lack of cooling may be caused by a refrigerant leak from the evaporator. There are no safety concerns for you or your passengers. The refrigerant in your vehicle is environmentally friendly and will not cause any harm.

If you are not experiencing any problems with your vehicle's air conditioning system, no action is required. In the event you experience an air conditioning problem, please contact your dealer for diagnosis. Repairs involving the replacement of your air conditioning evaporator will be completed at no charge to you within the 7-year or 115,000-km warranty limits.

If you previously paid for a repair involving replacement of the evaporator, you may be eligible for reimbursement. To request reimbursement consideration, please send us the enclosed *yellow* card and the *original* paid repair bill (keep a copy for your records). A postage-paid envelope is provided for your convenience. The yellow card may also be used to change or correct your name or address information.

If you have any questions concerning this letter, please contact your servicing Chrysler Canada dealership.

Chrysler is taking this action to demonstrate our commitment to your continued satisfaction.

Sincerely,

Chrysler Canada

Chrysler Canada Ltd.
CIMS 240-01-10
P.O Box 1621
Windsor, Ontario N9A 4H6

Use this Chrysler letter as leverage for goodwill refunds on other AC components and for other models and years. The fact that it was issued by Chrysler Canada is inconsequential; the same policy applies in the States.

The 4-speed LE42 automatic transmission is a spin-off of Chrysler's failure-prone A604 version—and owner reports show it to be troublesome as well. Owners tell of chronic glitches in the computerized transmission's shift timing and computer malfunctions, which result in driveability problems (stalling, hard starts, and surging).

Body problems abound, with lots of interior noise, uneven fit and finish, poor quality trim items that break or fall off easily, exposed screw heads, faulty door hinges that make the doors rattle and hard to open, distorted windshields, windows that come off their tracks or are misaligned and poorly sealed, power window motor failures, and steering wheel noise when the car is turning. Other body defects specifically addressed in dealer service bulletins include the following: noisy front suspension; glue oozing out at the back center brake-light-and-windshield molding; water collecting in the park/turn lights; noisy rear upper strut mounts; water draining into the trunk when the deck lid is raised; and water entering into the AC/heater housing.

Dealer service bulletins: 1993—AC operates erratically (covered by a secret warranty). • Automatic temperature control (ATC) works poorly in warm weather. • An ominous clicking noise comes from the passenger compartment, and the 3.3L engine emits a ticking sound when cold. • Hard starting and long crank times when the engine is hot. • Ignition noise on the AM band. • Malfunctioning AC ducts, which blow different temperatures of air. **1993–95**—Upgraded spark plugs will improve cold starting; ask for part #56027275. **1994**—Acceleration shudder. • Faulty engine timing belts. • The transmission wiring harness bracket could break, transmission wires could short-circuit, and the floor shifter knob could stick. • The radio often "locks up." **1995**—Glitches in the computerized transmission's shift timing cause driveability problems (stalling, hard starts, and surging). Amazingly, the 4-speed LE42 automatic transmission—a spin-off of Chrysler's failure-prone A604—appears to be just as problem-plagued as its predecessor. • AC refrigerant leaks. • Heater/AC housing leaks water and there's moisture in headlights. • Excessive engine noise is likely caused by carbon buildup on the top of the pistons. • Engine mount rattles. • Transmission clicks and clunks. • Fuel line rattles caused by faulty fuel rail assembly. • Squeaking front or rear brakes require upgraded brake linings. • A-pillar wind noise. • Rattling C-post appliqué or poor fit of the appliqué to the back glass. • Front hub clicks and clunks. • B-pillar and rear spring rattles. • Upper strut mount squeaks. • Excessive road noise from the front wheels and rear seat requires reduced tire pressure and the addition of foam/sealer insulation to the front upper load beam or the C-pillar. **1996**—3.3L/3.5L lower engine oil leaks. • Reduced transmission limp-in default sensitivity. • Shuddering on upshift or whenever the torque converter is engaged. • Upgraded Overdrive clutch hub. • Front suspension clunking or rattling. • Metallic knocking from front of vehicle when passing over bumps. • High-speed windshield washer spray knockdown. • Water leaks into trunk (see "Secret Warranties/Service Tips"). • Polycast wheel center falls off. • Cupholder improvements.

1997—Tips on troubleshooting noisy brakes. • AC evaporator leaks. • AC suction line failure. • Warped or poor-fitting passenger-side airbag door. • A metallic popping noise might be heard coming from the front of the vehicle. • Sticking sunroof or sunshade. • Rear drum brake ticking. • Water ingestion into heater/AC housing.

Upscale LHS and New Yorker versions haven't escaped Chrysler's notorious poor-quality body components and sloppy assembly. In addition to the above-mentioned owner and bulletin-related problems, additional service bulletins for these cars indicate that they're likely to have their own persistent problems—such as faulty fuel pumps causing stalling, reduced power, or erratic transmission shifting; radio lockups; water leaks coming from the heater/AC housing; and moisture in the headlights. Bulletins also address how to silence a noisy AC compressor, a squeaking or creaking noise coming from the rear window when travelling at slow speeds over rough roads, and a high-pitched whistling noise caused by a defective idle air control motor.

Safety summary/Recalls: All models: 1993—Models with 3.3L V6 engines may have a faulty O-ring in the engines' fuel-injection system that may harden and let fuel escape. **1993–95**—Models with 3.5L engines may have faulty fuel-injector components that could cause an engine compartment fire. • Headlights are too dim for safe motoring, and some owners report that the headlights sometimes cut out completely. This problem also affects post-1995 versions. Defrosting is inadequate on some 1993s, allowing ice and moisture to collect at the base of the windshield. Chrysler has a fix for these two problems that requires the installation of a new headlight lens and small foam pads into the defroster outlet ducts. • Both ABS and non-ABS brakes perform poorly, resulting in excessively long stopping distances—more so than for other cars in this class, as the following Canadian owner's email confirms:

> I recently had an accident in my 1997 Intrepid with ABS brakes. On bone dry pavement I was unable to do more than slow the car down. Lots of room to stop. Both feet on the pedal pushing like hell! No tire skid and no ABS ratcheting. Air bags in my face and $7500 damage. I've been trying to find others that have had the same experience....
>
> Brian Hyndman
> Port Coquitlam, BC

• The overhead digital panel is distracting and forces you to take your eyes from the road. • The emergency brake pedal catches pant cuffs and shoelaces as you enter or exit the vehicle. • A high rear windowsill obstructs rear visibility. • These cars have safety-related peculiarities that you wouldn't believe. The owner of a 1993 Intrepid recounts his unforgettable experience:

I started having trouble getting the key out of the ignition after I shut the car off. This happened on a Saturday afternoon. I called the dealer and was told I was pretty much out of luck until a mechanic was available on Monday. If I had been smart, I would have left the keys in the ignition and prayed some stupid thief would steal the car. I finally had to call a friend who works at Transport Canada's Road Safety department here in Ottawa. He had the answer—you have to smack the gearshift lever from right to left so the internals under the button on the gearshift lever pop out. Lo and behold, this worked. Nifty feature on a $27,000-plus car. I still have to do this to this day, especially during colder weather...The power remote locks would not work and the driver's side door could not even be unlocked with the key (some rod was broken). The only way I could get into the car was to unlock the passenger door with the key and crawl across the front seat! Who is the brainiac who decided the location of the horn button? The horn is impossible to locate in an emergency.

1994–97—NHTSA is looking into reports that the front suspension may collapse, causing the driver to lose control of the vehicle. This government agency knows of 26 complaints and 105 warranty claims for 1994 models, and another 49 complaints covering 1995–97 years that used an upgraded suspension. Broken welds or cracks where the lower control arm attaches to the front cradle may be the cause of the failures. **1996**—Sudden acceleration when starting out in Drive. • Airbags fail to deploy. • Driver's pant leg gets caught on the parking brake assembly upon entering the vehicle. • Many reports that while the vehicle is being driven at 60 mph, there's a sudden loss of power, the engine shuts down, power steering and brakes become inoperative, and the Check Engine light comes on. • High pressure fuel lines between the two cylinder heads leak gas onto the engine. • When shifting into Reverse from Park, automatic transmission acts as if it's in Neutral, and the engine races when the accelerator is pressed. • ABS brake failures. • Brake rotors rust prematurely, warp easily, and pads have to be changed every 10,000 miles. • Vehicle shakes violently when ABS brakes are applied. • Inadequate headlight illumination. • Dashboard reflection in the windshield hampers visibility. • Horn buttons difficult to access in emergency situations. • Stuck right rear door lock won't allow door to open. • Door hinges don't hold door open securely, causing injury to occupants when door closes unexpectedly. • Frequent water pump, AC, and battery failures. **1997**—Fire ignited in trunk. • Fuel line hoses disconnected from the engine, spilling fuel into the engine area. • ABS brake failures. • Airbags failed to deploy. • Engine hesitates and surges. • Vehicle decelerates while driving. • Premature wearout of front brake pads and rotors (rotors warp or become rust-pitted). • Excessive brake noise. • Several reports that Goodyear Eagle tires tend to hydroplane. • Steering linkage failure causes vehicle to wander all over the roadway. • Power steering failure—extremely hard to turn. • Many reports of sudden transmission failures, many due to cracked transmission casings. • Transmission fluid leakage caused by defective transmission casing bolt. • Seat backrest failure. • Frequent windshield replacements due to distortion—particularly annoying at night when combined with poor headlight illumination. • Intermittent turn signal operation. • Flawed interior door panels. • Frequent instrument panel malfunctions: lights, gauges, AC all go out at once. • Cigarette lighter shoots out so hard it shoots under driver's seat—while red hot. **1998**—Several reports of sudden acceleration when shifting into Reverse. • When transmission relay fails, it causes a harsh downshift to second gear while at highway speeds. • Airbags failed to deploy. • Rear brakes improperly adjusted by Chrysler result in overloaded front brakes and warped front brake rotors. • Windshield distortions. **Recalls: All models: 1993**—Dealers will reroute the wiring harness to prevent shorting. **1994**—Faulty transmission wiring might cause the car to allow starting when not in the Park position. **Intrepid and Vision: 1993**—Defective lower control arm washers could cause loss of steering. **Concorde, Intrepid, LHS, and Vision: 1993–97**—Models with 3.5L V6 engines may have a faulty O-ring in the engines' fuel-injection system that may harden and let fuel escape.

Secret Warranties/Service Tips

All models/years—A rotten-egg odor coming from the exhaust is probably caused by a malfunctioning catalytic converter; this is covered by Chrysler's original warranty *and* the emissions warranty. Don't take "no" for an answer. The same advice goes for all the squeaks and rattles and the water and wind leaks that afflict these vehicles. Don't let Chrysler or the dealer pawn these problems off as maintenance items. They're all factory related and should be covered for at least five years. **All models: 1993**—Failure of the fuel pump check valve could cause start-up die-out, reduced power, or erratic shifting. • Doors that are hard to open or close or that make a snapping sound likely need four-check door straps, which Chrysler will provide free of charge. • More importantly, AC evaporator failures will be covered under a special seven-year program, according to Chrysler service honchos. Although limited to 1993s, it's logical (to me, at least) that this warranty extension sets up a benchmark that owners of other, more recent models can rely upon to get their ACs repaired under warranty (even if the evaporator isn't the cause of the failure). **1993–94**—Acceleration shudder could be caused by automatic transmission front pump leakage. • A-pillar wind noise requires sealing the upper load beam and A-pillar or sealing the roof rail body seam. • AC belt rollover requires the installation of a revised AC belt and idler pulley. • Exchange the base body control module (BCM) for an upgraded version if dash instruments and gauges suddenly quit working. • Upgraded disc brake linings will help reduce front or rear squeaking noises. • AM radio static (poor reception of distant stations) can be corrected by installing a supplemental engine-suppression strap to the left side of the engine. • Engine mount rattles signal the need to replace the engine mounts (always replace in pairs). • Cold-start piston knocking noise

can be eliminated by replacing the piston and connecting rod assembly.
• No-starts, poor engine performance, and loud noises when attempting to
start can be corrected by installing a snubber over the timing-belt tensioner
plunger (this applies to the 3.5L engine only). • Dealers will exchange
small head restraints for larger ones free of charge. • A heater/AC housing
that leaks water into the passenger compartment can be plugged by enlarg-
ing the right plenum drain hole. • Rear disc brake noise can be stopped by
installing upgraded rear disc brake adapters. • Rear glass rattling is likely
caused by a loose back light. • Excessive rear road noise can be reduced by
indexing the spring to the upper strut mount; in cases where indexing
doesn't work, you may have to replace the rear upper strut mounts with
revised mounts. • A transmission buzz or rattle can be stopped by replacing
the transfer chain snubber and attaching screws. • If water leaks or dust
accumulates inside the trunk, try sealing the quarter panel to the outer
wheel house panel seam. **1993–97**—The blower motor could seize or freeze
from water seeping into the heater/AC housing. • AC evaporator leaks
caused by premature corrosion can be prevented by installing a cowl
plenum screen; Chrysler confirms this is a warranty repair.

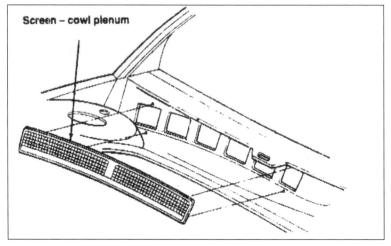

Both the screen and its installation are covered by Chrysler's warranty.

1994—Harsh, erratic, or delayed transmission shifts can be corrected by
replacing the throttle position sensor (TPS) with a revised part. **1994–95**—
The intermittent or total loss of air conditioning can be corrected by
installing a revised AC pressure transducer. **1995–96**—More troubleshooting tips are offered on diagnosing and fixing trunk water leaks.

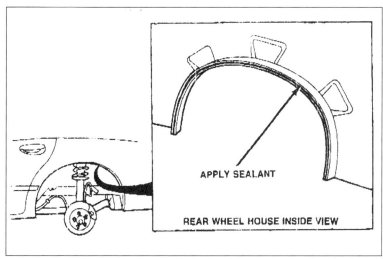

APPLY SEALANT

REAR WHEEL HOUSE INSIDE VIEW

A Chrysler trademark for the past three decades (like the 6-cylinder engine's stalling on rainy days): water leaks often lead to premature trunk and wheelwell rusting.

1995–97—If the AC suction line fails, replace it and install a revised right-side engine ground strap; the original ground strap probably caused the failure. **1996–97**—If you hear a metallic popping noise coming from the front of the vehicle when you accelerate from a stop, install two new upper and two new lower cradle mounting isolators. • Rear drum brake ticking can be silenced by burnishing the rear brakes.

Concorde/Intrepid/LHS/New Yorker (1994–98)/Vision Profile

	1993	1994	1995	1996	1997	1998
Cost Price ($)						
Concorde	19,720	21,020	21,090	19,990	20,980	21,855
Intrepid	18,000	19,100	19,230	18,990	19,950	20,235
LHS	—	30,870	30,190	30,850	30,850	—
New Yorker	—	26,125	26,190	27,890	—	—
Vision	18,725	20,272	20,232	19,795	20,860	—
Used Values ($)						
Concorde ↑	8,500	10,000	11,000	13,500	15,500	19,000
Concorde ↓	7,000	9,000	10,000	12,000	14,000	18,000
Intrepid ↑	7,500	9,000	10,500	12,000	14,000	17,500
Intrepid ↓	6,000	7,500	9,000	10,500	12,500	16,000
LHS ↑	—	12,500	14,000	16,000	18,500	—
LHS ↓	—	10,500	13,000	14,500	16,500	—
New Yorker ↑	—	11,000	13,000	14,500	—	—
New Yorker ↓	—	9,000	11,500	13,500	—	—
Vision ↑	7,000	8,500	10,000	11,500	13,000	—
Vision ↓	6,000	7,000	8,500	10,000	12,000	—

Extended Warranty	Y	Y	Y	Y	Y	Y
Secret Warranty	Y	Y	Y	Y	Y	Y
Reliability	❶	❶	❶	❷	❷	❷
Air conditioning	❶	❶	❶	❷	❷	③
Automatic transmission	❶	❶	❶	❷	③	③
Body integrity	❶	❶	❶	❷	❷	❷
Braking system	❷	❷	❷	❷	❷	③
Electrical system	❶	❶	❷	❷	❷	③
Engines	③	③	③	④	④	④
Exhaust/Converter	③	④	④	④	④	④
Fuel system	③	③	③	③	④	④
Ignition system	❷	❷	③	④	④	④
Rust/Paint	③	④	④	④	④	④
Steering	③	④	⑤	⑤	⑤	⑤
Suspension	❷	❷	❷	③	③	④
Crash Safety						
Concorde	④	④	④	④	④	—
Intrepid	④	④	④	④	④	—
LHS	—	④	④	④	④	—
New Yorker	—	④	④	④	—	—
Vision	④	④	④	④	④	—
Side Impact						
Concorde	—	—	—	—	④	—
Intrepid	—	—	—	—	④	—
Vision	—	—	—	—	④	—

Note: All these vehicles are practically identical and should have similar crash-worthiness scores, even though not every model was tested each year.

Dynasty, Fifth Avenue, Imperial, New Yorker (1988–93)

Rating: Not Recommended (1985–93). The 1994 and later New Yorkers are completely different cars from previous New Yorkers and are rated on the previous pages. Even though the top-of-the-line Imperial has a rapid depreciation rate, it's no bargain at any price. **Maintenance/Repair costs:** Higher than average; repairs aren't dealer dependent. **Parts:** Higher-than-average cost, but can be bought for much less from independent suppliers. Body parts are often back-ordered. Imperial body parts are rare and costly.

Strengths and weaknesses: These relatively fuel-efficient four-door sedans handle and ride like the average mid-sized car popular two decades ago. Compared to large rear-drives equipped with V6 or V8 engines, they can't tow as much weight, their unit-body construction makes for a noisier ride, and long-term reliability is way below average.

The base 2.5L engines are a major source of mechanical woes and, when turbocharged, can cost you a small fortune to repair. Owners complain of substandard piston rings, faulty oil seals, and a failure-prone timing-chain mechanism that can lead to severe engine damage unless it's checked and adjusted frequently.

The Mitsubishi 3.0L V6 engine, offered since 1988, has generated complaints concerning oil leaks, electronic malfunctions, and fuel system problems. Chrysler's 3.3L V6, available as of the 1990 model year, is more reliable. The electronic 4-speed automatic has elicited a number of complaints about erratic and noisy shifting. The A604 automatic transmission is a nightmare, and Chrysler is replacing it by the ton, paying the warranty deductible and compensating consumers for consequential damages.

Front suspension components and brakes wear out quickly. The electrical system is bug-plagued; avoid the electronic dashboard. Air conditioning malfunctions occur all the time, accompanied by the evaporator freezing up. Windshield wiper motors short-circuit, and often the motor is replaced unnecessarily. Owners report erratic horn operation and leaky radiators. Knobs and levers break very easily. Front seats lack lower-back support, and the middle passenger is punished by the hard edges of the split seat and folded armrest. Mediocre heating (when the Dynasty accelerates, there isn't enough engine vacuum to operate the actuators that maintain a consistent heat range); there aren't any ducts to distribute warm air to the rear. When going over bumps, these cars shake and rattle like old taxicabs. Many owners report water infiltration, especially around the windshield and into the trunk. Surface rust is common, especially around windshields, door bottoms, and the rear lip on trunk lids.

Safety summary/Recalls: All models: 1993—Sudden acceleration while in Reverse or forward gear; brakes wouldn't respond. • Inadvertent airbag deployment. • Airbag failed to deploy. • Short drivers feel uneasy having to sit so close to the airbag housing. • Airbag warning light stays lit for no reason. • When started, vehicle leaps forward. • Defective fuel-injectors cause vehicle to jerk and lunge. • Engine serpentine belt and belt tensioner failures, causing complete loss of power. • Premature head gasket failures and engine mount breakage. • Chronic stalling at any speed. • Fuel pumps often need replacing and may be part of the cause of stalling. • Frequent transmission failures. • When weather turns cold, transmission won't shift properly. • Faulty ECM (computer module) makes the automatic transmission downshift at irregular intervals. • When travelling at high speeds with cruise control engaged, automatic transmission may suddenly downshift from fourth into second gear. • Transmission cooling lines often leak. • Transmission whines and growls. • Sudden steering wheel lockup when driving. • Steering column fails to lock when key is removed. • Power-steering belt tensioner failures. • Brake failures continued after ABS recall repairs carried out.

• Brake master cylinder leaks fluid. • Noisy brakes. • Shock absorbers failed • Leaky MacPherson struts. • Chronic battery failures. • Courtesy light mounted above rear view mirror can interfere with driver's vision. • Gas line from tank to fuel filter rubs on framing, thus wearing a hole in the line. **Recalls: All models: 1990**—The dealer will install a free by-pass valve to prevent automatic transmission damage in cold weather. **1990-91**—The high-pressure hose could leak in models with ABS. **1991**—The front outboard seatbelt latch is faulty. **1992**—The coupling bolts for the steering column shaft are faulty. **Dynasty: 1989-90**—The dealer will install a free by-pass valve to prevent automatic transmission damage in cold weather. **Fifth Avenue: 1990**—The airbag could be defective on cars with gray interior. **1991**—Pin bolts for the front disc brake caliper guide could be too loose. • A short circuit in the heater blower motor could cause a fire in the cowl area.

Secret Warranties/Service Tips

All models/years—Defective valve springs on the 3.3L V6 engine will be replaced free of charge (DSB R#466). • There is excessive air conditioner noise with 3.3L engine (DSB #24-8-89). • Most model years with the notori-ously failure-prone A604 automatic transmission suffer clutch slippage (DSB #21-09-90). Ask for a repair refund for this or any other transmission failure that occurs within 7 years/100,000 miles. • A rotten-egg odor coming from the exhaust is probably caused by a malfunctioning catalytic converter and might be covered under the emissions warranty. **All models: 1988-93**—3.0L engines that burn oil or produce a smoky exhaust at idle can be fixed by installing snap rings on the exhaust valve guides and replacing all of the valve guide stems or the cylinder head. **1990-93**—Harsh automatic shifts can be tamed by installing the following revised parts: kickdown, accumulator, reverse servo cushion springs, and accumulator piston. **1991-92**—Engines with a rough idle and stalling following a cold start could require a new single board engine controller (SBEC). **1991-93**—Poor AC performance while the AC blower continues to operate is likely due to the evaporator freezing; the evaporator freezes when the powertrain control module (PCM) isn't prop-erly disengaging the AC clutch via the relay. • An engine that stalls follow-ing a cold start might need an upgraded Park/Neutral/start switch. • The serpentine belt could come off the pulley after driving through snow; install an upgraded shield, screw, and retainers to overcome this problem. **1992**—Long crank times, a rough idle, and hesitation can be corrected by replac-ing the intake manifold assembly or ECT and sensor connector. **1992-93**—Eliminate a deceleration shudder by replacing the PCM with an upgraded version. • Rough idling after a cold start with 2.5L engines can be corrected by installing an upgraded PCM. **1993**—Acceleration shudder could be caused by a leaking automatic transmission front pump. • For improved automatic shifting, install an upgraded transmission control mod-ule. • Fuel pump check valve failure can cause start-up die-out, reduced power, or erratic shifting.

Dynasty, Fifth Avenue, Imperial, New Yorker (1988–93) Profile

	1988	1989	1990	1991	1992	1993
Cost Price ($)						
Dynasty	13,598	13,580	15,945	16,740	17,000	17,540
Fifth Avenue	—	—	23,990	23,405	23,906	22,725
Imperial	—	—	25,550	27,515	29,063	30,000
New Yorker	19,949	20,015	20,986	18,990	20,134	20,000
Used Values ($)						
Dynasty ↑	3,000	3,500	4,000	4,500	5,500	6,500
Dynasty ↓	2,500	3,000	3,500	4,000	4,500	5,500
Fifth Avenue ↑	—	—	6,500	7,500	8,000	9,500
Fifth Avenue ↓	—	—	5,500	6,000	7,000	8,000
Imperial ↑	—	—	7,000	8,000	9,000	10,500
Imperial ↓	—	—	6,000	7,000	7,500	9,000
New Yorker ↑	4,500	5,500	6,500	7,000	7,500	9,000
New Yorker ↓	3,500	4,500	6,000	6,500	6,000	7,500
Extended Warranty	Y	Y	Y	Y	Y	Y
Secret Warranty	N	N	N	Y	Y	Y
Reliability	❶	❶	❶	❶	❶	❶
Air conditioning	❶	❶	❶	❶	❷	❷
Automatic transmission	❷	❷	❶	❶	❶	❶
Body integrity	❷	❷	❷	❷	❷	❷
Braking system	❶	❶	❶	❷	❷	③
Electrical system	❷	❷	❷	❷	❷	③
Engines	❶	❶	❶	❷	❷	❷
Exhaust/Converter	❷	❷	❷	❷	❷	❷
Fuel system	❶	❶	③	③	③	③
Ignition system	❶	❶	❷	❷	❷	③
Rust/Paint	❷	❷	❷	③	③	③
Steering	❶	❶	❶	❷	❷	③
Suspension	❶	❶	❶	❷	③	③
Crash Safety						
Dynasty	—	—	—	—	—	④
Imperial	—	—	④	④	—	—
New Yorker	—	—	—	—	—	④

FORD

Cougar/Thunderbird

Rating: Above Average (1995–97); Below Average (1985–94).
Maintenance/Repair costs: About average, and repairs aren't dealer
dependent. **Parts:** Higher-than-average cost (independent suppliers
sell for much less), and not hard to find. Despite the fact that 1997 was
the last model year for both models, parts should remain plentiful.

Strengths and weaknesses: These are no-surprise, average-performing,
two-door luxury cars that have changed little over the years.
Nevertheless, they offer more performance and greater reliability than
GM rear-drives and most of the Big Three–produced front-drives.
Handling and ride are far from perfect, though, with considerable body
lean and rear-end instability when taking curves at moderate speeds.
   Overall reliability of these models has been average, as long as you
stay away from the turbocharged 4-cylinder engine. True, it offers lots of
power, but excessive noise and expensive repairs are the price you pay.
Front suspension components wear out quickly, as do power-steering
rack seals. Owners of recent models have complained of ignition module defects, electrical system bugs, premature front brake repairs, steering pump hoses that burst repeatedly (one owner of a 1994 Cougar
wrote that he replaced the hose twice in the same year), erratic transmission performance, early AC failures, defective engine intake manifolds, excessive vibrations when driving, numerous squeaks and rattles,
faulty heater fans, and failure-prone power window regulators.

Dealer service bulletins: 1993—Poor-performing AC systems are
caused by a slipping clutch at high ambient temperatures; AC cooling
may be insufficient at idle; and the AC compressor may moan from idle
to 1500 rpm. • Power-steering units may be noisy and power door locks
may not work. **1994**—Faulty 3.8L engine rocker arm assemblies may
cause squeaking, chirping, and knocking. • Rough idle, hesitation,
excessive fuel consumption, and poor heater output are likely caused
by a thermostat sticking in an open position or opening before it
should. • The transmission shudders under light to moderate acceleration. • There may be extraneous noise in radio speakers, caused by a
malfunctioning fuel pump. • Electric rear window defrosters may fail
prematurely and the floor ducts tend to leak water. • Moon roofs are
also plagued by excessive wind noise and buffeting. **1995**—Exhaust
moan or vibration. • Inefficient AC cooling or excessive clutch end
gap. • Intermittent loss of torque at 3–4 upshift. • No-crank due to
starter solenoid corrosion. • Faulty outside temperature display. •
Water intrusion of the MLP/TR sensor. • Brake roughness upon application and a clacking/thumping noise when braking. • Exhaust moan
or vibration, fuel pump buzz/whine heard through the radio speaker,

and rocker arm noise. • Warranty coverage for a bowed antenna. • Faulty temperature gauge. **1996**—Stalling or hard starts. • Squeal or hoot noise from the engine compartment. • Transmission valve body cross leaks. • Power steering requires increased effort at low speeds. • Chatter during turns. • Growling noise from the steering column while vehicle is turning. • Roughness during braking. • Fuel pump buzz/whine heard through radio speaker. • Musty and mildew-type odors. • Tape won't eject from cassette player. • Window won't go to full up position. • Water drips on floor from AC evaporator core. • Water leaks from the cowl vent screen. **1997**—AC emits musty odor. • Erratic or prolonged 1–2 shift. • Door latch stuck open. • Fog/film on windshield/interior glass. • Loose catalyst or muffler heat shields. • Shudder or vibration while in third or fourth gear. • Chirping or squeaking blower motor. • Radio AM static while driving. • Water in air inlet elbow. • Vibration while driving at highway speeds. • Inoperative remote keyless entry.

Safety summary/Recalls: All models: 1992–93—NHTSA is probing allegations that the headlight switches may be failure-prone. **1996**—Vehicle caught fire after being parked for 13 hours. • Airbags failed to deploy. • Airbag indicator light comes on for no reason. • Right rear wheel came off. • During inclement weather, design of engine allows water to saturate the air filter, causing engine to die out. • PCM chip defect causes engine to cut out and the Check Engine light to come on. • Malfunctioning crankshaft and oxygen sensors may cause chronic stalling and no-starts. • Cracked intake manifold allows coolant leakage. • Frequent motor mount failures. • Transmissions are noisy, won't shift properly, and frequently won't shift at all. • Excessive driveshaft vibrations. • Power steering works poorly at low speeds and sometimes cuts out completely when cruising on the highway. • Heater and AC compressor failures. • Defective AC fan switch. • Frequent reports of sudden brake failures, front brake rotor warpage, and noisy brakes. • Brake pedal sinks below the accelerator pedal level, causing driver to depress the accelerator. • Hood struts are too weak to keep hood in open position. • Crooked steering wheel replaced. • Power window regulator failures. • Electric door locks are failure-prone. • Doors fit poorly. • Headlights require constant adjustment and don't provide as much illumination as with other model years. • Seatbelt doesn't release properly. • Defective sunroof guides, and the gasket barely lasts two years. • Sun visor hits driver in the head when it's adjusted. • Speedometer and gauges work erratically. **1997**—Sudden acceleration while stopped at a traffic light. • Left vehicle in Park with engine running and it suddenly lurched into Reverse. • Car suddenly pulled to the left when braking, and steering locked up. • Excessive vibrations while cruising that increase in intensity when braking. • Premature front brake wear. • Headrests can't be raised high enough to protect the head. • Seat won't latch. • Brake caliper moves in its bracket.

• Transmission fluid leakage. • Water leaks onto passenger-side floor due to missing wiring harness plug. • Dash reflection on the windshield obstructs visibility. • Dealer can't correct windshield washer spray to prevent it from spraying the rear window. • Multiple Firestone tire failures. **Recalls: All models: 1988–93**—The ignition switch could experience an internal short circuit, creating the potential for overheating, smoke, and possibly fire in the steering column. **1989**—Rear suspension wheel knuckles could fracture. • There is excessive brake pedal travel. **1990–91**—Wiper motor nuts may loosen or fall off. • **1996**—The automatic transmission may disengage or fail to engage when shift lever is moved to Park. • Driver's door may not sustain the specified load when it's in the secondary latch position. • The semi-automatic temperature control blower may malfunction.

Secret Warranties/Service Tips

All models/years—Ford's "goodwill" warranty extensions cover fuel pumps and computer modules that govern engine, fuel-injection, and transmission functions. If Ford balks at refunding your money for a faulty computer module, say that you wish to have the 5-year/80,000 mile emissions warranty applied by either the company or the courts. There's nothing like a small claims court action to focus Ford's attention. The same advice applies if you notice a rotten-egg odor coming from the exhaust. It's likely the result of a malfunctioning catalytic converter. • Paint delamination, fading, peeling, hazing, and "microchecking" (see page 113 for details on claiming a refund). **All models: 1985–92**—A buzz or rattle from the exhaust system may be caused by a loose heat shield catalyst. **1989–94**—Water dripping from the floor ducts when the AC is working requires a relocated evaporator core. **1992–95**—A corroded solenoid may be the cause of starter failures. **1994**—Automatic transmissions with delayed or no forward engagement, or a higher engine rpm than expected when coming to a stop, are covered in DSB #94-26-9. • A no-crank condition in cold weather may be due to water freezing in the starter solenoid. • Hesitation or stumble in vehicles equipped with a 3.8L engine may be fixed by installing an upgraded PCM that allows for low-grade fuel. **1994–95**—A thumping or clacking noise heard from the front brakes signals the need to machine the front disc brake rotors; Ford will pay for this repair under its base warranty. **1994–97**—An erratic or prolonged 1–2 shift can be cured by replacing the cast aluminum piston with a one-piece stamped steel piston that has bonded lip seals, and by replacing the top accumulator spring. These upgraded parts will increase the transmission's durability, according to Ford.

Cougar/Thunderbird Profile

	1991	1992	1993	1994	1995	1996	1997
Cost Price ($)							
Cougar	16,890	17,790	17,830	18,360	18,960	18,450	19,690
T-bird	16,550	17,675	15,830	17,325	17,890	17,990	18,390
Used Values ($)							
Cougar ↑	5,500	6,500	8,000	9,000	11,000	13,300	15,000

Cougar ↓	4,800	5,500	6,500	8,000	9,500	11,000	13,500
T-bird ↑	5,500	6,500	7,500	9,000	10,500	12,500	14,500
T-bird ↓	4,500	5,500	6,000	8,000	9,000	11,000	13,000
Extended Warranty	Y	Y	Y	Y	Y	N	N
Secret Warranty	Y	Y	Y	Y	Y	Y	Y
Reliability	②	②	②	②	③	④	④
Air conditioning	②	②	②	②	③	③	④
Automatic transmission	②	②	②	②	②	③	③
Body integrity	②	②	②	②	③	③	③
Braking system	②	②	②	②	②	②	③
Electrical system	②	②	②	②	②	③	③
Engines	③	④	④	④	⑤	⑤	⑤
Exhaust/Converter	③	③	③	④	⑤	⑤	⑤
Fuel system	②	③	③	③	③	③	③
Ignition system	③	③	④	④	⑤	⑤	⑤
Rust/Paint	①	②	②	②	②	②	③
Steering	②	②	③	③	③	③	⑤
Suspension	②	③	③	④	④	④	⑤
Crash Safety	④	④	—	⑤	⑤	⑤	⑤
Side Impact	—	—	—	—	—	—	③

Crown Victoria/Grand Marquis

Rating: Recommended (1997–98); Above Average (1994–96); Average (1984–93). Overall, these cars aren't as reliable as Japanese luxury vehicles, but they're the best of the domestic crop when it comes to price, power, performance, and overall comfort. Don't waste your money buying a 1997 or 1998 version if you can find a low-mileage 1996 version. It'll cost much less and give you the same features. The Marquis is a slightly more luxurious version that costs more but gives little of consequence for the extra expense. **Maintenance/Repair costs:** Average, but some AC and electronic repairs can be carried out only by Ford dealers. **Parts:** Higher-than-average cost (independent suppliers sell for much less), but not hard to find.

Strengths and weaknesses: These cars are especially suited to people who need lots of room or who prefer the safety blanket provided by road-hugging, gas-guzzling weight. Handling is mediocre, but it's about average for cars this size. Both the 4.6L and 5.0L V8s provide adequate though sometimes sluggish power, with most of their torque found in the lower gear ranges. The fuel pump, sender, fuel filter, and fuel hose assemblies are failure-prone. There are many complaints of EEC IV ignition module malfunctions that cause hard starting and frequent stalling. Brakes, shock absorbers, and springs wear out more quickly than they should. Furthermore, there is such a high number of safety-related complaints concerning brake and fuel lines, suspension, and steering components that an undercarriage inspection is a prerequisite to buying any model year.

Dealer service bulletins: 1993—Poor performance of AC systems caused by a slipping clutch at high ambient temperatures. • Ticking, pinging, or popping when the AC clutch cycles, and a noisy FX-15 AC compressor. • Premature front brake rotor wear and vibrations when braking. • Noisy power-steering units. • Inoperative or malfunctioning cellular phones. • Power door locks that may not work. **1994**—Transmission shudder under light to moderate acceleration. • Radio speaker noise caused by a faulty fuel pump. • Defective electric rear window defrosters. **1995**—Delayed transmission engagement and shift errors, loose transmission connector, intermittent loss of torque at 3–4 upshift, irregular or no-torque converter operation, and shifts to Neutral at heavy throttle. • Insufficient AC cooling or excessive clutch end gap. • Water intrusion of the MLP/TR sensor. • A clacking/thumping noise when braking, and brake roughness upon application. • A fuel pump buzz/whine heard through the radio speaker. **1996**—Stalling or hard starts. • Delayed 1–2 shift. • Transmission valve body cross leaks. • Chatter during turns. • Fog/film on windshield/interior glass. • Musty and mildew-type odors. • Right front door window requires much effort to roll up. **1997**—ABS brakes may activate on their own or produce a grinding, pulsing, fluttering effect on the brake pedal. • AC emits musty odor. • Air rush and/or flutter noise from center register. • Erratic or prolonged 1–2 shift. • Spark knock during acceleration. • Door latch sticks open. • Driver-side seat cushion is uncomfortable, sags. • Fog/film on windshield/interior glass. • Front door panel crack on rear edge. • Loose catalyst or muffler heat shields. • Wind noise around doors. • Shudder or vibration while in third or fourth gear. • Steering wheel noise or vibration. • Suspension leans to right side. • Axle whine at 60 mph.

Safety summary/Recalls: One Canadian Marquis owner writes:

> Fuel is delivered from the gas tank to the engine via a pressurized fuel line. There is a gas return line that brings fuel back from the engine to the gas tank. At the location of the wheelwell, the return line is installed slightly higher than the fuel line. Because of this, the return line is exposed to intermittent rubbing from the chassis. Since the fuel line is metal, it will not wear right away. In my car, it took six years, but now the line is leaking gasoline. I don't know whether all Marquis cars have this problem; however, the Alberta Motor Association mechanic, the Canadian Tire mechanic and the City Ford dealer mechanic all indicated that the car came from the factory this way. There's a serious risk of both fire and explosion while driving the car.

All models: 1992–93—Ford has received 19 complaints of reduced power-steering assist during high-speed maneuvers with 1992–93 Crown Victoria police cars. Lawsuits have been filed and NHTSA is also involved. • There are reports of hoods suddenly flying up and shattering the windshield while vehicles are in motion. • There are also complaints of poor traction on ice, a hard-to-see shift indicator, and the instrument panel washing out in sunlight. **1996**—Fire caused by a short in the electrical system. • Airbag failed to deploy. • ABS brake failures. • Engine surges without warning or shuts down when brakes are applied. • Cruise control won't disengage when brakes are applied. • Oil pan/gasket leaks. • Many reports that the left frame bracket broke at weld, causing vehicle to pull sharply to the right when brakes were applied. • Inadequate lubrication caused the right lower ball joint to separate, causing an accident. • Other reports of ball joint and lower control arm failures say that the vehicle's front wheel assembly is also affected. • Police department inspectors report their vehicles have shown excessive play in the Pitman arms. • Brake lines are routed too close to the body and chafe excessively. • Brake pedal went to the floor due to failure of the stop switch and clip on pedal. • Frequent replacement of front brake components. • Steering locks up, will not return, or is so loose it won't steer vehicle. • Cracked intake manifolds cause loss of coolant. • Frequent catalytic converter failures. • Inoperative rear window defroster. • Seatbelt buckle doesn't stay latched. • Seatbelts failed to restrain occupants during a collision. **1997**—Fire caused by a faulty fuel line. • Other engine compartment fires reported, cause unknown. • Sudden acceleration due to a design flaw of the throttle linkage and bracket. • Floormats can shift under the gas or brake pedals, causing them to jam. • Vehicle left in Park position with engine on slipped into Reverse. • Many reports of brake failures caused by brake line rubbing against body components. • Collapsed body mounts allow undercarriage to rub flat spots on steel brake lines, causing brake failure. • Steering wheel lockup while driving. • Front suspension ball joint failure after having recall campaign correction done. • Lower passenger-side control arm fell off when vehicle was in first gear. • Sharp door edges have injured three people. • Engine intake manifold failures that cause anti-freeze to leak into the engine compartment. • Front doors are too large and difficult to maneuver around. **1998**—NHTSA investigators are looking into reports that the inertia fuel shutoff switch operates when it shouldn't, stalling the vehicle. • Vehicle caught fire in the engine compartment while parked in garage overnight. • Sudden acceleration after vehicle stalled and was restarted. • Airbags failed to deploy. • Sudden loss of power, stalling. • Traction control engages for no reason, causing loss of power and control. • Steering too sensitive when changing lanes, easy to lose control. • Dome light switch is poorly designed; it can only be activated by the driver due to its location. • Loss of lighting caused by sudden electrical system failure. • Rubber hose leading from the fuel tank is easily hit when going over a bump or pothole. **Recalls: All models: 1984**—Seatbelt anchors may not meet federal regulations. **1987**—Faulty fuel-injection tube assembly may cause fuel leakage and create a fire hazard. **1987–88**—Automatic seatbelt retractors in station wagons with dual-facing rear seats are faulty. **1988–89**—A faulty ignition module may cause a fire. **1991**—The car may roll away even though the automatic transmission lever says that it's in Park. **1992–93**—A short circuit could cause a front seat fire. • On non-ABS-equipped vehicles, an abraded rear brake line can cause loss of brake fluid and loss of braking power. **1992–97**—Hoods may fly open. **1995**—Fuel could leak from the tank and pose a fire hazard; dealer will replace the fuel-filler pipe seat. • Faulty headlight and power window circuit breakers may unexpectedly turn the headlights off. • Rear seatbelt attachments may be faulty. • Airbag may not inflate properly and the end cap could separate. **1996**—Driver's door may not sustain the specified load when in the secondary latch position. **1996–99**—Prematurely worn ball joint could break, causing loss of steering. **1995–96**—Pitman arm corrosion on fleet cars can cause abnormal wear. **Grand Marquis: 1994**—The metal cylinder that holds the airbag can be projected into the passenger area as the airbag deploys.

Secret Warranties/Service Tips

All models: 1987–90—Excessive oil consumption is likely caused by leaking gaskets, poor sealing of the lower intake manifold, defective intake and exhaust valve stem seals, or worn piston rings. Install new guide-mounted valve stem seals for a more positive fit and install new piston rings for improved oil control. **1989–90**—Program B89 provides for the inspection and replacement of the Overdrive gear and installation of a repair kit (#E9AZ-7L22B-A). • No Overdrive or an extended 3–4 shift may require a new Overdrive band, transmission separator plate kit, overhaul kit, and reverse drum. • Harsh or rough shifting may be caused by sticking control valves. • Poor AM radio reception due to ignition static can be improved by securing the antenna ground connection. **1990**—Excessive transmission noise, delayed shifts, or no engagements may be due to metal particles from the thrust washer that have plugged the filter, or burnt clutch plates. • Install a new "service only" EEC IV processor to correct driveline clunk when the throttle is closed. • If the AC blower won't change speed, consider installing a new switch assembly. If the blower sometimes cuts out, look for a loose connection at the variable-speed blower control. • If the front seats move in their tracks or make noise, Ford will install new seat tracks and a memory track on the driver's side free of charge. • A sluggish speed-control response can be remedied by installing a new EEC IV processor. • A loose or wobbly steering wheel requires putting in a new bearing tolerance ring service kit (#F0DZ-3L539-D). **1990–91**—Fuel pump whining can be reduced by adding tank insulation material. **1990–93**—Brake pedal and steering vibration when braking can be reduced by installing improved brake rotors (#F1VY-1125-A) and linings (#F3AZ-2001-A). **1992**—Premature brake wear and seizure due to overheating can be corrected by installing air scoops to cool the brakes. **1992–94**—A moaning or loud noise coming from the engine compartment of cars equipped with the 4.6L engine can be corrected by installing a new air-idle by-pass tube and resonator assembly. • Automatic transmissions with delayed or no forward engagement, or a higher-than-expected engine rpm when coming to a stop, are covered in DSB #94-26-9.

1992–97—An erratic or prolonged 1–2 shift can be cured by replacing the cast aluminum piston with a one-piece stamped steel piston that has bonded lip seals and by replacing the top accumulator spring. These upgraded parts will increase the transmission's durability, according to Ford. **1995–97**—ABS brakes that activate on their own or produce a grinding, pulsing, fluttering effect on the brake pedal probably need upgraded wiring connectors at the ABS sensors.

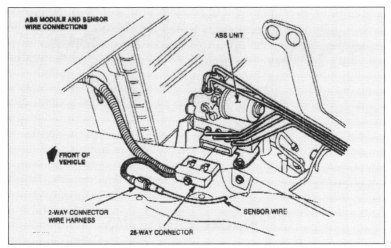

This three-hour job should fall under Ford's base warranty.

1996–97—Spark knock during acceleration can be silenced by replacing the MAF sensor and reprogramming the power control module. **All models/years**—Three components that frequently benefit from Ford "goodwill" warranty extensions are catalytic converters, fuel pumps, and computer modules. If Ford balks at refunding your money, apply the emissions warranty for a full or partial refund. • Paint delamination, fading, peeling, hazing, and "microchecking" (see page 113 for details on claiming a refund).

Crown Victoria/Grand Marquis Profile

	1991	1992	1993	1994	1995	1996	1997	1998
Cost Price ($)								
Crown S/LTD	18,776	21,051	21,250	19,350	21,320	21,780	21,430	21,725
Marquis GS	19,920	21,455	23,425	21,125	22,130	22,600	23,145	22,495
Used Values ($)								
Crown S/LTD ↑	6,000	8,000	9,000	10,500	12,500	14,500	17,000	19,000
Crown S/LTD ↓	5,000	7,000	8,000	9,000	11,000	13,000	15,500	17,500
Marquis GS ↑	6,500	8,500	9,500	11,500	13,000	15,000	17,500	19,500
Marquis GS ↓	6,000	7,500	9,000	9,500	11,500	13,500	16,000	18,000

Extended Warranty	Y	Y	Y	N	N	N	N	N
Secret Warranty	Y	Y	Y	Y	Y	Y	Y	N
Reliability	③	③	③	④	④	④	⑤	⑤
Air conditioning	②	②	②	②	③	③	③	④
Automatic transmission	①	①	②	②	②	②	④	④
Body integrity	①	①	①	①	②	②	②	③
Braking system	①	①	①	①	②	②	②	③
Electrical system	②	②	②	②	③	③	③	④
Engines	④	④	④	④	④	④	⑤	⑤
Exhaust/Converter	①	①	③	③	③	④	⑤	⑤
Fuel system	②	②	③	③	③	③	③	④
Ignition system	②	②	②	③	③	③	③	④
Rust/Paint	②	②	②	②	③	③	③	④
Steering	②	②	③	③	③	③	③	④
Suspension	②	②	②	②	②	②	③	③
Crash Safety	—	③	③	③	④	⑤	⑤	⑤
Side Impact	—	—	—	—	—	—	④	④

GENERAL MOTORS

Caprice, Impala SS, Roadmaster

Rating: Above Average (1995–96); Average (1994); Not Recommended (1985–93). This group of cars ceased production in 1996. A good alternative would be any rear-drive Buick LeSabre or a Ford Crown Victoria or Grand Marquis. **Maintenance/Repair costs:** Maintenance is inexpensive and easy to perform, plus repairs can be done by any corner garage. **Parts:** Average parts costs can be cut further by shopping at independent suppliers, who are generally well stocked.

Strengths and weaknesses: These cars are large, comfortable, and easy to maintain. The trunk is spacious. Overall handling is acceptable, but expect a queasy ride from the too-soft suspension. Gas mileage is particularly poor. Despite the many generic deficiencies inherent in these rear-drives, they still score higher than GM's front-drives for overall reliability and durability. The Impala SS is basically a Caprice with a 260-hp Corvette engine and high-performance suspension.

On 1988–91 models, engine problems include crankshaft and head gasket failures, cracked cylinder heads, injection pump malfunctions, and oil leaks. Engine knocking is another common problem on early models that's hard to correct inexpensively, due to the various possible causes that have to be eliminated. Early V8s, in particular, suffer from premature camshaft wear, and the 350-cubic-inch V8s often fall prey to premature valve guide wear caused by a faulty EGR valve. Cars equipped with the 5.7L diesel V8 should be approached with caution; they aren't very durable and cost an arm and a leg to troubleshoot and repair. The 4-speed automatic transmission was troublesome until 1991, with burnt-out clutches and malfunctioning torque converters being the most common failures.

The 1991–96 models have elicited few engine and transmission complaints, although they have shown the following deficiencies: chronic AC and ignition glitches; prematurely worn brakes (lots of corrosion damage), steering, and suspension components, especially shock absorbers and rear springs; serious electrical problems; and poor-quality body and trim items.

Body assembly is not impressive, but paint quality and durability is fairly good, considering the delamination one usually finds with GM's other models. Wagons often have excessive rust around cargo-area side windows and wheelwells, and hubcaps on later models tend to fly off.

Dealer service bulletins: 1993—Buzzing at idle coming from the 4L60E automatic transmission, along with a maladjusted shift linkage, causing loss of Reverse or lack of power in second gear. • Improperly adjusted automatic transmission shift linkage leading to a burnt out Low/Reverse clutch and increased rpms with downshifts. • Noisy power-steering units. • Intermittent cruise control operation. • Extreme temperature difference when the AC is put in a bi-level mode, and inoperative AC compressors. **1994**—Excessive oil consumption. • Faulty door-mounted radio speakers. • Poor AC performance. • Inadequate interior air flow. **1995**—Front brake pulsation. • An exhaust system moan or boom • Inadvertent horn honking • A low-voltage reading or dim lights at idle. • A steering system crunch or popping noise. • Wiper blade chatter. • Poor paint application and rust spots. **1996**—Engine noise (install new valve-stem oil seal). • 3–2 part throttle downshift flare and delayed transmission engagement. • Transmission chuggle/surge. • Transmission fluid leak from pump body (replace bushing). • Steering column noise. • Radio frequency interference diagnosis. • AC odors. **Caprice: 1995**—1–2 and 2–3 shifting malfunctions. **Roadmaster: 1995**—Automatic door lock may not work

Safety summary/Recalls: All models: 1994–96—NHTSA probes are looking into reports that coolant in vehicles with heavy-duty cooling systems may leak into the rear of the engine compartment, where it may ignite. **1996**—Left rear wheel came off while driving. • Airbags failed to deploy. • Airbag light stays lit for no apparent reason. • ABS brakes lock up. • Transmission torque converter/engine flywheel breakage. • Broken torque converter bolts. • Steering box loosens up despite new bolts. • Steering lockup. • Sometimes vehicle fishtails uncontrollably while at moderate speed. • Front coil spring failure. • Premature tire wear caused by faulty suspension components that can't be fixed by repeated alignments. • Fuel pump failure caused by wiring harness short. **Recalls: All models: 1985**—Leaking fuel feed and return pipe may cause a fire. • Cars equipped with a 4.3L engine could have a battery-cable short, which creates a fire hazard. **1985–88**—Faulty cruise control could lead to sudden acceleration. **1987**—Cars equipped with 200-4R automatic transmissions could start in gear or engage the wrong gear. **1989**—GM will inspect and replace the AC condenser inlet pipe. **1991**—Seatbelts malfunction because of defective shoulder belt guide loop. **1991–92**—Rear seatbelts that are uncomfortable will be changed for free by GM. • Corrosion could prevent the hood from latching properly, making it hard to open or causing it to fly open. **1992**—A rattling front door lock rod can be silenced by installing a corrective kit (#10222731). **1994**—A leaking oil cooler inlet hose is a fire hazard. • Fractured wheel studs may allow the wheel to separate from the car. • Faulty fuel tank strap fasteners. **1994–95**—Accelerator pedal may stick. **Roadmaster, Caprice: 1995–96**—Loose wheel lug nuts could cause the wheel to fall off.

Secret Warranties/Service Tips

All models/years—A rotten-egg odor coming from the exhaust is usually the result of a malfunctioning catalytic converter covered by the emissions warranty. • Paint delamination, peeling, or fading (see pages 73–75). **All models: 1982–91**—Hydramatic 4L60/700R4 automatic transmission may have no upshift or appear to be stuck in first gear. The probable cause is a worn governor gear. It would be wise to replace the retaining ring as well. **1982–93**—Vehicles equipped with a Hydramatic 4L60 transmission that buzzes when the car is in Reverse or at idle may need a new oil pressure regulator valve. **1985–87**—The 307-cubic-inch V8 is the most reliable and durable engine in this lineup. In 1985–86, it was plagued with camshaft/lifter problems due to the small offset from lifter bore to cam lobe. The problem was rectified on '88 models when GM adopted roller-lifters. The engine's aluminum intake manifold and gasket can be eaten away by extensive corrosion in each of the four corners where they contact a coolant port; serious coolant leaks result. Flush the radiator yearly and use a good-quality anti-freeze in order to extend the life of these components. **1987–91**—A bulletin lists the different types of tailpipe smoke signals that alert you to the need for different repairs: cars with V8 engines that emit blue or bluish-white smoke may require a valve seal kit (#12511890); models with port fuel-injection that emit black smoke after long starter cranks may have fuel leaking into the engine from the injectors; models with throttle body injection and port fuel-injection that emit white or bluish smoke and have normal oil consumption likely have poor sealing between the intake manifold joint and the cylinder head. **1989–91**—If the transmission won't go into Reverse or is slow to shift into Reverse, GM suggests that the Reverse input clutch housing be changed. **1991**—A poor-running 5.0L engine may require an EGR valve kit and PCV valve in addition to a new PROM. **1994**—Excessive oil consumption is likely due to delaminated intake manifold gaskets. Install an upgraded intake manifold gasket kit. • GM campaign 94C15 will adjust at no charge a misadjusted automatic transmission shift linkage that could, if left alone, burn out the Low/Reverse clutch. **1994–96**—Excessive engine noise can be silenced by installing an upgraded valve stem oil seal. • A chuggle or surge condition in vehicles with a with 5.7L engine will require a reflash calibration. **Roadmaster: 1991**—If the starter makes a grinding noise or won't engage the engine, the fault could be a weak starter spring. • Front doors that won't stay open on an incline or are hard to open need an improved hold-open door spring. **1992**—Water leaks into the trunk from the fixed mast antenna; install an upgraded antenna base (#25610633) and bezel (#25609129). • If the front seat doesn't have enough upward travel, GM will provide a special kit (#12520796) to raise it. • A chuggle or shudder at 44 mph on vehicles equipped with a 5.7L engine may be corrected by installing a new torque converter assembly. **1994**—Excessive oil consumption is likely due to delaminated intake manifold gaskets. Install an upgraded intake manifold gasket kit. • Poor AC performance can be improved by replacing the temperature control cable. • Delayed automatic transmission shift engagement is a common problem addressed in DSB #47-71-20A. **1995–96**—Delayed automatic transmission shift engagement may require the replacement of the pump cover assembly.

Caprice, Impala SS, Roadmaster Profile

	1990	1991	1992	1993	1994	1995	1996
Cost Price ($)							
Caprice	15,990	18,040	19,020	19,225	20,698	21,798	21,495
Caprice wagon	17,786	19,590	20,433	21,318	22,703	24,375	22,995
Roadmaster	—	—	24,255	25,895	27,224	28,425	28,595
Roadmaster wagon	—	24,642	25,110	27,895	29,078	30,370	30,250
Impala SS	—	—	—	—	23,360	24,390	24,995
Used Values ($)							
Caprice ↑	4,000	6,000	7,000	9,000	10,000	11,500	13,500
Caprice ↓	3,000	5,000	6,000	8,000	9,000	10,000	12,000
Caprice wagon ↑	4,500	7,000	9,000	10,500	12,000	14,500	16,500
Caprice wagon ↓	4,000	6,000	7,500	9,000	10,500	12,500	15,000
Roadmaster ↑	—	—	9,500	11,000	13,000	15,000	17,500
Roadmaster ↓	—	—	8,000	9,000	11,000	13,000	16,000
Roadmaster wagon ↑	—	9,500	11,000	13,000	15,000	17,500	20,000
Roadmaster wagon ↓	—	8,000	9,500	11,000	13,000	16,000	18,000
Impala SS ↑	—	—	—	—	19,000	21,500	23,500
Impala SS ↓	—	—	—	—	17,000	19,000	21,500
Extended Warranty	Y	Y	Y	Y	N	N	N
Secret Warranty	Y	Y	Y	Y	Y	Y	Y
Reliability	❷	❷	❷	❷	③	③	③
Air conditioning	❷	❷	❷	❷	③	③	④
Automatic transmission	❷	③	③	③	③	④	④
Body integrity	❷	❷	❷	❷	❷	③	③
Braking system	❷	❷	❷	❷	❷	❷	③

Electrical system	❷	❷	❷	❷	❷	❷	③
Engines	③	③	③	③	③	④	④
Exhaust/Converter	❷	❷	❷	❷	③	④	④
Fuel system	③	③	③	③	③	③	③
Ignition system	❷	❷	❷	❷	❷	❷	③
Rust/Paint	❷	❷	③	③	③	③	③
Steering	❷	❷	❷	❷	③	④	④
Suspension	❷	❷	❷	③	③	④	④
Crash Safety							
Caprice	—	④	④	④	④	④	④

Note: The 1995–96 Caprice models scored four stars for driver protection but only two for front passenger protection in government-run crash tests.

LUXURY CARS

Used luxury cars are attractive buys because they project a flashy image and can be bought for 50 percent of the new price after three years or so. If the selling price is reasonable, independent servicing is available, and used parts can be found, they can be bargains. On the downside, they're complicated to service and the cost of new parts can be horrendous.

And do remember this: spending more on a luxury car doesn't always mean you'll get more safety or reliability. You may simply get more headaches (see "Safety summary/Recalls" for General Motors, Ford, and Saab).

Traditionally, the luxury-car niche has been dominated by American and German automakers. During the past decade, however, buyers have gravitated towards Japanese models. This shift in buyer preference has forced Chrysler, GM, and Ford to downsize and adopt front-drives. It has also forced GM to drop its rear-drive Fleetwood. Despite these moves to better respond to buyers' preferences, American luxury cars are still seen by most consumers as overweight and unreliable land yachts.

You don't always have to spend big bucks to get true luxury and iron-clad reliability. Smart buyers can target the fully equipped Toyota Camry and Cressida, Honda Accord, Nissan Maxima, and Mazda 929, all of which offer the same equipment, reliability, and performance as Lexus, Infiniti, and Acura models, but for much, much less.

There are few used American luxury cars that can stand up to a six-year-old Japanese or German luxury vehicle. And this fact is reflected in the head-spinningly high depreciation rates seen with most large-cum-luxury cars put out by the Big Three. Chrysler's rear-drive New Yorker and Ford's Crown Victoria, Grand Marquis, and Lincoln Town Car come closest to meeting the imports in overall reliability and durability. On the other hand, the discontinued Chrysler Imperial was more show than go, and the front-drive large-luxury New Yorker and LHS are unremarkable and are plagued by serious powertrain reliability problems, as can be seen by the numerous dealer service bulletins I've intercepted. GM's Cadillacs aren't even in the running; in fact, *AutoWeek* magazine has dubbed the Catera a "lame duck."

Recommended

BMW 5 Series (1992–98)
Lexus ES 250, ES 300, GS 300,
  LS 400, SC 400 (1990–98)
Mercedes-Benz 300 Series, 400
  Series, 500 Series, E-Class (1993–98)

Mitsubishi Diamante (1992–98)
Nissan Maxima (1996–98)
Toyota Avalon (1995–98)
Volvo 850 Series (1995–97)
Volvo 900 Series (1995–97)

Above Average

Acura Legend (1989–95)
Audi A4, A6, A8, S4, S6, 80, 90,
  100, 200, 5000 (1995–98)
BMW 3 Series (1995–98)
Ford Lincoln Mark VII, Mark VIII
  (1995–98)
Ford Lincoln Town Car
  (1995–98)
GM Aurora (1995–98)
GM Brougham/
  Fleetwood RWD (1993–96)
Infiniti G20, I30, J30, Q45
  (1995–98)

Mazda 929 (1993–95)
Mazda Millenia (1995–98)
Mercedes-Benz 300 Series,
  400 Series, 500 Series,
  E-Class (1992)
Mercedes-Benz C-Class
  (1995–98)
Nissan Maxima (1989–95)
Toyota Cressida (1985–92)
Volvo 850 Series (1993–94)
Volvo 900 Series (1989–94)

Average

BMW 3 Series (1994)
BMW 5 Series (1985–91)
Ford Lincoln Continental
  (1996–98)
Ford Lincoln Mark VII, Mark
  VIII (1994)
Ford Lincoln Town Car
  (1988–94)
GM Brougham/
  Fleetwood RWD (1984–92)
GM 98 Regency, Park
  Avenue (1997–98)

GM Concours, DeVille,
  Fleetwood FWD (1995–98)
GM Riviera, Toronado,
  Trofeo (1995–98)
Infiniti G20, I30, J30, Q45
  (1991–94)
Mazda 929 (1988–92)
Mercedes-Benz 190 Series,
  C-Class (1988–94)
Nissan Maxima (1986–88)
Saab 900, 9000 (1998)

Below Average

BMW 3 Series (1984–93)
Ford Lincoln Continental
  (1984–95)
Ford Lincoln Mark VII, Mark VIII
  (1986–93)
GM 98 Regency, Park
  Avenue (1991–96)
GM Cadillac Allanté, Catera,
  Eldorado, Seville (1992–98)

GM Concours, DeVille,
  Fleetwood FWD (1985–94)
Mercedes-Benz 190 Series,
  C-Class (1984–87)
Mercedes-Benz 300 Series,
  400 Series, 500 Series
  E-Class (1985–91)
Saab 900, 9000 (1995–97)

Not Recommended

Acura Legend (1986–88)
Audi A4, A6, A8, S4, S6, 80, 90,
  100, 200, 5000 (1984–94)

GM Riviera, Toronado,
  Trofeo (1986–93)
Saab 900, 9000 (1985–94)

GM 98 Regency, Park   Volvo 700 Series (1985–92)
  Avenue (1985–90)
GM Cadillac Allanté, Catera,   ⟍
  Eldorado, Seville (1986–91)

ACURA

Legend

Rating: Above Average (1989–95); Not Recommended (1986–88). Resale value is high on all Legend models, and especially so on the coupe. Shop instead for a cheaper 1989 or later base Legend with the coupe's upgraded features. **Maintenance/Repair costs:** Higher than average, and most repairs are dealer dependent. To avoid costly engine repairs, check the engine timing belt every 2 years/30,000 miles and replace it every 60,000 miles. **Parts:** Higher-than-average cost (some independent suppliers sell for much less under the Honda name), but not hard to find, despite the fact that the Legend was dropped in 1995.

Strengths and weaknesses: Pre-1990 Legends were upscale, enlarged Accords that were unimpressive performers with either 6-cylinder power-plant. Dependability, acceptable road handling, and a spacious interior are the car's main advantages. In spite of occasional clutch malfunctions, the 5-speed manual gearbox is the transmission of choice. The automatic shifts harshly and its lockup torque converter is constantly cutting in and out, reducing both performance and fuel economy. An overly soft sus-pension gives the car a bouncy ride, and it easily bottoms out when the vehicle is loaded or traversing rough roads. Front-end components get noisier as time passes. Long-term durability is better than average, with the only problems centered on body hardware and accessory equipment malfunctions, notably poor radio performance.
  The 3.2L V6 that appeaared in 1991 is by far a better performer than the 2.5L and 2.7L engines of earlier models, although some drivers complain it runs hot. Ride quality is improved, power steering is more responsive, and rear seating is more spacious. Automatic shifting is still rough (especially during acceleration), fuel economy is disappointing, and the coupe's rear seat room is still a joke. Owners report that sus-pension struts soften quickly, minor electrical problems occur occasion-ally, AC performance is erratic, radio reception is poor, brake servicing is too frequent, and body hardware is unimpressive. The windshield washer pump frequently malfunctions on the 1991–92 versions.

Dealer service bulletins: All models: 1993—Faulty trunk-mounted CD changer magazines. **1994**—Lots of body-panel fit problems. • Poor radio reception. • Steering wheel shimmy. • Faulty power-steering

speed sensors. • Door window scratches. **1995**—Malfunctioning seatbelt. • Buzzing seatbelt anchor. • Steering wheel shimmy troubleshooting. • Erratic audio remote-control operation. • Gap in front door sill
molding at B-pillar. • Clicking noise while turning.

Safety summary/Recalls: 1986–87—Fuel tank over-pressurization may
result in fuel spewing out when the cap is removed. **1986–88**—These
Legends have one of the highest rates of accidental sudden acceleration reported by owners. **1992–93**—Inadvertent airbag deployment.
Recalls: 1986–90—Takata seatbelt replacement. **1991**—A faulty automatic transmission shift cable should be replaced. **1992**—Vehicles may
not have an igniter for the passenger-side airbag.

Secret Warranties/Service Tips

All models/years—Like Honda's, most of Acura's DSBs allow for special
warranty consideration on a "goodwill" basis even after the warranty has
expired or the car has changed hands. Referring to this euphemism will
increase your chances of getting some kind of refund for repairs that are
obviously factory defects. Acura will repair or replace defective steering
assemblies, constant velocity joints, and catalytic converters free of charge
for up to 5 years/80,000 miles on a case-by-case basis. There's no labor
charge or deductible. Used vehicles and repairs carried out by independent
garages aren't covered by this special program. But, since the converter is an
emissions component, it's almost always automatically covered under the
emissions warranty. • Steering wheel shimmy can be reduced by rebalancing the wheel/tire/hub/rotor assembly in the front end. • Poor radio
reception or interference is addressed in DSB #94-011, issued August 30,
1994. • The automaker will install air intake screens to keep debris away
from the blower motor. • Vertical scratches on the door window result from
the window making contact with the molding's metal clips. • Seatbelts that
fail to function properly during normal use will be replaced for free under
the company's lifetime seatbelt warranty. **All models: 1986–95**—A clicking
noise heard while the vehicle is turning means you need to replace the
constant-velocity joint. **1990**—Water collects in the spare tire well; diagnosis and repair DSB #89-021. • Malfunctioning security system control unit;
diagnosis and repair DSB #90-002. **1991**—Poor AM radio reception or
interference from the car's electrical equipment may be due to a poor
ground connection between the antenna collar and car body. **1991–92**—
Static on the AM radio band may also be caused by a faulty Bose amplifier
as well as poor antenna grounding due to loose mounting nuts. • If the
remote audio volume controls cause static or operate erratically, change
the volume control motor inside the audio unit. • Poor AC performance is
often caused by a misadjusted heater valve cable. **1991–93**—Engine knocking after a cold-start is likely due to carbon buildup in the piston ring land.
1991–94—To prevent the lower bumper face from pulling loose, Acura will
reinforce the mounting points and reverse the overlap of the lower bumper
face and the splash shield. • Power-steering speed sensor failures. **1995**—
You can correct the gap in the front door sill molding at the B-pillar by
trimming back the nylon carpet retainer.

Legend Profile

	1988	1989	1990	1991	1992	1993	1994	1995
Cost Price ($)								
Base	23,735	24,580	24,580	27,910	28,580	30,370	36,490	38,220
Used Values ($)								
Base ↑	6,500	7,500	8,500	9,500	13,500	15,000	17,000	21,000
Base ↓	5,500	7,000	8,000	8,500	12,000	13,500	15,500	19,000
Extended Warranty	N	N	N	N	N	N	N	N
Secret Warranty	N	N	N	N	N	N	N	N
Reliability	③	③	③	④	④	④	⑤	⑤
Air conditioning	③	③	③	④	④	④	⑤	⑤
Body integrity	③	③	③	③	③	③	③	③
Braking system	③	③	③	④	④	④	④	⑤
Electrical system	❷	❷	❷	③	③	③	③	④
Engines	❷	❷	❷	③	④	⑤	⑤	⑤
Exhaust/Converter	④	④	⑤	⑤	⑤	⑤	⑤	⑤
Fuel system	④	④	④	④	④	⑤	⑤	⑤
Ignition system	③	③	④	④	④	⑤	⑤	⑤
Manual transmission	③	❷	④	⑤	⑤	⑤	⑤	⑤
- automatic	③	③	③	③	③	④	④	⑤
Rust/Paint	❷	③	③	③	④	④	⑤	⑤
Steering	④	④	④	④	⑤	⑤	⑤	⑤
Suspension	③	③	③	③	④	⑤	⑤	⑤
Crash Safety	—	—	—	—	③	③	③	③

AUDI

A4, A6, A8, S4, S6, 80, 90, 100, 200, 5000

Rating: Above Average (1995–98); Not Recommended (1984–94). **Maintenance/Repair costs:** Higher than average, and almost all repairs have to be done by an Audi dealer. **Parts:** Way-higher-than-average cost, and independent suppliers have a hard time finding parts. Don't even think about buying one of these front-drives without a three- to five-year supplementary warranty backed by Audi.

Strengths and weaknesses: These cars are attractively styled, handle well, are comfortable to drive, and provide a spacious interior. Yet the pre-1993 models have a worse-than-average reliability record and are plagued by mechanical and electrical components that don't stand up to the rigors of driving in cold climates. Furthermore, it seems that Audi has written off these failure-prone cars in favor of the better built and more recent A4 and A6 models. The dealer body isn't strong enough to adequately service all of these vehicles when things go wrong, so owners of older models are generally left to independent garages to serve their needs. Premium fuel is required for vehicles equipped with the 6-cylinder engine.

A4, A6, A8, S4, S6, and Sport 90

Thess are the pick of the Audi litter starting with the 1995 model year. Although Audi continued its alphabet name game by grouping its 100 series under a new A6 heading, these cars were substantially improved. Packed with standard features, the A6 is a comfortable, spacious, front-drive or all-wheel-drive luxury sedan that comes with dual airbags and ABS. It uses the same V6 powerplant as the A4, its smaller sibling. The S4 is a limited-production, high-performance spin-off that carries a 227-hp turbocharged rendition of the old 5-cylinder powerplant.

These cars are conservatively styled, slow off the mark (in spite of the V6 addition when hooked to an automatic), and plagued by electrical glitches. The 4-speed automatic shifts erratically and the 2.8L V6 engine needs full throttle for adequate performance. Handling is acceptable, but the ride is a bit firm and the car still exhibits considerable body roll, brake dive, and acceleration squat when pushed. Handling is on a par with the BMW 300 series, and acceleration times beat out those of the Mercedes. Quattro's AWD is extended to entry-level models at a time when most automakers are dropping the option on passenger cars.

Overall quality control has really improved during the past several years, with fewer body, brake, and electrical glitches than exhibited by previous models. A perusal of this year's internal service bulletins shows a dramatic improvement in quality control over earlier versions.

80, 90, and 100 series

Launched in 1988, these entry-level Audis share the same wheelbase and front-drive and 4X4 components. Equipped with an efficient but wimpy 4-cylinder (dropped in 1991) or the more powerful 2.3L 5-cylinder engine, 4-wheel disc brakes, and galvanized body panels, these small sedans are leagues ahead of Audi's mid-1980s vehicles. The 1991 models are clearly a better choice; they use an improved 4-speed automatic transmission hooked up to a more powerful engine. 1992 was basically a carry-over year in which unsold 1991 models were recycled. Some of their more common problems include AC, electrical system, and brake malfunctions.

5000 and 5000 Quattro

Renamed the 100 and 200 in 1989, these sedans have had a terrible repair record. The diesel engine is a nightmare, as are the turbocharged gasoline engines coupled to automatic transmissions. Front-drive mechanicals are unreliable and very complex to troubleshoot. Steering racks aren't durable and the engine cooling and electrical systems require frequent repair. Front brake rotors and calipers wear out very quickly and exhaust system components have a short life span. Other common problems include electrical short circuits in the taillights, AC failures, hot-starting difficulties, and leaking transmission seals. The top of the front fenders and the front edge of the hood and rear-wheel housings are susceptible to rust perforations. Furthermore, the persistently poor alignment of lower side moldings is a common body problem. Resale value is much lower than average and owners who've been sucked into buying these vehicles because of their bargain-basement prices face frequent and outrageously expensive "routine" servicing that's anything but routine.

Dealer service bulletins: A4, A6, A8, S4, S6 and Sport 90: 1995—Oil leakage from the rear and upper engine. • Coolant circulation pump leakage. • Delayed first- and second-gear shift. • A malfunctioning climate control. • Inaccurate fuel gauge and temperature gauges. • Door lock key binding. • Skipping wiper blades. **1996**—ABS light comes on inadvertently. • Front speaker buzzing. • Cruise control won't maintain set speed. • Delayed 1–2 shift on cold-start warm-up. • Inaccurate Delta Bose radio display. • Friction noise from front and rear door seals. • Fuel gauge doesn't register full. • Carbon buildup in the intake valve and combustion chamber. • Exhaust popping and rasping noise. • Radio volume goes to maximum when adjusted. • Binding rear ashtray lid. • Rear differential noise and vibration while driving. • Loose rear reading light. • Tachometer sticking and erratic AC display. **1997**—False ABS light warning. • Delayed 1–2 shift on cold-start warm-up. • Friction noise from front and rear door seals. • Rasping noise from exhaust. **100 series: 1993**—Misaligned deck lids that are hard to close. • Noisy steering column and squeaking and rattling coming from the front seats and inside the B-pillar. • Excessive wind noise because of poor window sealing. • Smearing, chattering wiper blades. • The 1992–94 models have quirky AC systems that often malfunction and have to be constantly readjusted. The fresh air fan for the same model years will also misbehave, suddenly going into high-speed operation for no reason.

Safety summary/Recalls: A6 sedan and Quattro wagon: 1998–99—During refueling, gasoline spits back violently from the filler pipe. **90, 100: 1993**—Under-hood fires reported. **Recalls: A4: 1996**—A fuel gauge that won't register full signals a short circuit. • Inoperative horn is due to insufficient electrical ground contact. **1997–98**—Dealer will install a retaining ring to hold the air screen in place. **100 series: 1992**—Audi will modify the brake vacuum booster system to improve brake pedal assist. **5000 Quattro: 1984–89**—Hardened fuel-injector seals allow fuel to leak onto the engine. **1985–86**—A misadjusted fuel distributor may cause fuel vapors to collect in the air filter and ignite if the engine backfires. • Defective idle stabilizer valve on the 5-cylinder version with automatic transmission may cause the vehicle to surge and buck. **1985–91**—An extension of the previous recall to prevent bearing and gear failure from sapping power from the front wheels or locking them up. **1986**—Malfunctioning rear or right front seatbelt locks. **V8: 1990–91**—Cruise control may not return to idle. **A4, A6, 90: 1995–96**—If the cruise control won't maintain speed, add additional vacuum or change the vacuum servo unit. **1995–97**—Static electricity can set off driver airbag. **A6, 90, 100: 1994–96**—Defective ignition switches will cause malfunctioning turn signals, windshield wipers, lights, power windows, and air conditioners. **80, 90: 1984–90**—Dealers will fix leaky or cracked brake hoses. **1985–86**—Defective idle stabilizer valve on the 5-cylinder version with automatic transmission may cause the vehicle to surge and buck. **1985–91**—Evaporation of the differential oil could result in bearing and gear failure, which saps power from the front wheels or locks them up. **1986**—Rear or right front seatbelt locks may malfunction. **1990**—Faulty steering lock bolts may block steering wheel movement. A faulty idle control module may cause erratic or increased idle speed. **90, 100, all V6-equipped Cabriolets: 1993–95**—Leaky fuel-injectors will be replaced, free of charge. **100, 200, 5000 Quattro, V8: 1984–85**—A faulty idle control module may cause erratic or increased idle speed. **1984–86**—Audi will install a transmission/brake interlock. **1984–88**—Audi will install a vent line valve or modify the fuel-filler neck to prevent fuel vapor ignition on Turbo models.

Secret Warranties/Service Tips

All models/years—Defective catalytic converters that cause a rotten-egg smell may be replaced free of charge under the emissions warranty. **A4: 1996–99**—Audi will install upgraded brakes to "fix" problems related to premature corrosion (*Automotive News*, February 8, 1999). **100, 200, 5000 Quattro, V8: 1991–92**—A clacking noise occurring whenever the vehicle passes over a bump is caused by plastic-to-plastic contact between the door lock latch and the door wedge. **1992–94**—DSB #94-09 troubleshoots common AC problems. • DSB #94-05 recommends replacing the fresh air fan with an upgraded part. **1995–97**—Delayed 1–2 shift on cold-start warm-ups is a normal condition resulting from the emissions control settings, according to Audi.

A4, A6, A8, S4, S6, 80, 90 Profile

	1991	1992	1993	1994	1995	1996	1997	1998
Cost Price ($)								
80	21,400	23,055	—	—	—	—	—	—
90	26,045	—	26,295	28,265	26,115	—	—	—
A4	—	—	—	—	—	26,975	28,905	29,965
A6	—	—	—	—	31,045	32,775	33,100	34,250
A8	—	—	—	—	—	—	57,400	57,900
S4	—	44,155	47,295	51,615	—	—	—	—
S6	—	—	—	—	45,720	—	—	—

Used Values ($)

80 ↑	6,500	7,500	—	—	—	—	—	—
80 ↓	5,000	6,000	—	—	—	—	—	—
90 ↑	7,000	—	10,500	12,500	15,000	—	—	—
90 ↓	5,500	—	9,000	11,000	13,000	—	—	—
A4 ↑	—	—	—	—	—	21,000	25,000	27,000
A4 ↓	—	—	—	—	—	19,000	22,000	25,000
A6 ↑	—	—	—	—	19,500	22,000	26,000	31,000
A6 ↓	—	—	—	—	17,500	20,500	24,000	29,000
A8 ↑	—	—	—	—	—	—	45,000	50,500
A8 ↓	—	—	—	—	—	—	42,000	47,000
S4 ↑	—	20,500	23,500	27,000	—	—	—	—
S4 ↓	—	18,500	21,500	24,500	—	—	—	—
S6 ↑	—	—	—	—	32,000	—	—	—
S6 ↓	—	—	—	—	29,500	—	—	—

Extended Warranty	Y	Y	Y	Y	Y	Y	Y	Y
Secret Warranty	N	N	N	N	N	N	N	N

Reliability	➊	➊	➋	➋	③	④	④	④
Air conditioning	➊	➊	➊	➊	➋	➋	➋	③
Body integrity	④	④	④	④	④	④	④	④
Braking system	➋	➋	➋	➊	➋	➋	➋	③
Electrical system	➊	➊	➊	➊	➊	➋	➋	③
Engines	➊	➊	➊	➋	③	③	③	④
Exhaust/Converter	➋	➋	➋	➊	④	⑤	⑤	⑤
Fuel system	➊	➋	➋	⑤	④	④	④	④
Ignition system	➋	➋	➋	➊	③	③	③	③
Manual transmission	③	③	③	③	③	④	⑤	⑤
- automatic	➋	➋	④	④	④	⑤	⑤	⑤
Rust/Paint	➋	➊	④	④	④	④	④	④
Steering	➋	➋	③	③	③	③	③	④
Suspension	➋	③	③	③	③	③	③	③
Crash Safety								
A4	—	—	—	—	—	④	④	—
A6	—	—	—	—	—	⑤	⑤	⑤
A8	—	—	—	—	—	—	—	⑤

100, 200, 5000 Profile

	1988	1989	1990	1991	1992	1993	1994
Cost Price ($)							
100	—	25,315	27,235	28,505	28,105	30,845	35,565
100Q	—	31,140	29,805	30,865	36,805	41,395	43,465
200	—	33,340	33,740	34,935	—	—	—
200TQ	—	36,690	36,140	42,755	—	—	—
5000	23,535	—	—	—	—	—	—

5000Q	27,320	—	—	—	—	—	—
V8	—	—	47,785	50,555	53,505	58,945	59,145
Used Values ($)							
100 ↑	—	5,000	6,000	7,000	10,500	12,000	14,500
100 ↓	—	4,000	5,000	6,000	9,000	10,500	13,000
100Q ↑	—	7,500	8,500	9,100	14,000	16,000	18,500
100Q ↓	—	6,000	7,000	8,0000	12,000	14,000	17,000
200 ↑	—	7,000	8,000	9,000	—	—	—
200 ↓	—	5,500	6,500	7,500	—	—	—
200TQ ↑	—	9,000	10,000	11,000	—	—	—
200TQ ↓	—	7,000	8,500	9,500	—	—	—
5000 ↑	3,500	—	—	—	—	—	—
5000 ↓	3,000	—	—	—	—	—	—
5000Q ↑	4,000	—	—	—	—	—	—
5000Q ↓	3,500	—	—	—	—	—	—
V8 ↑	—	—	13,500	15,500	20,000	23,000	27,000
V8 ↓	—	—	11,500	13,500	17,000	22,500	24,000

Extended Warranty	Y	Y	Y	Y	Y	Y	Y
Secret Warranty	N	N	N	N	N	N	N
Reliability	❶	❶	❶	❷	—	❷	③
Air conditioning	❷	❷	③	③	—	③	③
Body integrity	④	④	④	④	—	④	⑤
Braking system	❷	❷	❷	❷	—	❷	③
Electrical system	❶	❶	❶	❶	—	❷	❷
Engines	❶	❶	❶	❷	—	④	⑤
Exhaust/Converter	❷	❷	❷	③	—	⑤	⑤
Fuel system	❶	❷	❷	❷	—	③	③
Ignition system	❷	❷	❷	❷	—	③	③
Manual transmission	④	④	④	—	—	⑤	⑤
- automatic	❷	❷	④	④	—	⑤	⑤
Rust/Paint	❷	③	④	④	—	④	⑤
Steering	❷	❷	❷	❷	—	④	④
Suspension	❷	❷	❷	③	—	⑤	⑤
Crash Safety							
100	—	⑤	—	⑤	—	—	—

BMW

3 Series, 5 Series

Rating: 3 series: Above Average (1995–98); Average (1994); Below Average (1984–93). **5 series:** Recommended (1992–98); Average (1985–91). These cars come with a reputation that far exceeds what they actually deliver. Don't take my word for it; look at the BMW Lemon websites at: *www.bssound.com.au/bmw/lemon.htm* and *www.bmwlemon.com.* Pre-'94 prices drop dramatically, making these years the bargain buys of the 3 series group. **Maintenance/Repair costs:** Higher than average, but many repairs can be done by independents who specialize in BMW repairs. Unfortunately, the specialists are concentrated around large urban areas. **Parts:** Higher-than-average cost, and often back-ordered.

Strengths and weaknesses: Pre-1991 3-series vehicles exhibit great 6-cylinder performance with the manual gearbox, and ride and handling are commendable. The 318's small engine is seriously compromised by an automatic transmission; the 325e is more pleasant to drive and delivers lots of low-end torque. The 4-cylinder engines that first appeared on the 1991 models aren't well suited to the demands of the automatic gearbox. These cars are fun to drive as long as you keep in mind that the rear end is unstable on slippery pavement. Rear passenger and cargo room is limited and overall reliability is average. Whenever a problem arises, however, repair costs are particularly high, due to the small number of dealers, the relative scarcity of parts, and the acquiescence of affluent owners.

The electrical system is the source of most complaints. The automatic transmission isn't durable and front brakes require frequent attention. Owners also report chronic surging at idle and a rotten-egg smell from the exhaust (all models/years). Door seams, rocker panels, rear-wheel openings, and fender seams are particularly prone to rust. Early BMWs were poorly rustproofed and deteriorated very quickly, especially along the door bottoms and within the front and rear wheel-wells. Check the muffler bracket for premature wear, and weather seals and door adjustments for leaks.

Models after 1991 provide peppy 4-cylinder acceleration only with high revs and a manual transmission. Keep in mind that city driving requires lots of manual gear shifting characterized by an abrupt clutch. If you must have an automatic, look for a used model with the 6-cylinder engine or see if you can get by with the larger 1.9L 4-cylinder that went into the mid-'96 models. 1997 models came with traction control.

There is no problem with rear seat or cargo room with the 5-series Bimmer. Handling and ride are superb, although these weighty upscale models do strain when going over hilly terrain if they have the automatic gearbox. There was no 1996 version.

5-series owners report numerous electrical and fuel glitches, faulty turn signal indicators, starter failures, self-activating emergency flashers, rotten-egg odors from the exhaust, and excessive steering wheel/brake vibration.

Dealer service bulletins: 3 series: 1994—Coolant leakage from the timing case profile gasket. • A binding/sticking ignition leading to starter failures. • Sagging convertible headliners. • Water leaking into the driver-side footwell and the E-box area, flooding the DME control module. • Self-activating emergency flashers and flickering instrument lighting. • A rotten-egg smell caused by faulty catalytic converters. **1995**—Excessive brake squealing. • Insufficient interior air distribution. • Leaking door contact switches; binding air-distribution knobs; and noisy, ineffective wipers. **1996–97**—AC evaporator ices up. • ABS warning light glows for no reason. • CD skips when road surface is rough. • Delayed gear engagement or adapter case leak. • Electrical troubleshooting tips. • Electronic mobilizer malfunctions. • False alarms caused by glass breakage sensor. • General module malfunctions. • Noise from AC expansion valve on 318ti. • Noise from AC compressor area. • Sun visor pops out of clip. • Sunroof fails to close. • Transmission shudders. • Whistle noise when cooling fan runs on high speed. • Wind noise troubleshooting tips. **5 series: 1995**—AC belt tensioner noise. • Leaking door contact switches. • Faulty trunk lock actuator. • Noisy, ineffective wipers. **528, 540: 1997**—Brakes momentarily won't release. • CD skips when road surface is rough. • Electronic mobilizer malfunctions. • Glove-box lock broken. • Radio with DSP switches off intermittently. • Right front door won't lock. • Wind noise troubleshooting tips.

Safety summary/Recalls: 318: 1995—During an accident, the driver-side seatbelt and airbags failed to operate as they should. • Other reports of airbags not deploying. • Sudden steering lockup. • AC expansion valve failures. • Noisy exhaust manifold. • Erratic automatic transmission shifting: hesitation and jerky shifts. • Transmission slips when accelerating, causing vehicle to stall. • Clutch pressure plate failures. • Electrical system malfunctions. **1996**—Airbags failed to deploy. • AC failures. **1997**—Gas and brake pedals are too close together. • Airbag safety light keeps coming on. **1998**—Sudden acceleration. **Recalls: All models: 1984**—Sudden acceleration on 318i models may be caused by a faulty engine idle control valve. • A binding heater control valve can cause the solenoid to malfunction, resulting in an instrument panel fire. **1984–91**—Leaks caused by a cooling system malfunction will be corrected at no charge. **1985–86**—Supporting plates will be installed to reinforce the steering column. **1985–90**—Fuel pump relay failures that cause no-starts require a new relay, which may be replaced free under the emissions warranty. **1986–87**—Faulty center-mounted brake light switch needs to be replaced. **318: 1991–92**—Ice buildup in the throttle housing can lead to increased idle speed or impaired deceleration. **1992**—A faulty cooling system may spray hot water into the interior.

325C: 1994—Brake light switch may fail. **325i: 1991**—Faulty windshield wiper switch ground screw. **325iX: 1988**—A bent oil dipstick tube could prevent the throttle from returning to idle when the accelerator is released. **1988–95**—All 3- and 5-series models will have their radiator caps replaced free of charge. Original caps failed to relieve excess pressure, causing heater cores or hoses to rupture. **1991**—The transfer case leaking at the weep hole signals the need to revise the depth of the inner seal; repair may be covered under BMW's emissions warranty. **318i, 318iS, 325i, 325iS: 1992**—Airbag may not deploy. **1992–93**—Fuel lines can harden and "set" over time. **318, 325: 1991**—Erratic wiper operation caused by an electrical short circuit. **318i, 325iS: 1991**—The knee booster will be relocated so that it won't interfere with the steering column's absorption of crash forces. **325i, 325iS: 1992–94**—Brake light switch may fail. **1993–94**—Defective front transmission crossmember support.

Secret Warranties/Service Tips

All models/years—According to BMW, a rotten-egg smell coming from the exhaust is due to fuel impurities and can't be resolved by changing the catalytic converter. The company says that it won't pay for any converters replaced for this reason. **3 series: 1986–89**—A cracked intake manifold purge valve is a common problem. **Models with E34 or M50 engines: 1990–91**—Cylinder head cover leaks require a new, upgraded cover (#11-12-1-722-385, or #11-12-738-171 for later models). **1990–93**—Vehicles equipped with Jurid 506 brake pads may exhibit a steering vibration. **1992**—If the heater blower performs erratically, chances are the blower resistor unit needs replacing. **1994**—A starter motor failure may be caused by a faulty steering lock and electrical switch. • A sagging convertible headliner requires reinforced plastic clips that hold the headliner bracket to the bow. • Water intrusion into the driver's footwell area and the subsequent corrosion of the X13 and X14 connectors can be prevented by sealing off the hood's mounting flange just inboard of the left gas strut. • Water leaks into the E-box can be prevented by installing an improved capacity air intake drain hose in the right side drain, in addition to installing another drain hose. **1996**—Transmission shuddering requires the installation of a modified transmission control module. **1996–97**—Delayed gear engagement or adapter case leak requires the installation of a new transmission seal kit (#21-41-422-762). **5 series: 1989**—A fusible link could fail, shorting out all electrical power. **1990–93**—Change the Jurid 506 brake pads. **525i: 1990–94**—Brake light switch may fail. **1991**—Inoperative power accessories may require the installation of a Reinshagen general module (version 5.2 or later). **525iT: 1992–94**—Brake light switch may fail. **525i, 535i: 1991–92**—Airbag may not deploy. **1993–94**—Emergency flashers may self-activate. • Tips on fixing starter motor failures. **530I, 530iT: 1994**—Brake ligth switch may fail.

3 Series Profile

	1991	1992	1993	1994	1995	1996	1997	1998
Cost Price ($)								
318ti	—	—	—	—	25,295	26,180	26,535	26,685
318i 4d	20,275	23,275	25,420	26,720	27,645	30,120	30,745	31,045
Convertible	28,875	29,245	—	31,945	33,965	35,745	36,145	—
325i/328	26,700	30,265	32,055	33,350	34,120	36,410	36,845	36,870
Convertible	35,650	37,495	36,725	40,150	40,970	42,875	42,935	44,495
Used Values ($)								
318ti ↑	—	—	—	—	16,000	18,000	20,500	23,000
318ti ↓	—	—	—	—	14,000	16,500	18,500	21,000
318i 4d ↑	8,500	12,000	14,000	17,500	19,000	21,500	24,000	26,500
318i 4d ↓	7,000	11,000	12,500	16,500	17,000	19,500	22,000	24,500
Convertible ↑	10,500	13,500	—	21,000	23,500	26,000	29,000	—
Convertible ↓	9,000	11,500	—	18,500	21,000	23,500	26,500	—
325i/328 ↑	10,500	15,500	17,000	20,500	23,500	26,000	29,000	32,000
325i/328 ↓	8,500	13,500	14,500	18,500	21,000	24,000	27,000	30,000
Convertible ↑	14,000	17,500	19,500	27,000	29,000	33,000	36,000	38,000
Convertible ↓	12,000	15,000	17,500	24,500	27,000	29,500	34,000	36,000

Extended Warranty	Y	N	N	N	N	N	N	N
Secret Warranty	N	N	N	N	N	N	N	N

	1991	1992	1993	1994	1995	1996	1997	1998
Reliability	②	②	③	③	③	③	③	④
Air conditioning	②	②	②	②	③	④	④	④
Body integrity	②	②	②	③	③	③	③	④
Braking system	②	②	②	③	③	③	③	③
Electrical system	②	②	②	②	②	②	②	③
Engines	②	②	②	③	④	④	④	⑤
Exhaust/Converter	②	②	②	③	③	③	③	④
Fuel system	②	②	③	③	③	③	④	④
Ignition system	③	③	③	③	④	④	④	④
Manual transmission	③	③	③	④	⑤	⑤	⑤	⑤
- automatic	③	③	③	③	③	③	④	④
Rust/Paint	②	②	③	④	④	⑤	⑤	⑤
Steering	③	③	③	④	④	⑤	⑤	⑤
Suspension	④	④	④	④	④	⑤	⑤	⑤
Crash Safety								
325i 2d	③	—	—	—	—	—	—	—
325i 4d	—	④	④	—	④	—	—	—
328i	—	—	—	—	—	④	④	—

5 Series Profile

	1989	1990	1991	1992	1993	1994	1995
Cost Price ($)							
525i		37,325	34,245	35,600	37,975	38,355	39,775	40,125
535i		44,775	44,775	43,625	45,725	45,755	—	—

Used Values ($)

525i ↑	12,500	14,500	16,000	18,500	20,500	23,000	26,000	
525i ↓	11,000	12,500	14,000	16,000	18,500	21,500	23,000	
535i ↑	14,500	16,500	18,500	20,500	22,500	—	—	
535i ↓	12,500	14,000	16,000	19,000	19,500	—	—	

Extended Warranty	Y	Y	Y	Y	Y	Y	Y	Y
Secret Warranty	N	N	N	N	N	N	N	N

Reliability	②	③	③	③	④	⑤	⑤	⑤
Air conditioning	②	③	④	④	⑤	⑤	⑤	⑤
Body integrity	②	②	②	③	③	③	③	④
Braking system	②	②	②	③	③	③	③	④
Electrical system	②	②	②	②	③	③	③	③
Engines	②	③	③	③	④	④	⑤	⑤
Exhaust/Converter	③	③	③	③	③	③	④	⑤
Fuel system	③	③	③	③	④	④	⑤	⑤
Ignition system	③	③	③	④	④	④	⑤	⑤
Manual transmission	③	③	④	⑤	⑤	⑤	⑤	⑤
- automatic	②	③	③	③	④	⑤	⑤	⑤
Rust/Paint	②	③	④	④	④	④	⑤	⑤
Steering	③	③	③	③	④	④	⑤	⑤
Suspension	④	④	④	④	⑤	⑤	⑤	⑤

Note: The above models haven't been crash-tested.

FORD

Lincoln Continental, Mark VII/Mark VIII, Town Car

Rating: Lincoln Continental: Average (1996–98); Below Average (1984–95). **Lincoln Mark VII, Mark VIII:** Above Average (1995–98); Average (1994); Below Average (1986–93). **Lincoln Town Car:** Above Average (1995–98); Average (1988–94). Redesigned for 1998. **Maintenance/Repair costs:** Higher than average, and they must be done by a Ford or Lincoln dealer. **Parts:** Higher-than-average cost, but not hard to find (except for electronic components and body panels).

Strengths and weaknesses: These large luxury cruisers are proof that quality isn't proportional to the money you spend. Several designer series offer all the luxury options anyone could wish for, but the two ingredients most owners would expect to find—high quality and consistent reliability—are sadly lacking, especially when it comes to the automatic transmission, electrical system, brakes, body hardware, and fit and finish.

These cars aren't lemons (at least the later models aren't), but they don't offer the kind of trouble-free driving one would normally expect in a new vehicle selling for over $40,000. The automatic leveling air-spring suspension system makes for a stiff ride (especially on early models), while still allowing the Continental to "porpoise" due to its heavy front end. The Continental's anemic V6 powertrain is poorly suited to a car of this heft. The engine hesitates in cold weather and the automatic transmission shifts roughly due to malfunctioning computer modules.

Major mechanical defects affect the engine (frequent flywheel replacements), transmission, ABS, electrical, suspension, and steering systems, as well as the electronic modules. The mass of electrical gadgets increases the likelihood of problems as the cars age. For example, automatic headlight doors fail frequently, and the electronic antenna seldom rises to the occasion. The computerized dashboard is particularly failure-prone.

Other reliability complaints concern transmission fluid leakage due to misplaced bolts, rough upshifting caused by a defective valve body, and air conditioning and heating that sometimes work in reverse order (you often get heat when opening the AC, and air conditioning frequently comes on when the heater is engaged).

Continental (front-drive)
When the Continental went front-drive in 1988, it made a bad situation worse. The frequency and cost of repairs increased considerably, and parts became more difficult to find. The automatic transmission continued to malfunction, particularly on 1988–91 models; electrical components became even less reliable; stopping performance was compromised by premature brake wear and rear wheel lockup; and body hardware continued to be second class. The redesigned 1995 Continental featured a new V8 powerplant, more aerodynamic styling, and fiberglass panels. However, powertrain, electrical system, and brake problems remained.

Town Car
The rear-drive Town Car is the pick of the Lincoln litter. Thanks to its rear-drive configuration, it's relatively inexpensive to repair and parts aren't hard to find. Nevertheless, it's still afflicted by the Lincoln's generic problems: transmission, AC, and electrical glitches, and body hardware deficiencies. Try to find a 1991 or better version with the 4.6L engine to optimize performance and economy.

Dealer service bulletins: Continental: 1993—Poorly performing AC systems caused by a slipping clutch at high ambient temperatures, and AC FX-15 compressor growling. • Service Engine light may go on for no apparent reason. • A-pillars may make cracking noises in cold weather. • Power-steering units may be noisy and power door locks may not work. • Frequent under-hood squeaks, chirps, and knocks. • Premature wear on the inner edge of the rear tires, corrected by a new camber kit. **1994**—Faulty 3.8L engine rocker arm assemblies could cause squeaking, chirping, and knocking. • Inadequate AC operation caused by a faulty cold engine lockout switch and hose assembly. • Faulty electric rear window defrosters. **1995**—Engine misfires, no-start, hard start, and spark plug fouling. • Faulty in-tank fuel delivery modules causing the engine to stall and not restart will be replaced for free under Ford Program #95B71. • The Virtual Image Cluster will also be replaced at no charge under Program #95B71. (Ford will pay for a loaner car at $30 per day whenever carrying out these Program repairs.) • Harsh shifts, no 3–4 shift, erratic shifts, delayed transmission engagement and shift errors, low transaxle fluid level improperly setting the DTC and causing serious transmission malfunctions, and clicking noise when shifting into Reverse. • Insufficient AC cooling or excessive clutch end gap. • Brake roughness upon application or a thumping, clacking noise when braking. • Power-steering grunt or groan. • Rocker arm noise. • A ticking noise from the cooling fan or AX4N transaxle. **1996**—Stall or hard start after 1–4 hour soak. • Vehicle drifts or pulls while driving. • Transaxle click noise during Reverse engagement. • Transaxle driveline noises. • Case breaks at rear planet support. • Air suspension leaks down overnight. • Fog/film on windshield/interior windows. • Musty and mildew-type odors. **1997**—Harsh automatic shifting. • Chronic dead battery. • Excessive blower motor noise. • Acceleration or deceleration clunk. • Front suspension clunk. • A-pillar creaking noise. • Front end accessory drive belt (FEAD) may slip during wet conditions, causing a reduction in steering power-assist. • Steering wheel grunt or honk noise. • Loose catalyst or heat shields. • Stall or surging with automatic transmission engagement. **Mark VIII: 1994–97**—An erratic or prolonged 1–2 shift can be cured by replacing the cast aluminum piston with a one-piece stamped steel piston with bonded lip seals and by replacing the top accumulator spring. These upgraded parts will increase the transmission's durability, says Ford. **1995**—Intermittent loss of torque at 3–4 upshift, shifts to Neutral at heavy throttle, delayed transmission engagement and shift errors, and irregular or no torque converter operation. • Brake roughness upon application. • Insufficient AC cooling or excessive clutch end gap. • Faulty fuel gauge. • Hard start in low temperatures. **1996**—Stall or hard start after 1–4 hour soak. • Transmission valve body cross-leaks and shudder/downshift bump. • Growling noise from steering column when vehicle turns. • Squealing noise from the engine compartment. • Fog/film on windshield/interior windows. • Musty and mildew-type odors. **1997**—Erratic transmission shifting, especially the 1–2 shift. • Chirping and squeaking from blower motor. • No-start or crank; anti-theft system not responding. • Radio AM band static while driving. • Troubleshooting wind noise around doors. **Town Car: 1994**—A rough idle, hesitation, excessive fuel consumption, and a poor heater output that's likely caused by a thermostat sticking in an open position or opening before it should. • Transmission shudder under light to moderate acceleration. • Radio speaker noise caused by fuel pump malfunctions. • Faulty electric rear window defrosters. **1995**—Problems with the 1995 Town Car are identical to those listed for the Crown Victoria (see page 304). **1996**—Stall or hard start after

1–4 hour soak. • Squealing noise from the engine compartment. • Transmission valve body cross-leaks. • Chatter during turns. • Creaking from A-pillar area. • Rough idle or stalling at high altitudes. • Inoperative power-assisted deck lid. • Fog/film on windshield/interior windows. • Musty and mildew-type odors. **1997**—Erratic transmission shifting, especially the 1–2 shift. • Spark knock upon acceleration. • Door latch stuck open. • Fog/film on windshield/interior windows. • Loose catalysts or muffler heat shields. • Diagnosing and correcting wind noise around doors. • Shudder or vibration while in third or fourth gear. • Steering wheel noise and vibration. • Suspension leans to right side. • Whining noise from rear axle at highway speeds.

Safety summary/Recalls: Continental: Investigators are looking into reports of fires erupting in the engine compartment or wheelwells. **1995**—While parked, vehicle rolled backwards and suddenly accelerated forward. • Steering locks when driving through deep puddles. • Frequent reports of seatbelts failing to retract during an accident. • Defective inner tie-rod and strut causes severe steering shake. • Brake failures due to premature wear of rear drums and rotor warpage. • Inadequate defogging leaves two small circles to see through. • Console lights reflect into driver's portion of windshield and rear view mirror. • Rear deck stereo hump obstructs rear visibility. **1996**—Sudden acceleration while driving on the highway. • While parked, vehicle suddenly jumped out of Park and rolled forward and hit another car. • Several reports that the front suspension collapsed. • Front strut failures. • Clock spring broke causing loss of steering. • Steering wheel jams intermittently. • Power steering is inoperative when it rains. • Transmission jumped out of gear while driving. • Power seats malfunction. • Vehicle cannot be properly aligned, causing premature tire wear. **Town Car: 1992–93**—Engine compartment fires near the left front wheelwell or brake master cylinder. **1996**—Vehicle fires reportedly ignited in the engine compartment wiring. • Frequent reports of sudden acceleration. • Many reports of sudden acceleration while in Reverse, leading to the replacement of the speed control servo and servo cable. • Frequent complaints of chronic stalling. • ABS brakes often malfunction. • Airbag failed to deploy during collision. • Airbag packing gets hard in cold weather, leaving horn inoperative. • Trunk lid flew open on highway. • Many incidents where seatbelts either are too short for adults, won't retract, or ratchet tighter while being worn. • Two front seatbacks collapsed rearward when vehicle was rear-ended. • Excessive noise when braking. • Wind noise comes in through windshield. **1998**—Fuel may spit out of filler pipe when refueling. **Recalls: Continental: 1986**—Throttle may fail to return to idle. • Defective brake master cylinder warning sensor. **1986–87**—Fuel-line coupling may leak. **1987–88**—Body mounts will be inspected and a reinforcement plate installed. • Faulty transmission shift cable. • Power-steering pump pulley could separate from engine. **1988–93**—Advanced front subframe fastener corrosion. **1989**—Faulty left rear seatbelt retractor.

1992–94—Engine cooling fan motor may overheat and cause a fire. **1994**—Missing or improperly installed brake pedal push rod retainer. **1995–96**—"Autolamp" control module may fail. **1996–97**—Transmission may not engage; PRNDL may give a false reading. **Town Car: 1988–89**—Faulty ignition switches may be a fire hazard. **1988–94**—Subframe engine and transmission mounts could fail due to excessive corrosion, which could cause the subframe to drop and make steering difficult. **1990**—Ford will install new seat tracks and a memory track on the driver's side. **1990–91**—Hood can pop open during highway driving. **1991–92**—Secondary hood latch may not engage. **1991–94**—Faulty cruise control units and speed control cable. **1992–94**—Overheated engine cooling fan may start a fire. **1994**—Rear brake adapter to axle housing flange could loosen or separate. • Missing or improperly installed brake pedal push rod retainer. **1995**—Fuel could leak from tank. • Passenger airbag may not deploy properly. **1996**—Driver's door may not sustain specified load. • Seatbelts with switchable retractors for child restraints may not have the right components. **1997**—Driver's airbag may malfunction.

Secret Warranties/Service Tips

All models/years—Three components that frequently benefit from Ford "goodwill" warranty extensions are catalytic converters, fuel pumps, and computer modules. If Ford balks at refunding your money, apply the emissions warranty for a full or partial refund. • Paint delamination, fading, peeling, hazing, and "microchecking" (see page 113 for details on claiming a refund). **Continental: 1984–94**—A hum from the air suspension system can be corrected by replacing the compressor isolators with upgraded parts. **1988–90**—Hard cold-start, hesitation, and stalling during idle or when decelerating may be corrected by removing excessive sludge deposits or an oil film from the throttle body bore and plate or from the idler air by-pass valve. • High effort during wide turns at highway speeds signals the need to install a new power-steering short rack. • The intermittent loss of the AC may be due to a defective suction accumulator (#E6VY-19C836-A). **1988–94**—A squeak or chirp coming from the blower motor can be stopped by installing an upgraded blower motor with improved brush-to-commutator friction. • A cracked forward clutch piston may cause forward/reverse problems; install an improved clutch piston. • A speaker whine or buzz caused by the fuel pump can be stopped by installing an electronic noise RFI filter. **1989**—A rough idle or lean fuel flow may require the installation of deposit-resistant injectors. **1989–93**—A persistent fuel odor in the interior when the AC is running signals the need to install a new auxiliary vapor tube kit and relocate the tube near the rear bumper. **1991**—When Ford modified the automatic transmission for easier shifting, it also made it less reliable. In fact, *Consumer Reports'* annual member survey shows that almost 20 percent of the owners of the 1991 Sable, Taurus, and Lincoln Continental said that they had experienced a serious transmission failure in the preceding 12 months—four times the average for 1991 vehicles, according to *Consumer Reports.* Ford has extended the warranty on these transmissions to up to six years. • Delayed transaxle 3–2 downshifts may require a new, more durable spring retainer clip (#F1DZ-7F194-A).

1991–94—A sloshing noise from the fuel tank when accelerating or stopping requires the installation of an upgraded tank. Cost is covered under the emissions warranty. **1992–94**—A corroded solenoid may be the cause of starter failures. **1993–94**—An inoperative AC blower probably needs an improved cold engine lockout switch and hose assembly. • Stalling or hard starts in high ambient temperatures or high altitudes may be due to fuel tank contamination damaging the fuel pump. Ford paid for a fuel tank flush and a new fuel pump/sender and in-line fuel filter until May 31, 1997, under Service Program 94B48. **1994–95**—A thumping or clacking heard from the front brakes signals the need to machine the front disc brake rotors. Ford will pay for this repair under its base warranty. **1995–97**—An acceleration or deceleration clunk is likely caused by the rear lower subframe isolators allowing movement between the mounts and the subframe. • A front suspension clunk may signal premature sway bar wear. **Mark VII, Mark VIII: 1985–92**—An exhaust buzz or rattle may be caused by a loose heat shield catalyst. **1986–94**—The in-tank fuel pump is the likely cause of radio static. Install an electronic noise RFI filter (#F1PZ-18B925-A). **1993–94**—A squeak or chirp coming from the blower motor can be stopped by installing an upgraded blower motor with improved brush-to-commutator friction. • Automatic transmissions with delayed or no forward engagement, or a higher engine RPM than expected when coming to a stop, are covered in DSB #94-26-9. **Town Car: 1983–90**—A buzzing or humming from the fuel pump when the engine is shut off, a low battery, and hard or no-starts signal the need to install an upgraded pump relay (#F19Z-9345-A). **1987–90**—Excessive oil consumption is likely caused by leaking gaskets, poor sealing of the lower intake manifold, defective intake and exhaust valve stem seals, or worn piston rings. Install new guide-mounted valve stem seals for a more positive fit and new piston rings with improved oil control. **1989–90**—No Overdrive or an extended 3–4 shift may require the installation of a new Overdrive band, transmission separator plate kit, overhaul kit, and reverse drum. **1990**—A no-start condition may be caused by a defective Neutral start switch. • A pull to the right when braking can be corrected by installing a new brake pad and lining kit (#F1VY-20001-A). **1990–92**—Brake pedal and steering vibration when braking can be reduced by installing improved rotors (#F1VY-1125-A) and linings (#F3AZ-2001-A). **1991–92**—Secondary hood latch may not engage. **1992–94**—Automatic transmissions with delayed or no forward engagement, or a higher engine rpm than expected when coming to a stop, are covered in DSB #94-26-9. **1993–94**—A speaker whine or buzz caused by the fuel pump can be stopped by installing an electronic noise RFI filter. **1997**—Driver-side airbag may lack two mounting bolts.

Lincoln Continental Profile

	1991	1992	1993	1994	1995	1996	1997	1998
Cost Price ($)								
Continental	32,175	34,237	33,918	34,375	41,370	42,440	37,850	38,500
Used Values ($)								
Continental ↑	6,000	8,000	9,500	12,000	15,000	18,000	22,500	27,000
Continental ↓	5,000	6,500	8,500	10,000	13,000	15,500	20,000	25,000

Extended Warranty	Y	Y	Y	Y	Y	Y	Y	Y
Secret Warranty	Y	Y	Y	Y	Y	Y	Y	N

Reliability	❶	❷	❷	❷	❷	③	③	④
Air conditioning	❶	❶	❶	❶	❷	③	③	③
Automatic transmission	❶	❷	❷	❷	❷	③	③	③
Body integrity	❷	❷	❷	❷	❷	③	③	③
Braking system	❶	❶	❶	❶	③	③	③	④
Electrical system	❶	❶	❶	❷	❷	❷	❷	③
Engines	❶	❶	❷	❷	③	③	④	④
Exhaust/Converter	③	④	④	⑤	⑤	⑤	⑤	⑤
Fuel system	❷	③	③	③	④	④	④	④
Ignition system	❶	❷	③	③	③	③	④	④
Rust/Paint	③	③	③	④	④	④	④	④
Steering	❷	③	③	④	④	④	④	④
Suspension	❶	❶	❶	❷	❷	❷	③	④
Crash Safety	③	③	③	③	—	—	—	—

Lincoln Mark VII/Mark VIII Profile

	1991	1992	1993	1994	1995	1996	1997	1998
Cost Price ($)								
Mark VII/VIII	30,942	32,746	37,230	38,675	39,425	40,290	36,950	37,500
Used Values ($)								
Mark VII/Mark VIII ↑	8,000	9,500	11,000	13,000	16,000	19,000	22,000	26,000
Mark VII/Mark VIII ↓	6,000	8,000	9,500	12,000	14,000	17,000	20,000	24,000

Extended Warranty	Y	Y	Y	Y	Y	Y	Y	Y
Secret Warranty	N	Y	Y	Y	Y	Y	Y	N

Reliability	❷	❷	❷	❷	❷	③	③	③
Air conditioning	❷	❷	❷	③	③	③	③	③
Automatic transmission	❷	❷	❷	❷	❷	③	④	⑤
Body integrity	❷	❷	❷	❷	❷	❷	❷	③
Braking system	❷	❷	❷	❷	❷	③	④	④
Electrical system	❷	❷	❷	❷	❷	❷	❷	❷
Engines	④	④	③	③	④	④	④	④
Exhaust/Converter	❷	❷	③	④	④	④	⑤	⑤
Fuel system	③	③	③	③	③	③	④	④
Ignition system	③	③	③	③	③	③	④	③
Rust/Paint	❷	❷	❷	❷	③	③	③	④
Steering	❷	❷	③	④	④	④	⑤	⑤
Suspension	❷	❷	❷	③	③	③	③	④

Note: The Mark series hasn't been crash-tested.

Lincoln Town Car Profile

	1991	1992	1993	1994	1995	1996	1997	1998
Cost Price ($)								
Town Car	31,909	33,585	35,350	35,930	37,595	38,120	38,720	38,330
Used Values ($)								
Town Car ↑	7,000	9,000	10,500	13,000	17,000	20,000	24,000	29,000
Town Car ↓	5,500	7,500	9,000	11,500	15,000	18,000	22,000	26,000
Extended Warranty	N	N	N	N	N	N	N	N
Secret Warranty	Y	Y	Y	Y	Y	Y	Y	N
Reliability	2	2	2	3	4	4	4	4
Air conditioning	1	2	2	3	3	3	3	4
Automatic transmission	3	2	2	2	3	3	4	4
Body integrity	1	3	3	3	3	3	3	3
Braking system	1	1	1	1	1	2	3	3
Electrical system	1	1	1	2	2	3	3	3
Engines	4	4	4	4	4	5	5	5
Exhaust/Converter	3	3	4	4	4	5	5	5
Fuel system	2	2	3	3	3	3	3	4
Ignition system	1	2	2	3	3	3	3	3
Rust/Paint	2	2	3	3	3	3	4	5
Steering	2	2	3	4	4	3	3	4
Suspension	3	3	3	3	3	4	4	4
Crash Safety	5	5	5	5	5	4	4	—

GENERAL MOTORS

98 Regency, Park Avenue

Rating: Average (1997–98); Below Average (1991–96); Not Recommended (1985–90). Although a new Park Avenue commands a higher price than a new 98 Regency, the value of a used Park Avenue trails slightly. **Maintenance/Repair costs:** Higher than average, but repairs aren't dealer dependent. **Parts:** Higher-than-average cost (independent suppliers sell for much less), but not hard to find. Nevertheless, don't even think about buying one of these front-drives without a three- to five-year extended warranty backed by the automaker.

Strengths and weaknesses: These attractive, luxurious cars are billed as six-seaters, but only four passengers can ride in comfort. Although the 1991–96 Park Avenue and 98 Regency were improved over the years, they've compiled the worst repair history among large cars. Main problem areas are the engine, automatic transmission, fuel system, brakes, electrical system (including defective PROM and MEMCAL modules), starter and alternator, and badly assembled, poor-quality body hardware. The 3.0L V6 engine is inadequate for cars this heavy, and the 3.8L has been a big quality disappointment. Stay away from the failure-prone diesel engine. Under-hood servicing is complicated. Automatic transmission and engine computer malfunctions are common. The fuel-injection system is temperamental. Window mechanisms are poorly designed. The power-steering assembly is failure-prone. There are frequent electrical failures. Front brake pads and rotors require frequent replacement. Shock absorbers leak or go soft very quickly. Extensive surface corrosion has been a problem because of poor and often incomplete paint application at the factory.

Like the LeSabre, the 1997 Park Avenue and Ultra (its fully dressed version) were redesigned to include a reworked powertrain, a stiffer body, improved interior amenities, upgraded four-wheel disc brakes, and an upgraded ventilation system.

Aficionados of full-sized luxury sedans love the flush glass, wraparound windshield and bumpers, and clean body lines that lend the latest makeover an aerodynamic and pleasing appearance. But these cars are more than just pretty packages; they provide lots of room, luxury, style, and (dare I say) performance. Plenty of power is available with the 205-hp 3.8L V6 engine and the Aurora's 240-hp supercharged powerplant. It does 0–60 mph in under 9 seconds (impressive, considering the heft of these vehicles), and improves low- and mid-range throttle response. Power is transmitted to the front wheels through an electronically controlled transmission that features "free-wheeling" clutches designed to eliminate abrupt gear changes. Both the Park Avenue and Ultra use a stretched version of the more rigid Riviera and Aurora platform.

The revised 1997 Park Avenue models have had fewer complaints, perhaps because of the short time they've been out and the fact that GM's warranty is still in effect. Nevertheless, the main problem areas continue to be the following: powertrain malfunctions; engine and transmission leaks; a concerto of squeaks, rattles, moans, and whines; AC not performing properly; and numerous body and trim defects. Since the 1998 returned relatively unchanged, don't expect any major improvements quality-wise.

Dealer service bulletins: 1993—3.8L engines frequently stall when decelerating or lead to extended cranking; also, they often stall after a cold start. • Excessive front-end vibration when passing over bumps. • Whistling when the AC is in recirculate mode. **1994**—Lots of bulletins address automatic transmission and heater/AC problems. **1995**—Noise while driving up medium grades or accelerating. • Stall upon deceleration. • Cold-start rattle with the 4T60E automatic transmission. • Grinding/growling when in Park on an incline. • A coolant leak from the belt tensioner assembly. • Throttle body noise upon acceleration from stop. • Brake vibration and/or pedal pulsation. • Whistle coming from the heater/AC unit. • Low voltage reading or dim lights at idle. •

Headlights/parking lights remain on. • Squeak/creak from rear of vehicle. • Poor paint application and rust spots. **1996**—Second-gear starts, poor shifting 1–3. • AC defrost valve creaks when changing modes. • AC odor at start-up in humid climates. • AC flutter or moan. • Noisy steering column. • Cold-start rattle. • Engine cranks but won't start. • Engine oil leaks. • Excess vibration of electrochromatic rear view mirror. • Exterior light condensation. • Fluttering, popping, ticking, and clunking noises. • Inoperative door locks. • AC thump noise upon start-up. • Intermittent Neutral/loss of Drive at highway speeds. • Instrument panel buzz or rattle when the brakes are applied. • Popping noise from front of vehicle when turning. • Troubleshooting radio frequency interference. • Rattle in rear door when closing. • Transaxle gear whine. • Whistle noise from HVAC (climate control system). • Wind noise around front and rear doors. **1997**—AC thump noise. • Driver's seat rocks. • Noisy front brakes. • Engine oil leaks. • Engine oil level indicates over-full. • Harsh shift from Reverse to Drive. • Excess vibration of electrochromic rear view mirror. • Erratic wiper operation in automatic mode. • Spontaneous horn activation or inoperative horn. • Instrument panel buzz or rattle when the brakes are applied. • Popping noise from front of vehicle when turning. • Growl or vibration when turning or accelerating. • Paint chips on rear compartment lid. • Roof panel running front to back has a wavy/dimpled appearance and transmits excessive rain noise. • Steering vibration/moan when parking. • Transaxle gear whine.

Safety summary/Recalls: Recalls: All models: 1986—Faulty headlight switches. • Power-steering hose leaks could cause an under-hood fire. • ABS may suddenly fail due to fluid leaking from system. **1987**—A faulty fusible link could cause an under-hood fire. • Some throttle cables may not return to idle position. **1991**—Parking brakes might not hold. • Console shift lever could disengage. **1992–93**—Transmission-cooler line could separate at low temperatures. **Park Avenue: 1997**—Center seatbelt anchor bolts were improperly installed. • Brake/Traction Control Module could cause ABS to lose its effectiveness and make for longer stopping distances. **98 Regency: 1994–95**—Headlight switch may not work. **1995**—Current leakage in models with Twilight Sentinel can cause loss of headlights and parking lights, or the lights may suddenly come on while the car is parked. **1996**—Damaged capacitor could cause confusing electronic warnings to be displayed. • Backfire upon start-up can damage the intake manifold and cause hard starting or a fire.

Secret Warranties/Service Tips

All models/years—A rotten-egg odor coming from the exhaust is probably caused by a malfunctioning catalytic converter and may be covered under GM's emissions warranty. • The THM 44C-T4 automatic transaxles on front-drive models equipped with V6 engines are particularly failure-prone: their pinched or kinked vacuum lines result in low oil pressure. • Paint delamination, peeling, or fading (see pages 73–75). **All models: 1988–93**—Vehicles equipped with a 3800 engine that stalls upon deceleration or is hard to start may need a new air control motor (IAC). **1991–94**—Harsh automatic transmission upshifts can be corrected by installing an upgraded accumulator valve in the control valve body. • Loss of Drive or erratic shifts may be caused by an intermittent short to ground on the A or B shift solenoid or an electrical short circuit in the transaxle. • Water leaking from the doors into the passenger compartment has a number of causes and remedies (DSB #431003). **1993–94**—Owners who complain of automatic transmission low-speed miss, hesitation, chuggle, or skip may find relief with the improved MEMCAL module that GM developed to remedy the problem. **1994**—Inadequate heating, ventilation, and AC operation is addressed in DSB #431219. **1995–96**—Wind noise around front and rear doors; diagnosis and repair. **1995–97**—Transmission gear whine means the final drive assembly may have to be replaced.

98 Regency, Park Avenue Profile

	1991	1992	1993	1994	1995	1996	1997	1998
Cost Price ($)								
98 Regency	25,129	25,943	25,839	26,695	26,695	28,800	28,600	29,000
Park Avenue	25,595	26,570	26,650	27,625	28,880	28,850	30,650	31,340
Used Values ($)								
98 Regency ↑	7,500	8,500	9,500	11,500	14,000	16,000	18,000	20,500
98 Regency ↓	6,500	7,000	8,500	10,000	12,000	14,000	16,000	18,500
Park Avenue ↑	8,000	9,500	11,000	13,000	15,000	17,000	21,500	24,000
Park Avenue ↓	7,000	8,000	9,500	11,500	13,000	15,500	19,000	22,000
Extended Warranty	Y	Y	Y	Y	Y	Y	Y	Y
Secret Warranty	Y	Y	Y	Y	Y	Y	Y	Y
Reliability	❷	❷	❷	❷	❷	❷	③	③
Air conditioning	❷	❷	❷	❷	❷	③	③	③
Automatic transmission	❷	❷	❷	❷	❷	③	③	③
Body integrity	❶	❶	❶	❶	❶	❶	❶	③
Braking system	❷	❷	❷	❷	❷	③	③	③
Electrical system	❷	❷	❷	❷	❷	❷	❷	❷
Engines	❷	❷	❷	③	③	③	③	③
Fuel system	❷	❷	❷	❷	❷	❷	③	③
Ignition system	❷	❷	❷	❷	③	③	③	③
Rust/Paint	❶	❶	❶	❶	❶	❶	❷	③
Steering	❶	❶	❶	❶	❷	❷	❷	③
Suspension	❷	❷	❷	❷	❷	③	③	③
Crash Safety								
98 Regency	⑤	⑤	⑤	—	—	—	—	—

Cadillac Allanté, Catera, Eldorado, Seville

Rating: Below Average (1992–98); Not Recommended (1986–91).
Maintenance/Repair costs: Higher than average, but repairs aren't
dealer dependent. **Parts:** Higher-than-average cost (independent suppliers sell for much less), but not hard to find. Don't buy one of the
front-drives without a three- to five-year supplementary warranty.

Strengths and weaknesses: The early Cadillacs are luxury embarrass-
ments and later models barely pass muster. Even though most use the
same mechanical components with the same deficiencies as the Riviera
and Toronado models, they're far more failure-prone due to the complexity of their different luxury features.

Allanté
Introduced in 1987, the Allanté was essentially a "kit car" Cadillac two-seat
roadster with body components flown in from Italy and mechanicals assembled in Detroit. This car got the more powerful Northstar V8 in 1993—the
same year the car was discontinued. Originally selling for $77,475, a 1987
model would fetch no more than $9,000 today. Does it have any value as a
collector's item? Not a chance.

Owners report many reliability problems—especially with brake,
electronic control, and powertrain glitches—and woefully poor-quality
body assembly. Also, the convertible top is a chore to put up or down.
Allanté owners have expressed a few other concerns: chronic and costly
ABS brake repairs; emergency brake rattles, particularly if the emergency brake is not used often (the cause is prematurely worn rear brake
pads, or defective brake "springs" or clips); turn signals sticking (simply squirt TV Tuner Cleaner from Radio Shack into the assembly);
defective intake manifolds; and faulty alarms. For more detailed information from Allanté owners who both love and hate their car, access
www.allante.org on the Internet.

Catera
Assembled in Germany and based on the Opel Omega, the rear-drive,
mid-sized Catera comes with a 200-hp V6 engine, 4-speed automatic
transmission, 16-inch alloy wheels, 4-wheel disc brakes, a limited-slip differential, traction control, and standard dual front airbags. The conservatively styled 1997 Catera (the uninspired styling has Lumina written all
over it) was designed to compete with the BMW 328i, Lexus ES 300, and
Mercedes Benz C280. GM hoped not to drive away its more traditional
"empty-nesters" (I guess that's a polite term for "old folks"), while lur-
ing more baby boomers to its higher-performance variations.

The last time Cadillac introduced an entry-level model was 1981, when
the automaker launched the Cimarron, a fully loaded, Chevrolet
Cavalier–derived Cadillac that carried a $4,000 premium over the compa-
rably equipped Cavalier. Back then, most auto critics and consumer advocates considered the Cimarron to be at the rear of the pack as far as

performance and quality control were concerned. The Catera, on the other hand, has received good reviews from the European press for its quiet, spacious, and comfortable interior, responsive handling, precise steering, fine-tuned suspension, and almost nonexistent lean or body roll when cornering. Without a doubt, this is one Cadillac that's meant to be driven. On the downside, though, the controls aren't easy to figure out, some gauges are hard to read, and the driver's rear view is hindered by the large rear head restraints and narrow back windshield. Furthermore, owners report chronic stalling and hard starts, possibly due to a malfunctioning idle control valve, constant warning-light illuminations, poor AM radio reception (requiring an additional amplifier), and loose interior panels. Two other performance problems reported by owners: when you pass over a large expansion joint, the floorpan vibrates annoyingly; if you drive over a bump when turning, the steering wheel kicks back in your hands.

A few other points you may wish to consider: GM dealers are notoriously bad when it comes to understanding and repairing European-transplanted cars (just ask any Saab owner). As well, low-volume cars generally don't have an adequate supply of replacement parts in the pipeline until they've been on the market for a while. Add in the Catera's European connection and you'd best be ready to endure long service waits and high parts costs for those repairs not covered under warranty.

Finally, the fact that Cateras are European built doesn't necessarily mean that these Cadillacs will be reliable or durable. Based on the past performance of Big Three European imports, it's a safe bet that these cars will be less reliable and more troublesome than the competition. GM first learned that lesson with the British-built Vauxhall Firenza it unleashed on an unsuspecting Canadian public in the '70s. A few years later, it settled out of court on several class actions that I piloted, and paid a $20,000 fine to the federal government for misleading advertising. (On a nationally advertised roadtrip across Canada, GM said the cars excelled. Truth is, they were a mess. They required a team of engineers just to get started.)

Eldorado and Seville
From 1992 on, the Eldorado's styling became more distinctive, even though the vehicle shares most powertrain and chassis components with the Seville. Although the base 4.9L V8 provides brisk acceleration, the 32-valve Northstar V8, first found on the 1993 Touring Coupe, gives you almost 100 more horses with great handling and a comfortable ride. Overall, the Touring Coupe or Sport Coupe will give you the best powertrain, handling, and braking features. Of course, you'll have to contend with poor fuel economy, rear visibility that's obstructed by the huge side pillars (a Seville problem, as well), confusing and inconvenient climate controls, and a particularly complex engine compartment.

Sitting on the same platform as the Eldorado, the Seville has European-style allure with a more rounded body than the Eldorado. Apart from that, since its redesign in 1992, its engine, handling, and braking upgrades have followed in lockstep fashion the Eldorado's improvements.

Whether you buy a used Eldorado or Seville, keep in mind that the improved versions came out with the 1995 models, which carried on unchanged until their redesign for 1998. So, if you must buy one of these models, remember that the only distinguishing feature between them is styling, not performance.

The 4.1L V8 is best avoided. It may be simpler to work on, but it too is fuel thirsty and easily overpowered by the Eldorado's weight.

These cars have generic deficiencies that fall into common categories: poorly calibrated and failure-prone engines, transmissions, and fuel and ignition systems; a multiplicity of electrical short circuits; and sloppy body assembly using poor-quality components. Specifically, engines and fuel systems often produce intermittent stalling, rough idling, hesitation, and no-starts; the Overdrive automatic is prone to premature failure; oil pumps fail frequently; front brakes and shock absorbers wear out quickly; often, paint is poorly applied, fades, or peels away prematurely; fragile body hardware breaks easily; and there are large gaps between sheet-metal panels and doors that are poorly hung and not entirely square. Other body problems include cracking of front outside door handles, door rattles (Eldorado), poor bumper fit, loose sun visor mounting, rear taillight condensation, fading and discoloring appliqué moldings (Seville), interior window fogging, "creaking" body mounts, water leaking into trunk from licence-plate holder (Eldorado), noisy roof panels and seatback lumbar motors, and a creaking noise at the front-door upper hinge area.

Dealer service bulletins: All models with 4.9L engines: 1993—May be hard to start, frequently stall, and lose power; and may not maintain the cruise control set speed. • Condensation in the taillights. • Radio static. • Excessive front-end vibrations when passing over bumps. • Faulty engine oil pumps (Allanté). • Transmission gear whine and rear suspension noise. **Catera: 1997**—Brake squealing. • Clunk noise from engine compartment on vehicles with cruise control. • Ignition key binds, drags, or sticks in ignition. • Loose fuel cap. • Low-voltage reading or dim lights at idle. • Noise in radio AM band when rear defogger on. • Oil leak from engine timing cover. • Inoperative power door locks. • Inoperative rear defogger. • Windshield wiper slap/flop noise. **Eldorado: All years**—Squeaks and squealing after a cold start. • Warped windshield and rear-window molding. **1994**—Faulty engine oil pumps and noisy fuel pumps. • Engine oil leaks. • 4.6L engines may run roughly, miss, surge, or hesitate. • Engine accessory belt noise. • An inoperative cruise control or brake/transmission interlock. • Erratic shifting. • AC hissing noise and rear suspension noise. • Condensation dripping from the heater duct and poor heat distribution (driver's feet get cold). • Doors won't stay open on slight grades and parking brake binds. **1995**—Engine cranks but won't start; no fuel pressure; loss of oil pressure or lack of power. • Engine oil leak at the rear main seal or T joint. • Starter motor runs continuously. • Metallic knocking sound from the engine. • A grinding or scraping noise in Park or Neutral. • Front brake vibration and/or pedal pulsation. • Annoying AC odor. • A low-voltage reading or dim lights at idle. • Remote keyless entry malfunctions. • Rattle noise from front of vehicle, front-seat clicking noise, clicking noise from under the hood or dash, and rubbing noise when the front wheels are turned all the way. • Door window slaps or rattles when closing door. • Excessive radio static. • Wet or smelly carpet from water leaks. • Poor paint application and rust spots. **1996**—Engine oil leaks from upper to lower crankcase joint. • Loss of oil pressure and/or lack of power. • Oil leakage from the oil pan to lower crankcase attaching bolts. • Second-gear starts, poor 1–3 shifting. • Steering column noise. • Poor AC cooling in traffic and high ambient temperatures. • Insufficient heat distribution or lack of air flow. • Coolant temperature gauge always reads hot. • Erratic or inaccurate instrument panel displays and gauges. • Insufficient remote keyless entry operating range. • Positive battery cable won't tighten properly. • Radio clock stuck on 12:00. • Radio frequency interference diagnosis. • Whistle noise from HVAC. • Exhaust rattles. • Rattling heard when vehicle goes over bumps. • Clicking noise from front seats. • Squawk noise from rear of vehicle in cold temperature. • Slow parking brake release or slow HVAC mode changes. • Water leak from rear-door side-window area. • Wet or smelly carpet from water leaks. • Abnormal condensation in taillights and other lights. • Faulty cup holders. **1997**—Front brake noise. • Remote won't open doors or trunk. • Excessive vibration of electrochromatic mirror. • Fuel tank won't fill to capacity/always reads full. • Horn hard to operate when cold. • Inoperative power door locks. • Metallic buzz or rattle at the instrument panel when the brakes are applied. • No warning light or driver information center message. • Power window inoperative after express down feature is used. • Torque converter clutch buzz or moan.

Safety summary/Recalls: Allanté: 1989–92—NHTSA is investigating Allantés for brake problems following a petition from a 1989 Allanté owner who collected 29 complaints from his website (Allante Appreciation Group, *www.allante.org*). The government is looking primarily into reports of the brakes failing or malfunctioning. **Seville: 1994**—Owners report that the throttle may stick in the open or closed position. Dealers will modify the throttle control cable to secure it in place. Drivers also complain that the shoulder belt chafes at the neck. NHTSA is looking into dash-trim panels that fly apart when the airbag is deployed. **Recalls: All models: 1986–87**—Faulty headlight circuit. **1989**—ABS may be defective. **1990**—Gear indicator may be poorly aligned. • Faulty rear seatbelt shoulder retractors. **1990–91**—Front outer shoulder belt web may stick in retractor. **1992**—Possible loss of steering control. **All models with 4.6L engine: 1993**—Fuel leakage in engine compartment. **1993–94**—Leaking engine oil cooler hose may cause a fire. **1994**—Faulty throttle cable. **Eldorado, Seville: 1995–96**—Excessive moisture (due to a window left open when it rains, for example) may cause the airbag to deploy when the ignition is switched on. There have been 70 reported incidents, 39 of them with injuries to drivers, passengers, or both. Before NHTSA forced this recall, GM sent notices to owners advising them to take precautions if their vehicle interiors became wet. (No, I haven't read the letter and I can't imagine what kind of precautions one should take.) A short circuit caused by wet carpets could cause the airbags to deploy suddenly.

Secret Warranties/Service Tips

All models: 1990–94—A rear suspension squawk can be eliminated by installing upgraded stabilizer shaft insulators. **All models with 4.9L engines: 1991–95**—GM will install a new computer chip that reduces stalling, pursuant to an agreement with the U.S. Justice Department and EPA. **1993**—DSB #476506 gives lots of tips on fixing 4.6L engines that run roughly, miss, surge, or hesitate. **1993–94**—DSB #476003 goes into great detail about troubleshooting the various engine oil leaks afflicting 1993–94 models. • Noisy fuel pumps can be silenced only by installing an upgraded fuel pump under warranty. • Poor heat distribution (driver's feet get cold) can be fixed by replacing the floor outlet assembly. **1994**—Condensation dripping from the heater duct requires the installation of a watertight dam in the HVAC case. • An inoperative cruise control or brake/transmission interlock may signal a misadjusted stop-light switch assembly. • A binding parking brake may need a new park-brake vacuum-release switch. **1996–97**—A torque converter clutch buzz or moan requires the installation of an upgraded case-cover-assembly spacer plate and the upper-control-valve body. **1997**—Excessive front brake noise can be cured by installing upgraded front brake pads. **Catera: 1997**—Brake squealing can be silenced by installing redesigned calipers. • Oil leakage from the engine timing cover can be corrected by installing a new oil pump gasket.

Cadillac Allanté, Catera, Eldorado, Seville Profile

	1991	1992	1993	1994	1995	1996	1997	1998
Cost Price ($)								
Allanté	55,250	58,470	61,675	—	—	—	—	—
Catera	—	—	—	—	—	—	33,635	34,250
Eldorado	32,380	33,720	35,240	38,565	39,505	41,020	39,883	39,945
Seville	34,975	36,225	38,240	42,265	43,220	44,420	41,883	43,160
Used Values ($)								
Allanté ↑	18,000	21,000	30,000	—	—	—	—	—
Allanté ↓	16,000	19,000	26,000	—	—	—	—	—
Catera ↑	—	—	—	—	—	—	23,500	27,000
Catera ↓	—	—	—	—	—	—	21,500	25,000
Eldorado ↑	9,000	12,500	15,000	17,000	20,000	23,000	28,000	33,000
Eldorado ↓	7,500	10,500	13,000	15,000	18,500	21,000	25,000	30,000
Seville ↑	11,500	14,500	17,000	19,000	22,000	25,000	29,000	35,000
Seville ↓	10,000	12,500	15,500	17,000	19,500	22,500	26,000	33,000
Extended Warranty	Y	Y	Y	Y	Y	Y	Y	Y
Secret Warranty	Y	Y	Y	Y	Y	Y	Y	Y

Reliability	②	②	②	②	②	②	③	③
Air conditioning	②	②	②	②	②	③	③	④
Automatic transmission	②	②	②	②	③	③	③	④
Body integrity	②	②	②	②	②	②	②	②
Braking system	②	②	②	②	②	②	③	③
Electrical system	②	②	②	②	②	②	②	③
Engines	②	②	②	②	③	③	③	③
Exhaust/Converter	②	②	②	③	③	④	④	⑤
Fuel system	②	②	②	③	③	③	④	④
Ignition system	②	②	②	②	③	③	③	③
Rust/Paint	②	②	②	②	②	②	③	③
Steering	②	②	②	②	④	④	④	④
Suspension	②	②	②	②	②	②	③	④
Crash Safety								
Seville	—	④	—	—	—	—	—	—

Note: Reliability figures apply to the Eldorado and Seville only; Allanté and Catera reliability information is given in the text.

Aurora, Riviera, Toronado, Trofeo

Rating: Riviera, Toronado, Trofeo: Average (1995–98); Not Recommended (1986–93). GM skipped the 1994 model year and introduced an all-new 1995 version. **Aurora:** Above Average (1995–98). **Maintenance/Repair costs:** Higher than average, but repairs aren't dealer dependent. **Parts:** Higher-than-average cost (independent suppliers sell for much less), but not hard to find. Nevertheless, don't even think about buying one of the earlier front-drives without a three- to five-year supplementary warranty.

Strengths and weaknesses: Although the redesigned 1988–93 cars got performance, handling, and ride upgrades, they kept the same low level of quality control with multiple design and manufacturing defects, including serious fuel-injection, engine computer, and electrical system problems. One particularly poor design was the complex Graphic Control Center, which used an oversensitive video screen and small push buttons. It's both distracting and expensive to repair. The automatic transmission is notoriously failure-prone, and brakes wear out prematurely and perform poorly. Surface rust and poor paint quality are the most common body complaints on all years. Shock absorbers wear out quickly and the diesel engine seldom runs properly. Mechanical parts are easy to find, but body panels have to be ordered from GM at a premium.

The 1995–98 models offer many more luxury features but continue their checkered repair history. GM improved the quality over the years, but generic deficiencies affecting the automatic transmission, engine, computer modules, suspension, and fit and finish make these cars less than luxury from a quality-control standpoint.

Aurora

This front-drive luxury sedan is aimed at the Acura, Infiniti, and Lexus crowd. It uses the same basic design as the Riviera but doesn't share the same major mechanical features or popular styling.

The Aurora's main advantages are its sporty handling and unusual aero styling. In contrast to the Riviera and Toronado, the Aurora seats five only and uses a 4.0L V8 derived from the Cadillac 4.6L V8 Northstar engine. Acceleration is underwhelming (this is a heavy car) but adequate for highway touring. Road and wind noise is omnipresent and the rear trunk's small opening compromises the large trunk's ability to handle odd-sized objects.

Dealer service bulletins: All models: 1995—Engine misfires, rough idle, white exhaust smoke, and a continuous spark knock. • Excessive oil consumption. • A cold-start rattle with the 4T60E automatic transmission. • A starter motor that runs continuously. • Reduced heater performance on the driver's side. • Brake vibration and/or pedal pulsation. • Instrument panel trim may separate from the upper trim pad. • Low-voltage reading or dim lights at idle. • A scraping noise and increased effort needed to open the doors. • Inoperative fuel-filler door. • ABS/traction light stays on. • Poor paint application and rust spots. **1996**—Second-gear starts and erratic 1–3 shifts. • AC odor in humid climates. • Steering column noise. • Cold-start rattle noise. • Engine cranks but won't start. • Engine oil leaks. • Excessive vibration of electrochromatic mirror. • Exterior light condensation. • Troubleshooting tips for fluttering, popping, ticking, and clunking noises. • Gap between door opening weather strip and roof line. • Inoperative power door locks. • Intermittent Neutral/loss of Drive at highway speeds. • Instrument panel buzz or rattle when the brakes are applied. • Popping noise, growl, or vibration when making a right turn. • Reduced heater performance on the driver's side. • Reduced retention of door trim lace. • Roof panel running front to back has a wavy/dimpled appearance and transmits excessive rain noise. • Underbody noise from rear of vehicle. • Wet or smelly carpet from water leaks. **1997**—Front brake noise. • Engine cranks but won't start. • Engine oil leaks. • Engine oil level indicates over-full. • Excessive vibration of electrochromatic mirror. • Harsh shift from Reverse to Drive. • Inoperative power door locks. • Instrument panel buzz or rattle when the brakes are applied. • Popping noise, growl, or vibration when making a right turn. • Steering vibration, shudder, or moan when parking. • Roof panel running front to back has a wavy/dimpled appearance and transmits excessive rain noise. **Aurora: 1995**—White exhaust smoke, engine oil leak at the rear main seal or T joint, and loss of oil pressure or lack of power. • A popping noise is heard during cranking, or the starter motor continues to run or crank after shutoff. • Reduced heater performance on the driver's side. • Brake vibration and/or pedal pulsation. • A clicking noise emanating from the dash or hood, creak noise at the right side of vehicle, and a thumping from the rear of the vehicle. • Loose, rattling headliner and clicking emanating from the sunroof. • Excessive radio static. • Instrument panel trim that may separate from the upper trim pad. • Wet, smelly carpet from water leaks. • Wind noise at the front door A-pillar. **1996**—Engine oil leaks from upper to lower crankcase joint. • Oil leakage from the oil pan to lower crankcase attaching bolts. • Loss of oil pressure and/or lack of power. • Steering column noise. • Popping noise from front of vehicle when turning. • Underbody noise from rear of vehicle. • Reduced heater performance. • Rear compartment lid-assist rod separating from lid. • Gap between door opening weather strip and roof line. • Reduced retention of door trim lace. • Condensation on exterior light. • Wet or smelly carpet from water leaks.

Safety summary/Recalls: Recalls: All models: 1986–87—The power-steering pump hose may leak, creating the possibility of an engine fire. **1989**—ABS brakes may fail due to a faulty brake line. **1990**—Faulty transmission cable may indicate that the wrong gear is engaged. **1991–93**—Front shoulder seatbelt may stick in retractor. • Poorly aligned rear shoulder seatbelt retractor assemblies. **1992**—Possible steering loss due to the disengagement of the steering shaft. **1996**—Driver warning alarms and displays may malfunction. • Backfire can break the intake manifold and cause a fire.

Secret Warranties/Service Tips

All models/years—A rotten-egg odor coming from the exhaust is likely the result of a malfunctioning catalytic converter covered by GM's emissions warranty. • Paint delamination, peeling, or fading (see pages 73–75). **All models: 1989–90**—Stalling from a cold start and a chuggle at 30 mph require a new MEMCAL. **1991–93**—Loss of Drive or erratic shifts may be caused by an intermittent short circuit to ground on the A or B shift solenoid, or an electrical short circuit in the transaxle. • Harsh automatic transmission upshifts can be corrected by installing an upgraded accumulator valve in the control valve body. • A front-end engine knock troubleshooting chart and extensive diagnostic tips are found in DSB #306001. **1995–96**—Intermittent Neutral/loss of Drive at highway speeds can be fixed by replacing the control valve body assembly. **Riviera: 1990–91**—A revised headrest guide loop will be installed on Rivieras if the shoulder seatbelt rests uncomfortably on the neck. **1990–93**—An engine ticking at idle can be traced to rattling piston pins, which must be replaced with upgraded parts. **Toronado, Trofeo: 1990–92**—A body-mount creak that occurs whenever the vehicle passes over a bump may be due to one or more of the body mounts being poorly positioned in the frame; correct by installing a new, lower insulator. • Chronic wind noise coming from the front door window can be corrected by reinstalling the run channel retainer. • A shake or vibration in the front end when going over smooth roads may be caused by an internal leak in the engine mount.

Aurora Profile

	1995	1996	1997	1998
Cost Price ($)				
Aurora	43,020	43,695	46,045	36,625
Used Values ($)				
Aurora ↑	14,000	18,000	21,500	25,500
Aurora ↓	12,500	16,500	19,500	22,500
Extended Warranty	Y	Y	Y	Y
Secret Warranty	Y	Y	Y	Y
Reliability	④	④	④	④
Crash Safety	③	③	③	③

Riviera, Toronado, Trofeo Profile

	1991	1992	1993	1995	1996	1997	1998
Cost Price ($)							
Riviera	26,250	27,080	28,120	28,857	30,715	31,375	33,165
Toronado	25,579	26,539	—	—	—	—	—
Trofeo	27,075	27,895	—	—	—	—	—
Used Values ($)							
Riviera ↑	8,500	9,000	10,500	15,000	17,000	20,500	24,000
Riviera ↓	7,500	8,500	9,500	12,500	15,500	18,500	22,000
Toronado ↑	6,000	8,500	—	—	—	—	—
Toronado ↓	4,500	7,000	—	—	—	—	—
Trofeo ↑	6,500	8,900	—	—	—	—	—
Trofeo ↓	4,900	7,400	—	—	—	—	—
Extended Warranty	Y	Y	Y	Y	Y	Y	Y
Secret Warranty	Y	Y	Y	Y	Y	Y	Y
Reliability	❷	③	③	③	③	④	④
Air conditioning	③	③	④	④	④	④	④
Automatic transmission	❷	❷	③	③	③	③	③
Body integrity	❷	❷	❷	❷	③	③	③
Braking system	❷	❷	❷	❷	❷	③	③
Electrical system	❷	❷	❷	❷	❷	❷	③
Engines	③	③	③	④	④	④	④
Exhaust/Converter	④	④	④	⑤	⑤	⑤	⑤
Fuel system	❷	③	③	③	③	③	④
Ignition system	③	③	③	③	③	③	④
Rust/Paint	❷	❷	❷	❷	❷	❷	③
Steering	③	③	③	④	④	④	④
Suspension	❷	③	③	③	③	④	④

Note: These vehicles haven't been crash-tested.

Brougham/Fleetwood (RWD)

Rating: Above Average (1993–96); Average (1984–92). A smart car for retirees, it's on par with the Ford Crown Victoria and Grand Marquis when it comes to comfort and reliability. **Maintenance/Repair costs:** Average, and repairs aren't dealer dependent. **Parts:** Reasonably priced (independent suppliers sell for much less) and not hard to find, despite the fact that these rear-drives were dropped in '96.

Strengths and weaknesses: The quintessential land yacht, these cars emphasize comfort over handling with their powerful engines and large chassis. Nevertheless, with their spacious interior and many convenience features, these large cars are ideal for vacationing and light trailer pulling.

The most serious problem areas are the fuel-injection system, which frequently malfunctions and costs an arm and a leg to repair; automatic transmissions that shift erratically; a weak suspension; computer module glitches; poor body assembly; and paint defects. From a reliability/durability standpoint, the rear-drives are much better made than their front-drive counterparts.

GM dealer service bulletins show that these vehicles also have noisy power-steering units and cooling fans, the AC bi-level mode produces extreme temperature differences, the instrument panel squeaks and rattles, there are rear quarter-panel gaps and rusting at the rear side door window molding, and water leaks into the passenger side of the front compartment.

Safety summary/Recalls: 1995—Dashboard reflects into windshield. • Vehicle accelerated while braking. • Frequent stalling. • Trunk lid opened while driving. • Brakes require extended stopping distances. **1996**—Airbags failed to deploy. • Seatbelts didn't restrain driver and passenger during a collision. • Chronic stalling due to fuel sending unit failure. • Engine head gaskets failures. • Transmission pounds when shifting gears. • Water pump leakage on the serpentine belt may cause steering to lock up. • Power-steering hose and pump failure. • Brakes often lock up when applied. • Excessive brake noise caused by the premature wearout of brake rotor and drum. • AC cooling switch and high pressure hose failures. • Instrument cluster hard to read in daylight. • Power door locks and trunk lock frequently fail to operate properly. • Loose windshield molding. • Defective keyless entry module. **Recalls: All models: 1984–88**—A sticking throttle could lead to sudden acceleration. **1986**—Vehicles with a 5.0L engine could also have a sticking throttle. **1987**—Cars equipped with an automatic transmission could start in gear or engage the wrong gear. **1993**—Passenger-side airbag may have a defective igniter. **1994**—Oil-cooler inlet hose leaks. • Lug nuts may loosen. • Fuel-tank strap fasteners can detach. **1994–95**—Throttle control spring may stick in low temperatures.

Secret Warranties/Service Tips

All models/years—Defective catalytic converters that cause a rotten-egg smell in the interior may be replaced free of charge under the emissions warranty. • Paint delamination, peeling, or fading (see pages 73–75). **All models: 1994**—Intermittent loss of power door locks, seats, and mirrors due to a short circuit in the door lock circuit. **1995**—A popping noise during cranking, the engine cranks but won't start, no fuel pressure, or extended crank time after cold soak. • Lack of power. • Engine oil leak at the rear main seal or T joint. • Low oil pressure, loss of oil pressure, or lack of power. • AC odor. • Grinding or scraping noise in Park or Neutral • A cold-start rattle with the 4T60E automatic transmission. • Front-brake vibration and/or pedal pulsation. • A rubbing noise when the front wheels are turned all the way. • Door window scraping noise or sticking, rattle noise from front of vehicle, and excessive radio static. • A clicking noise from under the dash or hood • A front-seat clicking noise. • Erroneous fuel gauge readings, a low-voltage reading or dim lights at idle, and frequent blown fuse or battery drain. • Malfunctioning remote keyless entry. • Wet or smelly carpet from water leaks. • Poor paint application and rust spots. **1996**—3–2 part throttle downshift flare. • Engine noise (install new valve stem oil seal). • Transmission chuggle/surge. • Transmission fluid leak from pump body (replace bushing). • Crunch/pop noise in steering system. • AC odors. • Radio frequency interference diagnosis. **Fleetwood (RWD): 1993**—Noisy transmissions, power-steering units, and cooling fans. • AC bi-level mode produces extreme temperature differences. • Instrument panel squeaks and rattles. • Rusting at the rear side door window molding. • Water leaks into the passenger side of the front compartment.

Brougham/Fleetwood (RWD) Profile

	1990	1991	1992	1993	1994	1995	1996
Cost Price ($)							
Brougham/Fleetwood (RWD)	30,128	31,375	32,910	35,160	35,185	37,015	38,420
Used Values ($)							
Brougham/Fleetwood (RWD) ↑	7,000	8,500	11,000	13,000	15,500	18,000	21,000
Brougham/Fleetwood (RWD) ↓	6,000	7,500	9,000	11,500	13,500	16,500	19,000
Extended Warranty	Y	Y	Y	Y	Y	Y	Y
Secret Warranty	N	N	N	Y	Y	Y	Y
Reliability	③	③	③	③	③	④	④
Air conditioning	③	③	③	③	③	④	④
Automatic transmission	③	③	③	③	③	④	④
Body integrity	❷	❷	❷	③	③	④	④
Braking system	❷	❷	❷	③	③	③	③
Electrical system	❷	❷	❷	❷	❷	❷	❷
Engines	③	③	③	③	④	④	④
Exhaust/Converter	❷	❷	❷	❷	③	③	④

Fuel system	②	②	②	③	③	③	③
Ignition system	②	②	②	③	③	③	③
Rust/Paint	②	②	②	③	③	③	③
Steering	②	②	②	③	④	④	④
Suspension	②	②	②	③	③	③	③

Note: The Brougham and Fleetwood (RWD) haven't been crash-tested.

Concours, DeVille, Fleetwood (FWD)

Rating: Average (1995–98); Below Average (1985–94). **Maintenance/ Repair costs:** Higher than average, and most repairs must be done by a dealer. **Parts:** Higher-than-average cost (independent suppliers sell for much less), but not hard to find. All of these front-drives require a three- to five-year supplementary warranty.

Strengths and weaknesses: Although they have better handling and are almost as comfortable as the old series, the early models of these luxury coupes and sedans aren't worth considering because of their dismal reliability and overly complex servicing. Redesigned 1995–98 versions have posted fewer complaints; however, they are still far below the industry norm for quality and reliability. As with the Eldorado and Seville, you get the best array of handling, braking, and performance features with the 1996 and later versions. They do ride more quietly and comfortably, but fuel economy is still poor, the dash controls and gauges are confusing and not easily accessible, and the rear view is obstructed by the high trunk lid and large side pillars.

The 4.3L V6, 4.1L V8, and 4.5L V8 engines and 4-speed automatic transmission suffer from a variety of terminal maladies including oil leaks, premature wear, poor fuel economy, and excessive noise. The electrical system and related components are temperamental. The suspension goes soft quickly, and the front brakes often wear out after only 18 months/20,000 miles. Problems with the digital fuel-injection and engine control systems are very difficult to diagnose and repair. Poor body assembly is characterized by premature paint peeling and rusting, excessive wind noise in the interior, and fragile trim items.

Dealer service bulletins: DeVille: 1993—Buzzing or whining 4L60 automatic transmissions. • Fuel tank popping during start-up. • Noisy fuel pumps and faulty engine oil pumps. • A noisy cooling fan, power-steering moaning, and rattles from the rear strut area. • Rear quarter-panel gaps. • Squeaks and squealing after a cold start, and whistling when the AC is in recirculate mode. **Concours, DeVille: 1994**—4.6L engines may run roughly, miss, surge, or hesitate. • Engine oil leaks. • Engine accessory belt noise and AC hissing. • Erratic shifting. • Inoperative cruise control or brake/transmission interlock. • Parking brake binding. • Condensation dripping from the heater duct and poor heat distribution (driver's feet get cold). • Doors won't stay open on slight grades. • Rear compartment water leaks. **1995–96**—Engine oil leaks from upper to lower crankcase joint. • Loss of oil pressure and/or lack of power. • Oil leakage from the oil pan to lower crankcase attaching bolts. • Poor AC cooling in traffic and high ambient temperatures. • AC defrost creaking noise. • AC odors. • Steering column noise. • Insufficient heat distribution or lack of air flow. • Erratic or inaccurate instrument panel displays and gauges. • Insufficient remote keyless entry operating range. • Inaccurate fuel gauge. • Exhaust rattles. • Rattling heard when vehicle goes over bumps. • Clicking noise from front seats. • Squawk noise from rear of vehicle in cold temperature. • Slow parking brake release or slow HVAC mode changes. • Vertical seat height adjustment tips. • Abnormal condensation in taillights and other lights. • Wet or smelly carpet from water leaks. **1997**—Fuel tank won't fill to capacity/always reads full. • Front brake noise. • Remote won't open doors or trunk. • Excessive vibration of electrochromatic mirror. • Front-door front auxiliary weather strip loose. • Uncomfortable front seatback. • Horn hard to operate when cold. • Inoperative power door locks. • Metallic buzz or rattle at the instrument panel when the brakes are applied. • No warning light or driver information center message. • Power window inoperative after express down feature is used. • Torque converter clutch buzz or moan.

Safety summary/Recalls: DeVille: 1994–97—Rear turn signal lights may not flash. **DeVille, Concours: 1995–96**—A short circuit caused by wet carpets could cause the airbags to suddenly deploy. Excessive moisture in the vehicles—for example, due to a window left open when it rains—may cause the airbag to deploy when the ignition is switched on. **Recalls: All models:1986**—Faulty headlight switch. **1986–87**—Anti-lock brake fluid may leak onto the pump motor and cause partial or complete loss of front or rear braking. **1994**—Engine oil cooler inlet hoses may be too close to the steering gear, causing it to leak and creating a fire hazard. **1994–95**—Accelerator pedal may stick. **1996**—Hood may fly up. **1997**—Faulty Brake Traction Control module could increase stopping distance. **All models with 4.9L engines: 1991–95**—GM will install a new computer chip that also reduces stalling, pursuant to an agreement with the U.S. Justice Department and EPA. **DeVille with 4.9L engines: 1991–93**—Upper transaxle oil cooler hose could come loose and create a fire hazard.

Secret Warranties/Service Tips

All models/years—Defective catalytic converters that cause a rotten-egg smell in the interior will be replaced free of charge under the emissions warranty. • Paint delamination, peeling, or fading (see pages 73–75). **All models: 1991–94**—Loss of Drive or erratic shifts may be caused by an intermittent short to ground on the A or B shift solenoid, or an electrical short circuit in the transaxle. **1994**—Condensation dripping from the heater duct requires the installation of a watertight dam in the HVAC case. • An inoperative cruise control or brake/transmission interlock may signal a misadjusted stop-light switch assembly. • DSB #476003 goes into great detail about how to troubleshoot the various engine oil leaks afflicting 1994 models. • Doors that won't stay open on slight grades require upgraded door springs. • Noisy fuel pumps can be silenced only by installing an upgraded fuel pump under warranty. • DSB #476506 gives lots of tips on fixing 4.6L engines that run roughly, miss, surge, or hesitate. • Poor heat distribution (driver's feet get cold) can be fixed by replacing the floor outlet assembly. • Rear compartment water leaks are addressed in DSB #311510. **All models with 5.7L engine: 1994–96**—A chuggle or surge condition will require a reflash calibration. • Excessive engine noise can be silenced by installing an upgraded valve-stem oil seal. **1995**—Intermittent Neutral/loss of Drive at highway speeds can be fixed by replacing the control valve body assembly. **1996–97**—A torque converter clutch buzz or moan requires the installation of an upgraded case-cover-assembly spacer plate and the upper-control-valve body.

Concours, DeVille, Fleetwood (FWD) Profile

	1991	1992	1993	1994	1995	1996	1997	1998
Cost Price ($)								
DeVille	31,925	32,910	34,160	34,440	36,320	37,420	38,445	39,145
Concours	—	—	—	37,215	40,935	41,135	42,660	42,960
Fleetwood (FWD)	36,095	37,530	—	—	—	—	—	—
Used Values ($)								
DeVille ↑		8,500	10,500	12,000	14,000	18,000	22,000	25,000	29,000
DeVille ↓		7,000	9,000	10,500	12,500	16,500	20,000	23,000	27,000
Concours ↑	—	—	—	18,500	22,000	24,500	26,500	31,000
Concours ↓	—	—	—	16,000	18,500	22,000	24,500	28,000
Fleetwood (FWD) ↑	9,500	11,000	—	—	—	—	—	—
Fleetwood (FWD) ↓	8,000	9,000	—	—	—	—	—	—

	1991	1992	1993	1994	1995	1996	1997	1998
Extended Warranty	Y	Y	Y	Y	Y	Y	Y	Y
Secret Warranty	N	N	N	Y	Y	Y	Y	Y

	1991	1992	1993	1994	1995	1996	1997	1998
Reliability	❷	❷	❷	❷	❷	③	③	③
Air conditioning	❷	❷	❷	③	③	③	④	④
Automatic transmission	④	④	④	④	④	⑤	⑤	⑤
Body integrity	❷	③	③	❷	❷	❷	③	③
Braking system	❷	❷	❷	❷	❷	❷	❷	③
Electrical system	❷	❷	❷	❷	❷	❷	③	③
Engines	❷	❷	❷	③	③	③	④	④
Exhaust/Converter	③	③	④	④	④	④	⑤	⑤
Fuel system	❷	❷	❷	❷	③	③	③	③
Ignition system	❷	❷	❷	❷	③	③	③	③
Rust/Paint	❷	③	③	③	④	④	④	⑤
Steering	❷	❷	❷	❷	③	④	④	④
Suspension	❷	❷	③	③	③	③	④	④
Crash Safety								
DeVille	⑤	⑤	⑤	④	—	③	④	④
Side Impact								
DeVille	—	—	—	—	—	—	④	④

INFINITI

G20, I30, J30, Q45

Rating: Above Average (1995–98); Average (1991–94). The fully equipped Maxima, Accord, Camry, Avalon, Millenia, and 929 are better buys from a price/quality standpoint, but they don't have the same luxury cachet. The 1997–98 Q45s were "decontented" by Infiniti, meaning they sold for less because they were made more cheaply, came with fewer standard features, and were equipped with a smaller, less powerful engine. **Maintenance/Repair costs:** Higher than average, and repairs must be done by either an Infiniti or a Nissan dealer. This is worrisome inasmuch as Nissan dealers have had a string of poor sales years and may be tempted to make up the profit loss through their service bays. **Parts:** Higher-than-average cost, but not hard to find (except for body panels).

Strengths and weaknesses: With its emphasis on sporty handling, the Infiniti series takes the opposite tack from the Lexus, which puts the accent on comfort and luxury. Still, the Infiniti comes fully equipped and offers owners the prestige of driving a comfortable, reliable, and nicely styled luxury car. One serious weakness, however, is the 1994 airbag-equipped J30's poor crash rating—all the more surprising when one considers that the 1992 Nissan Maxima passed the NHTSA 35 mph crash tests with flying colors.

G20

The least expensive Infiniti, the G20 is a front-drive luxury sports sedan that uses a base 2.0L 140-hp 16-valve, twin-cam, 4-cylinder powerplant to accelerate smoothly, albeit noisily, through all gear ranges. Dual airbags came on line midway through the 1993 model year and ABS is standard. Towing capacity is 1,000 lb. Cruise control is a bit erratic, particularly when traversing hilly terrain. Unlike the engine, the automatic transmission is silent and power is reduced automatically when shifting. Steering is precise and responsive on the highway. However, the rear end tends to swing out sharply following abrupt steering changes. Early Infiniti G20s rode a bit too firmly, which led to the suspension being softened on the 1994 model. Now drivers say that the suspension tends to bounce and jiggle occupants whenever the car goes over uneven pavement or the load is increased.

Overall, however, the Infiniti G20s aren't as refined as their entry-level Lexus counterparts in interior space, drivetrain, or convenience features. Owners have complained that the engine's lack of low-speed torque means that it has to work hard above 4000 rpm—while protesting noisily—to produce brisk engine response in the higher gear ranges. The automatic transmission shifts roughly, particularly when passing (a problem corrected in the 1994 models); the power steering needs more assist during parking maneuvers; and the dealer-installed fog lights cost an exorbitant $500 to replace. Poorly thought-out control layout is best exemplified by the hard-to-reach heat/vent controls, an armrest-mounted trunk and filler release that's inconvenient to operate, and center-console-mounted power window switches that are difficult to find while driving. Tall drivers will find the leg room insufficient. The trunk is spacious, but its small opening is limited by the angle of the rear window.

There are three helpful bulletins containing troubleshooting tips for AC compressor leaks and noise, Code 45 driveability alerts, and brake shudder and steering wheel shimmy.

I30, J30

Resembling the 929 Serenia, the rear-drive, four-door J30 and its high-performance variant, the I30, are sized and priced midway between the G20 and the top-of-the-line Q45. The J30 uses a modified version of the Nissan 300ZX's 3.0L 210-hp V6 engine. Although the vehicle is replete with important safety features and accelerates and handles well, its engine is noisy, passenger and cargo room have been sacrificed to styling, and fuel economy is underwhelming. The more spacious, better-performing I30 replaced the J30 in 1997.

The J30 comes with a standard airbag (or dual airbags, depending on the model year), ABS, and traction control. It's changed very little over the years, meaning that there's no reason to choose a more recent model over a much cheaper older version. Or consider buying an Acura Legend, Lexus ES 300, or a fully equipped Accord, Maxima, 929, Cressida, or Camry.

Dealer service bulletins list the following two defects affecting the '95s: a front seat rattling noise and a loose B-pillar lower finisher. For all J30 model years, there are a number of other helpful bulletins containing troubleshooting tips for AC compressor leaks and noise, brake clunking noises and pedal pulsation, hard starts, rough idle, water leaks, Code 45 driveability alerts, and brake shudder and steering wheel shimmy.

Q45

This luxury sedan provides performance while its chief rival, the Lexus ES 400, provides luxury and quiet. Faster and glitzier than other cars in its category, the Q45 uses a 32-valve 278-hp 4.5L V8 tire burner not frequently found on a Japanese luxury compact. It accelerates faster than the Lexus, going 0–60 mph in 7.1 seconds without a hint of noise or abrupt shifting. Unlike the base engine of the G20, though, the Q45's engine supplies plenty of upper-range torque as well. The suspension was softened in 1994, but the car still rides much more firmly than its Lexus counterpart. The four-wheel steering is precise, but the standard limited-slip differential is no help in preventing the car's rear end from sliding out on slippery roads, due mainly to the original equipment "sport" tires designed mainly for 120 mph autobahn cruising. There's not much foot room for passengers, and cargo room is disappointing. Fuel economy is nonexistent. ABS is standard, but a passenger-side airbag wasn't available before 1994. A redesigned 1994 version got a restyled front end, a chrome grille, and an updated instrument panel. Three years later, the car was again made over with the addition of a downsized 4.1L V8 set on a smaller platform.

Owners report excessive wind noise around the A-pillars, sunroof wind leaks, tire thumping noise, cellular telephone echoing, faulty CD players, and a popping sound from the radio.

Dealer service bulletins list the following defects affecting the 1994–96 models: AC not blowing cold, front brake pad noise, low or rough idle, doors locking/unlocking themselves, and windshield cracking. You may also be interested in reviewing other helpful bulletins that contain troubleshooting tips for AC compressor leaks and noise, brake clunking noises and pedal pulsation, booming/drone noise and vibration, cold-weather hard starts, rough idle, suspension noise, Code 45 driveability alerts, and brake shudder and steering wheel shimmy.

Bulletins for the 1997 model don't cover much that's new, concerning themselves principally with clunking noises and pedal pulsation, cold-weather starting tips, hard starting, and rough idle and suspension noise diagnostic tips.

Safety summary/Recalls: G20: 1995—Driver seriously injured by airbag deployment when vehicle was pushed into a wall at low speed. • Faulty cruise control wouldn't disengage, brakes failed, and collision ensued. • Defective fuel-filler tube/fuel vent tube. • Frequent stalling. • Large sun visor blocks driver's view of stoplights. • Passenger-side power windows operate erratically. • Defective speaker amplifier. • Center console handle broke. **1996**—Violent deployment of airbag during collision resulted in permanent eye damage. • Brakes were applied to disengage cruise control and vehicle suddenly accelerated. • Noisy brakes; dealer cannot fix the problem. • Oil pressure switch failure. **J30: 1995**—Airbag failed to deploy. • Airbags deployed during low speed (7 mph) fender-bender, causing extensive injuries to occupants. • Rear end swings out when accelerating. • Excessive vibrations when accelerating make vehicle difficult to steer. • Driver's seatbelt won't retract. **Q45: 1995**—Sudden acceleration when coming to a stop. • Gas and brake pedals are set too close together. • Failure of driver's power seat adjuster motor. • Hood flew up while driving along the highway at about 60 mph. **1996**—Airbag indicator flashes due to ECM failure. • Premature failure of the shock absorber and power window. **1997**—Owner alleges that vehicle design causes the vehicle to hydroplane where other cars wouldn't. **Recalls: G20: 1991–92**—Rear seatbelt buckle may only partially engage. **1991–96**—Possible fuel leakage from a corroded fuel-filler tube. **1993–95**—Harness connector protector near seatbelt pre-tensioner can ignite. • Cabin may catch fire in a collision. **J30:**

1993–94—Cabin may catch fire in a collision. **Q45: 1991–92**—On models with Bose speakers, circuit board may short out, overheat, and burn. **1997–98**—Key can be removed when shift lever is not in Park and engine is shut off; dealers will replace the shift lock control unit.

Secret Warranties/Service Tips

All models/years—Troubleshooting tips to correct hard starts. • Vehicles with sunroofs may have wind noise coming from the sunroof area because of a small pinhole in the body sealer at the rear C-pillar. • Windshield cracking. • Erratic operation of the power antenna requires that the antenna rod be replaced. **G20: 1991**—An intermittent slip of the sunroof motor requires the installation of an improved motor assembly. • Noisy 2–3 shifting requires the installation of a countermeasure input shaft and an improved high clutch assembly with less free play. • Reverse gear blocking can be corrected by installing an improved Reverse idle gear set. **1991–92**—If the engine's timing chain rattles, install an upgraded chain tensioner (#13070-53J03). • If the air conditioner emits a stale odor or blows out small white flakes, Infiniti will install an improved evaporator core that should correct the problem. **1991–94**—Condensation may prevent the CD player from reading the CD. The only recourse is to wait until the optic sensor dries (10–20 minutes; longer for trunk-mounted players). **Q45: 1990**—An idle vibration felt through the steering, floor, and seat can be corrected by adjustments to the idler. • Air and wind noise coming from the windshield, dash, or A-pillar may be corrected by resealing the problem areas. • The following noises require the following repairs, according to DSB #ITB90-039: valve ticking—replace valves/guides; front engine block knocking—replace tensioners; tapping from valves during warm-up—replace pivot/rocker; tapping from valves at all times—check cam bearings. **1990–91**—Front-suspension clicking may require that the shock absorber upper bushing be regreased. • A driveline vibration or drone at moderate speeds can be eliminated by installing a new balance propshaft assembly. • Takata seatbelt replacement. **1991**—Reports of transmission overheating and failures have forced Infiniti to extend the warranty to 7 years in order to compensate owners whose transmissions have insufficient cooling and filtration. Furthermore, the company will install an external cooler and filter at no charge. **1994–96**—Doors that intermittently lock by themselves require the installation of countermeasure front door lock actuators (DSB #NTB96-027).

G20, I30, J30, Q45 Profile

	1991	1992	1993	1994	1995	1996	1997	1998
Cost Price ($)								
G20	18,650	19,585	22,750	25,625	26,625	27,630	—	—
I30	—	—	—	—	—	32,000	30,395	30,695
J30	—	—	34,450	37,400	39,000	40,400	36,245	—
Q45	40,385	42,385	45,850	50,900	52,850	54,000	48,395	48,395
Used Values ($)								
G20 ↑	7,500	8,500	10,000	11,000	12,500	14,500	—	—
G20 ↓	6,500	7,500	9,000	9,500	11,000	13,000	—	—
I30 ↑	—	—	—	—	—	17,500	20,500	24,500

I30 ↓	—	—	—	—	—	15,500	18,500	22,000
J30 ↑	—	—	12,500	14,500	16,500	19,000	22,000	—
J30 ↓	—	—	10,500	12,500	14,500	17,000	19,000	—
Q45 ↑	11,000	12,500	14,500	18,500	22,000	24,500	32,500	36,500
Q45 ↓	9,500	10,500	12,500	16,500	19,000	22,500	29,500	34,000
Extended Warranty	N	N	N	N	N	N	N	N
Secret Warranty	N	N	N	N	N	N	N	N
Reliability	②	②	②	④	④	⑤	④	④
Air conditioning	②	③	③	③	④	⑤	④	⑤
Automatic transmission	②	②	②	③	④	④	④	⑤
Body integrity	②	②	②	③	③	③	②	③
Braking system	②	②	②	②	③	③	②	③
Electrical system	②	②	②	③	③	③	②	③
Engines	②	③	④	④	⑤	⑤	④	④
Exhaust/Converter	④	④	④	④	⑤	⑤	⑤	⑤
Fuel system	②	②	③	④	④	④	④	④
Rust/Paint	③	③	④	⑤	⑤	⑤	⑤	⑤
Steering	②	③	④	④	④	⑤	③	⑤
Suspension	③	③	③	④	⑤	⑤	③	⑤
Crash Safety								
I30	—	—	—	—	—	④	④	④
J30	—	—	—	④	④	④	—	—
Side Impact								
I30	—	—	—	—	—	—	④	—

LEXUS

ES 250, ES 300, GS 300, LS 400, SC 400

Rating: Recommended (1990–98). A bit more reliable and better built than the Infiniti, but more costly too. A fully equipped Legend, Accord, Maxima, or Camry will provide airbags, comparable highway performance, and reliability at far less initial cost. But, if you do pay top dollar for a used Lexus, its slow rate of depreciation virtually guarantees that you'll get much of your money back. Keep in mind Lexus airbags pack a mighty wallop and may cause severe injuries; install an off-switch or look for depowered airbags starting with the 1997 models. Keep in mind that the LS 400 depreciates much more slowly than the SC 400, resulting in the SC 400 costing far less used, despite the fact it sold originally for almost as much as the LS 400. **Maintenance/Repair costs:** Higher than average, and repairs must be done by either a Lexus or a Toyota dealer. **Parts:** Higher-than-average cost, but not hard to find (except for body panels).

Strengths and weaknesses: Like the Acuras and Infinitis, Lexus models all suffer from some front brake, electrical, body, trim, and accessory deficiencies that are confirmed by confidential dealer service bulletins.

ES 250

The ES 250's base engine gives exceptional, smooth acceleration and gets 19 mpg. The 4-speed Overdrive transmission makes subtle changes by reducing the engine power just before shifting. Trailers of up to 2,000 lbs can be towed by cutting out Overdrive. The ES 250 is one of the best riding front-drive cars money can buy, and its seating offers plenty of support and a comfortable driving position that can be automatically adjusted for two drivers. Braking and handling, though, aren't very impressive. 1991 was its last model year.

ES 300

Resembling an LS 400 dressed in sporty attire, the ES 300 was launched in 1992 to fill the gap between the ES 250 and the LS 400. In fact, the ES 300 has many of the attributes of the LS 400 sedan for much less money. A five-passenger sedan based on the Camry, it comes equipped with a standard 3.0L 24-valve engine that produces 181 horsepower coupled to either a 5-speed manual or a 4-speed electronically controlled automatic transmission. Unlike the Infinitis, the ES 300 accelerates smoothly and quietly, while averaging about 20 mpg in mixed driving. The suspension is soft and steady. Passenger and cargo room are plentiful, with lots of leg and head room (except on sunroof-equipped versions). ABS is standard, but a second airbag is available only on the 1994 model.

Surprisingly, for a vehicle this well made, government-reported safety-related defects are legion. Airbag-induced injuries, sudden acceleration, ABS and Goodyear tire failures, interior window fogging, and AC toxic emanations are only a few of the ES 300 complaints that carried over many years and have been reported with other Lexus models.

GS 300

The rear-drive GS 300 is a step up from the front-drive ES 300 and just a rung below Lexus's top-of-the-line LS 400. It carries the same V6 engine as the ES 300, except it has 20 more horses. This produces sparkling performance at higher speeds, though the car is a bit sluggish from a start. Fuel economy is sacrificed for performance, however, and the base suspension and tires pass noisily over small bumps and ruts. Visibility is also less than impressive, with large rear pillars and a narrow rear window restricting the view. There's not much usable trunk space either, and the liftover is unreasonably high.

LS 400

The Lexus flagship, the LS 400 rear-drive outclasses all other luxury sedans in reliability, styling, and function. The base engine is a 242-hp 4.0L V8 that provides smooth, impressive acceleration and superior highway passing ability at all speeds. Its transmission is smooth and efficient. The suspension gives an easy ride without body roll or front-end plow during emergency stops, thereby delivering a major comfort advantage over other luxury compacts. There's an absence of engine and wind noise. ABS and dual airbags are standard.

Owners have complained that the brakes don't inspire confidence, owing to their mushy feel and average performance. Furthermore, there's limited rear foot room under the front seats, and the rear-middle passenger has to sit on the transmission hump. This car is a gas guzzler that thirsts for premium fuel.

SC 300, SC 400

These two coupes are practically identical, except for their engines and luxury features. The cheaper SC 300 gives you the same high-performance 6-cylinder engine used by the GS 300 and Toyota Supra, while the SC 400 uses the same 4.0L V8 engine found in the LS 400. You're likely to find fewer luxury features with the SC 300 because they were sold as options. Nevertheless, look for an SC with traction control for additional safety during poor driving conditions. On the downside, V8 fuel consumption is horrendous, rear seating is cramped, and trunk space is unimpressive. Also, invest in a good anti-theft device, or your Lexus relationship will be over almost before it begins.

Dealer service bulletins: 1996—Ambient temperature displays –220°C. • Front brake groan. • Static noise on weak AM stations. **ES 300: 1995–96**—CD changer won't eject magazine. • Direct clutch improvements. • Front brake groan. • Moon roof panel wind noise. • Static noise on weak AM stations. **LS 400: 1995**—Engine knocking, front seat cushion noise, front stabilizer bushing noise, strut bar cushion noise, and sun visor rattling. **SC 300, SC 400: 1995**—Rear suspension rattling or clacking, probably caused by a faulty rear spring bumper (replace with an upgraded spring bumper).

Safety summary/Recalls: 1994—Airbags failed to deploy. • During collision, driver's seat and shoulder belts did not retract, but released. • Driver-side seatbelt buckle released after vehicle hit on the left side. • Accelerator pedal fell off and jammed under the accelerator bar. • Frequent reports that the interior windows fog up, causing reduced visibility. • Frequent reports of Goodyear tire blowouts and ABS brake failures. • Rear brake pad failures. • Transmission pan leaks and failures. • Inadequate middle console illumination. **1995**—Airbags failed to deploy. • Both front seatbelts failed to lock during a collision. • Seatbelt failed to restrain passenger during collision. • Goodyear Eagle tire blowout. • Premature failure of the electronic control unit. • Transmission leaks. • Brake pedal design makes it difficult for someone with a shoe size larger than men's nine to use the brakes. • Excessive noise when braking. • Faulty windshield moldings cause excessive wind noise. **1996**—Fire in the engine compartment. • Frequent reports that the airbag failed to deploy. • Weak seatback collapsed rearward in a collision. • Entire vehicle shimmies. • Sudden steering failure when turning. **1997**—Vehicle left in Park rolled backwards and hit another car. Same thing occurred with a vehicle parked in a garage, but this time cause was isolated to a failure of the shift lock actuator fuse. • Owner says airbags are a hazard for short people. • Also, floor pedals are located too high and are too far apart for short people. • Middle rear shoulder belt locks up, making it very difficult to get occupant out; owner had to cut the belt. • Instrument cluster lights aren't bright enough for night driving. • AC assembly panel failure. **1998**—Vehicle accelerated as brakes were applied. • Premature front brake pad wearout. • Seat adjustment motor failure. **ES 300: 1993**—Engine compartment fire. • Airbags fail to deploy. • Airbag deployed and caught on fire. • Airbag deployment burned driver severely. • Airbags deployed when vehicle at a standstill, causing severe burns to driver's nose and hands. • In another incident, car was bumped slightly, airbags deployed 10 seconds later, and driver received severe facial injuries. • ABS system failures. • Goodyear tires experience blowouts and are worn out prematurely at 10,000 miles. • Steering tie rod broke while driving, causing loss of steering and an accident. • Transmission doesn't engage right away, but when it does engage, it jumps forward. • When vehicle goes over a bump, the steering wheel jumps out of hand. • Foul odor from AC caused occupants to fall ill with bronchial infection. • Several reports that dashboard emits fumes that fog inside window glass. • Headlights provide poor illumination. • Driver can't read speedometer when sun shines onto dash. • Seatback collapsed backwards when vehicle was rear-ended. **Recalls: ES 250: 1990–91**—Fuel tank leak. **GS 300: 1993–94**—Premature ball joint wear could affect steering and handling. An upgraded ball joint socket will be installed. **LS 400: 1990**—Cruise control may not return to its former position. • Prolonged illumination of the center-mounted brake light. **1995–97**—A faulty starter-motor magnetic switch may cause a fire or render the starter inoperative. **SC 400: 1996–97**—A faulty starter-motor magnetic switch may cause a fire or render the starter inoperative.

Secret Warranties/Service Tips

ES 250: 1990—To reduce front brake squeaks, Lexus has changed the rotors (#43517-32020). **1990–91**—Front brake squeaking can also be reduced by using revised brake pads (#04491-32390). **1991**—Cellular telephone antenna wind noise can be eliminated by installing a newly designed antenna. • A cruise control that cancels after setting needs a filter circuit added to the cruise control ECU. **ES 300: 1992**—Inaccurate fuel gauges require an improved indicator needle. **1992–93**—Sun visor rattles can be fixed by using the Lexus Squeak and Rattle Repair Kit. • Rear brake squeaks can be reduced by using upgraded rear brake pads. • Rear stabilizer bar bushing noise can be eliminated by installing upgraded bushings.

1993—Problems with hot start or poor engine performance when going downhill require the installation of an upgraded ECM. • Front seat headrest rattles can be corrected by installing an improved headrest support. **LS 400: 1990**—Front brake popping can be corrected by installing a modified pad support plate and applying new adhesive. • Moon roof wind noise may be corrected by realigning the roof panel. • Faulty cruise control assemblies will be replaced with an improved assembly (SSC 901). • Warped center high-mounted brake-light housings will be replaced free under a goodwill program (SSC 902). **1990–91**—A difficult-to-open rear door may be helped by modifying the rear door check arm. • To prevent transmission clicking when shifting from Neutral to Drive or Reverse, reduce the depth of the flange yoke assembly. • Windshield upper molding noise requires that the molding be changed and a thicker adhesive tape be applied. • AC groaning can be eliminated by reducing the expansion valve flow rate and adding an O-ring to the EPR piston. **SC 300, SC 400: 1992**—Popping from the Nakamichi radio has been eliminated with an upgraded model containing improved volume control resistors.

ES 250, ES 300, GS 300, LS 400, SC 400 Profile

	1991	1992	1993	1994	1995	1996	1997	1998
Cost Price ($)								
ES 250	24,500	—	—	—	—	—	—	—
ES 300	—	28,650	31,030	31,070	34,180	34,895	33,045	33,935
GS 300	—	—	40,130	40,370	45,380	48,445	48,595	40,025
LS 400	41,650	43,600	48,030	50,370	52,680	54,445	54,495	54,515
SC 400	—	39,100	42,730	45,570	49,780	53,845	52,295	54,315
Used Values ($)								
ES 250 ↑	8,500	—	—	—	—	—	—	—
ES 250 ↓	7,500	—	—	—	—	—	—	—
ES 300 ↑	—	14,000	16,000	18,000	20,500	22,500	26,500	29,500
ES 300 ↓	—	13,000	14,000	16,000	18,500	20,500	24,500	27,500
GS 300 ↑	—	—	19,000	22,000	25,000	29,000	32,000	35,000
GS 300 ↓	—	—	17,500	20,000	22,500	27,500	30,000	32,500
LS 400 ↑	16,500	19,000	22,000	25,000	32,000	36,000	41,000	44,000
LS 400 ↓	15,000	16,500	19,500	23,500	29,000	33,500	38,000	40,000
SC 400 ↑	—	18,000	21,000	24,500	29,000	33,000	37,000	40,000
SC 400 ↓	—	15,500	19,500	22,500	26,000	30,000	34,000	36,000
Extended Warranty	N	N	N	N	N	N	N	N
Secret Warranty	N	N	N	N	N	N	N	N
Reliability	③	④	④	⑤	⑤	⑤	⑤	⑤
Air conditioning	❷	❷	③	④	⑤	⑤	⑤	⑤
Automatic transmission	③	④	⑤	⑤	⑤	⑤	⑤	⑤
Body integrity	❷	❷	③	④	⑤	⑤	⑤	⑤
Braking system	❷	❷	❷	❷	❷	③	④	④
Electrical system	❷	❷	③	③	④	④	④	④
Engines	❷	③	③	③	⑤	⑤	⑤	⑤
Exhaust/Converter	④	④	⑤	⑤	⑤	⑤	⑤	⑤

Fuel system	④	④	⑤	⑤	⑤	⑤	⑤	⑤
Ignition system	③	④	⑤	⑤	⑤	⑤	⑤	⑤
Rust/Paint	⑤	⑤	⑤	⑤	⑤	⑤	⑤	⑤
Steering	④	④	⑤	⑤	⑤	⑤	⑤	⑤
Suspension	❷	❷	③	④	⑤	⑤	⑤	⑤
Crash Safety								
ES 250	③	—	—	—	—	—	—	—
ES 300	—	—	—	—	—	⑤	—	④
GS 300	—	—	—	③	③	③	③	—
Side Impact								
ES 300	—	—	—	—	—	—	—	⑤

MAZDA

929

Rating: Above Average (1993–95); Average (1988–92). The only real negative is the 929's consistently poor crash test scores. **Maintenance/Repair costs:** Higher than average, and they must be done by a Mazda dealer. **Parts:** Higher-than-average cost, but not hard to find through cheaper independent suppliers, despite '95 being its last model year.

Strengths and weaknesses: The key word for the 929 is understatement: the engine is unobtrusive, the exterior is anonymous, and the interior is far from flashy. In spite of its lack of pizzazz and imprecise power steering, the 929 will accelerate and handle curves as well as the best large European sedans. The 929 has proven to be fairly reliable.

In addition to poor crashworthiness, the car's main drawbacks are its limited interior room and trunk space. The driver's seat doesn't have enough rear travel for tall drivers, and head room is tight. Owners report some problems with premature disc brake wear, electrical glitches, exhaust system rust-out, electronic shock absorber durability (particularly with the 1989–91 models), and fit and finish deficiencies.

Redesigned in 1992, the 929 got a more rounded body and a longer wheelbase that added to interior room while sacrificing trunk space. Despite these improvements, tall occupants will still feel cramped.

Shocks are very expensive to replace. Manual transmission isn't offered, and the automatic's many settings can be confusing. Furthermore, the transmission's lockup feature frequently cuts in and out. The rear end sometimes wants to slide out a bit on slippery surfaces, and the front end bounces around on bumpy roads. The optional automatic adjusting suspension does little to improve the car's ride or handling.

Dealer service bulletins: 1995—Heater and AC unit noise after long storage. • Rattling sunroof and outer door handles. • A slightly off-center steering wheel. • Brake pulsation repair. • Inoperative rear door window. •

Brake shudder repair. • Scratched or peeling B-pillar trim.
• Troubleshooting various causes of engine noise.

Safety summary/Recalls: Recalls: 1988–91—Mazda will replace door handles with ones that won't break as easily. • Takata seatbelt replacement.

Secret Warranties/Service Tips

All models/years—DSB #006/94 covers all the possible causes and remedies for excessive vibrations when braking. • Water intrusion into the lock actuator connectors may cause the unintended operation of the rear defroster. **All models: 1988–91**—Cold-engine piston slapping requires replacement pistons to fix the problem. • Constant brake pulsation or shudder is likely caused by an uneven rotor surface or excessive rotor run-out. • Hard shifting after cold-weather starts can be corrected by installing upgraded synchronizer rings and clutch hub assemblies. **1988–92**—Valve train noise occurring just after start-up may be caused by air trapped in the hydraulic lash adjuster. Correct by installing redesigned rocker arm shafts that promote better oil flow. **1989**—Mazda has modified the bushing assembly to reduce shudder and make for a more comfortable ride. The new assembly part is #H260-34-230C. **1990**—A power seat that won't adjust up or down smoothly likely has a broken gear in the seat motor. **1990–91**—Difficult starts in hot weather can be corrected by installing an upgraded cold-start thermo-switch (#JE27-18-870). **1992–94**—Freezing door and hatch lock cylinders are addressed in DSB #021/94.

929 Profile

	1988	1989	1990	1991	1992	1993	1994	1995
Cost Price ($)								
Sedan	19,534	22,189	23,579	23,799	28,150	29,550	31,895	36,235
Used Values ($)								
Sedan ↑	5,000	5,500	6,000	7,000	9,000	10,500	12,000	14,500
Sedan ↓	4,500	5,000	5,500	6,500	7,500	9,000	10,500	12,500
Extended Warranty	Y	Y	Y	Y	N	N	N	N
Secret Warranty	N	N	N	N	N	N	N	N
Reliability	②	②	③	③	③	④	⑤	⑤
Air conditioning	②	②	②	②	③	④	⑤	⑤
Automatic transmission	②	②	②	③	④	④	⑤	⑤
Body integrity	②	②	②	②	②	②	③	③
Braking system	②	②	②	②	②	②	②	③
Electrical system	②	②	②	②	②	③	③	③
Engines	②	③	③	④	⑤	⑤	⑤	⑤
Exhaust/Converter	②	②	②	②	③	③	④	⑤
Fuel system	③	③	③	④	④	④	④	④
Ignition system	②	③	④	⑤	⑤	⑤	⑤	⑤
Rust/Paint	③	③	④	④	⑤	⑤	⑤	⑤
Steering	③	③	③	③	④	⑤	⑤	⑤
Suspension	②	②	②	③	④	⑤	⑤	⑤
Crash Safety	②	—	—	—	—	—	—	—

Millenia

Rating: Above Average (1995–98). Lots of power and sophisticated mechanicals make this luxury tourer a winner. From a performance standpoint, the Camry V6 with its less complicated powertrain outruns the Millenia. **Maintenance/Repair costs:** Higher than average, and repairs must be done by a Mazda dealer. **Parts:** Higher-than-average cost, but parts are easily found.

Strengths and weaknesses: Smaller than the Mazda 929, the front-drive Millenia carries the same 2.5L 170-hp V6 used by the 626. An optional 2.3L Miller-Cycle "S" 6-cylinder engine, although smaller than the base powerplant, still manages to pump out 210 horsepower. Both engines use a standard 4-speed automatic transmission that shifts a bit harshly when pushed. As with all luxury cars, the Millenia comes with a wide array of standard features that would normally cost thousands of dollars more. Although billed as a five-passenger car, the middle occupant in the rear seat is cramped and has to sit on a hump—a problem that 929 owners are familiar with.

Assembly and component quality are fairly high; however, there have been reports of powertrain failures, front brake failures, and electrical glitches. Among the powertrain problems, owners cite transmission failures and defective engine head gaskets.

Dealer service bulletins: 1995—Cruise control surging. • Transmission position indicator light failure. • AC evaporator freeze-up. • Battery discharge due to the trunk light staying on. • Snap noise around the A-pillar. • Steering wheel may be off-center. • Roof insulator peeling off. **1996**—Brake pulsation repair. • Cracked center sun visor holder. • Creaking or knocking noise from rear of vehicle. • Rattle noise from rear package tray. **1997**—Brake pulsation repair.

Safety summary/Recalls: 1995—Many complaints that vehicle surges when shifted into Reverse. • Inadvertent airbag deployment; failure to deploy. • Steering wheel back is open, allowing objects to jam the steering mechanism. • Driver's automatic seatbelt came loose when vehicle was rear-ended. • While vehicle was being driven on the highway, engine locked up due to leakage from the oil pan. • ABS brake failures. • Many reports of cracked engine valve cover gaskets, which allowed oil to leak onto the wiring and spark plugs. • Because the engine intake valve is set so low, whenever it comes in contact with water, the car stalls. • Premature AC and CV joint failures. • Sudden electrical system failure. • Defroster doesn't do an adequate job in cold weather; collects water or quits altogether. • When AC is on, the headlights go dim. • Low-beam lights are inadequate for night driving. • Battery connections become loose, making it impossible to unlock or start vehicle. • When driver turned the ignition switch, the battery cable popped off. This caused the automatic door locks to become inoperative, trapping occupants. •

Trunk won't open with inside latch release. • The location of the cup holder allows drinks to be spilled into the shifter mechanism, causing the shifter to lock up. • Cup holder doesn't always release. • Seatbelt buckle on passenger's side fell completely apart in driver's hand. • Aluminum alloy wheel cracked. **1996**—Airbag failed to deploy. • Transmission failures. • Intermittent starting problems. • Loose dashboard and interior trim. • It's easy to hit your head on the low trunk lid and latch. **1997**—Traction control system failure. **Recalls:** N/A.

Secret Warranties/Service Tips

All models: 1995–96—A creaking or knocking noise from the rear of the vehicle is likely caused by loose diagonal braces behind the rear seat.

Millenia Profile

	1995	1996	1997	1998
Cost Price ($)				
Base	29,335	28,445	29,446	33,445
Used Values ($)				
Base ↑	14,000	15,500	17,500	20,000
Base ↓	12,500	13,500	16,000	18,000
Extended Warranty	N	N	N	N
Secret Warranty	N	N	N	N
Reliability	③	④	⑤	⑤
Crash Safety	④	④	④	—

MERCEDES-BENZ

190 Series, C-Class

Rating: Above Average (1995–98); Average (1988–94); Below Average (1984–87). Although these cars are above average in reliability and comfort, every model—other than the 300 series—is overpriced and overrated. The 190 version is not recommended. Consider buying a 1997 C-class only if you feel you need the 2.3L engine's 12 additional horses and improved automatic gearbox. Keep in mind, though, that you'll have to keep the car much longer to amortize its higher cost. **Maintenance/Repair costs:** Higher than average, and most repairs must be done by a Mercedes dealer if you don't live in an area where independent shops have sprung up. **Parts:** Higher-than-average cost. Parts supply and servicing have become problematic now that the 190 series has been off the market since 1993.

Strengths and weaknesses: Mercedes introduced the 190 "baby" Benz in 1984 in an effort to downsize its entry-level compact and make it more affordable. It never caught on due to its serious drivetrain deficiencies, cramped interior, and rounded styling (a real departure from Mercedes's traditional squared-off look). The best choice from a quality/price standpoint is any post-1989 version equipped with the in-line 6-cylinder powerplant.

The 1994 models were renamed the C-class, and gained interior room and more powerful engines. The standard 2.6L 6-cylinder motor is a real powerhouse in this small car, and its power is used effectively when coupled to the manual 5-speed transmission. The 4-speed automatic is a big disappointment—it requires a lot of throttle effort to downshift and prefers to start out in second gear. The 1994 versions add much-needed horsepower, but lack the manual 5-speed transmission that would set those extra horses free. Rear seat room is limited and a lot of road noise intrudes into the passenger compartment.

The base 2.3L engine is acceptable around town, but highway cruising requires more grunt to handle the car's heft and accessories. And speaking of grunt, the 2.8L engine is ideally suited to these small cars. Although its power is used most effectively when coupled to the new 5-speed manual transmission, its performance with the 5-speed automatic is quite good. On 1996 models, some owners have complained that the 4-speed automatic requires a lot of throttle effort to downshift.

Keep in mind that owner surveys give the entry-level C-class cars a *just-*better-than-average rating, while the 300 and higher series have always scored way above average in owner satisfaction. The 190's reliability is a notch below that of other Mercedes vehicles; the 1994 model C-class is the better buy from a quality and reliability standpoint, although 1995 and later models will have fewer bugs. Nevertheless, owners report frequent problems with drivetrain noise and vibration, and slipping or soft shifts. Brakes, AC, and the electrical system, are also failure-prone.

Dealer service bulletins: 190: 1993; C220: 1994—Drivetrain noise and vibration. • Harsh shifts or erratic shift quality. • High coolant temperature. • Rough reverse release. • Handling of fuel system complaints. **C-class: 1995**—Drivetrain noise and vibration. • High coolant temperature. • Slipping or soft shifts.

Safety summary/Recalls: All models: 1993—Vehicle stalled while on the highway. • After vehicle was towed home, fire ignited in the engine compartment. • ABS brake failures cause the brakes to lock up. • Premature replacement of the front wheel bearings. • Climate control module failures. • Hard starting. • Driver's master door lock failed to unlock other doors. • Power door lock vacuum control pump failure. • Bent upper control arm/camber MIKE link caused right rear wheel to turn out. **1995**—Check Engine light remains on for no apparent reason. • Frequent stalling due to defective idle speed control unit. •

Missing left rear wheelwell inside panel allows tire to spray debris into area. **1996**—Airbags failed to deploy. • Airbag light stays on for no apparent reason. • After parking the vehicle and turning off the ignition, the vehicle lurches forward or rocks backwards. • In another incident, vehicle was put in Park on an incline and keys were removed; vehicle rolled backwards down the hill. • Brakes are noisy when applied and don't brake well. • While car is being driven, engine light comes on for no apparent reason. • Complete electrical system failure. • Windshield washer fluid sensor failure. **1997**—While in Reverse, vehicle suddenly accelerated in reverse. **C280: 1994**—Vehicle suddenly accelerated forward in garage. • Another report that while coming to a stop at an intersection, vehicle will accelerate when foot is on the brake. • Airbag failed to deploy. • Upon braking, ABS pedal went to the floor, resulting in extended stopping distance. • Extreme pressure is needed to push horn button. • Cruise control failure. • Premature rear wheel bearing failure. • Windshield wiper is inadequate; poor visibility. **Recalls: All models: 1994–95**—Secondary hood latch may not work properly.

Secret Warranties/Service Tips

All models/years—Excessive engine valve train noise may be caused by a stretched timing chain. After 30,000 miles the camshaft and timing chain drive should be checked carefully, especially if excessive noise is heard. **All models: 1989–92**—Excessive oil consumption may be corrected by replacing the valve stem seals with upgraded Viton seals. **1990–91**—A jerking that occurs when driving downhill with the cruise control engaged can be corrected by installing a relay to disable the deceleration fuel shut-off switch.

190 Series, C-Class Profile

	1991	1992	1993	1994	1995	1996	1997	1998
Cost Price ($)								
190E 2.3	31,260	30,200	33,930	—	—	—	—	—
190E 2.6	34,050	35,250	36,865	—	—	—	—	—
C220	—	—	—	31,085	32,000	33,055	—	—
C230	—	—	—	—	—	—	33,235	33,235
C280	—	—	—	37,105	38,400	37,815	37,985	37,815
Used Values ($)								
190E 2.3 ↑	11,000	12,000	14,000	—	—	—	—	—
190E 2.3 ↓	9,500	10,000	12,500	—	—	—	—	—
190E 2.6 ↑	13,500	15,000	17,000	—	—	—	—	—
190E 2.6 ↓	11,500	13,000	14,500	—	—	—	—	—
C220 ↑	—	—	—	19,500	22,000	25,000	—	—
C220 ↓	—	—	—	17,500	20,000	22,500	—	—
C230 ↑	—	—	—	—	—	—	26,000	29,000
C230 ↓	—	—	—	—	—	—	24,000	27,000
C280 ↑	—	—	—	23,000	25,000	28,000	31,000	34,000
C280 ↓	—	—	—	20,500	23,000	26,000	29,000	32,000

Extended Warranty	Y	Y	Y	Y	Y	Y	Y	Y
Secret Warranty	N	N	N	N	N	N	N	N
Reliability	②	②	②	③	③	④	④	⑤
Air conditioning	②	②	②	③	③	④	④	⑤
Automatic transmission	④	④	⑤	⑤	⑤	⑤	⑤	⑤
Body integrity	②	②	②	②	③	③	③	③
Braking system	②	②	②	②	③	④	⑤	⑤
Electrical system	②	②	②	②	②	③	③	③
Engines	②	③	③	④	④	⑤	⑤	⑤
Exhaust/Converter	④	④	④	⑤	⑤	⑤	⑤	⑤
Fuel system	②	③	③	③	④	⑤	⑤	⑤
Ignition system	④	④	④	④	④	⑤	⑤	⑤
Rust/Paint	④	④	④	④	④	④	⑤	⑤
Steering	③	③	④	④	⑤	⑤	⑤	⑤
Suspension	③	③	④	④	⑤	⑤	⑤	⑤
Crash Safety								
190	③	—	—	—	—	—	—	—
C220/C230	—	—	—	④	④	④	④	④
Side Impact								
C230	—	—	—	—	—	—	—	③

300 Series, 400 Series, 500 Series, E-Class

Rating: Recommended (1993–98); Above Average (1992); Below Average (1985–91). The 1994 and later models are referred to as E-class with the entry-level model a 300 diesel. **Maintenance/Repair costs:** Higher than average, and repairs must be done by a Mercedes dealer. **Parts:** Higher-than-average cost and limited availability.

Strengths and weaknesses: These cars are ideal mid-sized family sedans. They're reliable, depreciate slowly, and provide all the interior space that the pre-1994 190 series and C-class leave out. Their only shortcomings are a high resale value that discourages bargain hunters and a weak dealer network that limits parts distribution and drives up parts costs. The 300 series offers a traction control system that prevents wheel spin upon acceleration—somewhat like ABS in reverse.

Another interesting feature is a 24-valve 220-hp high-performance version of the in-line 6-cylinder engine that powers the 300 series. All this has its price, though. If, ironically, you'd like to drive one of these cars but are of an economical frame of mind, choose the 260E—it offers everything the 300 does, but for much less. The 300CE is a coupe version, appealing to a sportier crowd, while the 300TE is the station wagon variant.

Dealer service bulletins: Bulletins show that the 1995 300 series may have transmission gasket leaks, in addition to drivetrain noise and vibration, and slipping or soft shifts. The 1996–97 models have no bulletins listing factory-related problems or troubleshooting tips.

Safety summary/Recalls: 300 series: 1994—Sudden acceleration caused accident and injuries. • Defective ABS brakes; brakes locked up and caused driver to lose control of vehicle. • Emergency brake cable failed twice. • Vehicle rolls backwards when stopped on a hill. • Driver's seatbelt failed. • Accelerator pedal is too hard to press, causes fatigue in driver's leg. • Frequent power door lock and automatic antenna failures. • Front panels were cracked and loose. • Rear axle and fuel pump failures. **1995**—Sudden acceleration caused an accident. • Brake rotor and caliper failure. • Headlights cast dark shadows. • Windshield wipers fail to keep glass clean. • Automatic transmission slips or shifts erratically, as if hunting for the right gear. **1996**—Check Engine light flashes on and off at will. • AC fan starts and stops intermittently. • Door rattles. • Failure prone headlight bulbs. **Recalls: 300 series, E-class: 1992–95**—Front passenger's footrest could abrade the wiring harness underneath. The ensuing short circuit could stall the engine or deploy the airbag.

Secret Warranties/Service Tips

All models: 1987–90—A cruise control that surges or maintains a speed that's 4–6 miles above the set speed may have a faulty amplifier or reference resistor gasket. **1987–92**—Excessive brake vibrations can be reduced by installing upgraded Jurid 226 front brake pads. **1988–90**—A gurgling heater core noise can be silenced by Mercedes's "gurgling kit." **1990–91**—Excessive exhaust noise between the exhaust manifold flange and rear muffler may be caused by a leak at the O_2 sensor or the clamped joints. If this isn't the cause, change the catalytic converter.

300 Series, 400 Series, 500 Series, E-Class Profile

	1991	1992	1993	1994	1995	1996	1997	1998
Cost Price ($)								
300E	41,350	43,300	46,115	—	—	—	—	—
300CE	57,700	60,750	61,400	—	—	—	—	—
300D	41,350	43,300	46,115	—	—	—	—	—
E300D	—	—	—	—	43,100	42,465	42,475	45,200
E420/E430	—	—	—	51,475	52,975	—	51,585	52,305
E500/S500	—	—	—	82,975	89,675	88,095	89,795	89,795
Used Values ($)								
300E ↑	16,500	20,000	23,000	—	—	—	—	—
300E ↓	14,500	18,000	21,500	—	—	—	—	—
300CE ↑	22,000	24,000	28,000	—	—	—	—	—
300CE ↓	19,500	22,500	25,000	—	—	—	—	—
300D ↑	17,000	19,500	21,500	—	—	—	—	—
300D ↓	15,000	17,500	19,000	—	—	—	—	—

E300D ↑	—	—	—	—	27,000	33,000	36,000	39,000
E300D ↓	—	—	—	—	24,500	29,500	34,000	37,000
E420/E430 ↓	—	—	—	28,000	33,000	—	44,000	48,000
E420/E430 ↑	—	—	—	24,000	29,000	—	41,000	45,000
E500/S500 ↑	—	—	—	45,000	54,000	59,000	64,000	70,000
E500/S500 ↓	—	—	—	53,000	50,000	55,000	60,000	65,000

Extended Warranty	N	N	N	N	N	N	N	N
Secret Warranty	N	N	N	N	N	N	N	N
Reliability	③	③	③	③	④	④	⑤	⑤
Air conditioning	❷	③	③	③	③	④	⑤	⑤
Automatic transmission	③	③	③	④	④	⑤	⑤	⑤
Body integrity	③	④	⑤	⑤	⑤	⑤	⑤	⑤
Braking system	❷	③	③	③	③	③	③	③
Electrical system	❷	❷	❷	❷	❷	❷	③	③
Engines	❷	❷	❷	❷	③	④	⑤	⑤
Exhaust/Converter	③	④	④	④	⑤	⑤	⑤	⑤
Fuel system	③	③	④	④	⑤	⑤	⑤	⑤
Ignition system	③	③	④	⑤	⑤	⑤	⑤	⑤
Rust/Paint	④	④	④	④	④	④	⑤	⑤
Steering	③	③	③	③	④	④	④	⑤
Suspension	③	③	③	③	⑤	⑤	⑤	⑤

Note: The above model years haven't been crash-tested by NHTSA.

MITSUBISHI

Diamante

Rating: Recommended (1992–98). Think of the Diamante as an upscale Camry with lots of electronic gadgets. **Maintenance/Repair costs:** About average; best of all, repairs aren't dealer dependent. **Parts:** Parts are easily found and relatively inexpensive.

Strengths and weaknesses: The Diamante is an excellent family-car buy because of its spacious, comfortable interior, fair fuel economy, and impressive reliability. Virtually unchanged, the 1992–95 wagons and sedans targeted the sports sedan buyer, while the revamped 1996–97 models moved up into the luxury sedan niche where they now compete against BMW, Lexus, and Nissan's Maxima.

1992–95 models have few problems, although they're far from perfect. Main areas of concern are a failure-prone automatic transmission on the '93 models, and electrical shorts and brake problems plaguing all model years. Early models also may have excessive wind noise coming from the side windows, fragile trim items that break or fall off, premature paint peeling, and sound system glitches.

1996–97 model Diamante deficiencies reported by owners include brake vibrations, premature brake pad wear, and electrical system malfunctions.

Safety summary/recalls: 1995—Automatic transmission suddenly shifted into Neutral. • Airbag deployment caused severe injuries to occupants. **1996**—Sudden ABS failure. • Transmission failure. • Electronic control unit failure causes excessive hesitation when shifting gears. • Premature wear of the front brake rotors. • Windows leaking, mirror falling off, door locks freezing too easily. **Recalls: All models: 1992–95**—Right front wheel-side brake hose can crack, resulting in leakage. A revised brake hose will be installed. **1993**—The rear outboard lower safety belt attachment bolt may have been inadequately torqued.

Secret Warranties/Service Tips

All models/years—Troubleshooting tips to correct excessive valve noise at startup are included in DSB #95-11-001. **All models: 1994–95**—Horn buttons tend to pop out due to their holding claws being too short. Mitsubishi will replace the horn buttons and switch under its "goodwill" warranty on a case-by-case basis.

Diamante Profile

	1992	1993	1994	1995	1996	1997	1998
Cost Price ($)							
Base/ES	21,375	22,842	25,995	28,370	27,550	26,370	28,120
Used Values ($)							
Base/ES ↑	8,000	9,500	11,000	13,000	14,500	17,000	21,000
Base/ES ↓	6,500	8,000	9,500	11,000	13,000	15,000	19,000
Extended Warranty	N	N	N	N	N	N	N
Secret Warranty	N	N	N	N	N	N	N
Reliability	③	③	③	④	④	⑤	⑤
Air conditioning	④	④	⑤	⑤	⑤	⑤	⑤
Automatic transmission	⑤	④	❷	③	④	⑤	⑤
Body integrity	③	③	③	③	④	④	④
Braking system	❷	❷	③	③	③	④	④
Electrical system	❷	❷	❷	❷	④	④	⑤
Engines	④	④	④	⑤	⑤	⑤	⑤
Exhaust/Converter	④	④	④	④	⑤	⑤	⑤
Fuel system	③	④	④	③	④	④	⑤
Ignition system	③	④	④	④	④	⑤	⑤
Rust/Paint	❷	③	③	④	④	⑤	⑤
Steering	③	③	③	④	⑤	⑤	⑤
Suspension	④	④	④	④	⑤	⑤	⑤
Crash Safety	⑤	❷	—	—	—	—	—

NISSAN

Maxima

Rating: Recommended (1996–98); Above Average (1989–95); Average (1986–88). The redesigned 1995–98 version offers a peppier engine, more rounded styling, and a bit longer wheelbase. **Maintenance/Repair costs:** Higher than average, but repairs can be done practically anywhere. **Parts:** Higher-than-average cost, but easy to find.

Strengths and weaknesses: These front-wheel drive sedans are very well equipped and nicely finished, but cramped for their size. Although the trunk is spacious, only five passengers can travel in a pinch (in the literal sense). The 6-cylinder engine, borrowed from the 300ZX, offers sparkling performance; the fuel injectors, however, are problematic. Early Maximas are less expensive to buy, but more costly to maintain—for example, the exhaust manifold, a component that commonly fails, will set you back $300–$500 to replace. Owners report that the '95 Maxima's suspension was cheapened to the detriment of both the ride and the handling.

Minor electrical and front suspension problems afflict early Maximas. Brakes and engine timing belts need frequent attention in all years. Newer models have a weak automatic transmission and the ignition system can malfunction. There have also been reports of "cooked" transmissions. This is due to a poorly designed transmission cooler. Mechanics say that this breakdown can be avoided by installing an externally mounted transmission cooler with a filter and replacing the transmission filter cooler at every oil change.

Owners report that the V6-equipped Maxima is sometimes hard to start in cold weather due to the engine's tendency to flood easily. The cruise control unit is another problematic component. When it's engaged at moderate speeds, it hesitates or "drifts" to a lower speed, acting as if the fuel line were clogged. It operates correctly only at much higher speeds than needed. Incidentally, owners say that a new fuel filter will *not* correct the problem. Additionally, though warped manifolds were once routinely replaced under a "goodwill" warranty, Nissan now makes the customer pay. The warpage causes a manifold bolt to break off, thereby causing a huge exhaust leak. Most fuel-injector malfunctions are caused by carbon clogging up the injectors; there are additives you can try that might reduce this buildup. There have also been internal problems with the coil windings on the fuel-injectors. Your best bet is to replace the entire set.

Nissan has had problems with weak window regulators for some time. If the window is frozen, don't open it. The rubber weather stripping around the window is also a problem. It cuts easily and causes the window to go off track, which in turn causes stress on the weak regulators. Driver-side window breakage is common and can cost up to $300 to repair. Costly aluminum wheels corrode quickly and are easily damaged by road hazards. There have been a few reports of surface rust and paint problems. Pre-1990 Maximas suffer from rust perforation on the sun-roof, door bottoms, rear wheelwells, front edge of the hood, and bumper supports. The underbody should also be checked carefully for corrosion damage. Premature wearout of the muffler is a frequent prob-lem; it's often covered by Nissan's "goodwill" warranty, wherein the company and dealer will contribute 50 percent of the replacement cost.

1995–98 models

These redesigned Maximas have a longer wheelbase (adding to inte-rior room), a new 3.0L engine, and more rounded styling. They com-pete well with fully equipped Camrys, entry-level Infinitis, and Lexus models. Nevertheless, tall passengers will find the interior a bit cramped, and the automatic transmission is often slow to downshift and isn't always smooth. Quality control and overall reliability are apparently much better with these more recent iterations.

Dealer service bulletins: 1995—Hard cranking, no or low line pressure rise (control valve), and poor driveability (Code 45). • Clutch slippage. • AC compressor leaks or is noisy. • Troubleshooting excessive front and rear brake noise. • Rear brake, spare tire cover, and exhaust heat shield rattling. • Faulty center console lid latch. • Wind noise around the front door. • Certain windshield cracks are covered under warranty. **1996**—Brake squeak or squeal. • Center console lid latch replacement. • Hard starts or no-starts. • Timing chain noise.

Safety summary/Recalls: 1996—Fire ignited from shorted wires under the passenger-side seat. • Airbag failed to deploy. • ABS failures. • Vehicle constantly pulls to the right. • Engine warning light flashes for no apparent reason. • Sudden loss of power resulting in inoperative brakes and steering. • Chronic stalling. • Power steering failure. • Erratic transmission performance. • Hard to shift transmission out of Park. • Key can be taken out of ignition while vehicle isn't in Park. • Power door locks failed. • Defective AC expansion valve. • Several reports of headlight explosions. **1997**—Door latch won't engage in cold weather. • Front wheel suddenly locked up while driving. • Power steering leaks fluid. • Trunk lid opened while driving. • Pedal went to the floor when brakes were applied, resulting in extended stopping dis-tance. **1998**—Vehicle intermittently accelerates while braking. • Defective AC compressor. • Hazy, milky pattern on glass exterior causes poor visibility. • Frequent windshield wiper failures. **Recalls: 1986**—Windshield may detach in a collision. **1992–93**—Dealers will install a new airbag sensor so that the airbags won't inadvertently deploy when-ever the car passes over a speed bump. **1993–94**—Loose wheel nuts on aluminum wheels could allow wheels to fall away.

Secret Warranties/Service Tips

All models/years—Defective catalytic converters that cause a rotten-egg smell may be replaced free of charge under Nissan's emissions warranty. • Bulletin P195-006 looks at the many causes and remedies for excessive brake noise. **All models: 1985–91**—Excessive brake noise can be corrected with upgraded front and rear pads, caliper pins, and baffle plates. **1989**—Insufficient heating may be caused by air bubbles trapped in the heater core. • Ice-induced heater motor failure requires a new blower (#27200-85E02). **1989–91**—Starting difficulties can often be traced to a connector that is not fully seated in the ECU. **1989–92**—Nissan has developed a variety of brake pads to respond to a number of customer complaints regarding excessive noise when braking. • Clutch shudder can be eliminated by installing an upgraded pressure plate release lever. **1995–96**—Timing chain rattling noise can be silenced by replacing the timing chain tensioner and slack guide. • Brake squeak or squeal can be corrected by installing front and rear brake kits.

Maxima Profile

	1991	1992	1993	1994	1995	1996	1997	1998
Cost Price ($)								
Base	18,975	19,997	23,525	22,579	21,989	23,084	23,665	23,739
Used Values ($)								
Base ↑	7,500	9,000	10,500	11,500	13,000	14,000	16,500	18,000
Base ↓	6,000	8,000	9,500	10,000	11,500	12,500	14,500	16,500
Extended Warranty	N	N	N	N	N	N	N	N
Secret Warranty	N	N	N	N	N	N	N	N
Reliability	③	④	④	④	④	④	⑤	⑤
Air conditioning	③	④	④	⑤	⑤	⑤	⑤	⑤
Body integrity	❷	❷	❷	③	④	④	④	④
Braking system	❷	❷	❷	❷	③	③	④	④
Electrical system	❷	❷	❷	❷	③	③	④	④
Engines	③	④	④	④	⑤	⑤	⑤	⑤
Exhaust/Converter	❷	③	③	③	③	⑤	⑤	⑤
Fuel system	③	③	③	③	③	④	⑤	⑤
Ignition system	③	③	③	③	③	④	⑤	⑤
Manual transmission	❷	❷	③	③	③	⑤	⑤	⑤
- automatic	③	③	③	④	④	⑤	⑤	⑤
Rust/Paint	③	③	③	④	④	⑤	⑤	⑤
Steering	③	③	④	④	④	⑤	⑤	⑤
Suspension	③	③	④	④	④	⑤	⑤	⑤
Crash Safety	③	③	③	③	④	④	④	④
Side Impact	—	—	—	—	—	—	④	④

374

Lemon-Aid

SAAB

900, 9000

Rating: Average (1998); Below Average (1995–97); Not Recommended (1985–94). Interestingly, the upscale 9000 series isn't as crashworthy as the cheaper 900 versions, nor is it more reliable, exhibiting similar generic deficiencies as its entry-level brother. **Maintenance/Repair costs:** Higher than average, and repairs must be done by a GM or Saab dealer. **Parts:** Higher-than-average cost and limited availability.

Strengths and weaknesses: These Swedish-built luxury cars don't offer the refinement and ride comfort of most other cars in their class; the redesigned 1999 models will, however. They do combine excellent handling and great interior ergonomics (one of the few imports with the EPA's "large car" label), but without all the bells and whistles found in domestic luxury breeds. Convenience items like a fuse box in the glove box, a toolbox in the hatchback, and easy-to-replace bulbs, etc., add to your comfort.

Unfortunately, Saabs don't live up to the Swedish reputation for exceptional reliability and are quirky in design. Servicing is inadequate and will probably get much worse in the future. Parts are already costly and hard to find outside major urban areas. Take the tires, for example. Those for the 1992 9000 aren't a common size (205/50ZR16), and therefore command a not-so-common price—about $250 per tire, depending on the manufacturer.

Generally, the 900 and 9000 series have similar deficiencies affecting the engine cooling—biodegradable water pumps and electrical systems, brakes, automatic transmission (clutch O-rings), and body hardware. The 9000 is assembled with greater care, but owner reports show only a marginal improvement in overall reliability and durability.

Short circuits are legion and run the gamut from minor annoyances to fire hazards (see "Safety summary/Recalls"). Electrical glitches in the Traction Control System's relay module give a false reading that the tires are spinning, which shuts the engine down.

Turbos produce much stronger acceleration and better handling than other 9000s without compromising their overall reliability. Nevertheless, they should be approached with caution because owner abuse or poor maintenance can quickly lead to turbocharger deterioration. Air conditioners and exhaust system parts have a short life span, and leaky seals and gaskets are common. Rust perforations tend to develop along door bottoms and the rocker panels. The underbody, especially the floor, should be inspected for corrosion damage on older models.

Dealer service bulletins: 900: 1995—Battery drain due to climate control system. • Excessive exhaust vibration. • Loose center cover on rear belt member. • Rear floor duct noise. • Creaking noise in right-hand

A-pillar. • Evaporative loss system leaks. • Excessive clutch pedal freeplay. • Hard brake pedal when starting a cold engine. • Binding ignition switch contacts. • Inoperative blower motor. • Leaking sunroof or wet headliner. • Loosening seat upholstery. • Noise from rear speaker, secondary air injection pump, vacuum pump, dash, or front seat. • Pedal raising kit. • AM band radio interference. • Airbag warning light comes on. • Sulfur smell from exhaust. • Vibration caused by tires or rims. **1996**—Rear floor duct noise. • Excessive clutch pedal play. • Inoperative blower motor. • Leaking sunroof or wet headliner. • Loosening seat upholstery. • Front seat or dash noise. • Pedal raising kit. • AM band radio interference. • Clutch plate rattling. • Sulfur smell from exhaust. **9000: 1995**—Poor EDU illumination. • Loose dome light. • Evaporative loss system leaks. • Excessive fuel line pressure. • Failing fan control. • Secondary air injection pump noise. • Noise when shifting from second to third gear (automatic). • Rain or washer fluid running over rear window. • Dashboard squeaks and rattles. • Smell from climate control system. • Inoperative speedometer. • Airbag warning light comes on for no apparent reason. • Sulfur smell from exhaust. • Tire or rims causing excessive vibration. • Whistling noise from windshield. **1996**—Failing fan control. • Interior lights won't go out. • Noise when shifting from second to third gear (automatic). • Rattling noise from clutch plate. • Climate system smells. • Whistling noise from windshield. • Inoperative speedometer.

Safety summary/Recalls: 900: 1996—Under-hood fire ignited as vehicle was idling with transmission lever in the Park position. • Several reports that when shifting from Reverse to Drive, vehicle suddenly accelerated forward without braking or steering control. • Airbags failed to deploy, and the warning light comes on for no apparent reason • Fuel filter failures caused fuel leak. • Car drifts to the right while driving. • Defective exhaust check valve lifters. • Transmission failures and excessive vibrations. • Repeated gear shifting problems cause the shifter bushings and motor mount housing to be prematurely worn. • Sundry electrical system shorts and failures affecting the stereo and CD player, anti-theft system, and battery. • Frequent trunk latch release, door handle, and passenger seat adjuster failures. • Glass headlight cover is often broken. • Left sideview mirror can't be adjusted properly to see blind spots to left rear of vehicle. **9000: 1986–91**—Reports of passenger compartment fires. The government is investigating reports that Saab officials destroyed key documents that described the problem. A class action suit has been filed in Los Angeles, and a second suit has been filed in Atlanta, Georgia. **Recalls: All models with 2.3L engines: 1995**—Faulty electronic system. **900: 1989**—Recall No. 274 provides for the free replacement of the fuel filter. • Front seats may not lock into position properly. **1994**—Hatchbacks show fatigue cracks which could allow seat to suddenly fold backwards. **1995**—Convertibles may experience a possible loss of steering control due to a misaligned steering shaft. **900 (Turbo): 1985**—Flexible fuel hose may leak. **1986**—

376   *Lemon-Aid*

Steering shaft could pull out of joint. **1986–87**—Fuel hose may rupture. **1987–88**—Wiring harness may chafe, creating a fire hazard. **1988**—Front lower control arm may fail. **1989**—Leaking fuel filter may create a fire hazard. • Heater fan resistor may overheat. **1993**—Front brakes are very vulnerable to salt and slush, which compromises braking. **1994–95**—Transmission may be in Neutral when shifter is in Reverse. • Car could roll away if it's parked with the parking brake disengaged. **1996**—Seatbelt anchorage may not hold. **5d, Coupe (manual transmissions):** **1994–95**—A shift linkage defect may cause an unexpected movement if transmission is in gear. **9000: 1986**—Wiring harness may short-circuit, creating a fire hazard. **1986–91**—Fire may be caused by a short circuit in the driver console. **1988**—Faulty cruise control may lead to unintended acceleration. • Recall No. 272 provides for the free replacement of the lower control arm attachment bolts. **1988–89**—Fluid leakage may compromise braking effectiveness. **1988–90**—Fire may erupt in the backup light circuit. **1989**—Leaking fuel filter may create a fire hazard. **1991**—Car may be started in gear. **1992–93**—Dealers will install a new fuel filler and fuel-filler vent hose to prevent fuel leakage. • Vehicles equipped with an engine oil cooler may catch fire in a collision. **1992–94**—ABS corrosion can lead to loss of full braking power. **1993–94**—Brake lights may operate erratically.

Secret Warranties/Service Tips

900: 1988–91—Cold weather starting problems may be fixed with service kit #8819070. **1990–91**—A new valve and new O-rings will correct starting problems caused by a sticking fuel pump check valve. **1993–94**—Binding ignition switch contacts can lead to electrical failures. **1994**—A-pillar wind noise is addressed in DSB #08194-0486. • DSB #88/94-0480 lists the causes and remedies of AC malfunctions. **9000: 1992–94**—A noisy climate control unit may have excess pressure building up at the fresh air intake. **1993–94**—A stuck shift lever may be caused by a blown #3 fuse. A faulty sun visor/vanity mirror causes the short circuit.

900, 9000 Profile

	1991	1992	1993	1994	1995	1996	1997	1998
Cost Price ($)								
900	19,812	20,435	21,400	22,750	24,545	24,490	25,520	27,505
9000	24,077	26,175	28,570	30,670	32,695	32,695	35,360	32,695
Used Values ($)								
900 ↑	5,000	7,000	8,500	12,000	15,000	17,500	20,000	22,500
900 ↓	4,500	6,000	7,500	11,000	13,500	16,000	18,500	20,000
9000 ↑	7,000	10,000	11,500	15,000	19,000	22,000	25,000	28,000
9000 ↓	6,000	8,500	10,000	13,000	17,500	19,000	23,000	25,000
Extended Warranty	Y	Y	Y	Y	Y	Y	Y	Y
Secret Warranty	N	N	N	N	N	N	N	N

Reliability	❷	❷	❷	❷	❷	❷	③	③
Air conditioning	❷	❷	❷	❷	③	③	③	③
Body integrity	❷	❷	❷	❷	③	③	④	④
Braking system	❷	❷	❷	❷	❷	❷	❷	③
Electrical system	❶	❶	❶	❷	❷	❷	❷	③
Engines	❷	❷	❷	③	③	③	④	④
Exhaust/Converter	❷	❷	❷	❷	③	③	④	④
Fuel system	③	③	③	③	③	③	③	③
Ignition system	❷	❷	③	③	③	③	③	③
Manual transmission	③	③	③	④	④	⑤	⑤	④
- automatic	❷	❷	❷	❷	❷	③	③	④
Rust/Paint	③	③	③	③	③	③	④	⑤
Steering	③	③	④	⑤	⑤	⑤	⑤	⑤
Suspension	❷	❷	③	③	③	③	④	④
Crash Safety								
900	—	—	—	—	④	④	④	④
9000	—	—	④	—	—	—	—	—

TOYOTA

Avalon

Rating: Recommended (1995–98). A Camry knock-off; if you want a more driver-involved experience in a Toyota, consider a Lexus ES 300 or GS 300. **Maintenance/Repair costs:** Higher than average. Repairs must be done by a Toyota dealer. **Parts:** Higher-than-average cost and limited availability.

Strengths and weaknesses: This near-luxury four-door offers more value, interior space, and reliability than do other cars in its class that cost thousands of dollars more. A front-engine, front-drive mid-sized sedan based on a stretched Camry platform, the Avalon is bigger than the rear-drive Cressida it replaced and similar in size to the Ford Taurus. Sure, there's a fair amount of Camry in the Avalon, but it's quicker on its feet than the Camry, better attuned to abrupt maneuvers, and two inches longer. In fact, there's more rear-seat leg room than you'll find in either the Taurus or the new Chevrolet Lumina. It's close to the Dodge Intrepid in this respect.

Quality control is above reproach. Owners have some performance gripes, however. They include numerous electrical system glitches, premature front brake repairs, power steering that's a bit too light, excessive body lean, and under-steer when cornering. Body construction and assembly are solid, although the first two model years exhibited more deficiencies than the last few years.

Dealer service bulletins: 1995–96—Air conditioning odors. • AM band radio static on vehicles with an automatic antenna. • Front brake groan and rear brake moan. • Rear seat popping noise. • Wind noise from front door A-pillar area.

Safety summary/Recalls: 1995—Researchers are looking into 20 incidents of turn signal failures after the hazard warning lights have been activated. **1997**—Brakes may fail due to freezing vacuum hose.

Secret Warranties/Service Tips

All models: 1995–96—Use an upgraded rear brake pad material to eliminate rear brake moan. • To reduce wind noise from the front door A-pillar area, consult DSB #B0010-97. **1996**—Use an upgraded brake pad material to eliminate brake groan noise. • Tips on reducing engine noise, front door wind noise, front suspension, and rear popping noise. • Upgraded hazard switch. **1997**—AC odor troubleshooting. • Fixing front suspension crunch.

Avalon Profile

	1995	1996	1997	1998
Cost Price ($)				
XL	23,155	23,838	23,958	24,698
XLS	27,085	27,868	27,468	28,548
Used Values ($)				
XL ↑	14,500	17,000	19,000	21,000
XL ↓	13,000	15,500	17,500	19,500
XLS ↑	17,500	19,000	21,000	23,000
XLS ↓	15,000	17,500	19,500	21,500
Extended Warranty	N	N	N	N
Secret Warranty	N	N	N	N
Reliability	⑤	⑤	⑤	⑤
Crash Safety	—	④	④	④
Side Impact	—	—	—	③

Cressida

Rating: Above Average (1985–92). The Cressida was dropped in 1992 and then replaced with the Avalon for the 1995 model year. **Maintenance/Repair costs:** Higher than average, but repairs can be done by an independent garage. **Parts:** Higher-than-average cost and limited availability.

Strengths and weaknesses: The Cressida ages well and offers an excellent combination of dependable, no-surprise, rear-drive performance, comfort, and luxury. There is little to find at fault when it comes to overall reliability, and the engine is a model of smooth power. Its only shortcomings: a bit less interior and trunk space than one would find with the Nissan Maxima or Acura Legend, inconvenient and confusing dash controls, and poor fuel economy.

The later models are more crashworthy, reliable, and trouble-free than earlier versions, but they're also much more expensive. Two complaints, however, continue to surface throughout the years: premature front brake wear and excessive brake pulsation/vibration. Toyota has issued a drawer full of bulletins to eliminate the problems, but they seem to reappear each year in some form or another. AC glitches and electrical short circuits are also commonplace. Exhaust system parts rust quickly.

Safety summary/Recalls: N/A.

Secret Warranties/Service Tips

All models/years—Older Toyotas with stalling problems should have the engine checked for excessive carbon buildup on the valves before any more extensive repairs are authorized. • The brake pulsation/vibration problem is fully outlined and corrective measures are detailed in DSB #BR94-002, issued February 7, 1994. **All models: 1989**—Speaker static when the power mirror is activated requires a noise filter in the power-mirror circuit.

Cressida Profile

	1985	1986	1987	1988	1989	1990	1991	1992
Cost Price ($)								
Base	15,690	16,130	20,475	21,238	21,753	21,763	22,473	23,783
Used Values ($)								
Base ↑	4,500	5,000	5,500	6,000	7,000	8,000	9,000	10,000
Base ↓	4,000	4,500	5,000	5,500	6,000	7,000	8,000	9,000
Extended Warranty	N	N	N	N	N	N	N	N
Secret Warranty	N	N	N	N	N	N	N	N
Reliability	②	②	②	②	③	③	③	③
Air conditioning	①	①	①	②	②	②	③	③
Body integrity	④	④	④	④	④	④	④	④
Braking system	②	②	②	②	②	③	③	③
Electrical system	②	②	③	③	③	③	③	④
Engines	④	④	④	④	④	④	④	④
Exhaust/Converter	②	②	②	②	②	②	②	③
Fuel system	④	④	④	④	④	④	④	④
Ignition system	③	③	③	③	③	③	③	④
Manual transmission	③	③	③	③	—	—	—	—
- automatic	④	④	④	④	④	④	④	④
Rust/Paint	④	④	④	④	④	④	④	④
Steering	③	③	③	③	③	④	④	④
Suspension	①	①	①	②	③	③	③	④
Crash Safety	①	—	—	—	①	③	③	—

VOLVO

700 Series

Rating: Not Recommended (1985–92). Actually, the 700 series has fewer defects than other cars; however, the components that do fail are hard to diagnose and also cost a great deal to correct. As these cars age, these problems become more severe and dealers become more reluctant to invest their time in fixing them. **Maintenance/Repair costs:** Higher than average. Repairs must be done by a Volvo dealer. **Parts:** Higher-than-average cost and limited availability.

Strengths and weaknesses: The 700 series is more spacious, luxurious, and crashworthy than the entry-level 240. Its standard engine and transmission perform well, but aren't as refined as the 850. Furthermore, the 700 series suffers from the same generic brake, electrical, engine cooling, air conditioning, and body problems as does its cheaper cousin. Brakes tend to squeak or grind, wear rapidly, and require expensive service. Exhaust systems usually need replacing after a few years.

Owners complain of hard cold starts on 1987–92 models. Power windows fail to operate as a result of either dirt getting into the mechanism or the wiring short-circuiting. Air conditioning units that emit a musty odor or fail to work properly when the car is idling are a common problem. Body and interior trim pieces are fragile—dashboard cracks often appear after the third year. The windshield wiper motor malfunctions after two years. There have been some complaints of sunroof rattles, premature surface rust (the paint chips easily), and rusted-out exhaust systems.

Safety summary/Recalls: 1986–91—Front seat/center console fires. **Recalls: All models: 1985**—Water pump pulley may be defective. **1985–87**—Possible engine wiring harness short circuit. **1985–88**—On vehicles with B230F engines, the driveshaft could separate from the transmission. **1988**—Headlight switch may short-circuit. **1989–90**—Fuel may seep from fuel tank. Cars are eligible for new fuel tanks. **1992**—Faulty front seatbelts could detach from anchors. • The seatbelt webbing guide may break. **Wagons: 1986**—Locked tailgate can be opened from inside the vehicle.

Secret Warranties/Service Tips

All models/years—Check the valve cover nuts at every servicing interval to prevent oil leakage. **All models: 1988–90**—Brake pulsation, a common problem, is addressed in DSB #51/111. • If you're having problems starting your Volvo on cold mornings, see DSB #23/135 and DSB #23/21A. **1989–90**—Service Campaign No. 54 calls for the free installation of a cable harness. **1989–92**—To improve cold starting, Volvo will install an improved fuel-injection control module gratis if the emissions warranty applies. Under another program, Volvo will replace the MFI E PROM to improve cold starting.

1990–91—AM band radio interference will be stopped with kit #3533250-1.
1992—Volvo Special Service Campaign No. 59 provides for the free replacement of AC pressure switches and harness, the Regina fuel control units, and Rex ignition control units. These repairs are to be carried out regardless of vehicle mileage or the number of previous owners. • A decrease in idling speed when the AC engages can be corrected by installing a capacitor kit.

700 Series Profile

	1985	1986	1987	1988	1989	1990	1991	1992
Cost Price ($)								
740 GLE/GL	17,240	18,240	21,485	22,330	20,335	22,050	23,135	24,680
Used Values ($)								
740 GLE/GL ↑	3,500	4,500	5,500	6,000	7,000	8,000	9,000	11,000
740 GLE/GL ↓	3,000	4,000	5,000	5,500	6,000	7,000	8,000	9,500
Extended Warranty	Y	Y	Y	Y	Y	Y	Y
Secret Warranty	N	N	N	Y	Y	Y	Y
Reliability	③	③	③	③	③	③	④
Air conditioning	❶	❶	❶	❷	❷	③	④
Body integrity	❷	❷	❷	❷	❷	❷	③
Braking system	❶	❶	❶	❶	❶	❶	❷
Electrical system	❶	❶	❶	❶	❶	❶	❷
Exhaust/Converter	❶	❶	❶	❷	③	④	④
Fuel system	③	③	③	③	③	③	④
Ignition system	③	③	④	③	③	③	③
Manual transmission	③	③	③	③	③	③	④
- automatic	❷	❷	④	③	③	③	④
Rust/Paint	③	③	③	③	③	③	④
Steering	③	③	③	③	③	③	③
Suspension	③	③	③	③	③	③	④
Crash Safety	—	—	❶	—	—	⑤	⑤

850 Series

Rating: Recommended (1995–97); Above Average (1993–94). Surprisingly, for a car company that emphasizes its commitment to safe cars, the 850 series has quite a few safety-related defects reported by owners, including engine fires, loss of steering, sudden acceleration, transmission failures and tire blowouts. Don't waste your money on a 1997 850: the 1996 models are virtually identical to the more expensive 1997 versions and are a real bargain if the selling price has been reduced sufficiently. **Maintenance/Repair costs:** Higher than average. Repairs must be done by a Volvo dealer. The 1998 model 850s were redesignated the S70/V70. **Parts:** Costs are reasonable and parts are not hard to find.

Strengths and weaknesses: Bland, but practical to the extreme, with plenty of power, good handling, and lots of capacity. For 1997, the 850 GLT got a bit more lower-end torque, while the turbo version was upgraded with electrically adjusted front passenger seats and an in-dash CD player. The base 850 sedan uses a 2.4L 24-valve 168-hp 5-cylinder engine hooked to a front-drive powertrain. (An all-wheel drive version is available in only Canada and Europe.) Wagons use the same base powerplant, hooked to a 5-speed manual or optional 4-speed electronic automatic. GLTs have a torquier, turbo variant of the same powerplant that boosts horsepower to 190.

The "sports" sedan T5 is a rounder, sportier-looking Volvo that delivers honest, predictable performance but comes up a bit short on the "sport" side. Volvo's base turbo boosts horsepower to 222, but its new T-5R variant uses an upgraded turbocharger that boosts power to 240 horses—for up to seven seconds.

Passenger space, seating comfort, and trunk and cargo space are unmatched by the competition. Braking on dry and wet pavement is also exemplary. The ride of both the sedan and the wagon deteriorates progressively as the road gets rougher and passengers are added. Turbo versions are particularly stiff, and passengers are constantly bumped and thumped.

The 850 hasn't escaped the traditional AC, electrical system, and brake problems that afflict its predecessors. Additionally, owners have complained that the early models have uncomfortable seatbelts, insufficient rear travel for the front seats, and some body hardware deficiencies, resulting in excess noise invading the interior.

Dealer service bulletins: 1993–94—Faulty engine accessory mounting brackets. • Electrical short circuits. • Water contamination of the accessory drive belt. • Poor radio reception on the FM band. **1995**—Faulty cruise control. • Climate control system odor. • Steering knock at full lock, rattle from tailgate lock, sunroof rattling, doorstop and interior fittings noise, and auxiliary belt noise. • Poor performance of the engine belt tensioner, and prematurely worn crankcase ventilation hoses. **1996**—AM band radio interference. • Cruise control won't engage. • Damage to tailgate by tailgate handle. • Generator noise in the loudspeakers. • High oil consumption. • Starting difficulties. • Improvements to ventilation and defrosting. • New shims to reduce rear resonance vibrations. • Remedies for noise from evaporative canister hose. • Repair tips for loose door stops in A and B posts. • Repair tips for roof panel unevenness. • Loose windshield upper trim strip.

Safety summary/Recalls: 1996—A handful of reports that while vehicle was being driven, it suddenly lost all power and the engine compartment caught fire. • Inadvertent airbag deployment injured driver. • ABS brake failures. • Vehicle suddenly downshifts while cruising on the highway. • Transmission slipped out of Park, rolled down incline, and hit a house. • During rainy periods, the steering wheel locks up or the dashboard suddenly lights up. • Repeated tire blowouts. • Premature failure of the engine cooling fan and the evaporator pump fan relay for the exhaust manifold. Owners also cite cruise control, power steering pump, and front seatbelt failures. • Electrical glitches affect the speedometer, radio cassette player, and battery. • Broken driver-side door hinge. **1997**—Pirelli (205/45-17) tires blew out; the design and size for this vehicle is inappropriate. • Vehicle drifts left when being driven, even after the steering mechanism was replaced. • Gas odor in the interior after driving a short distance. • Driver's seatbelt retractor locks up. **Recalls: All models: 1993–96**—Block heater could loosen and overheat, seriously damaging the engine. **1994**—Frozen throttle linkage could result in erratic engine operation. **1995**—The threaded insert that attaches the seatbelt catch to the front seat was incorrectly manufactured. • Some jacks may fail. **1996–97**—Throttle may not return to idle when foot is taken off the accelerator pedal.

Secret Warranties/Service Tips

All models/years—Check the valve cover nuts at every servicing interval to prevent oil leakage. **All models: 1993**—A jerking sensation while accelerating may be caused by electrical interference between the rpm sensor wiring and the secondary ignition system. • Accessory drive belt noise due to water infiltrating into the system can be corrected by installing a special right front fender liner extension manufactured by Volvo to fix the problem. • Headlight wiper and washer motors may cause radio interference on the FM band. Eliminate this noise by installing suppressed wiper motors and a suppressor between the washer pump and the existing wiring. • Under Service Campaign No. 62, Volvo dealers will install at no charge an improved engine accessory mounting bracket. **1993–94**—Steering column spring noise can be silenced by using upgraded bolts to secure the upper bracket to the airbag retaining plate. **1993–96**—Tips on repairing roof panel unevenness. **1995**—If the cruise control won't engage, check the vacuum supply and vacuum supply pipe first. **1997**—Correct high oil consumption. • New shims will minimize low-speed braking vibrations. • Tips on correcting hard starting. • AC odor troubleshooting tips. • Measures for improved ventilation and defrosting. • Uneven panel above roof arches. • Engine may run too lean.

850 Series Profile

	1993	1994	1995	1996	1997
Cost Price ($)					
Base	24,495	24,725	25,540	26,620	28,180
Turbo	—	31,900	32,000	33,145	33,525
TLA/AWD	—	—	—	37,380	36,190
Used Values ($)					
Base ↑	15,500	17,500	18,500	21,000	23,000
Base ↓	14,000	16,000	17,500	19,500	22,000
Turbo ↑	—	21,500	24,000	27,000	28,500
Turbo ↓	—	20,000	22,500	25,000	27,000
TLA/AWD ↑	—	—	—	29,000	31,000
TLA/AWD ↓	—	—	—	27,500	29,000

Extended Warranty Secret Warranty	Y Y	Y N	Y N	Y N	Y N
Reliability	③	④	⑤	⑤	⑤
Air conditioning	❷	❷	③	③	④
Automatic transmission	❷	③	④	⑤	⑤
Body integrity	❷	❷	③	④	④
Braking system	③	③	③	③	③
Electrical system	❷	❷	❷	❷	③
Engines	⑤	⑤	⑤	⑤	⑤
Exhaust/Converter	⑤	⑤	⑤	⑤	⑤
Fuel system	④	④	④	⑤	⑤
Ignition system	③	③	④	⑤	⑤
Rust/Paint	③	④	⑤	⑤	⑤
Steering	⑤	⑤	⑤	⑤	⑤
Suspension	③	④	⑤	⑤	⑤
Crash Safety	—	⑤	⑤	⑤	⑤
Side Impact	—	—	—	—	④

900 Series

Rating: Recommended (1995–97); Above Average (1989–94). The 1998 model 900s were renamed the S90/V90 and have apparently inherited similar brake and electrical deficiencies. It's interesting to note that the 960 series becomes cheaper to acquire than the 940 as the years progress. **Maintenance/Repair costs:** Higher than average, and repairs must be done by a Volvo dealer. **Parts:** Higher-than-average cost and limited availability.

Strengths and weaknesses: Essentially repackaged 760s, these flagship rear-drive sedans and wagons have a much better reliability record than do the 240 and 700 series, and are on par with the 850 over the last five model years. Both the 940 and 960 offer exceptional roominess and comfort, and are capable of carrying six people with ease. The wagon provides lots of cargo space and manages to do it in great style. Some owner gripes: the base 114-hp 2.3L engine is overpowered by the car's weight, excessive fuel consumption with the turbo option, and excessive road and wind noise at highway speeds. These cars come with reinforced sides, which Volvo claims exceed federal regulations.

Dealer service bulletins: 1993–94—Hard starting and stalling caused by low fuel volatility. • Excessive vibrations when idling on vehicles equipped with an automatic transmission. • Whistling from the bulkhead and wiper-well cover panel. **1995**—Evaporator odor treatment. • Front brake squealing. • Poor AC performance.

Safety summary/Recalls: 1986–91—Front seat/center console fires. **1991**—Sudden airbag deployment. **1994–95**—Airbags deploy for no reason. **Recalls: All models: 1989–90**—Fuel may seep from fuel tank. **1992–93**—Front seatbelts may detach from anchorage. • The seatbelt webbing guide may break. **1995**—Driver-side airbag may not deploy properly. **1996–97**—Throttle may not return to idle when foot is taken off the accelerator pedal. **Turbo 944, 945: 1991**—Throttle may jam. • Child car seat may not conform to federal safety standards. **1993**—Erratic throttle operation.

Secret Warranties/Service Tips

All models/years—Check the valve cover nuts at every servicing interval to prevent oil leakage. **All models: 1989–93**—To improve cold starting, Volvo will install an improved fuel-injection control module free of charge if the emissions warranty applies. Under another program, Volvo will replace the MFI E PROM to improve cold starting. **1992**—Volvo Special Service Campaign No. 59 provides for the free replacement of AC pressure switches and harness, the Regina fuel control units, and Rex ignition control units. These repairs are to be carried out regardless of the vehicle mileage or the number of previous owners. **1992–94**—A decrease in idling speed when the AC engages can be corrected by installing a capacitor kit.

900 Series Profile

	1991	1992	1993	1994	1995	1996	1997
Cost Price ($)							
940 GLE	28,265	25,390	25,390	23,325	24,315	—	—
960	—	34,370	36,070	33,875	30,360	34,455	34,795
Used Values ($)							
940 GLE ↑	11,000	13,000	10,000	12,500	15,000	—	—
940 GLE ↓	10,000	11,500	9,000	10,500	13,500	—	—
960 ↑	—	11,00	13,000	17,000	18,000	20,000	23,500
960 ↓	—	9,500	11,000	15,000	16,500	18,000	21,000
Extended Warranty	Y	Y	Y	Y	Y	N	N
Secret Warranty	Y	Y	Y	N	N	N	N
Reliability	③	③	④	⑤	⑤	⑤	⑤
Air conditioning	❷	❷	❷	③	④	⑤	⑤
Automatic transmission	❷	③	③	④	⑤	⑤	⑤
Body integrity	❷	❷	❷	❷	③	③	③
Braking system	❷	❷	❷	❷	❷	③	③
Electrical system	❷	❷	❷	❷	❷	③	③
Engines	④	④	④	④	⑤	⑤	⑤
Exhaust/Converter	⑤	⑤	⑤	⑤	⑤	⑤	⑤
Fuel system	④	④	⑤	⑤	⑤	⑤	⑤
Ignition system	③	④	④	⑤	⑤	⑤	⑤
Rust/Paint	⑤	⑤	⑤	⑤	⑤	⑤	⑤
Steering	⑤	⑤	⑤	⑤	⑤	⑤	⑤
Suspension	③	③	④	⑤	⑤	⑤	⑤

SPORTS CARS

The average sports car model, like the Mazda Miata, should be able to go from 0 to 60 mph in under 10 seconds and top 80 mph at the end of a quarter mile. Meanwhile, luxury sports sedans, like the Infiniti Q45 and Lexus LS 400, have produced exceptional acceleration times of 60 mph in less than 8 seconds and have exceeded 90 mph after a quarter mile. But most sports cars, or "high-performance vehicles" as they're euphemistically named, don't offer the comfort or reliability of an Infiniti or Lexus. Instead, they sacrifice reliability, fuel economy, interior space, and comfortable suspension for speed, superior road handling, and attractive styling. They also need a whole slew of expensive high-performance packages, because many entry-level sports cars aren't very sporty in their basic form.

By carefully browsing through classified ads and dealer car lots, you should find many fully loaded offerings at a fraction of their original cost. Remember that models that have been taken off the market, like the Toyota Supra, Nissan 300ZX, and Chevrolet Corvette ZR1, aren't likely to become collectors' cars with soaring resale values. In fact, discontinued Japanese sports cars like the Nissan 1600 haven't done nearly as well as some of the British roadsters taken off the market at about the same time.

Recommended

Chrysler Stealth/Mitsubishi
  3000GT (1993–97)
Ford Cobra, Mustang (1996–98)
Ford Probe (1995–97)
GM Camaro/Firebird,
  Trans Am (1996–98)
Honda Prelude (1993–98)

Mazda MX-3 Precidia (1994–95)
Mazda MX-5 Miata (1996–98)
Mazda RX-7 (1991–95)
Nissan 240SX (1995–98)
Toyota Celica (1995–98)
Toyota MR2 (1991–93)

Above Average

Chrysler Avenger/Sebring
  (1998)
Chrysler Laser/Talon/Mitsubishi
  Eclipse (1997–98)
Chrysler Stealth/Mitsubishi
  3000GT (1992)
GM Corvette (1996–98)
Honda Prelude (1985–92)
Hyundai Scoupe (1995)
Hyundai Tiburon (1997–98)

Mazda MX-3 Precidia (1992–93)
Mazda MX-5 Miata (1990–95)
Mazda RX-7 (1985–90)
Nissan 200SX (1995–98)
Nissan 240SX (1989–94)
Nissan 300ZX (1994–96)
Toyota Celica (1986–94)
Toyota MR2 (1988–89)
Toyota Supra (1995–97)

Average

Chrysler Avenger/Sebring
(1995–97)
Chrysler Stealth/Mitsubishi
3000GT (1991)
Ford Probe (1993–94)
GM Camaro/Firebird,
Trans Am (1994–95)

GM Corvette (1994–95)
Nissan 300ZX (1993)
Toyota MR2 (1986–87)
Toyota Supra (1994)

Below Average

Chrysler Daytona, Laser, Shelby
(1990–93)
Ford Cobra, Mustang (1980–95)
Ford Probe (1989–92)

GM Camaro/Firebird
Trans Am (1992–93)
Hyundai Scoupe (1991–94)
Nissan 300ZX (1988–92)
Toyota Supra (1986–93)

Not Recommended

Chrysler Daytona, Laser, Shelby
(1984–89)
Chrysler Talon/Laser/Mitsubishi
Eclipse (1990–96)

GM Camaro/Firebird,
Trans Am, (1982–91)
GM Corvette (1980–93)

CHRYSLER

Avenger/Sebring

Rating: Above Average (1998); Average (1995–97). The Avenger and its more luxuriously appointed Sebring twin have had fewer factory-related defects than other new Chrysler designs, probably because they're built by Mitsubishi at its Illinois plant. V6-equipped versions cost about $2000 more than the base models. **Maintenance/Repair costs:** Higher than average. Repairs must be done by a Chrysler dealer. **Parts:** Higher-than-average cost and limited availability.

Strengths and weaknesses: Like the Eagle Talon and Mitsubishi Eclipse, the Avenger and Sebring are both surprisingly agile—which isn't actually that surprising considering they share many of the same components. The convertible, made in Mexico, is six inches longer than the Sebring coupe and is powered by a standard 2.0L twin cam, while the upscale JXi gets a performance injection with the 2.5L 6-cylinder powerplant.

Acceleration is fairly good with the base engine, but the optional V6 powerplant is the engine of choice to overcome the power-hungry automatic transmission. Engine, tire, and road noise at higher speeds can be disconcerting. Rear seat access can be a pain, literally, and rear seating may be uncomfortable for long trips.

Sports Cars

Although its vehicles are better built than what Chrysler offers, Mitsubishi quality control has slipped somewhat as of late, with owners singling out the brakes, electrical system, ignition, and body construction as the areas most needing attention.

Dealer service bulletins: 1995—Poor engine performance, hard starts, and stalling caused by a faulty powertrain control module. • Tendency to drift to the left requires upgraded compression lower arm assemblies. • Loss of air conditioning (corrected by installing a revised AC pressure transducer). • Headliner sagging. • Difficulty in closing the sunroof owing to a faulty lever mechanism. • Whistle from front windshield. **1996**—Troubleshooting excessive brake noise. • Door buzz and rattle. • Hard start, misfire, or rough idle. • Interior window film buildup. • No-start condition. • Poor driveability. • Engine compartment popping or knocking. • Power seat switch can stick. • Ratcheting sound when coming to a stop. • Rear shock noise. • Sag or hesitation on acceleration. • Shudders during upshift. • Sunroof inoperative or opens by itself. • Sunroof ratcheting sound or jerky operation, binding, or coming off its track. • Speed control undershoot or overshoot. • Engine compartment ticking noise. • Transaxle shudder. • Vehicle drift or lead. Whistle from front windshield. **1997–98**—Delayed transaxle engagement. • Excessive cold-crank time, start die-out, or weak run-up. • Knocking noise in engine compartment, possible oil pump damage. • Light knocking noise from the rear shock area. • Squeaking or rubbing noise from the rear shock area. • Transaxle desensitization to intermittent faults. • Whistle from front windshield.

Safety summary/Recalls: All models: 1995—Front ball joints fail, suspension collapses. **1996–97**—Sebring convertible top flies off. • Small horn buttons on the steering wheel spokes may be hard to reach in an emergency. **Recalls: All models: 1996**—Faulty power mirror switch. • Power brake booster hose mislocated. **1997**—Front passenger head restraint support bracket may break. Dealers must replace the entire seatback assembly. **Sebring: 1996–98**—Faulty ignition switches, console shifter, and cables in convertible models may cause the vehicle to roll away or render the ignition-park interlock system inoperative.

Secret Warranties/Service Tips

All models: 1995—One of the causes of premature brake wear, shudder, and noise is a misadjusted brake light switch. **1995–96**—Engine compartment ticking can be silenced by replacing the duty cycle purge solenoid with a quieter solenoid assembly. **1995–97**—Engine compartment popping or knocking may require an upgraded EGR valve. • Tips for reducing transaxle shudder are found in DSB #21-05-97. **1995–98**—Wind noise coming from the front windshield area is caused by wind lifting the windshield molding at the glass. Add sealant the full length of the windshield.

Avenger/Sebring Profile

	1995	1996	1997	1998
Cost Price ($)				
Avenger	16,309	17,008	18,857	18,685
Sebring	17,636	18,418	18,541	18,850
Convertible	—	25,210	21,555	25,575
Used Values ($)				
Avenger ↑	10,000	12,000	14,000	16,000
Avenger ↓	8,500	10,500	13,000	14,500
Sebring ↑	10,000	12,000	14,000	15,700
Sebring ↓	8,500	10,500	13,000	14,200
Convertible ↑	—	14,000	16,000	20,000
Convertible ↓	—	12,500	14,000	18,000
Extended Warranty	Y	Y	Y	Y
Secret Warranty	N	N	N	N
Reliability	③	③	④	④
Crash Safety				
Avenger	—	⑤	⑤	—
Sebring	—	—	⑤	—

Daytona, Laser, Shelby

Rating: Below Average (1990–93); Not Recommended (1984–89). Sports car thrills combined with wallet-busting bills. **Maintenance/Repair costs:** Higher than average, but repairs can be done by any garage. **Parts:** Higher-than-average cost and limited availability.

Strengths and weaknesses: The high-performance Daytonas—Turbo Z, Pacifica, and Shelby Z—can run with the best of them for a little while, and then the service bills start piling up. Without the failure-prone turbocharged engine and sport suspension, these coupes provide mediocre handling and acceleration.

All engines are troublesome. If they're not maintained meticulously from the very beginning, the turbocharger is likely to fail around the 50,000-mile mark and cause serious damage to the engine and your wallet. Fuel system problems are common on all versions, requiring the frequent replacement of electronic computer modules. The manual transmission has a sloppy shift linkage and a heavy clutch that doesn't stand up to hard use. Models loaded with electrical accessories have a higher failure rate than stripped-down versions. Electronic instrument panels and other electrical items are temperamental. The body is particularly poorly assembled, and water/wind leaks are common.

Safety summary/Recalls: Recalls: All models: 1985—Fatigue cracks could allow the seat to suddenly move backwards. **1985–87**—Fire hazard caused by fuel supply hose leak in models with turbo engines. **1987–89**—Exhaust system heat may melt carpet. Install free heat shield kit #4549356. **1989–90**—Leaking cylinder heads and gaskets will be replaced free of charge under Recall No. 467. **1990**—Airbag may be defective on cars with a gray interior. **1991**—Front disc brake caliper guide pin bolts may be too loose. **1992**—Coupling bolts on steering column shaft may be faulty. **1992–93**—Dealers will install additional bolts to better secure the dash panel. Inadequate spot welds attaching the front rails to the dash panel could cause structural damage, including door-opening interference and sheet metal cracking.

Secret Warranties/Service Tips

All models/years—A rotten-egg odor coming from the exhaust is probably caused by a defective catalytic converter. **All models: 1989**—Leaking fuel-injectors are a common problem. • Corrosion of the oxygen sensor connector is a common problem. **1989–90**—Defective valve stem seals are the likely cause of high oil consumption with 2.2L and 2.5L engines (DSB #HL-49-89C). **1990–92**—Erratic idle speeds occurring after deceleration from a steady cruising speed can be corrected by replacing the idle air control motor with a revised motor. **1991–92**—Engines with a rough idle and stalling following a cold start may require a new single board engine controller (SBEC). **1992**—If the heater and ventilation system change to the defrost mode during acceleration, trailer towing, or hill climbing, the installation of a revised vacuum check valve should cure the problem. • Long crank times, a rough idle, and hesitation may be corrected by replacing the intake manifold assembly. • A leak in the oil filter area may be corrected by installing a special oil filter bracket gasket (#MD198554). **1992–93**—Some 41TE transaxles may produce a buzzing noise when shifted into Reverse. Replace the valve body assembly or valve body separator plate.

Daytona, Laser, Shelby Profile

	1986	1987	1988	1989	1990	1991	1992	1993
Cost Price ($)								
Daytona	10,070	11,524	11,807	11,045	12,589	12,428	12,918	13,500
IROC	—	—	—	—	—	15,687	15,254	15,980
Laser	11,051	—	—	—	—	—	—	—
Shelby	—	14,474	15,176	14, 634	16,066	15,752	15,254	—
Used Values ($)								
Daytona ↑	1,800	2,400	2,800	3,500	4,000	4,500	5,000	6,000
Daytona ↓	1,500	2,000	2,400	3,000	3,500	4,000	4,500	5,000
IROC ↑	—	—	—	—	—	5,500	6,000	7,000
IROC ↓	—	—	—	—	—	5,000	5,000	6,000
Laser ↑	2,500	—	—	—	—	—	—	—
Laser ÿ	2,000	—	—	—	—	—	—	—
Shelby ↑	—	3,000	3,500	4,500	5,000	6,000	6,500	—
Shelby ↓	—	2,500	3,000	4,000	4,500	5,500	6,000	—

Extended Warranty	Y	Y	Y	Y	Y	Y	Y	Y
Secret Warranty	N	N	N	N	N	N	N	N
Reliability	❷	❷	❷	❷	③	③	③	③
Crash Safety								
Daytona	—	—	—	⑤	⑤	⑤	⑤	⑤

Laser/Talon/Mitsubishi Eclipse

Rating: Above Average (1997–98); Not Recommended (1990–96). The '95 models offer fresh styling, dual airbags, and a more powerful engine. The 1996 versions are identical to the more expensive, restyled '97 versions, and are the better buy if they're substantially cheaper. **Maintenance/Repair costs:** Higher than average, but repairs can be done practically anywhere. **Parts:** Good parts availability. Dealers have had some trouble adequately servicing these high-tech vehicles, and parts are a bit more expensive than other cars in this class.

Strengths and weaknesses: These sporty Mitsubishi-made cars combine high performance, low price, and reasonable durability. The base 1.8L engine is adequate and the suspension is comfortable, although a bit soft. The optional 16-valve, turbocharged 2.0L comes with a firmer suspension and gives more horsepower for the dollar than most other front-drive sports coupes, without much turbo lag. The 5-speed manual is the gearbox of choice. Torque steer makes the car appear to try to twist out of your hands when all 195 turbocharged horses are unleashed. The 4-speed automatic transmission cuts into the Laser's highway performance. Overall handling is impressive, with the 4X4 system giving sure-footed foul weather stability. Keep in mind that the all-wheel drive (AWD) model has a smaller trunk area than the front-drive.

The '97 Talon was dramatically restyled with wide air openings under the front bumper, new body cladding, and a redesigned rear end which includes a spoiler housing the center-mounted brake light. A new, "decontented" (a fancy word that means it lacks many of the bells and whistles of the ESi, TSi, and TSi AWD) base model was also added. The TSi got 17-inch wheels and better high-performance tires.

The ESi comes with a 140-hp 2.0L engine (borrowed from the Neon Sport), while the TSi is powered by a 210-hp 2.0L Mitsubishi-bred engine. Two additional powerplants are available: a 2.0L double overhead cam with 135-hp, and a turbocharged version of the same engine rated at a sizzling 195-hp. A manual 5-speed is standard, and an optional 4-speed automatic is available on all models except the Turbo RS. AWD is offered on both '96 car models, but only the '97 TSi offers AWD.

All high-performance models cost thousands of dollars less than their Japanese competitors, without compromising quality or performance.

The 16-valve Talon and its 4X4 variant are at the top of the trim list and provides five more horses than the turbocharged TSi.

Mitsubishi products have an above-average reliability record, as several decades of Colts have shown. Nevertheless, beginning with the 1990–94 models, owners report glitches with the 1.8L engine and electrical system, driveline vibrations, premature brake wear and excessive noise, and poor fit and finish. Some problems reported with 1995–97 versions were unstable idling, poor idling, and reduced rpm when the AC is running; cold weather hard starts and stalling; cold weather transmission shift delays (2–3 and 3–4) that take up to two minutes; transmission defaults into second gear (limp-in mode); a tendency to drift or lead to the right; speed control undershoot or overshoot; false theft alarm; center exhaust pipe heat shield buzz; door buzz and rattle; misadjusted door glass causing water leaks and wind noise; noisy clutch pedal; interior window film buildup; headliner sagging; power seat switch sticking; stress marks on the quarter trim panel; buzz or rattle from the rear quarter trim; inoperative, noisy, and jerky sunroof operation; faulty lever latch pin; and reports that the sunroof may open by itself.

Dealer service bulletins: 1994—Turbocharger bolts may be poorly torqued (Chrysler will re-torque them for free—DSB JE-41-89). • Excessive engine noise caused by carbon buildup on the top of the pistons. • Excessive driveline vibration. • Rear brake squeak, and standard brakes often lock up or require long stopping distances. **1995**—Poor idling and reduced rpm when the AC engages (requires an upgraded powertrain control module). • Cold-weather hard starts and stalling, and cold-weather transmission shift delays (2–3 and 3–4) that take up to two minutes. • Vehicle tends to drift or lead to the right, requiring upgraded compression lower arm assemblies. • Center exhaust pipe heat shield buzz and noisy clutch pedal. • Headliner sagging. • Stress marks on the quarter trim panel. • Faulty sunroof lever latch pin. **1996**—No-start due to faulty neutral safety switch. • Hard start, misfire, or rough idle. • Erratic idle. • Single cylinder misfire. • Driveability improvements. • Shuddering during upshifts or when torque converter is engaged. • Reduced limp-in default sensitivity. • Difficulty going into second gear or Reverse after a cold start. • Speed control overshoots or undershoots. • Vehicle drifts or leads at high speeds. • Excessive brake noise. • Intermittent theft alarm activation. • Power seat switch can stick. • Ratcheting sound when coming to a stop. • Sunroof is inoperative or opens by itself. • Sunroof operation produces a ratcheting sound or is jerky. • Sunroof or sunshade binds or comes off its track. • Door buzz and rattle. • Rear quarter trim buzz or rattle. • Engine compartment ticking noise. • Interior window film buildup. **1997**—Excessive brake noise. • Inoperative CD player. • Poor driveability. • Transmission shudder. • Loose side body moldings.

Safety summary/Recalls: Standard brakes often lock up or require long stopping distances. Choose the optional ABS. • Three deficiencies that compromise comfort and safety on many of these cars are the absence of airbags and ABS on the Laser; a small, shallow trunk with a high sill; and head restraints that block rear visibility. **Recalls: All models: 1990**—Sunroof glass may detach from roof. • Poor windshield retention during a collision. **1990–91**—Takata seatbelt replacement. **1995–96**—Incorrectly installed fuel gauge/pump gaskets may cause a fire. Requires a new fuel tank. **Laser: 1990**—Headlight wiring harness may short, causing the lights to fail. **Talon/Talon 4X4: 1990**—Early production oxygen sensors that can't withstand the turbo engine's high temperatures will be replaced for free under an emissions recall. **Talon/Talon 4X4, Eclipse: 1997**—Front passenger head restraint support bracket may break. Dealers must replace the entire seat back assembly.

Secret Warranties/Service Tips

All models/years—A rotten-egg odor coming from the exhaust may be the result of a malfunctioning catalytic converter, which may be covered by the emissions warranty. **All models: 1991–92**—Tappet/lash adjuster noise is a common problem that's covered by DSB 09-53-91. **1990–91**—A loose rear-quarter trim panel may require new clips. **1990–94**—Driveline vibrations on smooth roads can be eliminated by installing upgraded engine and transmission mounting brackets. **1992–94**—Rear brake squeaks can be silenced with a Mitsubishi shim kit. **1997**—Tips available on repairing loose side body moldings. **Laser: 1990**—To correct transmission case gasket leaks, use gasket kit #MD730803. **Talon: 1990**—Turbocharger bolts may be poorly torqued. • Warping of the headliner molding can be fixed by installing an improved molding. • If the headlights won't retract when the switch is turned off, replace the passing control relay, heat shrink tube, and tie straps. • Hard shifting/gear clash can be prevented by installing a modified 1–2 synchronizer sleeve, spring, and 3–4 spring.

Laser/Talon/Mitsubishi Eclipse Profile

	1991	1992	1993	1994	1995	1996	1997	1998
Cost Price ($)								
Eclipse	12,655	12,894	13,399	13,686	15,891	15,135	15,821	17,775
Laser	12,958	13,398	13,876	14,042	—	—	—	—
Turbo RS	16,150	17,110	17,680	17,887	—	—	—	—
Talon	14,906	15,854	13,910	14,080	16,927	15,954	16,701	16,400
Talon 4X4	18,429	19,382	20,034	20,270	20,758	21,695	21,666	21,000
Used Values ($)								
Eclipse ↑	4,500	6,000	6,500	7,500	9,000	11,500	12,500	13,500
Eclipse ↓	4,000	5,000	6,000	6,500	7,500	10,000	11,500	12,500
Laser ↑	3,500	4,500	5,500	6,500	—	—	—	—
Laser ↓	3,000	4,000	4,500	5,500	—	—	—	—
Turbo RS ↑	5,000	5,500	6,500	7,500	—	—	—	—
Turbo RS ↓	4,500	5,000	5,500	6,000	—	—	—	—

Talon ↑	5,500	6,000	7,000	8,000	9,000	10,000	12,000	14,000
Talon ↓	5,000	5,500	6,000	7,000	8,000	9,000	10,500	12,500
Talon 4X4 ↑	5,500	6,500	7,500	8,500	9,500	11,000	14,000	16,000
Talon 4X4 ↓	4,500	5,500	6,500	7,500	8,500	9,500	12,500	14,500
Extended Warranty	Y	Y	Y	Y	Y	Y	N	N
Secret Warranty	N	N	N	N	N	N	N	N
Reliability	②	②	②	②	②	②	④	⑤
Air conditioning	③	③	④	⑤	⑤	⑤	④	④
Body integrity	②	②	②	②	②	②	③	③
Braking system	②	②	②	②	②	②	③	④
Electrical system	②	②	②	②	②	②	②	③
Engines	①	②	②	②	②	②	③	④
Exhaust/Converter	③	③	③	④	⑤	⑤	⑤	⑤
Fuel system	①	②	②	③	③	③	④	④
Ignition system	③	②	②	③	③	④	⑤	⑤
Manual transmission	③	③	③	④	④	④	⑤	⑤
- automatic	②	②	②	②	②	②	③	③
Rust/Paint	②	③	③	③	③	③	③	④
Steering	③	③	③	④	④	④	④	⑤
Suspension	③	③	③	③	④	④	④	④
Crash Safety	④	④	④	④	④	④	④	—
Side Impact	—	—	—	—	—	—	—	①

Stealth/Mitsubishi 3000GT

Rating: Recommended (1993–97); Above Average (1992); Average (1991). The Mitsubishi 3000GT and Dodge Stealth are serious, reasonably priced sports cars that are as much go as show. **Maintenance/Repair costs:** Average, and repairs must be done by a Chrysler or Mitsubishi dealer. **Parts:** Higher-than-average cost and limited availability. The small engine compartment means that some of the simplest jobs will require special tools and take an inordinate amount of time to complete.

Strengths and weaknesses: An impressive highway performer with a good reliability record, except for some persistent transmission problems. The base V6 engine accelerates well and provides more than enough power for all driving conditions. The awesome twin turbo power on the R/T Turbo rivals the engine performance of sports cars selling for far more. Power steering is crisp and predictable and provides just the right amount of road feel. Standard disc brakes work very well, but the ABS is particularly impressive in stopping the car in a short distance without any loss of steering stability or fading after repeated application. Where the Stealth disappoints is in its limited driver head room (a Ford Probe problem, too), confusing and hard-to-find interior instrumentation and controls, hard-to-service engine compartment, and mediocre quality control when it comes to body hardware, fit, and finish. The Stealth isn't a car for short drivers, since they may have trouble seeing over the hood or reaching the clutch pedal. When the seat is moved forward, short drivers may be unable to see the overhead lights. Rear seating is very cramped—the norm with most sports cars. The dash control that adjusts the exhaust system sound is more gimmick than innovation. The Turbo's excessive weight taxes fuel economy.

Dealer service bulletins and a small number of owner complaints show that the first-year (1991) Stealth had an unusually large number of factory defects that were mostly corrected in the second year. For example, owners report frequent gearbox and fit problems, including drivetrain noise, grinding noise when shifting, gear clash, hard shifting into all gears, difficulty shifting into Reverse, door glass rattling, excessive wind noise along door glass, water leaks, and sluggish window operation. Other problems reported by owners and confirmed by dealer service bulletins: cruise-control failure due to improper wiring connection, noisy engine lash adjuster and prematurely-worn crankshafts on turbo-equipped versions, power transfer unit and viscous coupling failure, 1–2 gear clash, faulty exhaust manifold nuts, noisy steering column, rear suspension tapping noise, and faulty turn signals. The Getrag transmission on post-'93 models is unreliable, expensive to repair, and not easily found.

Safety summary/Recalls: 1992–93—Sunroof glass shattering. **Recalls: All models: 1991**—Takata seatbelt replacement. **1991–94**—Front-wheel brake hoses may crack. **R/T Turbo: 1991**—Oil leaking from the AWD transfer case may cause bearing damage/failure.

Secret Warranties/Service Tips

All models/years—A rotten-egg odor coming from the exhaust is probably the result of a malfunctioning catalytic converter, which may be covered by the emissions warranty. **All models: 1991–94**—Rear cargo cover rattling or failure to stay in the holder requires a new clip. **1992**—Vehicles that won't start may have corroded wiring in the A-67 12-connector. **1994**—Door glass weather stripping may pull out, requiring the installation of upgraded weather stripping.

Stealth/Mitsubishi 3000GT Profile

	1991	1992	1993	1994	1995	1996	1997	1998
Cost Price ($)								
Base 3000GT	21,161	21,826	24,102	27,645	28,920	31,110	28,400	28,240
Turbo	32,265	34,288	37,693	41,370	43,520	46,878	45,060	46,700
Base Stealth	18,484	19,525	20,863	23,659	24,572	25,651	—	—
RT	24,443	25,868	27,766	26,404	27,756	29,207	—	—
RT Turbo	30,438	32,096	34,350	38,785	38,785	35,355	—	—

Used Values ($)

Base 3000GT ↑	8,000	9,500	11,000	13,000	15,000	17,500	20,000	23,000
Base 3000GT ↓	6,500	8,000	9,500	11,000	13,500	16,000	18,500	22,000
Turbo ↑	12,000	13,500	16,000	18,500	21,000	23,000	27,000	30,000
Turbo ↓	10,500	12,500	14,000	16,500	18,500	22,000	25,000	28,000
Base Stealth ↑	7,000	8,500	10,000	11,000	13,500	15,000	—	—
Base Stealth ↓	6,000	7,000	8,500	10,000	12,500	14,000	—	—
RT ↑	8,000	10,000	12,000	14,000	15,000	16,000	—	—
RT ↓	7,000	8,500	10,000	12,000	14,000	15,000	—	—
RT Turbo ↑	11,500	13,500	15,000	18,000	20,000	23,000	—	—
RT Turbo ↓	10,500	12,500	14,000	16,000	18,000	22,000	—	—

Extended Warranty	N	N	N	N	N	N	N	N
Secret Warranty	Y	Y	Y	Y	Y	Y	Y	Y

Reliability	③	③	④	④	⑤	⑤	⑤	⑤
Air conditioning	③	③	⑤	⑤	⑤	⑤	⑤	⑤
Body integrity	❷	❷	❷	❷	③	③	③	④
Braking system	③	③	❷	③	③	④	④	④
Electrical system	❷	❷	❷	❷	③	③	③	③
Engines	❷	❷	③	④	④	⑤	⑤	⑤
Exhaust/Converter	❷	③	④	⑤	⑤	⑤	⑤	⑤
Fuel system	④	⑤	⑤	⑤	⑤	⑤	⑤	⑤
Ignition system	❷	③	④	④	⑤	⑤	⑤	⑤
Manual transmission	❷	❷	③	③	③	③	③	③
- automatic	❷	❷	③	③	③	③	③	③
Rust/Paint	③	③	③	③	③	④	④	⑤
Steering	④	⑤	⑤	⑤	⑤	⑤	⑤	⑤
Suspension	③	③	③	④	④	⑤	⑤	⑤
Crash Safety	—	—	⑤	—	—	—	—	—

FORD

Cobra, Mustang

Rating: Recommended (1996–98); Below Average (1980–95). Unfortunately, Mustangs don't perform well in rough weather and they have had a frighteningly high number of safety-related mechanical failures. GM's Camaro and Firebird are the Mustang's traditional competition as far as performance is concerned. Ford has the price advantage, with a base Mustang costing a bit less than the cheapest Camaro, but it lags from a performance standpoint—10 horses with the V6 and 60 horses with the V8. The GM models also offer more sure-footed acceleration, crisper handling, standard ABS, a 6-speed transmission, and more comfortable rear seats. Don't waste your money on a 1997 Mustang if a 1996 version, in good condition, is available. The 1996 models were substantially improved and can be a real bargain if the price is right. All 4-cylinder versions should be shunned. **Maintenance/Repair costs:** Average, particularly because repairs can be done anywhere. **Parts:** Average cost, and parts are often sold for much less through independent suppliers.

Strengths and weaknesses: As stated earlier, rear-wheel drive Mustangs remain popular because they offer sporty styling and high-performance thrills, usually for less money than GM's Camaro and Firebird, the Mustang's main domestic rivals. The 4-cylinder engine, used through 1993, isn't just failure-prone—it also doesn't carry half the horses of the 5.0L V8 and has no redeeming qualities. A limited edition Cobra sporting a 245-hp V8 debuted in 1993. Unfortunately, the 1993 Mustang fell behind the GM competition when the Camaro and Firebird were radically restyled that year, gaining additional safety features, a more rigid and dent-resistant body, better body fit and finish, and a more powerful base engine.

1994–98 models
Ford fought back with its own redesign of its 1994 model, replacing the 4-banger with a V6, adding four-wheel disc brakes, making the chassis more rigid (especially the convertible version), and dropping the hatchback. Mustangs now carry a base 3.8L V6 and an optional 4.6L V8. In addition, the high-performance limited edition Cobra variation delivers 90 more horses than the stock 4.6L V8 offers. The single and twin cam V8 options make the Mustang a powerful—if a bit unsophisticated—street machine. V6 models are an acceptable compromise, even though the engines fail to deliver the gobs of power most performance enthusiasts expect from a Mustang and, up to the 1995 model year, they have a propensity for blowing up their head gaskets.

Base models come equipped with a host of luxury and convenience items, which can be a real bargain once the base price has sufficiently depreciated, say, after the first three or four years. Off-lease models are particularly good buys these days.

This is definitely not a family car. For example, a light rear end makes the car dangerously unstable on wet roads or when cornering at high speeds. But for those who want a sturdy and stylish second car, or who don't need room in the back or standard ABS, the 1996–98 Mustang is a pretty good sports car buy. And if GM carries out its threat to drop its rear-drive Camaro and Firebird after the year 2000, the Mustang will be the main alternative for rear-drive sports car enthusiasts.

Like Camaros, Mustangs have never been very reliable cars. The first Mustang, launched in 1964 and now worth more than $25,000, had serious rusting, electrical, and suspension problems. And guess what? Thirty-five years later, Mustangs still have electrical systems and electronic modules that are constantly breaking down, transmissions that jump from Park to Reverse, and a base suspension and front brakes that wear out in the blink of an eye.

The less said about the infamous 2.3L 4-cylinder engine, the better. The V6 is also failure-prone (head gaskets, again), leaving the V8 engine with a definite performance and reliability edge. Turbocharged models aren't recommended because of their frequent and expensive mechanical breakdowns. If you want high-performance action, you'll have to pay a premium—and be prepared for some monstrous repair bills and white-knuckle acceleration on wet roadways. Sport trim models feature an upgraded suspension and wheel package that improves handling considerably.

Keep in mind that the electronic modules that govern engine and transmission performance are often on the fritz, producing chronic hard starts, stalling, and overall poor city and highway performance. Furthermore, the 3.8L 6-cylinder engine has begun to tally up a record number of head gasket failures around the 100,000-mile mark. Other problem areas: the front brakes, fuel pumps and front suspension remain consistent weak spots, and MacPherson struts and various steering components are likely to wear out before their time. The parking brake cable also seizes easily. The EEC IV engine computer can be temperamental, and electrical problems are common. Assembly quality is still not on par with Japanese vehicles.

Dealer service bulletins: 1995—Misaligned or worn accessory drive belt. • Delayed transmission engagement and shift errors, intermittent loss of torque at 3–4 upshift, and shifts to Neutral during heavy throttle. • Insufficient AC cooling or excessive clutch end gap. • Rear brake squeak, brake roughness upon application, and a thumping/clacking sound when braking. • Water intrusion of the MLP/TR sensor. • Faulty rear view mirror, loose rocker panel moldings, a temperature control knob that doesn't reach full cool position, and a malfunctioning temperature gauge. • Fuel pump buzz/whine heard through the radio speaker in addition to poor radio reception. **1996–97**—Stalling or hard starts. • Noisy 4.6L engine. • Transmission valve body cross leaks. • Erratic or prolonged 1–2 shift. • Squeal or hoot noise from engine compartment. Accessory belt damaged or comes off. • Coolant leaks from upper radiator hose. • Chatter during turns. • Front suspension rattle. • Fuel pump buzz/whine heard through the radio speaker. • Musty and mildew-type odors. • Blower motor noisy or inoperative in cold weather. • Convertible top leaks. • Sticking or clicking odometer/trip odometer. • Overheating; AC shuts off. • Hard starting, long crank, stalling. • Loose catalyst or muffler heat shields. • Fog/film on windshield/interior glass. **1998**—Loose rocker panel moldings. • Excessive clutch vibrations. • Buzz or rattle from the exhaust system. • Musty odors from the AC. • Radio speaker whine or buzzing.

Safety summary/Recalls: Regularly equipped Mustangs, like most rear-drive Fords, don't handle sharp curves very well. The rear end swings out suddenly, and the car tends to spin uncontrollably. Furthermore, the car loses traction easily on wet roads and braking is barely adequate. **1995—** Fuel line failure caused several fires. • Front fan belt caught on fire with no warning. • Several reports of sudden acceleration due to a stuck throttle. • Airbag failed to deploy. • Airbag deployment caused severe injuries. • Inadvertent airbag deployment. • Several reports that when driver applied the brakes, the airbag deployed. • ABS brake failures, warped rotors, and frequent pad replacement. • Engine head gasket failures. • Power steering fails; steering wheel is off-center or locks up. • Chronic stalling thought to be caused by defective fuel pump. • Transmission failure while driving caused accident. • Torque converter failure causes transmission to slip. • Many reports of vehicle jumping from Park to Reverse and rolling away. • Rear axle broke during normal driving conditions. • Front-end alignment doesn't hold, causing premature wear of steering and tie-rods. • On one occasion, tie-rods broke and caused vehicle to go out of control, resulting in several fatalities. • Front struts suddenly collapsed. • Weak rear struts allow vehicle to "bottom out." • Front stabilizer bar rusted and cracked. • Driver's door hinge broke. • Fuel gauge inoperative or gives an inaccurate reading. • Gas tank too small and requires frequent fillups. • Trunk leaks cause premature rusting. • Fog lights fill with water and blow their bulbs. • Frequent AC failures. • Seatbelt failed to restrain driver. **Recalls: All models: 1984–85—**Front seatbelt buckles may break and separate from the belt webbing. **1985—**Defective ignition module. • Faulty plastic sleeve in front seatbelt tongue assembly. • Power brake booster could come apart. **1986–87—**Fuel line coupling may leak fuel. **1987—**Faulty fuel-injection tube assemblies may cause fuel leakage and create a fire hazard. **1988–93—** Faulty ignition module may pose a fire hazard. **1991—**Vehicle could roll away with the shift lever in Park position. **1994–96—**Hood may be defective. **1995—**Defective tie-rod ends could cause an excessive shake or shimmy, resulting in an accident. **1998—**Cruise control may stick. • Steering may fail. • Fuel leak may cause a fire. **Mustang GT: 1995—**Front seat cushion supports could abrade wiring harness, posing a fire hazard.

Secret Warranties/Service Tips

All models/years—Three components that frequently benefit from Ford "goodwill" warranty extensions are catalytic converters, fuel pumps, and computer modules. If Ford balks at refunding your money, apply the emissions warranty for a full or partial refund. • Paint delamination, fading, peeling, hazing, and "microchecking" (see page 113 for details on claiming a refund). **All models: 1980–88—**Inoperative power door locks need an upgraded retainer clip assembly (#E8AZ-5421952-A). **1982–86—**Wind noise and water leaks with T-roofs and convertibles are usually caused by misaligned doors. Install door alignment kit #E72Z-6123042-A or -B. **1982–90—**An unusual engine metal-to-metal noise may be caused by the flexing of the torque converter. Install six new flywheel bolts with reduced head height to provide additional clearance. **1985–97—**A buzz or rattle from the exhaust system may be caused by a loose heat shield catalyst. **1986–94**—The in-tank fuel pump is the likely cause of all that radio static you hear. Stop the noise by installing an electronic noise RFI filter (#F1PZ-18B925-A). **1987–90**—Excessive oil consumption is likely caused by leaking gaskets, poor sealing of the lower intake manifold, defective intake and exhaust valve stem seals, or worn piston rings. Install new guide-mounted valve stem seals for a more positive fit and new piston rings with improved oil control. **1988–92**—Cold hesitation when accelerating, rough idle, long crank times, and stalling may all signal the need to clean out excessive intake valve deposits. These problems also may result from the use of fuels that have low volatility, such as high-octane premium blends. **1990**—Excessive transmission noise, delayed shifts, or no engagements may be due to thrust washer metal particles that have plugged the filter or burnt out the clutch plates. **1990–93**—Noise heard from the power-steering pump may be caused by air in the system. **1991**—A rough idle or lean fuel flow may require the installation of deposit-resistant injectors. **1994**—Automatic transmissions with delayed or no forward engagement, or a higher engine rpm than expected when coming to a stop, are covered in DSB #94-26-9. • A cracked cowl top vent grille should be replaced with an upgraded version. • A driveline boom can be silenced by replacing the rear upper control arms. • A noisy fuel pump needs to be replaced by an improved "guided check valve" fuel pump. • Models with laser-red paint may have serious paint decay problems, requiring a repainting of the entire body. • A ticking or tapping sound coming from the engine at idle can be silenced by installing an improved fuel hose/damper assembly. **1994–95**—A thumping or clacking heard from the front brakes signals the need to machine the front disc brake rotors. Ford may pay for this repair under its base warranty. • Loss of torque during or just after 3–4 shift may be caused by a hydraulic condition in the transmission or an intermittent signal from one of the powertrain system sensors. **1994–97**—An erratic or prolonged 1–2 shift can be cured by replacing the cast aluminum piston with a one-piece stamped steel piston with bonded lip seals, and by replacing the top accumulator spring. These upgraded parts will increase the transmission's durability, says Ford. **1994–98**—Loose rocker panel moldings will be fixed under the bumper-to-bumper warranty. **1996**—Stalling or hard starts may be due to the idle air control valve sticking. **1996–98**—Engine oil mixed with coolant or coolant loss signals the need for revised lower intake manifold side gaskets and/or front cover gaskets (covered by the emissions warranty). **1998–99**—Tips on spotting abnormal ABS braking noise.

Cobra, Mustang Profile

	1991	1992	1993	1994	1995	1996	1997	1998
Cost Price ($)								
Cobra	—	—	19,935	22,425	23,060	26,645	27,195	26,155
Mustang LX/Coupe	12,321	12,343	12,847	16,455	17,550	18,485	18,810	17,805
Convertible	18,271	18,873	19,706	22,840	23,610	23,935	23,710	22,305
Used Values ($)								
Cobra ↑	—	—	10,500	13,000	16,000	18,500	21,000	23,500
Cobra ↓	—	—	9,000	11,000	14,500	16,500	19,000	21,500
Mustang LX/Coupe ↑	4,000	5,500	6,000	7,000	10,000	12,000	13,500	15,000
Mustang LX/Coupe ↓	3,500	4,500	5,000	6,000	8,500	10,000	12,000	14,000

Convertible ↑	5,500	7,000	7,500	8,500	12,500	14,500	16,000	18,000
Convertible ↓	5,000	5,500	6,500	7,000	11,000	13,000	15,000	16,500
Extended Warranty	Y	Y	Y	N	N	N	N	N
Secret Warranty	Y	Y	Y	Y	Y	Y	Y	N
Reliability	❷	❶	❷	❷	❷	③	③	④
Air conditioning	❶	❶	❶	❶	❶	❷	④	⑤
Body integrity	❶	❶	❷	❷	❷	❷	③	③
Braking system	❶	❶	❷	❷	❷	❷	③	③
Electrical system	❶	❶	❶	❶	❷	❷	③	④
Engines	③	❷	❶	❶	❶	③	④	④
Exhaust/Converter	❷	③	③	③	③	④	⑤	⑤
Fuel system	❷	❷	❷	③	③	③	③	④
Ignition system	③	③	③	③	④	④	④	④
Manual transmission	③	③	③	③	④	⑤	⑤	⑤
- automatic	❷	❷	❷	❷	③	③	③	④
Rust/Paint	❶	❶	❶	❶	❶	③	③	④
Steering	❷	③	③	③	③	④	⑤	⑤
Suspension	❷	③	③	③	③	④	⑤	⑤
Crash Safety								
Base	—	—	—	④	④	④	④	⑤
Convertible	④	④	④	—	—	⑤	⑤	—
Side Impact								
Base	—	—	—	—	—	—	—	③

Probe

Rating: Recommended (1995–97); Average (1993–94); Below Average (1989–92). **Maintenance/Repair costs:** Average, and repairs can be done by independent garages or Mazda dealers. Nevertheless, the under-hood layout is crowded, making for high routine maintenance costs. **Parts:** Despite the fact that 1997 was the Probe's last model year (Mazda's MX-6 bit the dust as well), parts should remain plentiful and reasonably priced.

Strengths and weaknesses: The four-seater Probe sporty coupe was launched in May 1988 as the front-wheel drive replacement for the aging Mustang. Don't get the impression that the Mazda MX-6 and Probe are twins because they share most mechanical features. In fact, they differ markedly in handling and appearance. Ford engineers took more control of the chassis tuning and suspension geometry to give the car a smoother and firmer sporty demeanor, and its stylists chopped and pulled the body to give it a more aerodynamic, aggressive personality.

Available only as a two-door hatchback, there are two models, each with its own powerplant: a 2.0L 4-cylinder and a 2.5L V6 engine. These engines give the car much-needed power and smoothness not found in the anemic and brutish powertrains used in the past.

Mazda's mechanicals are above reproach, but despite gobs of torque, the GT doesn't give the muscle-car performance found in the less refined 5.0L Mustang GT. Performance is sapped considerably by the automatic transmission. Early models are beset by severe "torque steer," a tendency for the chassis to twist when the vehicle accelerates. Nevertheless, overall handling is precise and predictable on all models without sacrificing ride quality, which is a bit on the hard side.

Refinements of the 1993 and later versions include two new Mazda-designed engines that give the car a small horsepower boost, more interior room, all-disc brakes on the GT, and less torque steer.

The Probe's overall mechanical reliability is fairly good, but like its Mustang cousin, body assembly is the pits (no surprise here—Mazda did the mechanicals; Ford did the body work.) Paint quality and rust protection are mediocre at best. The turbocharged engine has been relatively trouble-free, but owners have complained of frequent stalling and stumbling with the base 2.2L powerplant. Many experience excessive ABS noise and vibrations when braking, and the front brakes tend to wear out very quickly. AC components have a short lifespan of three to five years and are outrageously expensive to troubleshoot and repair.

The car is essentially a 2+2 with the rear reserved for children or cargo. The interior is short on head room for tall drivers (especially on vehicles equipped with a sunroof), but cargo room is increased with the folding rear seatbacks. Multiple squeaks and rattles, wind and water leaks, and cheap interior appointments are the most common body complaints. The digital read-outs are distracting and often incorrect.

Dealer service bulletins: 1993—Poorly performing 4EAT automatic transmissions produce harsh 3–2 downshifts. • The Service Engine light may go on for no apparent reason. **1994–95**—Fluid leak from the transaxle pump seal. • Brake roughness upon application. • Inaccurate fuel gauge. • Erratic headlight door operation. • Off-center steering wheel. **1996–97**—Engine misses, stalls, runs rough, or has reduced power. • Excessive engine noise. • Upper engine noise service tip. • Hesitation, low power, rough idle. • 3–4 shift hunt. • CD4E transmission shifts harshly, seeps fluid from the vent, and produces a buzz or a clicking vibration. It may also make a whistling noise in Park. • Fluid leaks at axle shaft. • Inaccurate fuel gauge reading when the tank is full. • Loose catalyst or muffler heat shields. • Fog/film on windshield/interior glass. • Door glass makes a pop or snap noise when rolled up or down. • Musty and mildew-type odors.

Safety summary/Recalls: The driver's motorized shoulder belt is literally a pain in the neck. It rides high on the neck, fails to retract properly, tangles easily, and often hangs too loose. It also requires that the driver attach the lapbelt separately. Beware of coil spring corrosion causing the spring to suddenly break. Ford will pay for the repair on a case-by-case basis. **Recalls: All models: 1985**—A defective ignition may make for hard starting. • Defective plastic sleeve in front seatbelt tongue assembly. • Power brake booster could come apart. **1986–87**—Fuel line coupling could leak fuel. **1990–92**—Motorized shoulder belts may not work. **1991**—Vehicle could roll away when in Park. **1993**—A faulty rear hatch strut may cause the hatch to drop without warning. Dealer will replace rivets that have undersized heads on the strut pivot pins. **1994–95**—Passenger-side airbag may not inflate properly. **1996**—Incorrect warning regarding rear-facing child safety seats. **1997**—Timing belt tensioner spring may break and jam the belt. **GL: 1991**—There's a free fix for welds that anchor the front shoulder belt retractors.

Secret Warranties/Service Tips

All models/years—Three components that frequently benefit from Ford "goodwill" warranty extensions are catalytic converters, fuel pumps, and computer modules. If Ford balks at refunding your money, apply the emissions warranty for a full or partial refund. • Paint delamination, fading, peeling, hazing, and "microchecking" (see page 113 for details on claiming a refund). **All models: 1989**—2.2L engines with hairline cracks in the cylinder head must have the head replaced. • Hard cold-starts or chronic stalling may require a cold stall pressure regulator kit (#900809A). • No-starts/ low battery may mean that you need a new alternator pulley and belt kit (#E92Z-10344-D). **1989–91**—Constant fogging and moisture condensation on the interior windows and windshield signals the need to adjust the recirculation/fresh control cable. **1989–92**—An exhaust buzz or rattle may be fixed by installing new clamps to secure the heat shield. **1989–94**—A no-start condition, or inoperative heater or lights, may be caused by water and corrosion in the wiring connector, or a short-to-ground at splice 102 (circuit 9). **1990–91**—Rear disc brake squeal can be corrected by installing revised brake pads (#E92Z-2200-A). • Taillight condensation can be prevented by installing a new outer lens kit. • Engine knocking at idle may require the installation of a thicker thrust plate. **1990–94**—A speaker whine or buzz caused by the fuel pump can be stopped by installing an electronic noise RFI filter. **1993–94**—A clunk or knock from the steering assembly when turning the steering wheel is likely due to an insufficient yoke plug (pinion) preload. • Wind/water leaks require the readjustment of the front door glass, as outlined in DSB #994-5-4. • Inoperative power door locks may have a corroded wiring harness connection. • Frozen door locks, a common problem, are addressed in DSB #94-8-6. • A ticking noise coming from the 2.0L engine's hydraulic lash adjusters can be stopped by a longer oil pump control plunger that prevents air from passing through to the oil pump. **1994**—A rough idle affecting 2.0L engines could be caused by spark leakage from a damaged number 1 or number 2 spark plug wire. **1994–97**—Transaxle fluid seepage can be corrected by servicing with a remote vent kit or by replacing the main control cover. **GT: 1990**—Service Program No. 96 provides for the rerouting of the wiring harness and hose clamp to prevent transmission failure.

Probe Profile

	1990	1991	1992	1993	1994	1995	1996	1997
Cost Price ($)								
Base	13,434	13,680	14,140	15,119	15,975	15,890	16,240	16,235
GT	16,570	17,016	16,740	17,687	19,105	19,485	19,545	18,735
Used Values ($)								
Base ↑	3,500	5,000	5,500	6,000	7,500	8,500	10,000	11,000
Base ↓	2,800	4,000	4,500	5,000	7,000	7,500	8,500	9,500
GT ↑	4,000	5,000	6,000	7,000	9,000	10,000	11,000	12,500
GT ↓	3,500	4,500	5,500	6,500	8,000	9,000	10,000	11,000
Extended Warranty	Y	Y	Y	N	N	N	N	N
Secret Warranty	Y	Y	Y	Y	Y	Y	Y	Y
Reliability	③	③	③	③	④	④	⑤	⑤
Air conditioning	❷	❷	❷	❷	❷	③	③	③
Body integrity	❶	❶	❶	❶	❶	❶	❷	❷
Braking system	❶	❶	❶	❶	❶	❷	❷	❷
Electrical system	❶	❶	❷	❷	❷	❷	❷	③
Engines	③	③	③	④	⑤	⑤	⑤	⑤
Exhaust/Converter	❷	❷	❷	③	⑤	⑤	⑤	⑤
Fuel system	③	③	③	③	④	⑤	⑤	⑤
Ignition system	❷	③	③	⑤	⑤	⑤	⑤	⑤
Manual transmission	④	④	④	④	⑤	⑤	⑤	⑤
- automatic	③	③	③	④	④	⑤	④	⑤
Rust/Paint	❶	❶	❶	③	③	③	③	③
Steering	③	③	③	③	④	④	④	⑤
Suspension	③	③	③	③	④	④	④	⑤
Crash Safety	—	④	④	③	⑤	⑤	⑤	⑤

Note: Although the 1990 Probe wasn't crash-tested, the 1989 crash test results showed minimal injury would be sustained by the driver and front-seat passenger.

GENERAL MOTORS

Camaro/Firebird, Trans Am

Rating: Recommended (1996–98); Average (1994–95); Below Average (1992–93); Not Recommended (1982–91). As with the Mustang, the Camaro and Firebird have elicited many safety-related complaints, including airbag deployment injuries, sudden acceleration, brake failures, and steering loss. The 1996 Camaro and Firebird are essentially the same as the more expensive 1997 versions. A V8-equipped Camaro or convertible is the best choice for retained value a few years down the road. But you can do quite well with a used base coupe equipped with the performance handling package and high-performance tires. GM has announced it may drop the Camaro and Firebird after the year 2000. If it does, this move is unlikely to affect the cars' resale values or parts supply. **Maintenance/Repair costs:** Average, and repairs can be done by any independent garage. **Parts:** Reasonably priced and easy to find.

Strengths and weaknesses: When compared with the Mustang, Camaros and Firebirds are better performing rear-drive muscle cars that produce excellent crash protection scores and high resale values. They also take the lead over the Mustang with their standard ABS and slightly better reliability record. However, brute power is combined with almost-as-brutal repair charges. The Camaro's and Firebird's overall performance varies a great deal depending on the engine, transmission, and suspension combination in each particular car. Base models equipped with the V6 powerplant accelerate reasonably well, but high-performance enthusiasts will find them slow for sporty cars. Handling is compromised by poor wet-road traction, minimal comfort, and a suspension that's too soft for high-speed cornering and too bone-jarring for smooth cruising. The Z28, IROC-Z, and Trans Am provide smart acceleration and handling, but at the expense of fuel economy.

1982–93

Much like Ford's embarrassing 4-banger, the puny and failure-prone 2.5L 4-cylinder powerplant was the standard engine up to 1986—part of the legacy of an earlier fuel crisis and the subsequent downsizing binge. The turbocharged V8 offered on some Trans Am models should be viewed with caution because of its many durability problems.

Body hardware is fragile, poor paint quality and application is common and leads to premature rusting, and squeaks and rattles are legion. Body integrity is especially poor on cars equipped with a T-roof. Areas particularly vulnerable to rusting are the windshield and rear wheel openings, door bottoms, and rear quarter panels. The assorted add-on plastic body parts found on sporty versions promote corrosion by trapping moisture along with road salt and grime. Also note that the Camaro's flat seats don't offer as much support as the better-contoured Firebird seats.

These cars are also plagued by chronic fuel-system problems, especially on the Cross-Fire and multi-port fuel-injection controls. Automatic transmissions, especially the 4-speed, aren't durable. The standard 5-speed manual gearbox has a stiff shifter and a heavy clutch. Clutches fail frequently and don't stand up to hard use. The 2.8L V6, used through 1989, suffers from leaky gaskets and seals and premature camshaft wear. The larger 3.1L 6-cylinder has fewer problems. Malfunctioning dash gauges and electrical problems are common. Exhaust parts rust quickly. Dual outlet exhaust systems on V8 engines are expensive to replace. Front suspension components and shock absorbers wear out very quickly.

1994–98

Of this grouping, you should stick with the 1996–98 models for the best quality and price. Nevertheless, all of these cars are much better overall performers, with a more powerful and reliable base engine; increased body rigidity that hushes some of the squeaks and rattles so prevalent with previous years; a redesigned, easier-to-read dash; a bit more rear head room; and additional standard safety features. A more powerful 3.8L V6 arrived in spring 1995 and became standard for 1996.

On 1997 models, GM offered a 30th birthday styling package for the Camaro and some interior upgrades, V6 engine dampening for smoother running at high speeds, optional Ram Air induction, and racier-looking ground-effects body trim for the Firebird.

These sporty convertibles and coupes are almost identical in their pricing and in the features they offer (the Firebird has pop-up headlights, a more pointed front end, a narrower middle, and a rear spoiler). As noted above, both cars got a complete make-over in 1995, making them more powerful and aerodynamic with less spine-jarring performance. They were given new plastic skins, dual airbags, standard anti-lock brakes, new suspension and steering systems, a new 5-speed manual transmission, a reworked interior, and minor cosmetic improvements.

As one moves up the scale, overall performance improves considerably. The V8 engine gives these cars lots of sparkle and tire-spinning torque, but there's a fuel penalty to pay. A 4-speed automatic transmission is standard on the 5.7L-equipped Z28; other versions come with a standard 5-speed manual gearbox or an optional 6-speed. Many of these cars are likely to have been ordered with lots of extra performance and luxury options, including a T-roof package guaranteed to include a full assortment of creaks and groans.

Both the Camaro and the Firebird may be equipped with an impressively effective passkey theft-deterrent system similar to the one used successfully in the Corvette. A resistor pellet in the ignition disables the starter and fuel system when the key code doesn't match the ignition lock.

Not everything is perfect, however. Owners report that the base engine is noisy, though the 3.8L doesn't have the head gasket failures seen with Ford's 3.8L powerplant. Fuel economy is practically nonexistent, the air conditioner malfunctions (but not to the same extent as Ford-produced units), front brakes and MacPherson struts wear out quickly, servicing the fuel-injection system is an exercise in frustration, and body problems are worse than with the Mustang and just won't go away.

These cars are still afflicted by door rattles, misaligned doors and hatch, a sticking hatch power release, and poor fit and finish. Owners also complain that the steering wheel is positioned too close to the driver's chest, the low seats create a feeling of claustrophobia, visibility is limited by wide side pillars, and trunk space is sparse with a high liftover.

Dealer service bulletins: 1994—Poor radio reception. • A rough-running AC compressor on V8-equipped vehicles requires an upgraded compressor pulley. **1995**—Transmission fluid leak from the pump body. • Excessive rear axle noise. • Steering pull, usually to the right. • Front brake vibration and/or pedal pulsation and unevenly worn rear brake pads. • A low-voltage reading or dim lights at idle. • Rear compartment lid leaks water. • Door glass rattles. • Poor paint application and rust spots. **1996**—Engine rpm flare during gear shifts. • Engine oil leak at rear of engine near flywheel cover, and spark knock at idle. • 3–2 part throttle downshift flare and delayed transmission engagement. • Transmission fluid leak from pump body (replace bushing). • Steering column noise. • Steering lead or pull, usually to the right. • Steering column click or snap noise. • Uneven brake pad wear. • Convertible top leaks water. • Coolant leak at engine coolant heater assembly. • AC odors. • Radio frequency interference diagnosis. • Condensation on exterior light. • Water leaks at rear compartment lid when vehicle is parked on an incline. • Water leak diagnostic guide. • Cannot remove ignition key. • Anti-theft alarm may sound if vehicle gets wet. • Inoperative power door locks. • Rattle or buzz from parking brake handle release button. **1997**—Oil leaks between the intake manifold and engine block. • Troubleshooting a malfunctioning convertible top. • Erratic headlight or turn signal operation. • Inoperative power door locks. • Low-voltage reading or dim lights at idle. • Premature burnout of rear taillight/brake light bulbs. • Rattle or buzz from parking brake handle release button.

Safety summary/Recalls: All models: 1995—Four reports that car caught fire on the left rear side near the fuel tank. • Other fires ignited near the radio and in the engine compartment. • Many reports claiming sudden acceleration. • Airbag failed to deploy. • Inadvertent airbag deployment. • Severe injuries caused by airbag deployment. • Airbag deployed, projecting dash panel into the passenger's face. • Airbag deployed and caught fire. • Frequent ABS brake failures; pedal goes to the floor. • ABS particularly ineffective in rainy weather. • Rear brakes rusted out. • Left rear caliper grabs when making turns. • On one occasion, the rear brake caliper bolt came off, causing the brakes to fail. • Emergency brake fails frequently, allowing car to roll away even though shift lever is placed in Park. • Faulty cruise control. • Fuel line retaining clamp could fail, causing the plastic fuel lines to come into contact with the exhaust manifold cover. • The tie-rod broke while driving, forcing the car off the road. • In wet conditions, or when passing over a puddle, the power-steering pump fails, resulting in steering lockup. • Broken gas tank weld. • Stabilizer bar failure. • Care must be taken when shifting the floor shifter to avoid cutting hand on the dash. • Frequent transmission failures while driving. • Transmission bolts came off. • Trunk latch failure allows trunk to open while driving. • Two reports that double-locking T-top flew off from passenger side while driving with both locks engaged. • In another incident, the sunroof flew off. • Convertible top latch failure. • Door windows leak. • Inadequate defroster; causes windows to fog. • Headlight dimmer switch failures. • Driver's seatbelt failed during accident. **Recalls: All models: 1985**—Shoulder seatbelt may not retract. **1985–86**—For vehicles with rear disc brakes and manual transmissions, the parking brake adjuster may not hold the vehicle when parked on an incline. **1985–90**—Defective seatbelt buckle assemblies may not latch. **1986**—Faulty push-pull headlight switch. **1988**—GM will inspect and repair the power-steering pump support brace and mounting bracket. **1988–89**—On vehicles equipped with a 2.8L V6 engine, fuel feed hoses may leak. **1989**—Rear seatbelts in convertibles may be too long. **1990**—Fuel return hoses may leak on vehicles equipped with a V8 engine. **1991**—Poor windshield retention in an accident. Defective seatbelt latch plates will be fixed for free. • Defective front seats. **1991–92**—Fuel-filler neck may leak. **1992**—The automatic transmission shift control cable may separate and hamper shifting. **1994**—Fuel line on V8-equipped cars may leak fuel into the engine compartment. **1995**—Faulty lower steering shaft coupling could lead to loss of steering. **1997**—Seatbelt retractor may fail.

Secret Warranties/Service Tips

All models/years—A rotten-egg odor coming from the exhaust is probably the result of a malfunctioning catalytic converter, which may be covered by the emissions warranty. • Paint delamination, peeling, or fading (see pages 73–75). **All models: 1982–93**—Vehicles equipped with a Hydramatic 4L60 transmission that buzzes when the car is in Reverse or idle may need a new oil pressure regulator valve. **1985–91**—Hydramatic 4L60/700R4 automatic transmission may have no upshift or appear to be stuck in first gear. The probable cause is a worn governor gear. It would be wise to also replace the retaining ring. **1989**—If the rear brakes moan when they're applied slightly while backing up or turning, a redesigned caliper mounting plate may be needed (DSB #89-162-5). • Knocking from a cold 5.0L engine means that the PROM module has to be replaced (DSB #89-284-6E). • No-start or stalling may be caused by a disconnected fuel pump coupler. **1989–90**—Campaign 90-C-11 provides for free convertible top latch handles. **1990**—Cold-start stalling with the 3.1L engine may be corrected by replacing the MEMCAL. **1992**—Oil leaks from the rear of a 5.0L or 5.7L engine may be caused by insufficient sealing around the camshaft plug. **1993–94**—DSB #431028 covers all aspects of securing loose door outer panels. • A loose, rattling instrument panel or upper trim panel requires new dual lock riveted fasteners. • Rear brake squeal can be silenced by installing upgraded disc brake pads. **1993–96**—Uneven rear brake pad wear or premature wear can be corrected by replacing the caliper anchor bracket, guide pins, and the brake pads with upgraded parts. **1993–97**—Oil leaks between the intake manifold and engine block are most often caused by insufficient RTV bonding between the intake manifold and cylinder block. **1994**—Excessive oil consumption is likely due to delaminated intake manifold gaskets. Install an upgraded intake manifold gasket kit. • Delayed automatic transmission shift engagement is a common problem addressed in DSB #47-71-20A. • Install a new "flash" PROM to cure engine surging or hesitation and stalling upon acceleration for cars with automatic transmissions. **1997**—Tips on correcting parking brake handle noise. • New switches will fix inoperative door locks. • Fixing automatic transmission slippage. • Engine oil leak diagnosis. • Theft alarm sounds when vehicle gets wet. • Diagnosing engine miss and poor driveability. **Models with 2.5L engines: All years**—Spark knock can be fixed with the free installation of a new PROM module (#12269198) if the emissions warranty applies. • Frequent stalling may require a new MAP sensor (DSB #90-142-8A). **1990–91**—Stalling on deceleration or at stops requires a new MEMCAL that refines idle speed control and throttle follower operation. **1991**—Poor starting may be caused by the spring in early starter drives compressing too easily. Install an upgraded starter motor drive assembly (#10473700). **1995–96**—Delayed automatic transmission shift engagement may require the replacement of the pump cover assembly. **3.8L V6: 1996–98**—These engines have a history of low oil pressure caused by a failure-prone oil pump. A temporary remedy is to avoid low-viscosity oils and use 10W-40 in the winter and 20W-50 for summer driving.

Camaro/Firebird, Trans Am Profile

	1991	1992	1993	1994	1995	1996	1997	1998
Cost Price ($)								
Camaro Base	14,496	14,132	16,385	16,250	17,536	18,411	18,786	19,196
Z28	18,276	18,112	20,125	19,900	21,236	21,951	22,721	22,571
Convertible	20,134	23,405	—	25,351	26,388	27,016	28,091	27,975
Firebird	14,624	15,070	16,710	16,735	17,764	19,408	19,209	20,380
Trans Am	19,174	19,840	22,480	21,005	22,344	22,709	23,339	26,400
Used Values ($)								
Camaro Base ↑	5,500	6,500	7,500	9,000	10,000	11,000	13,000	15,000
Camaro Base ↓	4,500	5,500	6,500	7,500	8,000	10,000	11,500	13,500
Z28 ↑	6,500	7,500	9,000	11,000	12,000	14,000	16,000	18,000
Z28 ↓	5,000	6,500	7,500	9,000	10,000	12,000	14,000	16,000
Convertible ↑	8,500	9,000	—	13,500	15,000	17,000	19,000	22,000
Convertible ↓	7,000	8,000	—	12,500	13,000	15,500	17,000	20,000
Firebird ↑	5,500	6,500	8,000	9,000	11,500	12,500	13,500	15,000
Firebird ↓	4,500	5,500	7,000	7,500	10,000	11,500	12,500	14,000
Trans Am ↑	6,000	7,500	9,000	11,500	13,000	15,000	17,000	19,500
Trans Am ↓	5,000	6,500	7,500	10,000	11,500	13,000	15,500	18,000
Extended Warranty	Y	Y	Y	N	N	N	N	N
Secret Warranty	Y	Y	Y	Y	Y	Y	Y	Y
Reliability	❶	❷	❷	③	③	④	④	⑤
Air conditioning	❷	③	③	③	④	⑤	⑤	⑤
Body integrity	❶	❶	❶	❶	❷	❷	❷	③
Braking system	❷	❷	❷	❷	❷	③	③	④
Electrical system	❶	❶	❶	❶	❶	❶	❷	❷
Engines	❷	④	④	③	③	③	③	❷
Exhaust/Converter	❶	❶	③	③	③	④	④	⑤
Fuel system	❶	❷	❷	③	③	④	④	⑤

Ignition system	②	②	②	②	③	③	④	④
Manual transmission	③	③	③	④	④	⑤	⑤	⑤
- automatic	③	③	③	④	④	⑤	⑤	②
Rust/Paint	❶	❶	③	③	③	④	⑤	⑤
Steering	③	③	③	③	③	③	④	⑤
Suspension	④	③	④	④	④	④	④	⑤
Crash Safety								
Camaro	⑤	⑤	⑤	⑤	⑤	⑤	⑤	④
Side Impact								
Camaro	—	—	—	—	—	—	③	③

Note: Although the 1990 Camaro wasn't crash tested in a frontal collision, the 1987 crash test results showed minimal injury would be sustained by the driver and front-seat passenger.

Corvette

Rating: Above Average (1996–98); Average (1994–95); Not Recommended (1980–93). The cheaper 1996 Corvette won't have the cachet or the mechanical and body refinements of the redesigned 1997 version. If you choose the 1997 model, try to get a second-series car that was made after June 1997. Keep in mind that premium fuel and astronomical insurance rates will further drive up your operating costs. **Maintenance/Repair costs:** Higher than average, although most repairs can be done by any independent garage. **Parts:** Expensive, but easy to find. Surprisingly, it is often easier to find parts for older Corvettes, through collectors' clubs, than to find many of the high-tech components used today.

Strengths and weaknesses: Corvettes made in the late '60s and early '70s are acceptable buys, due mainly to their value as collector cars and their uncomplicated repairs. The Corvette's overall reliability has declined over the years as its price and complexity have increased. This is due in large part to GM's updating its antiquated design with high-tech, complicated add-ons, rather than coming up with something original. Consequently, the car has been gutted and then retuned using failure-prone electronic circuitry. Miles of emissions plumbing have also been added to make it a fuel-efficient, user-friendly, high-performance vehicle. Unfortunately, the Corvette has missed these goals by a large margin.

The electronically controlled suspension systems have been glitch-plagued over the past several years. Servicing the different sophisticated fuel-injection systems isn't easy—even (especially) for GM mechanics. The noisy 5.7L engine frequently hesitates and stalls, there's lots of transmission buzz and whine, the rear tires produce excessive noise, and wind whistles through the A- and C-pillars. These, and the all-too-familiar fiberglass body squeaks, continue to be unwanted standard features throughout all model years. The electronic dash never works quite right (speedometer lag, for example).

On the other hand, Corvette ownership of more recent models does have its positive side. For example, the ABS vented disc brakes, available since 1986, are easy to modulate and fade-free. The standard European-made Bilstein FX-3 Selective Ride Control suspension can be preset for touring, sport, or performance. Under speed, an electronic module automatically varies the suspension setting, finally curing these cars of their earlier endemic over-steering, wheel spinning, breakaway rear ends, and other nasty surprises.

If you're planning to buy a used Corvette, be wary of any model made 1979–93—and make sure that you get a GM-backed supplementary warranty with later models! The frequency of repairs and the high repair costs make maintenance outrageously expensive on all but the more recent versions. Although older cars are likely to be junked or already restored, the following are some of the things that can put a large dent in your wallet if they haven't been fixed already.

1977–83
Major mechanical failings affect the air conditioning, transmission, clutch, shift linkage, camshaft lifters and rear half-shaft soft yokes, carburetor, steering, rear brakes, and starter and electrical system, including the lights. As far as body assembly goes, the major deficiencies are poor panel fits, faulty and fragile interior/exterior parts and trim items, quirky instruments, cheap upholstery, and defective window lifts. Owners also complain of poor workmanship/shoddy assembly causing a cacophony of squeaks and rattles, poor dealer servicing, unavailable and expensive parts, and excessive labor charges.

1984–90
These models are incredibly difficult to service. One *Lemon-Aid* reader had a faulty engine bearing at 10,000 miles and spent $1,800 to remove the engine. It takes half a day to change the spark plugs on the passenger side. Likely mechanical problem areas are the emission-control system (injectors, computer-controlled sensors, fuel-injection, and engine gaskets), air conditioning, and ignition/distributor. Owners also experience engine and drivetrain failures, Bosch radio malfunctions, and the need to make frequent wheel alignments. Fragile body hardware, poor fit and finish, wind/road noise, and water intrusion into the interior are still major weaknesses. Owners complain of faulty controls and window lifts, and defective paint (base coat comes through the finish), interior/exterior parts and trim, glass and weather stripping, instruments, lights, door locks, upholstery, and carpeting.

1991–97
Though the restyled 1991 Corvette remained the same mechanically, all models got the convex tail and square taillights previously used only on the upscale ZR-1 coupe. A new LTI engine with 55 more horses came on the scene with the 1992 'Vette, and the following year the ZR-1

got a 405-hp variant of the same powerplant, shortly before the model
was replaced in the spring of 1995 by the Grand Sport. A more substantial redesign was carried out for the 1997 model year.

Owners rave about the redesigned models' improved performance,
better handling, and additional safety features, but continue to find
fault with the stiff ride, poor fuel economy, and excessive interior noise.
From a reliability standpoint, 1993 and later models are much
improved, with problems affecting mostly the electronic and electrical
system, body hardware, fit and finish, suspension, and air conditioning.

Dealer service bulletins: 1995—A high effort to shift into gear in cold,
wet weather; high shift effort into Reverse. • A 3–2 downshift flare and
erratic downshifting with the automatic transmission. • Starter clicks
but won't start engine. • Front brake pulsation. • A low-voltage reading
or dim lights at idle. • Right-hand wiper blade chatter • Excessive radio
static. • Door glass scratches. • Poor paint application. **1996**—Oil leaks
between the intake manifold and engine block. • 3–2 part throttle
downshift flare and delayed transmission engagement. • Transmission
fluid leak from pump body (replace bushing). • Steering column noise.
• Radio frequency interference diagnosis. • Low-voltage reading or dim
lights at idle. • Door trim armrest lid hard to open. • Water leak diagnostic guide. • Condensation on exterior light. **1997**—Air temperature
from HVAC outlets doesn't change. • Erratic fuel gauge readings. •
Low-voltage reading or dim lights at idle. • Hatch won't pop up when
activated in cold weather. • Water drips into rear compartment.

Safety summary/Recalls: Recalls: 1988–89—The rear wheel tie-rod
end could fracture. GM will replace any defective tie-rod assembly
free of charge. **1990**—Inoperative parking brakes will get a new brake
lever assembly. • The fuel feed and return line connectors may leak
fuel. **1992–93**—Power-steering hose leakage may cause an engine
compartment fire.

Secret Warranties/Service Tips

All models/years—A rotten-egg odor coming from the exhaust is probably caused by a defective catalytic converter, which may be covered by the
emissions warranty. • Clearcoat paint degradation, whitening, and chalking, long a problem with GM's other cars, is also a serious problem with
the fiberglass-bodied Corvette, says DSB #331708. It too is covered by a
secret warranty for up to six years. **All models: 1982–91**—Hydramatic
4L60/700R4 automatic transmission may have no upshift or appear to be
stuck in first gear. The probable cause is a worn governor gear. It would be
wise to replace the retaining ring as well. **1982–93**—Vehicles equipped
with a Hydramatic 4L60 transmission that "buzzes" when the car is in
Reverse or idle may need a new oil pressure regulator valve. **1987–89**—
Revised cylinder head gaskets provide better sealing (DSB #89-283-6A).
1990–91—Engine wiring short circuits may be caused by an abraded electrical harness at the mounting clamp just below the oil pressure sensor.

1992—5.7L engines may develop leaks at the oil filter area. GM Campaign 92COS has covered the repair cost in the past. • 5.7L engines may backfire excessively when shifting from first to second gear with the throttle wide open. Correct by changing the MEMCAL module. • Oil leaks from the rear of a 5.7L engine may be caused by insufficient sealing around the camshaft plug. Replace the plug and reseal. **1992–96**—Oil leaks between the intake manifold and engine block are most often caused by insufficient RTV bonding between the intake manifold and cylinder block. **1994**—Excessive oil consumption is likely due to delaminated intake manifold gaskets. Install an upgraded intake manifold gasket kit. • Delayed automatic transmission shift engagement is a common problem, and is addressed in DSB #47-71-20A. **1995–96**—Delayed automatic transmission shift engagement may require the replacement of the pump cover assembly. **1997**—Correcting water leaks into the rear compartment. • Inadequate heating, defrosting. • Correcting drivebelt noise.

Corvette Profile

	1991	1992	1993	1994	1995	1996	1997	1998
Cost Price ($)								
Base	33,999	35,270	36,230	37,345	37,955	38,400	38,365	38,365
Convertible	40,305	41,780	42,830	44,120	44,835	46,235	—	45,295
ZR-1	64,668	72,378	66,828	67,993	68,603	—	—	—
Used Values ($)								
Base ↑	13,500	15,000	17,000	19,000	21,000	25,000	35,000	39,000
Base ↓	11,500	13,500	15,000	17,000	19,000	22,500	33,000	36,000
Convertible ↑	15,500	17,500	19,500	22,000	25,500	28,000	—	41,000
Convertible ↓	13,500	18,000	17,500	19,500	22,500	25,000	—	39,000
ZR-1 ↑	27,000	30,000	33,000	36,000	48,000	—	—	—
ZR-1 ↓	24,000	27,000	30,000	33,000	46,000	—	—	—

Extended Warranty	Y	Y	Y	Y	Y	Y	Y	Y
Secret Warranty	N	N	N	Y	Y	Y	Y	N

	1991	1992	1993	1994	1995	1996	1997	1998
Reliability	②	②	②	③	③	④	④	④
Air conditioning	②	②	②	③	③	③	③	④
Body integrity	②	②	②	②	②	②	②	③
Braking system	②	②	②	②	②	②	③	③
Electrical system	②	②	②	②	②	②	③	④
Engines	②	②	③	③	③	③	③	④
Exhaust/Converter	②	②	②	③	③	④	④	⑤
Fuel system	②	②	②	②	②	③	③	④
Ignition system	②	②	②	②	②	③	④	⑤
Manual transmission	②	②	③	③	③	④	④	⑤
- automatic	②	②	②	②	③	③	③	③
Rust/Paint	②	②	②	②	③	③	③	④
Steering	②	②	②	③	③	④	④	④
Suspension	②	②	②	②	②	③	④	④

Note: The Corvette hasn't been crash-tested.

HONDA

Prelude

Rating: Recommended (1993–98); Above Average (1985–92).
Maintenance/Repair costs: Average. Repairs aren't dealer dependent.
To avoid costly engine repairs, check the engine timing belt every
2 years/30,000 miles and replace it every 60,000 miles ($300). **Parts:**
Higher-than-average cost, but independent suppliers sell parts for
much less.

Strengths and weaknesses: Unimpressive as a high-performance sports
car, the Prelude instead delivers a stylish exterior, legendary reliability,
and excellent resale value.

The 1978–87 first-generation Preludes were described as luxury,
sporty cars, but didn't offer much of either. They should be inspected
carefully for engine problems and severe underbody corrosion, particularly near the fuel tank. Noisy front brakes, premature disc warpage,
high oil consumption, and worn engine crankshaft/camshaft lobes are
the main problem areas with these models. They're also prone to
extensive rusting around wheel openings, door bottoms, the trunk lid,
fenders, rear taillights, bumper supports, chassis members, suspension
components, and the fuel tank.

The 1988–91 models offer more and smoother engine power, excellent handling, and improved reliability. There are some generic complaints that continue to crop up, including rapid front brake wear,
scored and warped front brake rotors, automatic transmission failure,
defective constant velocity joints, premature exhaust system rust-out,
and a warping hood.

The 1992–96 models are shorter, wider, and heavier. They're not very
fast. The four-wheel steering found on the 1992 4WS version is more
gimmick than anything else. It was dropped after 1994. The automatic
transmission is smoother, although it still saps some of the Prelude's
power. Both the rear seating and tiny trunk are inadequate for most
people. You can expect fewer but all-too-familiar glitches, including
minor electrical problems, body and accessory defects, brake squealing,
and prematurely warped front brake rotors. Most independent mechanics are ill equipped to service these cars because Preludes have become
increasingly complicated to repair.

The year for big Prelude changes was 1997. The car was restyled,
repowered, and given handling upgrades that make it a better performing, more comfortably riding sports coupe: an additional five horses
for the base 2.2L VTEC engine, a new Automatic Torque Transfer
System (ATTS), an upgraded suspension, standard ABS, air conditioning, 16-inch wheels, and a CD player with six speakers. The Sequential
SportShift automatic transmission (a variation of the one used in the
NSX) equips the base Prelude. Overall, the car is roomier (the

extended wheelbase gives added stability and provides more room in the rear seating area), has a more solid body structure, and includes a totally redesigned, user-friendly dash with analogue gauges.

Owners report that air conditioner condensers frequently fail after a few years and often need cleaning to eliminate disagreeable odors. Other problems include minor electrical glitches, brake squealing, and prematurely warped front brake rotors. A host of new technical features adds to the Prelude's complexity and guarantees that you'll never stray far from the dealer's service bay. In fact, most corner mechanics are poorly equipped to service these cars and the Automatic Torque Transfer System (ATTS) won't make their job any easier. Parts are a bit more expensive than for other cars in this class.

Dealer service bulletins: 1993—Poor radio reception on the AM band. • Excessive steering wheel vibrations. • CD changer in trunk won't eject. • Noisy window regulators. **1994**—Buzzing in the driver's door. • Cup holders that don't stay closed. • Fuel filler doors that won't stay open. • Noise from the driver's seat track. • Steering wheel shimmy continues to be a problem. **1995**—Creaking clutch pedal. • A jingling in the left side of the dashboard. • A slow-to-retract seatbelt. • A warped console. **1996**—Headliner rattles. • The seatbelt is slow to retract.

Safety summary/Recalls: Recalls: 1978-85—Severe chassis corrosion around fuel tank and body seams prompted Honda to provide free chassis repairs and replace suspension/steering components and fuel tanks under a "silent" recall campaign. **1983-87**—Road salt could cause the fuel filler and/or breather pipe to rust through, resulting in leaks. A recall campaign has been organized to fix this defect. **1986-91**—Takata seatbelt replacement. **1988**—Corroded coil spring breakage could cause loss of control. • Power-steering hose leaks could cause a fire.

Secret Warranties/Service Tips

All models/years—Steering wheel shimmy can be reduced by rebalancing the wheel/tire/hub/rotor assembly in the front end. • Seatbelts that fail to function properly during normal use will be replaced for free under Honda's lifetime seatbelt warranty. • Honda will also repair or replace defective steering assemblies, constant velocity joints, and catalytic converters free of charge up to 5 years/80,000 km on a case-by-case basis. There's no labor charge or deductible. Used vehicles and repairs carried out by independent garages aren't covered by this special program. The converter is almost always covered under the emissions warranty. • Most Honda DSBs allow for special warranty consideration on a "goodwill" basis for most problems even after the warranty has expired or the car has changed hands. **All models: 1988-93**—Poor AM reception or popping from the speakers is likely due to a poor ground connection between the antenna collar and car body. Correct the reception by improving the ground connection and tightening the antenna assembly mounting nuts in the proper sequence. • Creaking from the window regulator can be corrected by installing an upgraded regulator spiral spring. **1990**—Defective AC compressor pickup sensors are a common problem. **1992**—A rattle from the front of the car that occurs when driving over rough surfaces but goes away when brakes are lightly applied can be corrected by installing new front brake pad retainers. **1994–96**—Silence rear headliner rattling by applying EPT sealer 5T to the rear headliner where it contacts the wiring harness.

Prelude Profile

	1991	1992	1993	1994	1995	1996	1997	1998
Cost Price ($)								
Base/S	15,955	16,540	17,330	18,450	19,930	20,340	23,595	23,695
Used Values ($)								
Base/S ↑	8,000	9,500	10,500	11,500	13,500	15,000	17,000	20,500
Base/S ↓	6,500	8,000	9,000	10,000	12,000	13,500	15,000	18,500
Extended Warranty	N	N	N	N	N	N	N	N
Secret Warranty	N	N	N	N	N	N	N	N
Reliability	⑤	⑤	⑤	⑤	⑤	⑤	⑤	⑤
Air conditioning	③	③	③	④	⑤	⑤	⑤	⑤
Body integrity	③	③	③	③	③	③	③	④
Braking system	❷	③	③	③	③	③	④	⑤
Electrical system	❷	❷	③	③	④	④	④	⑤
Engines	③	③	④	⑤	⑤	⑤	⑤	⑤
Exhaust/Converter	❷	③	⑤	⑤	⑤	⑤	⑤	⑤
Fuel system	④	④	④	④	⑤	⑤	⑤	⑤
Ignition system	④	④	⑤	⑤	⑤	⑤	⑤	⑤
Manual transmission	⑤	⑤	⑤	⑤	⑤	⑤	⑤	⑤
- automatic	③	③	④	⑤	⑤	⑤	⑤	⑤
Rust/Paint	③	❷	③	③	④	⑤	⑤	⑤
Steering	❷	❷	③	③	③	③	④	④
Suspension	③	③	④	⑤	⑤	⑤	⑤	⑤
Crash Safety	❶	④	④	—	—	—	—	—

HYUNDAI

Scoupe

Rating: Above Average (1995); Below Average (1991–94). An Excel cross-dressing as a sports car. **Maintenance/Repair costs:** Higher than average, although most repairs can be done by any independent garage. **Parts:** Higher-than-average cost, with limited availability, due partly to the discontinuation of the model after '95.

Strengths and weaknesses: This is essentially a cute coupe with an engine more suited to high gas mileage than hard driving. Except for its lighter weight, less luggage space, and shorter overall length, the Scoupe is really an Excel clone, and there are better performing and more reliable sports coupes available. Plenty of interior room up front, but the roof is too angular; if you're short and have to pull the seat up, your head almost touches the roof. The rear interior room is inadequate. The Scoupe is fuel efficient and has a good heating and ventilation system.

This is far from a performance car, mainly due to the Excel's under-pinnings and drivetrain. The 4-speed automatic transmission robs the base engine of much-needed horsepower, making for poor acceleration on inclines and constant shifting between 2500 rpms and 3500 rpms when pushed. Suspension may be too firm for some. There's plenty of body roll in turns, and mediocre steering. Brakes are hard to modulate.

Customer service has improved, if only because dealers have more factory support. Body construction is sloppy, giving rise to wind/water leaks, rattles, and breakage. Lots of engine and road noise intrude into the interior. Owners also report frequent electrical system shorts and brake and wheel bearing problems.

Dealer service bulletins: 1993—Engine has difficulty reaching recommended operating temperature (MPI fault code #21), low fuel pressure, and possible fuel leak at fuel gauge connection valve. • Harsh shifting with the automatic transmission when accelerating or coming to a stop. • Excessive disc brake noise. **1994**—Starting difficulties. • Transmission glitches. • AC failures. • Noisy shock absorbers and radio malfunctions. **1995**—Automatic transmission won't engage Overdrive. • Exhaust system releases a rotten-egg odor. • Rear suspension squeaks. • Trunk water leaks. • Troubleshooting tips for locating and plugging other interior water leaks.

Safety summary/Recalls: 1994—Vehicle suddenly accelerated and would not shut off when key was taken from the ignition. • Airbag failed to deploy. • Complete brake failure. • Loss of power steering when turning. • Idle speed control module failure caused erratic idling along with acceleration and deceleration problems. • While car is being driven at high speeds, the transmission slips into Neutral without warning. • Driver's seat doesn't lock into place. • Seatback collapsed when vehicle was rear-ended. • Cylinder head failures. • Check Engine light comes on for no reason. • Leaky shock absorbers. • Wiper blades don't clean windshield properly. **1995**—Corrosion caused the front inner tie-rod to break, allowing the wheel to fall inward.

Secret Warranties/Service Tips

All models/years—An automatic transmission that won't engage Overdrive may need the oil temperature sensor replaced or may have faulty wiring or a defective Transmission Control Module. **All models: 1991**—Stalling when shifting into gear immediately after starting a cold engine may be corrected by installing a Cold Start Enrichment Kit (#39901-24Q00D). **1991–92**—A difficult-to-engage Reverse gear needs an upgraded part. • A harsh shift when coming to a stop or upon acceleration may be due to a misadjusted accelerator switch TCU. **1992–94**—Hyundai has a field fix for manual transaxle gear clash/grind (DSB #9440-004). **1993–94**—Hyundai has also developed an improved spark plug (painted yellow on the tip) for better cold-weather starting. **1994**—Hyundai may replace the AC discharge hose for free under a special service campaign (DSB #94-01-010).

Scoupe Profile

	1991	1992	1993	1994	1995
Cost Price ($)					
Base	10,030	10,569	10,879	11,409	11,905
LS/GLS	10,815	11,174	11,414	11,889	12,735
Used Values ($)					
Base ↑	2,900	3,500	4,500	5,500	6,500
Base ↓	2,200	3,000	3,500	4,500	5,500
LS/GLS ↑	3,500	4,200	5,000	6,000	7,000
LS/GLS ↓	3,000	3,000	4,000	5,000	6,000
Extended Warranty	Y	Y	Y	Y	Y
Secret Warranty	N	N	N	N	N
Reliability	②	②	②	②	③
Air conditioning	②	②	④	④	④
Automatic transmission	②	②	②	②	③
Body integrity	②	②	②	②	③
Braking system	②	②	②	②	②
Electrical system	②	②	②	②	②
Engines	④	④	④	④	⑤
Exhaust/Converter	⑤	⑤	⑤	⑤	⑤
Fuel system	③	③	③	③	④
Ignition system	②	②	②	③	④
Rust/Paint	②	②	②	③	③
Steering	③	③	③	③	④
Suspension	③	③	③	④	④
Crash Safety	④	④	④	④	④

Tiburon

Rating: Above Average (1997–98). A high performance Elantra. Keep in mind that for about $1,000 more you can get the better performing FX model. **Maintenance/Repair costs:** Higher than average, although most repairs can be done by any independent garage. **Parts:** Higher-than-average cost with limited availability.

Strengths and weaknesses: This is a fun-to-drive, reasonably sporty car that's based on the Elantra sedan. Although it's too early to have a definitive opinion, overall reliability looks promising. The Tiburon is a credible alternative to the Ford Probe, Nissan 200SX, Mitsubishi Eclipse, or Toyota Celica. The base 16-valve 1.8L 4-cylinder engine is smooth, efficient, and adequate when mated to the 5-speed manual transmission. Put in an automatic transmission and performance heads south, and engine noise increases proportionally. Overall handling is crisp and predictable, due mainly to the Tiburon's long wheelbase and sophisticated suspension.

The FX gets the more sprightly 2.0L engine along with optional ABS. Standard brakes are adequate though sometimes difficult to modulate. As with most sporty cars, interior room is cramped for average-sized occupants. Tall drivers, especially, might find rearward seat travel insufficient, making head room a bit tight.

Although no serious defects have been reported, be on the lookout for body deficiencies (fit, finish, and assembly), harsh shifting with the automatic transmission, oil leaks, and minor brake glitches.

Dealer service bulletins: 1997—Automatic transmission won't engage Overdrive. • Clutch pedal squeaking. • Tapping noise coming from the passenger-side dash panel/engine compartment area. • Exhaust system buzz. • Improved shifting into all gears. • Improved shifting into Reverse. • Clutch drag.

Safety summary/recalls: Recalls: 1997—A faulty wiper motor will be replaced.

Secret Warranties/Service Tips

All models/years—Hyundai has a new brake pad kit (#58101-28A00) that the company says will eliminate squeaks and squeals during light brake application. Hyundai also suggests that you replace the oil pump assembly if the engine rpm increases as the automatic transmission engages abruptly during a cold start. **1997**—A tip on eliminating clutch pedal squeaking is offered. • Tips on eliminating clutch drag are offered.

Tiburon Profile

	1997	1998
Cost Price ($)		
Base	15,609	16,217
FX	17,539	17,717
Used Values ($)		
Base ↑	9,500	11,000
Base ↓	8,000	9,500
FX ↑	10,500	12,000
FX ↓	9,000	10,500
Extended Warranty	N	N
Secret Warranty	N	N

Reliability	④	⑤
Air conditioning	⑤	⑤
Automatic transmission	③	③
Body integrity	③	③
Braking system	③	③
Electrical system	③	③
Engines	⑤	⑤
Exhaust/Converter	⑤	⑤
Ignition system	⑤	⑤
Rust/Paint	⑤	⑤
Steering	⑤	⑤
Suspension	⑤	⑤

Note: The Tiburon hasn't been crash-tested.

MAZDA

MX-3 Precidia

Rating: Recommended (1994–95); Above Average (1992–93).
Maintenance/Repair costs: Higher than average, and most repairs have
to be done by a Mazda dealer. **Parts:** Higher-than-average cost, with limited availability. Mazda has promised to reduce parts prices.

Strengths and weaknesses: The base 1.6L engine supplies plenty of
power for most driving situations. When equipped with the optional
1.8L V6 powerplant (the smallest V6 on the market at the time) and
high-performance options, the MX-3 Precidia transforms itself into a
130-hp pocket rocket. In fact, the MX-3 Precidia GS sports coupe easily
outperforms the 4-cylinder Honda del Sol, Toyota Paseo, and Geo
Storm for comfort and high performance thrills. It does fall a bit short
of the Saturn SC due to its limited low-end torque, and fuel economy
is disappointing. Reverse gear is sometimes hard to engage.

Brake and wheel bearing problems are commonplace. Most of the
MX-3 Precidia's parts are used on other Mazda cars, so their overall
reliability should be outstanding.

Body assembly is average and rattles/squeaks are common. Owners
have complained of paint defects and sheet metal that's too thin above
the door handles (dents in the metal appear where you would ordinarily place your thumb when closing the door). Some owners report
wind and water leaks around the doors and windows. Moderate engine
noise increases dramatically above 60 mph.

Small door openings are a hardship for tall occupants when entering and exiting. Steering wheel rubs against thighs even when the seat
is pushed as far back as it will go. Rear head room and leg room are limited. A high beltline and cowl add to the claustrophobic feeling. The
trunk has a high liftover.

Dealer service bulletins: 1995—Complaints about shift feel. • Brake pulsation troubleshooting tips. • Heater and AC unit noise after long storage. • Breakage of luggage compartment hinge holder. • A slightly off-center steering wheel.

Safety summary/Recalls: The car's tendency to under-steer can be unnerving when taking corners at moderate speed. **Recalls: 1990–91**—Malfunctioning automatic shoulder belts will be replaced, gratis.

Secret Warranties/Service Tips

All models/years—DSB #006/94 gives all of the possible causes and remedies for brake vibrations. **All models: 1992**—A front-end snapping noise during tight turns at walking speed is probably caused by excessive clearance between the wheel bearing and steering knuckle. Install modified wheel bearings. • Idle fluctuation when applying an electrical load during idle, or after deceleration from a high rpm, can be corrected by installing a new Electronic Control Unit. • Poor AC performance may be due to insufficient airflow across the AC condenser. • A noisy rear hatch can be silenced by changing the rear hatch glass, hinge, or molding. • Squeaking noise from the rear pillars is due to interference between the rear inner pillar and its reinforcement. • A sulfur odor coming from the exhaust can be eliminated by installing an upgraded catalytic converter. **1992–94**—Freezing door and hatch lock cylinders are addressed in DSB #021/94. • Clutch squealing can be silenced by installing an upgraded part with a thicker clutch cushioning plate. **1994**—Timing belt noise can be silenced by replacing the tensioner pulley with an upgraded part.

MX-3 Precidia Profile

	1992	1993	1994	1995
Cost Price ($)				
Base	12,630	13,055	14,840	15,780
GS	15,430	15,825	17,340	—
Used Values ($)				
Base ↑	5,000	5,500	6,500	7,500
Base ↓	4,000	5,000	5,500	6,500
GS ↑	6,000	7,000	8,000	—
GS ↓	5,000	6,000	6,500	—
Extended Warranty	N	N	N	N
Secret Warranty	N	N	N	N
Reliability	③	③	④	⑤
Air conditioning	❷	③	③	④
Automatic transmission	③	④	⑤	⑤
Body integrity	❷	❷	④	④
Braking system	❷	❷	❷	❷
Electrical system	❷	❷	❷	❷

Engines	⑤	⑤	⑤	⑤
Exhaust/Converter	③	④	④	⑤
Fuel system	⑤	⑤	⑤	⑤
Ignition system	⑤	⑤	⑤	⑤
Rust/Paint	③	③	④	⑤
Steering	⑤	⑤	⑤	⑤
Suspension	③	③	⑤	⑤
Crash Safety	③	③	—	—

MX-5 Miata

Rating: Recommended (1996–98); Above Average (1990–95). The 1998 version is merely a carryovered 1997. **Maintenance/Repair costs:** Higher than average, and dealer dependent. **Parts:** Higher-than-average cost, with limited availability (save money with an aftermarket gel battery).

Strengths and weaknesses: The base 1.6L engine delivers adequate power and accelerates smoothly with a top speed of 115 mph. Acceleration from 0 to 60 mph is in the high 8-second range. The 5-speed manual transmission shifts easily and has well-spaced gears. The vehicle's lightness and 50/50 weight distribution make this an easy car to toss around corners, but it's quite jittery on uneven roads.

Owners' top gripes target the same characteristics that make other sports car enthusiasts swoon: inadequate cargo space, cramped interior for large adults, excessive interior noise, and limited low-end torque, which makes for frequent shifting.

Owners also say it's important to change the engine timing chain every 60,000 miles. Other reported problems: 1990–91 model crankshaft failures, leaky rear end seals and valve cover gaskets, torn drive boots, electrical system glitches, brake pulsation, valvetrain clatter on start-up (changing oil may help), prematurely worn-out shock absorbers and catalytic converter, a leaking or squeaky clutch, and minor body and trim deficiencies.

Dealer service bulletins: 1995—Brake pulsation troubleshooting tips. • Clutch release bearing squeal. • Steering wheel may be off-center. • Clogged side sill drain holes. • Heater unit noise after long storage. **1996**—Brake pulsation repair. • Side sill paint damage from scuff plate. **1997**—Brake pulsation repair.

Safety summary/Recalls: Eighty percent of used Miatas are estimated to have some collision damage. Check your choice before signing the contract. **1995–96**—Inadvertent airbag deployment. • Engine and horn failure. • Roof leaks. • Accelerator pedal cut a slit in the carpet, allowing the gas pedal to jam. **Recalls: 1990–93**—The optional hardtop's hoist accessory kit may have plastic buckles that break and allow the hardtop to suddenly fall. **1991**—Faulty ABS.

Secret Warranties/Service Tips

All models/years—DSB #006/94 gives all of the possible causes and remedies for brake vibration. **All models: 1990**—A hard-to-close trunk lid requires an upgraded rubber cushion (#B48156786). • Poor AC performance is likely caused by the misalignment of the AC harness. • A rattling noise coming from the exhaust manifold may require the replacement of the insulator bracket. • Water may damage door speakers unless a speaker cover assembly (#B4Y5 7696X) is installed. • A musty odor coming from the AC system can be cured by installing an upgraded resin-coated evaporator core (#NA0J 61II0A). **1990–91**—Hard shifting into second gear before the vehicle has warmed up can be corrected by installing an upgraded second gear synchronizer ring and clutch hub sleeve (#JM1NA351-M-232720). **1990–95**—Dirt and debris can clog up side sill drain holes, allowing water to collect and corrosion to occur. Drill larger drain holes. **1992–94**—If the window won't open fully, install a new cable fastener. **1994**—Timing belt noise can be silenced by replacing the tensioner pulley with an upgraded part.

MX-5 Miata Profile

	1991	1992	1993	1994	1995	1996	1997	1998
Cost Price ($)								
Base	14,499	15,150	15,650	17,045	17,940	18,900	20,775	21,000
Used Values ($)								
Base ↑	6,500	8,000	9,000	10,000	11,000	12,000	14,000	17,000
Base ↓	5,000	7,000	8,000	9,000	10,000	11,000	12,000	15,500
Extended Warranty	N	N	N	N	N	N	N	N
Secret Warranty	N	N	N	N	N	N	N	N
Reliability	④	④	④	④	④	⑤	⑤	⑤
Air conditioning	④	④	④	⑤	⑤	⑤	⑤	⑤
Body integrity	❷	❷	③	③	③	④	④	④
Braking system	❷	❷	③	③	④	④	⑤	⑤
Electrical system	❷	❷	❷	③	③	④	④	④
Engines	❷	❷	③	④	④	⑤	⑤	⑤
Exhaust/Converter	④	④	④	④	④	④	⑤	⑤
Fuel system	③	④	④	⑤	⑤	⑤	⑤	⑤
Ignition system	❷	❷	③	③	③	④	④	④
Manual transmission	⑤	⑤	⑤	⑤	⑤	⑤	⑤	⑤
Rust/Paint	❷	❷	③	③	③	④	④	⑤
Steering	⑤	⑤	⑤	⑤	⑤	⑤	⑤	⑤
Suspension	⑤	⑤	⑤	⑤	⑤	⑤	⑤	⑤
Crash Safety	③	③	③	—	—	④	④	—

RX-7

Rating: Recommended (1991–95); Above Average (1985–90). There was no 1992 model. **Maintenance/Repair costs:** Higher than average, and most repairs have to be done by a Mazda dealer. **Parts:** Higher-than-average cost, with limited availability. Parts shortage may become chronic now that the RX-7 has been discontinued.

Strengths and weaknesses: The RX-7 is an impressive performer that goes from 0 to 60 mph in 8 seconds and covers the same distance in 6.2 seconds when equipped with a turbocharger. The ride can be painful on bad roads, though, due primarily to the car's stiff suspension. The GSL and Turbo models are very well equipped and luxuriously finished. Except for some oil-burning problems, apex seal failures, and leaking engine O-rings, the RX-7 has served to dispel any doubts concerning the durability of rotary engines.

Nevertheless, careful maintenance is in order, since contaminated oil or overheating will easily damage the rotary engine. Clutches wear quickly if used hard. Disc brakes need frequent attention paid to the calipers and rotors. The MacPherson struts get soft more quickly than average. AC malfunctions and fuel, exhaust system, and electrical glitches are also common. Be wary of leaky sunroofs. Radiators have a short life span. Rocker panels and body seams are prone to more serious rusting. The underbody on older cars should be inspected carefully for corrosion damage. Fuel economy has never been this car's strong suit.

Age has improved the RX-7's reliability. In fact, dealer service bulletins list only two possible problems with the 1995 RX-7: AC unit noise after long storage and a slightly off-center steering wheel. The Mazda RX-7 Lemon Site on the Internet (*scuderiaciriani.com/rx7/lemon_site/sources.htm*) is a treasure trove of maintenance tips, common defects, copies of service bulletins and good specific buying and selling information.

Safety summary/Recalls: 1995—Wide tires compromise the car's stopping ability in the rain. One driver's RX-7 slipped off the highway and hit a tree. **Recalls: 1979–83**—Idler arms may corrode, freeze, or break after prolonged exposure to road salt. **1986–87**—Road salt may also cause excessive front brake disc pad liner corrosion. **1989–91**—Shoulder belts may fail. **1991–95**—Fuel hoses may crack and leak fuel. • Poor braking after an overnight park is caused by engine oil mist clogging the brake vacuum check valve. **1993–94**—Engine heat could make fuel hoses deteriorate and leak prematurely, posing a fire hazard.

Secret Warranties/Service Tips

All models/years—DSB #006/94 gives all of the possible causes and remedies for brake vibration. **All models: 1985–91**—Hard shifting into second gear before the vehicle has warmed up can be corrected by installing an upgraded second gear synchronizer ring and clutch hub sleeve

(#JM1NA351-M-232720). **1986–88**—A hard-to-start cold engine can be fixed by switching to air gap spark plugs and disconnecting the sub-zero starting assist device. • Misfire and hesitation over 6000 rpm can be corrected by installing an upgraded air flow meter. • A rough idle may be caused by a short circuit in the water temperature switch wiring. • Erratic power window operation may require a new regulator guide assembly, motor bracket, and sprocket. **1987–88**—Turbo models with a rough idle or cold-starting problems may need a new air control valve (#N332 13990). **1993–94**—To eliminate slipping clutch problems, Mazda may install, at no charge, an improved clutch disc.

RX-7 Profile

	1988	1989	1990	1991	1992	1993	1994	1995
Cost Price ($)								
RX-7	17,938	19,178	19,768	20,799	—	—	—	—
Convertible	22,668	27,478	28,418	29,199	—	—	—	—
Turbo	23,509	26,219	26,809	28,149	—	32,850	36,395	37,950
Used Values ($)								
RX-7 ↑	4,000	4,500	5,500	6,000	—	—	—	—
RX-7 ↓	3,500	4,000	4,500	5,000	—	—	—	—
Convertible ↑	6,500	7,500	8,500	9,500	—	—	—	—
Convertible ↓	5,500	6,500	7,500	8,500	—	—	—	—
Turbo ↑	6,000	7,000	8,000	9,500	—	15,000	18,000	20,500
Turbo ↓	5,000	5,500	6,500	7,500	—	13,500	16,000	18,500
Extended Warranty	Y	Y	Y	Y	Y	Y	Y	Y
Secret Warranty	N	N	N	N	N	Y	Y	N
Reliability	③	③	④	⑤	⑤	⑤	⑤	⑤
Air conditioning	❷	❷	③	③	③	③	③	③
Body integrity	③	③	③	③	③	③	④	⑤
Braking system	❷	❷	③	③	③	③	③	③
Electrical system	❷	❷	❷	❷	③	③	③	③
Engines	⑤	⑤	⑤	⑤	⑤	⑤	⑤	⑤
Exhaust/Converter	③	③	③	④	⑤	⑤	⑤	⑤
Fuel system	③	⑤	⑤	⑤	⑤	⑤	⑤	⑤
Ignition system	③	③	③	④	⑤	⑤	⑤	⑤
Manual transmission	③	③	③	④	④	④	④	⑤
- automatic	❷	❷	❷	③	③	③	④	⑤
Rust/Paint	❷	❷	③	④	⑤	⑤	⑤	⑤
Steering	④	④	④	⑤	⑤	⑤	⑤	⑤
Suspension	❷	③	④	⑤	⑤	⑤	⑤	⑤
Crash Safety	❷	—	—	—	—	—	—	—

NISSAN

200SX

Rating: Above Average, if you're not a real high-performance enthusiast (1995–98). The '98 SE-R offered standard AC and ABS in addition
to its peppy 140-hp 2.0L engine. **Maintenance/Repair costs:** Average,
and most repairs can be done by any garage. **Parts:** Reasonably priced,
but hard to find.

Strengths and weaknesses: Nissan calls this front-drive compact their
sporty coupe class leader, but the 200SX is merely a Chrysler Neon
fighter that has a sports car flair without the substance. The interior is
unnecessarily cramped, and you get only average power and handling
with the base powerplant. Later models are much sportier and have
more passenger room. Prices are reasonable, though, and the repair
history for these cars is average.

   All engines have performed reasonably well, although the SE-R's
2.0L has been the most suitable for hard-driving thrills. The clutch has
been the source of some complaints, along with occasional electrical
malfunctions. Rapid front brake wear and rotor damage are common
problems. Body construction is much better than average.

Dealer service bulletins: 1995—AC system shuts off. • AC compressor
leakage. • Brake noise. • Cold-weather starting tips. • C-pillar finisher
lifting. • Engine cranks but won't start. • Front window misalignment.
• Fuel gauge not indicating full tank. • Horn activates randomly. •
Squeak and rattle troubleshooting tips. • Wind noise field fix procedure. • Windshield cracking may be covered under the warranty.
1996—Engine cranks but won't start or is hard to start. • Squeak and
rattle repair.

Safety summary/Recalls: 1996—Inadvertent airbag deployment. •
Dual airbags failed to deploy. • Airbag indicator and Check Engine
lights come on intermittently for no reason. • Shoulder seatbelt retractors lock up whenever occupant makes the slightest movement. •
Clutch makes grinding, chattering noise when fully depressed. • When
the weather turns cold, the emergency brake freezes and won't release.
• Faulty sunroof. **Recalls: 1995**—On vehicles with ABS, the hydraulic
actuator may malfunction, increasing the stopping distance.

Secret Warranties/Service Tips

All models/years—DSB #006/94 gives all of the possible causes and remedies for brake vibration. • 1994 and earlier models equipped with RE4RO1A
transmissions may experience repeated planetary failure due to poor cooler
flow in the fin-type cooler. Apparently, cooler line flushing machines can't
flush clear this type of cooler. In the past, the entire radiator would need to

be replaced to upgrade the cooling system. Nissan now has a spiral cooler replacement kit (#21606-15V25) that can be used instead.

200SX Profile

	1995	1996	1997	1998
Cost Price ($)				
Base	13,874	14,303	14,418	14,638
Used Values ($)				
Base ↑	7,000	8,000	9,000	10,000
Base ↓	6,000	7,000	8,000	9,000
Extended Warranty	N	N	N	N
Secret Warranty	N	N	N	N
Reliability	⑤	⑤	⑤	⑤
Crash Safety	—	—	⑤	—

240SX

Rating: Recommended (1995–98); Above Average (1989–94). Only the convertible version was carried over in 1994. **Maintenance/Repair costs:** Average. Most repairs can be done by any garage. **Parts:** Reasonably priced and easy to find.

Strengths and weaknesses: Although this rear-drive sport coupe carried a 2.4L 4-cylinder engine to differentiate it from its 2.0L weaker cousin, the 200SX, it still falls far short of producing high-performance thrills. Its 140-hp base engine provides more than enough torque to handle most driving needs—just don't expect fast acceleration times or a comfortable ride. Handling is impressive, though, thanks to the car's independent suspension. The redesigned 1995 coupe features a longer wheelbase, 15 additional horses, and optional ABS/traction control. It still provides a harsh ride and poor traction on slippery roadways. Head room remains limited, cargo space is practically nil, and the trunk is barely large enough to carry your lunch—as long as you eat light and can fit it through the small opening.

This car doesn't have any serious shortcomings apart from a cramped interior and excessive engine noise. The few deficiencies reported concern electrical malfunctions, early AC burnout, premature clutch wear, noisy brakes that wear out quickly, exhaust system rust-out, and fit and finish deficiencies.

Dealer service bulletins: 1995—Engine overheating and poor driveability (Code 45). • AC compressor leaks or is noisy. • Excessive brake noise. • Particular windshield cracks are covered under warranty. **1996**—Engine cranks, but won't start.

Safety summary/Recalls: 1996—ABS brake failure; pedal went to the floor and brakes failed to stop the vehicle. **Recalls: 1989–91**—Takata seatbelt replacement. **1995**—Faulty brake warning light.

Secret Warranties/Service Tips

All models/years—DSB #006/94 gives all of the possible causes and remedies for brake vibration. **All models: 1989**—Doors that won't lock from the outside may need a door rod clip modification. • A special service campaign covers the free replacement of the engine timing belt and tensioner. It's worth a fight for a partial refund. **1989–91**—Starting difficulties can often be traced to a connector not fully seated in the ECU. **1990**—Excessive squeaking from the front brakes can be fixed by increasing the front brake pad chamfer.

240SX Profile

	1991	1992	1993	1994	1995	1996	1997	1998
Cost Price ($)								
Base	15,539	16,495	16,785	25,344	19,758	20,563	20,628	20,648
Used Values ($)								
Base	6,000	7,500	8,500	12,000	13,000	11,500	13,500	15,000
Base	5,000	6,000	7,000	11,000	12,000	10,500	12,500	13,500
Extended Warranty	N	N	N	N	N	N	N	N
Secret Warranty	N	N	N	N	N	N	N	N
Reliability	③	③	③	④	④	⑤	⑤	⑤
Air conditioning	❷	③	④	④	④	⑤	⑤	⑤
Automatic transmission	③	③	③	⑤	⑤	⑤	⑤	⑤
Body integrity	❷	❷	③	③	③	④	④	⑤
Braking system	❷	❷	❷	❷	③	③	④	④
Electrical system	❷	❷	❷	❷	③	③	④	④
Engines	④	④	④	④	⑤	⑤	⑤	⑤
Exhaust/Converter	❷	❷	③	③	③	③	④	⑤
Fuel system	❷	③	③	③	④	④	⑤	⑤
Ignition system	③	③	③	③	④	④	⑤	⑤
Rust/Paint	③	③	③	③	④	④	⑤	⑤
Steering	❷	❷	③	④	④	④	⑤	⑤
Suspension	③	④	④	④	④	⑤	⑤	⑤
Crash Safety	⑤	⑤	⑤	—	③	③	③	—

Note: A high-priced convertible was the only '94 model available.

300ZX

Rating: Above Average (1994–96); Average (1993); Below Average
(1988–92). Nissan's answer to the Corvette, this car has everything:
high-performance capability, a heavy chassis, complicated electronics,
and average depreciation. Turbocharged 1990 and later models are
much faster than previous versions and better overall buys.
Interestingly, the '89 models cost almost half as much as the '90 versions. **Maintenance/Repair costs:** Way higher than average, and only a
Nissan dealer can repair these cars. Just replacing the air cleaner and
spark plugs is a task. Turbocharger repairs can put a big dent in your
wallet, as well. **Parts:** Expensive and hard to find.

Strengths and weaknesses: Now Nissan's talking high performance with
this weighty rear-drive that offers a high degree of luxury equipment
along with a potent 300-hp engine. Traction is poor on slippery surfaces, however, and the rear suspension hits hard when going over
speed bumps.

The complexity of all the bells and whistles on the 300ZX translates
into a lot more problems than you'd experience with either a Mustang
or a Camaro—two cars that have their own reliability problems, but are
far easier and less costly to repair. The best example of this is the electrical system, long a source of recurring, hard-to-diagnose shorts. Fuel-
injectors are a constant problem and lead to poor engine performance.
The manual transmission has been failure-prone, clutches don't last very
long, front and rear brakes are noisy and wear out quickly, and the aluminum wheels are easily damaged by corrosion and road hazards. The
exhaust system is practically biodegradable. The glitzy digital dash with
three odometers and weird spongy/stiff variable shock absorbers are
more gimmicky than practical. Body assembly is mediocre.

Dealer service bulletins: 1995—Poor driveability (Code 45). • The AC
compressor leaks or is noisy. • Excessive brake noise. • Particular windshield cracks are covered under warranty. **1996**—Engine cranks but
won't start.

Safety summary/Recalls: 1996—Vehicle suddenly accelerated uncontrollably. **Recalls: 1979–87**—Nissan will install, at no charge, a shift interlock to prevent sudden acceleration on earlier models, although the
same problem persists on later versions, due to other suspected causes.

Secret Warranties/Service Tips

All models/years—Premature rear brake pad wear may be caused by poorly
adjusted brakes or rusty rear rotors. Rear brake pad kit (#D4060-01P90) will
help to correct the problem. DSB #006/94 gives all of the possible causes
and remedies for brake vibration. • 1994 and earlier models equipped with
RE4RO1A transmissions may experience repeated planetary failure due to

poor cooler flow in the fin-type cooler. Apparently, cooler line flushing machines can't flush clear this type of cooler. In the past, the entire radiator would need to be replaced to upgrade the cooling system. Nissan now has a spiral cooler replacement kit (#21606-15V25) that can be used instead. **All models: 1990**—Clunking when braking in Reverse can be eliminated by installing a retainer on each front brake pad. **1990–91**—Starting difficulties can often be traced to a connector not fully seated in the Electronic Control Unit. **1991**—An automatic transmission that shifts poorly or slips out of gear can be fixed by retorquing the band servo retainer bolts. **1992**—An oil leak from the drive pinion oil seal can be fixed by installing an upgraded seal.

300ZX Profile

	1989	1990	1991	1992	1993	1994	1995	1996
Cost Price ($)								
Base	23,309	28,960	30,175	31,490	30,445	34,080	35,399	37,845
Used Values ($)								
Base ↑	5,000	9,500	11,500	13,000	14,500	17,000	19,000	22,000
Base ↓	4,000	8,500	10,000	11,500	13,000	15,000	17,000	20,000
Extended Warranty	Y	Y	Y	Y	Y	Y	Y	Y
Secret Warranty	N	N	N	N	N	N	N	N
Reliability	②	②	③	④	④	④	④	④
Air conditioning	①	①	③	③	④	④	⑤	⑤
Body integrity	①	①	①	①	①	①	②	③
Braking system	①	①	①	①	①	①	②	②
Electrical system	①	①	①	①	②	②	③	③
Engines	③	③	③	③	③	④	④	⑤
Exhaust/Converter	①	③	③	③	④	④	④	⑤
Fuel system	②	②	③	③	③	③	④	④
Ignition system	②	②	③	③	③	③	④	④
Manual transmission	③	④	④	④	④	⑤	⑤	⑤
- automatic	②	②	③	③	③	④	④	④
Rust/Paint	②	②	③	③	③	④	⑤	⑤
Steering	③	③	③	③	④	④	④	⑤
Suspension	③	③	③	③	④	④	④	⑤
Crash Safety	—	—	③	③	③	—	—	—

TOYOTA

Celica

Rating: Recommended (1995–98); Above Average (1986–94). The 1996 and 1997 models are practically identical; choose the cheapest version. Keep in mind that the GT and GTS have a firmer suspension, a better equipped interior, ABS, and a more sporting feel than do other versions. All handle competently and provide the kind of sporting performance expected from a car of this class. The extra performance in the higher-line versions does come at a price, but this isn't a problem given the high resale value and excellent reliability for which Celicas are known. **Maintenance/Repair costs:** Average, and most repairs can be done at any garage. **Parts:** Reasonably priced and easy to find.

Strengths and weaknesses: The pre-1986 Celicas weren't very sporty. Their excessive weight and soft suspension compromised handling and added a high fuel penalty. With the 1986 make-over, Celicas gained more power and much better handling—especially in the GT and GTS versions—but they're still more show than go, with limited rear passenger room.

Redesigned 1994 models are full of both show and go, with more aerodynamic styling, an enhanced 1.8L that gives more pickup than the ST's 1.6L, and better fuel economy. Among the upgraded models available, smart buyers should choose a used 1994 ST for its more-reasonable price, smooth performance, quiet running, and high fuel economy.

All Celicas offer exceptional reliability and durability. Servicing and repair are straightforward, and parts are easily found. The front-wheel drive series performs very well and hasn't presented any major problems to owners. Prices are high for Celicas in good condition, but some bargains are available with the base ST model.

Owner gripes target the excessive engine noise, limited rear seat room, and inadequate cargo space. Pre-1994 models get the most complaints regarding brakes, electrical problems, AC malfunctions, and premature exhaust wearout. The 1994 models may have a manual transmission that slips out of second gear, and hard starts caused by a faulty air flow meter (#22250-74200). Areas vulnerable to early rusting include rear wheel openings, suspension components, the area surrounding the fuel-filler cap, door bottoms, and trunk or hatchback lids.

Safety summary/Recalls: Even if your vehicle has 4X4 capability, it's imperative that snow tires be fitted in order to avoid dangerous control problems on snow and ice. **1990**—Campaign L03 provides for the free replacement of the instrument panel light control switch. • Faulty airbag inflator. **1996**—Sudden brake failure. • Broken brake caliper bolt. • Clogged up idle control valve makes for hard starts. **Recalls: 1988–89 All-Trac Turbos**—The radiator and coolant will be replaced for free by Toyota.

Secret Warranties/Service Tips

All models/years—Older Toyotas with stalling problems should have the engine checked for excessive carbon buildup on the valves before any more extensive repairs are authorized. • Owner feedback and dealer service managers (who wish to remain anonymous) confirm the existence of Toyota's secret warranty that will pay for replacing front disc brake components that wear out before 2 years/30,000 miles. • The decade-old problem of brake pulsation/vibration is fully outlined and corrective measures are detailed in DSB #BR94-002, issued February 7, 1994. • To reduce front brake squeaks on ABS-equipped vehicles, ask the dealer to install new, upgraded rotors (#43517-32020). **All models: 1986–89**—Reduce excessive engine ping and jerking by installing an upgraded TCCS Electronic Control Unit under the emissions warranty. **1986–91**—Rattling headrests are a common problem addressed in DSB #B091-010.

Celica Profile

	1991	1992	1993	1994	1995	1996	1997	1998
Cost Price ($)								
Base	14,232	15,063	15,983	18,628	19,410	19,638	19,703	20,531
Used Values ($)								
Base ↑	7,000	8,000	9,500	10,500	12,500	14,500	16,500	17,500
Base ↓	5,500	7,000	8,000	9,500	11,500	13,000	15,000	16,500
Extended Warranty	N	N	N	N	N	N	N	N
Secret Warranty	N	N	N	N	Y	Y	Y	Y
Reliability	③	③	④	④	④	⑤	⑤	⑤
Air conditioning	❶	❶	❷	③	③	③	③	④
Body integrity	❷	❷	❷	❷	③	③	⑤	⑤
Braking system	❶	❶	❷	❷	❷	❷	③	③
Electrical system	❶	❶	❶	③	③	④	⑤	⑤
Engines	③	③	③	③	③	③	④	⑤
Exhaust/Converter	❷	❷	❷	❷	③	③	⑤	⑤
Fuel system	④	④	④	④	④	④	④	④
Ignition system	④	④	④	④	④	④	⑤	⑤
Manual transmission	③	④	④	④	④	④	⑤	⑤
- automatic	③	③	③	④	④	④	④	⑤
Rust/Paint	❷	④	④	④	④	④	④	⑤
Steering	④	④	④	④	④	④	⑤	⑤
Suspension	④	④	④	④	④	④	⑤	⑤
Crash Safety	③	③	③	—	—	—	—	—

MR2

Rating: Recommended (1991–93); Above Average (1988–89); Average (1986–87). There was no 1990 model. The best choice is the 1993 model, which had handling and engine performance improved. **Maintenance/Repair costs:** Average. However, most repairs have to be done by a Toyota dealer, and engine repairs can get quite expensive due to the limited access to the engine compartment. **Parts:** Reasonably priced, but not easily found.

Strengths and weaknesses: The MR2 does everything a sports car should, without fuss or surprises. Except for vague steering and some front-end instability, handling is practically flawless. The standard 16-valve 4-cylinder motor is smooth and adequate. The supercharged and turbocharged engines, though overpriced, produce more power than even a sports car driver would want to use. They also have a bit of turbo lag and require deft handling. The engine's placement behind the driver's seat also produces excessive noise and vibration, which make long trips very uncomfortable.

In order of frequency, the most common complaints on all MR2s are as follows: the brakes, electrical glitches, and body hardware (fit and finish) deficiencies.

Safety summary/Recalls: 1993—Seatbelt and airbag failed during accident, resulting in multiple injuries. • Windshield and windows are coated with a fog-like film, reducing visibility.

Secret Warranties/Service Tips

All models/years—Toyota has a secret warranty that will pay for replacing front disc brake components that wear out before 2 years/30,000 miles. • The brake pulsation/vibration problem is fully outlined and corrective measures are detailed in DSB #BR94-002, issued February 7, 1994. **All models: 1991**—Front brake squeal can be reduced by using new anti-squeal springs (#47743-32030). • Sound system interference can be eliminated by changing the alternator.

MR2 Profile

	1988	1989	1991	1992	1993	1994	1995
Cost Price ($)							
Base	13,843	14,848	16,848	17,813	20,208	23,613	24,655
Used Values ($)							
Base ↑	4,000	5,000	6,500	7,500	9,000	13,000	14,500
Base ↓	3,000	4,000	5,500	6,500	7,500	10,500	13,000
Extended Warranty	Y	Y	Y	Y	Y	Y	Y
Secret Warranty	Y	Y	Y	Y	Y	Y	Y

Reliability	③	③	③	③	④	④	④
Air conditioning	❷	❷	③	④	⑤	⑤	⑤
Body integrity	❷	❷	③	③	③	③	③
Braking system	❷	❷	❷	❷	③	③	③
Electrical system	❷	❷	❷	❷	③	③	③
Engines	⑤	⑤	⑤	⑤	⑤	⑤	⑤
Exhaust/Converter	❷	❷	③	③	③	④	⑤
Fuel system	④	④	④	④	④	④	④
Ignition system	③	③	③	③	③	④	④
Manual transmission	③	③	③	③	③	⑤	⑤
- automatic	③	③	④	④	④	④	④
Rust/Paint	③	③	⑤	⑤	⑤	⑤	⑤
Steering	③	③	③	③	③	⑤	⑤
Suspension	③	③	③	③	③	③	③

Note: The MR2 hasn't been crash-tested.

Supra

Rating: Above Average (1995–97); Average (1994); Below Average (1986–93). 1997 was the last model year, although some '97 Supras were recycled as '98s. These are average sports cars that are overpriced and overweight. **Maintenance/Repair costs:** Way higher than average. Only a Toyota dealer can repair these cars. **Parts:** Expensive and frequently back-ordered.

Strengths and weaknesses: This is a nicely styled sports car that has caught the Corvette/Nissan 300ZX malady: cumulative add-ons that drive up the car's price and weight, and drive down its performance and reliability. The 6-cylinder engines are smooth and powerful, when they are running properly. Handling is sure and precise—better than the Celica because of the independent rear suspension. The Supra has limited rear seating, fuel mileage is marginal around town, and insurance premiums are likely to be much higher than average. Owners report major engine problems, frequent rear differential replacements, electrical short circuits, AC malfunctions, and premature brake, suspension, and exhaust system wear. The engine is an oil-burner at times, and cornering is often accompanied by a rear-end growl. Seatbelt guides and the power antenna are failure-prone. Body deficiencies are common.

Safety summary/Recalls: 1994—Sudden acceleration resulting in collision with a tree. • Airbag failed to deploy. • Electrical system retards the timing of the engine, causing extreme lack of power with AC on. • Passenger's window intermittently fails to shut. • Oil-plug drain gasket failure. • Transmission, brake, and AC failures. • Several Michelin tire blowouts. **Recalls:** None that are recent.

Secret Warranties/Service Tips

All models/years—Older Toyotas with stalling problems should have the engine checked for excessive carbon buildup on the valves before any more extensive repairs are authorized. • Toyota will pay for replacing front disc brake components that wear out before 2 years/30,000 miles. • The brake pulsation/vibration problem is fully outlined and corrective measures are detailed in DSB #BR94-002, issued February 7, 1994. **All models: 1985–88**— Starter/ring gear clash can be corrected with an upgraded starter assembly (#28100-62011 or -62021). **1986–88**—Excessive brake squeak and groaning can be reduced by installing revised brake pads (#04491-14240). **1989–90**— Cold driveability and startability is improved with a modified TCCS Electronic Control Unit. **1990–91**—A new front brake pad material is now used (#04491-14280) to improve brake pad durability.

Supra Profile

	1990	1991	1992	1993	1994	1995	1996	1997
Cost Price ($)								
Base	23,875	24,845	25,575	34,225	36,185	31,497	39,020	30,340
Used Values ($)								
Base ↑	7,000	8,500	9,500	11,000	18,000	19,500	23,000	25,500
Base ↓	5,500	7,000	8,500	9,500	16,000	17,500	21,000	23,000
Extended Warranty	N	N	N	N	N	N	N	N
Secret Warranty	N	N	N	N	N	N	N	Y
Reliability	②	③	③	③	③	④	④	④
Air conditioning	②	②	③	③	③	④	④	④
Body integrity	②	②	②	②	③	③	③	③
Braking system	②	②	②	②	②	②	③	③
Electrical system	②	②	②	②	②	③	③	③
Engines	③	③	③	③	④	④	④	⑤
Exhaust/Converter	②	②	②	③	③	③	③	④
Fuel system	②	②	②	③	③	③	④	④
Ignition system	③	③	③	④	④	④	④	⑤
Manual transmission	③	③	③	③	③	③	④	⑤
- automatic	③	③	③	③	③	④	⑤	⑤
Rust/Paint	②	②	③	④	④	④	⑤	⑤
Steering	③	③	③	③	③	④	⑤	⑤
Suspension	③	③	③	③	③	③	③	④

Note: The Supra was never crash-tested.

MINIVANS

Chrysler launched the minivan concept with its 1984 Caravan and Voyager. Although poorly assembled and riddled with deficiencies, the tall, boxy vehicle was an instant success because it combined fuel efficiency, carlike maneuverability, and increased cargo/passenger space in a smartly styled "garageable" van. On the other hand, Volkswagen's minivan—morphed into the EuroVan in the early '90s—had been on sale for over 35 years and never did very well. Used mostly as a camper, it suffered from decades-old styling, poor dealer support, insufficient heating, glacial acceleration, and a reputation for being reliably unreliable.

Fortunately, while Chrysler and VW have apparently stood still from a quality improvement standpoint, the competition has caught up and, in the case of Honda and Toyota, surpassed the two originators of the minivan concept. In fact, vehicles produced during the past few years use more powerful engines; offer a greater variety of powertrains; and have better crash ratings, more safety features (airbags, etc.), more responsive road handling, better quality control, more competitive prices, and greater parts availability.

If you must buy a minivan, remember that, much like sport-utilities, they usually fall into two categories: up-sized cars and down-sized trucks. The up-sized cars are "people movers." They're mostly FWD, handle like a car, and get great fuel economy. The Mercury Villager, Nissan Quest, and GM's Lumina, Silhouette, Trans Sport, and Venture are the best examples of this kind of minivan. In fact, their road performance and reliability surpass both Chrysler and Ford's front-drive minivans. GM's Astro/Safari and the Ford Aerostar, on the other hand, are down-sized trucks. Using rear-wheel drive, 6-cylinder engines, and heavier mechanical components, these minivans handle cargo as well as passengers. Towing capacity varies between 3,000 and 5,000 lb. On the negative side, fuel economy is no match for the FWD minivans, and highway handling on rear-drives is also more trucklike. Nevertheless, post-1995 rear-drive GM and Ford minivans are more reliable performers than the Ford Windstar or Chrysler offerings.

Minivan ownership costs are quite reasonable, according to the American management consulting firm Runzheimer International, which has concluded that it costs less to operate a minivan than it does many compact cars. Still, most minivans are overpriced, and motorists needing a vehicle with large cargo- and passenger-carrying capacity should consider a cheaper GM Vandura or Chevy Van, even if it means sacrificing some fuel economy and convenience features (they can be added by most conversion shops at competitive prices). You just can't beat the excellent forward vision and easy-to-customize interiors that these large vans provide.

Recommended

Ford Mercury Villager/
  Nissan Quest (1997–98)

Above Average

Ford Mercury Villager/Nissan
  Quest (1995–96)
GM Silhouette/Trans Sport/
  Venture (1997–98)

Honda Odyssey (1995–98)
Toyota Previa (1991–97)
Toyota Sienna (1998)

Average

Ford Aerostar (1995–97)
GM Astro/Safari (1996–98)
GM Lumina/Lumina APV/
  Silhouette/Trans Sport (1995–96)

Mazda MPV (1996–98)

Below Average

Chrysler Caravan/Voyager,
  Grand Caravan/Grand Voyager/
  Town & Country, (1997–98)

Ford Windstar (1996–98)
Mazda MPV (1988–95)

Not Recommended

Chrysler Caravan/Voyager,
  Grand Caravan/Grand Voyager/
  Town & Country (1984–96)
Ford Aerostar (1986–94)
Ford Mercury Villager, Nissan
  Quest (1993–94)
Ford Windstar (1995)

GM Astro/Safari (1985–95)
GM Lumina/Lumina APV/
  Silhouette/Trans Sport
  (1990–94)
Toyota LE (1984–90)

CHRYSLER

**Caravan/Voyager, Grand Caravan/Grand Voyager/
Town & Country**

Minivans

Rating: Below Average (1997–98); Not Recommended (1984–96). Don't consider any model year without being armed with the longest powertrain warranty you can afford. Other minivans you may wish to consider: the GM front-drive minivans, Ford Mercury Villager, Nissan Quest, or Toyota Sienna. Major generic defects affecting the 1984–96 models make these minivans very risky buys. In spite of the poor reliability of the early versions, Chrysler minivans remained popular because Chrysler's comprehensive 7-year warranty paid for their shortcomings. But that warranty's gone and the defects remain. **Maintenance/Repair costs:** Higher than average, but any garage can repair these minivans. **Parts:** Expensive (especially for paint, AC, transmission, and ABS components, which are covered under a number of "goodwill" warranty programs and several recall campaigns).

There's presently an abundance of used Chrysler minivans on the market; however, very few have any of their original warranty coverage left. Count on spending at least another $1,000 for a supplementary warranty to protect yourself from Chrysler's costly generic defects. Just ABS and transmission repairs alone could cost you $5,000. One radio listener recently asked me if my advice to get the extended warranty on the Caravan or Ford's Windstar should be seen as a "red flag" as to the reliability of these vehicles. Yes, that's exactly what it is.

Strengths and weaknesses: Chrysler's minivans dominate the new- and used-minivan market because they offer pleasing styling and lots of convenience features. They also ride and handle better than most truck-based minivans (although there's lots of room for improvement) and can carry up to seven passengers in comfort. Cargo hauling capability is more than adequate, with a 3,000 lb. maximum towing range.

On the downside, these minivans pose maximum safety risks due to their poor crashworthiness and chronic mechanical failures. Worse still, owners report of experiencing a host of bizarre "happenings" with their minivans, suggesting that these vehicles require the services of an exorcist rather than a mechanic (seatbelts that may strangle children, airbags that deploy when the ignition is turned on or the floor gets wet, and stalling when within radar range of airports or military installations).

Powertrain problems
These minivans are way underpowered with the base 4-cylinder engine. It has a history of head gasket failures, but it outshines the larger Mitsubishi 2.6L, which is guaranteed to self-destruct just as the warranty expires. The timing belt, piston rings, and valves are particular weak points on the 2.6L powerplant. The two-piece camshaft oil seals are also prone to sudden leaks. The Chrysler-built 2.5L engine is fairly dependable but sluggish, and the 3.3L V6 is the most reliable. The Mitsubishi 3.0L V6 is much more reliable than its smaller 2.6L version, but it lacks power on long climbs, has multiple fuel-injection and oil leak problems, and produces a loud piston "slapping" noise during cold starts. Cold climates present additional problems for Chrysler minivan owners: one 1989 Voyager owner from Red Deer, Alberta, says that dealers in his area claim that his 3.0L engine seized because of poor cold-weather oil lubrication. If this is true, it spells trouble for the many owners who have to drive in cold-weather conditions and are now nearing the end of Chrysler's original warranty coverage.

Automatic transmissions built over the past decade are a nightmare (see "Safety summary/Recalls"): imagine having to count to three in traffic before Drive or Reverse will engage, or "limping" home on the highway in second gear at 30 mph. The disastrous A604 4-speed automatic was particularly troublesome on 1988–91 models. Then it was renamed—and continued to pile up complaints. Chrysler, stung by critics' charges that these transmissions were lemons, pledged that a free oil cooler by-pass valve would be installed on 1989–90 minivans to prevent transmission damage in cold temperatures. This program is outlined in Customer Satisfaction Notification #281T.

Automatic transmissions on the post-1991 versions continue to leak, gear down to a limp-in mode, shift noisily, and hunt for the proper gear—the likely cause of some of the poor gas mileage claims. These factory-related defects on recent minivans and other models are listed in DSB #18-24-95.

NO: 18-24-95
DATE: June 23, 1995
SUBJECT: Improved Transmission Shift Quality
MODELS:

1989 – 1995	(AA) Acclaim/Sprint/LeBaron Sedan
1989 – 1993	(AC) Dynasty/New Yorker/New Yorker Salon
1990 – 1993	(AG) Daytona
1990 – 1995	(AJ) LeBaron Coupe/LeBaron Convertible
1993 –1994	(AP) Sundance/Shadow/Shadow Convertible
1990 – 1991	(AQ) Chrysler TC
1989 – 1995	(AS) Caravan/Voyager/Town & Country
1990 – 1993	(AY) Imperial/New Yorker Fifth Avenue
1995	(FJ) Sebring/Avenger/Talon**
1995	(JA) Cirrus/Stratus
1993 – 1995	(LH) Concorde/Intrepid/Vision/LHS/New Yorker

NOTE:
THIS BULLETIN APPLIES TO VEHICLES EQUIPPED WITH THE 41TE OR 42LE TRANSAXLE.
SYMPTOM/CONDITION:
Vehicles that operate at speeds where EMCC usage is engaged (vehicle speeds between 34 and 41 MPH), may experience early deterioration of the transmission fluid (15,000 to 30,000 miles), exhibit a pronounced shudder during EMCC operation, harsh upshifts/downshifts, and/or harsh torque converter clutch engagements. Performing REPAIR PROCEDURE # 2, which includes updates to the Transmission Control Module (TCM) calibration and eliminates EMCC, will resolve these symptom/conditions.
The TCM calibration used in the 1995 model year 41TE arid 42LE TCM is being made available for all vehicles dating back to the 1989 model year. The shift quality improvements and default issues that will be corrected by the new TCM calibration are:

1. COASTDOWN TIP-IN BUMP: Vehicle is decelerated almost to a stop (less than 8 MPH), then the driver tips back into the throttle to accelerate a noticeable bump may be felt.
2. COASTDOWN SHIFT HARSHNESS: Harsh coastdown shifts on some 4–3, 3–2 and 2–1 downshifts.
3. 1995 LH WITH 42LE TRANSAXLE — SLUGGISHNESS/LACK OF RESPONSE: On some early 1995 LH vehicles built prior to Oct. 24, 1994, a perceived lack of power or transmission responsiveness may be encountered under normal operating conditions. The transmission may not release the converter clutch as desired with increased throttle. This occurs in 4th gear from 35 MPH to 50 MPH.
4. 1989–1994 WITH 41TE & 42LE TRANSAXLES: Harsh shifts and/or vehicle shudder during 3–2 or 2–1 kickdowns at speeds less than 25 MPH.
5. 1993 WITH 41TE TRANSAXLE: Harsh 3–4 upshifts may occur, especially at highway speeds, while using the speed control.
6. 1989–1994 WITH 41TE TRANSAXLE — HARSH/DELAYED GARAGE SHIFTS: Delay is less than 2 seconds and the shift is harsh after the brief delay. NOTE: Delays greater than 2 seconds are caused by transmission hardware malfunction, i.e., valve body, pump, failed lip seals or malfunctioning PRNDL or neutral start switch.
7. 1989–1994 WITH 41TE & 42LE TRANSAXLES—POOR SHIFT QUALITY AFTER A BATTERY DISCONNECT: All transmission learned values are reset to the factory default values if battery power is lost to the TCM. The new 1995 calibration will now retain all learned values in memory after battery disconnect. However, if a transmission is rebuilt or a new transmission or TCM is installed. the Quick Learn procedure must be performed to calibrate Clutch Volume Indexes (CVI)on 1993 and later vehicles. (1992 and prior vehicle cannot be Quick Learned).
8. EARLY 1993 WITH 41TE & 42LE TRANSAXLE — INTERMITTENT SPEED CONTROL DROP OUT: The new service calibration change corrects this condition (this condition was also covered in Technical Service Bulletin 08-09-93 dated Mar. 12, 1993).
9. 1989–1993 WITH 41TE & 42LE TRANSAXLES — New fault code 35 (failure to achieve pump prime) has been added for improved diagnostic capability and fault codes 21, 22 and 24 are de-sensitized to reduce erroneous limp-in conditions.
POLICY: Reimbursable within the provisions of the warranty.

```
DATE: Feb. 17, 1995
SUBJECT: Delayed Transaxle
MODELS:
1993 – 1995      (AA)    Spirit/Acclaim/LeBaron Sedan
1993             (AC)    Dynasty/New Yorker/New Yorker Salon
1993             (AG)    Daytona
1993 – 1995      (AJ)    LeBaron Coupe/LeBaron Convertible
1993 – 1994      (AP)    Shadow/Shadow Convertible/Sundance
1993 – 1995      (AS)    Town & Country/Caravan/Voyager
1993             (AY)    Imperial/New Yorker Fifth Avenue
1993 – 1995      (ES)    Chrysler Voyager (European Market)
1993 – 1995      (LH)    Concorde/Intrepid/LHS/New Yorker/Vision
SYMPTOM/CONDITION: Intermittent delayed transmission engagement at vehicle start up (garage shift) in excess of 3 sec-
onds. The transaxle may be cold or hot.
Other possible conditions that may cause delayed transaxle engagement are a sticking or frozen PRNDL switch, or a transaxle
front pump with excessive gear clearances.
PARTS REQUIRED:
AR 4659085       Valve Body, 41TE
AR 4504048       Package, Oil Filter 41TE
AR 4659084       Valve Body, 42LE
AR 4796730       Package, Oil Filter 42LE
AR 4467721       Fluid, Mopar Automatic Transmission — Type 7176
REPAIR PROCEDURE: This bulletin involves replacing the transaxle valve body and oil filter.
```

These bulletins clearly show that Chrysler is well aware of its automatic transmissions' propensity for shuddering, delayed engagement, and eventual self-destruction.

Other mechanical weaknesses in early models include the premature wearing out of front suspension components, wheel bearings, front brake discs, brake master cylinder, water pump, air conditioning unit, engine cooling system, and manual transmission clutch. Fuel-injectors on all engines have been troublesome, and engine supports may be missing or not connected.

Overall fit and finish has gotten worse, not better, over the years (see "Secret Warranties/Service Tips"). Body hardware and interior trim are fragile and tend to break, warp, or fall off (door handles are a good example). After about a year's use, the Caravan and its various spin-offs become veritable rattle boxes, with poorly anchored bench seats being a major player. Finish problems can be summed up in three words: paint, paint, paint. The paint tends to discolor or delaminate after the second year. Chrysler knows about this problem and often tries to get the owner to pay half the cost of a repainting job (about $1,500 on a $3,000 job), but will eventually agree to pay the total cost if the owner stands fast, threatens small claims court action, or belongs to a consumer protection group like Vancouver-based CLOG (Chrysler Lemon Owners Group). Moreover, minivan owners fed up with Chrysler's refusal to repaint their vehicles have filed a class action in Washington state, seeking damages for owners of 1986–97 cars, sport-utilities, minivans, and trucks (see Part Two for the full text of the lawsuit).

Mechanical weaknesses on later models include the premature wearing out of the engine tensioner pulley, motor mounts, starter motor, front brake discs and pads (the brake pad material crumbles in your hands), brake master cylinder, suspension components, exhaust system components, ball joints, wheel bearings, water pumps, fuel pumps and pump wiring harnesses, radiators, heater cores, and AC units. Fuel-injectors on all engines have been troublesome, the windshield wiper washers freeze up in cold temperatures, sliding doors malfunction, engine supports may be missing or not connected, and there are frequent power-steering pump leaks. Two further problems are batteries that last 9–12 months and factory-installed tires that fail prematurely (at 20,000–25,000 miles) and are hard to find—especially in the LT rating.

Cold-weather problems abound. One owner says that her 1992 Voyager's rear heater coolant tubes were so badly corroded that they had to be replaced after two years at a cost of $160. Radiators and AC lines also quickly succumb to corrosion.

Dealer service bulletins: 1996—3.3L and 3.8L lower engine oil leaks. • Coolant seepage from rear heater hose connections. • Cold-start stumble. • Rough idle, hesitation, or sags after fuel tank is filled (see "Secret Warranties/Service Tips"). • Intermittent driveability problem near radar (again, explained more fully in "Secret Warranties/Service Tips"). • Intermittent powertrain shudder. • Transmission limp-in caused by a faulty speed sensor. • Reduced limp-in default sensitivity. • Excessive transmission downshifting/upshifting in cruise control. • Dealers will install an upgraded overdrive clutch hub. • Difficulty going into second gear or Reverse after a cold start. • Upshift shuddering. • ABS activates below 10 mph.• Front wipers activate while driving or will not turn off. • Vehicle drifts or leads at high speeds. • Underbody squeaks, buzzes, and rattles. • Exhaust drone at 2500–2800 rpm. • B-post area rattling. • Blower motor whine and AC-related moan/whine. • Power steering produces a clunk or popping noise at highway speeds. • Steering noise during parking lot maneuvers. • Front door squeak/creak noise. • Ratcheting sound when coming to a stop. • Rear wheel rattle or click noise. • Rattling rear bench seat. • Rear brake noise (see "Secret Warranties/Service Tips"). • Integrated child safety seat seatbelt retractor may restrict seatbelt travel. Dealer will replace assembly at no charge under Customer Satisfaction Note #650. • Child seat shoulder harness won't pull out. • Discolored cowl grille or outside rear view mirrors. • Poor cowl cover fit. • Dust intrusion into rear of vehicle. • False info on fuel tank capacity and inaccurate fuel gauge. • Hard to unlatch rear bench seats. • HVAC control knobs or buttons may stick. • Interior window film buildup. • Intermittent operation of sliding door locks. • Liftgate-to-rear-fascia gap too small. • Paint chips at the upper front corner of the sliding doors. • Poor AM radio reception and RAS radio cassette malfunctions. • Faulty power vent windows. • Loose quad seats. • Roof panel is wavy or has depressions. • Inoperative sliding door and liftgate power lock motor; the sliding door may be difficult to open from the outside. • Suction-cup marks on door glass. • Unexplained theft alarm activation or dead battery. • Water leaks onto carpet from HVAC housing. • White stress marks on interior trim panel. • Flying hubcaps (see "Secret Warranties/Service Tips"). **1997**—The defects affecting the newest minivans are similar to those failures we've seen for over a decade (see following DSB). All the more reason to be skeptical of Chrysler's claims that its quality control has improved since the 1996 model was redesigned.

DSB SUMMARY	1997 CHRYSLER CARAVAN
1. MAY-97	41TE/42LE TRANSMISSION SERVICE INFORMATION
2. OCT-96	A/C ERROR STARTER, EATX, CRUISE CONTROL...
3. JUL-97	A/C EVAPORATOR ODORS
4. JUN-97	A/C SUCTION AND/OR DISCHARGE LINE SERVICE
5. FEB-97	AIR BAG WARNING LABELS
6. OCT-96	BRAKE NOISE
7. FEB-97	CHALKY RESIDUE ON BLACK PLASTIC BODY COMPONENTS
8. JAN-97	COMPASS (CMTC) AND/OR INSTRUMENT CLUSTER MALFUNCTION
9. MAR-97	COOLANT SEEPAGE AT UNDERBODY AUXILIARY REAR HEATER LINE
10. APR-97	CUSTOMER NOTIFICATION #712—PASSENGER AIR BAG SAFETY
11. JUL-97	CUSTOMER SATISFACTION NOTICE #721—CHILD SAFETY SEAT
12. SEP-96	DINGS FROM INSIDE-OUT AT SLIDING DOOR(S) LATCH AREA
13. MAY-97	ENGINE COOLANT USAGE
14. JAN-97	ERRONEOUS M L ON WITH HEX CODE S29, S2A, S2B
15. MAY-97	FRONT HVAC BLOWER MOTOR RESISTOR CONNECTOR SERVICE
16. JAN-97	FUEL TANK SERVICE
17. MAY-97	HIGH EFFORT REQUIRED TO UNLATCH REAR BENCH SEATS
18. DEC-97	HONK NOISE DURING LOW SPEED MANEUVERS
19. SEP-97	INOPERATIVE CD PLAYER/SALES CODE RAZ RADIO
20. OCT-97	INTERMITTENT MOMENTARY LOSS OF POWER ASSIST
21. NOV-96	INTERMITTENT/INOPERATIVE RADIATOR FANS
22. MAY-97	LEAK DETECTION PUMP (LDP) DEALER TEST MODE
23. SEP-97	NHTSA AUTHORIZED AIRBAG DEACTIVATION / MEDICAL NECESSITY
24. NOV-97	POOR DRIVEABILITY WITH HIGH DI FUEL
25. FEB-97	REAR BRAKE CYCLIC RUBBING NOISE
26. FEB-97	REAR BRAKE MOAN/HOWL NOISE
27. NOV-97	REMOTE KEYLESS TRANSMITTER BATTERY FAILURE
28. NOV-96	REPAIR OF FALLOUT DAMAGED PAINT
29. APR-97	SAFETY RECALL #714/MASTER CYLINDER PRIMARY PISTON
30. MAY-97	SAFETY RECALL #724 — STAMPED STEEL ROAD WHEELS
31. NOV-97	SERVICE MANUAL REVISION
32. JUN-97	SERVICE MANUAL, REVISIONS
33. MAR-97	SLIDING DOOR — POOR FIT AT REAR
34. OCT-97	THUMPING NOISE AT REAR OF VEHICLE DURING COLD OPERATIONS
35. JUN-97	TIRE & WHEEL RUNOUT
36. MAR-97	TRANSAXLE SHUDDER DURING EMCC SHIFT
37. JUN-97	TRANSMISSION FLUID AUXILIARY COOLER
38. JAN-97	UNDER BODY CREAK OR KNOCK SOUND
39. SEP-97	WATER LEAKS ONTO FLOOR FROM HVAC HOUSING
40. JUN-97	WIPERS DON'T PARK OR WIPE IN INTERMITTENT MODE

Déjà vu, all over again!

Safety summary/Recalls: Chrysler continues to downplay the seriousness of its minivan safety defects, whether in the case of ABS failures, inadvertent airbag deployments, or faulty rear latches. Nevertheless, the company has recently lost several important lawsuits concerning airbag dangers (a $69 million U.S. class action) and faulty minivan rear latches (see Part Two). Following a sustained Internet campaign against Chrysler—led by irate car and minivan owners and buttressed by thousands of complaints registered by safety investigators on both sides of the border—the automaker has announced a safety recall of 1991–93 minivans and passenger cars in order to correct life-threatening ABS malfunctions and extend the base warranty to 10 years/100,000 miles on ABS components (not calipers, pads and shoe linings, or other maintenance items). Two other ABS components, piston seals (excessive wear) and the pump motor (deterioration), will be repaired free of charge at any time during the life of the vehicle. Drivers of these defective minivans that experience any kind of ABS malfunction should go to the nearest Chrysler dealer and demand the ABS be checked at Chrysler's expense. **All models/years**—Owners report that cruise control units often malfunction, accelerating or decelerating the vehicle without any warning, and that sudden stalling and transmission failures also create life-threatening situations. The owner of a 1993 Caravan SE equipped with a 3.3L engine calls the transmission malfunction a safety hazard:

> I have experienced a transmission control module failure where the vehicle immediately dropped into second gear. This could have been tragic if it had occurred in heavy traffic.

All models: 1991–93—Seatbelts may become unhooked from the floor anchor. **1994**—Airbags deploy when the vehicle is started. **1994–95**—Airbags and wiper motor share the same fuse; if the wiper motor fails, the airbags are deactivated. **1995**—Engine fires. • Thieves love the door lock design. • Broken spare tire suspension cable allows tire to fall away while driving. • Right-side rear door suddenly flies open when vehicle passes over a small bump. • Seatbelt buckles jam or suddenly release. • Child shoulder harness clip easily pulls out. • Roof drip rails allow water to leak inside. • Open glove box back section allows for papers to be sucked into the AC blower. • Inoperative horn. **1995–96**—Brake failures, lockup, excessive noise, and premature wear. • Airbag fails to deploy or accidentally deploys. • Injury from airbag. • Sudden acceleration, stalling. • No steering. • Seatbacks fall backwards. • Fuel tank is easily damaged. • Park won't hold vehicle. • Transmission fails, suddenly drops into low gear, won't go into Reverse, delays engagement, or jumps out of gear. • Rear windows fall out or shatter. • Power window and door lock failures. • Sliding door jams, trapping occupants. • Weak headlights. **1996**—Driver's side airbag deploys when the ignition is turned on. • Child safety seat harness over-retracts, trapping children or catching their hair. • Fuel tank leaks from tank top and fuel rail. • Incorrect fuel gauge. • Fuel sloshes around (no baffle), deforms tank, and makes noise. • Fuel leaks from vapor-recovery canister. • Broken steering belt tensioner causes the sudden loss of power steering and power brakes. • Wipers self-activate. • Sliding door falls off. • Faulty power door locks. • Cracked axle/drive shaft. • Cruise control drops speed and then surges to former setting. • With AC engaged, vehicle stalls, then surges forward. • Power-steering failure, excessive noise. • Vehicle parked with gear in Park and with emergency brake applied rolled into a lake. **Recalls: All models: 1984–95**—All minivans are subject to a voluntary service campaign that will fix a rear liftgate latch that may fail in a collision. **1985**—Dealers will install a protective cover over the brake proportioning valve. • The fuel supply tube leaks in vehicles equipped with a 2.2L engine. **1986–88**—On passenger models, first rear seats may detach in an accident. **1988**—Possible fuel tank leakage. **1988–89**—Notification #281T, applicable to vehicles with a trailer towing package, provides for a free oil cooler by-pass valve to prevent transmission failure in cold weather. **1989–90**—Engine valve cover gasket may leak oil, creating a fire hazard. • Notification #466 provides for a free engine valve spring. • Safety recall #314T provides for the free installation of a reinforcing plate on the front seatbelt strap. **1990**—An incorrectly mounted proportioning valve may increase the chance of skidding. • Notification #281T extends the free oil cooler by-pass valve program to 1990 minivans. **1991**—Faulty turn-signal flasher. • ABS hydraulic fluid leakage. **1991–92**—Steering wheel cracks may cause wheel to loosen. **1991–93**—Recall to fix two kinds of seatbelt problems: faulty buckle cover may prevent seatbelt from being fully latched; and seatbelt anchor hook could become detached from the anchor. • Chrysler ABS recall calls for the installation of a new pump and seal kit, if needed. The kit comes with a lifetime warranty, while all other ABS components will henceforth be covered for 10 years/100,000 miles. **1992**—Replace liftgate supports, which may break from fatigue. • Safety recall #326T requires the replacement of all brake pedals that have been found to lack sufficient strength. • Faulty steering column shaft coupling bolts. • Improperly bent fuel tank flanges could cause a fire. **1993–94**—Rear liftgate struts and bolts will be replaced to prevent liftgate from falling down. **1994–95**—A wiring harness short may cause the driver-side airbag to deploy when the minivan is started. **1995–98**—Airbags may deploy for no reason. **1996**—Faulty bench seat attaching bolts. • Filler tube rollover valve. • Installation of a fuel-filler ground strap. • Improved retractors for child safety seats (service action) and upgraded seat module bolts (recall). • Defective engine cylinder head plug could cause a fire. **1997**—Goodyear Conquest tires will be replaced. • Dealers will clean the child safety seat latch and add a belt extender for anchoring the belts. • Brake master cylinder seals may be defective, allowing fluid to be drawn into the power-assist reservoir. • Wheels may have been damaged during mounting. **1998**—Install upgraded child safety seat belts.

Secret Warranties/Service Tips

All models/years—If pressed, Chrysler will pay the full cost of correcting paint defects during the first six years of ownership (see Part Two). • A rotten-egg odor coming from the exhaust may be the result of a malfunctioning catalytic converter, probably covered under the emissions warranty. • Front brakes tend to wear out quickly on front-drive minivans. Owners say that Chrysler has paid half the cost of brake repairs for up to 2 years/ 25,000 miles. **All models: 1987–92**—The heater and air conditioning system may suddenly change to the defrost mode during a low vacuum condition, which can occur during trailer towing, hill climbing, and acceleration. Install a revised vacuum check valve to correct this problem. **1987–94**—3.0L engines that burn oil or produce a smoky exhaust at idle can be fixed by installing snap rings on the exhaust valve guides and replacing all of the valve guide stems or the cylinder head. **1988–90**—Intermittent rough running at idle signals a need for a new EGR. **1988–94**—A sticking AC heater blend door can be corrected by spraying an anti-rust penetrant into the assembly. **1989–90**—Oil leaks from the cylinder head cover with 2.5L engines are caused by poor sealing. The original cylinder head cover must be replaced with one that uses silicone sealant (RTV) instead of a gasket (DSB #09-17-89). • Defective valve stem seals are the likely cause of high oil consumption with 2.5L engines (DSB #HL-49-89C). • A604 automatic transmission clutch slippage is a common problem addressed in DSB #21-09-9. • A surge/buck at 35–55 mph with an automatic transmission can be corrected by installing driveability kit #4419447. **1989–95**—An excellent summary of Chrysler's transmission glitches and corrections covering these seven model years can be found in DSB #18-24-95. **1989–96**—Acceleration shudder that may be accompanied by a whine is likely the result of leakage in the transmission front pump, caused by a worn pump bushing. **1990–92**—Erratic idle speeds occurring after deceleration from a steady cruising speed can be corrected by replacing the idle air control motor with a revised motor. **1990–94**—Harsh automatic shifts can be tamed by installing the following revised parts: kickdown, accumulator, reverse servo cushion springs, and accumulator piston. • Cold-start piston knocking noise can be eliminated by replacing the piston and connecting rod assembly. • Erratic fuel gauge operation can be fixed by installing a revised sender assembly or fuel pump/sender assembly. **1991**—Loss of fuel pressure causing fuel-pump noise, erratic transmission shifting, engine power loss, or engine die-out may be due to a defective fuel pump. • An erratic idle with 2.5L engines can be cured by using an improved SMEC/SBEC engine controller. • Faulty power door locks may have a short circuit, need a new fuse, or require a new door latch with power door lock assembly. **1991–92**—If the engine knocks when at full operating temperature and during light to medium acceleration, it may mean that the single board engine controller (SBEC-Powertrain Control Module) needs replacing. • Engines with a rough idle and stalling following a cold start also may require a new SBEC. • The airbag warning light may continuously illuminate when the vehicle's ignition is in the ON position. This malfunction may be due to corrosion caused by water in the airbag's six-way connector. **1991–93**—Engines that stall following a cold start may need an upgraded Park/Neutral/Start switch. **1991–94**—The serpentine belt may come off the pulley after driving through snow. Install upgraded shield, screw, and retainers. • Noisy fuel pumps need to be replaced with upgraded pump, wiring harness, fuel tank isolators, and fuel tank straps. • Noise when shifting into Reverse or when turning is addressed in DSB #09-14-94. **1991–95**—Poor AC performance while the AC blower continues to operate is likely due to a frozen evaporator. • DSB #24-05-94 looks at all the causes of, and remedies for, poor heater performance. • If the vehicle tends to drift left, cross-switch the tire and wheel assemblies, readjust the alignment, or reposition the front crossmember. **1992**—The brake pedal may not return to its fully released position, causing the brake lights to remain illuminated. Install a pedal return kit (#4723625). • Front door forward hem separation (the door seems to sag) can be corrected by welding the inner door panel to the outer door panel along the front door forward hem. • Long crank times, a rough idle, and hesitation may be corrected by replacing the intake manifold assembly. • A vehicle that's hard to start may have a corroded ECT/sensor connector. • An oil leak in the oil filter area may be corrected by installing a special oil filter bracket gasket (#MD198554). • If the heater and ventilation system change to the defrost mode during acceleration, trailer towing, or hill climbing, the installation of a revised vacuum check valve should cure the problem. • Intermittent failure of the power door locks, chimes, wipers, gauges, and other electrical devices can be corrected by replacing defective relays with revised relays (#4713737). **1992–93**—Some 41TE transaxles may produce a buzzing noise when shifted into Reverse. This problem can be corrected by replacing the valve body assembly or valve body separator plate. • A deceleration shudder can be eliminated by replacing the powertrain control module with an upgraded version. • Rough idling after a cold start with 2.5L engines can be corrected by installing an upgraded powertrain control module (PCM). **1992–94**—AC duct odors are addressed in DSB #24-21-93. • Poor heater performance may be the result of a misadjusted clip on the blend air door cable. **1993**—A fuel pump check valve failure can cause start-up die-out, reduced power, or erratic shifting. **1993–94**—Improved automatic shifting can be had by installing an upgraded transmission control module. • AC evaporator whistling requires the installation of upgraded AC expansion valves and gaskets. • An AC moan may be silenced by installing an AC clutch plate with a damper ring. **1993–95**—Delayed automatic transmission engagement may be due to low fluid, a stuck or frozen PRNDL switch, or a transaxle front pump with excessive ground clearance. • Harsh low-speed automatic transmission shifting, accompanied by a fluctuating digital speedometer reading. This may be corrected by covering the wiring harness with aluminum wire, which prevents the spark plug wires from sending false signals to the outport speed sensor wiring that connects to the TCM. • Constant upshifting/downshifting on vehicles equipped with cruise control has a variety of causes as set out in DSB #08-15-95. • An exhaust that smells like rotten eggs can be corrected by installing an upgraded catalytic converter (see following bulletin).

No: 11-03-96
GROUP: Exhaust
DATE: June 17, 1996
SUBJECT: Excessive Sulphur Odor
MODELS:
1992-1995 (AA) Acclaim/Spirit/LeBaron Sedan
1992-1993 (AC) Dynasty/New Yorker/ New Yorker Salon
1992-1993 (AG) Daytona
1992-1995 (AJ) LeBaron Coupe/LeBaron Convertible
1992-1994 (AP) Sundance/Shadow/Shadow Convertible
1993-1995 (AS) Caravan/Voyage/Town & Country
NOTE: THIS BULLETIN APPLIES TO VEHICLES EQUIPPED WITH 2.2L OR 2.5L ENGINES ONLY.
SYMPTOM/CONDITION: New catalytic converters are now available to address customer complaints of excessive hydrogen sulfide odor (rotten egg smell) coming from the tailpipe of their vehicles at idle. These catalysts were specially manufactured with a revised internal coating which minimizes sulphur odor.

1	4882530	Catalytic Converter	(AS 2.5L ATX/MTX FED/CAL)
1	4882531	Catalytic Converter	(AA,AG,AP 2.2L/2.5L MTX FED/CAL) 1992-1994
1	4882532	Catalytic Converter	(AA,AC,AG,AJ,AP 2.2L/2.5L ATX FED) 1992-1995
1	4882533	Catalytic Converter	(AA,AC,AG,AJ,AP 2.2L/2.5L ATX CAL) 1992-1995
			(AA, 2.5l ATX FED) 1994)
			(AA, 2.5L FFV) 1992
1	4882534	Catalytic Converter	(AA, 2.5L FFV) 1993-1994

PARTS REQUIRED:
REPAIR PROCEDURE: This bulletin involves the replacement of the catalytic converter with a revised part.
Replace the catalytic converter following the repair procedures given in group 11 of the appropriate service manual.
POLICY: Reimbursable within the provisions of the warranty.
TIME ALLOWANCE:
Labor Operation No: 11-50-01-91   0.7 Hrs.
FAILURE CODE: P8-New Part

If your minivan stinks, blame Chrysler, not your passengers. Repair costs should be covered by the emissions warranty.

1994—Harsh, erratic, or delayed transmission shifts can be corrected by replacing the throttle position sensor (TPS) with a revised part. • A creaking left B-pillar can be silenced by repositioning the metal portion of the left B-pillar baffle. **1994–95**—Intake valve deposits are frequently the cause of poor driveability complaints. • Intermittent no-cranks can be corrected by modifying the battery-to-starter cable terminal insulator at the starter connection. • A front suspension rapping noise heard when going over bumps can be corrected by providing additional clearance between the front coil springs and strut towers. **1996**—Poor engine performance near military installations or airports is caused by radar interference. Correct by installing a "hardened" crankshaft position sensor and/or reprogramming (flashing) the PCM with new software calibrations. • Rear brake noise that occurs at any time can be silenced by replacing the rear brake shoes and rear wheel cylinders. Another possibility is the addition of rear brake shoe springs. • Rough idle, hesitation, or sags after the fuel tank is filled can only be corrected by the installation of a new fuel tank, according to DSB #18-28-95. The repair is covered under warranty and should take about an hour. The dealer should also give you your gas back. • Steering noise during parking lot maneuvers may be fixed by installing a new power-steering gear and left-side attaching bolt. • Chrysler minivan wheel covers tend to take flight (and I thought that was only a Chevy Caprice problem). Chrysler will install upgraded covers under warranty. **1998**—You may silence a chronic squeaking noise coming from underneath the vehicle by installing a new strut pivot bearing (see following bulletin).

NO: 02-10-98
GROUP: Suspension
DATE: Sept. 25, 1998
SUBJECT:
Squeaking Noise From Strut Bearing(s)
MODELS:
1998–1999 (NS) Town & Country/Caravan/Voyager
1998–1999 (GS) Chrysler Voyager (International Market)
NOTE:
 THIS BULLETIN APPLIES TO VEHICLES BUILT THROUGH OCT. 1, 1998.
SYMPTOM/CONDITION:
A squeaking/chirping noise is heard (inside or outside the vehicle) from the strut tower area(s) when turning the steering wheel or when the vehicle is driven over any irregularities in the road surface.
DIAGNOSIS:
With the vehicle on a level surface, hold a front suspension coil spring with your hands near 180° apart, and try to rotate the spring right and left. If a squeaking/chirping noise is heard from the top of the strut tower, perform the Repair Procedure. Repeat for the opposite side strut tower.
Parts Information:
AR (2) 04684418   Bearing, Strut Upper Pivot
POLICY: Reimbursable within the provisions of the warranty.

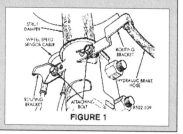

FIGURE 1

This repair should take about an hour for each side and is covered by Chrysler's base warranty.

Caravan/Voyager, Grand Caravan/Grand Voyager/ Town & Country Profile

	1991	1992	1993	1994	1995	1996	1997	1998
Cost Price ($)								
Caravan/Voyager	12,806	13,360	14,106	14,972	16,705	18,510	19,570	20,535
G. Caravan/G.Voy.	17,472	18,723	18,140	19,595	20,025	21,810	23,325	23,060
Town & Country	24,425	25,160	26,080	27,845	28,240	25,865	28,070	28,150
Used Values ($)								
Caravan/Voy. ↑	4,500	6,500	8,500	9,500	10,500	13,500	15,000	16,500
Caravan/Voy. ↓	4,000	5,500	7,500	8,000	9,500	11,500	13,500	15,500
G. Caravan/G.Voy. ↑	6,500	8,500	9,500	12,500	13,500	15,000	16,500	18,500
G. Caravan/G.Voy. ↓	5,500	7,000	8,000	10,500	12,500	13,500	15,000	17,000
Town & Country ↑	9,000	10,000	11,000	13,000	14,000	19,000	21,000	23,000
Town & Country ↓	7,500	8,000	10,000	10,500	12,500	17,500	18,500	21,000
Extended Warranty	Y	Y	Y	Y	Y	Y	Y	Y
Secret Warranty	Y	Y	Y	Y	Y	Y	Y	Y
Reliability	❶	❶	❷	❷	❷	❷	❷	③
Air conditioning	❶	❶	❷	❷	❷	❷	③	③

Automatic transmission	①	①	①	①	①	①	①	①
Body integrity	①	①	①	①	①	①	②	②
Braking system	①	①	①	①	①	①	①	②
Electrical system	①	①	①	①	①	①	②	③
Engines	①	①	②	②	②	③	③	③
Exhaust/Converter	②	②	②	②	③	③	③	③
Fuel system	①	①	①	②	③	③	③	④
Ignition system	②	②	②	②	②	②	③	④
Rust/Paint	①	①	①	①	①	①	①	①
Steering	③	③	③	③	③	④	④	④
Suspension	③	③	③	③	③	③	③	③
Crash Safety								
Caravan	—	④	④	④	④	—	④	③
Grand Caravan	—	—	—	—	—	③	③	③
Town & Country	—	④	④	④	④	—	④	③
Town & Country LX	—	—	—	—	—	③	③	③

FORD

Aerostar

Rating: Average (1995–97); Not Recommended (1986–94). More brawny and more reliable than Chrysler's minivans. The Aerostar's last model year was 1997. **Maintenance/Repair costs:** Average, and any garage can repair an Aerostar. **Parts:** Plentiful, but not durable (especially AC; brake calipers, pads, and rotors; and electrical components).

Strengths and weaknesses: The 1986–94 models are at the bottom of the evolutionary scale as far as quality control is concerned. However, the last three model years have shown lots of improvement. Repair costs are reasonable (except for high AC costs), but mainly because the Aerostar's myriad mechanical and body defects are covered by Ford warranty extensions (see "Secret Warranties/Service Tips"). The Aerostar's modern, swoopy shape belies its limited performance capabilities: the 3.0L and 4.0L engines are unreliable through the 1991 model year, and the 3.0L is a sluggish performer. Older 2.3L and 2.8L engines can barely pull their own weight. The 4-speed automatic transmission often has a hard time deciding which gear to choose, and the power steering transmits almost no road feel to the driver. The ride is bouncy, handling is sloppy, and braking performance is poor. Reliability problems on all models make early Aerostars risky buys, especially if the previous owner has been less than fastidious in maintenance and repairs.

Valve cover and rear main oil seal leaks are frequent, and leaks from the front axle vent tube often require the replacement of the front axle assembly. Even oil pans, which you wouldn't normally associate with leaks, tend to leak as a result of premature corrosion. Fuel-injectors are either faulty or plugged. Other problems include expensive automatic transmission failures; electronic and electrical system glitches; power steering, suspension, and brake defects; and premature and chronic air conditioner breakdowns involving AC condensers and compressors that tend to fail after the first three years of use. (Ford has consistently produced failure-prone AC systems in the Aerostar van since its birth in 1986; according to *Consumer Reports*, their failure rate was almost three times that of other vehicles in its class.) Auto air conditioning experts refer to the problem as the "Black Death"—in reference to the sludge these Ford ACs produce that leads to massive internal component failures. One AC specialist describes the problem in these terms:

> The biggest problem is the original FX-15 compressor that came with the truck and the rebuilt replacement, which will likely be another FX-15. These compressors are bad news. When they go bad they fall to pieces internally and contaminate your system. The "gook" settles in your condenser and is hard to get rid of. We sometimes end up having to flush as many as three times, operating the system for 30 to 45 minutes between flushes and changing the orifice tube each time. This allows the heat and pressure to break loose the "gook" in the condenser. When we replace an FX-15 compressor, we will not use a remanufactured FX-15...they simply do not hold up.
>
> Motorcraft's FS-10/FX-15 compressors are especially sensitive to high pressures. Faulty fan clutches are one of the reasons why so many late-model Ford ('89 and newer) compressors fail. This also applies to FWD cars with weak or inoperative radiator cooling fans. FS-10 compressor design is excellent. However, something could be done about their fan clutch durability. We have noted an above normal incidence in Aerostars ('91 and up), Explorers ('91 and up), Ford Taurus, Sable (up to 1994), T-Bird/Cougar ('89 and up), and F-series ('92 and up).

A grinding/growling coming from the rear signals that the in-tank electric fuel pump is defective. Many mechanics find that the electronic engine controls are difficult to diagnose if problems arise. Routine repairs are very awkward because most components are buried under the windshield and dashboard. Windshield wipers are badly designed for winter driving. They freeze at the bottom of the windshield and wear out the wiper motor. Body hardware and integrity have earned low marks as well.

Safety summary/Recalls: 1986–90—A draft of a January 20, 1993, Ford internal document lists "known incidents which are attributed to the ignition switch." It includes the 1986 Aerostar and Econoline full-sized vans. NHTSA documents show that the Aerostar has almost the highest rate of ignition switch fires of any Ford truck, second only to the 1988

Bronco. State Farm Insurance has filed an action against Ford to cover its payouts to policyholders whose Aerostars caught fire from an over-heated ignition switch. • The hefty B-pillar (where the edge of the door meets the body behind the front seat) obstructs peripheral vision. • Some Aerostars don't have front seat head restraints, unless the vehi-cles are equipped with the optional captain's chairs, and even then the restraints sit far too low for the average person. • Owners complain that the brake master cylinder and daytime running lights module may sud-denly fail, and that 1990 Aerostars' rear brakes sometimes lock up in wet weather. **1988–90**—Cracked fuel tanks. **1993–94**—NHTSA is look-ing at electrical malfunctions that may cause overheating and/or fires at the fuel sender assembly on fuel tanks. **Recalls: 1986**—The rear sus-pension separating from the axle could cause steering loss. • Recall #90S04 provides for a free fuel tank replacement. • Lumbar seat wiring could short-circuit, creating a fire hazard. **1986–87**—Possible fuel line leaks. • Captain's chair may cut into seatbelt webbing. **1986–88**—Trailer towing package taillight wires may short-circuit, creating a fire hazard. **1987–89**—The rear liftgate may fail due to defective ball studs attaching the lift cylinders to the body. **1988–91**—The ignition switch could experience an internal short circuit, creating the potential for overheating, smoke, and possibly fire in the steering column area of the vehicle. **1989–90**—Quad Bucket seat assemblies may fail. **1990**—Ford will replace, gratis, faulty brake master cylinders. **1990–91**—Models with the A4LD automatic transmission may slip out of Park and roll as if in Neutral. **1992–94**—Vehicles may have a defective rear anti-lock brake control module. **1992–97**—Ford will fix wiring shorts that could cause a fire. • On models with AWD, the transmission or transfer case may crack or break. Dealers will install a new rear transfer case exten-sion and a new aluminum rear driveshaft. **1995**—Spare tire may frac-ture the brake line. • Defective brake rotors. • Fuel pump and wiring electrical shorts. **1996**—Driver's door may not sustain specified load in the secondary latched position. • Defective brake rotors. • Defective electrical relay ignition switch. **1997**—Aftermarket brake rotors may crack. Call 1-800-264-3414 for Aimco manufacturer's free replacement.

Secret Warranties/Service Tips

All models/years—Press Ford for "goodwill" warranty coverage if your AC is afflicted by the "Black Death" within 5 years/80,000 miles. • Use the emissions war-ranty to cure rotten-egg odors caused by a defective catalytic converter. • Two com-ponents that benefit from Ford's "goodwill" warranty extensions are fuel pumps and the computer modules that govern engine, fuel injection, and transmission functions. If Ford balks at refunding your money for a faulty computer module or fuel pump, apply the emissions warranty for a full or partial refund. • Paint delam-ination, fading, peeling, hazing, and "microchecking" (see page 113 for details on claiming a refund). **All models: 1986–91**—3.0L engine knocking at idle may require the installation of a new, thicker thrust plate to reduce camshaft end play. • Hard cold starts, hesitation, and stalling may be caused by sludge in the throttle body and/or an idle by-pass valve. Install an idle air by-pass service kit (#F2DZ-9F939-A). **1986–94**—A speaker whine or buzz caused by the fuel pump can be stopped by installing an electronic noise RFI filter. • Rust perforations may occur in the front and/or rear lower rocker panel areas because the panels weren't coated with primer. Ford will replace the panel at no charge for up to 6 years/100,000 miles (see following bulletin).

95-6-12
03/27/05
ROCKER PANEL - FRONT AND/OR REAR - RUST PERFORATION - SERVICE TIPS
LIGHT TRUCK:
1986–94 AEROSTAR
ISSUE:
Rust perforation may occur in the front and/or rear lower rocker panel area(s) on some vehicles. This may be due to the lower rocker panels having no electrodeposition primer (E-Coat) on the inside surface, for vehicles built from 1985–94.
ACTION:
Weld on lower rocker panel covers and blend to body with body filler. Paint rocker panel(s) to match the vehicle. Refer to the following procedures for service details.

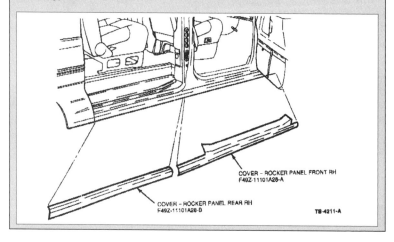

COVER – ROCKER PANEL FRONT RH
F49Z-11101A28-A

COVER – ROCKER PANEL REAR RH
F49Z-11101A28-B

TB-4211-A

1987–92—Brakes that stick or bind may have corroded brake caliper slide pins. Install corrosion-resistant pins (#E8TZ-2C150-B). **1988**—Delayed Reverse engagement can be corrected by installing a new separator plate. **1989–92**—If there's a popping or clunking and floorboard vibration when braking, it's likely caused by the front brake caliper suddenly springing away from the caliper abutment and returning. Adjusting the front brake pads and knuckle clearance will correct this problem. **1989–96**—A chatter noise during sharp turns is likely due to an insufficient friction modifier, or over-shimming of the clutch packs within Traction-Lock differentials. **1990**—Delayed upshift or no upshift can be corrected by installing a new #4 thrust washer. • AC compressor shaft seal leaks can be best fixed by installing a new seal (#E9SZ-19D665-A). **1990–92**—A 4.0L engine oil leak may occur around the rocker gasket because of variations in the gasket quality. Install two new rocker cover gaskets (Carrier type), along with conical spring screws. • Automatic transmission fluid leakage may be caused by a faulty or loose transfer case rear output seal. **1990–96**—Noisy power steering is likely caused by a pressure spike in the serpentine tube of the power-steering cooler. **1993–95**—A squeak or chirp coming from the blower motor can be stopped by installing an upgraded blower motor with improved brush-to-commutator friction. • An automatic transmission whine heard upon light acceleration can be silenced by replacing the front and rear planetary assembly and the front and rear sun gear. • Overheating or binding rear brakes can be corrected by backing off the self-adjusters. **1995–96**—Hard starts and stalling can be corrected by installing an upgraded idle air control valve under the emissions warranty. **1995–97**—Coolant leakage from the engine block heater requires the replacement of the block heater with an upgraded one that attaches better. **1997**—Delayed transmission engagement or constant shifting may be caused by an improper torque converter apply-and-release schedule (reprogram the powertrain control module).

Aerostar Profile

	1990	1991	1992	1993	1994	1995	1996	1997
Cost Price ($)								
Cargo	12,542	13,310	14,478	14,977	15,796	17,486	17,966	17,995
Wagon	14,487	15,466	15,881	15,682	16,302	17,895	18,375	18,405
Used Values ($)								
Cargo ↑	3,500	4,500	5,500	6,000	6,500	7,500	8,500	9,500
Cargo ↓	3,000	4,000	5,000	5,000	5,500	6,500	7,000	8,500
Wagon ↑	4,500	5,500	6,500	7,000	8,000	9,000	10,000	12,000
Wagon ↓	4,000	5,000	6,000	6,000	6,500	7,500	8,500	10,000
Extended Warranty	Y	Y	Y	Y	Y	Y	N	N
Secret Warranty	Y	Y	Y	Y	Y	Y	Y	Y
Reliability	❶	❷	❷	❷	③	③	④	④
Air conditioning	❶	❷	❷	❷	❷	③	④	④
Body integrity	❷	❷	❷	❷	❷	❷	❷	❷
Braking system	❶	❶	❶	❶	❶	❷	❷	❷
Electrical system	❶	❶	❶	❷	❷	③	③	③
Engines	❷	❷	❷	④	④	⑤	⑤	⑤
Exhaust/Converter	❶	❶	❶	❷	③	④	④	⑤
Fuel system	❶	③	③	③	③	④	④	④
Ignition system	❷	❷	③	③	④	④	⑤	⑤
Manual transmission	③	③	③	③	③	③	④	⑤
- automatic	❶	❷	③	③	③	③	④	④
Rust/Paint	❶	❶	❶	❶	❷	❷	③	③
Steering	❷	❷	③	③	③	④	④	④
Suspension	❷	❷	❷	③	③	③	③	④
Crash Safety	—	—	④	④	④	④	④	④

Mercury Villager/Nissan Quest

Rating: Recommended (1997–98); Above Average (1995–96); Not Recommended (1993–94). More carlike than most of their competitors. The Quest, engineered by Nissan and built by Ford in Ohio, is practically identical to the Villager, except for some slight styling differences, more standard equipment, and a slightly lower rate of depreciation. By choosing a Villager cargo van over a wagon, you can save between $1,500 and $2,000. **Maintenance/Repair costs:** Higher than average. Any garage can repair these minivans. **Parts:** Both Mercury and Nissan dealers carry parts, and auto club surveys show that parts are less expensive than those of most other minivans in this class. The exception to this rule: broken engine exhaust manifold studs (a frequent problem), AC, and electrical components. There are plenty of two- and three-year-old models on the market that have just come off lease; the Nissan may cost a bit more, however, because it depreciates more slowly than the Villager. Other minivans you may wish to consider: the GM front-drives or Toyota Sienna.

Strengths and weaknesses: The Villager's and the Quest's strongest features are their impressive highway performance (as long as you're not carrying a full load) and easy, no-surprise, carlike handling. Additional assets are a 4-speed automatic transmission that's particularly smooth and quiet, and mechanical components that have been tested for years on the Maxima and various Ford vehicles. The ride on both smooth and uneven highways is comfortable, overall highway stability is above reproach, and braking performance is quite good, aided by standard ABS, which improves directional control by eliminating wheel lockup.

These fuel-thirsty minivans are heavier than the Aerostar by about 700 pounds, and the 3.0L engine has only 6–16 additional horses to carry the extra weight. GM's 2.8L engines produce more torque than what the Villager and Quest can deliver. Precise steering makes the Villager feel more responsive at highway speeds and in emergency maneuvers than it really is. The control layout can be a bit confusing.

Interior space is impressive. The Villager is nearly a foot longer and two inches wider and higher than Chrysler's short-wheelbase minivans. There's better seating for three adults in the rear than with the Caravan, middle seatbacks fold flat, and the rear seats have tracks that allow them to slide forward all the way to the front or fold flat and convert to a serving area for tailgate parties.

There have been many reports of engine exhaust manifold stud failures (through 1994), electrical problems, brake failures, premature wear of the front disc brakes, and chronic stalling, possibly due to faulty fuel pumps or a shorted electrical system. One owner of a 1993 Villager GS tells of chronic vibrations at 60 mph that can't be dampened even after frequent tire replacements and suspension retuning. Body integrity on model years up to 1996 is sub-par, with doors opening and closing on their own and poor fit and finish, allowing lots of wind noise to enter the interior. (Yes, Ford got the body work, while Nissan handled the mechanicals. You can tell, can't you?) There have also been some reports of panel and paint defects and premature rusting on the inside sliding door track.

Dealer service bulletins: 1994—Transaxle whine in Overdrive. • Insufficient AC cooling or excessive clutch end gap. • Chirp/squeak from the blower motor, and blower motor running after shutoff. • Coolant leaks at the radiator hose (replaced for free at 3 years/60,000 miles under Ford's 94B42 Program). • Inoperative heater backlight. • Rattling or chucking noise from the sliding door, and sub-woofer rattling noise in the radio speakers. **1995**—Knocking noise in lower engine. • Coolant leak from the engine below the camshaft. • AC compressor failure. • Insufficient AC cooling or excessive clutch end gap. • Brakes binding and/or overheating. • Front brake squeal or groan. • Fuel pump buzz/whine through radio speaker. • Rear bench seat squeaks or rattles when the vehicle is underway. • Sliding door squeaks, rattles, or is hard to close. • Rear suspension makes a crunch/grunt noise. • Body side window won't stay closed. • Inoperative rear wiper motor. • Fog/film on windshield/interior glass. • Carpet lifts at right sliding seat track. • Sulfur smell from the exhaust system. • Musty and mildew-type odors. **1996**—Knocking noise in lower engine continues for another model year. • AC compressor failure is still a problem. • Intermittent operation of remote keyless entry system. • Sliding door squeaks, rattles, or requires great effort to close. • Rear bench seat squeaks or rattles when the vehicle is moving. • Rear suspension makes a crunch/grunt noise. • Airbag light flashes constantly. • Body side window won't stay closed. • Fog/film on windshield/interior glass. • Fuel pump buzz/whine through radio speaker. • Inadvertent horn operation. • Carpet lifts at right sliding seat track. • Musty and mildew-type odors. **1997**—Hard starts or no-starts in cold temperatures or high altitudes. • Shift lever hard to move from Park. • Front door windows bind. • Broken third-row right-hand seatbelt guide. • Fuel odor in passenger compartment when refueling. • Intermittent operation of remote keyless entry system. • Airbag light flashes constantly. • Chirping/squeaking noise from blower motor at low speeds. • Hissing from B-pillar area. • Noise during light brake application and release. • Rear suspension noise. • Tips on preventing brake vibration. • Fog/film on windshield/interior glass.

Safety summary/Recalls: 1994–96—NHTSA is looking into fuel leaks into the engine compartment and gas fumes that infiltrate the interior. • Vehicle suddenly accelerated forward. • Inadvertent airbag deployment. • Sudden stalling due to faulty fuel pump. • Both steering and brakes failed when turning into an intersection. • Steering wheel locked up while making a right turn. • Chronic ABS brake failures; brake pads and rotors need replacing every 10,000 miles; and drums often need turning. • Loose exhaust system heat shield. • Alarm system will lock and unlock the doors on its own. •Remote control door locks often won't respond, trapping occupants inside. • Faulty rear door latch and lock allow the door to come open while driving. • The sliding door opens for no apparent reason. • Power windows often jam. • Seatbelts don't retract properly and ratchet too tightly. • Shoulder belt got caught around child's neck and had to be cut away. • Frequent rear windshield wiper failures. • Solar window at certain angles distorts vision by reflecting images. **Recalls: All models: 1993**—A faulty brake master cylinder or leaking fuel-filler hoses will be replaced for free. • Defective automatic seatbelt anchor bolts. • Leaves or other debris can accumulate in the fresh-air intake of the heating and AC system, creating a possible fire hazard. **1994–95**—A faulty electrical socket may cause the rear light to fail to operate. • Defective third-row sliding bench seat. **1996**—Power windows aren't in compliance with safety regulations. **1997**—Fuel line hoses could crack or split. **Villager: 1997–98**—Faulty batteries may rupture or cause a fire.

Secret Warranties/Service Tips

All models/years—A rotten-egg odor coming from the exhaust is probably caused by a malfunctioning catalytic converter, which is covered by Ford's original warranty and the 5-year/80,000 mile emissions warranty. • Two components that benefit from Ford's "goodwill" warranty extensions are fuel pumps and computer modules that govern engine, fuel-injection, and transmission functions. • Paint delamination, fading, peeling, hazing, and "microchecking" (see page 113 for details on claiming a refund). **All models: 1993**—Harsh automatic transmission upshifts may be caused by metal contamination in the solenoid assembly. • Excessive exhaust manifold noise is likely due to a broken stud. Install upgraded studs. • An inoperative air conditioning blower motor can be fixed by installing a new blower motor resistor. • Stalling whenever the vehicle is shifted from Park to Drive to Reverse may mean that the torque converter is stuck in the "lockup" mode. Install an upgraded valve body assembly (#F3XY-7A100-D) and a transaxle oil pan gasket to fix the problem. • A ticking or clicking from the suspension strut area signals the need for an upgraded front strut spacer (#F3XY-3A120-A). • Fogging or frosting of the side windows may be caused by a misconnected C261 electrical connector. • If the liftgate light/door ajar light flickers intermittently or the vehicle won't start, the rear liftgate latch may need to be changed. • A rear suspension clunk or thump when passing over bumps is likely caused by improperly calibrated rear shock absorbers. • Install an upgraded speed control module (#F3XY-9FS12-B) if the vehicle loses 3–5 mph on hills or grades with the present module. • A clicking or ticking noise when accelerating can be corrected by installing a new EGR tube with a redesigned fitting. • A shudder or vibration that occurs during the 1–2 shift can be corrected by replacing the automatic transaxle valve body with an upgraded valve body and transaxle oil pan gasket. **1993–94**—Ford will cover defective engine exhaust manifold studs on a case-by-case basis up to 5 years/80,000 miles (see following bulletin).

Classification: EM94-002
Section: Engine Mechanical
Reference: TECHNICAL BULLETIN NTB94-041
Models: See below
Date: April 14, 1994
BROKEN EXHAUST MANIFOLD STUD
APPLIED MODELS:
- Pathfinder (WD21)
- Maxima (J30 and U11)
- Truck (D21)
- 300ZX (Z31)
- 200ZX (S12)
SERVICE INFORMATION: The exhaust manifold stud has been changed for improved durability. Use the following procedure to repair vehicles that exibit excessive exhaust noise due to exhaust manifold stud breakage.
REPAIR PROCEDURE:

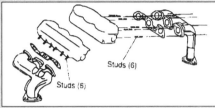

Studs (6)

Studs (6)

Figure 1

1. Remove the exhaust manifold on the side of the engine with broken stud(s). (Figure 1)
2. Replace the broken stud(s) and the front and rear studs DWI using the improved part, P/N 14065-V5003
3. Replace the exhaust manifold gasket and the exhaust manifold with new parts.
WARRANTY INFORMATION:
Please reference Section "AT-Manifolds (V6 Engine)" of the current "Nissan Flat Rate Manual" and select the appropriate right/left manifold gasket replacement OpCode with the indicated combination OpCode for the replacement of the right/left exhaust manifold stud. Use PNC 14006 and the indicated FRT's for the applicable vehicle.

Nissan will argue they've never heard of this stud problem and then relent and offer some compensation. Ford is easier to deal with.

• A squeak or chirp coming from the blower motor can be stopped by installing an upgraded blower motor with improved brush-to-commutator friction. • Sliding door noise may need a new service spring in the upper hinge and a readjustment of the dovetail. • A speaker whine or buzz caused by the fuel pump can be stopped by installing an electronic noise RFI filter. • Body squeaks and rattles are thoroughly discussed in DSB #04-86-94. **1993–95**—The rear wiper motor may quit or stop intermittently because water has gotten into the motor printed circuit board. • Replace front brake pads that cause excessive brake squeaking or groaning with upgraded pads. **1993–96**—A crunch/grunt noise from the rear suspension may be caused by rear shackle bushings that need lubrication. **1993–97**—Front door windows that bind may have the glass rubber improperly installed into the door sheet metal channel. **1994–98**—If there's a strong fuel odor in the passenger compartment when refueling, it's likely there's a missing sealer between the fuel-filler opening upper flange and the fuel-filler base assembly. **1995–96**—Ford has replaced, at no charge, 3.0L V6 engine blocks that produce excessive engine knock following a cold start. **1995–99**—Tips for correcting windshield water leaks. **1996–98**—Power door locks that intermittently self-activate (help, let me out!) are a common occurrence that's covered in DSB #98-22-5 (see following bulletin).

Article No.:
98-22-5
11/09/98
POWER DOOR LOCK - INTERMITTENT
SELF-ACTIVATION
LIGHT TRUCK:
1996–98 VILLAGER
This TSB article is being republished in its entirety to revise the Power Door Lock Signal and Wiring Check Procedure and provide an Actuator Assembly part number.
ISSUE
Intermittent self-activation of the power door locks may occur on some vehicles. This may be caused by any of the following:
- All 1996–98 Model Year Vehicles:
  - Adjustment of the front door lock rod linkage
  - Water/moisture collecting in the left front door window switch potentially causing an internal short or ground
  - Power door lock wiring
- All 1996-98 Model Year Vehicles Equipped With Anti-Theft:
  - Water/moisture collecting in the front door key lock cylinders potentially causing a grounding condition in the circuit
  - Water/moisture collecting in driver's door key cylinder switch-to-harness connector
- 1996 Vehicles Only:
  - Smart Entry Control (SEC) timer module
ACTION
Replace front window switch, module, adjust front door lock rod linkage, and grease switch and harness connections on anti-theft vehicles.
WARRANTY STATUS: Eligible Under the Provisions of Bumper to Bumper Warranty Coverage.

Talk about being a captive customer…!

1997—Hard starts or no-starts in cold temperatures or at high altitudes can be corrected by replacing the power control module (PCM) under the emissions warranty.

Mercury Villager/Nissan Quest Profile

	1993	1994	1995	1996	1997	1998
Cost Price ($)						
Villager GS	17,401	18,325	18,995	19,940	20,540	22,885
Villager LS	22,683	22,975	24,650	25,595	27,595	27,485
Quest XE	17,895	18,909	20,229	21,304	21,699	23,589
Quest GXE	21,800	23,419	24,999	26,104	26,469	26,539
Used Values ($)						
Villager GS ↑	8,500	9,500	10,500	11,500	13,000	15,000
Villager GS ↓	7,500	8,500	9,500	10,500	11,500	12,500
Villager LS ↑	10,000	11,500	13,000	14,000	16,000	17,000
Villager LS ↓	8,500	9,500	11,500	12,500	14,000	15,500
Quest XE ↑	9,000	11,000	12,000	13,000	14,500	16,000
Quest XE ↓	8,000	9,500	11,000	12,000	13,000	14,500
Quest GXE ↑	10,500	12,000	13,000	14,500	16,000	17,500
Quest GXE ↓	9,000	11,000	12,000	13,000	14,500	16,000
Extended Warranty	Y	Y	N	N	N	N
Secret Warranty	Y	Y	Y	Y	Y	N

Reliability	③	③	③	④	④	⑤
Air conditioning	③	③	③	③	⑤	⑤
Automatic transmission	④	⑤	⑤	⑤	⑤	⑤
Body integrity	❶	❷	❷	❷	③	③
Braking system	❷	❷	❷	❷	❷	③
Electrical system	❶	❷	❷	❷	❷	③
Engines	❷	③	③	⑤	⑤	⑤
Exhaust/Converter	❶	❷	③	④	⑤	⑤
Fuel system	④	④	⑤	⑤	⑤	⑤
Ignition system	④	④	⑤	⑤	⑤	⑤
Rust/Paint	❷	❷	③	④	④	④
Steering	④	⑤	⑤	⑤	⑤	⑤
Suspension	③	③	④	④	⑤	⑤
Crash Safety	④	④	④	④	④	—

Windstar

Rating: Below Average (1996–98); Not Recommended (1995). Don't go anywhere near this minivan without an extended powertrain warranty. Other, more-reliable minivans you may wish to consider: a late-model GM front-drive, a Mercury Villager/Nissan Quest, or a Toyota Previa or Sienna. Sure, the Windstar combines an impressive five-star safety rating, plenty of raw power, an exceptional ride, and impressive cargo capacity. But the self-destructing 3.8L engine and erratic automatic transmission are black holes that will suck your wallet into their vortex (see "Dead Ford Page" and "Ford Windstar Engine Head Gasket Automatic Transmission" website links in the Appendix. And, as a counterpoint to Ford's well-earned Windstar crashworthiness boasting, take a look at the following summary ("Safety summary/Recalls") of safety-related complaints recorded by the U.S. Department of Transportation. Scary, isn't it? **Maintenance/Repair costs:** Average while under warranty; higher than average thereafter (figure on $200 tie-rod replacements every two years). **Parts:** Reasonably priced parts aren't as hard to find as they once were, mainly due to the entry of independent suppliers.

Strengths and weaknesses: Launched as a 1995 model in March 1994, the Windstar is a front-drive minivan that looks a bit like a stretched Mercury Villager. It's longer, larger, and lower than most other minivans. It's also one of the few minivans not built on a truck platform (it uses the Taurus platform instead), and as a result, it has some of the carlike handling distinctions of Chrysler's minivans. It's offered in two body styles—a seven-passenger people-hauler and the less-expensive, basic cargo van.

    There are a number of powertrain deficiencies that cut dramatically into the Windstar's performance and overall reliability. The automatic transmission, for example, is anything but smooth and has a scarlet history for running away when unattended, or simply packing it in early due to a failure-prone forward clutch piston, among other defective components. At the best of times, it pauses before downshifting or shifts roughly into a higher gear.

The 3.0L engine is overwhelmed by the Windstar's heft and struggles to keep up, but opting for the 3.8L V6 may get you into worse trouble. Owners of recently minted Windstars report that the 3.8L engine head gaskets need replacing shortly after the 50,000-mile mark. And if all these problems get you hot under the collar, too bad, you'll also have to contend with an air conditioning system that's generically dysfunctional and is reportedly also biodegradable.

But what's gotten many owners steaming in the past has been Ford's arrogant mishandling of their calls and letters, as this Canadian owner of a '95 Windstar LX with 40,000 miles relates:

> We have purchased a 1995 Ford Windstar LX which is inadequate and unsuitable for its intended purpose—namely, reliable family transportation...together, the warranty work and retail work that directly relates to recalls, engine failures, transmission failures, and the like are in excess of $9,000...
>
> As recently as last week, our van stalled out at an intersection when we were attempting a left hand turn, in front of traffic. Fortunately there was no accident and nobody was injured. The engine stalled out completely and would not start for a minute or two...
>
> My concerns with Ford are twofold.
>
> 1) They have sold us a vehicle which is inadequate.
>
> 2) Ford's total failure to deal with the correspondence that I have sent.
>
> In my conversation with the Ford Customer Service Representative, I asked why, after sending five letters to Ford, we at that time received only one written reply...That letter was not responsive to the issues raised in my correspondence...Your Representative then replied that, "I don't see any reason why a written response is needed."
>
> With respect, the Corporate arrogance of your Customer Assistance Representative inflames a rather unsatisfactory relationship we have with Ford Canada. Further, to send us the identical form letter twice does little to assure us that Ford is at all responsive to our concerns, or for that matter, even reading our correspondence...
>
> I have done what I can, absent litigation, to bring this matter to Ford's attention. Whatever you do, do not send me a third copy of your form letter.

Dealer service bulletins: 1995—Insufficient AC cooling or excessive clutch end gap. • Condensation leak at the auxiliary AC unit requires the installation of upgraded hose clamps. • Malfunctioning Forward/ Reverse engagement, intermittent loss of torque at 3–4 upshift, and low transaxle fluid improperly setting the DTC causes major transmission malfunctions. • Solenoid corrosion causes a no-crank condition. • Chirp or squeak from the blower motor at low speeds. • Radio static, minor dash rattles, and false Door Ajar warnings. **1996**—Stall or hard start after 1–4 hour soak. • Case breakage at rear planet support. • Transaxle driveline noises. • Steering drift or pull diagnostic tips. • Clunk in floor pan when accelerating/decelerating. • Clunk when moving gearshift out of Park. • Faulty power door locks. • Fuel gauge won't read over three-quarters. • Fog/film on windshield/interior glass. • Objectionable carpet odor. • AC musty odor. • Windshield wiper chatter/ streaking. **1997**—Harsh automatic transmission at 1–2 shift. • Intermittent Neutral condition when coming to a stop. • Parking brake may not release. • Tips on preventing brake vibration. • Water dripping onto floor from AC drain tube. • Inoperative rear auxiliary AC blower. • AC compressor moan. • Chirp or squeak from the blower motor at low speeds. • Clunking noise when moving gear shift lever out of Park. • Squeaking, creaking noise from upper A-pillar on turns. • Static noise heard at the low end of AM radio band. • Right rear quarter panel black soot deposits. • Fog/film on windshield/interior glass.

Safety summary/Recalls: Base models don't have head restraints for all seats, and the digital dash can be confusing. Fuel tank leaks. **1996**— Sudden acceleration and chronic stalling. • Severe injuries caused by airbag deployment. • Control arm and inner tie-rod failures cause the wheel to fall off. • Chronic ABS brake and transmission failures. • Almost a dozen reports that the vehicle jumps out of Park and rolls away when on an incline or slips into Reverse with the engine idling. • Faulty fuel pump. • Built-in child safety seat is easy to get out of, yet securing seatbelts are too tight; child almost strangled. • Engine head gasket failures. • Faulty rear liftgate latches. **1997**—Sudden accelera-tion. • ABS and transmission failures. • Steering wheel lockup. **1998**— Sudden acceleration and chronic stalling. • Loose or missing front brake bolts could cause the wheels to lock up or a loss of vehicle con-trol. • Frequent ABS brake and transmission failures. • Transmission and axle separation. • Vehicle jumps out of Park and rolls away when on an incline or slips into Reverse with the engine idling. • Trunk lid can fall on one's head. • Faulty fuel pump, sensor, and gauge. **Recalls: All models: 1995**—Hood may be defective. • A loose connection within the electrical power distribution box could ignite the electrical wiring under the hood. • A pinched instrument panel wire harness could cause a short circuit and start an electrical fire. • The passenger airbag may not deploy properly. • An alternator wiring short circuit could cause a fire. **1996**—Hood may be defective. • Transmission may not engage; PRNDL may give a false reading. **1997–98**—Servo cover can leak, creating a fire hazard. **1998**—Defective steering assembly.

Secret Warranties/Service Tips

All models: 1995—Blower motor squeaking or chirping can be silenced by installing an upgraded blower motor. **1995–96**—Intermittent no-starts may be caused by microscopic cracks on the fuel pump relay cover located inside the Constant Control Relay Module (CCRM); install a new CCRM. **1995–98**—The front-end accessory drive belt (FEAD) slips during wet conditions, causing a reduction in steering power-assist. Ford suggests the belt be replaced. • Water leakage onto carpet or headliner in rear cargo area is a factory-related defect covered in DSB #98-5-5 (see following bulletin).

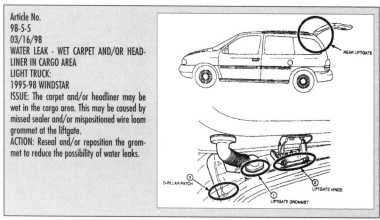

Article No.
98-5-5
03/16/98
WATER LEAK - WET CARPET AND/OR HEAD-
LINER IN CARGO AREA
LIGHT TRUCK:
1995-98 WINDSTAR
ISSUE: The carpet and/or headliner may be
wet in the cargo area. This may be caused by
missed sealer and/or mispositioned wire loom
grommet at the liftgate.
ACTION: Reseal and/or reposition the grommet to reduce the possibility of water leaks.

Ford says the resealing of the rear liftgate area or roof rack holes is covered by its bumper-to-bumper warranty.

1995–99—Tips for correcting side door wind noise and windshield water leaks. **1996–98**—Harsh automatic shifting from 1 to 2 may be caused by a malfunctioning electronic pressure control or the main control valves sticking in the valve body. • An intermittent Neutral condition when coming to a stop signals the need to replace the forward clutch piston and the forward clutch cylinder. • Black soot deposits on the right rear quarter panel can be avoided by installing an exhaust tailpipe extension under Ford's base warranty. • Engine oil mixed with coolant or coolant loss signals the need for revised 3.8L or 4.2L engine lower intake manifold side gaskets and/or front cover gaskets (covered by the emissions warranty). **1998–99**—Tips on spotting abnormal ABS braking noise.

Windstar Profile

	1995	1996	1997	1998
Cost Price ($)				
GL	19,995	20,785	23,070	24,025
LX	24,080	25,340	26,195	28,365

Used Values ($)

GL ↑	11,500	13,000	15,000	16,500
GL ↓	10,500	12,000	14,000	15,500
LX ↑	12,500	15,000	16,500	18,000
LX ↓	11,000	14,000	15,500	17,000

Extended Warranty	Y	Y	Y	Y
Secret Warranty	Y	Y	Y	Y

Reliability	❷	❷	❷	③
Crash Safety	⑤	⑤	⑤	⑤

GENERAL MOTORS

Astro/Safari

Rating: Average (1996–98); Not Recommended (1985–95). These vehicles are more minitruck than minivan. Believe it or not, these run-of-the-mill minivans are beginning to look quite good when compared to the powertrain-challenged Chrysler and Ford minivans. **Maintenance/Repair costs:** Average. Any garage can repair these rear-drive minivans. **Parts:** Plentiful and reasonably priced. As with the Aerostar, the classified ads are jam-packed with sellers wanting to unload their Astros and Safaris simply because their vehicles have got high mileage or the owners are small businesses whose needs have moved up to a larger van. Whatever the reason, you can find some real bargains if you're patient. Other choices you may wish to consider: the later-model Ford Aerostar or a full-sized GM or Ford van.

Strengths and weaknesses: Introduced during the 1985 model year, these minivans are basically trucks dressed in minivan garb. Nevertheless, these spacious vans can be fitted to tow up to 6,000 lb. and carry eight people. The base 4.3L V6 gives acceptable acceleration, but the High Output variant of the same engine (first available in the 1991 model) is a far better choice, particularly when it's mated to a manual gearbox. The full-time AWD versions aren't very refined, have a high failure rate, and are expensive to diagnose and repair. The 1995 models got a minor facelift, a bit more horsepower, and extended bodies.

Early versions suffer from failure-prone automatic transmissions, a poor braking system, and fragile steering components. The early base V6 provides ample power, but also produces lots of noise, consumes excessive amounts of fuel, and tends to have leaking head gaskets and failure-prone oxygen sensors. These computer-related problems often rob the engine of sufficient power to keep up in traffic. Even though the 5-speed manual transmission shifts fairly easily, the automatic takes forever to downshift on the highway. Handling isn't particularly agile on these minivans, and the power steering doesn't provide the driver with enough road feel. Unloaded, the Astro provides very poor traction, the ride isn't comfortable on poor road surfaces, and interior noise is rampant. Many drivers find the driving position awkward (no left-leg room) and the heating/defrosting system inadequate. Many engine components are hidden under the dashboard, making repair or maintenance awkward.

Even on more recent models, highway performance and overall reliability remain mediocre. The 4-speed automatic transmissions are clunky, but much more reliable than the Ford or Chrysler gearboxes. Excessive rear-end clunking and clanging occurs whenever the transmission shifts or downshifts while under load. One worker at GM's Oshawa, Ontario, plant—a 1993 Safari owner—wrote GM's president the following angry letter:

> Do you as CEO really know what's going on or does middle management filter out the bad news? GM's policy on warranty service is atrocious, your service representative was rude and your parts are substandard...Your bulletin 93-4A-101, "Discouraging dealers from attempting to repair driveline clunk," is weaseling out on your responsibilities to the customer.

Other owners report that the front suspension, steering components, computer modules, and catalytic converter can wear out within as little as 40,000 miles. There have also been lots of complaints about electrical, exhaust, cooling, and fuel system bugs; inadequate heating/defrosting; and axle seals wearing out every 12–18 months. Many owners write that they've had to endure a rotten-egg smell coming from the exhaust. Body hardware is fragile, and fit and finish is the pits. One 1994 Safari owner, frustrated by chronic water leaks, replaced the rear hatch molding three times without any improvement. Squeaks and rattles are legion and hard to locate. Sliding door handles often break off and the sliding door frequently jams in cold temperatures. The hatch release for the Dutch doors occasionally doesn't work and the driver's side vinyl seat lining tears apart. Premature paint peeling/delamination and surface rust are fairly common.

Dealer service bulletins: 1996—Engine noise (install new valve stem oil seal). • Hard start or no-start. • Intermittent hesitation, low power, and rough running. • Lack of power and early, late, or erratic shifts. • Transmission fluid leak from pump body. • 3–2 part throttle downshift flare and delayed transmission engagement. • Clutch chatter or shudder. • Driveline clunk noises. • Steering column snap or clicking noise. • Fuel tank lines may have insufficient torque. • Insufficient AC performance and/or noisy clutch. • AC odors. • No heat from air ducts. • Abnormal condensation in taillights and other lights. **1997**—Bench seat squeak or squawk noise. • Driveline clunk noises. • Engine noise.

• Rough engine performance. • Insufficient heat to driver's side, and cold air comes from the left-side kick panel. • Low-voltage reading or dim lights at idle.

Safety summary/Recalls: 1990–91—There were 31 complaints of dashboard fires. **1995**—Fire ignited under the dashboard. • Headlight switch shorted out, resulting in a fire. • Driver-side airbag failed to deploy. • Vehicle continues to accelerate after foot is removed from accelerator. • Frequent stalling. • Erratic engine performance due to blocked catalytic converter. • Engine leaks oil. • Loose fan belts cause belts to come off, causing loss of power steering and brakes. • Frequent brake failures. • Loss of braking when going over a bump. • ABS failed to engage. • ABS suddenly engaged for no reason and then wouldn't disengage. • ABS hesitates when applied. • Defective brake calipers. • Power brake hose fell off, causing loss of power brakes. • Front brake hoses collapsed, causing sudden brake failure. • Premature front brake wear. • Power-steering lockup. • Power-steering hose fell off, causing loss of power steering. • Power-steering fluid leaks. • Vehicle jerks to one side when braking. • Front wheels lock up when turning the steering wheel to the right from a stop while in gear. • Steering stuck when turning. • Seatbelts fail to work properly. • Shoulder belt failed to restrain driver in collision. • When the middle seat is removed, the seatbelt that is attached permanently to the headliner swings freely in the passenger compartment. • There is no room to latch the seatbelt. • Passenger-side seatbelt tightens up with every movement. • Seatbelt locks up unexpectedly. • Bench seatbelts are too short and cannot be adjusted. • Fresh-air ventilation system allows fumes from other vehicles to enter interior compartment. • With jack almost fully extended, wheel doesn't lift off of ground. • Spare tire not safe for driving over 35 mph. • Design of horn makes it difficult to use. • Horn buttons require excessive pressure to activate them. • Driver-side window failure. • Sliding door suddenly fell off. • Faulty door hinges allow the door to fall off. • Sliding door rattles. • Front passenger door won't close. • Passenger-side door glass fell out. • Rear hatch latch release failed. • Rear hatch hydraulic rods are too weak to support hatch. • Front passenger's seat reclining mechanism failed. • Poor traction. • Parked in gear and rolled downhill. • Transmission failures. • Left rear axle seal leaks, causing lubricant to burn on brake lining. • Excessive rear-end axle noise. • Sudden wheel bearing failure. • AC clutch fell apart. • Alternator bearing failure. • Windshield wipers fail intermittently. **Recalls: 1985**—The steering gear may crack or break free, causing sudden steering loss. **1985–91**—The seatback may recline suddenly. **1989**—GM will install and relocate a new AC line. **1990**—GM will repair the fuel return line fitting crimp for free. **1995**—Possible separation of control arm from the frame. • Vehicles with the L35 engine may have fuel line leakage. **1996–97**—Outboard seatbelt webbing on right rear bucket seat can separate during a crash. **1996–98**—Defective child safety seat attaching belts. **1997**—Defective right-hand rear bucket seatbelt webbing.

Secret Warranties/Service Tips

All models/years—Defective catalytic converters that cause a rotten-egg smell will be replaced free of charge under the vehicle's emissions warranty. • Paint delamination, peeling, or fading (see pages 73–75). **All models: 1985–93**— Vehicles equipped with a Hydramatic 4L60 transmission that buzzes when the car is in Reverse or idle may need a new oil pressure regulator valve. • A power-steering hiss can be silenced by replacing the power-steering valve assembly. **1988–92**—Hydramatic 4L60/700R4 automatic transmission may click or whine in third or fourth gear. There may also be a rattling noise coming from the rear of the transmission. Correct by installing five new fiber plates in the Low and Reverse clutch. The new plates have a differ-ent groove configuration that prevents third and fourth gear vibration. **1989–91**—THM 700-R4 automatic transmissions may exhibit a no-Reverse or delayed Reverse condition in cold weather. This problem can be cor-rected by replacing the piston outer seal with a long lip design. If this design is already being used or there's no improvement, change the Reverse input clutch housing. • A binding sliding door requires the replacement of the center track rolling bracket, the center track assembly, and the lower track striker/bumper assembly. **1992–94**—The PCV hose may freeze, causing oil starvation to the engine and leading to engine fail-ure. Alaska owners are eligible for free higher-flow calibrated PCVs under the emissions warranty. All other cold-weather operators are supposed to be told of the problem and given free servicing on a case-by-case basis. **1993–94**—A faulty speedometer, inability to shift down into second gear, or a transmission stuck in second gear may all be corrected by replacing the C240 connector. • Poor cold starting can be traced to a defective fuel pump relay. **1993–95**—Malfunctioning gauges and driveability problems may be the result of a short circuit caused by the C110 connector wire rubbing against the AC accumulator pipe. • GM says that a chronic driveline clunk can't be silenced and is a characteristic of its late-model vehicles. **1996–97**— Excessive engine noise can be curtailed by installing an upgraded valve stem oil seal. **1996–98**—Rough engine performance may be caused by a water-contaminated oxygen sensor.

Astro/Safari Profile

	1991	1992	1993	1994	1995	1996	1997	1998
Cost Price ($)								
Cargo	14,081	14,636	15,336	15,985	18,340	19,152	19,583	19,925
CS/base	17,145	16,726	17,146	17,819	19,886	19,736	20,167	21,628
Used Values ($)								
Cargo ↑	5,000	6,000	7,000	8,000	9,000	10,500	12,000	13,000
Cargo ↓	4,000	5,000	6,000	7,000	8,000	9,000	10,500	11,500
CS/base ↑	6,000	8,000	9,000	10,000	11,500	13,000	15,000	16,500
CS/base ↓	5,000	7,000	7,500	8,500	10,000	12,000	13,500	15,000
Extended Warranty	Y	Y	Y	Y	Y	Y	N	N
Secret Warranty	Y	Y	Y	Y	Y	Y	Y	Y
Reliability	❶	❷	❷	❷	❷	③	③	④

Air conditioning	②	②	②	②	②	③	④	④
Automatic transmission	①	②	③	③	③	③	③	③
Body integrity	①	①	①	①	①	①	②	②
Braking system	①	①	①	②	②	②	②	③
Electrical system	①	①	①	①	①	①	③	③
Engines	①	②	③	④	④	④	⑤	⑤
Exhaust/Converter	②	③	③	③	④	④	④	④
Fuel system	④	④	④	④	④	④	④	④
Ignition system	①	①	②	②	②	③	④	④
Rust/Paint	①	①	①	①	①	①	②	②
Steering	②	③	③	③	③	④	④	④
Suspension	②	②	②	②	②	③	③	④
Crash Safety	—	①	①	①	—	③	③	③

Lumina/Lumina APV/Silhouette/Trans Sport/Venture

Rating: Above Average (1997–98); Average (1995–96); Not Recommended (1990–94). The Lumina's last model year was 1996; the Trans Sport was carried over to the 1998 model year. The Venture debuted as a 1997 model. The 1997–98 model ratings have been raised because fewer powertrain problems have been reported by owners. **Maintenance/Repair costs:** Higher than average, but any garage can repair these minivans. **Parts:** Plentiful, but costly. Plastic body panels may soon be in short supply. There are plenty of reasonably priced two- and three-year-old models that have just come off lease on the market. Other minivans you may wish to consider: the Mercury Villager, Nissan Quest, or Toyota's Previa and Sienna.

Strengths and weaknesses: Although the 1994 and later models have less of a Dustbuster look, GM's plastic-bodied, front-drive minivan resembles more a swoopy station wagon than the traditional minivan (like the popular, boxy Chrysler Caravan). These vehicles use the Chevrolet Lumina platform, and therefore have more carlike handling than GM's Astro and Safari. Seating is limited to five adults in the standard models (two up front and three on a removable bench seat), but this can be increased to seven if you order optional modular seats. Seats can be folded down flat, creating additional storage space. Incidentally, be careful not to drop your keys between the windshield and the dash because you'll need a fishing rod to get them back.

The chassis and mechanical components on early models come from GM's W-bodies (Lumina, Regal, Cutlass Supreme, and Grand Prix), which explains why these minivans had so many of the same factory-related defects as their smaller cousins—notably, electronic module (PROM) and starter failures, short circuits, automatic transmission breakdowns, abysmal fit and finish, chronic sliding door malfunctions, and faulty rear seat latches. Other problems include a 4-speed automatic transmission that isn't as durable as the less fuel-efficient 3-speed automatic; a poorly mounted sliding door; side door glass that pops open; squeaks, rattles, and clunks in the instrument panel cluster area and suspension; and a wind buffeting noise around the front doors. By the way, don't trust the towing limit listed in GM's owner's manual. Automakers publish tow ratings that are on the optimistic side—and sometimes they even lie. Also, don't be surprised to find that the base 3.1L engine doesn't handle a full load of passenger and cargo, especially when mated to the 3-speed automatic transmission. The ideal powertrain combo would be the 4-speed automatic coupled to the optional "3800" V6 (first used on the 1996 versions).

The large dent- and rust-resistant plastic panels are robot-bonded to the frame with unique new adhesives, and they absorb engine and road noise very well, in addition to having an impressive record for durability. Some body shops complain, however, that the innovative panels are in short supply and that damaged panels can't be recycled. This drives up the cost of repairs and tempts insurance adjusters to simply write off repairable vehicles.

Dealer service bulletins: 1996—Intermittent Neutral/loss of Drive at highway speeds. • Second-gear starts; poor 1–3 shifting. • Insufficient AC performance, and AC odor at start-up in humid climates. • Steering column click, snapping noise. • Rattles from second- and third-row seat assemblies and in rear compartment area of the roof console. • Radio frequency interference diagnosis. • Erratic fuel gauge needle. • Low-voltage reading or dim lights at idle. • Condensation on exterior lights. • Water leak at the top of the sliding door. **1997**—Engine coolant weeping from coolant recovery reservoir. • Intermittent Neutral/loss of Drive at highway speeds. • Brakes are inoperative, drag, heat up, or wear out early. • Front brake squealing or grinding and rear brake clicking or squealing. • Air temperature from climate control system doesn't change. • Cold-start rattling. • Engine noise in passenger compartment. • Rattle at rear of vehicle or upon closing liftgate. • Rear suspension thud/clunk. • Inoperative power door locks. • Low-voltage reading or dim lights at idle. • Inoperative power window auto-down feature. • Movement of captain's chairs during cornering and turns. • Troubleshooting tips for sliding door malfunctions.

Safety summary/Recalls: Some front door–mounted seatbelts cross uncomfortably at the neck, and there's a nasty blind spot on the driver's side that requires a small stick-on convex mirror to correct. • NHTSA has closed an investigation of transaxle hose separation in exchange for GM's promise to conduct a regional recall. **Recalls: 1990**—Defective modular rear seat latches. **1993–94**—The rear seatbelt may not retract on vehicles with power sliding doors. **1995**—The throttle cable support bracket needs to be replaced in order to enable the engine to decelerate. • Steering could fail. • Brake pedal arm could fracture. **1998**—Vehicle may roll away while in Park. • Install safety guards on seat latches. **Trans Sport: 1990–91**—The upper glove box door may not stay closed in an accident.

Secret Warranties/Service Tips

All models/years—Defective catalytic converters that cause a rotten-egg smell in the interior may be replaced free of charge under the emissions warranty. **All models: 1990–91**—Hydramatic 4L60/700R4 automatic transmission may have no upshift or appear to be stuck in first gear. The probable cause is a worn governor gear. It would be wise to replace the retaining ring as well. **1990–92**—Vehicles with a 3T40 automatic transmission may slip in Low or Reverse gear. Correct by replacing the Low/Reverse clutch components, including the Low/Reverse release spring, clutch spring retainer, and piston snap ring. • A shudder or vibration at low speeds in vehicles equipped with a 3.1L engine may be caused by a faulty PROM electronic module. • A power-steering shudder can be corrected by replacing the power-steering return hose/pipe assembly with a revised assembly and internal tuning cable (#26030907). **1990–94**—An engine ticking at idle can be traced to rattling piston pins, which must be replaced with upgraded parts. **1991**—On vehicles with 3.1L engine, hesitation or stalling may require a new service calibration PROM that revises tip-in fuelling. If the problem is reduced power, it may signal the need to replace the electronic spark control (ESC). **1991–92**—A delayed shift between Drive and Reverse is likely caused by a rolled or cut input clutch piston outer seal. **1992**—Power-steering shudder can be reduced by installing an upgraded power-steering outlet hose/pipe assembly (#260337593). **1992–93**—No Reverse gear or slipping in Reverse can be corrected by installing an upgraded Low/Reverse clutch return spring and spiral retaining ring. **1992–94**—Loss of Drive or erratic shifts may be caused by an intermittent short to ground on the A or B shift solenoid, or an electrical short circuit in the transaxle. • A front-end clunking noise when driving over rough roads may require the repositioning of the diagonal radiator support braces. • A front-end engine knock troubleshooting chart is found in DSB #306001. **1993–94**—Owners who complain of automatic transmission low-speed miss, hesitation, chuggle, or skip may find relief with an improved MEMCAL module that GM developed to remedy the problem. **1993–95**—An engine coolant leak from the throttle body assembly may require an upgraded service seal kit. **1994**—Front door glass window scraping/chattering can be eliminated by relocating the front lower guide attachment. • Lazy front seatbelt retractors will be replaced free of charge. • A liftgate that fails to lock may have a loose or missing lock cylinder lock-out pin. • Manual sliding side doors that stick shut require a lock replacement. **1995**—A thud/clunk noise occurs when the fuel tank is more than three-quarters full. GM will replace the fuel tank and sender assembly. **1995–96**—Intermittent Neutral/loss of Drive at highway speeds can be fixed by replacing the control valve body assembly. **1997**—Rear brake clicking or squealing may be caused by a misadjusted parking brake cable. • Brakes that don't work, drag, heat up, or wear out early may have a variety of causes, all outlined in DSB #73-50-27. • A rear suspension thud or clunk may be silenced by installing upgraded rear springs.

Lumina/Lumina APV/Silhouette/Trans Sport/Venture Profile

	1991	1992	1993	1994	1995	1996	1997	1998
Cost Price ($)								
Lumina Cargo	14,102	14,905	15,225	16,015	16,775	18,415	—	—
Passenger	16,045	16,930	17,255	18,178	19,625	20,435	—	—
Silhouette	18,705	19,625	20,029	20,625	20,795	21,900	22,245	24,535
Trans Sport	17,609	17,585	18,049	18,279	19,965	21,595	21,049	22,950
Venture	—	—	—	—	—	—	20,495	21,999
Used Values ($)								
Lumina Cargo ↑	4,000	5,000	5,500	7,000	8,000	9,000	—	—
Lumina Cargo ↓	3,500	4,000	4,500	5,500	6,500	7,500	—	—
Passenger ↑	4,800	5,500	6,500	8,000	9,000	10,000	—	—
Passenger ↓	4,200	4,500	5,500	6,500	8,000	9,000	—	—
Silhouette ↑	5,500	7,000	8,000	9,000	10,500	12,000	16,500	18,000
Silhouette ↓	5,000	6,000	6,500	8,000	9,000	10,500	14,500	16,500
Trans Sport/SE ↑	5,000	6,000	7,000	8,000	9,500	11,000	15,500	17,000
Trans Sport/SE ↓	4,500	5,000	5,500	7,000	8,000	9,500	13,500	15,500
Venture ↑	—	—	—	—	—	—	14,500	16,000
Venture ↓	—	—	—	—	—	—	13,000	14,500
Extended Warranty	Y	Y	Y	Y	Y	Y	Y	Y
Secret Warranty	Y	Y	Y	Y	Y	Y	Y	Y
Reliability	❶	❷	❷	❷	③	③	④	④
Air conditioning	③	③	③	④	④	④	④	⑤
Automatic transmission	❷	❷	❷	③	③	③	④	⑤
Body integrity	❶	❶	❶	❷	❷	❷	❷	③
Braking system	❶	❷	❷	❷	❷	❷	③	③
Electrical system	❶	❶	❶	❷	❷	❷	③	③
Engines	③	④	④	④	④	④	④	⑤
Exhaust/Converter	③	④	④	④	④	④	④	⑤
Fuel system	④	④	④	④	⑤	⑤	⑤	⑤
Ignition system	❶	❷	❷	③	④	⑤	⑤	⑤
Rust/Paint	❶	❶	❶	❷	❷	❷	❷	③
Steering	④	④	④	④	④	④	④	⑤
Suspension	③	③	③	④	④	④	④	④
Crash Safety	④	④	④	④	⑤	⑤	④	④

HONDA

Rating: Above Average (1995–98). An Accord masquerading as a mini-van. The only reason the Odyssey doesn't get a recommended rating is its small engine and interior. Consider these smartly styled, fuel-efficient vehicles as full-sized, urban station wagons rather than highway-hauling minivans. The 1999 Odyssey is a much larger, more powerful vehicle that's a far better buy. **Maintenance/Repair costs:** Higher than average, but any garage can repair these minivans. **Parts:** Limited supply and costly. There aren't many reasonably priced three-year-old Odysseys on the market. If you can't afford to wait, consider the Mercury Villager, Nissan Axxess and Quest, or the Toyota Sienna.

Strengths and weaknesses: One can sum up the strengths and weak-nesses of the Odyssey (and its American twin through the 1998 model, the Isuzu Oasis) in three words: performance, performance, and performance. You get carlike performance and handling, responsive steering, and a comfortable ride, offset by slow-as-molasses-in-January acceleration with a full load, a raucous engine, and limited passenger/cargo space due to the narrow body.

The Odyssey has proven to be more reliable and gives better hand-ling than the American rear-drive, truck-inspired minivans. But its high price on the used-car market, weak 2.2L 4-cylinder engine, and small dimensions can't compete with Chrysler and Ford's newest versions. About the same size as the Mercury Villager/Nissan Quest twins, the Odyssey has four sedan-type doors, second-row bench seating, and a third seat that folds flat. With its four sedan-style doors and relatively compact size, this car is more like a tall station wagon.

Like the Accord, component quality and assembly are first class. Nevertheless, potential problem areas are the front brakes (pre-mature wear and noise) and trim and accessory items that come loose, break away, or malfunction. The timing chain may also have to be replaced frequently.

Dealer service bulletins: 1995—The front door panels may creak. • Speedometer buzzing. • Instrument panel buzz when the brake pedal is depressed. • Fuel gauge may read less than full. • The temperature control lever may be hard to move. • A product update warns owners that the 1995 models may have loose front suspension nuts, causing a pulling to the side, or excessive noise when braking. • Seatbelts are slow to retract. • Steering wheel shimmy. **1996**—Seatbelts that are slow to retract. • Warped wheel cov-ers. • Loose cigarette lighter socket.

Safety summary/Recalls: Cannot secure a child safety seat with the vehicle's seatbelts; too much play in the lapbelt. **1995**—Airbag failed to deploy. • Front two wheels separated from car while driving. • When vehicle is going over a hill, the cruise control has a tendency to overshoot the set speed by almost 6 mph. • AC doesn't cool the vehicle sufficiently and it puts out a nasty odor. • Defroster can't clear up fogged windows. • Due to its design, the muffler can suddenly fly off while the vehicle is underway. • Far rear restraint retracted so tightly it had to be cut to free the passenger. • Rear middle seatbelt slips and won't stay snug around the lap. **1996**—Airbags failed to deploy. • While backing out the vehicle, occupant turned AC on, and vehicle shot forward with no brakes. • Cruise control failed while vehicle was going uphill. **1997**—Sudden acceleration upon brake application. • Minivan was put in Drive, and AC was turned on; vehicle suddenly accelerated, brakes failed, and the minivan hit a brick wall. • Both front airbags failed to deploy in a head-on collision. **1999**—Sliding door is difficult to close. • Design of the gear shifter interferes with the radio controls. **Recalls: 1997–98**—Faulty ball joints may cause sudden deceleration or loss of steering control.

Secret Warranties/Service Tips

All models: 1995–96—Warped wheel covers are caused primarily by bent tabs. **1995–97**—In a settlement with the Environmental Protection Agency, Honda paid fines totaling $17.1 million and extended its emissions warranty on 1.6 million 1995–97 models to 14 years/150,000 miles. This means that costly engine components and exhaust system parts like catalytic converters will be replaced free of charge, as long as the 14-year/150,000 mile limit hasn't been exceeded. Additionally, the automaker will provide a full engine check and emissions-related repairs at 50,000–75,000 miles and will give free tune-ups at 75,000–150,000 miles. The settlement was first reported on page 6 of the June 15, 1998, edition of *Automotive News*.

Odyssey Profile

	1995	1996	1997	1998
Cost Price ($)				
LX	23,380	23,955	23,955	24,205
Used Values ($)				
LX ↑	12,500	14,500	16,500	18,000
LX ↓	11,000	12,000	15,000	16,500
Extended Warranty	N	N	N	N
Secret Warranty	Y	Y	Y	N
Reliability	⑤	⑤	⑤	⑤
Crash Safety	④	④	④	—

MAZDA

MPV

Rating: Average (1996–98); Below Average (1988–95). The MPV is a good performer hobbled by poor reliability and servicing. The 1997–98 models have lots of potential, if they don't fall apart as they age. **Maintenance/Repair costs:** Higher than average, but any garage can repair these minivans. **Parts:** Limited supply and costly. There are plenty of reasonably priced two- and three-year-old models that have just come off lease on the market. Be wary of earlier high-mileage versions, though; they tend to deteriorate fairly rapidly after the first few years. Other minivans you may wish to consider: a late-model GM Trans Sport, Mercury Villager, Nissan Quest, or Toyota's Previa and Sienna.

Strengths and weaknesses: Handling and overall highway performance put the MPV in the top third of the minivan pack, but the poor winter handling, below-average reliability of early models that are no longer under warranty, a "take it or leave it" attitude when handling warranty claims, mediocre servicing, and high fuel and parts costs make pre-1996 versions below-average buys when it comes to overall operating costs.

The 5-speed manual transmission shifts easily and has well-spaced gears, but it's relatively rare. The automatic performs fairly well but sometimes hesitates before going into gear at about 15 mph and again at 35 mph. Steering is crisp and predictable. Rear-drive setup makes for easy load-carrying and trailer-towing. The base 2.6L 16-valve 121-hp 4-cylinder engine is a dog, especially when hooked up to the automatic 4-speed transmission that robs it of what little power it has. The 3.0L 6-cylinder engine, on the other hand, delivers snappy acceleration with the front-drive, and impressive acceleration with the 4X4.

Overheating and head gasket failures are commonplace with the 4-banger, and the temperature gauge warns you only when it's too late. Some cases of chronic engine knocking in cold weather with the 3.0L have been fixed by installing tighter-fitting, Teflon-coated pistons. Valve lifter problems are also common with this engine. Winter driving is compromised by the MPV's light rear end and mediocre traction, and low ground clearance means that off-road excursions shouldn't be too adventurous.

Owners report that the electronic computer module (ECU), automatic transmission driveshaft, upper shock mounts, front 4X4 drive axles and lash adjusters, AC core, and radiator fail within the first three years. Cold temperatures tend to "fry" the automatic window motor, and the paint is easily chipped and flakes off early, especially around the hood, tailgate, and front fenders. Premature brake caliper and rotor wear and excessive vibration/pulsation are chronic problem areas (repairs are needed about every 8,000–10,000 miles).

474 *Lemon-Aid*

Dealer service bulletins: 1994—Rough idle on warm restart. • Tips for troubleshooting excessive engine noise. • Loose, rattling outer door handles. • Tips for troubleshooting premature automatic transmission planetary failures. • Soft shifts • Gear slips under heavy throttle. • Brake pulsation repair tips. • Steering column squeaks. • Slightly off-center steering column. **1995**—Brake pulsation repair. • Loose, rattling outer door handles. • Slightly off-center steering wheel. • Tips for troubleshooting excessive engine noise. **1996–97**—Brake pulsation repair tips.

Safety summary/Recalls: 1991–93—Liquid-vapor separator may fail, causing fuel leaks. • The front brake calipers may suddenly grab and then release, losing their efficacy, and the rear brakes may occasionally lock up in emergency situations. • Some models have head restraints and rear seatbelts that are too slack. • Lots of buffeting about by strong winds. **Recalls: All models: 1989**—Rear brake shoes may fail. **1989–91**—Takata seatbelt replacement. **1990–91**—Rear brakes may be too aggressive when braking at low speeds, causing the rear wheels to lock up with a possible loss of vehicle control. • The shoe linings on the rear brakes can change over time and increase friction, causing the rear-wheel ABS to activate prematurely.

Secret Warranties/Service Tips

All models/years—DSB #006-94 looks into all the causes and remedies for excessive brake vibrations, and DSB #11-14-95 gives an excellent diagnostic flow chart for troubleshooting excessive engine noise. • Serious paint peeling and delaminating will be fully covered for up to six years under a Mazda secret warranty, say owners. **All models: 1988–91**—Hard shifting after cold-weather starts can be corrected by installing upgraded synchronizer rings and clutch hub assemblies. **1989–91**—Cold-engine piston slapping requires replacement pistons to fix the problem. **1989–93**—AC refrigerant leaks may be caused by a failed O-ring at the block fittings. **1989–94**—Leaking fuel vapor separator that allows fuel vapors to enter the passenger compartment will be fixed up to 11 years from date of purchase, says the October 4, 1999, edition of *Automotive News*. In addition to paying a $900,000 fine, Mazda agreed to extend its warranty as part of a settlement with the federal Environmental Protection Agency. **1990–92**—If parking on an incline makes your MPV impossible to start, install an upgraded inhibitor switch and manual plate. **1992–93**—DSB #007/94 describes Mazda's upgraded head cylinder gasket. **1992–94**—A rough idle following a warm restart can be corrected by installing an upgraded two-stage fuel regulator.

MPV Profile

	1991	1992	1993	1994	1995	1996	1997	1998
Cost Price ($)								
Base	18,073	17,844	19,255	20,900	22,500	22,845	24,370	24,370
4X4	20,743	21,394	22,960	24,700	26,000	—	—	—
Used Values ($)								
Base ↑		6,000	8,000	9,000	10,000	11,000	12,500	14,500	16,500

Base ↓	5,000	6,500	7,500	8,500	9,500	11,000	13,500	15,000
4X4 ↑	7,500	8,500	9,500	11,000	12,500	—	—	—
4X4 ↓	6,500	7,500	8,500	9,500	11,000	—	—	—
Extended Warranty	Y	Y	Y	Y	Y	N	N	N
Secret Warranty	N	N	N	N	N	N	N	N
Reliability	❷	❷	❷	❷	❷	③	③	③
Air conditioning	❷	❷	❷	③	③	③	④	④
Automatic transmission	❷	❷	❷	③	③	③	④	④
Body integrity	❷	❷	❷	❷	❷	❷	❷	❷
Braking system	❶	❶	❶	❷	❷	❷	❷	③
Electrical system	❶	❶	❶	❷	❷	❷	❷	③
Engines	❷	❷	❷	❷	③	③	④	④
Exhaust/Converter	❷	❷	③	③	④	④	⑤	⑤
Fuel system	③	③	③	④	④	④	⑤	⑤
Ignition system	③	③	③	④	④	④	⑤	⑤
Rust/Paint	❷	❷	❷	③	③	③	③	④
Steering	❷	❷	③	③	④	⑤	⑤	⑤
Suspension	❷	❷	❷	❷	③	④	④	④
Crash Safety	③	—	—	—	④	④	④	④

TOYOTA

LE, Previa, Sienna

Rating: LE: Not Recommended (1984–90). **Previa:** Above Average (1991–97); the Previa has high-priced reliability and mediocre road performance. **Sienna:** Above Average (1998). Hopefully the 1999 Sienna has corrected many of the safety-related complaints recorded by the government relating to poor headlight illumination, brake malfunctions, and faulty sliding doors. **Maintenance/Repair costs:** Higher than average, and only Toyota dealers can repair these minivans, particularly when it comes to troubleshooting the supercharged 2.4L engine and All-Track. **Parts:** Limited supply, but reasonably priced. There are plenty of reasonably priced two- and three-year-old Previas that have just come off lease on the market. Other minivans you may wish to consider: the Mercury Villager or Nissan Quest. If you have the patience, the new Honda Odyssey is worth a two-year wait.

Strengths and weaknesses: When you look at Toyota's used minivan offerings, you're faced with the choice of buying an early-model, poorly performing LE Van; the more refined, though recently discontinued, Previa; or the hard-to-come-by 1998 Sienna.

The LE uses a conventional mechanical layout borrowed from the Toyota truck line. This means that, with its short wheelbase, it has an unusually high center of gravity and a tendency to tip precariously in tight turns. Add to this the brakes' tendency to lock on hard application and you have a recipe for disaster. The engine's placement under the front seats takes first prize for poor design and makes routine maintenance an all-day affair. Furthermore, the only way to go from the front of the vehicle to the rear is to get out and get back in. The LE is also extremely vulnerable to side winds flinging it about, and the short wheelbase accentuates the discomfort experienced when going over bumpy roads.

LE reliability isn't very good either, with owners reporting lots of premature fuel pump and air conditioning failures, faulty engine oil pressure sensors and cruise control mechanisms, excessive front brake vibrations and pad and disc wear, and poorly engineered and rust-prone steering components.

The redesigned 1991 Previa's performance and reliability are so much improved over its predecessor that it almost seems like a different vehicle. Roomier and rendered more stable thanks to its longer wheelbase, equipped with a new 2.4L engine (supercharged as of the 1994 model year) and loaded with standard safety and convenience features, 1991–97 Previas are almost as driver-friendly as the Chrysler and Mazda competition. Still, it can't match Chrysler for responsive handling and a comfortable ride, and Toyota's small engine is overworked and doesn't hesitate to tell you so.

Previa owners have learned to live with excessive engine noise, poor fuel economy, premature front brake wear and excessive brake vibration and pulsation, electrical glitches, AC malfunctions, and fit and finish blemishes. Four-wheel drive models with automatic transmissions steal lots of power from the 4-cylinder powerplant.

Sienna

Toyota's new Camry-based front-drive minivan replaced the Previa for the 1998 model year. It's built in the same high-quality Kentucky assembly plant as the Camry and comes with lots of safety and convenience features, including side airbags, anti-lock brakes, and a low-tire-pressure warning system.

Sienna abandons the Previa's futuristic look in favor of a more conservative Chevrolet Venture styling. It seats seven, offers a power sliding door (an additional door was added with the 1999 version) with optional remote controls, and has a V6 powerplant (an engine the Previa sorely needed). As with most minivans and vans, you can save about $1,000 by buying the Sienna's cargo version, but you won't get as many features.

Some of the Sienna's strong points: standard ABS and side airbags (LE, XLE); a smooth-running V6 engine; a comfortable, stable ride; a fourth door; a quiet interior; easy entry/exit; and better-than-average fit and finish reliability. Its weak areas: V6 performance is compromised by AC and automatic transmission power drain; it lacks the

trailer-towing brawn of rear-drive minivans; although the rear seats fold
flat to accommodate the width of a 4' X 8' board, the tailgate won't
close, plus the heavy seats are difficult to reinstall (a two-person job,
and the center seat barely fits through the door). There's also no traction control, fuel economy (premium fuel) isn't impressive, the low-
mounted radio is hard to reach, and third-row seats lack a fore/aft
adjustment to increase cargo space.

Reliability problems include electrical shorts, brake noise and malfunctions, sliding door malfunctions, and various body glitches, including excessive creaks and rattles and paint that's easily chipped—not at
all unusual for a first-year minivan.

Dealer service bulletins: 1995–96—Tips for preventing AC evaporator
odors. • Tips for troubleshooting excessive brake vibration or pulsation. **1997**—Wind noise repair kit. • CD player does not accept or ejects
CDs. **Sienna: 1998**—Instrument panel squeak and rattle tips. • Sliding
door noise reduction and door handle improvements. • Reducing
brake noise.

Safety summary/Recalls: Wind buffeting makes the Previa wander, and
rear seat head restraints block visibility. **1996**—Defective brake booster. •
Brake master cylinder failure. • Multiple ABS failures. • Poor, noisy AC compressor performance. • Windshield wipers suddenly stopped working. •
Middle right bench seat lapbelt is impossible to adjust due to its poor
design. • Speed sensor failure. **1998**—Sudden acceleration, due to a defective throttle cable; vehicle hit a wall. • Brakes made a loud grinding noise,
pedal went to the floor, and vehicle failed to stop. • Extremely loud groaning or grinding noise when braking. • When vehicle is turning left, steering
wheel has to be manually returned to the straight-ahead position or vehicle
will continue turning. • Many owners have complained the vehicle pulls
sharply to one side or another when driving at moderate speeds. • Shape
and design of the Sienna creates severe blind spots. • Headlights give poor
illumination. • Windshields are distorted, exhibiting a "melted" image. •
Rear door doesn't shut tightly. • Sliding door won't latch in cold weather. •
Design of the inside sliding door lock release makes it difficult to operate,
requiring excessive force to activate. • Poor visibility due to the tinted window design. • Headrests and third-row back seats are loose and vibrate. •
Shoulder belts in the middle row lock up instantly when first put on and stay
locked up, binding the passenger. **Recalls: All models: 1991**—Dealers will
replace faulty electrical components in Fujitsu Ten radios to eliminate a fire
hazard. • Premature windshield wiper failure. **1997**—Oil leakage will result
in a sufficiently low oil supply to cause bearing damage to the front differential unit. This can lead to eventual seizure of the unit, increasing the risk
of a crash. Dealers will install a modified air breather plug to prevent such
oil loss.

Secret Warranties/Service Tips

All models/years—Owner feedback confirms that front brake pads and discs will be replaced under Toyota's "goodwill" policy if they wear out before 2 years/30,000 miles. Improved disc brake pad kits are described in DSB #BR94-004. Brake pulsation/vibration, another generic Toyota problem, is fully addressed in DSB #BR94-002, "Cause and Repair of Vibration and Pulsation." **LE Van: 1988–92**—In its U.S. memo to dealers, No. 89-11 issued 2/21/89, Toyota says that it will pay for the replacement of the oxygen sensor for up to 80,000 miles on all of its trucks and vans. • Transmission extension seal leaks require the installation of an upgraded seal (#24201470). **Previa: 1990**—If the sliding door makes a scraping noise as it travels, it signals the need to replace the center rail with an improved part (#68303-28020). **1991**—Under a Special Service Program, Toyota has replaced, at no charge, the radiator, fan, and fan shroud with improved parts. • Under Special Service Program LO5, Toyota has also replaced the cylinder head core plugs and gaskets with improved components. If your minivan requires these repairs, ask Toyota for a partial refund. **1992–93**—Panasonic CD players that skip or won't play were upgraded as of June 1993. **1994–96**—Excessive brake vibration or pulsation can be corrected by installing upgraded front brake pads.

Previa, Sienna Profile

	1991	1992	1993	1994	1995	1996	1997	1998
Cost Price ($)								
Previa	17,173	19,453	21,198	24,218	24,400	26,473	26,963	—
Sienna	—	—	—	—	—	—	—	21,560
Used Values ($)								
Previa ↑	8,000	9,000	10,000	11,500	14,500	16,000	18,000	—
Previa ↓	6,500	7,500	8,500	10,000	13,000	14,500	16,000	—
Sienna ↑	—	—	—	—	—	—	—	20,000
Sienna ↓	—	—	—	—	—	—	—	18,500
Extended Warranty	Y	Y	Y	Y	Y	Y	Y	N
Secret Warranty	N	N	N	N	N	N	N	N
Reliability	③	③	④	⑤	⑤	⑤	⑤	⑤
Air conditioning	❷	③	③	③	④	⑤	⑤	⑤
Automatic transmission	③	③	③	④	⑤	⑤	⑤	⑤
Body integrity	③	③	④	⑤	⑤	⑤	⑤	③
Braking system	❶	❷	❷	❷	❷	❷	③	③
Electrical system	❷	③	③	③	❶	❶	❷	③
Engines	③	③	④	⑤	⑤	⑤	⑤	⑤
Exhaust/Converter	③	③	④	④	⑤	⑤	⑤	⑤
Fuel system	③	③	④	⑤	⑤	⑤	⑤	⑤
Ignition system	③	③	③	④	⑤	⑤	⑤	⑤
Rust/Paint	④	④	④	⑤	⑤	⑤	⑤	③
Steering	④	④	③	④	④	④	⑤	⑤
Suspension	③	③	③	④	④	④	⑤	⑤
Crash Safety	❶	—	③	④	④	④	④	⑤

Appendix
30 BEST INTERNET GRIPE SITES

Websites come and go. Please email *lemonaid@earthlink.net* if you find a site has closed down or moved. Also let me know if you have discovered a website that should be included in next year's *Lemon-Aid* guide.

1. Lemon-Aid (*lemonaidcars.com*)
The official website sponsored by the *Lemon-Aid* guides. Quick, easy, and free access to confidential service bulletins, owner complaints, recalls, and defect investigations. The Secret Warranty Watch is updated monthly, paint delamination jurisprudence is supplied, and tips for making a successful claim are given (even a sample complaint letter is included).

2. The Lemon Aid Stand (*www.pond.net/~delvis/lemonlinks.html*)
Gosh, it seems like everybody's using my name these days. Nevertheless, this website, though not affiliated with the *Lemon-Aid* guides, provides lots of useful info relative to defects, state lemon laws (listed by state), pleading your own case in court, etc. Plus it has a comprehensive listing of other helpful sites.

3. "Lemon Aid or How to Get Car Manufacturers to Call You and Beg You for Mercy!" (*www.saabnet.com/aas/1997.W26/1344522661.26426.html*)
Although not affiliated with the *Lemon-Aid* guides, this site contains a hilarious listing of tactics to use in getting auto manufacturers to return your calls, listen to your complaints, and give you compensation.

4. Automobile Disputes (*photo.net/philg/litigation/automobile-disputes.html*)
Philip Greenspun prepared this legal primer for non-lawyers who own a car, in or out of the explicit warranty, that the manufacturer refuses to repair.

5. The Consumer Law Page (*consumerlawpage.com*)
This "know-your-rights" website is sponsored by the California-based Alexander Law Firm, specialists in consumer law and class actions. It contains well-researched articles of interest to consumers, hundreds of free consumer information brochures, and a Resources page that provides over one thousand links to other useful sites. I find the website both informative and entertaining in the manner it explains complex legal issues in everyday terms that any layperson can comprehend (reading the ins and outs of the fire-prone GM pickup class action is

479

particularly interesting). Plus, California residents can get a free legal
opinion as to the merits of their claim.

6. *Perez-Trujillo v. Volvo Car Corp.* (*www.law.emory.edu/1circuit/mar98/
97-1792.01a.html*)
This U.S.-initiated lawsuit provides an interesting, though lengthy, dissertation on the safety hazards that airbags pose and why automakers
are ultimately responsible for the injuries and deaths caused by their
deployment.

7. U.S. NHTSA (*www.nhtsa.dot.gov/cars/problems/*)
Run by the Big Daddy of federal government auto safety regulators, the
National Highway Traffic Safety Administration, this site has a comprehensive database covering owner complaints, recall campaigns, defect
investigations initiated by the department, and automaker service bulletins that may not be found in the ALLDATA database. Best of all, this
data is easily accessed by typing in your vehicle's year, make, and model.

8. Insurance Institute for Highway Safety (*www.hwysafety.org*)
A dazzling site that's long on crash photos and graphs that show which
vehicles are the most crashworthy.

9. Center for Auto Safety (*www.autosafety.org*)
Consumers Union and Ralph Nader founded the Center for Auto Safety
(CAS) in 1970 to provide consumers a voice for auto safety and quality
in Washington and to help lemon owners fight back across the United
States. CAS has a small budget but a big impact on the auto industry. It
collects complaints and provides a lawyer referral service to its members.

10. ALLDATA Service Bulletins (*www.alldata.com/consumer/tsb/yr.html*)
Automotive recalls and technical service bulletins are listed by year,
make, model, and engine option. Select a year, and then a manufacturer, to see a summary list of recalls and technical service bulletins for
your car or truck.

11. Kelley Blue Book Prices (*www.kbb.com*)
Providing over 9 million free reports every month, the Kelley Blue Book
site is an excellent price guide when you are ready to buy a car. It gives
you the information you need to make an informed choice, whether
you are buying a new or used car, selling, or trading in your own car.
New- and used-car pricing reports are free to car-buying consumers.

12. Autopedia (*autopedia.com/index.html*)
An automotive encyclopedia, Autopedia offers a compendium of
automotive-related information. Its legal section and lemon law listings by state are particularly helpful.

13. Automobile News Groups
These news groups are compilations of email raves and gripes and cover all makes and models. They fall into four distinct areas: *rec.autos.makers.chrysler* (you can add any automaker's name at the end); *rec.autos.tech*; *rec.autos.driving*; and *rec.autos.misc.*

The following news group bulletin board is particularly helpful to owners with minivan and van problems: *www.he.net/~brumley/family/vanboard.html.*

14. The Auto Channel (*www.theautochannel.com*)
This website gives you comprehensive information useful in choosing a new or used vehicle, filing a claim for compensation, or linking up with other owners. Lots of background info on ABS defects and paint delamination/peeling, with an update as to where the paint class actions are before the courts.

15. The Unofficial BMW Lemon Site (*www.bmwlemon.com*)
Everything you wanted to know, or maybe didn't want to know, about factory-related defects affecting the 3-series, 5-series, and 7-series, V8-equipped models. Plus a useful link to Dodge Dakota lemon sites (go figure).

16. Chrysler Products' Problem Web Page (*www.wam.umd.edu/~gluckman/Chrysler/*)
This page was designed to be a resource for Chrysler owners who have had problems in dealing with Chrysler on such issues as peeling paint, transmission failure, the Chrysler-installed Bendix-10 ABS, and other maladies.

17. Chrysler Jeep Paint Delamination/Peeling (*www.goofball.com/keane/badpaint/*)
Jeep paint and other body defects are covered. Useful links to other sites, including a place where Chrysler's 1990 paint defect service bulletin can be downloaded.

18. Ford Insider Info (*www.blueovalnews.com*)
Set up by a Ford Mustang enthusiast living in the Detroit area who has contacts with lots of Ford employee whistleblowers, this website is the place to go for all the latest insider info on the company's activities. The website is still operating although Ford got a temporary restraining order preventing it from publishing certain internal documents that Ford considers to be confidential. Why did Ford pick on this website when websites such as *Lemon-Aid*'s go unchallenged? Insiders tell me that Ford is particularly incensed over *www.blueovalnews.com* spilling the beans that the 1999 Mustang SVT Cobras have exhaust problems that cut as much as 50 horsepower from the 320 horsepower advertised. Ford had to recall 5,300 Cobras to fix the problem.

19. Dead Ford (*www.mindspring.com/~ics_mak/deadford.html*)
An amusing and informative gathering place for Ford car, truck, sport-utility, minivan, and van owners who discuss common problems and solutions. A fun site just to see the FORD VENT page, where an animated character walks across the screen, drops his shorts, and takes a leak up against a thinly disguised Ford logo.

20. Ford Contour/Mystique (*www.contour.org/FAQ/*)
This website provides a comprehensive listing of major problems affecting the Ford Contour and Mercury Mystique.

21. Ford Taurus, Sable, Windstar, and Lincoln Continental Faulty Engine Head Gaskets (*home.att.net/~ccatanese/ford/*)
This is the most recent and most complete site relating to faulty engine head gaskets on Ford's 3.8L engines. Plenty of technical help supported by internal service bulletins and extended warranties you can download. Many links to other helpful sites.

22. Ford Taurus, Sable Automatic Transmission Victims (*members.aol.com/MKBradley/index.html*)
A great site for learning about Ford's biodegradable automatic transmissions (1991–97).

23. Ford Windstar Engine Head Gasket/Automatic Transmission (*www.cartrackers.com/forums/lemon.html*)
This forum provides specific information, repair tips and advice for Windstar owners facing engine or transmission failures. Great links!

24. Ford Paint Delamination/Peeling (*www.ihs2000.com/~peel/*)
Everything you should know about the cause and treatment of Ford paint delamination. It has useful links to other sites and tips on dealing with Ford and GM paint problems.

25. GM Paint Delamination/Peeling (*www.geocities.com/ihategm/*)
There are many sites where the problem is discussed. Simply access Alta Vista or any other search engine and type in "GM paint delamination," or "GM peeling paint." The site listed here is one of the better ones.

26. GMAC Sucks (*www.gmacsucks.com*)
An online complaint forum about GMAC and General Motors set up by an Army veteran whose vehicle was repossessed while he was stationed in Kosovo. Lot of links to other gripe sites as well as complaint summaries relating to both GM and GMAC.

27. GM Saturn Exposed (*www.saturnexposed.com*)
Go beyond the GM Saturn hype and learn why Saturn owners call their car "a different kind of headache." Plenty of owner summaries, service tips, and links to other Saturn gripe sites.

28. GM Suburban Lemons (*www.gmclemon.com*)
Thrill to the excitement of faulty brakes. Experience the wonder of breaking down in Utah on a Sunday afternoon. Marvel at the cut and thrust of verbal duels with callous GM reps. Enter the "which piece of crap is going to fall off next" sweepstakes. Cringe in terror at a tale of driving around with a fuel leak, corroded battery cables and a short circuit.

Lot of links to other gripe sites, copies of service bulletins relating to Suburban defects (brakes, especially), and summaries of complaints from other owners. Incidentally, GM bought back the Suburban from this owner, shortly after this website went up.

29. Nissan Gripe Site (*129.22.253.156*)
For dissatisfied owners of most Nissan vehicles, this site lists common defects and is particularly helpful in providing useful links to groups and government agencies. It also covers in detail what it calls Nissan's "silent recall" of defective engines.

30. Sport-Utility Gripes, Blasts, Whines, and Guilt Trips (The Roadhog Info Trough: *www.suv.org*; Sport-Utility Vehicle Anti-Fan Club: *www.howard.net/ban-suvs.htm*)
These anti-SUV sites believe that sport-utilities and trucks are safety and environmental hazards, in addition to being just plain annoying. You'll find lots of important info and links on the environmental and safety downsides of sport-utility, truck, and van ownership, but keep in mind that much of it is one-sided, and some info is outdated. The Friends of the Earth's Roadhog site is a hoot to browse if only because of its Internet survey list of 22 questions and responses that show most respondents don't care much about those policies our Corolla-and-Prizm-hugging activists hold dear.